**W9-BTJ-386**

*When should I travel to get the best airfare?*
*Where do I go for answers to my travel questions?*
*What's the best and easiest way to plan and book my trip?*

# frommers.travelocity.com

**Frommer's,** the travel guide leader, has teamed up with **Travelocity.com**, the leader in online travel, to bring you an in-depth, easy-to-use resource designed to help you plan and book your trip online.

At **frommers.travelocity.com**, you'll find free online updates about your destination from the experts at Frommer's plus the outstanding travel planning and purchasing features of Travelocity.com. Travelocity.com provides reservations capabilities for 95 percent of all airline seats sold, more than 47,000 hotels, and over 50 car rental companies. In addition, Travelocity.com offers more than 2,000 exciting vacation and cruise packages. Travelocity.com puts you in complete control of your travel planning with these and other great features:

**Expert travel guidance from Frommer's** - over 150 writers reporting from around the world!

**Best Fare Finder** - an interactive calendar tells you when to travel to get the best airfare

**Fare Watcher** - we'll track airfare changes to your favorite destinations

**Dream Maps** - a mapping feature that suggests travel opportunities based on your budget

**Shop Safe Guarantee** - 24 hours a day / 7 days a week live customer service, and more!

Whether traveling on a tight budget, looking for a quick weekend getaway, or planning the trip of a lifetime, Frommer's guides and Travelocity.com will make your travel dreams a reality. You've bought the book, now book the trip!

 **Travelocity.com** A Sabre Company

 **Frommer's**®

## Other Great Guides for Your Trip:

*Frommer's Born to Shop Hong Kong, Shanghai & Beijing*

*Frommer's China*

*Frommer's Southeast Asia*

## Here's what the critics say about Frommer's:

"Amazingly easy to use. Very portable, very complete."

*—Booklist*

♦

"The only mainstream guide to list specific prices. The Walter Cronkite of guidebooks—with all that implies."

*—Travel & Leisure*

♦

"Complete, concise, and filled with useful information."

*—New York Daily News*

♦

"Hotel information is close to encyclopedic."

*—Des Moines Sunday Register*

# Hong Kong

## 6th Edition

by Beth Reiber

HUNGRY MINDS, INC.

New York, NY • Cleveland, OH • Indianapolis, IN

Chicago, IL • Foster City, CA • San Francisco, CA

## ABOUT THE AUTHOR

**Beth Reiber** worked for several years in Germany as a freelance travel writer writing for major U.S. newspapers and in Tokyo as the editor of the *Far East Traveler.* Now a freelance travel writer residing in Lawrence, Kansas, with her husband and two sons, she's the author of several Frommer's guides, including *Frommer's Japan* and *Frommer's Tokyo,* and is a contributor to *Frommer's Europe from $70 a Day* and *Frommer's Southeast Asia.*

Published by:
## HUNGRY MINDS, INC.
909 Third Ave.
New York, NY 10022
**www.frommers.com**

ISBN 0-7645-6257-6
ISSN 1045-9332

Editor: Alice Fellows
Production Editor: Jennifer Connolly
Photo Editor: Richard Fox
Design by Michele Laseau
Cartographer: John Decamillis
Production by Hungry Minds Indianapolis Production Department

## SPECIAL SALES

For general information on Hungry Minds' products and services please contact our Customer Care department; within the U.S. at 800-762-2974, outside the U.S. at 317-572-3993 or fax 317-572-4002. For sales inquiries and reseller information, including discounts, bulk sales, customized editions, and premium sales, please contact our Customer Care department at 800-434-3422.

Manufactured in the United States of America.

5  4  3  2  1

# Contents

## Appendix: Hong Kong in Depth    277

## Index    297

# List of Maps

## Acknowledgments

I would like to thank some fine and very special people who graciously extended their help in the preparation of this book: Peter Randall, Diana Budiman, and Mandy Lo of the Hong Kong Tourist Association; and Teresa Costa Gomes of the Macau Government Tourist Office.

## An Invitation to the Reader

In researching this book, we've discovered many wonderful places—hotels, restaurants, shops and more. We're sure you'll find others. Please tell us about them, so we can share the information with your fellow travelers in upcoming editions. If you were disappointed with a recommendation, we'd love to know that, too. Please write to:

*Frommer's Hong Kong,* 6th Edition
Hungry Minds, Inc.
909 Third Ave.
New York, NY 10022

## An Additional Note

Please be advised that travel information is subject to change at any time—and this is especially true of prices. We therefore suggest that you write or call ahead for confirmation when making your travel plans. The author, editors, and publisher cannot be held responsible for the experiences of readers while traveling. Your safety is important to us, however, so we encourage you to stay alert and be aware of your surroundings. Keep a close eye on cameras, purses, and wallets, all favorite targets of thieves and pickpockets.

## What the Symbols Mean

### ✪ Frommer's Favorites

Our favorite places and experiences—outstanding for quality, value, or both.

The following abbreviations are used for credit cards:

| | | | |
|---|---|---|---|
| AE | American Express | EC | Eurocard |
| CB | Carte Blanche | JCB | Japan Credit Bank |
| DC | Diners Club | MC | MasterCard |
| DISC | Discover | V | Visa |

## Find Frommer's Online

**www.frommers.com** offers up-to-the-minute listings on almost 200 cities around the globe—including the latest bargains and candid, personal articles updated daily by Arthur Frommer himself. No other Web site offers such comprehensive and timely coverage of the world of travel.

# Introducing Hong Kong

**E**very time I come to Hong Kong, I feel as though I've wandered onto a movie set. Maybe I'm an incurable romantic, but when I stand at the railing of the famous Star Ferry as it glides across the harbor, ride a rickety old tram as it winds its way across Hong Kong Island, or marvel anew at the stunning views afforded from atop Victoria Peak, I can't help but think I must have somehow landed in the middle of an epic drama where the past has melted into the present. So many images float by—wooden boats bobbing up and down in the harbor beside huge ocean liners; crumbling tenements next to ultra-modern high-rises; squalid alleys behind luxury hotels; old Chinese pushing wheelbarrows as Rolls-Royces glide by; market vendors selling chicken feet and dried squid while talking on cellular phones.

In fact, one of the most striking characteristics of Hong Kong is this interweaving of seeming opposites, this interplay of the exotic and the technically advanced. There are as many skyscrapers here as you're likely to see anywhere—built with bamboo scaffolding. In addition to historic trams, Hong Kong boasts one of the most efficient subways in the world, complete with the world's first "contactless" tickets, cards that are waved over a scanner. Hong Kong has what are arguably some of the best and most sophisticated restaurants in the world, as well as *dai pai dong,* streetside food stalls. Hong Kong boasts one of the world's largest shopping malls, but there are also lively street markets virtually everywhere.

Because of these dazzling contrasts, Hong Kong offers visitors something unique—the chance to experience a vibrant Chinese city without sacrificing the comforts of home. To be sure, much of Hong Kong's Western fabric comes from the legacy left by the British, who ruled the colony until 1997, when it was handed back to China as a Special Administrative Region. British influence is still evident everywhere, from its school system to its free-market economy, from its rugby teams to its double-decker buses, and from English pubs and tea in the afternoon to (my favorite) orderly queues. But though the city was molded by the British, it has always been at its heart Chinese, with Chinese medicine shops, street vendors, lively dim sum restaurants, old men taking their caged birds for walks in the park, and colorful festivals. Indeed, for the casual visitor, Hong Kong seems little changed since the 1997 handover. No doubt some visitors remain oblivious to even the most visible sign of that change: the replacement of the Union Jack and old flag of the Crown Colony of Hong Kong with the red, starred flag of China and the new red Hong Kong flag with its emblem of the bauhinia flower.

Hong Kong was founded as a place to conduct business and to trade, and it continues to do so aggressively and successfully. The world's fourth-largest banking and financial center, Hong Kong is the "Wall Street of Asia," with banking, international insurance, advertising, and publishing among its biggest concerns. Hong Kong also boasts the world's eighth-largest trading economy, and is one of the world's leading exporters of toys, garments, and watches.

Little wonder that as a duty-free port, Hong Kong attracts approximately 11 million visitors a year, making tourism one of its leading industries. Shopping is one of the main reasons people come here, and at first glance the city does seem rather like one huge department store. But there's much more to Hong Kong than shopping. There's wining, dining, and sightseeing, and there are even isolated places to get away from it all. For those who wish to journey farther afield, Macau, a former Portuguese colony handed back to China in 1999, is just an hour's boat ride away; and vast China itself lies just beyond Hong Kong's border, making it the perfect gateway for trips to Guangzhou, Shanghai, Beijing, and other mainland destinations.

The more you search, the more you'll find. Before long, you, too, may find yourself swept up in the drama.

## 1 Frommer's Favorite Hong Kong Experiences

- **Dining on Dim Sum:** Nothing conveys a sense of Chinese life more vividly than a visit to a crowded, lively Cantonese restaurant for breakfast or lunch, where trolleys of dim sum in bamboo steamers are wheeled from customer to customer. Simply peer into the passing bamboo baskets and choose what appears the most tempting. A great way to start the day.
- **Getting up Early to Watch Tai Chi:** Before breakfast, head to one of Hong Kong's many parks to watch Chinese going through the slow, graceful motions of tai chi, or shadowboxing. For the best viewing, go to Kowloon Park, Hong Kong Park, Victoria Park, or the Zoological and Botanical Gardens. You can even participate in free practice sessions, held three mornings a week in Hong Kong Park.
- **Riding the Star Ferry:** To reacquaint myself with the city, one of the first things I do on each return trip is to hop aboard the Star Ferry for one of the most dramatic and cheapest 5-minute boat rides in the world. Hong Kong's harbor is one of the world's busiest; beyond it rises one of earth's most breathtaking skylines.
- **Taking a Tram:** Take a double-decker tram ride from one end of Hong Kong Island to the other for an unparalleled view of life in the crowded city as you pass skyscrapers, street markets, traditional Chinese shops, and department stores.
- **Gazing upon Hong Kong from Victoria Peak:** You don't know Hong Kong until you've seen it from here. Take the tram to Victoria Peak, famous for its views of Central, the harbor, and Kowloon beyond, followed by a 1-hour circular hike and a meal with a view. Don't miss the nighttime view, one of the most spectacular and romantic in the world.
- **Visiting a Tailor:** Nothing beats the thrill of having something custom-made to fit you perfectly. If this is your dream, make a trek to a tailor one of your first priorities, so that you'll have time for several fittings.
- **Bargain-Hunting in Stanley:** Stall after stall of casualwear, silk clothing, bathing suits, tennis shoes, accessories, and souvenirs and crafts imported from China makes this a shopper's paradise. After a day of bargaining, I like to recuperate in one of Stanley's trendy yet casual restaurants.

- **Window-Shopping on Nathan Road:** Open-fronted clothing boutiques, jewelry stores, camera shops, tailors, tourists from around the world, international cuisine, huge neon signs, and whirling traffic combine to make this boulevard Hong Kong's most famous shopping street.
- **Shopping at Shanghai Tang:** This 1930s-style Chinese department store is oh-so-chic, with lime-green or fuchsia-colored jackets, Mao watches, 1930s reproduction home decor, and more. The shopping bag that comes with your purchase is a bonus—just way too cool. The shop's free postcards are also fab.
- **Browsing for Chinese Souvenirs:** In addition to Shanghai Tang, many other Chinese emporiums sell vases, vase stands, porcelain figurines, chinaware, calligraphy brushes, birdcages, jade, silk jackets, and various Chinese crafts and products; Stanley Market is also good for Chinese souvenirs.
- **Strolling Tsim Sha Tsui's Waterfront:** There's a pedestrian promenade that stretches from the Star Ferry eastward along Tsim Sha Tsui and Tsim Sha Tsui East, providing close-up views of the harbor and Hong Kong Island with its skyscrapers. After dark, this is a wonderful romantic stroll, with the lights of Hong Kong Island shimmering across the water.
- **Hearing the Birds Sing at Yuen Po Street Bird Garden:** See pampered birds at this unusual garden, brought by their owners so they can sing and communicate with other birds on their daily outing. Vendors sell wooden birdcages, porcelain bird dishes, and other paraphernalia.
- **Paying Respects at the Big Buddha:** Laze on the open aft-deck during the 45-minute ferry ride to Lantau Island (and enjoy great views of the harbor and skyline along the way), followed by a bus ride over lush hills to see the world's largest, seated, outdoor bronze Buddha, located at the Po Lin Monastery. Complete your pilgrimage with a vegetarian meal at the monastery.
- **Hiking Across Lamma:** An excursion to this outlying island will do your soul good. Start with the ferry trip, followed by an hour's hike across the island, perhaps some swimming at a beach, and finally a meal of fresh seafood at an open-air waterfront restaurant.
- **Expanding Your Cultural Horizons at the Hong Kong Art Museum:** Hong Kong's most important museum is a must-see for its vast collection of Chinese antiquities, including ceramics, jade, and lacquerware, as well as its gallery of old paintings depicting Hong Kong through the ages and its changing exhibition of contemporary Hong Kong art—all against the dramatic backdrop of Hong Kong's harbor outside its windows. If you see only one museum during your stay, this should be it.
- **Having Your Fortune Told:** Want to know about your future love life, marriage, family, or career? Consult one of Hong Kong's many fortune-tellers; those that speak English can be found at Wong Tai Sin temple, the Tin Hau Temple near the Temple Street Night Market, and the Middle Kingdom at Ocean Park.
- **Exploring the Western District:** Produce, bolts of cloth, snakes, ginseng, dried seafood, Chinese herbs and medicines, a historic temple, a museum dedicated to Chinese and Western medicine, and antiques and collectibles are just some of the things you'll see while strolling through one of Hong Kong's most fascinating neighborhoods.
- **Browsing Antiques Shops on Hollywood Road:** Whether you have several thousand dollars to spend on Ming dynasty heirlooms or just a couple of bucks for a snuff bottle, there's something for everyone in the dozens of antiques shops lining this famous Hong Kong Island road and from outdoor vendor stalls on nearby Cat Street. A sightseeing bonus is Man Mo Temple, Hong Kong's oldest temple, on Hollywood Road.

# Hong Kong Region

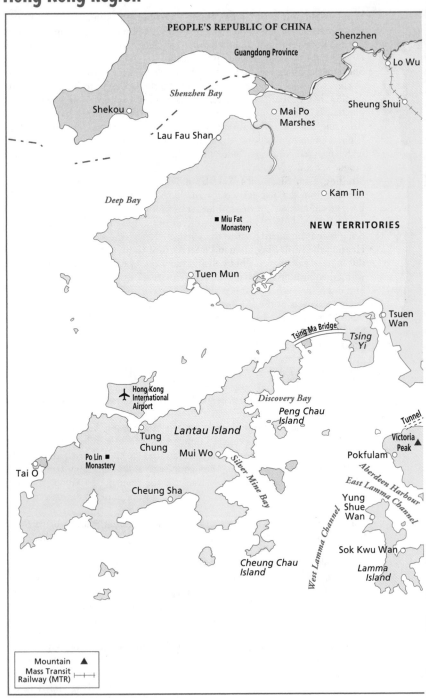

PEOPLE'S REPUBLIC OF CHINA

Shenzhen

Lo Wu

Guangdong Province

*Shenzhen Bay*

Shekou

Sheung Shui

Lau Fau Shan

Mai Po
Marshes

*Deep Bay*

Kam Tin

■ Miu Fat
Monastery

**NEW TERRITORIES**

Tuen Mun

Tsuen
Wan

Tsing Ma Bridge

*Tsing
Yi*

Hong Kong
International
Airport

*Discovery Bay*

*Peng Chau
Island*

Tunnel

Victoria
Peak ▲

Tung
Chung

*Lantau Island*

Mui Wo

Pokfulam

*Aberdeen Harbour*

Po Lin ■
Monastery

*Silver Mine Bay*

*East Lamma Channel*

Tai O

Yung
Shue
Wan

Cheung Sha

Sok Kwu Wan

*Lamma
Island*

*Cheung Chau
Island*

*West Lamma Channel*

Mountain ▲
Mass Transit
Railway (MTR) ├──┼──┤

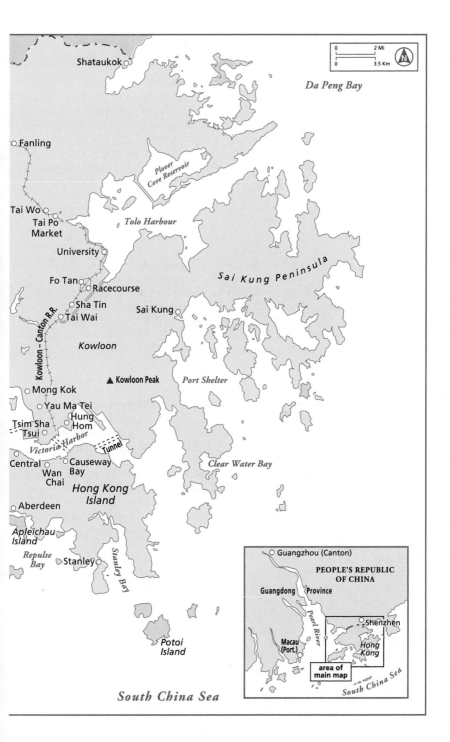

Shataukok

Da Peng Bay

Fanling

Plover
Cove Reservoir

Tai Wo
Tai Po
Market

Tolo Harbour

University

Sai Kung Peninsula

Fo Tan
Racecourse
Sha Tin
Tai Wai

Sai Kung

Kowloon

Kowloon – Canton R.R.

▲ Kowloon Peak

Port Shelter

Mong Kok

Yau Ma Tei
Hung
Hom

Tsim Sha
Tsui

Victoria Harbor

Tunnel

Clear Water Bay

Central
Wan
Chai

Causeway
Bay

Hong Kong
Island

Aberdeen

Apleichau
Island

Repulse
Bay

Stanley

Stanley Bay

Potoi
Island

South China Sea

Guangzhou (Canton)

PEOPLE'S REPUBLIC
OF CHINA

Guangdong Province

Pearl River

Macau
(Port.)

Shenzhen

Hong
Kong

area of
main map

South China Sea

0        2 Mi
0      3.5 Km

N

- **Taking High Tea at the Peninsula:** The British rulers may be gone, but their legacy lives on in the Peninsula's afternoon tea. Virtually all upper-class hotels offer afternoon tea, but none can compare with the experience in the lobby of Hong Kong's most venerable hotel, long a favored people-watching spot. Come for afternoon tea, listen to classical music, and gaze away.

- **Betting on the Horses:** Join thousands of spectators at Hong Kong's favorite sporting event, between September and May. Hong Kong boasts two sophisticated racing tracks, and if you need help in wagering bets, consider joining a special tour of the races offered by the Hong Kong Tourist Association.

- **Regressing to Childhood at Ocean Park:** Southeast Asia's largest oceanarium and fun park boasts one of the world's longest and fastest roller coasters, plus many other thrill rides, a great cable-car ride with breathtaking views of the South China Sea, playgrounds just for kids, a theater with seats that move with the action on the screen, and a re-created Chinese village depicting various dynasties of the past. If it's wildlife you're after, you'll find the world's largest reef aquarium, a shark tank with an underwater pedestrian tunnel, a fascinating collection of weird and wonderful goldfish, an aviary and butterfly dome, panda bears, and a dolphin and killer-whale show. A must for kids of all ages.

- **Imbibing at Happy Hour at a British Pub:** End a busy day of sightseeing and shopping by rubbing elbows with Hong Kong's working population as they take advantage of happy-hour prices in British pubs throughout the city. Most bars and pubs offer a happy hour that can stretch on for hours, with two drinks for the price of one, or drinks at reduced prices.

- **Celebrating Sundown with a Cocktail:** Many hotel lounges offer spectacular views of the city, as well as live music. As the sun disappears, watch the city explode in neon.

- **Stuffing Yourself at a Buffet Spread:** If you have a big appetite or like variety in your meal, there's no better bargain than Hong Kong's countless all-you-can-eat buffet spreads. Almost all hotels now offer buffet lunches and dinners; other restaurants may feature buffets for lunch. Many offer international cuisine, from Japanese sushi and Chinese dishes to pasta and carveries.

- **Relaxing at an Open-Air Seafood Restaurant:** Get rid of stress by relaxing over a meal of fresh seafood at one of Hong Kong's waterfront seafood restaurants; favorite places include Lamma island and Sai Kung in the New Territories.

- **Eating Your Way Through China:** There's no better place in the world to sample regional Chinese cuisine than Hong Kong, where you can eat everything from the ubiquitous Cantonese food to Szechuan, Shanghainese, Hunanese, Beijing, Chiu Chow, and Pekingese dishes.

- **Dining with a View:** Enjoy Chinese or continental cuisine at one of Hong Kong's many restaurants that offer spectacular views of either Kowloon (with its glowing neon lights) or Hong Kong Island (with its skyscrapers and Victoria Peak). In fact, Hong Kong boasts so many restaurants with views, the dilemma will be in the choosing. The absolute winners? Those atop Victoria Peak.

- **Bargaining at the Temple Street Night Market:** Highlights include shopping for casual clothing, music, toys, and accessories; enjoying a meal at a *dai pai dong* (roadside food stall); watching amateur street musicians; and having your fortune told.

- **Listening to the World's Largest Professional Chinese Orchestra:** Established more than 20 years ago, the 85-member Hong Kong Chinese Orchestra is the world's largest, playing traditional and modern Chinese instruments in orchestrations that combine Chinese and Western musical elements.

- **Partying Till Dawn at Lan Kwai Fong:** It's standing-room only at bars and pubs in Central's most famous nightlife district, where the action spills out onto the street and continues till dawn.
- **Zipping Over to Macau:** Macau, a Portuguese colony until it was handed back to the Chinese in 1999, is just an hour away by jetfoil and offers a fascinating blend of Chinese and Mediterranean lifestyles, evident in its spicy cuisine, colorful architecture, temples, churches, and handful of special-interest museums. Although you can "do" Macau in a day, I strongly urge you to spend at least a couple days in this tiny outpost. You'll save money doing so—Macau's hotels and restaurants cost a fraction of their Hong Kong counterparts.

## 2  Best Hotel Bets

Choosing a favorite hotel in Hong Kong can be a bit overwhelming, if not impossible, because the choices are so vast and there are so many competitors. Few cities offer such a large number of first-rate hotels, and few places can compete with the service that has made the Hong Kong hotel industry legendary. With apologies to the rest, here are my personal favorites (for full details, see chapter 4).

- **Best Historic Hotel:** This category has no competition: **The Peninsula,** Salisbury Road, Tsim Sha Tsui (☎ **852/2920 2888**), has long been the grand old hotel of Hong Kong. Built in 1928 and boasting the most ornate lobby in Hong Kong, it retains the atmosphere of a colonial past, even down to its restaurants, Gaddi's and The Verandah, both of which have changed little over the decades. Even its new tower, with high-tech rooms and trendy rooftop restaurant, only adds to the general aura.
- **Best for Business Travelers:** If you can afford it, spring for a room at **The Ritz-Carlton,** 3 Connaught Rd., Central District (☎ **852/2877 6666**), conveniently located right in the heart of Central's financial district. Small and intimate and filled with art and antiques, it seems more like an expensive apartment complex than a hotel; it offers rooms with sweeping harbor views, dual phone lines, and dataports; excellent service; a state-of-the-art business center; and a health club with heated outdoor swimming pool. For those who like to stay connected, there are also rooms that come with a computer hooked to the Internet, fax, printer, and scanner. For even more pampering, executive floors offer special privileges, including a private lounge with complimentary snacks and drinks throughout the day.
- **Best for Business Travelers Paying Their Own Way: Empire Hotel,** 33 Hennessy Rd., Wan Chai (☎ **852/2866 9111**), offers the room amenities, services, and facilities of a more expensive hotel but at moderate prices. Its location is convenient to Central, and guests can enjoy a heated rooftop pool large enough for laps, fitness room, business center, and in-room fax machines.
- **Best for a Romantic Getaway:** Go to Macau! The **Westin Resort Macau,** Estrada de Hac Sa on Colôane Island (☎ **853/871111**), has the perfect, idyllic setting for those who want to get away from it all, with large rooms (each with private terrace) overlooking the sea, landscaped grounds, indoor and outdoor pools, and a nearby beach for moonlit walks.
- **Best Trendy Hotel:** It may seem a contradiction in terms that Hong Kong's best historic hotel is also my pick for the best trendy hotel. But **The Peninsula**'s 32-story tower is a cut above Hong Kong's other hotels, with rooms to die for and its ultra-hip top-floor Felix, designed by Philippe Starck and featuring some of the most avant-garde fixtures this side of the Pacific. I'm ready to move in.

- **Best Lobby for Pretending That You're Rich:** The Peninsula has long been the favorite lobby for people-watching (no Japanese tourist misses it), but there's nothing that quite matches the overt extravagance of the **Grand Hyatt,** 1 Harbour Rd., Wan Chai (☎ **852/2588 1234**), which flaunts space and is decorated like a 1930s art deco ocean liner. Just walking down the curved staircase can make you feel like Greta Garbo.
- **Best Budget Hotel:** The **Eaton Hotel,** 380 Nathan Rd., Yau Ma Tei (☎ **852/2783 1818**), has more class and more facilities than most hotels in its price category, plus a few extras. With a good location near the Temple Street Night Market, it boasts friendly service, an outdoor terrace perfect for evening cocktails, a good Cantonese restaurant, a fitness room, a rooftop pool and sunning terrace, and rooms with all the comforts, as well as room service and same-day laundry service.
- **Best for Families:** The number-one choice for families in terms of price, facilities, and location is the **The Salisbury YMCA,** Salisbury Road, Tsim Sha Tsui (☎ **852/2369 2211**), located right next to the prestigious (and very expensive) Peninsula and just a short walk from the Star Ferry. It offers large suites great for families (and even views of the famous Victoria Harbour and Hong Kong Island), an inexpensive cafeteria serving buffet meals, two indoor swimming pools (including a children's pool), a play area on the fourth-floor terrace, and baby-sitting.
- **Best Service:** Other hotels may be just as good, but probably none can match the professional, unobtrusive service offered by **The Peninsula** (see address and telephone above); it has one of the highest staff-to-guest ratios in Hong Kong.
- **Best Location:** The **Mandarin Oriental,** 5 Connaught Rd., Central District (☎ **852/2522 0111**), a longtime landmark in the heart of Central, is just a few minutes' walk away from the Star Ferry, trams, and MTR. It's the best place to stay if you want to rub elbows with professionals who actually live and work in Hong Kong, but even better are its rooms with harbor views, which boast balconies and binoculars, making this a good location also for would-be spies pretending they're characters in a John Le Carré novel.
- **Best Health Club:** Most of Hong Kong's deluxe hotels boast state-of-the-art health clubs. But what I like most about the health club at the **JW Marriott Hotel,** Pacific Place in the Central District (☎ **852/2810 8366**), is that it's open 24 hours a day, which means you can work out when it fits *your* schedule. There's also an outdoor heated swimming pool, sauna, whirlpool, and steam room.
- **Best Hotel Pool:** The **Grand Hyatt** (see address and telephone above) and **Renaissance Harbour View Hotel Hong Kong,** 1 Harbour Rd., Wan Chai (☎ **852/2802 8888**), share one of Hong Kong's largest outdoor pools, surrounded by a lush, landscaped garden and with views of the harbor.
- **Best Views:** Most of Hong Kong's deluxe hotels boast harbor views, making this category the toughest. However, in my opinion, the best harbor views are from the Kowloon side, where you can feast your eyes not only on the boats plying the water but also on Hong Kong Island with its stunning architecture, Victoria Peak, and, at night, the shimmering of neon lights. And no hotel is as close to the water as **The Regent,** Salisbury Road, Tsim Sha Tsui (☎ **852/2721 1211**), built right over the harbor; as many as 70% of its rooms command sweeping views of the water and boast floor-to-ceiling and wall-to-wall windows, making the most of one of the world's most breathtaking city views.
- **Best for Those Addicted to the Internet:** The **Grand Hyatt** (see address and telephone above) offers rooms with cordless keyboards that access the Internet

and e-mail through an interactive TV at speeds 50 times faster than a conventional modem; views of the harbor are a bonus. The moderately priced **Kowloon Hotel,** 19–21 Nathan Rd., Tsim Sha Tsui (☎ **852/2929 2888**), impresses with its sophisticated "interactive telecenter," allowing access to such information as flight schedules and hotel bills, acting as a word processor, sending and receiving e-mail, interfacing with a fax machine (which also acts as a printer), and even containing video games. Other hotels with in-room computers giving access to the Internet include **The Regent** (see address and telephone above); **Regal Airport Hotel,** Chek Lap Kok (☎ **852/2286 8888**); and **Royal Pacific Hotel & Towers,** 33 Canton Rd., Tsim Sha Tsui (☎ **852/2736 1188**).

- **Best Hotel in a Chinese Neighborhood:** I'm partial to the **Hotel Concourse,** 22 Lai Chi Kok Rd., Mong Kok (☎ **852/2397 6683**), convenient to an MTR subway station yet far away from the tourists in Tsim Sha Tsui. The surrounding area is strictly Chinese (even hotel guests are primarily from mainland China), and the hotel is comfortable and the staff is friendly. Within walking distance are the Bird Market, the Ladies' Market, and a very local market on Fa Yuen Street.
- **Best Hotel for Dining:** Hong Kong boasts some of the best hotel restaurants in the world, but for an all-around winner, **The Peninsula** offers a variety of restaurants that never disappoint, from the long-time favorite Gaddi's serving traditional French cuisine to the over-the-top Felix designed by Philippe Starck, as well as restaurants serving Cantonese, Swiss, and Japanese food.

## 3  Best Dining Bets

I'm convinced Hong Kong has some of the best restaurants in the world—which makes it extremely difficult to choose the best of the best. These are my personal favorites (for full details, see chapter 5).

- **Best Spot for a Romantic Dinner: The Plume,** the Regent Hotel, Salisbury Road, Tsim Sha Tsui (☎ **852/2721 1211**), has all the makings of a special evening à deux: great harbor view, excellent service, and some of the best cuisine in Hong Kong—original creations that use Asian foods to enhance classical European dishes. You'll want to linger for some time here, savoring the food, the ambience, the view, and each other.
- **Best Spot for a Business Lunch:** Business travelers have long favored the **Mandarin Grill,** Mandarin Oriental Hotel, 5 Connaught Rd., Central (☎ **852/ 2522 0111**), conveniently located in the heart of Hong Kong's financial and business district. It offers drawing-room comfort and high-powered food, a winning combination for clinching those business deals.
- **Best Spot for a Celebration:** An elegant, colonial-age setting, attentive service, dependably good French haute cuisine, and an extensive wine list make **Gaddi's,** the Peninsula Hotel, Salisbury Road, Tsim Sha Tsui (☎ **852/2920 2888**), a natural for a splurge or special celebration. If, however, your idea of a celebration is more exuberant and youthful, you can do no better than **M at the Fringe,** 2 Lower Albert Rd., Central (☎ **852/2877 4000**), a Hong Kong favorite for its quirky interior, artsy crowd, and always excellent creative cuisine.
- **Best Decor:** The avant-garde **Felix,** the Peninsula Hotel, Salisbury Road, Tsim Sha Tsui (☎ **852/2920 2888**), was designed by Philippe Starck; in addition to providing Hong Kong's most unusual, innovative setting, the restaurant offers stunning views, one of the world's smallest discos, and exhibitionist bathrooms. Wear your trendiest duds—you, too, are part of the display.

- **Best View:** In a town famous for its views, you might as well go to the very top, where the curved facade of **Cafe Deco,** Peak Galleria, Victoria Peak (☎ 852/2849 5111), offers Hong Kong's best panorama, along with live jazz in the evening and moderately priced international cuisine. Request a harbor-view window seat a couple of weeks in advance.
- **Best Wine List:** Not only does **The Plume,** the Regent Hotel (see "Best Spot for a Romantic Dinner," above), offer great harbor views, some of the best European cuisine in Hong Kong, and impeccable service, but it also boasts the largest wine cellar in Asia, with 10,000 bottles and vintages from around the world.
- **Best Restaurant for Wine Lovers on Budgets:** If you can't afford a first-class restaurant, head to **Maman WineBar and Restaurant,** Regal Kowloon Hotel, 71 Mody Rd., Tsim Sha Tsui East (☎ 852/2313 8618), where you can choose from among 400 bottles of wine at close to retail prices and drink your purchase at the adjoining restaurant for a HK$100 ($13) corkage fee. There are also 50 wines by the glass, and a menu that revels in French homestyle cooking.
- **Best Cantonese Cuisine:** With some of the world's best Cantonese restaurants located in Hong Kong, this is obviously a tough call, but you can't go wrong at the very sophisticated and classy **Lai Ching Heen,** the Regent Hotel, Salisbury Road, Tsim Sha Tsui (☎ 852/2721 1211), where the emphasis is on stark simplicity, a view of the harbor, and traditional and creative dishes that border on Chinese nouvelle cuisine.
- **Best Chinese for the Uninitiated:** If you're unfamiliar with Chinese food beyond sweet-and-sour pork and feel—perhaps reluctantly—that Hong Kong is the place to widen your horizons, **Shang Palace,** Kowloon Shangri-La Hotel, 64 Mody Rd., Tsim Sha Tsui East (☎ 852/2733 8754), is a good introduction to the almost limitless variety of Cantonese food, all listed on an English menu. It's also a good place to try dim sum for the first time. The helpful staff is happy to make recommendations. The elaborately decorated lacquerware walls and Chinese lanterns all fit the fantasy of a Chinese restaurant in Asia.
- **Best Dim Sum Experience:** Its quaint ceiling fans, spittoons, and wooden booths evoke a 1930s ambience at **Luk Yu Tea House,** 24–26 Stanley St., Central (☎ 852/2523 5464). First opened in 1933, it's one of Hong Kong's oldest restaurants, famous for its dim sum and filled daily with regular customers. It's hard to find an empty seat here, but worth the effort.
- **Best American Cuisine:** There's no better place in town for a Caesar salad than **Napa,** Kowloon Shangri-La Hotel, 64 Mody Rd., Tsim Sha Tsui East (☎ 852/2733 8752), where you can follow your salad with Californian cuisine that includes pizzas and seafood. The great harbor views make it a perfect place for a relaxed lunch or dinner.
- **Best French Cuisine: Petrus,** Island Shangri-La Hotel, Supreme Court Road, Central (☎ 852/2820 8590), is the top French restaurant in more ways than one: It's located on the 56th floor and offers breathtaking harbor views. Decorated like a French castle, it offers contemporary French creations and one of Hong Kong's most definitive wine lists, delivered by a professional and discreet staff.
- **Best Italian Cuisine:** There are a lot of contenders in this category, but the harbor views, airy palatial setting, and traditional northern Italian home-style cooking combine to make **Grissini,** Grand Hyatt Hong Kong Hotel, 1 Harbour Rd., Wan Chai (☎ 852/2588 1234), a favorite choice for lunch or dinner.
- **Best Western/Asian Crossover Cuisine:** Trendy restaurants utilizing Western and Asian ingredients to create new dishes are the vogue in Hong Kong right

now, but few carry it off as masterfully as **Vong,** Mandarin Oriental Hotel, 5 Connaught Rd., Central (☎ **852/2522 0111**), offering what is arguably the best interpretation of Franco-Asian cuisine this part of the hemisphere, as well as great views of the harbor and a nattily dressed crowd.

- **Best Seafood:** Huge decorative seafood tanks and views of Victoria Harbour provide the perfect setting for a memorable seafood dinner at **Yü,** the Regent Hotel, Salisbury Road, Tsim Sha Tsui (☎ **852/2721 1211**). Lobster, crabs, prawns, abalone, mussels, and fish are kept alive until the decisive moment; colorful cards show the day's catch. Chefs prepare your food according to your wishes; there's also imported oysters and a sushi bar.

- **Best Buffet Spread:** Lots of hotels offer buffets, but none can match the changing vistas offered by the 30th-floor revolving **La Ronda,** Furama Kempinski Hotel, 1 Connaught Rd., Central (☎ **852/2848 7422**), which provides views of the harbor, Central, and the Peak along with a wide selection of Asian and Western dishes for both lunch and dinner. In fact, because the view is so different during the day and night, you may wish to come back twice. Nightly entertainment is a plus.

- **Best Steaks:** Juicy U.S. prime Midwestern beef, broiled to perfection, is the forte of American chain **Ruth's Chris Steak House,** 68 Mody Rd., Tsim Sha Tsui East (☎ **852/2366 6000**), along with side dishes of mashed potatoes, sautéed spinach, and Caesar salad. Guaranteed to satisfy the cravings of the most dedicated carnivore.

- **Best Burgers and Beer: Dan Ryan's Chicago Grill,** with two locations both sides of the harbor at 88 Queensway, Central (☎ **852/2845 4600**), and Ocean Terminal (☎ **852/2735 6111**), offers casual dining, good burgers (and other good American food), and drinks throughout the day; its Kowloon branch even provides a view of the busy harbor.

- **Best Pizza:** Located in Hong Kong's prime nightlife district, **Baci Pizza,** 1 Lan Kwai Fong, Central (☎ **852/2840 0153**), is a small casual pizzeria offering delicious, wafer-thin pizzas at reasonable prices, as well as pastas.

- **Best for the Body-Conscious:** Don your designer togs and join the well-dressed, good-looking professional crowd that has made **Joyce Cafe,** One Exchange Square, Central (☎ **852/2810 0807**), the number-one lunch choice for imaginative pasta, satisfying salads, sandwiches prepared with Asian and Western ingredients, and vegetarian fare. Fruit and vegetable juices win over afternoon martinis as the drink of choice.

- **Best Outdoor Dining:** Atop Victoria Peak, away from the constant drone of Hong Kong's traffic, is the delightful **Peak Cafe,** 121 Peak Rd., Victoria Peak (☎ **852/2849 7868**), with its outdoor terrace and lush foliage, where you can actually hear the birds sing. Some tables provide views of Hong Kong Island's southern coast. A jazz trio entertains on Thursdays.

- **Best People-Watching:** Although several restaurants in Hong Kong offer views of people parading past, **Vong** (see above) is the best place for observing your fellow diners. In fact, the place is so crowded and lively that you can't help but take in your neighbors, making this one of the hottest spots in town to be seen. By the way, the crossover food mixing East and West ingredients is probably the best around, and the views of the harbor are unbeatable, but is anyone noticing?

- **Best for Families: Marché Mövenpick,** Peak Tower, Victoria Peak (☎ **852/2849 2000**), is a cafeteria offering something for everyone (pizza and pasta for the kids, international fare and drinks for the parents), along with great views of Hong Kong. It's also one of the few restaurants to actually acknowledge the existence of kids, with a children's corner complete with a toddler slide, toys, crayons, and other diversions. For older kids, there's a Ripley's Believe It or Not! Odditorium and a motion-simulation theater in the same building on the Peak.

- **Best Restaurant for Shutterbugs:** Not only is **Jumbo Floating Restaurant,** moored in Aberdeen Harbour (☎ **852/2553 9111**), the largest floating restaurant in the world, but it's also one of Hong Kong's most ornate, and even offers its guests free, 20-minute sampan rides through the harbor with its boat population. Don't forget your camera.
- **Best Place to Chill Out:** If the stress of travel and the noise and crowds of Hong Kong have pushed you to breaking point, take a ferry to one of the open-air seafood restaurants on the waterfront of Sok Kwu Wan village on Lamma island, where you can dine on fresh seafood, drink a beer or two, and regain perspective. For even more relaxation, hike to one of the island's beaches.
- **Best Afternoon Tea:** For that most British institution, no place is more famous than the golden-age and unparalleled **Peninsula Hotel Lobby,** Salisbury Road, Tsim Sha Tsui (☎ **852/2920 2888**), where you can nibble on delicate finger sandwiches and scones, watch the parade of people, and listen to live classical music being played from an upstairs balcony.
- **Best Brunch:** You'll be spoiled forever—or at least for the rest of the day—if you begin your morning at **The Verandah,** the Peninsula Hotel, Salisbury Road, Tsim Sha Tsui (☎ **852/2920 2888**). Wonderfully reminiscent of the colonial era, it serves a delicious international brunch on Sundays. If ever there were a place that inspired champagne for breakfast, this is it.
- **Best Desserts:** I was born without a sweet tooth, but even I was tempted when the dessert cart was wheeled out at the end of a memorable dinner at **Sabatini,** Royal Garden Hotel, 69 Mody Rd., Tsim Sha Tsui East (☎ **852/2733 2000**). The sinfully rich creations were all lovingly described and looked equally delicious, but in the end I went for the tiramisu, and I can't imagine the meal without it.

# Planning Your Trip: The Basics

## 2

**M**uch of the anxiety associated with travel comes from a fear of the unknown—not knowing what to expect can give even seasoned travelers butterflies. This chapter will help you prepare for your trip to Hong Kong—but don't stop here. Reading through the other chapters before leaving will also help you in your planning. Just learning that Hong Kong has hiking trails and beaches, for example, may prompt you to pack your hiking boots or swimsuit. Keep in mind, however, that some of the information given here may change during the lifetime of this book.

## 1 Visitor Information

The **Hong Kong Tourist Association (HKTA)** is one of the best-organized and most efficient tourist offices I've come across. It offers a wealth of free information for travelers, including brochures on everything from hotels to sightseeing. See "Orientation" in chapter 3 for a complete listing of tourist offices in Hong Kong itself and a rundown of available booklets and brochures.

### HKTA OVERSEAS
Although the information stocked by HKTA offices abroad is sometimes not as up-to-date or as thorough as that available in Hong Kong itself or through the Internet (see below), it's worth contacting a local HKTA office before leaving home for general information and a map.

In the **United States:** 115 E. 54th St., 2nd floor, New York, NY 10022-4512 (☎ **212/421-3382;** fax 212/421-4285; e-mail: hktanyc@hkta.org); 401 N. Michigan Ave., Suite 1640, Chicago, IL 60611 (☎ **312/329-1828;** fax 312/329-1858; e-mail: hktachi@ hkta.org); 10940 Wilshire Blvd., Suite 2050, Los Angeles, CA 90024-3915 (☎ **310/208-4582;** fax 310/208-1869; e-mail: hktalax@ hkta.org).

In **Canada:** Hong Kong Trade Centre, 3rd floor, 9 Temperance St., Toronto, ON, Canada M5H 1Y6 (☎ **416/366-2389;** fax 416/ 366-1098; e-mail: hktayyz@hkta.org)

In the **United Kingdom:** 6 Grafton St., London W1X 3LB, England (☎ **0171/533-7100;** fax 0171/533-7111; e-mail: hktalon@ hkta.org).

In **Australia:** Hong Kong House, Level 4, 80 Druitt St., Sydney, NSW 2000, Australia (☎ **02/9283 3083;** fax 02/9283 3383; e-mail:

hktasyd@hkta.org); and P.O. Box 2120, Auckland, New Zealand (☎ **09/307-2580;** fax 09/307-2581; e-mail: hktaauk@hkta.org).

## HKTA ONLINE

You can have a virtual visit to Hong Kong by visiting HKTA's homepage at **www.hkta.org**. With exciting visuals, the site provides a comprehensive overview of Hong Kong—maps of the region, major attractions, a detailed weekly calendar of performing arts and festivals, listings for hotels and restaurants, and guided tours.

## 2 Entry Requirements & Customs

## ENTRY REQUIREMENTS

Entry formalities for most nationalities coming to Hong Kong have not changed since the 1997 handover. As we go to press, a valid passport is the only document most tourists, including Americans, need to enter Hong Kong, valid for at least 1 month beyond the planned departure date from Hong Kong. Americans can stay up to 1 month without a visa. Australians, New Zealanders, Canadians, and other British Commonwealth citizens can stay for 3 months without a visa. Citizens of the United Kingdom now can stay for 6 months without a visa; previously they were allowed a 12-month stay.

Once in Hong Kong, visitors must carry photo identification at all times, such as a passport or driver's license. Safeguard your passport in an inconspicuous, inaccessible place like a money belt. If you lose it, visit the nearest consulate of your native country as soon as possible for a replacement. As any extra safety precaution, it's a good idea to photocopy your passport.

If you plan to make an excursion into mainland China, you'll need a visa, which can be obtained in Hong Kong. Applications require one photo and generally take 3 working days to process (see section 3, "China," in chapter 10).

## CUSTOMS

**ENTERING HONG KONG**   Visitors are allowed to bring into Hong Kong duty free a 1-liter (34-ounce) bottle of alcohol, 200 cigarettes (or 50 cigars or 250 grams of tobacco), and a reasonable quantity of cosmetics and perfumes in opened bottles for personal use.

**GOING HOME**   Returning **U.S. citizens** who have been away for 48 hours or more are allowed to bring back, once every 30 days, $400 worth of merchandise duty free, including (for those 21 and older) 1 liter of wine or spirits. Beyond that, the next $1,000 worth of goods is assessed at a flat rate of 10% duty. Be sure to have your receipts handy. On gifts, the duty-free limit is $100. You're allowed to send up to $50 per package back by mail duty-free. You cannot bring fresh foodstuffs into the United States; tinned foods, however, are allowed.

**U.K. citizens** returning from Hong Kong have a customs allowance of: 200 cigarettes; 50 cigars; 250 grams of smoking tobacco; 2 liters of still table wine; 1 liter of spirits or strong liqueurs (over 22% volume); 2 liters of fortified wine, sparkling wine or other liqueurs; 60cc (ml) perfume; 250cc (ml) of toilet water; and £145 worth of all other goods, including gifts and souvenirs. People under 17 cannot have the tobacco or alcohol allowance.

**Canada** allows its citizens a $500 exemption, and you're allowed to bring back duty-free 200 cigarettes, 2.2 pounds of tobacco, 40 imperial ounces of liquor, and

50 cigars. In addition, you're allowed to mail gifts to Canada from abroad at the rate of Can$60 a day, provided they're unsolicited and don't contain alcohol or tobacco (write on the package "Unsolicited gift, under $60 value"). All valuables should be declared on the Y-38 form before departure from Canada, including serial numbers of valuables you already own, such as expensive foreign cameras. *Note:* The $500 exemption can be used only once a year and only after an absence of 7 days.

The duty-free allowance in **Australia** is A$400 or, for those under 18, A$200. Returning citizens can bring in 250 cigarettes or 250 grams of loose tobacco, and 1,125ml of alcohol. If you're returning with valuable goods you already own, such as foreign-made cameras, you should file form B263.

The duty-free allowance for **New Zealand** is NZ$700. Citizens over 17 can bring in 200 cigarettes, or 50 cigars, or 250 grams of tobacco (or a mixture of all three if their combined weight doesn't exceed 250 grams); plus 4.5 liters of wine and beer, or 1.125 liters of liquor. New Zealand currency does not carry import or export restrictions. Fill out a certificate of export, listing the valuables you are taking out of the country; that way, you can bring them back without paying duty.

## 3  Money

### CURRENCY

The basic unit of currency is the **Hong Kong dollar,** which is divided into 100 cents. Since 1983, when negotiations between Britain and China concerning Hong Kong's future sent public confidence and the value of the Hong Kong dollar into a nosedive, the Hong Kong dollar has been pegged to the U.S. dollar at a rate of 7.8 (which means that US$1 equals HK$7.8), giving the Hong Kong currency greater stability.

Three banks, the Hongkong and Shanghai Banking Corporation, the Bank of China, and, to a lesser degree, the Standard Chartered Bank, all issue their own colorful notes, in denominations of HK$10 (which is being phased out) HK$20, HK$50, HK$100, HK$500, and HK$1,000. As for coins, they're minted in bronze for 10¢, 20¢, and 50¢ pieces; in silver for HK$1, HK$2, and HK$5; and in nickel and bronze for HK$10. The HK$10 coins were issued in 1995 to replace HK$10 notes; the latter, though valid, are increasingly rare. Also valid are coins with the likeness of Britain's Queen Elizabeth, though these are also becoming rare (and are being snapped up by collectors) and have been replaced with coins depicting the bauhinia flower.

At any rate, throughout Hong Kong you'll see the dollar sign ("$"), which of course refers to Hong Kong dollars, not U.S. dollars. To prevent confusion, this guide identifies Hong Kong dollars with the symbol "HK$" (followed in parentheses by the U.S. dollar conversion). Although the official conversion rate is pegged at 7.8, you'll receive slightly less at banks, hotels, and currency exchange offices. During my last trip, I encountered exchange rates ranging from 7.77 (at a bank) to 7.25 (at a hotel). Some banks offer better exchange rates but charge a commission (worth it if you're exchanging large amounts of money); American Express offices may have lower exchange rates but do not charge a commission on American Express traveler's checks.

For the matter of convenience, therefore, all conversions in this book are based on HK$7.70 to $1 U.S. (and then rounded off). If the exchange rate changes drastically—i.e., it is no longer pegged to the U.S. dollar—plan your budget accordingly. According to figures released by the Hong Kong Tourist Association, North Americans spend an average of HK$1,600 ($208) per day on hotels, meals, shopping, and entertainment.

## The Hong Kong Dollar, the British Pound & the U.S. Dollar

**For American Readers**  At this writing, $1 U.S. = approximately HK$7.70 at banks and exchange offices (or HK$1 = 13¢), and this was the rate of exchange used to calculate the U.S. dollar values given in this book (rounded off). While stable since it's pegged to the U.S. dollar, this exchange rate may not be the same when you travel to Hong Kong. Therefore the following table should be used only as a guide.

**For British Readers**  At this writing, £1 = approximately HK$12.25 (or HK$1 = 6 pence), and this was the rate of exchange to calculate the pound values in the table below.

| HK$ | U.S.$ | U.K.£ | HK$ | U.S.$ | U.K£ |
|---|---|---|---|---|---|
| 0.25 | 0.03 | .02 | 150 | 19.48 | 12.24 |
| 0.50 | 0.06 | .04 | 200 | 25.97 | 16.32 |
| 1.00 | 0.13 | .08 | 250 | 32.47 | 20.41 |
| 2.00 | 0.26 | .16 | 300 | 38.96 | 24.49 |
| 3.00 | 0.39 | .23 | 350 | 45.45 | 28.57 |
| 4.00 | 0.52 | .24 | 400 | 51.95 | 32.65 |
| 5.00 | 0.65 | .41 | 450 | 58.44 | 36.73 |
| 6.00 | 0.78 | .49 | 500 | 64.94 | 40.81 |
| 7.00 | 0.91 | .57 | 550 | 71.43 | 44.90 |
| 8.00 | 1.04 | .65 | 600 | 77.92 | 48.98 |
| 9.00 | 1.17 | .73 | 650 | 84.42 | 53.06 |
| 10.00 | 1.30 | .82 | 700 | 90.91 | 57.14 |
| 15.00 | 1.95 | 1.22 | 750 | 97.40 | 61.22 |
| 20.00 | 2.60 | 1.63 | 800 | 103.90 | 65.31 |
| 25.00 | 3.25 | 2.04 | 850 | 110.39 | 69.39 |
| 30.00 | 3.90 | 2.49 | 900 | 116.88 | 73.47 |
| 35.00 | 4.55 | 2.86 | 1,000 | 129.87 | 81.63 |
| 40.00 | 5.19 | 3.26 | 1,250 | 162.34 | 102.04 |
| 45.00 | 5.84 | 3.67 | 1,500 | 194.80 | 122.45 |
| 50.00 | 6.49 | 4.08 | 1,750 | 227.27 | 142.86 |
| 75.00 | 9.74 | 6.12 | 2,000 | 259.74 | 163.26 |
| 100.00 | 12.99 | 8.16 | 2,250 | 292.21 | 183.67 |

## CREDIT CARDS

Credit cards are a safe way to carry money and provide a convenient record of all your expenses. Although many of the smaller shops in Hong Kong will give better prices if you pay in cash with local currency, most shops accept international credit cards, although some of the smaller ones do not. Look for credit-card signs displayed on the front door or in the shop. Readily accepted credit cards include American Express, Visa, and MasterCard. Note, however, that shops have to pay an extra fee for transactions that take place with a credit card—and they will try to pass on that expense to you. Keep this in mind if you're bargaining (see section 1 in chapter 8, "Shopping"), and make sure the shopkeeper knows whether you're going to pay with cash or plastic. All major hotels and better restaurants accept credit cards, but budget restaurants often don't. If you do pay with a credit card, check to make sure that "HK" appears before the dollar sign given for the total amount.

## ATMS

There are ATMs throughout Hong Kong, and one of the best reasons to carry a credit or a debit card is to obtain cash from an ATM. Not only do you eliminate the inconvenience of being able to exchange money only during banking hours, but the exchange rate is better. However, commission fees may be higher than those charged for exchanging cash or traveler's checks, so be sure you're going to change an amount that warrants the fee. To draw money from a Hong Kong ATM with either a credit or a debit card, you must have a four-digit personal identification number. If you're in doubt, ask your issuing bank for information before traveling to Hong Kong.

American Express cardholders have access to Jetco automated-teller machines and can withdraw local currency or traveler's checks at the Express Cash machines at both American Express offices (see "Fast Facts: Hong Kong" in chapter 3). Holders of MasterCard and Visa can use ATMs at the airport and various convenient locations around the city, including the Star Ferry concourses in Kowloon and Central, all major MTR (subway) stations, and major banks such as the Hongkong and Shanghai Banking Corporation.

## TRAVELER'S CHECKS

If you want to pay with cash, your money is safest in traveler's checks, which will be replaced if lost or stolen. Traveler's checks can be readily exchanged for Hong Kong dollars at banks, hotels, and currency-exchange offices (banks provide the most favorable rates). Traveler's checks also command a slightly better exchange rate than cash. Although Thomas Cook and other agencies can issue traveler's checks in Hong Kong currency, I don't think this offers any advantage. For one thing, Hong Kong shops, restaurants, and hotels are not as willing as their U.S. counterparts to accept traveler's checks for payment. Secondly, you can use leftover traveler's checks in U.S. dollars (or your own national currency) for future trips, but leftover traveler's checks in Hong Kong dollars must either be reconverted (not financially advantageous, because you lose money with each conversion) or saved for future trips to Hong Kong. You'll need your passport to exchange traveler's checks.

## 4  When to Go

Hong Kong's peak tourist season used to be in the spring and fall, but now tourists come to Hong Kong virtually year-round. Although the drop in tourism in recent years has translated to empty hotel rooms, it's always best to make hotel reservations in advance, particularly if you're arriving during the Chinese New Year or one of the festivals described below. In addition, major conventions and trade fairs can also tie up the city's best hotels.

## CLIMATE

Because of its subtropical location, Hong Kong's weather is generally mild in winter and uncomfortably hot and humid in summer, with an average annual rainfall of 89 inches. The most pleasant time of year is late September to early December, when skies are clear and sunny, temperatures are in the 70s, and the humidity drops to 70%. January and February are the coldest months, with temperatures often in the 50s, but it's still a pleasant time of year. You'll want a jacket during this time. In spring (March to May), the temperature can range between 60°F and 80°F and the humidity rises to about 84%, with fog and rain fairly common. That means there may not be much of a view from the cloud-enveloped Victoria Peak. By May, it can also be quite hot and muggy.

By summer, temperatures are often in the 90s, humidity can be 90% or more, and there's little or no relief even at night. If you're visiting Hong Kong this time of year, you'd be prudent to carry a hat, sunblock, sunglasses, and plenty of bottled water with you wherever you go. You'll also want an umbrella. This is when Hong Kong receives the most rain; it's also typhoon season. However, Hong Kong has a very good warning system, so there's no need to worry about the dangers of a tropical storm. The worst that can happen is that you may have to stay in your hotel room for a day or more, or that your plane may be delayed or diverted. It has never happened to me, but it did happen to a friend of mine (she was glad she was staying at the Regent instead of Chungking Mansion, since she was confined to her hotel for an entire weekend).

**Hong Kong's Average Monthly Temperatures and Days of Rain**

|  | Jan | Feb | Mar | Apr | May | June | July | Aug | Sept | Oct | Nov | Dec |
|---|---|---|---|---|---|---|---|---|---|---|---|---|
| Temp. (C°) | 15 | 15 | 18 | 22 | 25 | 27 | 29 | 29 | 27 | 25 | 21 | 18 |
| Temp. (F°) | 59 | 59 | 64 | 72 | 77 | 80 | 84 | 84 | 80 | 77 | 70 | 64 |
| Days of Rain | 5.6 | 8.9 | 10.1 | 11.1 | 14.9 | 14.2 | 17.5 | 17.3 | 14.4 | 8.6 | 5.9 | 3.9 |

## HOLIDAYS

Hong Kong has 17 public holidays a year, including some of the festivals described below. The majority are Chinese and are therefore celebrated according to the lunar calendar, with different dates each year. Since most shops, restaurants, and attractions remain open except during the Chinese New Year, the holidays should not cause any inconvenience to visitors. Banks, however, are closed.

**Public holidays for 2001 and 2002** are: New Year's Day (Jan 1), Lunar New Year (Jan 24–26, 2001; Feb 12–14, 2002), Easter (Good Friday, Saturday, Easter Sunday, and Easter Monday), Ching Ming Festival (Apr 5), Labour Day (May 1), Buddha's Birthday (Apr 30, 2001; May 20, 2002), Tuen Ng Festival (Dragon Boat Festival; June 25, 2001; June 15, 2002), Establishment Day of the Special Administrative Region (Hong Kong's return to China; July 2, 2001; July 1, 2002), day following Mid-Autumn Festival (Oct 2, 2001; Sept 21, 2002), National Day (Oct 1), Chung Yeung Festival (Oct 25, 2001; Oct 14, 2002), Christmas Day (Dec 25), the first weekday after Christmas (Dec 26).

## Hong Kong Calendar of Events

If you're lucky, your trip might coincide with one of Hong Kong's colorful festivals. Because most of them follow the Chinese lunar calendar, they don't fall on the same date each year. The only time shops and offices close at festival time is during the Chinese New Year, though some in Tsim Sha Tsui remain open to cater to tourists.

Below are the most popular events, including Chinese festivals and festivals of the arts. Your best source for additional information on all of these events is the Hong Kong Tourist Association (☎ **852/2508 1234** in Hong Kong), which can provide detailed information on where events are being staged and how to get there. For several of the festivals, HKTA even offers organized tours, which is one of the best ways to secure front-row seats without battling the crowds.

## January/February

○ **Chinese New Year.** The most important Chinese holiday, this is a 3-day affair, a time for visiting friends and relatives, settling debts, doing a thorough house-cleaning, consulting fortune-tellers, and worshipping ancestors. Strips of red paper with greetings of wealth, good fortune, and longevity are pasted on doors, and families visit temples. Most shops (except those in tourist areas) close down for at least 2 or 3 days; streets and building facades are decorated with elaborate light displays; flower markets sell peach trees, chrysanthemums, and other good-luck flowers; a parade winds its way along the waterfront, usually on the first day; and a dazzling display of fireworks lights up the harbor, usually on the second day of the holiday. Since this festival is largely a family affair (much like the Christian Christmas), it holds little interest for the tourist. In fact, if you're planning a side trip into China, this would be the worst time to go, since all routes to the mainland are clogged with Hong Kong Chinese returning home to visit relatives. Contact the Hong Kong Tourist Association at ☎ **852/2508 1234.** Late January or early February (Jan 24–26, 2001; Feb 12–14, 2002).

• **City Festival.** An alternative arts festival featuring lively fare from local and international artists, including theater, performance art, dance, music, and art exhibitions, held at various venues throughout Hong Kong. Contact the Fringe Theater at ☎ **852/2521 7251.** The month of January.

## February/March

○ **Hong Kong Arts Festival.** A 3-week-long celebration with performances by world-renowned orchestras, pop and jazz ensembles, opera, dance, and theater companies (including experimental theater and Chinese operas), and with ethnic music and art exhibitions. For a schedule of events, venues, and ticket information, call ☎ **852/2824 2430** or HKTA at ☎ **852/2508 1234,** or visit the Web site www.artsfestival.org. February/March.

## March

• **Hong Kong Sevens Rugby Tournament,** Hong Kong Stadium. Known as "The Sevens," this is one of Hong Kong's most popular and one of Asia's largest sporting events, with more than 20 teams from around the world competing for the Cup Championship. Contact the Hong Kong Rugby Football Union at ☎ **852/2504 8311** or www.hksevens.com.hk. Last weekend in March.

## April

• **Ching Ming Festival,** all Chinese cemeteries (especially in Aberdeen, Happy Valley, Chai Wan, and Cheung Chau Island). A Confucian festival to honor the dead, observed by sweeping ancestral graves, burning incense, offering food and flowers, and picnicking among the graves. Contact HKTA at ☎ **852/2508 1234.** Fourth or fifth day of the Third Moon, March/April.

○ **Tin Hau Festival,** all Tin Hau temples, especially in Joss House Bay and Yuen Long. One of Hong Kong's most colorful festivals, this celebrates the birth of Tin Hau, goddess of the sea and Hong Kong's most popular deity among fishing folk. The celebration stems from a 12th-century legend of a young girl who is believed to have saved her two brothers from drowning during a terrible storm. To pay her tribute, fishing boats are decorated with colorful flags, there are parades and lion dances, and family shrines are carried to shore to be blessed by Taoist priests. Contact HKTA, which organizes special tours of the events, at ☎ **852/ 2508 1234.** Twenty-third day of the Third Moon (usually Apr; Apr 16, 2001).

• **Hong Kong International Film Festival,** Hong Kong Arts Centre, Hong Kong Cultural Centre, City Hall, and other venues around town. More than 200 films from more than 40 countries are featured at this 2-week event, including new releases, documentaries, and archival films. Tickets cost HK$55 ($7.15). For more information, call ☎ 852/2734 2903 or 2734 9009 or check www. hkiff.com.hk. Two weeks in mid-April.

### April/May

☼ **Cheung Chau Bun Festival,** Pak Tai Temple, Cheung Chau Island. Unique to Hong Kong, this weeklong affair is thought to appease restless ghosts and spirits. Originally held to placate the unfortunate souls of those murdered by pirates, it features a street parade of lions and dragons and Chinese opera, as well as floats with children seemingly suspended in the air, held up by cleverly concealed wires. The end of the festival is heralded by three bun-covered scaffolds erected in front of the Pak Tai Temple. These buns supposedly bring good luck to those who receive them. HKTA organizes tours of the parade; call ☎ 852/2508 1234. Usually late April or early May, but the exact date is chosen by divination (check with the HKTA).

• **Buddha's Birthday,** Buddhist temples throughout Hong Kong. Worshippers flock to pay respect to Siddhartha Sakyamuni, founder of Buddhism, and to bathe Buddha statues. The Po Lin Monastery on Lantau Island is one of the most popular destinations on this day. Contact the HKTA at ☎ 852/2508 1234. Ninth day of the Fourth Moon (Apr 30, 2001; May 20, 2002).

### May/June

☼ **Dragon Boat Races** (Tuen Ng Festival). Races of long, narrow boats, gaily painted and powered by oarsmen who row to the beat of drums. It originated in ancient China, where legend held that an imperial adviser drowned himself in a Hunan river to protest government corruption. His faithful followers, wishing to recover his body, supposedly raced out into the river in boats, beating their paddles on the surface of the water and throwing rice to distract sea creatures from his body. There are two different races: The biggest is an international competition with approximately 30 teams, held along the waterfront in Tsim Sha Tsui East; the following weekend approximately 500 local Hong Kong teams compete, with races held at Stanley, Aberdeen, Chai Wan, Yau Ma Tei, Tai Po, and outlying islands. Contact HKTA at ☎ 852/2508 1234. Fifth day of the Fifth Moon (June 25, 2001; June 15, 2002) for international races; local races the following weekend.

### August

• **Yue Lan Festival (Festival of the Hungry Ghosts).** Released from the underworld, ghosts are believed to roam the earth for one lunar month each year. Religious ceremonies, street performances, and offerings of food and paper replicas of life's necessities are burned to appease the spirits of discontented ghosts (those who were murdered, died without proper funeral rites, or are without descendants to care for them), in an attempt to prevent the unhappy souls from seeking vengeance on humans. Contact HKTA for various venues (popular venues are King George V Memorial Park in Kowloon and Moreton Terrace Playground in Causeway Bay) at ☎ 852/2508 1234. Fourteenth day of the Seventh Moon (usually the end of Aug/Sept; Sept 2, 2001).

### September/October

☼ **Mid-Autumn Festival,** Victoria Park, Kowloon Park, and Victoria Peak. Held in early autumn, this major festival (sometimes referred to as the Moon Festival) celebrates the harvest and the brightest moon of the year. In honor of the event, local people light lanterns in the shapes of fish, flowers, and even ships and planes, gaze at the moon, and eat mooncakes (sweet rolls with sesame seeds, duck eggs, and ground lotus seeds). The mooncakes commemorate the 14th-century uprising against the Mongols, when written messages calling for the revolt were concealed in cakes smuggled to the rebels. Today the Urban Council organizes lantern carnivals in parks on both Hong Kong Island and Kowloon, where you can join the Chinese for strolls among hundreds of lanterns, making this one of Hong Kong's most charming and picturesque festivals. Contact HKTA at ☎ **852/2807 6177.** Fifteenth day of the Eighth Moon (Oct 1, 2001).

- **Chung Yueng Festival,** all Chinese cemeteries. The second time of year when ancestral graves are swept and offerings are made. Ninth day of the Ninth Moon (Oct 25, 2001).

# 5  Health & Insurance

## STAYING HEALTHY

No shots or inoculations are required for entry to Hong Kong from the United States, but you will need proof of a vaccination against cholera if you have been in an infected area during the 14 days preceding your arrival. Check with your travel agent or call the Hong Kong Tourist Authority if you are traveling through Asia before reaching Hong Kong.

If you're traveling during the hot and humid summer months, limit your exposure to the sun, especially during the first few days of your trip and particularly from 11am to 2pm. Use a sunscreen with a high protection factor and apply it liberally. To avoid dehydration, you should also carry a water bottle, especially when hiking.

Generally, you're safe eating anywhere in Hong Kong, even at roadside food stalls. Stay clear of local oysters and shellfish, however, and remember that many restaurants outside the major hotels and tourist areas use MSG in their dishes as a matter of course. See "A Taste of Hong Kong" in the appendix for more information.

Prescriptions can be filled at Hong Kong pharmacies only if they're issued by a local doctor. To avoid hassle, be sure to bring more of your prescriptions than you think you'll need, clearly labeled in their original packages; pack prescription medications in your carry-on luggage. Over-the-counter items are easy to obtain, though name brands may be different from those back home, and some ingredients allowed elsewhere may be forbidden in Hong Kong (and vice versa).

If you get sick, you may want to contact the concierge at your hotel—some upper-range hotels have in-house doctors or clinics. Otherwise, the U.S. embassy in Hong Kong can provide a list of area doctors who speak English. You can also contact the **International Association for Medical Assistance to Travelers (IAMAT)** (☎ **716/754-4883** or 416/652-0137; www.sentex.net/~iamat), an organization that lists many local English-speaking doctors. Otherwise, if you can't find a doctor who can help you right away, try the emergency room at the local hospital. Many emergency rooms have walk-in-clinics for cases that are not life-threatening.

## INSURANCE

There are three kinds of travel insurance: trip cancellation, medical, and lost-luggage coverage. Trip-cancellation insurance is a good idea if you have paid a large portion of your vacation expenses up front. The other two types of insurance, however, don't make sense for most travelers. Rule number one: Check your existing policies before you buy any additional coverage. In the case of medical insurance, your existing health plan may provide all the coverage you need; just be sure to carry your identification card in your wallet. And your homeowner's insurance, for example, should cover stolen luggage. However, airlines are responsible for only $1,250 on domestic flights if they lose your luggage and even less on international flights; keep valuable items it in your carry-on bag. You should also ask your homeowner's insurance whether your camera or video equipment is insured everywhere in the world. If you are not adequately covered, you may wish to purchase an extra policy to cover losses.

## 6　Tips for Travelers with Special Needs

### FOR TRAVELERS WITH DISABILITIES

Hong Kong can be a nightmare for travelers with disabilities. City sidewalks—especially in Central and Kowloon—can be so jam-packed that getting around on crutches or in a wheelchair is exceedingly difficult. Moreover, to cross busy thoroughfares, it's often necessary to climb stairs to a pedestrian bridge or use an underground tunnel. Also, most shops are a step or two up from the street, due to flooding during rainstorms.

However, a disability shouldn't stop anyone from traveling. There are more resources out there than ever before. You can join **The Society for the Advancement of Travel for the Handicapped (SATH),** 347 Fifth Ave., Suite 610, New York, NY 10016 (☎ **212/447-7284;** fax 212/725-8253; www.sath.org) for $45 annually, $30 for seniors and students, to gain access to its vast network of connections in the travel industry. The society provides information sheets on travel destinations and referrals to tour operators that specialize in traveling with disabilities. Its quarterly magazine, *Open World for Disability and Mature Travel,* is full of good information and resources. A year's subscription is $13 ($21 outside the U.S.).

In addition, if you are in a wheelchair, contact the Hong Kong Tourist Association for a free booklet called "Hong Kong Access Guide for Disabled Visitors." It provides information on more than 200 sites, including hotels, banks, cultural centers, museums, temples, and restaurants, with brief descriptions of accessibility in parking, how many steps there are at the entrance or whether there's a ramp, whether toilets are equipped for the handicapped, and more.

As for transportation, taxis are probably the most convenient mode of transportation, especially since they can load and unload passengers with disabilities in restricted zones under certain conditions and do not charge extra for carrying wheelchairs and crutches. Otherwise, the MTR (subway) has wheelchair access (elevators, ramps, or other aids) at 19 stations, as well as tactile pathways leading to platforms and exits for the visually impaired. Ferries are accessible to wheelchair users on the lower deck. For more information, contact the **Transport Department,** Floor 41, Immigration Tower on Gloucester Road in Wan Chai, for a booklet called "A Guide to Public Transport Services in Hong Kong for Disabled Persons."

### FOR GAYS & LESBIANS

There are only a handful of openly gay establishments in Hong Kong—the gay community is not a vocal one, and information in English is hard to come by. The **International Gay & Lesbian Travel Association (IGLTA)** (☎ **800/448-8550** or 954/776-2626; fax 954/776-3303; www.iglta.org), which has around 1,200 members, links travelers with the appropriate gay-friendly service organization or tour specialist. It offers quarterly newsletters, marketing mailings, and a membership directory that's updated quarterly. Membership often includes gay or lesbian businesses but is open to individuals for $150 yearly, plus a $100 administration fee for new members. Members are kept informed of gay and gay-friendly hoteliers, tour operators, and airline and cruise-line representatives. Contact the IGLTA for a list of its member agencies.

General gay and lesbian travel agencies include **Family Abroad** (☎ 800/ 999-5500 or 212/459-1800; gay and lesbian) and **Above and Beyond Tours** (☎ 800/397-2681; mainly gay men).

## FOR SENIORS

For the longest time seniors were given no discounts for sightseeing in Hong Kong. Yet those over 56 years of age account for more than 10% of Hong Kong's total visitor arrivals; these percentages are even higher for North American visitors, with seniors making up more than 20% of the visitor total. Hong Kong finally acknowledged this increasingly important segment of the tourism industry with half-price or free admission to most museums for those over 60. In addition, seniors can ride the cross-harbor ferry free of charge and receive reduced fares for ferries to the outlying islands, the trams (including the Peak Tram), and the subway system. Some discounts are available to seniors older than 60; others for seniors older than 65. In any case, seniors should carry identification for proof of age and should keep in mind that there are many stairs to climb in Hong Kong, including overhead pedestrian bridges and to subway stations. In addition, remember that it is *very* hot and humid in summer.

Before leaving home, consider becoming a member of the **American Association of Retired Persons (AARP),** 601 E St. NW, Washington, DC 20049 (☎ 800/ 424-3410 or 202/434-2277), which brings such benefits as *Modern Maturity* magazine and a monthly newsletter and discounts on airfares. The **National Council of Senior Citizens,** 8403 Colesville Rd., Suite 1200, Silver Spring, MD 20910 (☎ 301/ 578-8800), a nonprofit organization, offers a newsletter six times a year (partly devoted to travel tips); annual dues are $13 per person or couple.

If you want something more than the average vacation or guided tour, try **Elderhostel,** 75 Federal St., Boston, MA 02110-1941 (☎ 877/426-8056; www.elderhostel.org), or the University of New Hampshire's **Interhostel** (☎ 800/733-9753), both variations on the same theme: educational travel for senior citizens. On these escorted tours, the days are packed with seminars, lectures, and field trips, and the sightseeing is all led by academic experts. Elderhostel arranges study programs for those aged 55 and over (and a spouse or companion of any age) in the United States and around the world. Most courses last about 3 weeks and many include airfare, accommodations in student dormitories or modest inns, meals, and tuition. Write or call for a free catalog, which lists upcoming courses and destinations. Interhostel takes travelers 50 and over (with companions over 40), and offers 2- and 3-week trips, mostly international. The courses in both these programs are ungraded, involve no homework, and often focus on the liberal arts. They're not luxury vacations, but they're fun and fulfilling.

## FOR FAMILIES

Hong Kong is a great place for older kids, because so many of the attractions are geared for them and offer discounts for children, sometimes as much as 50%. In addition, public transportation is half price for children. As for very young children, keep in mind that there are many stairs to climb, particularly in Central with its elevated walkways, and at subway stations. Also, young children may not be welcome at the finer restaurants.

As for hotels, many allow children under a certain age (usually 12 but sometimes up to 18) to stay free of charge in their parents' room. Generally, only one child is allowed, or there's a maximum limit of three persons per room, and there's no extra charge only when no extra bed is required. Baby cots are usually available free of charge, and most hotels also offer baby-sitting. Refer to chapter 4, "Where to Stay," for individual listings of hotels that allow children free of charge and provide baby-sitting, as well as the section on "Family-Friendly Hotels."

## FOR STUDENTS

Students receive a slight discount to most museums in Hong Kong, but major attractions like Ocean Park do not offer discounts.

The best resource for students is the **Council on International Educational Exchange,** or CIEE (www.ciee.org). It can set you up with an ID card, and its travel branch, Council Travel Service (☎ **800/226-8624;** www.counciltravel.com), is the biggest student travel agency operation in the world, offering discounts on plane tickets and the like. From CIEE you can also obtain the student traveler's best friend, the $18 International Student Identity Card (ISIC). It's the only officially acceptable form of student identification, good for discounts to museums and attractions around the world. It also provides you with basic health and life insurance and a 24-hour help line. If you're no longer a student but are still under 26, you can get a GO 25 card from the same people, which will get you the insurance and some of the discounts (but not student admission prices in museums).

In Canada, **Travel CUTS,** 200 Ronson St., Ste. 320, Toronto, ONT M9W 5Z9 (☎ **800/667-2887** or 416/614-2887; www.travelcuts.com), offers similar services. **Campus Travel,** 52 Grosvenor Gardens, London SW1W 0AG (☎ **0171/730-3402;** www.campustravel.co.uk), opposite Victoria Station, is Britain's leading specialist in student and youth travel.

In Hong Kong, **Sincerity Travel,** operated by Hong Kong Student Travel Ltd., can help with visas and trips to China and cheap flights to other destinations. Even if you're not a student, you can still take advantage of some of the travel bureau's services. Among the half dozen or so offices spread throughout Hong Kong, one is especially convenient, on the 8th floor of the east wing (Room 835a) of Star House in Tsim Sha Tsui, next to the Star Ferry concourse (☎ **852/2730 3269**), open Monday through Friday from 9:30am to 7:30pm and Saturday from 9:30am to 6:30pm.

## FOR SINGLES

You shouldn't have any problems as a single traveler to Hong Kong. Almost every time I've come here, I traveled alone. The biggest problem is one of expense, since many hotels charge the same for both double and single occupancy. The other problem is with Chinese food—it's best when enjoyed with a group. Try fixed-price meals or all-you-can-eat buffets when dining alone, or join one of the organized tours where meals are often included.

An alternative is to register with **Travel Companion** (☎ **516/454-0880**), one of the nation's oldest roommate finders for single travelers, where you can find a trustworthy travel mate who will split the cost of the room with you and be around as little, or as often, as you like during the day.

Female travelers may also want to check out www.Journeywoman.com, an Internet-based magazine dedicated to travel for women, with a special section called "GIRLTALK Hong Kong," which carries tips on accommodations, restaurants, shopping, things to do, what to wear, and details of venues where solo female travelers will feel at home, submitted by women who have traveled to Hong Kong.

## 7 Getting There

With more than 40 airlines and half a dozen cruise lines serving Hong Kong from around the world, it's certainly not difficult to get there. Your itinerary, the amount of time you have, and your pocketbook will probably dictate how you travel. Below are some pointers to get you headed in the right direction.

## BY PLANE

Since the flying time to Hong Kong is about 14½ hours from Los Angeles, 16 hours from Chicago, and 20 hours from New York, you'll want to consider onboard services and even mileage programs (you'll earn lots of miles on this round-trip!) as well as ticket price when choosing your carrier.

**THE MAJOR AIRLINES**   Airlines that fly nonstop between North America and Hong Kong include **Canadian Airlines International** (☎ 800/426-7000), with daily flights from Vancouver; **Cathay Pacific Airways** (☎ 800/233-2742), with daily service from Los Angeles, Vancouver, and Toronto; **Singapore Airlines** (☎ 800/742-3333), with daily service from San Francisco; and **United Airlines** (☎ 800/241-6522; www.ual.com), with daily service from San Francisco, Los Angeles, and Chicago. Other airlines flying between North America and Hong Kong with stops en route include **Northwest Airlines** (☎ 800/225-2525), **Japan Airlines** (☎ 800/525-3663), **Korean Air** (☎ 800/438-5000), and **Philippine Airlines** (☎ 800/435-9725). Contact your travel agent or specific carriers for current information.

Of all the carriers, my first choice is Hong Kong's own Cathay Pacific Airways, one of Asia's premier airlines. It offers the most frequent nonstop service between North America and Hong Kong, with flights departing daily from Los Angeles and Vancouver (twice daily), and daily from Toronto, as well as direct flights daily from New York (with a stop in Vancouver). It was the first airline to install a personal TV into every economy-class seat in the fleet.

From the United Kingdom, Cathay Pacific (☎ 171/747 8888), **British Airways** (☎ 0845/773 3377), and **Virgin Atlantic Airways** (☎ 01293/747747) offer daily nonstop service from London to Hong Kong. From Australia, both Cathay Pacific (☎ 131747) and **Qantas** (☎ 131313) offer daily nonstop service from Sydney and Melbourne. From New Zealand, Cathay Pacific (☎ 0508/800454) offers daily nonstop service from Auckland.

See the box "Cyber Deals for Net Surfers" (later in this chapter) for Web sites and more information.

**AIRFARES**   Regardless of how you buy your ticket, there are certain regulations you should know about airfare pricing. While first-class, business-class, and regular economy fares (those with no restrictions) are the same year-round to Hong Kong, the cheapest fares (including Advance Purchase Excursion fares, described below) usually vary according to the season. The most expensive time to go is during the peak season (June through August) and the last couple of weeks in December. The lowest fares are available mid-January through March. Fares in between these two extremes, known as the shoulder season, are available in April and May and again from September to mid-January. To complicate matters, each season also has different rates for both weekday and weekend flights. There are also special promotional fares.

Listed below are some of the fare options from Los Angeles to Hong Kong aboard Cathay Pacific at the time of this writing. Be sure to contact the airlines or your travel agent for an update on prices once you've decided on your exact travel plans.

**Business & First Class**   Because the flight to Hong Kong is such a long one, comfort is a big consideration if you want to arrive at your destination in top form. Most carriers offer a separate **business class,** complete with separate check-in counters at the airport, a separate lounge at Hong Kong's international airport, pre-flight drinks, and more comfortable seating than in economy class. Amenities vary from carrier to carrier, but Cathay Pacific's business class, for example, offers a 50-inch seat pitch on long hauls and comfortable seating that can be adjusted to suit passengers of different heights and builds through such improvements as two footrests, a "winged headrest" to support the neck, and a lumbar airbag that can be inflated or deflated for lower-back comfort. In addition, a personal TV installed in the armrest provides eight channels of entertainment, including a choice of first-run movies and TV shows. Meals of both Asian and Western cuisine, served from trolleys where passengers can see the food before choosing, allow choices of four main courses and two desserts, as well as a cheese board. One cabin attendant for every nine passengers assures a high level of personal attention. Cathay Pacific's business-class round-trip fares from Los Angeles to Hong Kong range from $3,972 for tickets with some restrictions to $4,816 for unrestricted fares.

All airlines provide extra luxuries for their **first-class** passengers. Cathay Pacific's royal treatment, for example, begins as soon as you step up to its first-class check-in counter, where specially trained staff members are on hand to offer personal assistance and customers receive priority baggage clearance. At major gateways, first-class passengers are also treated to an exclusive first-class lounge, with free alcoholic drinks, coffee, and soda; at Hong Kong's new international airport, Cathay Pacific's first-class lounge is the largest in the world, complete with an extensive buffet with snacks and drinks, a business service center and Internet facilities, a relaxation area with sleeper sofas and electronic massage chairs, showers, and wash rooms. Onboard, passengers benefit from upgraded services, including electronically controlled seats upholstered in damask with a 62- to 74-inch seat pitch and individual video units offering a choice of in-flight entertainment, with up to 22 different first-run movies available each month. Meals are served at times chosen by each passenger, and, according to individual preference, range from full, five-course meals to light refreshments. Lead-free crystal, bone china, Asian lacquerware, silver-plated cutlery, and fine Irish linens round out the dining experience. As we went to press, Cathay's first-class round-trip fare from Los Angeles to Hong Kong was $8,646.

**Economy Class & Advance-Purchase Excursion Fares (APEX)** The key to obtaining the best prices at the dates you wish to travel is to book early. More specifically, you can cut the cost of your flight to Hong Kong by purchasing your ticket in advance, allowing some flexibility on the days you travel, and complying with certain restrictions. These are known as **APEX** (Advance Purchase Excursion) fares, and the restrictions may vary with the airline but usually require an advance purchase, require minimum and/or maximum stays, and are nonrefundable. Cathay Pacific's APEX fare, for example, requires that you purchase your ticket at least 7 days before departure and stay in Hong Kong no longer than 6 months. In addition, rates vary according to the season, with weekend flights costing more than weekday flights. At press time, Cathay Pacific's round-trip fares from Los Angeles to Hong Kong ranged from $1,313 on a weekend in the summer to $823 on a weekday in winter.

A more flexible (but more expensive) option is the **regular economy fare,** which carries no minimum stay and allows changes in travel dates. Regular round-trip economy fares—those with no restrictions—are $2,374 from Los Angeles to Hong Kong.

**FINDING THE BEST AIRFARES** Passengers within the same airplane cabin are rarely paying the same fare for their seats. You'll save money by purchasing your ticket in advance, and flying on a weekday. Here are a few other easy ways to save.

- Check newspapers or call airlines for promotional fares. Periodically airlines lower prices on their most popular routes. Check the travel section of major newspapers (especially those on the West Coast such as the *Los Angeles Times*), since they often carry advertisements for low fares. Call the airlines directly to ask whether any promotional rates or special fares are available. If your schedule is flexible, ask if you can secure a cheaper fare by staying an extra day or by flying midweek. (Many airlines won't volunteer this information.) If you already hold a ticket when a sale breaks, it may even pay to exchange your ticket, which usually incurs a $50 to $75 charge. Note, however, that the lowest-priced fares are often nonrefundable, require a 21-day advance purchase, and carry penalties for changing dates of travel.

- Look for discount fares. Some companies provide deeply discounted tickets—sometimes savings of more than 50% on economy fares and around 30% on APEX fares—with no restrictions, depending on availability. You can buy your ticket through them well in advance or, if you're lucky, at the last moment. Among the firms that deal with travel to Hong Kong (usually with a stop in Tokyo) are **Nippon Travel,** 5028 Wisconsin Ave. NW, Suite 403, Washington, DC 20016 (☎ **202/362-0039**); **Japan Associates Travel,** 2000 17th St. NW, Washington, DC 20009 (☎ **202/939-8853**); and **Euro-Asia Express** of Millbrae, California (☎ **800/878-8538** or 415/692-4892).

- **Consolidators,** also known as bucket shops, are a good place to find low fares. Consolidators buy seats in bulk from the airlines and then sell them back to the public at prices below even the airlines' discounted rates. Their small boxed ads usually run in the Sunday travel section of your newspaper at the bottom of the page. Before you pay, however, ask for a confirmation number from the consolidator and then call the airline itself to confirm your seat. Book your ticket with a different consolidator—there are many to choose from—if the airline can't confirm your reservation. Also be aware that bucket shop tickets are usually non-refundable or rigged with stiff cancellation penalties, often as high as 50%–75% of the ticket price. **Council Travel** (☎ **800/226-8624;** www.counciltravel.com) caters especially to young travelers, but their bargain basement prices are available to people of all ages. Other reliable consolidators include **1-800-FLY-CHEAP** (www. 1800flycheap.com) and **TFI Tours International** (☎ **800/745-8000** or 212/736-1140), which serves as a clearinghouse for unused seats.

## BY TRAIN

It's unlikely that you'll arrive in Hong Kong by train, unless of course you've been traveling the length of China. Such travel became easier with the completion of the Beijing-Kowloon Railway, providing a direct link between the two cities in approximately 28 hours and costing HK$1,191 ($155) for a bed in a deluxe, two-bed cabin, HK$934 ($121) for a "soft bed" in a four-bed cabin, and HK$601 ($78) for a "hard bed" in a six-bed cabin, one-way. Service is also available from Shanghai in a little more than 28 hours, costing HK$530 to HK$1,039 ($68.85 to $135) one-way, and from Guangzhou (formerly Canton), costing HK$190 to HK$230 ($24.65 to $29.85) and taking approximately 2 hours.

In any case, if you're traveling to Hong Kong via train, you'll pass through Customs at Shenzhen/Lo Wu, the border station, before continuing on the KCR East Rail to the KCR Kowloon-Canton Railway Station in Hung Hom. The KCR Railway Station is practically right in the middle of the city, though you'll probably want to take a taxi to your hotel. Expect to spend about HK$30 ($3.90) for a taxi from the KCR Kowloon-Canton Railway Station to a hotel in Tsim Sha Tsui or Tsim Sha Tsui East. An alternative is to disembark the KCR at Kowloon Tong Station, changing there to the Mass Transit Railway (Hong Kong's subway system), which will take you straight to Tsim Sha Tsui or Central.

# Cyber Deals for Net Surfers

It's possible to get some great deals on airfare, hotels, and car rentals via the Internet. So go grab your mouse and start surfing before you take off—you could save a bundle on your trip. The Web sites highlighted below are worth checking out, especially since all services are free. A good place to start is **Arthur Frommer's Budget Travel Online** (www.frommers.com), where you'll find lots of up-to-the-minute information—including the latest bargains and candid articles updated daily by Arthur Frommer himself.

Now incorporating Preview Travel, **✪ Travelocity** (www.travelocity.com; www.previewtravel.com; www.frommers.travelocity.com) is Frommer's online travel planning/booking partner. Travelocity uses the SABRE system to offer reservations and tickets for more than 400 airlines, plus reservations and purchase capabilities for more than 45,000 hotels and 50 car-rental companies. An exclusive feature of this system is its **Low Fare Search Engine,** which automatically searches for the three lowest-priced itineraries based on a traveler's criteria. Last-minute deals and consolidator fares are included in the search. If you book with Travelocity, you can select specific seats for your flights with online seat maps and also view diagrams of the most popular commercial aircraft. The **hotel finder** provides street-level location maps and photos of selected hotels. With the **Fare Watcher** e-mail feature, you can select up to five routes and receive e-mail notices when the fare changes by $25 or more. Travelocity's **Destination Guide** includes updated information on some 260 destinations worldwide—supplied by Frommer's.

**Expedia** (www.expedia.com) is Travelocity's major competitor. It offers several ways of obtaining the best possible fares: **Flight Price Matcher** service allows your preferred airline to match an available fare with a competitor; a comprehensive **Fare Compare** area shows the differences in fare categories and airlines; and **Fare Calendar** helps you plan your trip around the best possible fares. Its main limitation is that like many online databases, Expedia focuses on the major airlines and hotel chains, so don't expect to find too many budget airlines or one-of-a-kind B&Bs here.

**TRIP.com** began as a site geared toward business travelers, but its innovative features and highly personalized approach have broadened its appeal to leisure travelers as well. It is the leading travel site for those using mobile devices to access Internet travel information. TRIP.com includes a trip-planning function that provides the average and lowest fare for the route requested, in addition to the current available fare. An on-site **newsstand** features breaking news on airfare

## ORGANIZED TOURS

**ESCORTED TOURS**    If you're the kind of traveler who doesn't like leaving such arrangements as accommodations, transportation, and itinerary to chance, you may wish to join an escorted tour that includes Hong Kong. Among the many companies offering group tours are **Pacific Bestour,** 228 Rivervale Rd., Rivervale, NJ 07675 (☎ **800/688-3288** or 201/664-8778; www.bestour.com); and **TBI Tours,** 53 Summer St., Keene, NH 03431 (☎ **800/223-0266** or 603/357-5033; www.generaltours.com).

Luxury cruise liners are also a common sight in Hong Kong's harbor, anchored conveniently right next to the territory's largest shopping mall at Ocean Terminal on the sales and other travel specials. Among its most popular features are **Flight TRACKER** and **intelliTRIP.** Flight TRACKER allows users to track any commercial flight en route to its destination anywhere in the United States, while accessing real-time FAA-based flight monitoring data. intelliTRIP is a travel search tool that allows users to identify the best airline, hotel, and rental-car rates in less than 90 seconds. In addition, the site offers e-mail notification of flight delays, plus city resource guides, currency converters, and a weekly e-mail newsletter of fare updates, travel tips, and traveler forums.

**Yahoo!** (www.travel.yahoo.com) is currently the most popular of the Internet information portals, and its travel site is a comprehensive mix of online booking, daily travel news, and destination information. The **Best Fares** area offers what it promises, plus provides feedback on refining your search if you have flexibility in travel dates or times. There is also an active section of **message boards** for discussions on travel in general and specific destinations.

Here's a partial list of airlines and their Web sites, where you can not only get on the e-mailing lists, but also book flights directly:

- British Airways: **www.britishairways.com**
- Canadian Air International: **www.cdnair.ca**
- Cathay Pacific Airways: **www.cathaypacific.com**
- Japan Airlines: **japanair.com**
- Korean Airlines: **koreanair.com**
- Northwest Airlines: **www.nwa.com**
- Qantas Airways: **www.qantas.com.au**
- Singapore Airlines: **singaporeair.com**
- United Airlines: **www.united.com**
- Virgin Airways: **www.virgin.com**

One caveat: You'll get frequent-flier miles if you purchase one of these fares, but you can't use miles to buy the ticket.

**Smarter Living (www.smarterliving.com)**   If the thought of all that surfing and comparison shopping gives you a headache, then head right for Smarter Living. Sign up for its newsletter service, and every week you'll get a customized e-mail summarizing the discount fares available from your departure city. Smarter Living tracks more than 15 different airlines, so it's a worthwhile time-saver.

Kowloon side. Information on package tours and cruises can be obtained from your travel agent.

**PACKAGE TOURS**   Package tours are not the same thing as escorted tours. They are simply a way to buy airfare and accommodations at the same time. For destinations like Hong Kong, they are a smart way to go, because they save you a lot of money. That's because packages are sold in bulk to tour operators—who resell them to the public at a cost that drastically undercuts standard rates.

Packages, however, vary widely. Some offer a better class of hotels than others, while others offer the same hotels for lower prices or a range of hotel choices at different prices. Some offer flights on scheduled airlines, while others book charters. In some

# Tips for Flying in Comfort

A major consideration for visitors flying to Hong Kong, especially on long flights from North America, is jet lag. To minimize its adverse effects—primarily fatigue and slow adjustment to your new time zone—avoid drinking carbonated drinks, coffee, or alcohol during the flight. In addition, eat light meals high in vegetable and cereal content the day before, during, and the day after your flight, and drink plenty of water to prevent dehydration. Exercise during the flight by walking around the cabin and by flexing your arms, hands, legs, and feet. It also helps to set your watch (and your mental clock) to the time zone of your destination as soon as you board the plane.

Once you reach your destination, schedule your day according to your new time zone. Put in a normal day, even if you're tired. Go for a walk in the sunlight, and once in your hotel, turn on the lights as brightly as you can until it's time to go to bed in the evening. If you follow these instructions, your body should be back to normal within a couple of days.

Also note the following:

- You'll find the most legroom in a bulkhead seat, in the front row of each airplane cabin. However, you will have to store your luggage in the overhead bin, and you won't have the best seat in the house for the in-flight movie.

- When you check in, ask for one of the emergency-exit-row seats, which also have extra legroom. They are assigned at the airport, usually on a first-come, first-serve basis. In the unlikely event of an emergency, however, you'll be expected to open the emergency-exit door and help direct traffic.

- Ask for a seat toward the front of the plane so you'll be one of the first to disembark. If, however, you are traveling with a large carry-on, ask for a seat toward the back, so that you can be assured of boarding first and finding space in the overhead bin.

- Pack some toiletries for long flights. Airplane cabins are notoriously dry places. If you wear contact lenses, take them out before you get onboard and wear glasses instead. Sleep with a moist washcloth over your face, and take a travel-size bottle of moisturizer or lotion to refresh your face and hands as well as a toothbrush.

- If you're flying with a cold or chronic sinus problems, use a decongestant 10 minutes before ascent and descent, to minimize pressure buildup in the inner ear.

- If you're flying with kids, don't forget a deck of cards, toys and games, as well as pacifiers or chewing gum to help them relieve ear pressure buildup during ascent and descent. Most airlines provide amenities and services for children. Northwest, for example, provides bassinets (reserve in advance), warms baby bottles, and stocks baby food on all international flights.

packages, your choice of accommodations and travel days may be limited. Some packages let you choose between escorted vacations and independent vacations; others will allow you to add on just a few side trips or escorted day trips (also at lower prices than you could find on your own) without booking an entirely escorted tour.

The best place to start your search is the travel section of your local Sunday newspaper. Also check the ads in the back of national travel magazines like *Travel & Leisure,*

*National Geographic Traveler,* and *Condé Nast Traveler.* Pacific Bestour (see "Escorted Tours," above) offers combination flight/hotel packages. Another good resource is the airlines themselves, which often package their flights together with accommodations. **Northwest World Vacations** (☎ 800/800-1504) offers flight-and-hotel packages to Hong Kong that allow you to choose from a range of accommodations and provides options for additional nights as well as sightseeing tours. In addition, posted on Northwest's Web site every Wednesday is its Cyber Saver Bargain Alerts, offering special hotel rates, package deals, and discounted airline fares.

# 3

# Getting to Know Hong Kong

Hong Kong is an easy city to get to know—surprisingly compact, with streets clearly marked in English. Not only is public transportation well organized and a breeze to use, but also the Star Ferry and the trams are themselves sightseeing attractions. In general, however, walking is the best way to go, particularly in the narrow, fascinating lanes and alleys where vehicles can't go. This chapter describes the layout of the city, explains how best to get around it, gives practical advice, and tells you where to turn for additional information.

## 1 Orientation

### ARRIVING

No one who ever flew into Hong Kong's Kai Tak Airport in the past could ever quite forget the experience of landing in one of the world's most densely populated cities. The runway extended out into the bay, past apartments so close you could almost reach out and touch the laundry fluttering from the bamboo poles.

But Kai Tak, which ranked as the world's third busiest in 1996, was retired in 1998. Taking its place is the new **Hong Kong International Airport** (☎ **852/2181 0000**), four times the size of Kai Tak. Situated just north of Lantau island on Chek Lap Kok island and reclaimed land, about 20 miles from Hong Kong's central business district, the new, state-of-the-art airport is one of the world's most user-friendly. Two runways operate 24 hours a day; a shuttle train, moving walkways, and 124 immigration desks keep people flowing efficiently; and a baggage-handling system delivers bags in approximately 10 minutes.

After customs, visitors find themselves in the arrivals hall. One of the first things you should do is stop by the counter of the **Hong Kong Tourist Association (HKTA),** where you can pick up a map of the city, sightseeing brochures, and a wealth of other information, as well as get directions to your hotel. It's open during peak hours, generally daily 7am to 11pm.

Also in the arrivals hall is the counter of the **Hong Kong Hotel Association,** where you can book a room in one of its 60-some member hotels free of charge; open daily 6am to midnight. Note that while they do not have information on rock-bottom establishments, they can book rooms in several low-priced lodgings and the YMCAs.

If you plan on traveling to Macau, stop by the **Macau tourist information counter,** also in the arrivals lobby at 3B; it's open daily 9am to 1pm; 1:30 to 6pm; and 6:30 to 10:30pm.

You can **exchange money** at the arrivals hall, but since the rate here is rather unfavorable, it's best to exchange only what you need to get into town—about $20 (U.S.) should be enough.

At any rate, all passenger services, including the passenger terminal, arrivals hall, and transportation into the city, is on one level, which means you never have to use a staircase or elevator.

If you need to leave luggage at the airport, there is a **luggage-storage counter** on the departure floor.

**GETTING INTO TOWN**　　The quickest, most efficient way to get to downtown Hong Kong is via the sleek **Airport Express Line** (☎ 852/2881 8888), which is straight ahead after passing customs and entering the arrivals hall. Trains run every 10 minutes between 6am and 1am and take 20 minutes to reach Kowloon Station (off Jordan Street at the old Jordan Ferry Pier and near hotels in Tsim Sha Tsui and Yau Ma Tei) and 24 minutes to reach Hong Kong Station, on Hong Kong Island in the Central District (near Exchange Square, just west of the Star Ferry terminus). Fares are HK$60 ($7.80) to Kowloon and HK$70 ($9.10) to Central; if you're planning to return to the airport via the Airport Express Line, consider purchasing the stored-value Octopus card for $150 ($19.50)—see "Getting Around," later in this chapter, for more information. From both Kowloon and Hong Kong stations, free shuttle bus service deposits passengers at major hotels, departing every 20 minutes between 6am and 11pm.

In addition to the Airport Express, there are also dedicated airport buses that connect the airport with major downtown Hong Kong areas. Easiest—but most expensive—is the **Airport Shuttle** (☎ 852/2377 0733), which provides door-to-door service between the airport and major hotels. Tickets, available at a counter in the airport arrivals hall, cost HK$120 ($15.60), with buses departing every 30 minutes. It takes about 30 to 40 minutes to reach Tsim Sha Tsui, depending on the traffic.

Slower, with more stops, are **Cityflyer Airbuses** (☎ 852/2873 0818), also with ticket counters in the arrivals hall (if you pay onboard, you must have exact fare). Most important for tourists are Airbus A21, which travels through Mong Kok, Yau Ma Tei, Jordan, and Tsim Sha Tsui on its way to the Hung Hom Kowloon-Canton Railway Station; and Airbuses A11 and A12, which travel to Hong Kong Island. Buses depart every 10 to 15 minutes, with fares costing HK$33 ($4.30) to Kowloon and HK$40 ($5.20) to Central and Causeway Bay.

The easiest way to travel from the airport, of course, is to simply jump in a taxi, which is quite cheap in Hong Kong but expensive for the long haul from the airport. Depending on traffic and your final destination, a taxi to Tsim Sha Tsui costs approximately HK$300 ($38.95), while a taxi to Central District will cost about HK$350 ($44.45). There's also an extra luggage charge of HK$5 (65¢) per piece of baggage.

**NOTES ON DEPARTING**　　Passengers flying Cathay Pacific, United, Singapore Airlines, and a handful of other airlines (hopefully others will be added soon) offer the extra benefit of allowing you to check in for your return flight at one of two satellite stations—at Hong Kong Central Station near Exchange Square and at Kowloon Station, both served by the Airport Express Line (see above). Both allow you advance check-in any time from 24 hours to 90 minutes before your flight: You'll get your boarding pass, and your bags will be transferred to the airport. There's also checkroom service, useful if your flight is later in the day and you want to do some sightseeing before heading for the airport.

You can also travel directly to the airport and go through check-in there, which takes approximately 30 minutes (it's recommended, therefore, that you board the Airport Express Line for the airport at least 2 hours before your flight). Although most tickets now include airport departure tax in their price, you may be required to pay the tax (which is HK$50/US$6.50) if yours does not. At any rate, passengers waiting for flights can browse at the Hong Kong Sky Mall, with more than 100 outlets offering merchandise and food.

## VISITOR INFORMATION

The **Hong Kong Tourist Association (HKTA)** is an excellent source for tourist information, and one of your first stops upon arrival should be at the HKTA office in the arrivals hall of the Hong Kong International Airport, open daily 7am to 11pm.

In town, there are two HKTA offices conveniently located on both sides of the harbor ready to serve you. On the Kowloon side, there's a convenient office in Tsim Sha Tsui right in the Star Ferry concourse, open daily 8am to 6pm.

On Hong Kong Island, the larger, main HKTA office is located in the Central District at 99 Queen's Rd. Central, also open daily 8am to 6pm. It's rather inconvenient, however—about a 10-minute walk west of the Star Ferry pier and Central MTR station. If you have a question about Hong Kong, you can call the **HKTA Visitor Hotline** (☎ 852/2508 1234), available daily 8am to 6pm. After hours, a telephone-answering device will take your call and a member of HKTA will contact you.

The HKTA publishes a large assortment of free, excellent literature about Hong Kong. "The Official Hong Kong Guide," published monthly, is a booklet available at HKTA offices and in the guest rooms of most upper- and medium-range hotels. It contains a lot of practical information, including a short description of Chinese foods, shopping tips, a rundown of organized sightseeing tours, an overview of Hong Kong's major attractions, and a listing of festivals, events, and exhibits being held that month.

"Traveller's Guide" is a booklet that also gives general information on sightseeing, shopping, dining, and organized tours. Another useful booklet is "The Official Dining, Entertainment & Shopping Directory," which lists addresses and telephone numbers for hundreds of restaurants, nightlife venues, and shops. "Museums & Heritage" describes Hong Kong's most important historical monuments, architectural treasures, and museums dedicated to Hong Kong's past.

You can get a free map of Hong Kong from HKTA, providing close-ups of Tsim Sha Tsui, the Central District, Wan Chai, and Causeway Bay. There are also brochures outlining each of HKTA's organized tours. In addition, invaluable leaflets are available showing the major bus routes throughout Hong Kong, including Hong Kong Island, Kowloon, and the New Territories. Finally, if you plan to visit any of the outlying islands, be sure to get the current ferry schedules at HKTA.

To find out what's going on during your stay in Hong Kong, pick up "Hong Kong Diary," a HKTA leaflet published weekly which tells what's happening in theater, music, and the arts, including concerts and special exhibitions in museums. *HK Magazine,* distributed free at restaurants, bars, and other outlets around town and aimed at a young expat readership, is a weekly that lists what's going on at the city's theaters and other venues, including plays, concerts, exhibitions, the cinema, and events in Hong Kong's alternative scene. *Where Hong Kong* and *bc* are two other free magazines published monthly with information on Hong Kong. In addition, "Hong Kong Life," published as a supplement by the *Hong Kong Standard* newspaper on Sunday, describes what's going on in Hong Kong during next the week; the *South China Morning Post* carries an entertainment section on Friday.

## CITY LAYOUT

Hong Kong is located at the southeastern tip of the People's Republic of China, some 1,240 miles south of Beijing; it lies just south of the Tropic of Cancer at about the same latitude as Mexico City, the Bahamas, and Hawaii. Most people who have never

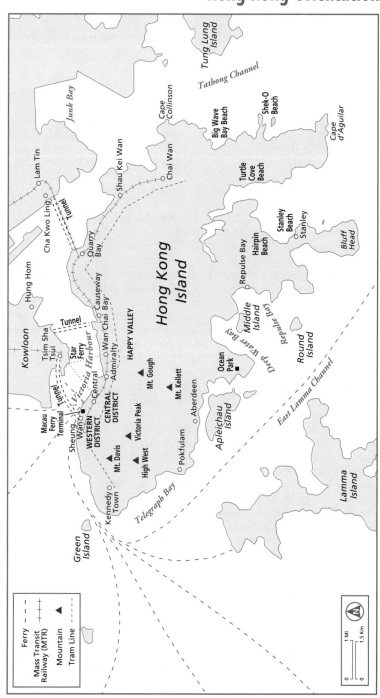

been to Asia probably think of Hong Kong as an island—and they'd be right if it were 1842. Not long after the colony was first established on Hong Kong Island, however, the British felt the need to expand, which they did by acquiring more land across Victoria Harbour on the Chinese mainland. Today Hong Kong Island is just a small part of the entire Special Administrative Region (SAR), which covers 404 square miles and measures 23½ miles north to south and 31 miles east to west—much of it mountainous.

Hong Kong can be divided into four distinct parts: Hong Kong Island, Kowloon Peninsula, New Territories, and the outlying islands. On **Hong Kong Island** are the Central District (Hong Kong's main financial and business district and usually referred to simply as Central), the Western District, Wan Chai, and Causeway Bay, all on the island's north side. On Hong Kong Island you'll also find such major attractions as Hong Kong Park, Victoria Peak, Stanley Market, Ocean Park, and the Zoological and Botanical Gardens.

Across Victoria Harbour, at the tip of **Kowloon Peninsula** is Tsim Sha Tsui and its many hotels, restaurants, museums, and shops, as well as KCR Kowloon-Canton Railway Station in Hung Hom, East Tsim Sha Tsui, and the Yau Ma Tei and Mong Kok districts.

The **New Territories** is by far the largest area, stretching north of Kowloon all the way to the Chinese border. Once a vast area of peaceful little villages, fields, and duck farms, the New Territories in the past couple of decades have witnessed a remarkable mushrooming of satellite towns with huge public-housing projects. Sha Tin, with a population approaching almost 700,000 and home of one of Hong Kong's two horse-racing tracks, is the largest; in all, the New Territories houses approximately half of the SAR's population. And yet, much of the New Territories remains open and uninhabited. Close to 70% of Hong Kong's total land mass is rural, with 23 country parks and 14 nature reserves accounting for more than 40% of Hong Kong's land area. The fact that Hong Kong is more than just a city surprises many first-time visitors.

As for Hong Kong's 260 **outlying islands,** most are barren and uninhabited; those that aren't lend themselves to excellent exploration into Hong Kong's past. Lantau, Lamma, and Cheung Chau are three of the region's best known and most easily accessible islands, where a gentler, slower, and more peaceful life prevails. Lantau, boasting the world's largest seated bronze Buddha (located at a monastery noted for its vegetarian meals), is the most popular destination. Lamma is famous for its open-air waterfront seafood restaurants, beaches, pleasant hiking trail, and expat community, while Cheung Chau makes for a pleasant half-day excursion with its lively, traditional village, boat population, and beach.

For the visitor, however, most hotels, restaurants, and points of interest are concentrated in four areas: **Tsim Sha Tsui** on the Kowloon side; and **Central District, Wan Chai,** and **Causeway Bay** on Hong Kong Island. Because these areas are so compact, the city must rank as Asia's most accessible and navigable city. I'd argue that Hong Kong is also the most stunning, given the ferries, cargo ships, fishing boats, and ocean liners bustling in Victoria Harbour, juxtaposed against many peaks that punctuate the cityscape.

**MAIN ARTERIES & STREETS**   Hong Kong Island's Central District is larger now than it was originally, thanks to massive land reclamation. **Queen's Road,** now several blocks inland, used to mark the waterfront, as did **Des Voeux Road** and **Connaught Road** in subsequent years. Today they serve as busy thoroughfares through Central, since the steep incline up Victoria Peak follows close on their heels. From the Central District, **Hennessy Road** and **Gloucester Road** lead east through Wan Chai to Causeway Bay.

It wasn't until 1972 that the first **cross-harbor tunnel** was built, connecting Causeway Bay on Hong Kong Island with Tsim Sha Tsui East in Kowloon. In 1989 a second tunnel was completed under Victoria Harbour; a third tunnel was completed in conjunction with Hong Kong's new International Airport.

On the Kowloon side, the most important artery is **Nathan Road,** which stretches north up the spine of Kowloon Peninsula and is lined with hotels and shops. **Salisbury Road** runs east and west at the tip of Tsim Sha Tsui from the Star Ferry through Tsim Sha Tsui East along the waterfront. Also on the waterfront is a promenade affording great nighttime views of neon-lit Hong Kong Island.

**FINDING AN ADDRESS**   With a good map, you should have no problem finding an address, since the system is the same as in North America. The streets are all labeled in English, and building numbers progress consecutively. For the most part, streets that run east to west (such as Des Voeux Road Central, Hennessy Road, Lockhart Road, and Salisbury Road) all have the even-numbered buildings on the north side of the street and the odd-numbered ones on the south. From Central, roads running through Wan Chai all the way west to Causeway Bay start with the lowest numbers near Central, with the highest-numbered buildings ending at Causeway Bay. On Nathan Road, Kowloon's most important thoroughfare, the lowest-numbered buildings are at the southern tip near the harbor; the numbers increase consecutively, with the evens on the east and the odds to the west.

Remember that the floors inside buildings follow the British system of numbering. What Americans would call the first floor, therefore, is called the ground floor in Hong Kong; the American second floor is numbered the first floor. In addition, if you're trying to find a specific office or factory outlet in a big building, it's useful to know that number 714 means it's on the seventh floor in Room 14, while 2312 means Room 12 on the 23rd floor.

**STREET MAPS**   You can get a free map of Hong Kong from the HKTA, which shows the major roads and streets of Tsim Sha Tsui, Yau Ma Tei, Mong Kok, the Central District, the Western District, Wan Chai, and Causeway Bay. It should be adequate for locating most hotels, restaurants, shops, and bars mentioned in this book. There are also free giveaway maps available at most hotels. If you want to explore Hong Kong in more detail, you can purchase an entire book with maps of the city region and areas in the New Territories called *Hong Kong Guidebook,* available at bookstores (see "Fast Facts" later in this chapter), but you'll probably need this only if you live here or are writing a guidebook. If you're Internet savvy, you can also view maps at www.hkta.org/map/index.html, though they aren't very detailed. At www.hkcitymap.com, however, you can search by street, building, or facility.

## Neighborhoods in Brief

### Hong Kong Island
**Central District**   This is where the story of Hong Kong all began, when a small port and community were established on the north end of the island by the British in the 1840s. Named "Victoria" in honor of the British queen, the community quickly grew into one of Asia's most important financial and business districts, with "godowns," or waterfront warehouses, lining the harbor. Today the area, known as the Central District but usually referred to simply as "Central," remains Hong Kong's nerve center for banking, business, and administration. If there is a heart of Hong Kong, it surely lies here, but there are few traces remaining of its colonial past.

The Central District boasts glass and steel high-rises representing some of Hong Kong's most innovative architecture, a couple of the city's posh hotels, expensive shopping centers filled with designer shops, office buildings, and restaurants and bars catering to Hong Kong's white-collar workers, primarily in the nightlife district known as Lan Kwai Fong. Although hotel choices in Central are limited to only a few upper-range hotels, staying here makes you feel like a resident yourself, as you rub elbows with the well-dressed professional crowd who work in Central's office buildings. Banks are so important to the Central District that their impact is highly visible—the Hongkong and Shanghai Bank, designed by British architect Norman Foster, and the Bank of China Tower, designed by I.M. Pei, are just two examples of the modern architecture that has dramatically transformed the Central District's skyline since the 1980s. Yet the neighborhood is also packed with traditional Chinese restaurants, outdoor markets, and the neon signs of family-run businesses. Rickety old trams— certainly one of Hong Kong's most endearing sights—chug their way straight through Central. There are also oases of greenery, at Chater Garden, popular with office workers for a lunchtime break, the Botanical Gardens, and Hong Kong Park with its museum of teaware, housed in Hong Kong's oldest colonial-age building.

**Lan Kwai Fong**    Named after an L-shaped street in Central, this is Hong Kong's premier nightlife and entertainment district, occupying not only Lan Kwai Fong but also neighboring streets like D'Aguilar, Wyndham, and other hillside streets. Filled with restaurants and bars in all price categories but popular mostly with people in their 20s and 30s, it's a good place to spend an evening.

**Victoria Peak**    Hong Kong's most famous mountaintop, Victoria Peak has long been Hong Kong's most exclusive address. Cooler than the steamy streets of Central below, Victoria Peak, often called simply The Peak, was the exclusive domain of the British and other Europeans—even nannies had to have the governor's permission to go there, and the only way up was by sedan carried by coolies or by hiking. Today Victoria Peak is much easier reached by the Peak Tram and affords Hong Kong's best views of Central, Victoria Harbour, and Kowloon. In fact, the view is nothing short of stunning. Also on The Peak are several attractions, some good restaurants, and multi-million-dollar mansions, glimpses of which can be had on a circular 1-hour walk around The Peak.

**Mid-Levels**    Located about halfway up Hong Kong's Victoria Peak, the Mid-Levels has long been a popular residential area, though not as posh as the villas on The Peak. Still, swank apartment buildings, grand sweeping views of Central, leafy trees and lush vegetation, and slightly cooler temperatures make it a much-sought-after address, and to serve the army of white-collar workers who commute down to Central every day, the world's longest escalator links the Mid-Levels with Central, an ambitious project with 20-some escalators and moving sidewalks.

**SoHo**    This new dining and nightlife district, flanking the Hillside Escalator Link that connects Central with the Mid-Levels, is popular with Mid-Levels residents and those seeking a quieter, saner alternative to the crowds of Lan Kwai Fong. Dubbed SoHo for the region "south of Hollywood Road," it has since blossomed into an ever-growing neighborhood of cafe-bars and intimate, small restaurants specializing in ethnic and innovative cuisine, making SoHo the most exciting addition to Hong Kong's culinary and nightlife map. Most establishments center on Elgin, Shelley, and Staunton streets.

**Western District**    Located west of the bustling Central District, the Western District is a fascinating neighborhood of Chinese shops and enterprises and is one of the oldest, most traditional areas on Hong Kong Island. Since it's one of my own personal favorites, I've spent days wandering its narrow streets and inspecting shops selling traditional herbs, ginseng, medicines, dried fish, antiques, and other Chinese products. The Western District is also famous for Hollywood Road, long popular for its many antiques and curio shops, and Man Mo Temple, one of Hong Kong's oldest temples. Unfortunately, modernization has taken its toll, and more of the old Western District seems to have vanished every time I visit, replaced by new high-rises and other projects. One of these projects is the Hillside Escalator Link, which snakes through Western as it connects the Mid-Levels with Central.

**Admiralty**   Actually part of the Central District, Admiralty is located just below Hong Kong Park, centered around an MTR subway station of the same name. It consists primarily of tall office buildings such as the Lippo Centre, the High Court Building, and Pacific Place, a classy shopping complex flanked by three deluxe hotels.

**Wan Chai**   Located east of Central, few places in Hong Kong have changed as dramatically or noticeably as Wan Chai. It became notorious after World War II for its sleazy bars, easy women, tattoo parlors, and sailors on shore leave looking for a good time. Richard Mason's 1957 novel *The World of Suzie Wong* describes this bygone era of Wan Chai; during the Vietnam War it also served as a popular destination for American servicemen on R&R. Although some of the nightlife remains, Wan Chai has slowly become respectable (and almost unrecognizable) with the addition of new, mostly business-style hotels, more high-rises, the Hong Kong Arts Centre, the Academy for Performing Arts, and the huge Hong Kong Convention and Exhibition Centre, an extension of which occupies reclaimed land and, with its curved roof and glass facade, is already a familiar sight on the Wan Chai waterfront. Wan Chai also boasts Central Plaza, Asia's second-tallest building and Hong Kong's tallest when it was completed in 1992.

**Causeway Bay**   Just east of Wan Chai, Causeway Bay is popular as a shopping destination, since shops stay open late and several department stores have branches here. The whole area was once a bay until land reclamation turned the water into soil several decades ago. Now it's a busy area of Japanese department stores; clothing, shoe, and accessory boutiques; street markets; nightclubs; and restaurants. On its eastern perimeter is the large Victoria Park.

**North Point**   Three subway stops east of Causeway Bay and served also by tram, North Point is emerging as a secondary business center, with headquarters for Kodak, IBM, American Express, and other international corporations. A few business hotels here serve visiting travelers on business and offer competitive rates, but otherwise there's little here to interest the short-term tourist.

**Happy Valley**   Once a swampland, Happy Valley's main claim to fame is its racetrack, built in 1846 and the oldest racetrack in Asia outside China.

**Aberdeen**   On the south side of Hong Kong Island, Aberdeen was once a fishing village but is now studded with high-rises and housing projects. However, it is still known for its hundreds of sampans, junks, boat people, and a couple of huge floating restaurants. Just to the east, in Deep Water Bay, is Ocean Park with its impressive aquarium, amusement rides, and a re-creation of an old Chinese village called Middle Kingdom. For more, see "Life on the Water in Aberdeen," in chapter 6.

**Stanley**   Once a fishing village, Stanley is now a lively center for discount markets selling everything from silk suits to name-brand shoes, casualwear, and souvenirs. It's located on the quiet south side of Hong Kong Island and boasts a popular public beach, a residential area popular with Chinese and foreigners alike, and, most recently, a growing number of trendy restaurants.

## Kowloon Peninsula

**Kowloon**   North of Hong Kong Island, across Victoria Harbour, is the Kowloon Peninsula. Kowloon gets its name from Gau Lung, which means "nine dragons." Legend has it that about 800 years ago a boy emperor named Ping counted eight hills here and remarked that there must be eight resident dragons, since dragons were known to inhabit hills. (The ninth "dragon" was the emperor himself.)

Today, the hills of Kowloon provide a dramatic backdrop for one of the world's most stunning cityscapes. Kowloon Peninsula is generally considered the area south of these hills, which means it also encompasses a very small part of the New Territories. However, "Kowloon" is most often used to describe its southernmost tip, the 4.8 square miles that were ceded to Britain "in perpetuity" in 1860. Its northern border is Boundary Street, which separates it from the New Territories; included in this area are the districts Tsim Sha Tsui, Tsim Sha Tsui East, Yau Ma Tei, and Mong Kok. Once open countryside, Kowloon has practically disappeared under the dense spread of hotels, shops, restaurants, and housing and industrial projects. It has also grown due to land reclamation.

**Tsim Sha Tsui**   At the southern tip of Kowloon Peninsula is Tsim Sha Tsui (also spelled "Tsimshatsui"), which, after Central, rates as Hong Kong's most important area. This is where most tourists stay and spend their money, since it has the greatest concentration of hotels, restaurants, and shops in Hong Kong. In fact, some of my acquaintances living in Hong Kong avoid Tsim Sha Tsui like the plague, calling it the "tourist ghetto." On the other hand, Tsim Sha Tsui does boast the Space Museum, a new cultural center for the performing arts, a great art museum, Kowloon Park, one of the world's largest shopping malls, a nice selection of international restaurants, a jumping nightlife, and Nathan Road, appropriately nicknamed the "golden mile of shopping." Although you'd be foolish to spend all your time in Tsim Sha Tsui, you'd also be foolish to miss it.

**Tsim Sha Tsui East**   Not surprisingly, this neighborhood is east of Tsim Sha Tsui. Built entirely on reclaimed land, the area has become increasingly important, home to a rash of expensive hotels, entertainment centers, shopping and restaurant complexes, science and history museums, a coliseum—and, on its eastern edge, the KCR Kowloon-Canton Railway Station, terminus for the Kowloon-Canton Railway that carries passengers through the New Territories and beyond to China. Although most hotels in this area are a bit of a walk from the Tsim Sha Tsui subway station, many provide free shuttle service to Tsim Sha Tsui, and a hoverferry service connects East Tsim Sha Tsui and Central.

**Yau Ma Tei**   If you get on the subway in Tsim Sha Tsui and ride two stations to the north (or walk for about 25 minutes straight up Nathan Road), you'll reach the Yau Ma Tei district (also spelled "Yaumatei"), located on Kowloon Peninsula just north of Tsim Sha Tsui. Like the Western District, Yau Ma Tei is also very Chinese, with an interesting produce market, a jade market, and the fascinating Temple Street Night Market. There are also several moderately priced hotels here, making this a good alternative to the tourist-oriented district of Tsim Sha Tsui.

**Mong Kok**   On Kowloon Peninsula north of Yau Ma Tei, Mong Kok is a residential and industrial area, home of the Bird Market, the Ladies' Market on Tung Choi Street, and countless shops catering to Chinese. Its northern border, Boundary Street, marks the beginning of the New Territories.

# 2  Getting Around

If you've just been to Tokyo or Bangkok, Hong Kong will probably bring a rush of relief. For one thing, English is everywhere—on street signs, on buses, in the subways. In addition, the city of Hong Kong is so compact, and its public transportation system so efficient and extensive, that it's no problem at all zipping from Tsim Sha Tsui to Causeway Bay or vice versa for a meal or some shopping. Even the novice traveler should have no problem getting around. Transportation is also extremely cheap. Just remember that cars drive on the left side of the street, English style, so watch it when stepping off the curb.

## BY PUBLIC TRANSPORTATION

Each mode of transportation in Hong Kong—bus, ferry, tram, and train/subway—has its own fare system and therefore requires a new ticket each time you transfer from one mode of transport to another. However, if you're going to be in Hong Kong for a few days and think you'll be traveling extensively on the subway, the Airport Express Line, and perhaps even the train (which services the New Territories), consider purchasing the **Octopus.** This electronic smart card allows users to hop on and off trains, subways, and most (but not all) buses and ferries without worrying about purchasing tickets each time or fumbling for exact change. It also gives a slight discount over regular fares—a regular HK$14 ($1.80) fare, for example, costs HK$12.50 ($1.65) using an Octopus. Sold at all MTR subway stations and some ferry piers, the Octopus costs HK$150 ($19.50), including a HK$50 ($6.50) refundable deposit, and can be reloaded in HK$100 ($13) units. Children and senior citizens pay HK$70 ($9.10) for the card, including deposit. To use it, simply sweep the card across a special pad at the entry gate; the fare is automatically deducted. The Octopus is valid for all subways, the Kowloon-Canton Railway (which runs northward from Kowloon through the New Territories), the Light Rail Transit system (which services the northwestern part of the New Territories), the Airport Express Line which runs between the airport and Kowloon and Central, most buses, and many ferries to a few outlying islands. In addition, the Octopus can be used for purchases at all 7-Eleven convenience stores. In the future, it's expected that the other forms of public transport in Hong Kong will join the Octopus system, including trams and minibuses.

**BY SUBWAY**   The Star Ferry and trams are so popular and at times so crowded that it's hard to imagine what they must have been like before Hong Kong's subway system was constructed to relieve the human crunch. Hong Kong's **Mass Transit Railway (MTR)** is modern, efficient, clean, and easy to use, and it's also much faster than the older modes of transportation (and sometimes even taxis). The only difficult thing about it is trying to remain seated on the slick, stainless-steel benches (you may laugh now, but wait till you've tried it), though bucket seats are slowly replacing these benches. Also, take note that there are no public toilets at any of the stations or on the trains, and that smoking, drinking, and eating are prohibited. However, mobile phones—each with their annoying rings, and even songs—work on the subways. The MTR operates daily 6am to 1am. For general inquiries, call the MTR Hotline at ☎ 852/2881 8888.

Built primarily to transport commuters in the New Territories to and from work and running under the harbor to link Kowloon with Hong Kong Island, the MTR serves 2.4 million passengers a day. You'll probably want to avoid rush hours, unless you enjoy feeling like a sardine in a can. There are only four lines on the 47-mile subway system, each is color-coded, and the stations are clearly marked in English, so you

## Public Transport Tips

Keep in mind that transportation on buses and trams requires the **exact fare.** It's therefore imperative to have a lot of loose change with you wherever you go. Even though the ferries and subways will give change, you'll find it more convenient if you have exact change, especially during rush hours. Alternatively, and especially if you're in Hong Kong for more than a couple of days, consider purchasing an Octopus card, good for travel on subways, the Kowloon-Canton Railway, the Airport Express Line to the airport, many buses, and some ferries to outlying islands.

shouldn't have any problem finding your way around. Stations are named for the areas they serve: Go to Central MTR station if you're looking for an address in the Central District, to Mong Kok MTR station if you're looking for a place in Mong Kok, Kowloon. Probably the most important line for tourists is the **red-coded Tsuen Wan Line,** which starts in Central on Hong Kong Island, goes underneath Victoria Harbour to Tsim Sha Tsui, and then runs north the length of Nathan Road, with stops at Jordan, Yau Ma Tei, and Mong Kok stations before heading northwest to the satellite town of Tsuen Wan in the New Territories. The **blue-coded Island Line,** with 14 stations, operates on the north side of Hong Kong Island from Sheung Wan (where you'll find the Macau Ferry Pier) east to Chai Wan, passing through Central, Wan Chai, and Causeway Bay. The other two lines, used mainly by commuters, are the **Kwun Tong Line,** which runs from Quarry Bay on Hong Kong Island and then goes under the harbor to arch across the New Territories before dropping south to Yau Ma Tei in Kowloon; and the **new Tung Chung Line,** which mirrors the Airport Express Line as it runs from Hong Kong Station in Central to Kowloon Station and onward to Tung Chung on Lantau island. Additionally, the Airport Express Line, serving airport passengers, runs between Hong Kong Station in Central and Hong Kong International Airport, with a stop at Kowloon Station.

Single-ticket, one-way fares range from HK$4 to HK$26 (50¢ to $3.40), depending on the distance, but the most expensive ride is the trip underneath the harbor, which costs HK$9 ($1.15) from Tsim Sha Tsui to Central (still cheap, but outrageous when compared to the Star Ferry). Fares for senior citizens 65 and older and children ages 3 to 11 range from HK$3 to HK$13 (40¢ to $1.70). Fares are posted in English above all vending machines, which accept HK$10, HK$5, HK$2, HK$1, and HK$0.50 coins and give back change. If you need coins, go to one of the change machines or to the ticket counter located at MTR stations.

In any case, your ticket is plastic, the size of a credit card, and you feed it into a slot at the turnstile. It disappears and then shoots up at the other end of the turnstile. *Be sure to save your ticket*—at the end of your journey you will again insert your ticket into the turnstile (only this time you won't get it back). Since these tickets are used again and again and have a magnetized strip, be careful not to bend or damage them.

As mentioned earlier, if you think you're going to be doing a lot of traveling on the MTR subway and perhaps even the KCR East Rail train (which services the New Territories), consider buying the Octopus, which saves you from having to buy another ticket each time you ride and gives a negligible discount.

**BY TRAIN**    In addition to the MTR and Airport Express Line, there are two other rail services in Hong Kong. Foremost is the **Kowloon-Canton Railway (KCR) East Rail** (☎ 852/2602 7799), which travels from the KCR Kowloon-Canton Railway Station in Hung Hom (near Tsim Sha Tsui East) up to Sheung Shui in the New Territories. That is, Sheung Shui is where you must get off if you don't have a visa to go

# Understanding the Deluge: Tropical Storm Warnings

It's not likely you'll experience a tropical storm during your stay in Hong Kong, but if you do, consider it part of your Asian experience. Called typhoons in this part of the world (after the Cantonese *dai fung,* which translates as "big wind") and hurricanes in the West, these severe tropical storms generally vent their fury between July and September. There's no need to worry that a storm may sneak up on you unawares—storms are tracked and monitored and are rated according to their strength. Their approach dominates local news, but even if you don't read the newspapers or listen to the evening news there are other telltale signs of a coming typhoon—MTR stations, hotel lobbies, and businesses post notices, and shopkeepers cover their windows with storm shutters.

Whenever a severe tropical rainstorm or typhoon is approaching Hong Kong, an alert is broadcast continuously on TV and the radio to keep you informed of the storm's movements. To keep people better informed of the severity of a storm, a system of numbers has been developed that begins at Typhoon Signal No. 1, continues to Typhoon Signal No. 3, and then jumps to Typhoon Signal No. 8 and up. (There used to be numbers in between, but these were dropped when the long range proved too confusing.)

Typhoon Signal No. 1 goes up when a tropical storm that could escalate into a typhoon has moved within a 460-mile radius of Hong Kong. Although public transportation and organized tours and outdoor activities continue as scheduled, this signal indicates that the public should be on alert. Most locals, however, are rather indifferent to a No. 1, especially since this condition can last for several days, with little physical indication of an approaching storm.

Typhoon Signal No. 3 is given when the winds have escalated, accompanied, perhaps, by heavy rains. By this time organized guided tours and harbor cruises have generally been suspended. Visitors should check with authorities before venturing on day trips to the outlying islands or Macau. Some businesses may close, as employees head for home while public transportation is still running.

Typhoon Signal No. 8 indicates that the gale has reached Hong Kong. Banks, offices, museums, and most shops and restaurants close, and road, ferry, and air transport are suspended. You should never take a Signal No. 8 lightly, but rather, remain in your hotel and celebrate with a typhoon party, which is pretty much what everyone else does. There's nothing like a tropical storm to set the adrenaline running.

Full details of Hong Kong's typhoon warning system can be found in the local telephone directory. For information during a storm, listen to TV or radio broadcasts or call the Hong Kong Observatory at ☎ **852/2835 1473.**

onward to China. If you do have a visa, you can continue to the border station of Lo Wu and travel onward all the way through China—and even Russia and Europe if you want to, ending up in London (but who knows how many years that would take). There are two different kinds of trains: the express through-train to Guangzhou, Shanghai, and Beijing; and the local commuter service for those going to towns in the New Territories.

At any rate, if you're taking the KCR East Rail commuter train, you'll make stops at Mong Kok, Kowloon Tong, Tai Wai, Sha Tin, Fo Tan, Sha Tin Racecourse (on horse-racing days only), University, Tai Po Market, Tai Wo, and Fanling before reaching Sheung Shui. The easiest place to board the KCR East Rail is at Kowloon Tong, since it's also a subway stop and transfer is easy. At any rate, the whole trip from Kowloon to Sheung Shui takes only a half hour on Hong Kong's new electric trains, so it's the easiest and fastest way to see part of the New Territories. It's also convenient, with trains running every 3 to 10 minutes daily from approximately 5:35am to midnight. Finally, it's also cheap, costing HK$9 ($1.15) for ordinary (second) class and HK$18 ($2.35) for first class if you go all the way to Sheung Shui. Fares to Lo Wu cost HK$33 ($4.30) and HK$66 ($8.50) respectively. Senior citizens 65 and older and children 3 to 12 pay half fare; those under 3 travel free. If you're curious about the New Territories, its scenery, and satellite towns, this is a fast, cheap, and painless way to see it.

In addition to the KCR East Rail, there's also a Light Rail Transit system, which operates in the northwestern part of the New Territories and links the two towns of Tuen Mun and Yuen Long. Fares range from HK$4 to HK$5.80 (50¢ to 75¢) and trains run from about 5:30 or 6am to midnight.

**BY BUS** Hong Kong buses are a delight—especially the British-style double-deckers. They're good for traveling to places where other forms of public transport don't go, such as to the southern part of Hong Kong Island like Stanley or up into parts of Kowloon and the New Territories. Bus numbers containing an "X" are for express buses, with limited stops. Depending on the route, buses run from about 6am to midnight, with fares ranging from HK$1.20 to HK$45 (15¢ to $5.85); half fare for children. Air-conditioned buses cost more than non-air-conditioned buses. *You must have the exact fare,* which you deposit into a box as you get on. Make sure, therefore, that you always carry a lot of spare change. Drivers often don't speak English, so you may want to have someone at your hotel write down your destination in Chinese, particularly if you're traveling in the New Territories. And if you're waiting for a bus in the New Territories or on an island, be sure to wave to flag it down.

Hong Kong's buses are operated by three companies: **New World First Bus** (☎ 2136 8888); **Kowloon Motor Bus** (KMB; ☎ 852/2745 4466); and the common yellow buses run by **Citybus** (☎ 852/2873 0818). There are two major bus terminals, located at or near both ends of the Star Ferry. On Hong Kong Island, most buses depart from Exchange Square in the Central District or from bus stops in front of the Outlying Islands Ferry Piers. Some buses also depart from Admiralty Station. In Kowloon, buses depart from in front of the Star Ferry concourse in Tsim Sha Tsui.

The HKTA has individual leaflets for Hong Kong Island, Kowloon, and the New Territories that show bus routes to most of the major tourist spots, indicating where you can catch the bus and its frequency, the fare, and where to get off. Keep in mind that buses can get very crowded at rush hours and that some buses look pretty ancient—which can make the winding trip to Stanley in a double-decker bus a bone-rattling and exciting experience.

**BY TRAM** Tramlines are found only on Hong Kong Island. Established in 1904 along what used to be the waterfront, these are old, narrow, double-decker affairs that clank their way in a straight line slowly along the northern edge of the island from Kennedy Town in the west to Shau Kei Wan in the east, with one branch making a detour to Happy Valley. Passing through the Central District, Wan Chai, and Causeway Bay on Des Voeux Road, Queensway Road, and Hennessy Road, they can't be beat for atmosphere and are easy to ride since most of them go only on one line (those branching off to Happy Valley are clearly marked). In the zeal to modernize Central, it's a wonder that these trams have survived at all. Since the advent of the subway there's been talk of getting rid of these ancient trams, but this has raised a storm of protest. Since their future is uncertain, be sure to ride them while you can. They are easily one of the most nostalgic forms of transportation in Hong Kong.

Enter the trams from the back and go immediately up the winding stairs to the top deck. The best seats in the house are those in the front row, where you have an unparalleled view of Hong Kong: laundry hanging from second-story windows, signs swinging over the street, markets twisting down side alleys, crowded sidewalks, and people darting in front of the tram you swear couldn't have made it. Riding the tram is one of the cheapest ways of touring Hong Kong Island's northern side, and the fare is the same no matter how far you go. Once you've had enough, simply go downstairs to the front of the tram and deposit the exact fare of HK$2 (25¢) into a little tin box next to the bus driver as you exit. Children and senior citizens pay half fare. If you don't have the exact amount, don't panic—no one will arrest you for overpaying a few cents. Trams run daily 6am to 1am.

In addition to the old-fashioned trams, there's also the **Peak Tram,** a funicular that transports passengers to one of Hong Kong's star attractions, Victoria Peak and its incomparable views. Its lower terminus is on Garden Road in Central, which you can reach via a HK$3 (40¢) shuttle bus departing from the Star Ferry concourse (next to City Hall) at 15- to 20-minute intervals daily 10am to 11pm (to 8pm Sundays and public holidays). The tram itself runs every 10 to 15 minutes 7am to midnight, with round-trip tickets costing HK$30 ($3.90) for adults and HK$9 ($1.15) for children. See "Hong Kong's Top Attractions" in chapter 6 for more information.

**BY STAR FERRY**    A trip across Victoria Harbour on one of the white-and-green ferries of the Star Ferry Company is one of the most celebrated rides in the world. Carrying passengers back and forth between Hong Kong Island and Kowloon ever since 1898, these boats have come to symbolize Hong Kong itself and are almost always featured in travel articles on Hong Kong Island. They all incorporate the word "star" in their names, for example, *Twinkling Star* or *Meridien Star.*

They're very easy to ride. Simply drop your coins into a slot on the ancient-looking turnstile, follow the crowd in front of you down the ramp, walk over the gangway, and find a seat on one of the polished wooden benches. A whistle will blow, a man in a sailor uniform will haul up the gangway, and you're off, dodging fishing boats, tugboats, and barges as you make your way across the harbor. Businesspeople who live in Hong Kong are easy to spot—they're usually buried behind their newspapers; visitors, on the other hand, tend to crowd around the railing, cameras in hand.

The whole trip is much too short, only 5 minutes across. But that 5-minute ride is one of the best in the world, and it's also one of the cheapest. It costs only HK$1.70 (22¢) for ordinary (second) class; if you really want to splurge, it's only HK$2.20 (28¢) for first class. First class is located on the upper deck, and it has its own entryway and gangway (follow the signs in the ferry concourse); if it's raining or cold, first class is preferable because there are glass windows in the bow. Otherwise I find ordinary class much more colorful and entertaining because it's the one the locals use and the view of the harbor is often better.

Star Ferries ply the waters daily 6:30am to 11:30pm between Hong Kong Island's Central District and the tip of Kowloon's Tsim Sha Tsui. Ferries depart every 3 to 5 minutes, except for early in the morning or late at night, when they leave every 10 minutes.

**BY OTHER FERRIES**    Besides the Star Ferry, there are also many ferries to other parts of the city. Ferries from the Central District, for example, also go back and forth to Kowloon's Hung Hom for HK$5.30 (70¢), convenient if you want to catch the train to China at KCR Kowloon-Canton Railway Station. There's also hoverferry service between Central and Tsim Sha Tsui East (near the Shangri-La Hotel), running at 20-minute intervals and costing HK$5.70 (75¢). From Wan Chai, there's also ferry service to Tsim Sha Tsui, running 7:30am to 11pm and costing HK$2.20 (28¢), and to Hung Hom, available 7am to 7pm and costing HK$5 (65¢).

In addition to ferries crossing the harbor between Kowloon and Hong Kong Island, a large fleet serves the many outlying islands and the northern part of the mainland. If you want to go to one of the outlying islands, you'll find that most of these ferries depart from the Outlying Islands Ferry Piers stretching west of the Star Ferry terminus in Central. Operated by the Hong Kong & Yaumati Ferry Company Ltd. (HKF), these boats vary in size; some even have outdoor deck areas in first class. The latest schedules and fares are available from the Hong Kong Tourist Association (HKTA) or by calling HKF (☎ **852/2542 3081** or 852/2542 3082). One thing to keep in mind is that on the weekends the ferries are unbelievably crowded with locals who want to escape the city. And on weekends the fares are higher, so it's best to travel on a weekday. Even so, the most you'll ever pay for a ferry, even on deluxe class on a weekend, is HK$31 ($4). See chapter 10, "Side Trips from Hong Kong," for more information on ferries to specific islands.

## BY TAXI

**REGULAR TAXIS**   As a rule, taxi drivers in Hong Kong are strictly controlled and are fairly honest. If they're free to pick up passengers, a red FOR HIRE flag will be raised in the windshield during the day and a lighted TAXI sign will be on the roof at night. You can hail them from the street, though there are some restricted areas, especially in Central. In addition, taxis are not allowed to stop on roads with a single yellow line between 7am and 7pm; they are not allowed to stop at all on roads with a double yellow line. Probably the easiest place to pick up a taxi is on side streets, at a taxi stand (located at all bus terminals), or at a hotel. Taxis are generally abundant anytime except when it's raining, during rush hour (about 5 to 8pm), during shift change (usually about 4pm), and on horse-racing days from September to May. Since many drivers do not speak English, it's a good idea to have your destination written in Chinese.

Taxis on Hong Kong Island and Kowloon are red. Fares start at HK$15 ($1.95) for the first 2 kilometers (1.24 miles), then are HK$1.40 (18¢) for each 200 meters (about 275 yards). Waiting time, incorporated in the meter, is HK$1.40 (18¢) per minute, luggage costs an extra HK$5 (65¢) per piece, and taxis ordered by phone add a HK$5 (65¢) surcharge. Extra charges, which include the driver's return trip, are also permitted for trips through tunnels: HK$20 ($2.60) for the Cross-Harbour Tunnel, HK$30 ($3.90) for the Eastern Harbour Crossing, HK$45 ($5.85) for the Western Harbour Tunnel, and HK$5 (65¢) for the Aberdeen Tunnel. Note, too, that there's an additional charge per bird or animal you might want to bring with you in the taxi! For a tip, simply round off your bill to the nearest HK$1 or add a HK$1. Although taxi drivers can service both sides of Victoria Harbour, they tend to stick to a certain neighborhood and often aren't familiar with anything outside their area.

Taxis in the New Territories are green, with fares starting at HK$12.50 ($1.60) at flag-fall. They cover only the New Territories and are not allowed to transport you back into Kowloon.

If you have a complaint about a taxi driver, call the police hotline (☎ **852/2527 7177**), but make sure you have the taxi's license number. The driver's name, photograph, and car number are displayed on the dashboard.

**MAXICABS & MINIBUSES**   These small, 16-passenger buses are the poor person's taxis; although they are quite useful for the locals, they're a bit confusing for tourists. For one thing, although the destination may be written in both Chinese and English, you almost need a magnifying glass to read the English, and by then the vehicle has probably already whizzed by. Even if you can read the English, you may not know the bus's route or where it's going.

There are two types of vehicles, distinguishable by color. The green-and-yellow ones, called **maxicabs,** follow fixed routes and charge fixed rates ranging from HK$2 to HK$22.50 (25¢ to $2.90), depending on the distance, and require the exact fare as you enter. The most useful ones on Hong Kong Island are probably those that depart from the Star Ferry concourse for Bowen Road and Ocean Park, as well as those that travel from Central's Lung Wui Road to Victoria Peak. In Kowloon, you can ride from the Star Ferry concourse in a maxicab to the Tsim Sha Tsui East shopping district.

The red-and-yellow **minibuses** are a lot more confusing, because they have no fixed route and will stop when you hail them from the street (except for some restricted areas in Central). However, they're useful for traveling along Nathan Road or between Central and Causeway Bay. Fares range from HK$2 to HK$20 (25¢ to $2.60), depending on the distance and demand (higher fares are charged on rainy days, race days, or cross-harbor trips), and you pay as you exit. Just yell when you want to get off.

## BY CAR

Rental cars are not advisable in Hong Kong and hardly anyone uses them, even businesspeople. For one thing, nothing is so far away that you can't get there easily, quickly, and cheaply by taxi or public transport. In addition, there probably won't be any place to park once you get to your destination. If you want a chauffeur-driven car, most major hotels have their own private fleet—you can even rent an air-conditioned limousine (a romantically minded friend of mine picked up her arriving boyfriend at the airport that way). If you're still determined to rent a car or plan to take a driving tour of the New Territories, self-drive firms—Avis, Budget, and Hertz—have branches here, along with a couple of dozen local firms. Your hotel concierge should be able to make arrangements; expect to pay about HK$850 ($110) for 1 day. A valid driver's license is required, and remember, traffic flows on the left-hand side of the street.

## BY RICKSHAW

Rickshaws hit the streets of Hong Kong in the 1870s and were once the most common form of transport in the colony. Now, however, they are almost a thing of the past—no new licenses are being issued. A couple of ancient-looking men hang around the Star Ferry terminal in the Central District, but they're usually either snoozing or reading the paper. I've never once seen them hauling a customer. Rather, they make money by charging up to HK$50 ($6.50) for tourists who want to take their pictures. If you do want to take a ride, they'll charge up to HK$100 ($13) to take you around the block, clearly the most expensive form of transportation in Hong Kong, and by their appearance that's probably about as far as they can go. But whether you're just taking a photograph or going for a ride, negotiate the price first.

## ON FOOT

One of the great things about Hong Kong is that you can explore virtually the entire city proper on foot. You can walk from the Central District all the way through Wan Chai to Causeway Bay in about an hour or so, while the half-hour walk up Nathan Road to Yau Ma Tei is recommended to all visitors. Unfortunately, land reclamation has been carried out so ambitiously, it may even be possible one day to walk from Hong Kong Island to Kowloon.

In the Central District there are mazes of covered, elevated walkways to separate pedestrians from traffic, connecting office buildings, shopping complexes, and hotels. In fact, some roads have no pedestrians because they're all using overhead passageways.

You can, for example, walk from the Star Ferry concourse to the Prince's Building, Alexandra House, and Landmark all via covered bridges. Likewise, you can walk from the Star Ferry concourse all the way to the Macau Ferry Pier via a walkway.

There's also an interesting "people-mover," the Central-Mid-Levels Escalator between Central Market on Des Voeux Road Central and the Mid-Levels on Victoria Peak. It's a series of moving walkways and escalators that snake their way through the Central District up the steep slope of the Peak. Constructed in the hope of alleviating traffic congestion for commuters who live in the Mid-Levels (about halfway up the Peak), the combination escalator/walkway has a total length of just less than a half mile and transports approximately 27,000 people a day, moving downward in the morning until 10am and then reversing uphill the rest of the day to accommodate those returning home.

## Fast Facts: Hong Kong

Your hotel concierge or guest relations manager is usually a valuable source of information, and the Hong Kong Tourist Association (HKTA) is also well equipped and eager to help visitors and answer their questions.

**Airport**    See "Arriving," earlier in this chapter.

**American Express**    There are two American Express offices, located on both sides of Victoria Harbour. On Hong Kong Island, you'll find an American Express on the first floor of the Henley Building, 5 Queen's Rd. Central, in the Central District (☎ 852/2110 2008). In Tsim Sha Tsui, it's at 48 Cameron Rd. (☎ 852/2311 3399). Both offices are open Monday to Friday 9am to 5pm and Saturday 9am to 12:30pm. American Express cardholders can withdraw local currency and traveler's checks 24 hours a day at the Express Cash automated-teller machines at both locations, as well as at Jetco ATMs throughout Hong Kong.

**Baby-sitters**    Most of the expensive and many of the medium-range hotels have baby-sitting services. Check chapter 4 for hotels that provide this service. For a full list of hotels with baby-sitters, contact the Hong Kong Tourist Association.

**Bookstores**    There are lots of English-language bookstores, particularly in Central and Tsim Sha Tsui. Ask your hotel concierge for the one nearest you. Otherwise, two of the largest are **Swindon Book Co.,** 13–15 Lock Rd., Tsim Sha Tsui (☎ 852/2366 8001), open Monday to Thursday 9am to 6:30pm, Friday and Saturday 9am to 7:30pm, and Sunday 12:30 to 6:30pm; and **Bookazine,** a small chain with several locations, including 20 Queen's Rd., Central (☎ 852/2521 1649), open Monday to Saturday 9am to 7pm and Sunday 10am to 6pm. Both carry books on Hong Kong and China, including special-interest topics ranging from art to history, as well as maps.

**Business Hours**    Although opening hours can vary among banks, banking hours are generally Monday to Friday 9am to 4:30pm and Saturday 9am to 12:30pm. Keep in mind, however, that some banks stop their transactions—including foreign currency exchange—an hour before closing time.

Most business offices are open Monday to Friday 9am to 5pm, with lunch hour from 1 to 2pm; Saturday business hours are generally 9am to 1pm.

Most shops are open 7 days a week. Shops in the Central District are generally open 10am to 6pm; in Causeway Bay and Wan Chai, 10am to 9:30pm; in Tsim Sha Tsui, 10am to 9 or 10pm (and some even later than that); and in Tsim

Sha Tsui East, 10am to 7:30pm. As for bars, most stay open until at least 2am; some stay open until the crack of dawn.

**Car Rentals**    See "Getting Around," earlier in this chapter.

**Climate**    See "When to Go," in chapter 2.

**Convention Center**    The **Hong Kong Convention & Exhibition Centre** is located on the harbor waterfront at 1 Harbour Rd., Wan Chai (☎ **852/2582 8888**).

**Currency**    See "Money," in chapter 2.

**Currency Exchange**    When exchanging money in Hong Kong, you'll get the best rate at banks. The exchange rate can vary among banks, however, so it may pay to shop around if you're exchanging a large amount. Some banks, for example, offer a better exchange rate but charge a commission of about HK$50 ($6.50); others many not charge commission but have lower rates. Most charge a commission on traveler's checks (unless, of course, you're cashing American Express checks at an American Express office), but the exchange rate is usually better for traveler's checks than cash. The three main banks in Hong Kong are the **Hongkong and Shanghai Banking Corporation** (usually shortened to Hongkong Bank or HSBC), 29 Queen's Rd. Central (☎ **852/2847 7222**); **Standard Chartered Bank,** 4 Des Voeux Rd. Central (☎ **852/2820 3333**); and **Bank of China,** 1 Garden Rd., Central (☎ **852/2826 6888**). Major banks are open Monday to Friday 9am to 4:30pm and Saturday 9am to 12:30pm. The Hang Seng Bank, which I find often offers good exchange rates, has branches virtually everywhere and is generally open Monday to Friday 9am to 5pm and Saturday 9am to 1pm.

Hotels give a slightly less favorable exchange rate but are convenient because they're open at night and on weekends. Money changers are found in the tourist areas, especially along Nathan Road in Tsim Sha Tsui. Avoid them if you can. They often charge a commission or a "changing fee," or give a much lower rate. Check exactly how much you'll get in return before handing over your money. If you exchange money at Hong Kong International Airport, change only what you need to get into town—$20 (U.S.) should be enough—because the exchange rate here is lower than what you'll get at banks in town.

There are also ATMs throughout Hong Kong, including MTR subway stations and the Star Ferry concourse in Tsim Sha Tsui. The Hongkong and Shanghai Banking Corporation has ATMs open 24 hours for Visa and MasterCard holders. American Express cardholders have access to Jetco ATMs and card machines located at both American Express offices (see "American Express," above).

**Dentists/Doctors**    Most first-class hotels have medical clinics with registered nurses, as well as doctors on duty at specified hours or on call 24 hours for emergencies. Otherwise, the concierge can refer you to a doctor or dentist. See chapter 4 for hotels with in-house physicians. The U.S. consulate can also provide information on English-speaking doctors. If it's an emergency, dial **999** or contact one of the recommendations under "Hospitals," below.

**Drugstores**    See "Pharmacies," below.

**Electricity**    The electricity used in Hong Kong is 220 volts, alternating current (AC), 50 cycles (in the U.S. it's 110 volts and 60 cycles). Most hotels are equipped to fit shavers of different plugs and voltages, but for other gadgets you'll need transformers and plug adapters (Hong Kong outlets take plugs with three rectangular prongs). Most laptop computers nowadays are equipped to deal with both 110 and 220 volts, though you'll still need an adapter. Except for budget accommodations, most hotels have hair dryers.

**Embassies/Consulates**    If you need to contact a consulate about application for a visa, a lost passport, tourist information, or an emergency, telephone first to find out the hours of the various sections. The visa section, for example, may be open only during certain hours of the day.

The **American Consulate,** 26 Garden Rd., Central District (☎ **852/2523 9011**), is open Monday to Friday 8:30am to noon and 1:30 to 4pm. The **Canadian Consulate,** 12th–14th Floor of Tower One, Exchange Square, 8 Connaught Place, Central District (☎ **852/2810 4321**), is open Monday to Friday 8:30am to 12:30pm and 1:30 to 5pm; closed Wednesday afternoon. Its passport section is open Monday to Friday 9am to noon.

The **British Consulate** at 1 Supreme Court Rd., Central District (☎ **852/2901 3000**), is open Monday to Friday 8:45am to 3pm. **The Australian Consulate** is on the 23rd and 24th floors of Harbour Centre, 25 Harbour Rd., Wan Chai, on Hong Kong Island (☎ **852/2827 8881**), and is open Monday to Friday 9am to 5pm. The **New Zealand Consulate** is on the 65th floor of Central Plaza, 18 Harbour Rd., Wan Chai (☎ **852/2525 5044**), and is open Monday to Friday 8:30am to 1pm and 2 to 5pm.

For information on visa applications to mainland **China,** contact a tour operator such as China Travel Service (see "China" in chapter 10).

**Emergencies**    All emergency calls are free—just dial **999** for police, fire, or ambulance. In addition, free ambulance service is provided by the **St. John Ambulance Brigade:** Call ☎ **852/2576 6555** on Hong Kong Island and ☎ **852/2713 5555** in Kowloon and the New Territories.

**Holidays**    See "When to Go" in chapter 2 for a list of Hong Kong's holidays and festivals.

**Hospitals**    The following hospitals can help you around the clock: Queen Mary Hospital, 102 Pokfulam Rd., Hong Kong Island (☎ **852/2855 4111**); Hong Kong Adventist Hospital, 40 Stubbs Rd., Hong Kong Island (☎ **852/2574 6211**); and Queen Elizabeth Hospital, 30 Gascoigne Rd., Kowloon (☎ **852/2958 8888**).

**Hotlines**    The Hong Kong Tourist Association's hotline is ☎ **852/2508 1234,** with service available Monday to Friday 8am to 6pm and on Saturday, Sunday, and holidays 9am to 5pm. The Police Crime Hotline (including complaints against taxi drivers) is ☎ **852/2527 7177.**

**Information**    See "Visitor Information," earlier in this chapter.

**Internet Access**    All upper-range and most medium-priced hotels in Hong Kong are equipped with dataports that allow guests to use laptop computers. Internet access is generally available upon purchase of an Internet access card for HK$100 ($13), valid for unlimited use for 5 days. Otherwise, many hotels offer business centers as well, most equipped with computers and Internet access (fees may be charged).

Outside hotels, **Shadowman,** 7 Lock Rd., Tsim Sha Tsui (☎ **852/2366 5262**), across from the Hyatt Regency, is a small cybercafe with a half-dozen computers, providing free Internet access for 20 minutes with the purchase of a drink or food and charging HK$10 ($1.30) per 15 minutes beyond that. It's open daily 8:30am to midnight. In addition, **Pacific Coffee** is a chain of coffee shops, several with a couple of computers that customers can access for free, including shop 1002 in the International Finance Center (IFC), above Hong Kong Station in Central (☎ **852/2868 5100**), open Monday to Saturday 7am to 10pm and Sunday 8:30am to 9pm; and in the Peak Tower on Victoria Peak (☎ **852/2849 6608**), open Monday to Thursday 8am to 10:30pm and Friday to Sunday 8am to 11pm.

**Languages**   English and Cantonese have long been Hong Kong's two official languages, but since the 1997 handover English and "Chinese" are listed as the two official languages. There is no one Chinese language, however. While most Hong Kong Chinese speak Cantonese, that's a foreign language in Beijing, where the official language is Mandarin (*Putonghua*). Perhaps the use of "Chinese" is the first step in an eventual change to Mandarin as the official language of Hong Kong. At any rate, while Mandarin and Cantonese differ widely, they use the same characters for writing. Therefore, while a Hong Kong Chinese and a mainland Chinese may not be able to communicate orally, they can read each other's newspapers. Chinese characters number in the tens of thousands; knowledge of at least 1,500 characters is necessary to read a newspaper. Chinese is difficult to learn primarily because of the tonal variations. Western ears may find these differences in pronunciation almost impossible to detect, but a slight change in tone changes the whole meaning. One thing you'll notice, however, is that Chinese is spoken loudly—whispering does not seem to be part of the language.

Despite the fact that English is an official language and is spoken in hotels and tourist shops, few Chinese outside these areas understand it. Bus drivers, taxi drivers, and waiters in many Chinese restaurants do not speak English and will simply shrug their shoulders to your query. To avoid confusion, have someone in your hotel write out your destination in Chinese so that you can show it to your taxi or bus driver. Most Chinese restaurants—and all those listed in this book— have English menus. If you need assistance, try asking younger Chinese, since it's more likely that they will have studied English in school.

**Liquor Laws**   The drinking age in Hong Kong is 18. The hours for bars vary according to the district, though those around Lan Kwai Fong and Tsim Sha Tsui stay open the longest, often till dawn.

**Lost Property**   If you've lost something in Hong Kong, your best bet is to contact the Hong Kong Police (☎ **852/2850 2000**). Items found on the street are generally turned in to that district's closest police station. Items left on subways and in subway stations end up in the MTR Lost and Found Office at Admiralty Station, Central (☎ **852/2881 8888** for information). For items left in taxis, call the Taxi Union Loss Report Service at ☎ **852/2385 8288**.

**Luggage Storage/Lockers**   The best and most convenient place to store luggage is at your hotel, even if you plan on traveling to Macau or China for a couple of days. Otherwise, there are luggage-checking services ("left-luggage") at Hong Kong International Airport, Kowloon Station, the Macau Ferry Terminal on Hong Kong Island, and the China Hong Kong Terminal on Canton Road, Tsim Sha Tsui.

**Mail**   Most hotels have stamps and can mail your letters for you. Otherwise, see "Post Offices" below. Mailboxes are a bright orange-red in Hong Kong. Airmail letters up to 20 grams and postcards cost HK$3.10 (40¢) to the United States or Europe. You can count on airmail letters to take about 5 to 7 days, sometimes longer, to reach the United States.

To mail a package via surface mail to the United States, it costs HK$251 ($32.65) for a package weighing 5 kilos (11 pounds) and HK$441 ($53.35) for a package weighing 10 kilos (22 pounds). A 5-kilo package sent airmail will cost HK$419 ($54.45), a 10-kilo package HK$799 ($103.85). Post offices sell boxes called Postpak that are handy for mailing items home; they come in three sizes costing HK$13.50 ($1.75) to HK$26 ($3.40). For general enquiries, call ☎ **852/2921 2222.**

If you don't know where you'll be staying in Hong Kong, you can still receive mail via the post office. Have it sent to you "Poste Restante" at the General Post Office, 2 Connaught Place, Central District, Hong Kong Island, which is located near the Star Ferry terminus. It will hold mail for 2 months; when you come to collect it, be sure to bring along your passport for identification.

**Newspapers**    The *South China Morning Post* and the *Hong Kong Standard* are the two local English-language daily newspapers. For a different perspective, you might also want to pick up the *China Daily,* from Beijing. The *Asian Wall Street Journal, Financial Times, International Herald Tribune,* and *USA Today International* are also available.

**Pharmacies**    There are no 24-hour drugstores in Hong Kong, so if you need something urgently in the middle of the night, you should contact one of the hospitals listed above. One of the best-known pharmacies in Hong Kong is Watson's, which dates back to the 1880s. Today there are more than 90 Watson's drugstores in Hong Kong, most of them open 9am to 10pm. Ask the concierge at your hotel for the location of a Watson's or drugstore nearest you.

**Police**    You can reach the police for an emergency by dialing ☎ **999,** the same number as for a fire or an ambulance. There's a crime hotline (☎ **852/ 2527 7177**), a 24-hour service that also handles complaints against taxis.

**Post Offices**    All major hotels will mail letters for you. Otherwise, there are plenty of post offices throughout the territory. Most are open Monday to Friday 9:30pm to 5pm and Saturday 9:30am to 1pm. The main post office is on Hong Kong Island at 2 Connaught Place, in the Central District near the Star Ferry concourse, where you'll find stamps sold on the first floor (what we would call the second floor in the United States). It's open Monday to Saturday 8am to 6pm and Sunday 8am to 2pm. On the Kowloon side, post offices are located at 405 Nathan Rd., between the Jordan and Yau Ma Tei subway stations, and at 10 Middle Rd., which is 1 block north of Salisbury Road. For more information, call ☎ **852/2921 2222.**

**Rest Rooms**    The best places to track down public facilities in Hong Kong are its many hotels. Fast-food restaurants and shopping malls are other good bets. There may be an attendant on hand, who will expect a small tip, about HK$2 (25¢). Note that there are no public facilities at any of the MTR subway stations. Hotels and tourist sites usually have Western toilets, but you may encounter Chinese toilets on ferries and on the islands. To use them, squat facing the hood.

**Safety**    Hong Kong is relatively safe for the visitor, especially if you use common sense and stick to such well-traveled nighttime areas as Tsim Sha Tsui, Lan Kwai Fong or Causeway Bay. The main thing you must guard against is pickpockets. Although on the decline, they often work in groups to pick men's pockets or slit open a woman's purse, quickly taking the valuables and then relaying them on to accomplices who disappear in the crowd. Favored places are Tsim Sha Tsui, Causeway Bay, and Wan Chai. You should also be on guard on crowded public conveyances such as the MTR. To be on the safe side, keep your valuables in your hotel's safety-deposit box. If you need to carry your passport or large amounts of money, it's a good idea to conceal everything in a moneybelt. Don't leave your passport in your hotel room unless it's in a safe or safety-deposit box.

**Taxes**   Hotels will add a 10% service charge and a 3% government tax to your bill. Restaurants and bars will automatically add a 10% service charge, but there is no tax. There's an airport departure tax of HK$50 ($6.50) for adults and children older than 12, but this is usually—though not always—included in your ticket price. If you're taking the boat to Macau, you must pay a Hong Kong departure tax of HK$19 ($2.45), which is already included in the price of your boat ticket.

**Taxis**   See "Getting Around," earlier in this chapter.

**Telephone/Fax**   The international country code for Hong Kong is 852.

In Hong Kong, local calls made from homes, offices, shops, restaurants, and some hotel lobbies are free, so don't feel shy about asking to use the phone. From hotel lobbies and public phone booths, a local call costs HK$1 (13¢) for each 5 minutes; from hotel rooms, about HK$4 to HK$5 (50¢ to 65¢). For directory assistance, dial ☎ **1081** for local numbers, **10013** for international inquiries. Two useful telephone directories are the White Pages for businesses and the Yellow Pages for residences, available in most hotel rooms.

Most hotels in Hong Kong will handle faxes and overseas calls and offer direct dialing. Otherwise, long-distance calls can be made from specially marked International Dialing Direct (IDD) public phones. The cheapest and most convenient method of making international calls is to use a PhoneCard, which comes in denominations ranging from HK$50 to HK$300 ($6.50 to $39) and is available at Star Ferry piers, HKTA information offices, machines located beside telephones, and other locations around Hong Kong. Simply insert the card into the slot and dial. You can also charge your telephone call to a major credit card by using one of about 100 credit-card phones in major shopping locations.

In 1999, Hongkong Telecom lost its exclusive telecommunications license, which is sure to bring more telephone companies offering competing services and lower rates. As this book goes to press, however, the cost of a direct-dial call to the United States, made by dialing 001-1-area code-telephone number, is HK$6.80 (90¢) per minute. Country codes include 1 for the United States and Canada, 44 for the United Kingdom, 61 for Australia, and 64 for New Zealand.

You can make a collect call from any public or private phone by dialing **10010.** You can also make cashless international calls from any telephone in Hong Kong by using Home Direct, which gives you immediate and direct access to an operator in the country you're calling. Calls can then be charged collect or charged to an overseas telephone card, making it cheaper than a regular international call from Hong Kong. Some designated Home Direct telephones in Hong Kong, located at the airport, Ocean Terminal in Tsim Sha Tsui, and other locations, even allow you to talk with an operator in your country with the push of a button. Home Direct numbers from Hong Kong are ☎ **800 96 0161** for Australia, ☎ **800 96 1100** for Canada, ☎ **800 96 0064** for New Zealand, and ☎ **800 96 0044** for the United Kingdom. For the United States, dial ☎ **800 96 1111** for AT&T, ☎ **800 96 1121** for MCI, and ☎ **800 96 1877** for Sprint. For more information on dial access numbers for Home Direct, phone locations, where PhoneCards can be purchased and operated, time zones, or other matters pertaining to international calls, call 10013.

**Television**    There are two English-language TV channels, TVB Pearl and ATV World, broadcasting weekday mornings, evenings, and all day weekends and holidays, with a choice of local programs and shows imported from Britain, America, and Australia. In addition, all first-class and most moderate hotels have satellite television (with imported British and American programming, a sports channel, and an Australian channel) or cable TV (movie channels, ESPN sports channel, Discovery channel, and BBC and CNN news channels), as well as in-house pay video movies. Many hotels also subscribe to the Hongkong Channel, which features short, 5-minute features on Hong Kong's history, transportation networks, traditional customs and festivals, cultural events, shopping tips, and other information.

**Time Zone**    Hong Kong is 13 hours ahead of New York, 14 hours ahead of Chicago, and 16 hours ahead of Los Angeles. Since Hong Kong does not have a daylight saving time, subtract 1 hour from the above times if it's summer. Because Hong Kong is on the other side of the International Date Line, you lose 1 day when traveling from the United States to Asia. Don't worry—you gain it back when you return to North America, which means that you arrive back home the same day you left Hong Kong.

**Tipping**    Even though restaurants and bars will automatically add a 10% service charge to your bill, you're still expected to leave small change for the waiter. A general rule of thumb is to leave 5%, but in most Chinese restaurants where meals are usually inexpensive it's acceptable to leave change up to HK$5 (65¢). In the finest restaurants you should leave 10%.

You're also expected to tip taxi drivers, bellhops, barbers, and beauticians. For taxi drivers, simply round up your bill to the nearest HK$1 or add a HK$1 (15¢) tip. Tip people who cut your hair 5% or 10%, and give bellhops HK$10 to HK$20 ($1.30 to $2.60), depending on the number of your bags. If you use a public restroom with an attendant, you may be expected to leave a small gratuity—HK$2 (25¢) should be enough. In addition, chambermaids and room attendants are usually given about 2% of the room charge.

**Water**    It's considered safe to drink Hong Kong's tap water, but most people prefer bottled water, which is widely available. In summer, it's wise to carry bottled water with you. Some hotels have their own purification systems. I always drink the water, and have never gotten ill. If you travel into China, however, drink only bottled water.

**Weather**    If you want to check the day's temperature and humidity level or the 2-day forecast, dial ☎ **18501** or 187 8066. Otherwise, if a storm is brewing and you're worried about a typhoon, tune in to one of the radio or television stations described above.

# Where to Stay

For many years hotel managers in Hong Kong were in the enviable position of having too many guests and not enough rooms to accommodate them. High demand and low supply caused hotel prices to skyrocket in the 1980s and most of the 1990s—many hotels raised their rates a whopping 15 to 20% a year. To keep up with the demand, new hotels mushroomed. In December 1985 the Hong Kong Tourist Association reported a total of 18,180 hotel rooms in the colony. By the end of 1997, the number had swelled to an incredible 33,425.

But then came the 1997 handover and the Asian financial crisis, and since then hotels have had to change their tune. Visitors declined more than 10% after the handover, in part because tourists began going elsewhere, but also because the once-lucrative Japanese market, hit by domestic financial woes, began seeking bargains in cheaper destinations like Bangkok. As a result, Hong Kong hotels have had to work hard to lure customers—many have kept the same rates since 1997; upper-end hotels have been offering special packages, including weekend getaways, off-season incentives, and upgrades; and lower-end hotels have slashed rates up to 50%, with special promotional rates that are valid through most of the year. From the bargain-hunter's point of view, there has never been a better time to visit Hong Kong.

Still, hotels are not cheap in Hong Kong, especially when compared with those in many other Asian cities. Rather, prices are similar to what you'd pay in major U.S. and European cities, and while $150 might get you the best room in town in Topeka, Kansas, in Hong Kong it will get you a small, undistinguished box not unlike a highway motel room. In other words, except for the cost of getting to Hong Kong, your biggest expenditure is going to be for a place to stay.

Although tourism is down, with hotel occupancy usually hovering around 79%, there are indications that tourist arrivals are increasing. Hong Kong's biggest hotel crunches have traditionally occurred twice a year, during Hong Kong's most clement weather: in March and April and again in October and November. Still, you'd be wise to reserve a hotel room at least 2 months in advance no matter when you plan to come, especially if you have a particular hotel, location, or price category in mind. Major trade fairs at Hong Kong's expanded convention center can wreak havoc on travelers who arrive without reservations—on my last visit, Hong Kong's hotels were fully booked.

As for trends in the hotel industry, Hong Kong's biggest markets nowadays are business travelers and group tours, primarily from mainland China. This translates into crowded elevators and lobbies in the

## Choosing a Place to Stay

No one area in this compact city is really more convenient for staying than any other. Public transportation is efficient and easy to use, and the attractions are spread throughout the city. However, most visitors do stay in Tsim Sha Tsui, on the Kowloon side, simply because that's where you'll find the greatest concentration of hotels as well as shops and restaurants. Business travelers often prefer the Central District, while those who want to avoid the tourist crowds may like the hotels strung along the waterfront of Wan Chai and Causeway Bay. Yau Ma Tei and Mong Kok, situated on the Kowloon Peninsula north of Tsim Sha Tsui, are great places to stay if you want to be surrounded by Chinese stores and locals, with hardly a souvenir shop in sight. See "Neighborhoods in Brief," chapter 3, for more information on these neighborhoods.

moderately priced hotels that Chinese tour groups frequent. Hotels catering to executive-level business travelers, meanwhile, have beefed up business services, from state-of-the-art business centers to in-room dataports for computer hookups, dedicated phone lines, and even fax machines or TVs with keyboards that double as computers for Internet access.

Hotels have also improved services and in-room amenities, so that even moderately priced rooms nowadays have hair dryers, room safes, and often cable or satellite TVs with in-house pay movies, as well as coffee/tea-making facilities. No-smoking floors are common in virtually all hotels now except for some of the inexpensive ones. Most hotels also have tour desks or can book tours for you. Unless otherwise stated, all hotels in this book have air-conditioning (a must in Hong Kong), private bathrooms, telephones with international direct dialing, clock-radios, and usually a stocked refrigerator with minibar. Room service (either 24 hours or until the wee hours of the morning), baby-sitting, and same-day laundry service are standard features of very expensive to moderate hotels, as are Western and Asian restaurants and business centers. Many also offer health clubs with swimming pools free for guests (though a few charge extra for their use). Some hotels even differentiate among their guests, charging health club fees, for example, for those who book through a travel agent but not for those who pay rack rates (the maximum quoted rates). Guests booking through travel agents may also receive fewer amenities.

It's darn near impossible to predict what might happen in the next few years. In 1997, it was expected that some 40 new hotels would open by the year 2000, pushing the number of rooms to 48,172. Instead, 38,265 rooms were available, with 45,295 expected by the end of 2002. Only one thing is certain: If the tourists do come back, hotels will be the first to happily raise their rates.

## PRICE CATEGORIES

The hotel prices listed in this book are the rack rates, since no one can predict what might happen during the book's lifetime. Rates will rise if the economy improves and tourists come back. During peak season when hotels are full, rack rates are often charged. Even so, it's *imperative* to ask about special packages, upgrades, or promotional fares when making reservations, particularly in off-season. Although I've included toll-free numbers in the United States and Canada for many of the listings below, I also recommend contacting the hotel directly to inquire about rates and special deals. During a summer promotional, for example, the Great Eagle Hotel offered rooms starting at HK$1,180 ($153) for a double, including buffet breakfast, compared with the standard rack rate of HK$2,300 ($298). Likewise, the Excelsior

## Best Hotel Bets

See chapter 1 for a list of my hotel favorites—the best for business travelers, the best for a romantic getaway, and more.

---

recently offered an "Executive Package" beginning at HK$1,350 ($175) for a double that included buffet breakfast, discounts at hotel restaurants, free local phone calls, free rental of a mobile phone, and free use of computers in the business center; otherwise, the standard rack rate is HK$1,900 ($247). The Holiday Inn Golden Mile sliced HK$1,000 ($130) off its rack rates for a summer promotion.

Generally speaking, the price of a room in Hong Kong depends upon its view and height rather than upon its size. Not surprisingly, the best and most expensive rooms are those with a sweeping view of Victoria Harbour, as well as those on the higher floors. Don't be shy about asking what price categories are available and what are the differences among them. Keep in mind that the difference in price between a room facing inland and a room facing the harbor can be staggering, with various price categories in between. There are, for example, "partial" or "side" harbor views, which means you can glimpse the harbor looking sideways from your window or between tall buildings. Double rooms that range from HK$2,000 to HK$3,000 ($260 to $390), for example, may include five different categories, beginning with a "standard" room on a lower floor facing inland and then increasing in cost to those on upper floors facing inland, those with side harbor views, those on lower floors facing the harbor, and, most expensive, "deluxe" rooms on higher floors with full harbor views. To save money, consider requesting the highest room available in the category you choose. If "standard" rooms, for example, run up to the 8th floor and deluxe rooms are on floors 9 to 20, you'll save money by asking for a standard room on floor 8. If you decide to spring for a full harbor view, be sure to ask for it when making your reservation, and request the highest floor available.

For moderately priced or inexpensive lodging, few of which offer any kind of view at all, rates are usually based on height, decor, and sometimes size, and it's prudent to inquire whether there's a difference in price between twin and double rooms; some hotels charge more for two beds in a room (more sheets to wash, I guess).

In any case, the wide range of prices listed below for double rooms in each of the listings reflects the various categories available. In moderately priced and inexpensive lodging, single rates are also usually available, but more expensive hotels often charge the same for double or single occupancy.

All of Hong Kong's expensive and moderately priced hotels and the best of the inexpensive hotels are members of the Hong Kong Hotel Association (HKHA) and the Hong Kong Tourist Association (HKTA). All hotels listed here belong to at least one of these organizations. The advantage of staying at a member hotel is that if you have a complaint, you can lodge it directly with the Hong Kong Tourist Association. Furthermore, the HKHA maintains a counter at Hong Kong International Airport where you can reserve a room at one of its member hotels at no extra charge.

The hotels in this chapter are arranged first by price and then by geographical location. The categories are based on rates for a double room (excluding tax and service) as follows: **Very Expensive,** HK$2,500 ($325) and up; **Expensive,** HK$1,700 to HK$2,500 ($220 to $325); **Moderate,** HK$900 to 1,700 ($117 to $220); and **Inexpensive,** less than HK$900 ($117).

Keep in mind that prices given in this book are for room rates only—a 10% service charge and 3% government tax will be added to your bill. Since a 13% increase can really add up, be sure to take it into account when choosing your hotel.

# Tips for Saving on Your Hotel Room

The rack rate is the maximum rate that a hotel charges for a room. Although a few deluxe hotels stick to their published rack rates year-round and many hotels charge rack rates during peak travel times in spring and autumn, you can probably strike a better bargain.

- Don't be afraid to bargain. Get in the habit of asking for a lower price than the first one quoted. Most rack rates include commissions of 10% to 25% or more for travel agents, which some hotels will cut if you make your own reservations and haggle a bit. In addition, always ask politely whether a less expensive room than the first one mentioned is available. In addition, ask whether there are any corporate discounts or any promotional packages.

- Rely on a qualified professional. Certain hotels give travel agents discounts in exchange for steering business their way, so if you're shy about bargaining, an agent may be better equipped to negotiate discounts for you.

- Dial direct. When booking a room in a chain hotel, call the hotel's local line as well as the toll-free number, and see where you get the best deal. Sometimes there are special packages, such as weekend honeymoon packages, that central reservations desks will not be aware of.

- Check hotel Web sites for promotional fares. You can also go to the Hong Kong Tourist Association's Web site www.hkta.org/hotels to search for room availability, find out about daily specials, and make reservations at HKTA's 60 member hotels.

- Remember the law of supply and demand. Avoid high-season stays—generally spring and autumn. Many hotels offer promotional fares through the summer. Business hotels may offer discounts over the weekend.

- Consider purchasing a package from an airline that includes hotel rooms. United Vacations and Northwest World Vacations, for example, offer a variety of discounted hotel rooms that can be purchased in conjunction with airfare to Hong Kong.

- Avoid excess charges. Find out before you dial whether your hotel imposes a surcharge on local or long-distance calls. A pay phone, however inconvenient, may save you money. Also, instead of using the minibar in your room, save money by buying drinks and snacks from convenience stores.

- If traveling with children, try to find a hotel that allows children to stay free in their parents' room. There's an age limit (generally anywhere 12 to 18 years of age), there's sometimes a maximum of three people to a room, and children are usually free only if no extra bed is required.

- Consider a suite. If you are traveling with your family or another couple, you can pack more people into a suite (which usually comes with a sofa bed), and thereby reduce your per-person rate.

## 1 Very Expensive

Hong Kong's top hotels are among the best in the world, with unparalleled service, state-of-the-art business and health-club facilities, guest rooms equipped with just about everything you can imagine, some of the city's best restaurants, and views of famous Victoria Harbour. They also offer the convenience of a concierge or guest-relations staff, on hand to help with everything from theater tickets to restaurant reservations. Among other extras are turndown service, 24-hour room service, voice mail, welcoming tea brought to your room shortly after your arrival, free newspaper delivered to your room, and many in-room conveniences and amenities. Many also offer executive floors, a "hotel-within-a-hotel" concept catering primarily to business executives with such added services as express check-in and checkout; use of a private executive lounge serving complimentary breakfast, snacks, and drinks; and an executive- floor concierge or attendant.

## KOWLOON

**Hyatt Regency Hong Kong.** 67 Nathan Rd., Tsim Sha Tsui, Kowloon, Hong Kong. ☎ **800/ 233-1234** in the U.S. and Canada, or 852/2311 1234. Fax 852/2739 8701. www. hongkong. hyatt.com. E-mail: general@hyattregency.com.hk. 723 units. A/C MINIBAR TV TEL. HK$2,800–HK$3,100 ($364–$403) single or double; HK$3,300–HK$3,600 ($429–$468) Regency Club; from HK$4,400 ($572) suite. Children under 12 stay free in parents' room (maximum: 3 persons per room). AE, DC, MC, V. MTR: Tsim Sha Tsui.

Established in 1969 as Hyatt's first property in Asia, this hotel occupies prime real estate on Nathan Road, but it is one of the few deluxe hotels in Hong Kong that does not offer harbor-view rooms. In my opinion, if you're going to spend this much on a room, it's a shame not to have a view of the famous Victoria Harbour. However, the Hyatt does have a convenient location in the midst of Nathan Road's so-called "golden mile of shopping," just a 5-minute walk from the Star Ferry and a 1-minute walk from the Tsim Sha Tsui MTR subway station. Appealing to American business and leisure travelers, it has undergone extensive renovation through the decades as tastes have changed, getting rid of its flamboyant red-and-gold lobby so popular in the 1970s in favor of a subdued, more sophisticated marble-and-teakwood reception area reflective of 1990s taste, and decorated with Chinese antiques.

As for rooms, hints of local culture are represented by the lacquered Chinese chests housing the TVs and Chinese brush paintings on the walls. Rooms facing Nathan Road are equipped with double-glazed windows and insulated walls to reduce outside noise. Pluses include safe-deposit boxes large enough for a briefcase and a voice-mail recording system in all rooms, but business travelers may find it worth paying for more expensive rooms equipped with multi-media workstations, including in-room fax machine, laser printer, computer loaded with business and communication software, and unlimited Internet access. The hotel's executive floor, the Regency Club, served by private elevator and with its own lounge and fitness room, offers the usual complimentary breakfast and evening cocktails, as well as rooms with dataports or complete workstations.

**Dining/Diversions:** The hotel boasts five food-and-beverage outlets, including **Hugo's** steakhouse and the trendy, elegant **Chinese Restaurant,** decorated in modern art deco style. There's nightly entertainment in the very popular **Chin Chin Bar.**

**Amenities:** Business center, shopping arcade, tour desk, concierge, free newspaper, 24-hour room service, baby-sitting, in-house nurse, beauty salon, limousine service, same-day laundry service, nightly turndown.

**✪ The Peninsula Hotel.** Salisbury Rd., Tsim Sha Tsui, Kowloon, Hong Kong. ☎ **800/ 262-9467** in the U.S., or 852/2920 2888. Fax 852/2722 4170. www.peninsula. com. E-mail: pen@peninsula.com. 300 units. A/C MINIBAR TV TEL. HK$2,900–HK$4,600 ($377–$598) single or double; from HK$5,200 ($656) suite. AE, CB, DC, MC, V. MTR: Tsim Sha Tsui.

This is Hong Kong's most famous hotel, the place to stay if you are an incurable romantic, have a penchant for the historical, and can afford its high prices. Built in 1928, it exudes elegance from its white-gloved doormen to one of the largest limousine fleets of Rolls-Royces in the world. Priding itself on service, it maintains one of the highest staff-to-guest ratios in Hong Kong. Its lobby, reminiscent of a Parisian palace with high gilded ceilings, pillars, and palms, has long been Hong Kong's foremost spot for people-watching.

Although The Peninsula lost its fabled view of the harbor following construction of the unsightly Space Museum on reclaimed land across the street, this problem was remedied in 1993 with the completion of a magnificent 32-story tower that rises just behind the present hotel. Although the tower looks rather unremarkable when viewed from across the harbor, its plain, white exterior is a perfect match to the old hotel, showing unusual restraint in a city known for its splashy architectural boldness. No holds were barred, however, with the tower's interior—its rooftop serves as a helipad, its top-floor restaurant was designed by Philippe Starck, the swimming pool, complete with sun terrace overlooking the harbor, is elegantly modeled on a classical Roman theme, and its guest rooms have amenities and facilities almost beyond belief, creating a new standard of excellence that will surely set off a flurry of renovations as other hotels try to compete. Even jaded travelers are likely to be impressed.

Spacious rooms are all equipped with a silent fax machine with a personalized phone number (written messages are sent via fax; telephone messages by voice mail); computer hookups; a telephone that shows time around the world, automatically displaying time in your home country; headphones for both radio and TV; and extremely focused bedside reading lights designed to keep sleeping partners happy. A display panel shows outdoor temperature and humidity, the TV has a laser-disc/CD player (free CDs and movies are available), and there are three telephones (and two lines) in the bedroom and a hands-free phone in the bathroom (local calls are free). Room safes, and a box in the closet where attendants can place your morning newspaper or take your dirty shoes for complimentary cleaning, round out the amenities. Requests for hotel services, as well as such functions as curtain control, are accomplished with the push of a button. Bathrooms are huge; they are equipped with their own TV, mood lighting, separate bath and shower stall, and two sinks, both with a magnifying mirror. It may be worth the extra money to spring for a harbor view, since the rooms facing the back are a disappointment and those in the older part of the hotel slightly claustrophobic.

**Dining/Diversions:** Every restaurant in The Peninsula comes highly recommended. For decades, the hotel's premier restaurant has been **Gaddi's,** offering traditional French cuisine as well as live music and dancing in the evening. But equally as popular is the tower's top-floor restaurant, **Felix,** which features Philippe Starck's avant-garde interior, innovative Pacific Rim crossover cuisine, dramatic views of Hong Kong, and even a bar and disco. Other good choices include **The Verandah** for Continental cuisine, the **Chesa** for traditional Swiss food, the **Spring Moon** for Cantonese specialties, and **Imasa** for traditional Japanese food. The Lobby is Hong Kong's best spot for afternoon tea.

**Amenities:** Free indoor swimming pool with sun terrace, health club with exercise equipment, Jacuzzis, saunas, steam rooms, solariums, rooftop helipad, soundproof music room with grand piano where guests can practice and rehearse, designer-brand shopping arcade, business center, beauty salon, barber, tour desk, concierge, 24-hour room service, Rolls-Royce limousine service, free newspaper, free shoe shines, nightly turndown, baby-sitting, same-day laundry service, in-house nurse, complimentary welcoming tea.

# Kowloon Accommodations

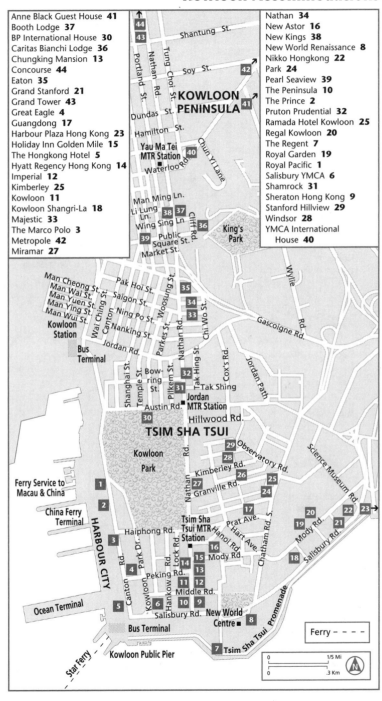

Anne Black Guest House **41**
Booth Lodge **37**
BP International House **30**
Caritas Bianchi Lodge **36**
Chungking Mansion **13**
Concourse **44**
Eaton **35**
Grand Stanford **21**
Grand Tower **43**
Great Eagle **4**
Guangdong **17**
Harbour Plaza Hong Kong **23**
Holiday Inn Golden Mile **15**
The Hongkong Hotel **5**
Hyatt Regency Hong Kong **14**
Imperial **12**
Kimberley **25**
Kowloon **11**
Kowloon Shangri-La **18**
Majestic **33**
The Marco Polo **3**
Metropole **42**
Miramar **27**

Nathan **34**
New Astor **16**
New Kings **38**
New World Renaissance **8**
Nikko Hongkong **22**
Park **24**
Pearl Seaview **39**
The Peninsula **10**
The Prince **2**
Pruton Prudential **32**
Ramada Hotel Kowloon **25**
Regal Kowloon **20**
The Regent **7**
Royal Garden **19**
Royal Pacific **1**
Salisbury YMCA **6**
Shamrock **31**
Sheraton Hong Kong **9**
Stanford Hillview **29**
Windsor **28**
YMCA International House **40**

# Central District Accommodations

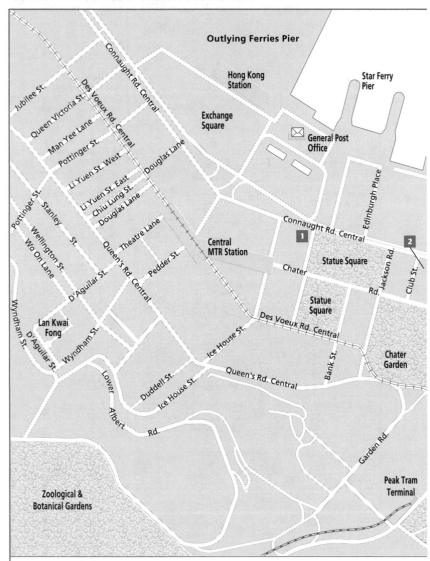

Conrad **6**
Furama **3**
Island Shangri-La **4**
JW Marriott **5**
Mandarin Oriental **1**
Ritz-Carlton **2**

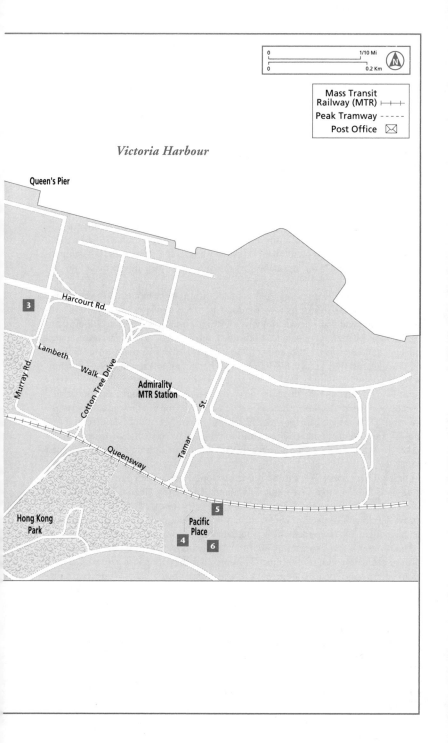

*Victoria Harbour*

Queen's Pier

Harcourt Rd.

3

Lambeth Walk

Murray Rd.

Cotton Tree Drive

Admirality
MTR Station

Tamar St.

Queensway

Hong Kong
Park

Pacific
Place

4

5

6

Mass Transit
Railway (MTR)
Peak Tramway
Post Office

0        1/10 Mi
0        0.2 Km

**The Regent Hong Kong.** 18 Salisbury Rd., Tsim Sha Tsui, Kowloon, Hong Kong. ☎ **800/545-4000** in the U.S. and Canada, or 852/2721 1211. Fax 852/2739 4546. www.rih.com. E-mail: reservations.rhk@fourseasons.com. 602 units. A/C MINIBAR TV TEL. HK$2,950–HK$4,250 ($383–$552) double; from HK$5,000 ($649) junior suite. Children under 19 stay free in parents' room. AE, CB, DC, MC, V. MTR: Tsim Sha Tsui.

The Peninsula's biggest rival, The Regent Hong Kong boasts what may well be the best views of Victoria Harbour from Tsim Sha Tsui. In fact, you can't get much closer to the water than this—the hotel is located on a projection of reclaimed land and sits on more than 120 pylons sunk into the harbor. Built in 1981 of polished rose granite and rising 17 stories, it has a bare lobby of polished granite and marble with the magnificent view of the harbor and Hong Kong Island as the focal point. The Regent also has some of Hong Kong's best restaurants, all with great views; an exclusive shopping mall; the world's largest fleet of Daimler limousines outside the United Kingdom; and a spectacular freestanding staircase of white Carrara marble leading to the hotel's ballroom. Even the outdoor pool's sun terrace and whirlpools overlook the harbor. The front desk staff, however, occasionally lacks the warmth and graciousness of competitor hotels. They border on the snobbish—the once-over I usually get makes me feel out of place.

Still, The Regent receives repeated accolades from more moneyed travelers than myself. As many as 70% of its rooms command sweeping views of the harbor, with floor-to-ceiling and wall-to-wall windows. The remaining (less expensive) rooms face the outdoor swimming pool and landscaped sun terrace. All rooms feature such updated facilities as room safes and cordless keyboards and TVs that provide Internet and e-mail access (fee: HK$158/$20.50 per 24 hours), as well as a dedicated dataport for quick computer link-up. Fax machines are available free of charge. But unlike most Hong Kong deluxe hotels, there are no designated executive floors, the underlying concept being that all rooms should offer the same degree of efficient and personalized service. There's a butler for every 12 rooms, on duty 24 hours a day. Notable features of the Regent are its spacious bathrooms, each fitted in Italian marble with a sunken bathtub and separate shower unit, and an air purification system in all guest rooms.

**Dining/Diversions:** The **Plume** is one of Hong Kong's finest French restaurants, while **Yü** is the city's trendiest seafood restaurant. **Lai Ching Heen** is an elegant Cantonese restaurant, while the **Harbour Side** offers a harbor view along with its inexpensive snacks and meals throughout the day. **Club Shanghai,** decorated like a 1930s Shanghai nightclub, offers live music and dancing.

**Amenities:** Outdoor swimming pool and whirlpools overlooking Victoria Harbour, business center, exercise studio (open 24 hours), health spa, upscale shopping arcade, beauty salon, concierge, 24-hour room service, house doctor, baby-sitting, free newspaper, free bottled water, nightly turndown, limousine service, same-day laundry service, complimentary welcoming tea and fresh fruit.

## CENTRAL DISTRICT

✪ **Island Shangri-La Hong Kong.** Pacific Place, Supreme Court Rd., Central, Hong Kong. ☎ **800/942-5050** in the U.S. and Canada, or 852/2877 3838. Fax 852/2521 8742. www.shangri-la.com. E-mail: isl@shangri-la.com. 565 units. A/C MINIBAR TV TEL. HK$2,300–$HK$3,450 ($299–$448) single; HK$2,500–HK$3,650 ($325–$474) double; from HK$5,600 ($727) suite. Children under 18 stay free in parents' room. AE, DC, MC, V. MTR: Admiralty.

Hong Kong Island's tallest hotel (measured from sea level) offers the ultimate in extravagance and luxury, rivaling the grand hotels in Paris or London. More than 700 Viennese chandeliers, lush Tai Ping carpets, artistic flower arrangements, and

## ❷  Did You Know?

The Hong Kong Housing Authority is one of the world's largest public landlords; more than one-third the population lives in public rental housing, and the world's largest public housing project is in Hong Kong.

more than 500 paintings and artworks adorn the hotel. The 17-story atrium, which stretches from the 39th to the 56th floor, features a marvelous 16-story-high Chinese painting, drawn on 250 panels of Chinese paper by 40 artists from Beijing and believed to be the largest landscape painting in the world. Also in the atrium is a private lounge open only to hotel guests and a two-story old world–style library, fitted with leather armchairs and classic lamps and stocked with reference materials, special-interest books, videotapes, and music compact discs. The hotel itself is enhanced by the connecting Pacific Place shopping center, with its many options in dining; across the street is Hong Kong Park.

Upon arrival, guests are personally escorted to their rooms (all of which ring the 17-story atrium) by a guest relations officer, who also explains features of the room. Rooms here, among the largest in Hong Kong and the largest on Hong Kong Island, face either the Peak or Victoria Harbour. They feature marble-topped desks, dataports and dual phone lines to accommodate personal computers, a hands-free phone, Chinese lacquerware TV cabinets and movies on demand, silk bedspreads, a room safe, and free bottled water. Oversize bathrooms are equipped with two sinks, separate tub and shower areas (harbor-view rooms only), bidet, bath scales, and even jewelry boxes. Bedside controls regulate everything from the opening of the curtains (it's great to wake up in the morning and have the city appear before you with a mere push of a button) to the "Do Not Disturb" light. Fresh flowers and teddy bears placed on pillows during nightly turndown are nice touches. Guests paying rack rates receive such additional services as free transportation from and to the airport, free laundry and dry cleaning throughout their stay, complimentary American or continental breakfast, free local telephone calls, and 6pm late checkout.

**Dining/Diversions:** **Petrus** is the hotel's signature restaurant, occupying a prime spot on the top floor and serving continental cuisine with a view. Next door is **Cyrano,** a lounge offering jazz entertainment every night and stunning views of the harbor. The **Lobster Bar** is *the* place to go for meals featuring the sea's best crustacean, but for casual dining with a breezy Californian atmosphere, highly recommended is the **Island Café,** specializing in buffets. Other restaurants serve Cantonese and Japanese fare.

**Amenities:** Outdoor heated swimming pool big enough for swimming laps, Jacuzzi, sauna, steam bath, health club, 24-hour business center, drugstore, barbershop, beauty salon, shopping arcade, concierge, free newspaper, 24-hour room service, same-day laundry service, nightly turndown, welcoming tea, limousine service, babysitting, medical clinic, free shuttle service to Queen's Pier in Central and the Convention Centre.

✪ **Mandarin Oriental.** 5 Connaught Rd., Central, Hong Kong. ☎ **800/526-6566** in the U.S. and Canada, or 852/2522 0111. Fax 852/2810 6190. www.mandarin-oriental.com. E-mail: reserve-mohkg@mohg.com. 542 units. A/C MINIBAR TV TEL. HK$2,800–HK$4,500 ($364–$584) single; HK$3,050–HK$4,750 ($396–$617) double; from HK$5,500 ($714) suite. AE, CB, DC, MC, V. MTR: Central.

With so many newer hotels on Hong Kong Island, the Mandarin, a 25-story landmark built in 1963, seems like a familiar old-timer. Famed for its service and consistently

# Causeway Bay & Wan Chai Accommodations

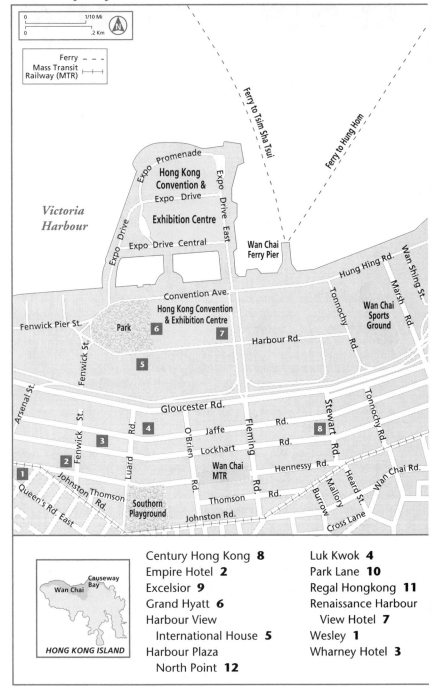

Century Hong Kong **8**
Empire Hotel **2**
Excelsior **9**
Grand Hyatt **6**
Harbour View
   International House **5**
Harbour Plaza
   North Point **12**

Luk Kwok **4**
Park Lane **10**
Regal Hongkong **11**
Renaissance Harbour
   View Hotel **7**
Wesley **1**
Wharney Hotel **3**

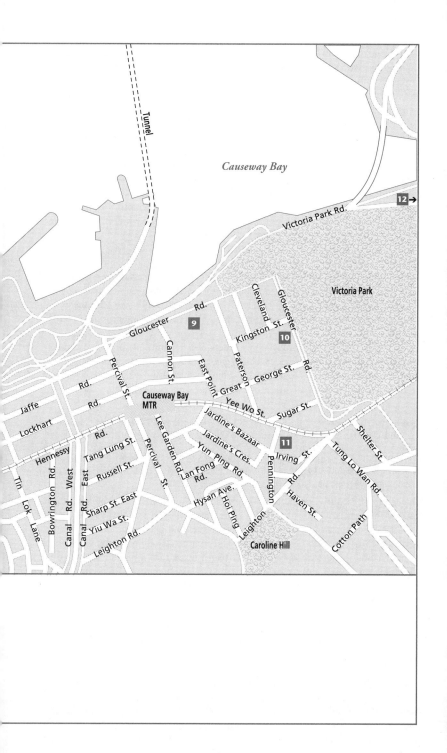

Causeway Bay

Tunnel

Victoria Park Rd.

Victoria Park

**12**→

Gloucester        Rd.        **9**

Cleveland

Gloucester    St.

Kingston St.        **10**

Paterson

Cannon St.

Percival St.

East Point    Great    George St.        Rd.

Causeway Bay
MTR

Jaffe        Rd.

Yee Wo St.        Sugar St.

Lockhart    Rd.

Jardine's Bazaar

Shelter St.

Jardine's Cres.

Hennessy    Rd.

Lee Garden Rd.

Yun  Ping  Rd.

Irving  St.

Tung Lo Wan Rd

Bowrington    Rd.

Tang Lung St.

Lan Fong
Rd.

Pennington

Russell St.

Percival    St.

Rd.

Haven St.

Tin    Lok    Lane

Canal    Rd.    East

Canal    Rd.    West

Sharp St. East

Hysan Ave.

Hoi Ping

Leighton

**11**

Yiu Wa St.

Leighton Rd.

Caroline Hill

Cotton Path

rated as one of the top hotels in the world, the Mandarin Oriental maintains a staff of 1,000 for its 540 rooms and suites; registration takes place in guest rooms rather than a front desk. Because of its great location in the heart of Hong Kong's business district (not far from Star Ferry), it attracts mostly a business clientele. For tourists, one advantage to staying in Central is that you're surrounded mostly by people who actually live and work in Hong Kong, as opposed to Tsim Sha Tsui, which is crowded largely with other tourists. In addition, the Mandarin's restaurants are among the best in Hong Kong, but its indoor pool is disappointingly small.

Spacious and decorated in an Asian theme with an understated elegance, most rooms offer balconies (rare in Hong Kong and admittedly a bit noisy) and face either the harbor or inland—those facing the harbor even come with binoculars. Rooms feature all the amenities and facilities you could possibly want, including two phone lines and dataports, and purified tap water for drinking, but if you are still in need of something, the staff will make every effort to fulfill your wishes.

**Dining/Diversions:** Several of the restaurants have a well-deserved reputation for excellent cuisine; there is the **Mandarin Grill** for seafood, the **Man Wah** for Cantonese food, and the very trendy **Vong** with its Asian-influenced French food and spectacular views. **The Captain's Bar,** just off the hotel lobby, is an intimate, cozy bar popular with Central's executive and professional crowd, while the **Chinnery,** with more than 100 single malt whiskies, remained off-limits to women until, incredibly enough, 1990.

**Amenities:** Indoor swimming pool, fitness center, sauna, whirlpool, art gallery, business center, shopping arcade, Cuban-style cigar divan, beauty salon, barbershop, tour desk, concierge, secretarial services, complimentary fruit basket, free newspaper, 24-hour room service, nightly turndown, same-day laundry service, house doctor, limousine service, baby-sitting.

✪ **The Ritz-Carlton.** 3 Connaught Rd., Central, Hong Kong. ☎ **800/241-3333** in the U.S. and Canada, or 852/2877 6666. Fax 852/2877 6778. www.ritz-carlton.com. E-mail: ritzrchk@hk.super.net. 216 units. A/C MINIBAR TV TEL. HK$2,850–HK$3,850 ($370.50–$500.50) single or double; HK$4,000–HK$4,200 ($520–$546) Ritz-Carlton Club executive floor; from HK$4,500 ($585) suite. Children under 13 stay free in parents' room (maximum: 3 persons per room). AE, DC, MC, V. MTR: Central.

Opened in 1993, the Ritz-Carlton occupies a smart-looking 25-story building in the heart of the Central District not far from the waterfront and Star Ferry. It follows the Ritz-Carlton tradition of excellent service and fine dining, and has an extensive collection of 18th- and 19th-century artwork and antiques. Its lobby is subdued and intimate, resembling more closely a wealthy person's home than a public place, with the reception desk tucked away in an alcove. All in all, the hotel, with its hushed, home-away-from-home atmosphere, is a far cry from the crowds at Hong Kong's more plebeian megahotels.

The low-key atmosphere prevails upstairs as well; since there are only 10 to 12 rooms on each floor, it seems more like an upscale apartment complex than a hotel, which obviously appeals to its overwhelmingly business clientele, many of whom are long-staying guests. The rooms are rather neutral in tone in an understated elegance, with half facing the harbor and offering great views; even those that face inland provide a nice view of lush Chater Garden and the Peak. All rooms feature pay movies on demand, dual phone lines and dataports, safes, free bottled water, and marble bathrooms with two sinks, separate toilet areas, and scales. Two floors are designed with business travelers in mind, complete with computers hooked up to the Internet, faxes, printers, and scanners. The top three floors serve as the Ritz-Carlton Club, where guests enjoy special services and amenities, as well as a private lounge offering five complimentary food-and-beverage presentations daily.

**Dining/Diversions:** The **Toscana** is the premier restaurant, specializing in regional Italian cuisine; other outlets serve Chinese, Japanese, and continental cuisine. The Chater Lounge, overlooking Chater Garden, has afternoon tea.

**Amenities:** Heated outdoor swimming pool, steam bath, sauna, whirlpool, fitness room, concierge, 24-hour room service, welcome tea, complimentary fruit basket, same-day laundry service, free newspaper, nightly turndown, baby-sitting, limousine service.

## CAUSEWAY BAY & WAN CHAI

**Grand Hyatt Hong Kong.** 1 Harbour Rd., Wan Chai, Hong Kong. ☎ **800/233-1234** in the U.S. and Canada, or 852/2588 1234. Fax 852/2802 0677. www.hongkong.hyatt.com. E-mail: info@grandhyatt.com.hk. 570 units. A/C MINIBAR TV TEL. HK$3,200–HK$3,500 ($416–$454) single; HK$3,450–HK$3,750 ($448.50–$487) double; HK$3,950–HK$4,250 ($513.50–$552.50) Regency Club executive floor double; from HK$5,500 ($715) suite. Children under 12 stay free in parents' room (maximum: 3 persons per room). AE, DC, MC, V. MTR: Wan Chai.

In a city with so many first-class hotels and such stiff competition, sooner or later a hotel had to exceed all the others in opulence and grandeur. Walking into the lobby of the Grand Hyatt is like walking into the Bavarian castle of a modern-day King Ludwig, a lobby so palatial in design that the word "understatement" has certainly never crossed its threshold. Decorated to resemble the salon of a 1930s art deco luxury ocean liner, it literally flaunts space, with huge black granite columns, massive flower arrangements, palm trees, bubbling fountains, and furniture and statuettes reminiscent of that era. It appears that no expense was spared in creating Hyatt International's Asian flagship hotel, and the service goes beyond expectations. Little wonder President Clinton chose the hotel's presidential suite during his 1998 visit.

Located on the waterfront near the Convention Centre and only a 5-minute walk from the Wan Chai Star Ferry pier that delivers passengers to Tsim Sha Tsui, it offers smart-looking, contemporary rooms, soothingly decorated to ease stress and invite relaxation. Pluses are the specially made beds with Egyptian cotton sheets, sliding clothes rack in the closet, and coffee table books. Rooms also have fax machines with personalized numbers, dataports, cordless keyboards to access the Internet and e-mail through an interactive TV at speeds 50 times faster than a conventional modem (fee: HK$85/$11 per 24 hours), voice mail, on-command movies, free bottled water, safes and marble bathrooms complete with 18-karat-gold fixtures, separate bathtub and shower areas, and bathroom scales and magnifying mirrors. Some 70% of the rooms provide a harbor view, while the rest have a view of the free-form pool and garden with partial glimpses of the harbor. Extra pampering is offered by the Regency Club's eight floors, serviced by private elevators, where complimentary continental breakfast, cocktails, and hors d'oeuvres are available and guest rooms are outfitted with DVD players.

**Dining/Diversions:** The bright and airy **Grissini** serves authentic Milanese cuisine, while **One Harbour Road** is a split-level upscale Cantonese restaurant. **JJ's** is one of the hottest and largest nightspots on the island, featuring live music, a disco, separate bar areas, and even a pizza parlor. More intimate is the Champagne Bar, with Hong Kong's most extensive list of the bubbly stuff and live entertainment.

**Amenities:** Huge outdoor swimming pool (shared with the adjacent Renaissance Harbour View Hotel and closed in winter), children's pool, two rooftop tennis courts, golf driving range, jogging track, Jacuzzi, fitness club, business center, beauty salon, concierge, free newspaper, 24-hour room service, limousine service, baby-sitting, nightly turndown, complimentary shuttle to Central and Admiralty MTR station, same-day laundry service.

## 2 Expensive

Many expensive hotels offer almost as much as Hong Kong's very expensive hotels, though only a few have great—if any—views of Victoria Harbour. In this category you can expect a guest-relations desk, 24-hour room service, health clubs, no-smoking floors, business centers, same-day laundry service, and comfortable rooms with hair dryers, cable or satellite TVs with in-room movies, and coffee/tea-making facilities. But since this category of hotels sometimes caters to large tour groups, they can also be noisier, with less personalized service than the deluxe hotels. On the other hand, many also have executive floors for business travelers.

### KOWLOON

**Grand Stanford.** 70 Mody Rd., Tsim Sha Tsui East, Kowloon, Hong Kong. ☎ **800/ 327-0200** in the U.S. and Canada, or 852/2721 5161. Fax 852/2732 2233. www.grandstanford.com. E-mail: gshv@netvigator.com. 580 units. A/C MINIBAR TV TEL. HK$2,100–HK$2,900 ($273–$377) single; HK$2,200–HK$3,000 ($286–$390) double; HK$2,700–HK$3,500 ($351–$454) executive floor double; from HK$4,000 ($519) suite. Children under 19 stay free in parents' room. AE, DC, MC, V. MTR: Tsim Sha Tsui.

Because of its location near Hong Kong's Coliseum in Tsim Sha Tsui East, a number of well-known personalities have stayed here, including David Bowie, Elton John, and John McEnroe. Formerly a Holiday Inn but now the flagship of Stanford Hotels International and completely renovated, it's right on the waterfront and offers the usual facilities and amenities expected of an upper-class hotel. Probably the biggest drawback is the 10-minute walk to the Tsim Sha Tsui MTR station, but it does offer hotel guests a free shuttle service to several locations in Tsim Sha Tsui every 30 to 45 minutes.

About half the rooms offer harbor views; unfortunately, the windows of the least expensive rooms open rather unceremoniously onto a windowless wall. All rooms, nicely renovated, feature double or king-size beds, dataports, voice mail, room safes, and magnifying mirrors; those with harbor views also have bathroom scales. The executive floors offer the usual amenities of complimentary newspaper, free breakfast, fruit basket, and free cocktails, as well as fax machines and trouser presses. One advantage here is the rooftop swimming pool, heated and open year-round.

**Dining:** The **Belvedere,** with views of the harbor, serves French cuisine, while the **Mistral** specializes in Italian foods. There are also a Cantonese restaurant and a cafe specializing in buffets.

**Amenities:** Outdoor heated swimming pool, fitness center, sauna, health spa, business center, beauty salon, concierge, 24-hour room service, same-day laundry service, baby-sitting, doctor and dentist on call, limousine service, nightly turndown, free shuttle service to Tsim Sha Tsui.

**Great Eagle Hotel.** 8 Peking Rd., Tsim Sha Tsui, Kowloon, Hong Kong. ☎ **800/457-4000** in the U.S. and Canada, or 852/2375 1133. Fax 852/2375 6611. www.gehotel.com. E-mail: resv@gehotel.com. 487 units. A/C MINIBAR TV TEL. HK$2,100–HK$2,600 ($273–$338) single; HK$2,300–HK$2,800 ($299–$364) double; HK$3,000–HK$3,600 ($390–$467) Club Floor double; from HK$4,000 ($520) suite. Children under 12 stay free in parents' room. AE, CB, DC, MC, V. MTR: Tsim Sha Tsui.

This 16-story hotel is located a couple of blocks inland from the harbor, just a few minutes' walk from the Star Ferry and the huge Harbour City shopping complex. Its lobby, bathed in warm gold tones, exudes a classic Italian atmosphere, with chandeliers, marble floor, a hand-painted dome ceiling, and glass art by American artist Dale Chihuly. It bills itself as an "intelligent" hotel. In each room, a sophisticated bedside control panel allows guests to operate lights, adjust air-conditioning levels, select a TV or radio program, call up messages or the hotel bill on the television screen, and switch on a "Do Not Disturb" light that automatically disconnects the door chime. As an added safety precaution, each guest receives an electronic key with a new combination, and staff keys are programmed for specific times only, thereby barring anyone from entering rooms after a shift ends. What's more, a printer records all hotel employee use, indicating when each key was used, where, and by whom. As if that weren't enough, the rooms are also equipped with electronic safes. Rooms also have voice mail, two hands-free speaker phones, and marble bathrooms with separate showers and tubs, and scales. The most expensive rooms are on higher floors with harbor views. Tourists account for about half the hotel's guests; the other half are business-people, many of whom stay on one of the four floors reserved for the Club, which can be reached only by inserting a special key in the elevator. Added amenities here include a private lounge where complimentary breakfast and cocktails are served, fax machines in all rooms, free local calls, free pressing and laundry services, and personalized stationery and name cards.

**Dining: T'ang Court,** serving Cantonese food in an elegant setting, is the premier restaurant, while the **Bostonian** is popular with locals for its fun atmosphere and American-style seafood.

**Amenities:** Rooftop outdoor heated swimming pool, health club, sauna, shopping arcade, business center, concierge, free newspaper, 24-hour room service, house doctor, welcome tea, baby-sitting, same-day laundry service, limousine service, nightly turndown.

**Harbour Plaza Hong Kong.** 20 Tak Fung St., Hung Hom, Kowloon, Hong Kong. ☎ 852/ **2621 3188.** Fax 852/2621 3311. www.harbour-plaza.com/hphk. E-mail: hp-book@ harbour-plaza.com.hk. 416 units. A/C MINIBAR TV TEL. HK$2,200–HK$2,900 ($286–$377) single; HK$2,350–$HK3,050 ($305–$396) double; HK$3,150–HK$3,450 ($409–$448) Club Floor double; from HK$4,500 ($584) suite. AE, DC, MC, V. Free shuttle from Tsim Sha Tsui.

Opened in 1995, this relatively new hotel is located in Hung Hom, known for its clothing factory outlets, the Whampoa Garden shopping center, and the KCR Kowloon-Canton Railway Station with service to China. Although it's a bit far from Tsim Sha Tsui, a free shuttle bus travels between the hotel and Tsim Sha Tsui every half hour. In addition, ferry service to Central and Wan Chai is just a couple of minutes' walk away. Although the hotel targets corporate business travelers, primarily Japanese and American, its enviable location right on the harbor waterfront gives it a resort-like atmosphere, as does its rooftop pool with great views of Hong Kong. Six of its seven food and beverage outlets boast harbor views, as do 66% of its guest rooms. Most face Causeway Bay or Quarry Bay (rather than the more fabled night lights of Wan Chai and Central), and glazed windows allow viewers to watch harbor activity without being seen. Rooms are equipped with safes, voice mail, two-line phones, dataports, on-command movies, bathroom scales, and magnifying mirrors. Two Harbour Club floors provide extra privileges like complimentary breakfast, cocktails, free local phone calls, an in-room fax machine, and personalized stationery.

**Dining/Diversions:** In addition to the usual Cantonese and Western restaurants, there's Hong Kong's only Japanese robatayaki restaurant (in which foods are grilled in front of you) and an Italian restaurant with al fresco dining. The Pit Stop is a bar with a racing theme, while the coffee shop has a computer with Internet access guests can use for free.

**Amenities:** Outdoor heated rooftop swimming pool open year-round with Jacuzzi, fitness center, sauna, steam bath, solarium, shopping arcade, business center, concierge, free newspaper, medical clinic, 24-hour room service, nightly turndown,

---

### ℍ Family-Friendly Hotels

**BP International House** *(see p. 82)* This inexpensive hotel offers "Family Rooms" with bunk beds that sleep four for US$170. Parents will appreciate the convenience of a laundry room. But best of all is the adjacent Kowloon Park, with its indoor and outdoor public swimming pools, children's playground, lake with flamingos and other birds, and plenty of romping space for active bodies.

**Grand Hyatt/Renaissance Harbour View** *(see pgs. 69 and 80)* These two hotels share one of Hong Kong's largest outdoor swimming pools, as well as a splash pool for smaller children. Both hotels also offer baby-sitting.

**Mandarin Oriental** *(see p. 65)* Beginning with check-in, children are invited to participate by entering their names and ages into a book reserved for younger guests. Children's menus are available at several of the hotel's restaurants and for room service. Chinaware features cartoon characters. Room amenities for babies include talcum powder, wet wipes, diapers, a teether, and an educational toy, while older children receive a coloring book with crayons and a reading book or puzzles and games. Items available on loan include cribs, bottle sterilizer units, baby baths, high chairs, board games, and computerized toys. Baby-sitting is available.

**Regal Airport Hotel** *(see p. 81)* You won't want to stay at the airport unless you have to, but this hotel has the best-equipped children's recreation room I've seen in Hong Kong, complete with electronic games, toys, table tennis, air hockey, and a toddler area. It's open weekends 11:30am to 9:30pm and during lunch and dinner the rest of the week. The hotel also offers baby-sitting.

**Salisbury YMCA** *(see p. 94)* The overwhelming choice for families in terms of price, facilities, and location (just a short walk to both the Star Ferry and the MTR), this Salisbury Road establishment offers large suites suitable for families, an inexpensive cafeteria serving buffet meals, two indoor swimming pools (including a children's pool), an indoor climbing wall, and a children's play area on the fourth-floor garden terrace. Baby-sitting is also available.

---

baby-sitting, same-day laundry service, limousine service, free shuttle service to Tsim Sha Tsui and the KCR Railway Station.

**Holiday Inn Golden Mile.** 50 Nathan Rd., Tsim Sha Tsui, Kowloon, Hong Kong. ☎ **800/ 465-4329** in the U.S. and Canada, or 852/2369 3111. Fax 852/2369 8016. www.goldenmile. com. E-mail: reserv@goldenmile.com. 600 units. A/C MINIBAR TV TEL. HK$1,900–HK$2,450 ($247–$318) single; $2,300–HK$2,550 ($299–$331) twin; HK$2,800 ($364) Executive Club twin; from HK$5,700 ($741) suite. Up to 2 children under 19 stay free in parents' room. AE, CB, DC, MC, V. MTR: Tsim Sha Tsui.

Named after the "golden mile of shopping" on Nathan Road, this Holiday Inn, built in 1975 and recently renovated from top to bottom, has a very good location right in the heart of Tsim Sha Tsui, about a 6-minute walk from the Star Ferry. The MTR is right across the street. Maybe that's why its lobby is used as a departure point for several sightseeing tours, which is convenient if you plan to take some organized tours during your stay, but can be rather noisy and bothersome if you don't (especially if you want to find an empty seat in the lobby). Needless to say, the hotel also caters to tour groups, mainly from Europe and North America. Rooms are very clean, modern, and fairly large for Tsim Sha Tsui, featuring either a king-size bed or two double beds, as well as cable and satellite TV, safes, and voice mail. Some rooms also have fax machines and Internet connections. Although boasting floor-to-ceiling windows, views are blocked by adjacent buildings; some even face the unsightly Chungking Mansion. Three floors of the 18-floor hotel are reserved for Executive Club rooms, which offer complimentary continental breakfast, discounts on laundry and dry cleaning, free local telephone calls, and free evening cocktails.

**Dining/Diversions:** Europe reigns in this Holiday Inn's restaurants, with continental foods served buffet-style in **Café Vienna** and intriguing, continental cuisine featured in the classy **Avenue** restaurant. There's also a Chinese restaurant and a delicatessen with a take-out counter offering home-smoked meats, sausages, and baked goods. **Hari's,** with live entertainment, is popular for its happy hour.

**Amenities:** Rooftop swimming pool open year-round, fitness room, sauna, beauty salon, shopping arcade, business center, tour desk, concierge, 24-hour room service, baby-sitting, same-day laundry service, doctor on call.

**The Hongkong Hotel.** Harbour City, 3 Canton Rd., Tsim Sha Tsui, Kowloon, Hong Kong. ☎ **800/524-0500** in the U.S. and Canada, or 852/2113 0088. Fax 852/2113 0011. www.marcopolohotels.com. E-mail: hongkong@marcopolohotels.com. 665 units. A/C MINIBAR TV TEL. HK$2,300–HK$3,530 ($299–$459) single; HK$2,400–HK$3,630 ($312–$472) double; HK$3,200–HK$4,270 ($416–$555) Continental Club executive floor double; from HK$3,960 ($515) suite. 1 child under 14 can stay free in parents' room. AE, DC, MC, V. MTR: Tsim Sha Tsui.

A member of the Marco Polo Hotel group and the best of three Marco Polo properties lining this street, this hotel is as close as you can get to the Star Ferry and is connected via air-conditioned walkway to the largest shopping complex in Asia, Harbour City. It is also close to the China Hong Kong Terminal with departures for Macau. Built in the 1960s and well maintained, it has a marble lobby that is spacious and comfortable. The most expensive rooms have unparalleled views of harbor activity, including the ocean liners that dock right next door, and are quite large, with walk-in closets and large bathrooms and vanities. The lowest-price rooms, which are also good-size, face the small courtyard swimming pool and other guest rooms, and can be quite dark. The guest rooms, most of which have queen- or king-size beds, combine Western and Eastern decor in muted colors and offer room safe, voice mail, and dual phone lines (dataports available in some rooms). The rooms on the Continental Club floors feature the usual complimentary breakfast, cocktails, welcome tea, and fruit basket, as well as free pressing service for one suit or dress.

**Dining/Diversions:** Among the hotel's seven restaurants and bars, **Tai Pan,** which features international cuisine served to the accompaniment of a piano, is the premier restaurant. Equally good are the **Golden Unicorn,** a Cantonese restaurant that serves an exceptional dim sum lunch; and **Gripps,** a casual American restaurant and bar.

**Amenities:** Tiny outdoor heated swimming pool, business center, beauty salon, barbershop, tour desk, concierge, 24-hour room service, baby-sitting, same-day laundry service, limousine service, house doctor, nightly turndown.

**Hotel Nikko Hongkong.** 72 Mody Rd., Tsim Sha Tsui East, Kowloon, Hong Kong. ☎ **800/645-5687** in the U.S. and Canada, or 852/2739 1111. Fax 852/2311 3122. www. hotelnikko.com.hk. E-mail: nikko@hotelnikko.com.hk. 460 units. A/C MINIBAR TV TEL. HK$2,360–HK$3,260 ($306–$423) single or double; HK$2,660–HK$3,560($346–$463) Nikko executive floor; from HK$5,850 ($760) suite. Children 14 and under stay free in parents' room. AE, DC, MC, V. MTR: Tsim Sha Tsui.

An affiliate of Japan Airlines and therefore catering heavily to the Japanese, the 15-story Nikko Hongkong is the farthest east of a string of hotels along the waterfront of Tsim Sha Tsui East. Opened in 1988, it's only a few minutes' walk from Kowloon

Station but at least a 15-minute hike to the Star Ferry to Central (closer is the hover-ferry service to Central, about a 7-minute walk away). Its rooms, more than half of which face the harbor, are decorated with furniture carved from American maple and with either Japanese works of art or Dutch maps of the Far East. An electronic bed-side panel enables guests to set the alarm, control the TV, and open or shut the cur-tains. Other features include computer hookups for both 110 and 200 volts and large room safes. Bathrooms, finished in black-veined white Italian Carrara marble, come equipped with separate bathtubs and showers as well as bathrobes and cotton kimonos. The Nikko executive floors occupy the top three floors of the hotel; ameni-ties here include complimentary continental breakfast, fruit basket, afternoon tea, cocktails, after-hours champagne, in-room computer/Internet service, and free local phone calls.

**Dining/Diversions:** Restaurants serve Chinese and Japanese cuisine and seafood, while the **Sky Lounge** on the 15th floor offers drinks and a view of Hong Kong's lights.

**Amenities:** Outdoor swimming pool, fitness room, sauna, business center, barber-shop, shopping arcade, concierge, free newspaper, 24-hour room service, house doc-tor, limousine service, baby-sitting, same-day laundry service.

✪ **Kowloon Shangri-La, Hong Kong.** 64 Mody Rd., Tsim Sha Tsui East, Kowloon, Hong Kong. ☎ **800/942-5050** in the U.S. and Canada, or 852/2721 2111. Fax 852/2723 8686. www.shangri-la.com. E-mail: ksl_reservations@shangri-la.com. 725 units. A/C MINIBAR TV TEL. HK$2,200–HK$3,200 ($286–$416) single; HK$2,400–HK$3,400 ($312–$441) double; HK$2,700–HK$3,700 ($351–$480) Horizon Club executive floor double; from HK$4,200 ($545) suite. Children under 18 stay free in parents' room. AE, CB, DC, MC, V. MTR: Tsim Sha Tsui.

The 21-story Kowloon Shangri-La, on the waterfront of Tsim Sha Tsui East, is a good choice for business travelers, who make up a large percentage of its clientele and the majority of whom are American. With a well-trained staff of 1,000, service here is ster-ling, which is probably one reason why repeat guests number more than 40% of hotel occupancy. Its two-story lobby is one of the most spacious in Hong Kong, with an expansive white Carrara marble floor, massive Viennese crystal chandeliers, a fountain, and Chinese landscape murals. The hotel, just a minute's walk from the hoverferry pier with service to Central, is within walking distance of Tsim Sha Tsui but some-thing of a hike from the nearest MTR station.

Rooms, offering either harbor views or rather mundane "garden views" (a popular euphemism for windows that face inland), are large and luxuriously appointed, with ceiling-to-floor bay windows and either a king-size bed or two double beds. Curtains, TV (with pay movies on demand), lights, and other appliances are controlled by bed-side panels. Messages are delivered via voice mail and can even be retrieved outside the hotel. Rooms also have dataports and room safes. If you pay rack rates, additional ben-efits include free airport transfer, free laundry and dry cleaning service, free American or continental breakfast, free local telephone calls, and a late 6pm checkout. The top two floors are the executive floors; called the Horizon Club, it offers a complimentary chauffeured limousine to and from the airport, an in-room fax, personalized sta-tionery, free laundry and dry cleaning, a pressing service, and complimentary break-fast and cocktails.

**Dining/Diversions:** The hotel's newest restaurant is **Napa** on the 21st floor, offer-ing innovative California cuisine and a stunning view of the harbor. The formal **Mar-gaux** is known throughout Hong Kong for its great French cuisine, while **Shang Palace** is an extravagantly decorated Cantonese restaurant. Other restaurants serve Japanese cuisine and steaks. **The Blue Note** features great jazz in an intimate setting.

**Amenities:** Small indoor swimming pool (with jets to help create resistance for lap swimming), free health spa with sauna, business center open 24 hours, beauty salon, tailor shop, concierge, 24-hour room service, free newspaper, complimentary welcoming tea, house doctor, limousine service, nightly turndown, baby-sitting, same-day laundry service.

**The Marco Polo, Hong Kong.** Harbour City, Canton Rd., Tsim Sha Tsui, Kowloon, Hong Kong. ☎ **800/524-0500** in the U.S. and Canada, or 852/2113 0888. Fax 852/2113 0022. www.marcopolohotels.com. E-mail: mphkgbc@wlink.net. 440 units. A/C MINIBAR TV TEL. HK$1,950–HK$2,200 ($253–$286) single; HK$2,050–HK$2,300 ($266–$299) double; from HK$3,450 ($448) suite. 1 child under 14 can stay free in parents' room. AE, DC, MC, V. MTR: Tsim Sha Tsui.

Not far from The Hongkong Hotel is its lower-priced companion, the Marco Polo. With a rather small and simple lobby, it caters mainly to business travelers, tourists, and occasional tour groups, and, for the money, does not offer as much as others in its price range. It's located in the Harbour City shopping complex, just a 5-minute walk from the Star Ferry. None of its comfortable, good-size rooms have harbor views; rather, the two price categories of rooms depend upon the floor, with the more expensive rooms on the 12th to 16th floors. If noise bothers you, ask for a room away from Canton Road, though these face another building and tend to be dark. Business travelers appreciate the desks with large work spaces, voice mail, and room safes; some rooms also have dataports. Although this hotel has no pool of its own, guests can use the one in The Hongkong Hotel.

**Dining:** Limited dining possibilities include a French restaurant, but Harbour City with its restaurants is just steps away.

**Amenities:** Business center, beauty salon, 24-hour room service, tour desk, same-day laundry service, baby-sitting, house doctor, and limousine service.

**The Prince, Hong Kong.** Harbour City, Canton Rd., Tsim Sha Tsui, Kowloon, Hong Kong. ☎ **800/542-0500** in the U.S. and Canada, or 852/2113 1888. Fax 852/2113 0066. www.marcopolohotels.com. E-mail: prince@marcopolohotels.net. 396 units. A/C MINIBAR TV TEL. HK$1,950–HK$2,200 ($253–$286) single; HK$2,050–HK$2,300 ($266–$299) double; HK$2,650 ($344) Continental Club double; from HK$3,950 ($402) suite. 1 child under 14 can stay free in parents' room. AE, DC, MC, V. MTR: Tsim Sha Tsui.

The third in a row of Marco Polo hotels on Canton Road (and therefore a slightly longer walk to and from Star Ferry), the Prince Hotel is also situated in the huge Harbour City shopping complex and caters to business travelers (mostly Japanese) and tour groups. Opened in 1984, it's a small hotel with rooms that feature either twin or queen-size beds, large working desks, room safes, and voice mail. The lowest-priced rooms are on the lower floors, and none of the rooms have harbor views. Continental Club executive rooms, on the top two floors, offer the usual private lounge and complimentary breakfast and cocktails, as well as complimentary pressing for one outfit. Again, guests staying here can use the outdoor heated swimming pool at The Hongkong Hotel (though it's a hike).

**Dining:** Hotel dining is limited to the **Spice Market,** which specializes in very good Asian buffets, but there are plenty of other restaurants nearby in Harbour City.

**Amenities:** Business center, beauty salon, room service (6am to 2am), house doctor, limousine service, free newspaper, baby-sitting, and same-day laundry service.

✪ **Royal Garden.** 69 Mody Rd., Tsim Sha Tsui East, Kowloon, Hong Kong. ☎ **852/2721 5215.** Fax 852/2369 9976. www.theroyalgardenhotel.com.hk. E-mail: htlinfo@rghk.com.hk. 422 units. A/C MINIBAR TV TEL. HK$2,100–HK$2,600 ($273–$338) single; HK$2,250–HK$2,750 ($292–$357) double; HK$2,900–HK$3,100 ($377–$403) Crown Club executive floor double; from HK$3,850 ($500) suite. 1 child under 12 can stay free in parents' room. AE, CB, DC, MC, V. MTR: Tsim Sha Tsui.

A member of The Leading Hotels of the World and a small hotel with a lot of architectural surprises, the Royal Garden features a 15-story inner atrium, a concept adapted from the traditional Chinese inner garden. Plants hang down from balconies ringing the soaring space, glass-enclosed elevators glide up the wall, a piano sits on an island in the middle of a pool, and the sound of rushing water adds freshness and coolness to the atmosphere. A wonderful 25-meter-long rooftop swimming pool is open overhead in summer, covered and heated in winter. All in all, it's the kind of hotel that invites exploration. The rooms, the most expensive of which have partial harbor views between two buildings, are decorated with Chinese furniture and feature movies on demand, room safes, voice mail, and a chilled water tap in the bathroom. (In case you're wondering, "partial harbor view" means either that other buildings are obstructing part of your view or that your windows do not squarely face the water.) Two floors serve as the Crown Club executive floors, which offer free transportation from the airport, a private lounge, complimentary continental breakfast and evening cocktails, free local telephone calls, dataport connections, and other special privileges. Although a bit of a hike to nearest MTR subway station, it's only a few minutes' walk to the hoverferry pier with service to Central.

**Dining: Sabatini** is the hotel's top restaurant, named after three Sabatini brothers who opened their first restaurant in Rome 3 decades ago, serving Italian food in an authentic Italian setting. There are also Chinese and Japanese restaurants, as well as an "open-air" restaurant in the atrium specializing in sumptuous buffets.

**Amenities:** Heated rooftop swimming pool and Jacuzzi open year-round, fitness room, putting green, tennis court, sauna, shopping arcade, business center, beauty salon, barbershop, concierge, 24-hour room service, same-day laundry service, free newspaper, house doctor, limousine service, baby-sitting, nightly turndown.

**Sheraton Hong Kong Hotel & Towers.** 20 Nathan Rd., Tsim Sha Tsui, Kowloon, Hong Kong. ☎ **800/325-3535** in the U.S. and Canada, or 852/2369 1111. Fax 852/2739 8707. www.sheraton.com/hongkong. E-mail: res_hongkong@sheraton.com. 805 units. A/C MINI-BAR TV TEL. HK$2,000–HK$2,400 ($260–$312) single, HK$2,200–HK$2,600 ($286–$338) double; Tower rooms HK$2,700–HK$3,100 ($351–$403) single, HK$3,000–HK$3,400 ($390–$442) double; from HK$3,000 ($390) suite. AE, CB, DC, MC, V. MTR: Tsim Sha Tsui.

The 20-some-year-old Sheraton has one of the most envied locations in Hong Kong—near the waterfront on the corner of Nathan Road and Salisbury Road. In fact, it's such a choice spot that for years rumors buzzed that the Sheraton would close down to make way for a more lucrative office building. Instead, the Sheraton underwent massive renovations in 1998 that upgraded its facilities and image, making it seem like a completely different hotel. Its lobby was previously plagued by overcrowding from Japanese tour groups and from locals who used it as a convenient waiting place to meet friends. Now it's been moved to the second floor to discourage foot traffic and updated with a sleek, contemporary look graced by Asian motifs and subdued lighting. A separate counter for group check-in alleviates the former front-desk crunch. A plus is the outdoor rooftop swimming pool, heated in winter, offering a spectacular view and more privacy than pools lower to the ground.

Comfortable guest rooms, all with in-room safes, range from those facing an inner courtyard (the cheapest) to those facing the harbor with great views. In between are those that overlook surrounding Tsim Sha Tsui, some of which face Nathan Road and even provide sideways glimpses of the harbor. Guests who require more peace and quiet can splurge for an executive room on the 16th or 17th floor of the Sheraton Towers, served by private elevator, where there's a private executive lounge and such privileges as complimentary breakfast and evening cocktails, free laundry and pressing, and in-room fax machine.

**Dining/Diversions:** One of the most popular drinking spots in Tsim Sha Tsui is **Someplace Else,** where it's elbow-to-elbow at the bar during happy hour. For more sophisticated and relaxed drinking, there's the **Sky Lounge** on the 18th floor, which can't be beat for its romantic view of the harbor. Sharing the 18th floor is the **Oyster and Wine Bar,** while **Morton's of Chicago** offers U.S. steaks. **Unkai** offers superb Japanese delicacies.

**Amenities:** Outdoor heated rooftop swimming pool and Jacuzzi, sauna, fitness room, golf simulator of the world's most famous courses, shopping arcade, business center, concierge, free newspaper, 24-hour room service, baby-sitting, beauty salon, same-day laundry service, limousine service, house doctor, nightly turndown.

## CENTRAL DISTRICT

✪ **Conrad International Hong Kong.** Pacific Place, 88 Queensway, Central, Hong Kong. ☎ **800/445-8667** in the U.S. and Canada, or 852/2521 3838. Fax 852/2521 3888. www. conrad.com.hk. E-mail: info@conrad.com.hk. 513 units. A/C MINIBAR TV TEL. HK$2,400–HK$2,800 ($312–$364) single or double; HK$2,900–HK$3,100 ($377–$403) executive floor double; from HK$5,200 ($675) suite. Children under 18 stay free in parents' room (maximum: 3 persons per room). AE, CB, DC, MC, V. MTR: Admiralty.

The 61-story Conrad, built in 1990, is one of a trio of exclusive hotels perched on a hillside above Pacific Place, an upscale shopping center located about halfway between the Central District and Wan Chai. One of the conveniences of staying here is that Pacific Place abounds in very good restaurants, greatly expanding dining options without having to venture far. Hong Kong Park is just steps away. The Conrad's facilities appeal to both businesspeople (who make up 70% of the hotel's clientele, the majority of whom are American or European) and well-heeled leisure travelers; there is a business center that never closes, an outdoor heated pool, and extra services and amenities designed to answer every need. Although the architecture is modern, the hotel's classic furnishings and interior design soften the modern effect, giving it a cozy atmosphere with wood paneling, polished granite, and comfortable furniture. I especially like the lighthearted touch of the larger-than-life butterflies and wildflowers on the murals of the massive lobby pillars.

Large-size rooms feature windows that extend the width of the room, offering views of either the Peak or the harbor (harbor-view rooms, of course, are better and cost more). All rooms have such conveniences as voice mail, fax machines, two phone lines, dataports, TVs that display messages and can be used for checking out, more than 100 pay movies that can be viewed any time on demand, free bottled water, safes, and separate shower and bathtub facilities. On a playful note, the bathrooms even feature a floating duck or other toy for a bit of fun in the bathroom, while a stuffed bear is placed on beds at turndown. If you really feel like splurging, four executive floors provide guests with an exclusive lounge, as well as complimentary breakfast, cocktails, clothes pressing, personalized stationery, fruit basket, free local telephone calls.

**Dining/Diversions: Nicholini's,** one of Hong Kong's best restaurants, specializes in authentic northern Italian cuisine, while **Brasserie on the Eighth** offers traditional French provincial cuisine. The **Golden Leaf** is a classy Cantonese restaurant; the **Garden Café** serves Western and Asian dishes in a casual, tropical setting.

**Amenities:** Heated outdoor swimming pool; health club with high-tech fitness room, sauna, and Jacuzzi; 24-hour business center; shopping arcade; concierge; free newspaper; 24-hour room service; nightly turndown; house doctor; baby-sitting; limousine service; same-day laundry service; welcome basket with tea, fruit, and chocolate; free shuttle bus to Central every half hour.

**Furama Hotel Hong Kong.** 1 Connaught Rd., Central, Hong Kong. ☎ **852/2525 5111.** Fax 852/2845 9339. www.furama.com.hk. E-mail: reservation@furama.com.hk. 517 units. A/C MINIBAR TV TEL. HK$1,850–HK$2,800 ($240–$364) single or double; from HK$3,000 ($390) suite. AE, DC, MC, V. MTR: Central.

Famous for its revolving restaurant on the 30th floor, the Furama is located in the heart of Central across from Chater Garden and only a 5-minute walk from the Star Ferry. Its cozy lobby faces the soothing, lush greenery of the garden, which gives the illusion of a tropical paradise rather than bustling Central, and which certainly is one of the best inland views from any hotel lobby in Hong Kong. Because of its location, approximately 70% of the hotel's clientele are business travelers, followed by leisure travelers (including tour groups). Opened more than 25 years ago, the hotel provides simple but comfortable guest rooms equipped with large room safes, bathroom scales, dataports, voice mail, and movies on demand. The highest-priced rooms feature very good views of the harbor, followed by views of Victoria Peak; the least expensive rooms look out over the surrounding buildings.

**Dining/Diversions: La Ronda,** a revolving restaurant that offers a lunch and dinner buffet of European and Asian cuisine, provides changing vistas of one of the world's most spectacular cityscapes. The Furama's Continental restaurant, the **Rôtisserie,** features live music in the evenings, as does the **Lau Ling Bar.** The **Island Restaurant** serves Cantonese cuisine, while Japanese specialties are available at **Agehan.**

**Amenities:** Fitness room, sauna, steam room, whirlpool, shopping arcade, business center, beauty salon, tour desk, concierge, 24-hour room service, same-day laundry service, house doctor, limousine service, baby-sitting, nightly turndown.

**JW Marriott Hotel.** Pacific Place, 88 Queensway, Central, Hong Kong. ☎ **800/228-9290** in the U.S. and Canada, or 852/2810 8366. Fax 852/2845 0737. www.marriott.com. E-mail: hotel@marriott.com.hk. 602 units. A/C MINIBAR TV TEL. HK$2,400–HK$3,000 ($312–$390) single or double; HK$2,800–HK$3,400 ($364–$442) executive floor single or double; from HK$6,000 ($780) suite. AC, DC, MC, V. MTR: Admiralty.

The 27-story Marriott, which opened in 1989 as the first of three hotels at Pacific Place, has already undergone major renovation. Its lobby, while not as grandiose as others in this category, is nonetheless the only one of Pacific Place's hotels to offer views of the harbor, though with ongoing land reclamation on the waterfront, taller buildings may soon block that view.

Rooms are all designed with right-angled "saw-tooth" windows to maximize views of the harbor or Peak and are outfitted with hand-painted bedspreads, large marbled bathrooms with separate tub and shower areas, bathroom scales, oversize desks equipped with office supplies, dual phone lines, voice mail, dataports, movies on demand, and bedside control panels that also operate the curtains. On the downside, rooms facing the harbor are subject to the slight din of traffic. On the other hand, rates are based on height, with the result that some of the cheapest rooms, from the 14th floor down, face the harbor. Four executive floors, with private access, offer the usual complimentary breakfast and cocktails.

**Dining/Diversions:** The **Man Ho** features gourmet Cantonese delicacies. **J.W.'s California** offers the best of the East and West. Light fare for breakfast, lunch, and dinner is served at the **Marriott Café.** There's also a sushi bar.

**Amenities:** Outdoor heated swimming pool open year-round, health club (open 24 hours!), sauna, steam room, whirlpool, indoor children's play area, beauty salon, business center (open 24 hours), concierge, free newspaper, 24-hour room service, limousine service, same-day laundry service, baby-sitting, welcoming tea, house doctor.

## CAUSEWAY BAY & WAN CHAI

**Excelsior.** 281 Gloucester Rd., Causeway Bay, Hong Kong. ☎ **800/526-6566** in the U.S. and Canada, or 852/2894 8888. Fax 852/2895 6459. www.mandarin-oriental.com. E-mail: booking@exhkg.com.hk. 887 units. A/C MINIBAR TV TEL. HK$1,900–HK$2,500 ($247–$325) single or double; HK$2,400–HK$2,600 ($312–$338) Executive Floor; from HK$3,800 ($493.50) suite. AE, DC, MC, V. MTR: Causeway Bay.

Located on the waterfront near a lively shopping area, the Excelsior, built in 1973, belongs to the Mandarin Oriental group of hotels. This is a good place to stay if you like to jog, since it's close to 50-acre Victoria Park, Hong Kong's largest city park. However, because up to 20% of the people staying here belongs to tour groups, the lobby is often overcrowded and buzzing with activity, sometimes making it difficult to get front-desk service or find an empty seat. The elevators are also crowded. All rooms are the same size with the same decor, and include room safes, movies on demand, and voice mail, but those that command a view of the harbor with the Hong Kong Yacht Club and Kowloon on the other side are the most expensive. Slightly cheaper are those with side harbor views or views of the park; the cheapest face inland toward the city. The guest rooms on the three top Executive Floors offer use of a private lounge, complimentary continental buffet breakfast, traditional afternoon tea, cocktails, and free local calls.

**Dining/Diversions:** Among several restaurants and bars that serve Western and Cantonese food, the classiest by far is **TOTT'S Asian Grill & Bar** on the top floor, with spectacular harbor views, outrageous red and zebra-striped decor, and East-meets-West cuisine. **Dickens Bar,** a comfortable and popular English-style pub/sports bar, offers live entertainment.

**Amenities:** Covered and air-conditioned rooftop tennis courts, fitness room, sauna, steam room, Jacuzzi, business center, beauty salon, shopping arcade, free newspaper, 24-hour room service, house doctor, limousine service, baby-sitting, and same-day laundry service.

**The Park Lane.** 310 Gloucester Rd., Causeway Bay, Hong Kong. ☎ **800/223-5652** in the U.S. and Canada, or 852/2293 8888. Fax 852/2576 7853. www.parklane.com.hk. E-mail: info@parklane.com.hk. 792 units. A/C MINIBAR TV TEL. HK$1,700–HK$2,800 ($220–$364) single or double; HK$3,000–HK$3,500 ($390–$454) Premier Club executive rooms; from HK$4,500 ($584) suite. Children under 12 stay free in parents' room (maximum: 3 persons per room). AE, DC, MC, V. MTR: Causeway Bay.

Although it's inland, I've always liked the location of this hotel—across from huge Victoria Park and close to many area restaurants, shops, and department stores. First opened in 1974, this 28-story hotel underwent extensive renovation in 1994; now its lobby has a more contemporary, brighter look and the guest rooms have been updated. Attracting primarily business travelers, the hotel offers rooms that vary in price according to floor level and view—the best are those facing Victoria Park with the harbor beyond. All rooms come with a king-size bed or two double beds, voice mail, room safes, and marble bathrooms. Extra perks are available to guests who stay on the two Premier Club executive floors, including complimentary breakfast, cocktails, shoe polishing, clothes pressing, fruit basket, fax machines, free local calls, and drinks.

**Dining/Diversions: 27 Restaurant & Bar,** located on the top floor with views of Victoria Park and the harbor, serves international cuisine with an Asian twist. **Stix** is a combination bar/American restaurant/dance club.

**Amenities:** Fitness center with exercise room, sauna, massage, steam bath, and Jacuzzi. Business center, hair salon, shopping arcade, tour desk, concierge, 24-hour room service, same-day laundry service, free newspaper, house clinic, baby-sitting, limousine service, same-day film processing, nightly turndown.

**Regal Hongkong Hotel.** 68 Yee Wo St., Causeway Bay, Hong Kong. ☎ **800/222-8888** in the U.S. and Canada, or 852/2890 6633. Fax 852/2881 0777. www.regal-hotels.com/ hongkong. E-mail: rhk@regal-hotels.com.hk. 420 units. A/C MINIBAR TV TEL. HK$2,100– HK$2,300 ($273–$290) single or double; HK$2,700 ($351) Regal Class double; HK$3,000 ($390) Regal Club double; from HK$6,000 ($780) suite. Children under 12 stay free in parents' room. AE, DC, MC, V. MTR: Causeway Bay.

Causeway Bay's newest deluxe hotel and the Regal Hotel Group's flagship property, the Regal Hongkong opened in 1993. The 32-story glass-facade building is just a stone's throw from Victoria Park, too far inland to provide anything more than glimpses of the harbor. In an attempt to bring old-world European grandeur to Asia, the hotel is decorated in an ornate French style, but for my taste it's a trifle overdone and borders on the gaudy. The lobby literally shimmers with chandeliers, imitation Louis XIV furniture, statues, a marble staircase, and an enormous European-style oil painting commissioned especially for the hotel. For my money, I'd stay elsewhere. The hotel appeals to a mainly Asian market.

In all, 1,700 paintings were commissioned—each guest room features one large painting above the bed, plus three smaller pieces (as my husband pointed out, the paintings are not nailed down). The rooms are comfortable, with bay windows (those facing Victoria Park provide the best view), sitting areas, room safes, alarm clocks displaying times around the world, TVs with on-line flight information, dataports, and separate tubs and shower stalls. Two floors constitute the Regal Class rooms, designed for business travelers and offering free breakfast, free local calls, and free bottled water, while four floors constitute the Regal Club, where guests can enjoy such extras as a private lounge and complimentary breakfast, evening cocktails, and free laundry service.

**Dining/Diversions: The Riviera,** located on the 31st floor overlooking Victoria Park, features Mediterranean cuisine with an emphasis on French and Italian fare. There are two Chinese restaurants—one serving Cantonese and the other Chiu Chow—and a cafe, lobby lounge, and sports bar.

**Amenities:** Rooftop outdoor swimming pool (closed in winter), fitness room, sauna, steam bath, business center, shopping arcade, concierge, 24-hour room service, limousine service, same-day laundry service, baby-sitting, free newspaper, nightly turndown, house doctor.

**Renaissance Harbour View Hotel Hong Kong (formerly New World Harbour View).** 1 Harbour Rd., Wan Chai, Hong Kong. ☎ **800/228-9898.** in the U.S. and Canada, or 852/2802 8888. Fax 852/2802 8833. www.renaissancehotels.com. E-mail: rhvhksal@hkstar. com. 862 units. A/C MINIBAR TV TEL. HK$1,900–HK$2,300 ($247–$299) single or double; HK$2,300–HK$2,600 ($299–$338) Renaissance Club executive floor; from HK$3,600 ($468) suite. AE, DC, MC, V. MTR: Wan Chai.

This large, 43-story hotel sits beside the Convention and Exhibition Centre on the Wan Chai waterfront, separated from the Grand Hyatt by one of Hong Kong's largest outdoor swimming pools and a garden, shared by the two hotels. Just a couple of minutes' walk from the Wan Chai Star Ferry that delivers passengers to Tsim Sha Tsui and Hung Hom, it provides some of the same facilities and advantages as the Hyatt, but at a lower price; obviously, it caters largely to those attending functions at the convention center, as well as business travelers. Its lobby is white and airy with views of the harbor, and more than 65% of the rooms also boast outstanding views of the water. All rooms feature fax machines, small safes, complimentary fruit baskets, flowers, voice mail, dataports, movies on demand, and TVs that double as message centers and checkout facilities. The top four floors comprise the Renaissance Club executive floors, where guest rooms are also equipped with laser/compact disc players and where complimentary breakfast, afternoon tea, and cocktails are available, as well as free use of a boardroom.

**Dining/Diversions:** The **Dynasty** serves classic Cantonese food, while **Scala** is the place to go for continental fare. The **Coffee Shop** offers snacks and breakfast and dinner buffets. **Oasis,** under a glass canopy, is the best place for cocktails.

**Amenities:** Huge outdoor swimming pool (closed in winter), children's pool, jogging track, two rooftop tennis courts, fitness center, Jacuzzi, golf driving range, business center, concierge, 24-hour room service, free newspaper, medical and dental consultants, baby-sitting, limousine service, same-day laundry service.

## AT THE AIRPORT

**Regal Airport Hotel.** 9 Cheong Tat Rd., Chek Lap Kok, Hong Kong. ☎ **800/222-8888** in the U.S. and Canada, or 852/2286 8888. Fax 852/2286 8686. www.regal-hotels.com. E-mail: regalrah@netvigator.com. 1,100 units. A/C MINIBAR TV TEL. HK$1,700–HK$2,400 ($221–$312) single; HK$1,850–HK$2,550 ($240–$331) double; HK$2,900 ($377) Regal Class double; HK$3,200 ($416) Regal Club double; from HK$6,800 ($883) suite. Children under 12 stay free in parents' room (maximum 2 children per room). AE, DC, MC, V. Airport Express Liner: Hong Kong International Airport.

Opened in autumn 1998 as Hong Kong's largest hotel and the only hotel at Hong Kong International Airport, this Regal chain hotel is only a 5-minute walk from the airport via covered walkway and is convenient for those with early-morning flights. Otherwise, because central Hong Kong is only a 20-minute train ride away, I think you're much better off staying in town, near the shops, restaurants, sights, and street-life vitality that make Hong Kong unique. In addition, even though the hotel makes a conscious effort to brighten its interior with lots of mirrors and glass, including a glass dome over the lobby and gleaming black floors that reflect light, it can't seem to escape its airport connection, and the futuristic decor (including a flying-saucer-shaped stage for live music in the lobby), reminds me of a space ship. Captain Kirk would feel right at home.

Guest rooms are quite large and soundproofed, with modern furniture in eye-popping colors of purple, red, or lime green, safes, and voice mail; all but the cheapest also have TVs with keyboards for Internet access and electronic games. Regal Club floors provide complimentary breakfast and cocktails, free pressing of one outfit, and other services, while Regal Class is geared toward business travelers.

**Dining/Diversions:** A half-dozen food-and-beverage outlets serve everything from Cantonese, Japanese, and continental cuisine. A 24-hour cafe offering Asian and Western fare is unique for its rotating art gallery, which moves through the restaurant on tracks.

**Amenities:** Indoor and outdoor swimming pools, Jacuzzi, health club, sauna, steam room, a very good children's play room, business center, 24-hour room service, concierge, limousine service, same-day laundry service, baby-sitting.

## 3 Moderate

Since tour groups have long been a mainstay of tourism in Hong Kong, you're most likely to encounter them at the moderately (and inexpensively) priced hotels, which account for the majority of hotels in Hong Kong. As for rooms, they tend to be rather small compared to American hotel rooms, with generally unexciting views, but usually have such amenities as hair dryers, minibars or empty refrigerators you can stock yourself, and instant coffee, as well as room service, bellhops, no-smoking floors, and sometimes a swimming pool and/or fitness room. Since harbor views are usually not available, rates are generally based on height and decor and sometimes on size.

# KOWLOON

**BP International House.** 8 Austin Rd., Tsim Sha Tsui, Kowloon, Hong Kong. ☎ **800/223-5652** in the U.S. and Canada, or 852/2376 1111. Fax 852/2376 1333. www. megahotels. com.hk. E-mail: bpi.reservations@megahotels.com.hk. 535 units. A/C TV TEL. HK$990–HK$1,450 ($129–$188) single; HK$1,100–HK$1,500 ($143–$195) double; HK$1,600–HK$1,800 ($208–$234) Corporate double room, from HK$3,100 ($403) suite. Children under 13 stay free in parents' room. AE, DC, MC, V. MTR: Jordan.

This is one of the newer moderately priced lodgings in Tsim Sha Tsui, built in 1993 and rising 25 stories above the north end of Kowloon Park. The word "House" in its name is misleading, since it is actually a rather large hotel, modern with a spacious but utilitarian lobby and catering mainly to tour groups, school excursions, and budget-conscious business travelers. In addition to a Chinese restaurant and coffee shop, there are vending machines that dispense beverages on each floor and a token-operated laundry (though laundry and dry-cleaning services are available). Within the same building is a full-line health club (for which guests pay extra), and the indoor and out-door public swimming pools in Kowloon Park are just a stone's throw away. The guest rooms, located on the 14th to 25th floors, are clean, pleasant, and modern, with satel-lite TV and voice mail. Although located inland, the best and priciest rooms offer great views of the harbor (with height limitations in Kowloon now gone, however, due to the relocation of the airport, you can expect that taller buildings will someday eclipse those views). Business travelers usually opt for one of the Corporate Rooms on the top three floors, which provide such extras as minibars, room safes, hair dryers, and radios. There are also very simple "Family Rooms" equipped with bunk beds that sleep four for HK$1,340 ($170).

**Kimberley Hotel.** 28 Kimberley Rd., Tsim Sha Tsui, Kowloon, Hong Kong. ☎ **800/223-5652** in the U.S. and Canada, or 852/2723 3888. Fax 852/2723 1318. www. kimberley.com.hk. E-mail: kh-rsvn@kimberley.com.hk. 546 units. A/C MINIBAR TV TEL. HK$1,100–HK$1,750 ($143–$227) single; HK$1,200–HK$1,850 ($156–$240) double; from HK$2,150 ($279) suite. AE, DC, MC, V. MTR: Tsim Sha Tsui.

Opened in 1991 and offering more facilities and amenities than many other hotels in its price range, the 20-story Kimberley Hotel is on the northern edge of Tsim Sha Tsui, about a 15-minute walk from the Star Ferry. It caters to both the tourist and business trade, including many Japanese. Guest rooms, constructed with V-shaped windows that let in more sunlight and allow for more panoramic—though unscenic—views, are equipped with hair dryers, very firm beds, phones in the bathroom, clotheslines, and coffee/tea-making facilities. The most expensive rooms are on higher floors and are larger, but even these are rather small. The suites represent an especially good deal since they occupy the top three floors and are equipped with kitchenettes and a loung-ing/dining area, making them ideal for long-term guests and families. There are two no-smoking floors. Facilities include two restaurants serving Japanese and Chinese food, a coffee shop offering lunch and dinner buffets, cocktail lounge, shopping arcade, business center, sauna (extra fee charged), fitness room, putting green, and golf cage. Services include free newspaper, room service (6am to midnight), same-day laun-dry service, house doctor, and baby-sitting.

✪ **Kowloon Hotel.** 19–21 Nathan Rd., Tsim Sha Tsui, Kowloon, Hong Kong. ☎ **800/262-9467** in the U.S., or 852/2929 2888. Fax 852/2739 9811. www.peninsula.com. E-mail: khh@peninsula.com. 736 units. A/C MINIBAR TV TEL. HK$1,300–HK$2,000 ($169–$260) sin-gle; HK$1,400–HK$2,100 ($182–$273) double; from HK$3,500 ($454) suite. AE, CB, DC, MC, V. MTR: Tsim Sha Tsui.

If you like high-tech hotels, this is the place for you. The Kowloon is a modern glass-walled structure right behind The Peninsula; they are both under the same management. Its location is great, just a few minutes' walk from the Star Ferry, but the rooms are minuscule; although they have V-shaped bay windows, allowing unobstructed views up and down the street, The Peninsula's new tower has robbed harbor views from all but the most expensive rooms. Still, the hotel has long offered the most technically advanced rooms in its price category (it even offered them long before upper-priced hotels jumped on the Internet bandwagon). Every room boasts an interactive telecenter (a multi-system TV linked to a central computer and offering satellite programming), which allows access to such information as up-to-the-minute flight details, incoming messages, and hotel bills; it also contains video games. The telecenter, with word-processing capability, also interfaces with in-room fax machines that double as printers; each has its own private number and even its own personalized e-mail address. Finally, guests can also retrieve voice mail messages electronically from outside the hotel, and best of all, Internet access is free. Other room features include an outdoor temperature reading, coffee/tea-making facilities, room safe, and hair dryer. There are no-smoking floors. The hotel lobby has a computerized street directory for consulates, points of interest, and other addresses; its printout is in both English and Chinese to instruct taxi drivers. Facilities include a business center, shopping arcade, and four restaurants, including a very good pizzeria and a restaurant specializing in international buffets. Services include free newspaper, limousine service, baby-sitting, same-day laundry service, and room service (6am to 2am).

**Majestic Hotel.** 348 Nathan Rd., Yau Ma Tei, Kowloon, Hong Kong. ☎ **800/44-UTELL** in the U.S. and Canada, or 852/2781 1333. Fax 852/2781 1773. www.majestichotel.com.hk. E-mail: info@majestichotel.com.hk. 387 units. A/C MINIBAR TV TEL. HK$1,450–HK$1,900 ($188–$247) single or double; from HK$3,500 ($455) suite. 1 child under 12 can stay free in parents' room. AE, DC, MC, V. MTR: Jordan.

This modern brick hotel, located in the colorful Yau Ma Tei district with its main entrance on Saigon Street, is just a few minutes' walk from the subway station and the Temple Street night market. It rises above the Majestic Centre complex, which includes a shopping arcade, food court, children's amusement center, and two small cinemas. The hotel offers good-size rooms, with a desk, sitting area, large windows (but unfortunately no exciting views), satellite television with in-house pay movies, room safe, hair dryer, coffee/tea-making facilities, and clothesline in the bathroom. The cheapest rooms occupy the lower floors and face another building. Unlike most hotels in Hong Kong, the Majestic offers ice machines on every floor. One restaurant serves breakfast, lunch, and dinner buffets, while the hotel bar overlooks Nathan Road and offers live entertainment. There's also a business center. Services include 24-hour room service, baby-sitting, same-day laundry service, and house doctor, and there are two no-smoking floors.

**Miramar.** 118–130 Nathan Rd., Tsim Sha Tsui, Kowloon, Hong Kong. ☎ **800/44-UTELL** in the U.S., or 852/2368 1111. Fax 852/2369 1788. www.miramarhk.com. E-mail: miramarhk@ hjhm-group.com. 525 units. A/C MINIBAR TV TEL. HK$1,000–HK$1,800 ($130–$234) single or double; HK$2,200 ($286) Miramar Club executive floor; from HK$3,800 ($493.50) suite. Children under 12 stay free in parents' room. AE, DC, MC, V. MTR: Tsim Sha Tsui.

Across from Kowloon Park, the Miramar is strategically located in the midst of a shopping area, including the Park Lane shopping arcade and Miramar Shopping Centre. An older family-owned hotel once known for its showy exterior and glitzy gold-colored decor, it toned down its public areas during a major renovation some years back, so the last trace of the Miramar's former flashy self can be seen in its stained-glass windows in the lobby's atrium ceiling. Since it caters largely to Asian tour groups, all but 22 of the rooms are twins and doubles. Each floor has its own attendant on duty 24 hours (once a feature of most Hong Kong hotels but now increasingly rare).

The rooms come equipped with a room safe and hair dryer. Some of the higher floor deluxe rooms offer views of Kowloon Park and the harbor in the distance. Executive floor rooms entitle guests to continental breakfast, evening cocktails, fruit baskets, free pressing of one outfit, free local telephone calls, and computer with Internet access. Other amenities include room service (6:30am to 1am), same-day laundry service, free newspaper, baby-sitting, and limousine service. Facilities include a business center, shopping arcade, fitness center with heated indoor pool and sauna, and restaurants serving Cantonese food (including dim sum) and East-meets-West crossover cuisine.

**New World Renaissance Hotel.** 22 Salisbury Rd., Tsim Sha Tsui, Kowloon, Hong Kong. ☎ **800/228-9898** in the U.S. and Canada, or 852/2369 4111. Fax 852/2369 9387. www.renaissancehotels.com. E-mail: nwhhkres@netvigator.com. 543 units. A/C MINIBAR TV TEL. HK$1,300–HK$1,600 ($169–$208) single; HK$2,000 ($260) Renaissance Club executive floor; from HK$3,000 ($390) suite. AE, DC, MC, V. MTR: Tsim Sha Tsui.

This hotel is tucked inside the New World complex, which includes more than 300 shops and boutiques. Modern in both decor and technology, the 20-year-old hotel nevertheless suggests an Asian atmosphere with its large flower arrangements and sleek black furniture, but I find the windowless lobby slightly claustrophobic. Furthermore, despite its prime location right on the waterfront, none its rooms faces the harbor. Rather, all rooms face Salisbury Road or the pool (which is quieter), with a few offering partial glimpses of the water. Otherwise, the rooms are comfortable enough, with modern Asian decor; fax machines; voice mail; room safes; dataports; TVs that display hotel information, travel news, and individual hotel accounts; coffee/tea-making facilities; and magnifying mirrors and hair dryers in the bathrooms. For those who want to splurge, there are four executive floors. Some rooms here do offer partial glimpses of the harbor, as well as complimentary breakfast and cocktails, free personalized stationery, free pressing of one outfit, and laser disc players. Four restaurants and bars include the Western-style Panorama with harbor views, while facilities include an outdoor swimming pool, fitness center, sauna, beauty salon, barbershop, and business center (open 24 hours). Guests appreciate the free newspaper, 24-hour room service, medical and dental services, limousine service, baby-sitting, same-day laundry service, and nightly turndown.

✪ **Park Hotel.** 61–65 Chatham Rd. S., Tsim Sha Tsui, Kowloon, Hong Kong. ☎ **800/44-UTELL** in the U.S. and Canada, or 852/2366 1371. Fax 852/2739 7259. www.parkhotel. com.hk. E-mail: hotel@parkhotel.com.hk. 423 units. A/C MINIBAR TV TEL. HK$900–HK$1,300 ($117–$169) single; HK$1,000–HK$1,400 ($130–$182) twin; from HK$2,000 ($260) suite. 1 child under 12 can stay free in parents' room. AE, DC, MC, V. MTR: Tsim Sha Tsui.

Built in 1961 and kept up-to-date with renovations, the Park Hotel has long been one of the best-known medium-priced hotels in Kowloon. It's a clean and comfortable establishment—you can't go wrong staying here. Especially popular with Australians and Asians, this hotel probably has the largest rooms in the moderate category, a plus if you're tired of cramped quarters, and all come with hair dryers, room safes, and coffee/tea-making facilities. The best rooms are on the upper floors of the 16-floor property; the lower floors can be noisy, especially those facing the street. There are two no-smoking floors. Facilities include Western and Cantonese restaurants, coffee shop, bar, shopping arcade, tour desk, and beauty salon. Services include room service (6:30am to 12:50am), medical service, baby-sitting, same-day laundry service, and limousine service. The location, on the border between Tsim Sha Tsui and Tsim Sha Tsui East, across from the Science Museum and Museum of History, is not as convenient as that of many other hotels in this category, though it is within walking distance of the MTR (about 6 min.) and hoverferry service to Central (about 8 min.).

**Pearl Seaview.** 268 Shanghai St., Yau Ma Tei, Kowloon, Hong Kong. ☎ **852/2782 0882**. Fax 852/2781 8800. www.pearlsea.com.hk. E-mail: pearlsea@netvigator.com. 257 units. A/C MINIBAR TV TEL. HK$880–HK$1,280 ($114–$166) single; HK$1,280–HK$1,580 ($166–$205) double; from HK$2,400 ($312) suite. AE, DC, MC, V. MTR: Yau Ma Tei.

This 19-story brick hotel opened in 1994, looking slightly out of place amidst the hustle and bustle of this Chinese neighborhood, just a stone's throw from a famous Tin Hau Temple and Temple Street's famous night market. Catering mainly to tour groups from mainland China, Singapore, and Malaysia, it has a tiny lobby (often packed) and one restaurant serving a selection of international dishes. Best is the cocktail lounge on the top floor offering views of a harbor (not the famous Victoria Harbour, but a working harbor nonetheless). Narrow corridors lead to small and clean rooms with pay movies, hair dryers, and coffee/tea-making facilities, the least expensive of which are on lower floors. Since rooms lack the convenience of a desk or large closet space, there's virtually no place to unpack or put your luggage. Services include room service (6am to midnight), same-day laundry service, baby-sitting, and house doctor. Basically, it's just a place to sleep.

**Ramada Hotel Kowloon.** 73–75 Chatham Rd. S., Tsim Sha Tsui, Kowloon, Hong Kong. ☎ **800/468-3571** in the U.S. and Canada, or 852/2311 1100. Fax 852/2311 6000. E-mail: hotel@ramada-kowloon.com.hk. 205 units. A/C MINIBAR TV TEL. HK$1,300–HK$2,050 ($169–$266) single or double; from HK$2,800 ($364) suite. 1 child under 12 can stay free in parents' room. AE, DC, MC, V. MTR: Tsim Sha Tsui.

Popular with individual business travelers, including many Americans, this no-nonsense hotel offers simple, clean rooms that feature safes (except in the cheapest units, which have glazed windows), satellite TVs with in-house pay movies, and hair dryers in addition to the usual amenities; more expensive rooms also have room safes and coffee/tea-making facilities. The highest-priced rooms face Chatham Road, which offers a better view but can be noisy. One restaurant serves Western and Asian food, including buffet meals, and there's also one bar and a business center. Services are limited to room service (6:30am to 10pm), limousine service, baby-sitting, and same-day laundry service. Its location on Chatham Road, near the science and history museums, is not as convenient as other business hotels in this category, though it is within walking distance of the MTR (about 8 min.), Star Ferry (about 15 min.), and hoverferry with service to Central (about 10 min.).

**Regal Kowloon Hotel.** 71 Mody Rd., Tsim Sha Tsui East, Kowloon, Hong Kong. ☎ **800/222-8888** in the U.S. and Canada, or 852/2722 1818. Fax 852/2369 6950. www.regal-hotels.com/kowloon. E-mail: rkh@regal-hotels.com.hk. 592 units. A/C MINIBAR TV TEL. HK$1,100–HK$1,800 ($143–$234) single or double; HK$2,200 ($286) Regal Class double; HK$2,700 ($351) Regal Club double; from HK$5,000 ($597) suite. 2 children under 12 can stay free in parents' room. AE, CB, DC, MC, V. MTR: Tsim Sha Tsui.

The 15-story Regal Kowloon does a smart job of blending East and West with reproduction 18th-century French antiques and Louis XV–style furniture standing alongside Chinese works of art. The guest rooms, all soundproofed, are rather middle of the road, equipped with room safes and most with sofas and dataports. The cheapest rooms face another building and provide no view whatsoever; most expensive rooms face a garden. Business travelers may opt for Regal Class rooms, which bring such privileges as free local calls, one free movie daily, and complimentary breakfast. Regal Club executive floors go a step further with a private lounge, complimentary cocktails, and late checkout. There are also no-smoking rooms. For dining, there's the acclaimed Maman WineBar and Restaurant, featuring French provincial home cooking and more than 50 wines by the glass, as well as other restaurants serving Cantonese,

American, and buffet meals. Facilities include a fitness room, shopping arcade, business center, beauty salon, and tour desk, while services include 24-hour room service, baby-sitting, house doctor, limousine service, same-day laundry service.

**Royal Pacific Hotel & Towers.** 33 Canton Rd., Tsim Sha Tsui, Kowloon, Hong Kong. ☎ **800/44-UTELL** in the U.S., or 852/2736 1188. Fax 852/2736 1212. www.royalpacific. com.hk. E-mail: res@royalpacific.com.hk. 673 units. A/C MINIBAR TV TEL. HK$980–HK$1,600 ($127–$208) single or double in the hotel, HK$1,600–HK$2,000 ($208–$260) single or double in the Towers, HK$2,300–HK$3,800 ($299–$493.50) Royal Executive room. 1 child under 14 can stay free in parents' room (Towers only). AE, CB, DC, MC, V. MTR: Tsim Sha Tsui.

Of the string of accommodations stretching along Canton Road, this gold-mirrored hotel is farthest north, across from Kowloon Park. It actually comprises two hotels—each with its own lobby, concept, and room rates. The Royal Pacific Hotel is more moderately priced and attracts tour groups from Asia and Europe (thankfully, there's a separate check-in counter for groups). Its rooms are rather small but offer all the usual comforts, including three phones (one in the bathroom), voice mail, safes, hair dryers, coffee/tea-making facilities, and interactive satellite TVs with access to pay movies on demand, e-mail and the Internet, computer games, and personal hotel bills. The cheapest rooms face another building, while the most expensive, called Premier Rooms and aimed at business travelers, overlook Kowloon Park and have fax machines and coffee/tea-making facilities. The Towers is more upscale, catering to individual travelers and executives with more luxurious furnishings and bathrooms with separate shower and tub areas. Only the highest-priced rooms in the Towers provide views of the harbor, as do some of the rooms on the Royal Executive Club floors, which offer the additional privilege of free breakfasts, cocktails, fresh fruit, and private lounge. The two hotels share one restaurant and a bar, business center, fitness room, sauna, and squash courts; they offer such guest services as room service (6am to 1am), same-day laundry service, baby-sitting, limousine service, and house doctor. The only disadvantage is the 10-minute walk from Star Ferry; on the other hand, it's located practically on top of the China Ferry Terminal, where boats depart for Macau and China.

**۞ Stanford Hillview Hotel.** 13–17 Observatory Rd., Tsim Sha Tsui, Kowloon, Hong Kong. ☎ **800/858-8471** in the U.S., or 852/2722 7822. Fax 852/2723 3718. www.stanfordhillview. com. E-mail: sfhvhkg@netvigator.com. 163 units. A/C MINIBAR TV TEL. HK$1,080–HK$1,480 ($140–$192) single or double. Long-term rates available. AE, DC, MC, V. MTR: Tsim Sha Tsui.

This small, intimate hotel, built in 1991, is near the heart of Tsim Sha Tsui and yet it's a world away from it too, located on top of a hill in the shade of some huge banyan trees, next to the Royal Observatory with its colonial building and greenery. Knutsford Terrace, an alley with trendy bars and restaurants, is just a couple of minutes' walk away. Its lobby is quiet and subdued (quite a contrast to most Hong Kong hotels) and its staff is friendly and accommodating. The hotel has a business center, a fitness room, and outdoor golf-driving nets, as well as a restaurant offering international buffets and à la carte menus of Western and Asian dishes. Rooms were all renovated in 1998 and have dataports and coffee/tea-making facilities. The most expensive rooms are on higher floors; ask for one that faces the Observatory. In addition to the rates and rooms above, there are two "economy" rooms that are smaller and are located on the second floor facing the back of the hotel; costing HK$880 ($114), these should be booked well in advance. Room service is available 7am to 11pm; there's also same-day laundry service and baby-sitting. All in all, a very civilized place, but it is a hike uphill to the hotel.

**Windsor Hotel.** 39–43A Kimberley Rd., Tsim Sha Tsui, Kowloon, Hong Kong. ☎ **800/537-8483** in the U.S. and Canada, or 852/2739 5665. Fax 852/2311 5101. www.windsorhotel.com.hk. E-mail: windsor@windsorhotel.com.hk. 166 units. A/C MINIBAR TV TEL. HK$950–HK$1,400 ($123–$182) single or twin. 1 child under 12 can stay free in parents' room. AE, DC, MC, V. MTR: Tsim Sha Tsui.

Although it's about a 15-minute walk from Star Ferry (but only a 5-minute walk to the MTR), this 15-story hotel is simple but pleasant, with a spotless white interior, small but functional (and usually crowded) marble lobby, and pastel-colored rooms offering such basics as coffee/tea-making facilities, hair dryers, free newspapers, data-ports, and in-room pay movies. Cheaper than the Kimberley across the street, its facilities are minimal—one Cantonese restaurant, a coffee shop, a bar (with a computer hooked up to the Internet), and a business center; services include room service (7am to 11pm), same-day laundry service, hotel doctor, and baby-sitting. Typical of most medium-range hotels throughout Hong Kong, it caters to both groups and individuals; the majority of guests hail from China, Japan, Germany, and Britain.

## CAUSEWAY BAY/WAN CHAI

**Century Hong Kong Hotel.** 238 Jaffe Rd., Wan Chai, Hong Kong. ☎ **800/537-8483** in the U.S. and Canada, or 852/2598 8888. Fax 852/2598 8866. www.centuryhotels.com/century. E-mail: booking@century.com.hk. 517 units. A/C MINIBAR TV TEL. HK$1,500–HK$1,700 ($195–$221) single; HK$1,600–HK$1,800 ($208–$234) double; HK$2,000 ($260) Royal Club executive floor double; from HK$3,200 ($416) suite. AE, DC, MC, V. MTR: Wan Chai.

Opened in 1992, this gleaming white 23-story hotel is a 7-minute walk via covered walkway from the Hong Kong Convention and Exhibition Centre and the Wan Chai Star Ferry terminus, with service to Tsim Sha Tsui and Hung Hom. Its airy, two-story lobby has floor-to-ceiling windows overlooking a busy intersection and is plagued by the constant hum of traffic, but since there are very few seats available you probably won't spend much time here anyway. Dull and unimaginative corridors lead to minuscule rooms, which are mercifully equipped with double-paned windows, safes, coffee/tea-making facilities, hair dryers, and "smart" telephones with voice mail and control panels (for displaying the time worldwide and for operating the TV, radio, lights, and "Do Not Disturb" sign). A few of the most expensive doubles offer a partial harbor view between buildings, as do some of the rooms on the three Royal Club executive floors, which also provide such extras as complimentary continental breakfast, afternoon tea, and cocktails. There are also non-smoking floors. In addition to an Italian restaurant, Shanghainese restaurant, cafe, and lounge, there are an outdoor pool, a wading pool, a fitness room, a steam room, a putting green, a business center, and a tour desk; services include 24-hour room service, same-day laundry service, nightly turndown, baby-sitting, limousine service, and house doctor.

✪ **Empire Hotel.** 33 Hennessy Rd., Wan Chai, Hong Kong. ☎ **800/830-6144** in the U.S. and Canada, or 852/2866 9111. Fax 852/2861 3121. www.asiastandard.com. E-mail: ehhresa@asiastandard.com. 345 units. A/C MINIBAR TV TEL. HK$1,400–HK$1,800 ($182–$234) single or double; HK$2,000 ($260) Empire Plus room; from HK$2,200 ($264) suite. AE, DC, MC, V. MTR: Wan Chai.

Nicely situated in the heart of Wan Chai and popular with mid-level business travelers for its convenience to Central, this business hotel offers good value, with many of the same amenities, services, and facilities found at higher-priced hotels, including a rooftop outdoor swimming pool (large enough for swimming laps), fitness room, sauna, business center, concierge, and tour desk. Rooms, with rates based on size (none provide a view of the harbor), are comfortable and pleasant, each equipped with a safe, coffeemaker/tea-making facilities, hair dryer, fax machine, and other amenities, including the Data View Information System, which allows guests to receive messages on their television sets, check flight schedules, check information (on stocks, finance, or shopping), play video games, and view the hotel services directory. There are also in-house pay movies and satellite programs. The top five floors, comprised of Empire Plus rooms, are geared toward business travelers with such extras as wall-mounted TVs (leaving more desk space) and a magnetic whiteboard. In addition to Western and Cantonese restaurants and a wine bar, there's a very popular and highly recommended Shanghainese restaurant called Wu Kong. Services include a free newspaper, room service (6:30am to midnight), same-day laundry service, free shuttle service to Hong Kong Station in Central, limousine service, medical and dental services, and baby-sitting.

✪ **Harbour View International House.** 4 Harbour Rd., Wan Chai, Hong Kong. ☎ **852/2802 0111.** Fax 852/2802 9063. www.harbour.ymca.org.hk. E-mail: hvihymca@netvigator.com. 320 units, all with bathroom. A/C MINIBAR TV TEL. HK$1,150–HK$1,650 ($149–$214) single or double. Children under 12 stay free in parents' room. AE, DC, MC, V. MTR: Wan Chai.

Opened in 1986, this modern YMCA occupies a prime spot on the Wan Chai waterfront, right next to the Hong Kong Arts Centre and not far from the convention center. Rooms, all twin or double beds, are simple but functional; facilities and services include a coffee shop, one restaurant with a view of the harbor serving Chinese and Western food, room service (7:15am to 11:30pm), baby-sitting, and laundry service. Best yet, more than half the rooms face the harbor with V-shaped windows, making this one of the least expensive places in Hong Kong with great views. Rooms that face inland are even cheaper.

**Luk Kwok Hotel.** 72 Gloucester Rd., Wan Chai, Hong Kong. ☎ **852/2866 2166.** Fax 852/2866 2622. www.lukkwokhotel.com. E-mail: lukkwok@lukkwokhotel.com. 196 units. A/C MINIBAR TV TEL. HK$1,460–HK$1,760 ($190–$229) single; HK$1,600–HK$1,900 ($208–$247) double; HK$2,200–HK$2,300 ($286–$299) executive floor double; from HK$3,200 ($416) suite. AE, DC, MC, V. MTR: Wan Chai.

The Luk Kwok was originally built in the 1930s on what was then the waterfront; seven stories in height, it was the tallest building in Wan Chai. It achieved its greatest fame, however, for its role in Richard Mason's fictional *The World of Suzie Wong,* when Wan Chai was the domain of prostitutes and sailors. How things have changed since then! After a complete demolition, the Luk Kwok reopened in 1990 as a totally new and remodeled larger hotel, slightly antiseptic, and appealing mainly to business travelers, probably because of its lack of facilities. Now located some 2 blocks inland due to land reclamation, not far from the Hong Kong Convention and Exhibition Centre, the new hotel is high-tech and modern, with a granite-and-marble lobby and updated rooms. The hotel's two restaurants, serving continental and Cantonese food, are on the first floor, while the next 17 floors are used for a parking garage and offices. Guest rooms, located on the 19th to 29th floors and including non-smoking floors, are a cut above those in other area business hotels, larger in size and equipped with room safes, voice mail, satellite TV with pay movies, coffee/tea-making facilities, dataports, and large counter space in the bathroom. The addition of plants in every bathroom is a nice touch, and some rooms even have a glimpse of the harbor between buildings. An executive floor offers such additional facilities as fax machines, free local telephone calls, and free American breakfast. In addition to a small cocktail lounge open to hotel guests only, there's a fitness room and a business center. Services include a free newspaper, tour desk, room service (6am to 1am), same-day laundry service, same-day photo processing, baby-sitting, limousine service, and house doctor.

**Wharney Hotel.** 57–73 Lockhart Rd., Wan Chai, Hong Kong. ☎ **852/2861 1000.** Fax 852/2529 5133. E-mail: wharney@wlink.net. 350 units. A/C MINIBAR TV TEL. HK$1,000–HK$1,600 ($130–$208) single; HK$1,200–HK$1,800 ($156–$234) double. 1 child under 12 can stay free in parents' room. AE, DC, MC, V. MTR: Wan Chai.

This pleasant business hotel is conveniently situated in the heart of Wan Chai, offering small but adequate rooms that feature hair dryers, coffee/tea-making facilities, and satellite TVs with pay in-house movies. There are five types of rooms, based on decor and floor level; the best rooms are located on higher floors in a newer addition, but there are no views. There are four no-smoking floors. Facilities include a coffee shop that serves Asian and Western buffet selections, Cantonese restaurant, bar with live evening entertainment, outdoor swimming pool, fitness room, steam room, sauna, and business center. There are also plans to open a waiting lounge for hotel guests whose flights leave later in the day, complete with sofas, magazines, and light refreshments. Services include baby-sitting, same-day laundry service, complimentary newspaper, limousine service, room service (6:30am to 1am), and house doctor.

## NORTH POINT

**Harbour Plaza North Point.** 655 King's Rd., North Point, Hong Kong. ☎ **852/2187 8888.** Fax 852/2187 8899. www.harbour-plaza.com/hpnp. E-mail: hpnp@harbour-plaza.com. 566 units. A/C MINIBAR TV TEL. HK$1,300–HK$1,750 ($169–$227) single; HK$1,400–HK$1,850 ($182–$240) double; HK$2,400 ($312) Harbour Club executive double; from HK$2,600 ($338) suite. AE, DC, MC, V. MTR: Quarry Bay (exit C).

Opened in 2000 in North Point, a fast-growing business district for international corporations, this hotel targets long-staying U.S. and European business travelers with such innovative concepts as goldfish placed into lone guests' rooms (so they won't feel lonely and to improve *fung shui*), flexible checkout (if available), laundry room, and an exercise gym that also offers classes in yoga, aerobics, and meditation. It also offers more standard features like an outdoor swimming pool and Jacuzzi, business center, free shuttle service to Causeway Bay and Hong Kong Station in Central, a Cantonese restaurant, a buffet restaurant (popular with area business executives for lunch), a bar, and a take-away counter for freshly brewed coffee and snacks. Rooms, the most expensive of which offer views of the harbor between buildings (ask for a room on a high floor), come with a large desk, dual phone lines, dataports, voice mail, coffee/tea-making facilities, hair dryers, and large safes. In addition to non-smoking floors, the Harbour Club executive floor, on the top floor, offers rooms with kitchenettes and CD/cassette players and such privileges as free breakfast, free cocktails, free transportation from the airport, and free local telephone calls. Services include same-day laundry service, room service (7am to 1am), free newspapers, and baby-sitting.

## 4 Inexpensive

Unfortunately, Hong Kong has more expensive hotels than it does budget accommodations. Hotels in this category generally offer small, functional rooms with a bathroom and air-conditioning, but they have few services or facilities. Some budget accommodations also offer rooms without private bathroom at cheaper prices (for hotels in this category, I've indicated whether rooms are with or without bathroom). Always inquire whether there's a difference in price between rooms with twin beds and those with double beds. If possible, it's best to *see* a room before committing yourself, since some may be better than others in terms of traffic noise, view, condition, and size. For the most part, however, you shouldn't have any problems with the inexpensive hotels recommended here.

## KOWLOON

**Anne Black Guest House (YWCA).** 5 Man Fuk Rd., Kowloon, Hong Kong. ☎ **852/2713 9211.** Fax 852/2761 1269. www.ywca.org.hk. E-mail: annblack@ywca.org.hk. 169 units, 127 with bathroom. A/C TV TEL. HK$440 ($57) single without bathroom, HK$490 ($64) single with bathroom; HK$490 ($64) twin without bathroom, HK$520–HK$580 ($68–$75) twin with bathroom. Monthly rates available. AE, MC, V. MTR: Yau Ma Tei.

This 20-story YWCA, built in 1972 and rather inconveniently located atop a hill about a 10-minute walk from the nearest MTR station, welcomes both men and women in its spotless rooms, most of which are twins with unstocked refrigerator and private toilet and shower. Six twin rooms have sinks but no baths nor refrigerators, so if you're on a budget be sure to book these rooms far in advance. The rooms are fairly plain in a no-nonsense dormitory kind of way; those that face the front offer slightly better views of the surrounding neighborhood. Ask for a room on a higher floor. There's one coffee shop offering simple Western and Cantonese food, a coin-operated laundry facility, and a fitness room (fee charged). The staff is friendly, making this a good choice despite its out-of-the-way location.

✪ **Booth Lodge.** 11 Wing Sing Lane, Yau Ma Tei, Kowloon, Hong Kong. ☎ **852/2771 9266.** Fax 852/2385 1140. 53 units, all with bathroom. A/C MINIBAR TV TEL. HK$620–HK$1,200 ($81–$156) single or double. Rates include breakfast. AE, MC, V. MTR: Yau Ma Tei.

About a 30-minute walk to the Star Ferry, but close to the Jade Market, Temple Street Night Market, and Ladies' Market, and only a 2-minute walk from the MTR station, Booth Lodge is located just off Nathan Road on the seventh floor of the Salvation Army building. Recently renovated, it has a comfortable lobby and an adjacent coffee shop offering à-la-carte dining and very reasonably priced lunch and dinner buffets with Chinese, Japanese, and Western selections. Best is the restaurant's outdoor brick terrace overlooking a wooded hillside, where buffet barbecues are held Friday, Saturday, and Sunday evenings. Rooms, all twins or doubles and either standard rooms or larger deluxe rooms, are clean; most have hair dryers. Some that face toward Nathan Road have views of a harbor in the distance, though those facing the hillside are quieter. There's laundry service, as well as a tour desk.

**Caritas Bianchi Lodge.** 4 Cliff Rd., Yau Ma Tei, Kowloon, Hong Kong. ☎ **852/2388 1111.** Fax 852/2770 6669. 90 units, all with bathroom. A/C MINIBAR TV TEL. HK$720 ($93.50) single; HK$820–HK$1,200 ($106.50–$156) double. Rates include continental or Chinese breakfast. Monthly rates available. AE, DC, MC, V. MTR: Yau Ma Tei.

Just down the street from Booth Lodge and also convenient to the jade and night markets and MTR station, this HKTA member is not as homey as Booth Lodge and has as much personality as a college dormitory. Still, most of its very simple rooms, with large desks and closets, face toward the back of the hotel, offering a view of a wooded cliff and a small park, certainly a nicer vista than most hotels can boast. Try to get a room on a higher floor. This establishment, under management of the Roman Catholic Church's social welfare bureau and popular with long-staying guests for its monthly rates, has one restaurant on the sixth floor and offers such services as laundry service and room service (7am to 9pm).

✪ **Eaton Hotel.** 380 Nathan Rd., Yau Ma Tei, Kowloon, Hong Kong. ☎ **800/44-UTELL** in the U.S. and Canada, or 852/2782 1818. Fax 852/2782 5563. www.eaton-hotel.com. E-mail: inquiry@eaton-hotel.com. 464 units. A/C MINIBAR TV TEL. HK$750–HK$2,600 ($97–$338) single or double. AE, DC, MC, V. MTR: Jordan.

This accommodation has more class and more facilities than most other hotels in this group, making it one of my top picks. A handsome, brick 21-story hotel, located above a shopping complex not far from the night market on Temple Street, features one of the longest hotel escalators I've ever seen—it takes guests straight up to the fourth-floor lobby. The lobby lounge is bright and cheerful, with a four-story glass-enclosed atrium that overlooks a garden terrace with a water cascade, where you can sit outside with drinks in nice weather. The guest rooms are small, but come with such comforts as a feather duvet, coffee/tea-making facilities, clothesline in the bathroom, hair dryer, pay movies, safe, voice mail, dataports, and "Do Not Disturb" button that lights up a signal outside the door. Rooms on the top floors and a new addition are more expensive, with fax machines, dataports, and fancier decor, including some innovatively designed rooms with views of a distant harbor. Otherwise, the best views are of Nathan Road. There are also no-smoking floors. Facilities include a very good Cantonese restaurant, coffee shop, cozy bar with a "colonial" atmosphere and terrace seating, nicely done though small rooftop pool with sunning terrace, fitness room, and business center. Guest services include complimentary newspaper, room service (7am to 2am), baby-sitting, and same-day laundry service.

**Grand Tower.** 627–641 Nathan Rd., Mong Kok, Kowloon, Hong Kong. ☎ 852/2789 **0011.** Fax 852/2789 0945. www.hanglung.com/grandtower. E-mail: gthotel@hanglung. com. 549 units. A/C MINIBAR TV TEL. HK$700–HK$1,400 ($91–$182) single or double; from HK$2,000 ($260) suite. 1 child under 12 can stay free in parents' room. AE, DC, MC, V. MTR: Mong Kok.

Part of the Grand Plaza shopping center, the Grand Tower is in Mong Kok at the northern end of Nathan Road, just a couple minutes' walk away from the Ladies' Market. It caters to a largely Asian clientele, split evenly between business and leisure travelers. Its bright, sixth-floor marble lobby lies beneath a skylight, in sharp contrast to the chaos and jumble of the streets below. Its rooms, equipped with hair dryers, coffee/tea-making facilities, and satellite TV with pay movies, are quite large and pleasant; the most expensive rooms are on upper floors and offer views of the city. Otherwise, rooms face either an inner courtyard or Nathan Road; while Nathan Road is noisier, it's also more entertaining—you could spend hours just staring out your window at its bustle. There is one no-smoking floor. Although it's a bit far from the tip of Tsim Sha Tsui, the hotel is close to both a subway station and bus stops and offers free, hourly shuttle service to Tsim Sha Tsui. Facilities include Cantonese and Chiu Chow restaurants, a coffee shop offering lunch and dinner buffets, a lobby lounge, a business center, and a shopping arcade. Services include a free newspaper, 24-hour room service, limousine service, house doctor, baby-sitting, and same-day laundry service.

**Guangdong Hotel.** 18 Prat Ave., Tsim Sha Tsui, Kowloon, Hong Kong. ☎ **852/2739 3311.** Fax 852/2721 1137. www.gdihml.com.hk/gdhk. E-mail: gdhotel@guangdonghotel. com.hk. 245 units. A/C MINIBAR TV TEL. HK$850–HK$1,300 ($110–$169) single or double; from HK$2,200 ($286) suite. 1 child under 12 can stay free in parents' room. AE, DC, MC, V. MTR: Tsim Sha Tsui.

The Guangdong, popular with both Asian business travelers and tour groups, is located in the heart of Tsim Sha Tsui, about a 10-minute walk from the Star Ferry. Its marble lobby is spacious and bare, reflecting the latest look in Hong Kong's hotels when it was built in the late 1980s. Two restaurants serve Cantonese and Western food. There's also a business center. The guest rooms, including no-smoking rooms, are small but clean and pleasant and offer satellite TV with in-house pay movies, safes, and hair dryers, with room rates based primarily on floor level. None of the rooms here offer views; most face other buildings. However, if you want to be away from the din of traffic, splurge for a room on a higher floor. Services you can expect include room service (7am to 11pm), baby-sitting, same-day laundry service, and limousine service.

**Hotel Concourse.** 22 Lai Chi Kok Rd., Mong Kok, Kowloon, Hong Kong. ☎ **852/2397 6683.** Fax 852/2381 3768. www.hotelconcourse.com.hk. E-mail: info@hotelconcourse. com.hk. 430 units. A/C MINIBAR TV TEL. HK$800–HK$1,460 ($104–$190) single or double; from HK$2,060 ($268) suite. 1 child under 13 can stay free in parents' room. AE, DC, MC, V. MTR: Prince Edward.

You'll find this hotel with a friendly staff at the northern end of Kowloon Peninsula, in an area known as Mong Kok. Since not many tourists venture this far north, this part of Kowloon has a much more local flavor than that of Tsim Sha Tsui and the hotel is popular with mainland Chinese, including many tour groups, since it's affiliated with China Travel Service, the official Chinese travel agency. For that reason, the lobby can be quite noisy and busy, as is the rest of Hong Kong. The hotel is simple, reminiscent of business hotels in Japan, and offers clean, functional rooms, including no-smoking rooms. The most expensive rooms are deluxe corner rooms, larger and brighter with large desks and fax machines. If you are just looking for an inexpensive room without such extras as swimming pool, business center, or shops, this may be the place for you. There's a casual Western restaurant specializing in buffet breakfast, lunch, and dinner, as well as a Cantonese restaurant renowned for its dim sum. Guest services include a free newspaper (upon request), same-day laundry service, room service 7am to 1am, baby-sitting, and a house doctor. The easiest way to reach the hotel from Hong Kong International Airport is via the hotel shuttle bus for HK$75 ($9.75) per person.

**Imperial Hotel.** 30–34 Nathan Rd., Tsim Sha Tsui, Kowloon, Hong Kong. ☎ **800/44-UTELL** in the U.S. and Canada, or 852/2366 2201. Fax 852/2311 2360. www.imperialhotel.com.hk. E-mail: imperial@imperialhotel.com.hk. 223 units, all with bathroom. A/C MINIBAR TV TEL. HK$750–HK$1,700 ($97.50–$221) single; HK$850–HK$2,000 ($110.50– $260) double. 1 child under 12 can stay free in parents' room. AE, DC, MC, V. MTR: Tsim Sha Tsui.

With the exception of The Salisbury YMCA (below), this simple, no-frills hotel has the best location of any of the inexpensive lodgings, right on Nathan Road between the Sheraton and Holiday Inn and near the MTR station. Its cheaper rooms face the back of Chungking Mansion, notorious for its cheap and often uninviting rooms. Although the view is not exactly stunning, it is enlightening, with laundry strung everywhere and garbage piled up below, apparently tossed unconcernedly from the windows above. If this view does not appeal to you, spring for a deluxe room that faces Nathan Road, although keep in mind that these rooms are subject to the noise of traffic; those on the top floors are high enough to offer glimpses of the harbor. In-room amenities include hair dryers, dataports, and pay movies, and no-smoking rooms are available. Facilities include one Chinese restaurant, a spaghetti restaurant, and a basement pub. Room service is available 7am to 11pm, and there's also same-day laundry service and baby-sitting.

**Metropole Hotel.** 75 Waterloo Rd., Yau Ma Tei, Kowloon, Hong Kong. ☎ **852/2761 1711.** Fax 852/2761 0769. www.metropole.com.hk. E-mail: hotel@metropole.com.hk. 487 units. A/C MINIBAR TV TEL. HK$850–HK$1,200 ($110–$156) single or double; HK$1,580 ($205) executive floor; from HK$3,200 ($416) suite. 1 child under 12 can stay free in parents' room. AE, DC, MC, V. MTR: Yau Ma Tei or Mong Kok.

Opened in 1989, this China-owned hotel caters both to groups and individuals, with separate lobbies for both to speed check-in. It offers a business center, small fitness room, outdoor rooftop swimming pool, and comfortable rooms complete with satellite TV with in-house pay movies, hair dryers, coffee/tea-making facilities, and two no-smoking floors. Guest rooms at the front of the hotel present a slightly better view of the surrounding neighborhood. Guest services include room service (6am to 1am), same-day laundry service, baby-sitting, house doctor, and limousine service. Two executive floors offer the following extras: an exclusive lounge, welcome champagne, fruit basket, and nightly turndown service. The hotel's main drawback is its location, about a 10-minute walk from the subway station. To compensate, the hotel offers free hourly shuttle service to Tsim Sha Tsui (near Star Ferry) and the Mong Kok MTR station. Otherwise, city bus no. 7 goes from the hotel to the Star Ferry. Among the hotel's several dining facilities, Porto is popular among locals for its very good Portuguese fare, while the House of Tang, serving Cantonese and Szechuan dishes, is also highly recommended.

**Nathan Hotel.** 378 Nathan Rd., Yau Ma Tei, Kowloon, Hong Kong. ☎ 852/2388 5141. Fax 852/2770 4262. E-mail: nathanhk@hkstar.com. 185 units, all with bathroom. A/C MINI-BAR TV TEL. HK$500–HK$950 ($65–$123) single; HK$600–HK$1,300 ($78–$169) twin. AE, DC, MC, V. MTR: Jordan.

More than 35 years old, the Nathan Hotel has been completely renovated and offers rooms that are not much different in decor than those in more expensive moderately priced hotels, though there are no frills outside the basics of hair dryers and room safes. One advantage is that since the hotel dates from an earlier era when land was less expensive, its rooms and bathrooms are quite large compared with those in most Hong Kong hotels; also, as in earlier days, there are attendants on duty on each floor around the clock (as had previously been the custom at all Hong Kong hotels). The hotel attracts business travelers from China and other Asian countries. Facilities are limited to one restaurant serving Cantonese and Western food and a business center. Services include complimentary newspaper (on request), room service (7am to midnight), same-day laundry service, baby-sitting, and limousine service. It's located north of Tsim Sha Tsui, near the Temple Street night market and about a 20-minute walk from the Star Ferry.

**New Astor.** 11 Carnarvon Rd., Tsim Sha Tsui, Kowloon, Hong Kong. ☎ **852/2366 7261.** Fax 852/2722 7122. www.newastor.com.hk. E-mail: hotel@newastor.com.hk. 148 units, all with bathroom. A/C MINIBAR TV TEL. HK$800–HK$1,180 ($104–$153) single or double. Monthly rates available. 1 child under 12 can stay free in parents' room. AE, DC, MC, V. MTR: Tsim Sha Tsui.

This is an older, small hotel that has undergone remodeling through the years to keep up with more modern competitors. Its facilities are almost nonexistent—just a business center and one restaurant serving mostly Western fare. Its simple rooms offer just the basics of TV with pay movies and hair dryer, though there is a no-smoking floor. Some of the cheapest rooms (mostly doubles) face another building, while the best rooms are corner rooms with large windows that face the street and such extras as safes and coffee/tea-making facilities. Guest services cover just the minimum—same-day laundry service and room service (7am to 11pm). Probably the hotel's best feature is its location, in the heart of Tsim Sha Tsui just off Nathan Road.

**New Kings Hotel.** 473 Nathan Rd. (entrance on Wing Sing Lane), Yau Ma Tei, Kowloon, Hong Kong. ☎ **852/2780 1281.** Fax 852/2782 1833. E-mail: newkings@netvigator.com. 72 units, all with bathroom. A/C TV TEL. HK$550–HK$600 ($71.50–$78) single; HK$650–HK$750 ($84.50–$97.50) twin. AE, MC, V. MTR: Yau Ma Tei.

This 30-year-old property underwent extensive renovation in 1997 and reopened as a completely new hotel, with rates that are only slightly higher than before, making it very good value. Located near the jade and night markets and a Tin Hau temple, it now sports a tiny but smart-looking lobby decorated with natural woods and jade colors. A coffee shop serves Western food. Rooms, though new, are rather plain, with empty refrigerators and small safes; tiled bathrooms lack counter space. There are only six rooms on each floor, a good thing since corridors are barely wide enough for one person. Expect to wait for the hotel's one elevator.

**Pruton Prudential Hotel.** 222 Nathan Rd. (entrance on Tak Shing St.), Tsim Sha Tsui, Kowloon, Hong Kong. ☎ **852/2311 8222.** Fax 852/2311 4760. E-mail: pruton@netvigator. com. 434 units. A/C MINIBAR TV TEL. HK$750–HK$1,500 ($97–$195) single or double; HK$1,800 ($234) Executive Club floor. 1 child under 12 stays free in parents' room. AE, DC, MC, V. MTR: Jordan.

This 1991 hotel, at the northern end of Tsim Sha Tsui, towers 17 stories above a six-level shopping complex and the MTR Jordan station, providing easy and direct access to the rest of Hong Kong. About a 20-minute walk from the Star Ferry and only minutes from the Temple Street Night Market, Jade Market, and a Tin Hau temple, it is topped by an observation tower 300 feet above street level, providing outstanding views of Kowloon, the harbor, and Hong Kong. Be sure to bring your camera to capture the view from here. Another plus is the 60-foot-long rooftop outdoor swimming pool. The guest rooms are tastefully modern, with sleek furniture, artwork, and Japanese moving panels framing the windows. The rates are based on the view; the cheapest rooms face the back of the hotel. All rooms have facsimile capability (fax machines are available for rent from the 24-hour business center), as well as hair dryers, room safes, and TVs with in-house movies. Deluxe rooms feature floor-to-ceiling bay windows, some with a partial glimpse of the harbor in the distance. In addition to a no-smoking floor, two Club Floors feature a separate hospitality desk and in-room fax machines. As the guests are predominantly Southeast Asian and Japanese business-people, there's a business center—open 24 hours a day. Although the hotel itself has only a coffee shop and a bar, there are several other restaurants within the shopping complex. Guest services include 24-hour room service, same-day laundry service, baby-sitting, and limousine service.

✪ **The Salisbury YMCA.** Salisbury Rd., Tsim Sha Tsui, Kowloon, Hong Kong. ☎ **852/2369 2211** (852/2268 7888 for reservations). Fax 852/2739 9315. www. ymcahk.org.hk. E-mail: room@ymcahk.org.hk. 365 units, all with bathroom. A/C. HK$660 ($86) single; HK$705–HK$865 ($92–$112) double; from HK$1,200 ($156) suite. Dormitory bed HK$190 ($25). AE, DC, MC, V. MTR: Tsim Sha Tsui.

For decades the overwhelming number-one choice among low-cost accommodations has been the YMCA on Salisbury Road, which has the good fortune of being right next to The Peninsula Hotel on the waterfront, just a 2-minute walk from both the Star Ferry and subway station. For years there was a fear that it might be torn down in the face of land-hungry developers, but instead the YMCA was completely rebuilt, with a spacious and cheerful lobby, additional rooms, and a sports facility added in 1991. Welcoming families as well as individual men and women, it has 19 single rooms (none with harbor view) and more than 280 twins (the most expensive twins provide great harbor views), as well as suites with and without harbor views that are great for families. Although simple in decor, these rooms (including no-smoking rooms) are on a par with those at more expensively priced hotels, with such in-room amenities as telephones with voice mail, satellite TVs with complimentary in-house movies, dataports, stocked refrigerators, coffee/tea-making facilities, safes, and hair dryers. For budget travelers, there are 14 dormitory-style rooms, each with two bunk beds, individual reading lights, private bathroom, and lockers, available only to visitors who have been in Hong Kong fewer than 10 days (write or fax for reservations; walk-ins are also accepted). There are three food and beverage outlets, including the **Salisbury Restaurant** serving buffet meals. The sports facility boasts two indoor swimming pools (one a lap pool, the other a children's pool, both free for all hotel guests except those in dormitory) and a fitness gym, two squash courts, and indoor climbing wall (fee charged). There's also a fourth-floor terrace with play equipment for children. Laundry service is available, as are baby-sitting and room service (7am to 11:30pm). Needless to say, the Salisbury is so popular that you should make reservations in advance, especially if booking for April or October. Although the Salisbury may seem expensive for a YMCA, the location and facilities are worth the price; here you have Tsim Sha Tsui's cheapest rooms with harbor views. Highly recommended.

**Shamrock Hotel.** 223 Nathan Rd., Yau Ma Tei, Kowloon, Hong Kong. ☎ **852/2735 2271.** Fax 852/2736 7354. www.yp.com.hk/shamrock. E-mail: shamrock@iohk.com. 148 units, all with bath. A/C TV TEL. HK$350–HK$500 ($45–$65) single; HK$400–HK$650 ($52–$84) double. AE, DC, MC, V. MTR: Jordan.

A pioneer member of HKHA and catering mainly to visitors from Southeast Asia, the Shamrock was built in the early 1950s and, despite recent lobby renovations that added marble floors and walls and artwork from Beijing, I don't think it's changed much since then. The most remarkable thing about this hotel is its lobby—although tiny, the ceiling is covered with about a dozen small chandeliers and lights of different designs. The guest rooms, equipped with empty refrigerators, are clean but a bit worn and rather small, though high ceilings (with small chandeliers!) give the rooms something of a spacious feeling. Some of the cheapest rooms are without windows (not for the claustrophobic). A restaurant on the 10th floor serves Western food, and there's room service (7am to 10pm), as well as laundry service. It's about a 20-minute walk from the Star Ferry.

**YMCA International House.** 23 Waterloo Rd., Yau Ma Tei, Kowloon, Hong Kong. ☎ **852/ 2771 9111.** Fax 852/2388 5926; reservation fax 852/2771 5238. www.ymcaintlhousehk.org. E-mail: ymcares1@netvigator.com. 407 units, all with bathroom. A/C TV TEL. HK$500–HK$760 ($65–$99) single; HK$620–HK$760 ($81–$99) twin. AE, DC, MC, V. MTR: Yau Ma Tei.

Located just off Nathan Road only a minute's walk from the MTR station, this YMCA recently renovated its old building and added a 25-story tower, transforming itself into a smart-looking establishment that can rival many of the more expensively priced hotels. The cheapest rooms occupy the older building, while the new tower rooms are similar in decor and comfort to modestly priced hotel rooms anywhere in the city. Ask for a room on a top floor, where it's brighter and you can look out over the city. All rooms have empty refrigerators and small safes, and no-smoking floors and laundry service are available. Facilities include one restaurant serving Western and Chinese fare and one lounge, as well as an indoor swimming pool (free to Y guests), fitness room (fee charged), sauna, tennis and squash courts, and business center.

# WAN CHAI

**Wesley.** 22 Hennessy Rd., Wan Chai, Hong Kong. ☎ **852/2866 6688.** Fax 852/2866 6633. E-mail: wesley@hanglung.com. 251 units. A/C MINIBAR TV TEL. HK$700–HK$1,800 ($91–$234) single or double. Monthly rates available. 1 child under 12 can stay free in parents' room. AE, DC, MC, V. MTR: Admiralty or Wan Chai.

This simple business hotel opened in 1992 on the former site of the famous Soldiers' & Sailors' Home, a Hong Kong landmark for more than a century. In keeping with Hong Kong's unofficial preferred decorating style, its small lobby is sparsely furnished, and the only hotel facilities are a business center, coffee shop, and Cantonese restaurant also serving dim sum. It reminds me of business hotels in Japan. All rooms are equally small, with V-shaped windows, and provide coffee/tea-making facilities and hair dryers. Rates are based on bed configurations, floor level and, to a small degree, room size: the cheaper rooms are on lower floors and are furnished with twin beds; the most expensive are slightly larger, with king-size beds and a small sitting area. Rooms facing the front of the hotel are noisier. The bathrooms are only large enough for one person, and the closets aren't tall enough to hang dresses. Services are limited to room service (7am to 10:30pm), same-day laundry service, baby-sitting, and house doctor.

## 5 Rock-Bottom Accommodations

### GUEST HOUSES

Hong Kong's cheapest accommodations aren't hotels and aren't recommended for visitors who expect cleanliness and comfort. Rather, these accommodations, usually called "guest houses," attract a young backpacking crowd, many of whom are traveling through Asia and are interested only in a bed at the lowest cost. They also attract laborers, mostly men from Asia, Africa, and the Middle East. At any rate, some guest houses offer rooms with a private bathroom; others are nothing more than rooms filled with bunk beds. Of Hong Kong's rock-bottom establishments, none is more notorious than **Chungking Mansion.** Although it occupies a prime spot at 40 Nathan Road, between the Holiday Inn Golden Mile and the Sheraton in Tsim Sha Tsui, Chungking Mansion is easy to overlook; there's no big sign heralding its existence. In fact, its ground floor is one huge maze of inexpensive shops.

But above all those shops are five towering concrete blocks, each served by its own tiny elevator and known collectively as Chungking Mansion. Inside are hundreds of little businesses, apartments, guest houses, eateries, and sweatshops. Some of the guest houses are passable; many are not.

I stayed at Chungking Mansion on my first trip to Hong Kong in 1983, living in a neon-colored cell that was furnished with two sagging beds, a night table, and closet. In the shared bathroom down the hall lived the biggest spider I have ever seen, a hairy thing that nevertheless behaved itself whenever I was there—it never moved an inch the whole time I took a shower, and when I returned each evening it was always motionless in another part of the room. I figured that it survived only by being unobtrusive, and I wouldn't be surprised if it's still there. I shared my room with another woman and we paid $5 (U.S.) each.

Chungking Mansion has changed a lot since then. Fifteen years ago there wasn't much choice among the guest houses within Chungking Mansion; most of them were on the borderline of squalor. Today there are literally dozens of new ones, and many of the older ones have cleaned up their act in their bid for the tourist's dollar. I myself counted about 60 guest houses here, though a security guard estimated that there were as many as 150 spread throughout the complex; many are very small with only a handful of rooms.

Still, Chungking is not the kind of place you'd want to recommend to anyone uninitiated in the seamier side of travel. The views from many room windows are more insightful than some guests might like—the backside of the building and mountains of trash down below. Even worse are the ancient-looking elevators filled to capacity with human cargo; you might want to stick to the stairs. In any case, sometimes the elevators don't work at all, making it a long hike up the dozen flights of stairs to the top floors. But the most compelling argument for avoiding Chungking Mansion is one of safety—it could be a towering inferno waiting to happen. However, for some budget travelers, it's a viable alternative to Hong Kong's high-priced hotels. And you certainly can't beat it for location.

If you insist on staying here, these are my recommendations. Chungking Mansion is divided into five separate blocks, from A Block to E Block. For the less daring, A Block is the best, since its elevator is closest to the front entrance to the building. It also contains the only guest house here that's a member of the Hong Kong Hotel Association (see below). The other elevators are farther back in the shopping arcade, which can be a little disconcerting at night when the shops are all closed and the corridors are deserted. I recommend that you begin your search in Block A. I also recommend that you stay on lower floors. If guest houses here are full or you want to save money, check the guest houses toward the back of the building in the other blocks. But no matter what the block, never leave any valuables in your room.

**Chungking House.** A Block, 4th and 5th floors, Chungking Mansion, 40 Nathan Rd., Tsim Sha Tsui, Kowloon, Hong Kong. ☎ **852/2366 5362.** Fax 852/2721 3570. 75 units, 67 with bathroom. A/C TV TEL. HK$230 ($30) single with shower only, HK$250 ($32) single with bathroom; HK$300–HK$380 ($39–$49) double/twin with bathroom. No credit cards. MTR: Tsim Sha Tsui.

This is the best-known guest house in Chungking Mansion—due primarily to the remarkable fact that it's a member of the Hong Kong Tourist Association (remarkable in that it's far shabbier than the other accommodations that belong to the association). It also has the best location at Chungking, in the A Block on a lower floor. There are front desks and lobbies on both the fourth and fifth floors, and these, too, are in desperate need of a good cleaning (just getting rid of the stacks of boxes holding supplies would be a good start). At any rate, the rooms are dreary and depressing, with wood paneling and ancient tiled bathrooms (ask for a room facing Nathan Road; though noisier, they are brighter and a tad more cheerful). The staff tends to be unconcerned and gruff. Still, you might want to try this place first before tackling the elevator or stairs to check out the guest houses on the upper floors.

## YOUTH HOSTELS

There are seven youth hostels in Hong Kong, including its islands and territories, and they offer the cheapest rates around. However, most are not conveniently located— indeed, some require a ferry ride and/or a 45-minute hike from the nearest bus stop, as they are located in country parks.

If you don't have a youth hostel card, you can still stay at a youth hostel by paying an extra HK$35 ($4.55) per night. After 6 nights, nonmembers are eligible for member status and subsequently pay overnight charges at members' rates.

The most conveniently located youth hostel is the 112-bed **Ma Wui Hall,** on the top of Mount Davis on Hong Kong Island (☎ **852/2817 5715**). It charges HK$65 ($8.45) per night for a dormitory bed for those aged 18 and over. There are also a few private rooms, with a double costing HK$220 ($28.60) and a triple costing HK$260 ($33.80). To reach it, take the Ma Mui Hall Shuttle Bus, which departs from the Macau Ferry Terminal (MTR: Sheung Wan) daily at 9:30am and 7, 9 and 10:30pm.

Alternatively, take bus no. 47A from Admiralty or minibus no. 54 from the outlying islands ferry terminal in Central, getting off near the junction of Victoria Road and Mt. Davis Path. Backtrack a few minutes from the bus stop and hike up Mt. Davis Path 35 minutes to the hostel (do not confuse Mt. Davis Path with Mt. Davis Road). A taxi from Central costs approximately HK$60 ($7.80). The hostel itself is open daily 7am to 11pm.

There are six other youth hostels on some of the outlying islands and in the New Territories; most charge HK$35 ($4.55) for those 18 and older. Check-in is from 4pm. There are kitchens and washing facilities, as well as camp sites. Since these hostels are not easily accessible, they are recommended only for the adventurous traveler. Of these, the **S.G. Davis Hostel,** on Lantau island near the Po Lin Monastery with its giant Buddha (☎ **852/2985 5610**), is the easiest to reach from the airport. For more information on Hong Kong's youth hostels, contact the **Hong Kong Youth Hostels Association,** Room 225–226, Block 19, Shek Kip Mei Estate, Sham Shui Po, Kowloon (☎ **852/2788 1638**). The Hong Kong Tourist Association also has a flyer on youth hostels.

# Where to Dine 5

**D**ining is one of *the* things to do in Hong Kong. Not only is the food excellent, but the range of culinary possibilities is nothing short of staggering. With an estimated 8,700 restaurants, Hong Kong has what may well be the greatest concentration of Chinese restaurants in the world. In a few short days, you can take a culinary tour of virtually every major region of China, dining on Cantonese, Szechuan, Shanghainese, Pekingese, Chiu Chow, and other Chinese specialties. Some restaurants are huge, bustling, family affairs, countless others are mere holes in the wall, and a few of the trendiest are Shanghai chic, remakes of 1930s salons and opium dens. (See "A Taste of Hong Kong" in the appendix for information on dining customs and a brief rundown on Chinese cuisines.)

But dining in Hong Kong is by no means limited to Chinese restaurants. Although various national cuisines have long been popular, particularly French, Italian, Thai, and Indian, ethnic restaurants have literally exploded onto the culinary scene in the past few years, offering even greater diversity, from tapas and tacos to sushi. Japanese food is especially the rage among locals, and you'll find Japanese offerings on virtually every international buffet spread in Hong Kong, along with sushi delivered via conveyor belts in an ever-growing number of sushi bars.

I'm convinced that you can eat as well in Hong Kong as in any other city in the world. And no matter where you eat or how much you spend, it's sure to be an adventure of the senses. Little wonder that a common greeting among Chinese in Hong Kong translates literally as "Have you eaten?" In Hong Kong, eating is the most important order of the day.

By far Hong Kong's most well-known, exclusive restaurants, both Chinese and Western, have long been located in the hotels. That's not surprising when you realize that first-class hotels are accustomed to catering to well-traveled visitors who demand high quality in service, cuisine, and decor.

In a welcome trend, however, enterprising, ambitious, and talented chefs have been opening neighborhood establishments, often in modest but imaginative surroundings. These include ethnic restaurants, as well as eateries offering innovative dishes, with limited but intriguing menus. A cluster of these restaurants has even created a whole new dining enclave, located on the steep hill alongside the Hillside Escalator

Link that connects Central with the Mid-Levels. Dubbed SoHo for the region "south of Hollywood Road," it has blossomed into an ever-growing dining and nightlife district, making it Hong Kong's most exciting addition to the culinary scene.

Other welcome trends are the inclusion of vegetarian and healthy foods on many menus and the growing popularity of crossover, East-meets-West cuisine, which capitalizes on ingredients and flavors from both sides of the Pacific Rim in the creation of innovative dishes.

---

## Tips on Ways to Save on Your Hong Kong Meals

The good news is that dining prices have dropped somewhat since the Chinese takeover. But you can still save a few Hong Kong dollars when eating out by keeping these tips in mind:

- **Eat your big meal at lunch.** Most Asian (excluding Chinese) and Western restaurants offer special fixed-price lunches that are much cheaper than evening meals; their menus often include an appetizer, main course, and side dishes. Don't neglect expensive restaurants just because you assume they're out of your price range. If you feel like splurging, lunch is the way to go. For example, you can eat lunch at Gaddi's (one of Hong Kong's most famous restaurants) for less than $40 per person.

- **Jump on the buffet bandwagon.** Buffet spreads are another great Hong Kong tradition. Almost all hotels offer buffets, often for breakfast, lunch, and dinner; independent restaurants are more likely to feature buffets at lunch. Some include a variety of both Asian and continental dishes, a real bonus for lone diners who want to sample a variety of cuisines at a reasonable cost. If you have a hearty appetite, buffets are one of the best bargains in town.

- **Eat early or late dinner to take advantage of special fixed-price meals.** A few restaurants offer early-bird or late-night specials. If you dine before 7pm at trendy Felix, for example, a three-course meal costs only $38 as opposed to the $78 to $100 usually spent on dinner here. At Vong, Hong Kong's best restaurant for French-Asian crossover cuisine, the Theatre Menu, available daily 6 to 7pm and again after 10:30pm, costs only $37; discounts are offered on fixed-price lunches ordered between noon and 12:30pm or 1:30 and 3pm. Marché Mövenpick, an inexpensive restaurant with great views from Victoria Peak, offers late-night buffets after 9:30pm, costing $14 Sunday to Thursday and $22 on weekends.

- **If you want to imbibe, stick with beer.** Wine is especially expensive. The estimated meal prices for the restaurants presented in this chapter do not include wine, since you could easily spend a fortune on drinks alone. To keep costs down, try the two most popular brands of beer: **San Miguel** (Filipino) and **Tsingtao** (Chinese). And speaking of beer, many bars and pubs mentioned in chapter 9, "Hong Kong After Dark," also serve food. In any case, remember that a 10% service charge will be added to your food and beverage bill. There is no tax, however.

- **Go the dim sum route.** Dim sum, served mainly in Cantonese restaurants, is another way to economize on breakfast or lunch. Dim sum are usually served four to a basket or plate; two or three baskets are usually filling enough for me, which means I can have breakfast or lunch for less than HK$100 ($13).

The restaurants listed below are grouped first according to location (the most popular areas are Kowloon, the Central District, and Causeway Bay/Wan Chai) and then according to price. Those in the **Very Expensive** category will cost more than HK$600 ($78) for a meal without drinks (some restaurants average HK$900 ($117) or more per person). In the **Expensive** category, meals average HK$300 to HK$600 ($39 to $78). **Moderate** restaurants serve meals ranging from HK$150 to HK$300 ($19.50 to $39), while **Inexpensive** restaurants offer meals for less than HK$150 ($19.50). Keep in mind, however, that these guidelines are approximations only.

I should add that Chinese restaurants often have very long menus, sometimes listing more than 100 dishes. The most expensive dishes will invariably be such delicacies as bird's nest, shark's fin, or abalone, for which the sky's the limit. In specifying price ranges for "main courses" under each Chinese establishment below, therefore, I excluded both these delicacies and the inexpensive rice and noodle dishes. In most cases, "main courses" refers to meat and vegetable combinations. Remember, since the price range is large, you can eat cheaply even at moderately priced restaurants by choosing wisely. Remember, too, that it's customary to order one main dish for each diner plus one extra, and to share.

The usual lunch hour in Hong Kong is 1 to 2pm, when thousands of office workers pour into the city's more popular restaurants. Try to eat before or after the lunch rush hour, especially in Central, unless you plan on an expensive restaurant and have a reservation.

Unless stated otherwise, the open hours given below are exactly that—the hours a restaurant remains physically open but not necessarily the hours it serves food. The last orders are almost always taken at least a half hour before closing. Restaurants that are open for lunch noon to 3pm, for example, will probably stop taking orders at 2:30pm. To avoid disappointment, call beforehand to make a reservation or arrive well ahead of closing time.

As for dress codes, unless otherwise stated, many upper-end restaurants have done away with the jacket-and-tie requirement. Rather, "smart casual" is nowadays appropriate for most of the fancier places, meaning that men should wear long-sleeved shirts and that jeans and sport shoes are inappropriate.

# 1 Restaurants by Cuisine

## AMERICAN

Al's Diner (p. 134)
Dan Ryan's Chicago Grill (p. 112)
Gripps (p. 115)
Napa (p. 109)
Planet Hollywood (p. 116)
Ruth's Chris Steak House (p. 110)

## ASIAN

The Spice Market (p. 117 )
TOTT'S Asian Grill & Bar (p. 138 )

## CANTONESE

China Lan Kwai Fong (p. 127)
The Chinese (p. 108)

City Hall Chinese Restaurant
 (p. 135)
Fook Lam Moon (p. 108)
Golden Unicorn Restaurant (p. 109)
Happy Garden Noodles & Congee
 Kitchen (p. 119)
Jade Garden Restaurant (p. 115)
Jumbo Floating Restaurant (p. 144)
Lai Ching Heen (p. 106)
Luk Yu Tea House (p. 131)
Man Wah (p. 124)
One Harbour Road (p. 138)
Shang Palace (p. 110)
The Square (p. 133)

Super Star Seafood Restaurant
(p. 117)
Treasure Inn Seafood Restaurant
(p. 145)
Tsui Hang Village Restaurant
(p. 118)
Yung Kee (p. 133)
Zen Chinese (p. 128)

## CHIU CHOW
City Chiuchow Restaurant (p. 112)
Golden Island Bird's Nest (p. 114)

## CONTINENTAL
Avenue Restaurant & Bar (p. 108)
Harbour Side (p. 115)
Hugo's (p. 104)
Jimmy's Kitchen (p. 130)
Landau's (p. 131)
M at the Fringe (p. 128)
Mandarin Grill (p. 124)
Pavilion (p. 132)
The Plume (p. 106)
Sammy's Kitchen (p. 144)
27 Restaurant & Bar (p. 138)

## CROSSOVER/EAST-MEETS-WEST/PACIFIC RIM
Felix (p. 103 )
Joyce Cafe (p. 130)
Tables 88 (p. 143)
TOTT'S Asian Grill & Bar (p. 138)
Vong (p. 125)

## FRENCH
Au Trou Normand (p. 108)
Cafe des Artistes (p. 127)
Gaddi's (p. 104)
Maman WineBar and Restaurant
(p. 109)
Margaux (p. 106)
Petrus (p. 125)
Stanley's French Restaurant (p. 143)

## GREEK
Bacchus (p. 139)

## HUNANESE
Hunan Garden (p. 129)

## INDIAN
The Ashoka (p. 134)
Banana Leaf Curry House (p. 118)
Gaylord (p. 113)
Koh-I-Noor (p. 120)
Stanley's Oriental Restaurant (p. 143)
The Viceroy (p. 140)
Woodlands (p. 103)

## INTERNATIONAL
Cafe Deco (p. 141)
The Greenery (p. 114)
Island Cafe (p. 130)
La Ronda (p. 127)
Marché Mövenpick (p. 142)
Open Kitchen (p. 141)
Peak Cafe (p. 142)
The Salisbury (p. 120)
The Verandah (p. 111)

## ITALIAN
Baci (p. 129)
Baci Pizza (p. 134)
Fat Angelo's (p. 119)
Grappa's (p. 129)
Grissini (p. 135)
Milano (p. 139)
Nicholini's (p. 124)
The Pizzeria (p. 116)
Sabatini (p. 110)
Spaghetti House (p. 120)
Tutto Bene (p. 111)
Va Bene (p. 128)

## JAPANESE
Benkay Japanese Restaurant (p. 126)
Genki Sushi (p. 119)
Hanagushi (p. 127)
Osaka (p. 116)
Tokio Joe (p. 133)
Unkai (p. 107)

## KOREAN
Arirang Korean Restaurant (p. 111)

## MALAYSIAN/SINGAPOREAN
Banana Leaf Curry House (p. 118)

## MEDITERRANEAN
Bacchus (p. 139)

## MEXICAN

Coyote Bar & Grill (p. 141)
I Caramba! (p. 135)

## PEKINGESE

American Restaurant (p. 140)
Peking Garden (p. 116)
Spring Deer Restaurant (p. 117)

## SEAFOOD

Lobster Bar (p. 121)
Super Star Seafood Restaurant
(p. 117)
Treasure Inn Seafood Restaurant
(p. 145)
Yü (p. 107)

## SHANGHAINESE

Great Shanghai (p. 114)
Lao Ching Hing (p. 139)
Shanghai Garden (p. 132)
Wu Kong (p. 118)
Ye Shanghai (p. 133)

## SPANISH

El Cid Spanish Restaurant (p. 112)

## SZECHUAN

Red Pepper (p. 140)
Sichuan Garden (p. 132)
Sze Chuen Lau Restaurant (p. 140)

## TEAS/CAKES

Clipper Lounge (p. 148)
Peninsula Hotel Lobby (p. 148)
Tiffin (p. 148)

## THAI

Chili Club (p. 141)
Golden Elephant Thai Restaurant
(p. 113)
Stanley's Oriental Restaurant
(p. 143)
Thai Lemongrass (p. 133)

## VEGETARIAN

Avenue Restaurant & Bar (p. 108)
Bo Kong (p. 141)
Joyce Cafe (p. 130)
Woodlands (p. 121)

## VIETNAMESE

Golden Bull (p. 113)
Indochine 1929 (p. 130)

## 2 Kowloon

### VERY EXPENSIVE

✪ **Felix.** In The Peninsula Hotel, Salisbury Rd., Tsim Sha Tsui. ☎ **852/2920 2888,** ext. 3188. Reservations required. Main courses HK$190–HK$280 ($24.70–$36.35). AE, CB, DC, MC, V. Daily 6pm–2am (last order 10:30pm). MTR: Tsim Sha Tsui. PACIFIC RIM/EAST-MEETS-WEST.

Located on the top floor of The Peninsula's new tower addition, this strikingly avant-garde restaurant comes as something of a shock in the otherwise staid and traditionally conservative hotel. But what else can you expect from a restaurant designed by Philippe Starck? He was given free rein to create one of Hong Kong's most unusual settings. Your first hint that Felix is not your ordinary dining experience begins with the elevator's wavy walls, which suggest a voyage to the world beyond. The wave pattern continues inside the restaurant in a huge aluminum wall, and two glass facades curve seductively to reveal stunning views of Kowloon. Two eye-catching zinc cylinders vaguely resemble gigantic snails and contain cocoon-cozy bars and what may be one of the world's tiniest discos, complete with a heat-sensitive floor that illuminates dancers' movements. Be sure to check out the rest room for the thrill of its slightly exhibitionist setting. The dining area itself is rather—what can I say—stark, with various styles of tables in marble, glass, and wood, all devoid of such "superfluous" decorations as table linen or flowers. The chair backs, also designed by Starck, are embellished with portraits of himself and his friends, but such details may be overlooked when the restaurant is full. Indeed, even the view from the windows tends to take second place in this self-conscious, people-watching setting. The food, featuring

Pacific Rim ingredients brought together in East-meets-West combinations, is quite good but also secondary to the setting. Dishes have ranged from a ginger-marinated sea bass on wasabi potatoes with Asian mustard to a hibachi filet of steak with a spicy crab glaze and a smoked chili-tomato sauce. At approximately HK$600 to HK$700 ($77.90 to $90.90) per person for a meal here excluding wine, Felix is almost a bargain considering it's a hotel restaurant, and in The Peninsula at that. True bargain hunters can save bundles, however, by dining early (before 7pm) and opting for the early-bird, three-course fixed-price dinner for HK$290 ($37.65). But clearly, the main reason for coming here is the experience—something to describe to the folks back home.

✪ **Gaddi's.** In The Peninsula Hotel, Salisbury Rd., Tsim Sha Tsui. ☎ **852/2920 2888,** ext. 3171. Reservations recommended at lunch, required at dinner. Jacket and tie required at dinner. Main courses HK$310–HK$550 ($39.85–$58.50); fixed-price lunch HK$280–HK$340 ($36.40–$44.20); fixed-price dinner HK$500–HK$800 ($65–$104). AE, CB, DC, MC, V. Daily noon–2:30pm and 7–10:30pm. MTR: Tsim Sha Tsui. FRENCH.

Opened in 1953 and named after a former general manager of The Peninsula, Gaddi's was long considered the best European restaurant in Hong Kong. Although that reputation has since been challenged by the birth of many other superb restaurants, the service is still excellent, the waiters are all professionals, and the food is always beyond reproof. Gaddi's is still a legend in Asia, the epitome of old Hong Kong. It's especially popular with an older, well-to-do crowd that prefers traditional French food without the culinary surprises of nouvelle cuisine.

The atmosphere, intended to evoke the hotel's original 1928 neoclassical architecture, is that of an elegant European dining room blended with the best of Asia; there are two crystal-and-silver chandeliers from Paris, a pure wool Tai Ping carpet in royal blue and gold, a Chinese coromandel screen dating from 1670, and Biedermeier-style chairs. As for the food, it's French haute cuisine at its finest, under the watchful eye of Gaddi's first British chef. The menu changes every 6 months, but it always includes steak and seafood, as well as a five-course dinner and a vegetarian menu. Signature dishes include raw-marinated goose liver with peeled white grapes set in a muscadet jelly, chilled tomato soup with deep-fried scampi tails; and steamed cod with lemon confit and sautéed cherrystone clams. The wine cellar is among the best and largest in Hong Kong, with a collection of rare vintages—but who could blame you if you get carried away and splurge on champagne? Dinner is likely to cost upwards from HK$1,000 ($129.85) per person excluding wine, even more if you order caviar followed by lobster. There's live, discreet music at night and a small dance floor. Lunch, especially the fixed-price two-course menu, which includes a glass of wine, is quite affordable, making this the top splurge for the money-conscious.

**Hugo's.** In the Hyatt Regency, 67 Nathan Rd., Tsim Sha Tsui. ☎ **852/2311 1234,** ext. 877. Reservations recommended. Jacket and tie required. Main courses HK$280–HK$450 ($36.40–$58.50); fixed-price lunch HK$240–HK$260 ($31.20–$33.80); fixed-price dinner HK$580–HK$850 ($75.40–$110.50). AE, DC, MC, V. Daily noon–3pm and 7–11pm. MTR: Tsim Sha Tsui. CONTINENTAL.

This was the first Hugo's opened by Hyatt in Asia; now there's a Hugo's in all their deluxe hotels. The rather masculine and slightly grim decor features swords on the walls and booths with iron partitions, little changed over the past decades. Popular with the locals and visiting businesspeople, it's a good choice for power lunches and a lively place for dinner, with Filipino musicians serenading evening diners. With an open charcoal grill, its specialty is U.S. prime rib of beef and Angus sirloin steak, as well as seafood flown in from around the world. The menu changes twice a year, but

# Kowloon Dining

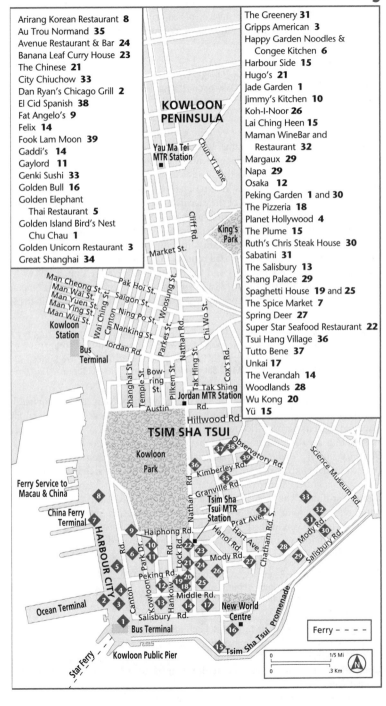

Arirang Korean Restaurant **8**
Au Trou Normand **35**
Avenue Restaurant & Bar **24**
Banana Leaf Curry House **23**
The Chinese **21**
City Chiuchow **33**
Dan Ryan's Chicago Grill **2**
El Cid Spanish **38**
Fat Angelo's **9**
Felix **14**
Fook Lam Moon **39**
Gaddi's **14**
Gaylord **11**
Genki Sushi **33**
Golden Bull **16**
Golden Elephant
  Thai Restaurant **5**
Golden Island Bird's Nest
  Chu Chau **1**
Golden Unicorn Restaurant **3**
Great Shanghai **34**

The Greenery **31**
Gripps American **3**
Happy Garden Noodles &
  Congee Kitchen **6**
Harbour Side **15**
Hugo's **21**
Jade Garden **1**
Jimmy's Kitchen **10**
Koh-I-Noor **26**
Lai Ching Heen **15**
Maman WineBar and
  Restaurant **32**
Margaux **29**
Napa **29**
Osaka **12**
Peking Garden **1** and **30**
The Pizzeria **18**
Planet Hollywood **4**
The Plume **15**
Ruth's Chris Steak House **30**
Sabatini **31**
The Salisbury **13**
Shang Palace **29**
Spaghetti House **19** and **25**
The Spice Market **7**
Spring Deer **27**
Super Star Seafood Restaurant **22**
Tsui Hang Village **36**
Tutto Bene **37**
Unkai **17**
The Verandah **14**
Woodlands **28**
Wu Kong **20**
Yü **15**

KOWLOON
PENINSULA

Yau Ma Tei
MTR Station

Chun Yi Lane

Cliff Rd.

King's
Park

Market St.

Man Cheong St.
Man Wai St.
Man Yuen St.
Man Ying St.
Man Wui St.
Kowloon
Station

Pak Hoi St.
Saigon St.
Ning Po St.
Nanking St.

Wai Ching St.
Canton

Parkes St.
Woosung St.
Nathan Rd.
Chi Wo St.

Bus
Terminal

Jordan Rd.

Shanghai St.
Temple St.
Bow-
ring
St.

Pilkem St.
Tak Hing St.

Cox's Rd.

Tak Shing
Jordan MTR Station
Rd.

Austin

Hillwood Rd.

TSIM SHA TSUI

Kowloon
Park

Observatory Rd.

Science Museum Rd.

Kimberley Rd.

Granville Rd.

Tsim Sha
Tsui MTR
Station

Prat Ave.

Hart Ave.

Chatham Rd. S.

Mody Rd.

Salisbury Rd.

Ferry Service to
Macau & China

China Ferry
Terminal

HARBOUR CITY

Rd.
Park Dr.
Haiphong Rd.

Nathan Rd.
Lock Rd.

Hanoi Rd.

Mody Rd.

Peking Rd.

Kowloon
Hankow

Middle Rd.

New World
Centre

Ocean Terminal

Canton

Salisbury
Rd.

Bus Terminal

Star Ferry

Kowloon Public Pier

Tsim Sha Tsui Promenade

Ferry - - - -

0            1/5 Mi
0          .3 Km

if the cognac flambée lobster bisque or baked artichoke hearts topped with lobster (house specialties) are on the menu, I would recommend them. The desserts are always spectacular, and the wine list is extensive.

✪ **Lai Ching Heen.** In the Regent Hotel, Salisbury Rd., Tsim Sha Tsui. ☎ **852/2721 1211,** ext. 2243. Reservations recommended (request a window seat). Main dishes HK$165–HK$560 ($21.45–$72.80). AE, DC, MC, V. Daily noon–2:30pm and 6–11:30pm. MTR: Tsim Sha Tsui. CANTONESE.

One of Hong Kong's top Cantonese restaurants, Lai Ching Heen envelops diners in a sophisticated, hushed environment, quite a contrast to the bright, noisy atmosphere typical of most Chinese restaurants. Its decor emphasizes the beauty of stark simplicity, with bonsai trees, flower arrangements, and a color scheme of rose and pale gray offsetting beautiful jade table settings and ivory and silver chopsticks. Large windows treat diners to a view of famous Victoria Harbour. Dishes are traditional Cantonese, as well as imaginative creations of the executive chef that border on Chinese nouvelle cuisine. The menu changes with each lunar month but always includes seafood, seasonal vegetables, and a wide selection of desserts. Examples are prawns with sesame and mayonnaise sauce, stir-fried shark's fin with crabmeat and Chinese chive, and sautéed diced pigeon and caramelized walnuts. Since most diners follow the Chinese custom of ordering several dishes and then sharing, the average dinner bill without wine here begins at HK$1,400 ($182) for two. For lunch an additional menu is offered that includes main dishes averaging about HK$100 to HK$120 ($13 to $15.60) in price, as well as dim sum.

**Margaux.** In the Kowloon Shangri-La Hotel, 64 Mody Rd., Tsim Sha Tsui East. ☎ **852/2721 2111,** ext. 8900. Reservations recommended. Main courses HK$210–HK$250 ($27.30–$32.50); fixed-price lunch HK$170–HK$200 ($22.10–$26); fixed-price dinner HK$588 ($76.44). AE, DC, MC, V. Mon–Sat noon–2:30pm and 6:30–10:30pm. MTR: Tsim Sha Tsui. FRENCH.

Small and intimate, with seating for only 58 lucky diners, Margaux is decorated in a style reminiscent of a château in southern France and exudes a warm, golden glow, imparted from its decor of rich fabrics, low lighting, and views of Hong Kong Island shimmering across the harbor. The menu, heavily influenced by the cuisines of Provence and the Mediterranean, is light and unpretentious, constantly changing to reflect seasonal foods. Fixed-price lunches, available as either two or three courses, may include such entrees as a roast of the day or steamed garoupa filet with soya-flavored butter. For dinner, the roast lobster is recommended if available. A selection of 250 wines represents some of the best regions from around the globe. With soft piano music serenading you in the background, this is a good choice for a romantic dinner (request a window seat when making reservations); female diners are even presented with a rose.

✪ **The Plume.** In the Regent Hotel, Salisbury Rd., Tsim Sha Tsui. ☎ **852/2721 1211,** ext. 2256. Reservations required (request a window seat). Main courses HK$270–HK$380 ($35.10–$49.40); fixed-price dinner HK$480–HK$720 ($62.40–$93.60). AE, DC, MC, V. Mon–Sat 7–11pm. MTR: Tsim Sha Tsui. CONTINENTAL.

Giving Gaddi's a run for its money is The Plume in The Regent Hotel. In fact, some people consider The Plume the best European restaurant in Hong Kong. Certainly it feels like a great restaurant, sitting right over the water with a grand view of Hong Kong Island and offering very interesting nouvelle cuisine served by an excellently trained staff.

It's open only for dinner, which begins with a complimentary serving of Indian bread and goose-liver pâté. The menu, which features only original creations that mix the best of the East and the West, changes every day but there's always the house specialty: a delicate cream of artichoke soup with beluga caviar. Other items have included caramelized bay scallops with lime oil and herb salad, and encrusted bresse pigeon and goose liver with Shanghai baby pak choi in perigord butter. One of the fixed-price meals is vegetarian. In any case, the food is so imaginative and full of surprises that epicures will want to set up camp. If you order à la carte, expect to spend at least HK$700 ($91) per person, without wine, though the wine is tempting: from one of the best wine lists in Asia.

**Unkai.** In the Sheraton Hong Kong Hotel and Towers, 20 Nathan Rd., Tsim Sha Tsui. ☎ **852/ 2369 1111,** ext. 2. Reservations recommended. Kaiseki fixed-price meals HK$500–HK$795 ($64.95–$103.25); teppanyaki fixed-price meals HK$750–HK$950 ($97.40–$123.40); fixed-price lunch HK$120–HK$300 ($15.60–$38.95). AE, CB, DC, MC, V. Daily noon–2:30pm and 6:30–10:30pm. MTR: Tsim Sha Tsui. JAPANESE.

The Hong Kong branch of a well-known group of restaurants in Japan, Unkai might well be the best Japanese restaurant in town. With chefs from Osaka, it caters to discerning Japanese, who make up a large proportion of the Sheraton's guests, with a variety of authentic dishes. True to Japanese form, the elegance of the restaurant is subtly understated, an aesthetic that is also carried into the food presentation. Foremost, of course, are the kaiseki courses, artfully arranged dishes that change according to the season. These are the most expensive fixed-price meals on the menu, but they are so huge that two can share. There's also tempura (meat and vegetables coated in batter and then deep-fried), teppanyaki (grilled foods), and sushi. Since ordering à la carte can be expensive, order a fixed-price meal (called a "course" on the menu) or come for lunch, when you have a choice of several fixed-price menus, including sushi courses, a tempura course, and an obento lunch box. The obento is especially charming, a small lacquered chest with dishes of food in each of the drawers. On weekends, all-you-can-eat buffets of sushi, sashimi, tempura, teppanyaki and more are available for HK$298 ($38.75).

**Yü.** In the Regent Hotel, Salisbury Rd., Tsim Sha Tsui. ☎ **852/2721 1211,** ext. 2340. Reservations necessary (request a window seat). Main courses HK$210–HK$330 ($27.25–$42.85). AE, DC, MC, V. Daily 6–11pm. MTR: Tsim Sha Tsui. SEAFOOD.

There's no mistaking what this restaurant serves—it's all right there in front of you, swimming blissfully in a 40-foot "bubble wall," unaware that the days are numbered. On the other side of the restaurant spreads a stunning view of Victoria Harbour. Located in the swank Regent Hotel but trendily low-key, the Yü offers a nice concept—fresh seafood for cautious diners reluctant to tempt fate by ordering locally caught fish in Hong Kong's cheaper, noisier, and more colorful seaside restaurants favored by Hong Kong Chinese. Of course, you also pay a mountain more to eat here, but from the looks of things there are plenty of takers. All the seafood, including a variety of garoupa, trout, other fish, lobsters, crabs, prawns, abalone, mussels, and oysters, are kept alive in tanks until the moment they're ordered; sometimes they have even been quarantined after being flown in to ensure quality. Colorful cards of fish are presented to diners to show the day's catch, which can be prepared in a variety of both Asian and Western ways, including grilled, poached, fried, or steamed. Many diners, however, stick to the imported oysters or begin their meals with the seafood platter—fresh seafood laid on a mountain of ice, including oysters, shrimp, prawns, mussels, and lobster, served with six different sauces. Another good choice is the lobster bisque or seafood basket, a variety of bamboo-steamed seafood. Sautéed lobster with black beans and fine noodles is the restaurant's signature dish. There's also a sushi bar, and, surprisingly, vegetarian choices. The wine list is limited, consisting mostly of whites, but a wider selection is available from The Plume's wine cellar.

# EXPENSIVE

**Au Trou Normand.** 63 Carnarvon Rd. (just north of Granville), Tsim Sha Tsui. ☎ **852/2366 8754.** Main courses HK$175–HK$250 ($22.75–$32.45); lunch buffet HK$120 ($15.60). AE, DC, MC, V. Daily noon–3pm and 6–11pm. MTR: Tsim Sha Tsui. FRENCH.

If you're hungering for traditional French food outside a hotel, this local favorite, in operation since 1964, is your best bet this side of the harbor. Decorated in the style of a cozy, inviting farmhouse, it offers unpretentious, classical French cuisine, including homemade goose liver mousse, homemade pork and liver terrine, onion soup, fresh frog legs sautéed in butter with parsley and garlic, snails in basil with garlic, burgundy beef stew, and sea scallops with lobster sauce. Most dinners average HK$400 ($51.95), without wine.

**Avenue Restaurant & Bar.** In the Holiday Inn Golden Mile, 50 Nathan Rd., Tsim Sha Tsui. ☎ **852/2315 1118.** Reservations recommended weekend evenings. Main courses HK$175–HK$258 ($22.75–$33.50); fixed-price lunch HK$178–HK$198 ($23.10–$25.70); fixed-price dinner HK$318–HK$358 ($41.30–$46.50). AE, DC, MC, V. Mon–Sat noon–2:30pm and 6–10:30pm (last order). MTR: Tsim Sha Tsui. CONTINENTAL.

The contemporary, upscale setting of this airy restaurant with its modern artwork, white-washed walls, palm trees, and greenhouselike dining area, together with its menu of modern European food, could easily mislead one into thinking that this trendy establishment is much more expensive than it is, making it very good value. It also overlooks Nathan Road, giving an unparalleled view of Hong Kong's bustling street life. Featuring modern European cuisine, the à-la-carte dinner menu offers an extensive selection tailored to various budgets and tastes, including a whole page devoted to vegetarian dishes. You might wish to start with an appetizer of crab and avocado with lemon mayonnaise, followed by grilled sole with spinach, new potatoes, poached egg, and grain mustard sauce, or pepper filet of beef with bourguignon sauce. For dessert try the chocolate souffle or the crème brûlée. There are also three- and four-course set dinners. For lunch, only fixed-price meals are available.

**۞ The Chinese.** In the Hyatt Regency, 67 Nathan Rd., Tsim Sha Tsui. ☎ **852/2311 1234,** ext. 2881. Reservations recommended at dinner. Main dishes HK$95–HK$170 ($12.35–$22.10); fixed-price lunch HK$310 ($40.30); fixed-price dinner HK$460–HK$740 ($59.80–$96.20). AE, DC, MC, V. Daily 11:30am–3pm and 6:30–11:30pm. MTR: Tsim Sha Tsui. CANTONESE.

Decorated in stark black and white with a blend of art deco and modern Chinese, this was Hong Kong's first Chinese restaurant to ignore the traditional red and gold. This trend-setting place remains one of Hong Kong's most refined Cantonese restaurants, with a small and intimate dining room reminiscent of Chinese teahouses of the 1920s. Traditional booth seating provides intimacy. The innovative menu combining Chinese ingredients with Western presentation changes with the seasons, but if available, the shark's fin served in papaya, deep-fried crispy chicken, minced pigeon with butter lettuce, drunken shrimp, and fried lobster balls are all equally delicious. Another great deal is the special dim sum available for lunch, costing HK$28 to HK$45 ($3.65 to $5.85) per basket.

**Fook Lam Moon.** 53–59 Kimberley Rd., Tsim Sha Tsui. ☎ **852/2366 0286.** Main dishes HK$90–HK$190 ($11.70–$24.70). AE, DC, MC, V. Daily 11:30am–2:30pm and 6–11:30pm. MTR: Tsim Sha Tsui. CANTONESE.

Upon entering this restaurant (look for the shrine to the kitchen god at the entrance), you immediately feel as if you've stepped back a couple of decades to a Hong Kong that has all but vanished. In years past there were a large number of indifferent, slow, and seemingly bored Chinese waiters standing around here, but on more recent visits

I've noticed that they have been replaced by an army of younger and more attentive employees. (Many Chinese restaurants are now hiring ambitious youths in an attempt to transform their image into that of a trendy establishment.) Some customers may find the service too attentive. In any case, Fook Lam Moon specializes in exotic dishes, including shark's fin, bird's nest, and abalone, served in a variety of ways, as well as more down-to-earth dishes such as fried crispy chicken and pan-fried lobster bars. Shark's fin, however, is the obvious number-one choice, with 19 different renditions listed on the menu. If you feel like splurging, prices for half a bowl of shark's fin with crab meat or shredded chicken begin at HK$250 ($32.50). If you are not careful, you could end up spending a small fortune (if you go for the exotic dishes, count on at least HK$1,000/$130 per person), but whatever you order, it's apt to be memorable. Indeed, some Hong Kong old-timers swear this restaurant serves the best Cantonese food in the world. Unlike many Chinese restaurants, this establishment provides both small (for two to four diners) and large tables.

There's another branch in Wan Chai at 35–45 Johnston Rd. (☎ **852/2866 0663;** MTR: Wan Chai), with the same hours.

**Golden Unicorn Restaurant.** In the Hongkong Hotel, 3 Canton Rd., Tsim Sha Tsui. ☎ **852/ 2730 6565.** Reservations recommended. Main dishes HK$110–HK$240 ($14.30–$31.20); fixed-price menu HK$388 ($50.40). AE, DC, MC, V. Daily noon–midnight. MTR: Tsim Sha Tsui. CANTONESE.

Opened in 1986, this sixth-floor restaurant was one of the pioneers in the trend to serve Chinese food in a more modern and formal setting. It features white tablecloths and flowers on each table and uses Wedgwood china and Christofle silverware. Some of its Cantonese selections have a Western flair bordering on *nouvelle Chinoise* cuisine. The menu includes drunken prawns, braised chicken with prawns and ham, and boneless duck with mashed taro. If you're by yourself you'll probably want to order the fixed-price menu, which changes monthly and allows you to sample several dishes. Otherwise, come for a lunch of dim sum.

**Maman WineBar and Restaurant.** In the Regal Kowloon Hotel, 71 Mody Rd., Tsim Sha Tsui East. ☎ **852/2313 8618.** Main courses HK$128–HK$198 ($16.60–$25.70); fixed-price lunch HK$148 ($19.20); fixed-price dinner HK$428 ($55.60). AE, DC, MC, V. Mon–Sat 11:30am–2:30pm and 6:30–10:30pm. MTR: Tsim Sha Tsui. FRENCH.

Although the floral design of the carpet is a bit over the top and there are no views, the Maman WineBar and Restaurant earns kudos for its adjoining wine shop, where diners can choose from among 400 bottles of wine sold at retail prices, take it in the restaurant, and pay a HK$100 ($13) corkage fee. For those who don't want an entire bottle, there are more than 50 wines by the glass. The cuisine celebrates the home cooking of southern France. Arriving dishes are placed in the center of the table for everyone to share; specialties include old-fashioned lamb stew, beef stew simmered in red Burgundy wine, confit of duck leg slowly cooked in a white bean stew, and roast rack of lamb with mustard, garlic, and rosemary sauce.

**Napa.** In the Kowloon Shangri-La Hotel, 64 Mody Rd., Tsim Sha Tsui East. ☎ **852/2733 8752.** Pastas HK$110–HK$132 ($14.30–$17.15); main courses HK$188–HK$290 ($24.40–$37.65); fixed-price lunch HK$168–HK$198 ($21.80–$25.70); fixed-price dinner HK$438 ($56.90). AE, CB, DC, MC, V. Daily noon–3pm and 6:30pm–midnight. MTR: Tsim Sha Tsui. AMERICAN/CALIFORNIAN.

Located on the top floor of the Kowloon Shangri-La Hotel and boasting great harbor views, this smart-looking restaurant is so upbeat it could make an optimist of even the most travel-weary diner. Crisply decorated with light-colored woods, modern art, and art deco–style fixtures (check out the naughty lamps in the bay windows), it offers what may well be the best Caesar salad in town, served in a Parmesan basket with sourdough croutons. Another good starter is the grilled eggplant cream soup; follow it with the king prawns on spinach with a seafood saffron emulsion and homemade potato gnocchi. For lighter appetites, there's also a limited selection of pastas.

**Ruth's Chris Steak House.** Empire Centre (opposite Regal Kowloon Hotel), 68 Mody Rd., Tsim Sha Tsui East. ☎ **852/2366 6000.** Main courses HK$180–HK$550 ($23.40–$71.45); fixed-price lunch HK$105–HK$148 ($13.65–$19.20); fixed-price dinner HK$450–HK$650 ($58.45–$84.40). AE, DC, MC, V. Daily noon–3pm and 6–11:30pm. MTR: Tsim Sha Tsui. STEAKS/AMERICAN.

Craving a big, juicy steak? This well-known American chain fits the bill with its U.S. prime Midwestern beef, available in cuts of filet, rib eye, strip, porterhouse, T-bone, and veal in various sizes and broiled to exact specifications. Other entrees include grilled tuna, lamb chops, and lobster; side dishes, which cost extra, range from mashed potatoes with roasted garlic to fresh sautéed spinach, seafood gumbo, and Caesar salad.

**✪ Sabatini.** In the Royal Garden, 69 Mody Rd., Tsim Sha Tsui East. ☎ **852/2733 2000.** Reservations required. Main courses HK$250–HK$490 ($32.45–$63.65); fixed-price lunch HK$150–HK$230 ($19.50–$29.85); fixed-price dinner HK$480 ($62.35). AE, DC, MC, V. Daily noon–2:30pm and 6–11pm. MTR: Tsim Sha Tsui. ITALIAN.

In 1954, three Sabatini brothers opened their first restaurant in Rome; their success led them to open branches in Japan and, in 1992, Hong Kong. The dining hall is rustic and cozy yet refined, with a brick and terra-cotta tile floor, wooden ceiling, and traditional Roman murals, giving it a more casual and relaxed ambience than most hotel Italian restaurants in the same price range. Its menu is a faithful replica of the original Roman fare (along with chef specialties), with liberal doses of olive oil, garlic, and peppers and featuring such popular dishes as baked snapper with seafood, veal escallop with mushrooms, and grilled lamb chops. The pasta, all handmade, ranges from linguine with lobster and asparagus to a classic spaghetti with tomato and basil. The antipasti buffet is so delicious, it's tempting to fill up just on its selections, but save room for the tiramisu. The list of mostly Italian wines is seemingly endless. Evenings feature guitar music; lunch is popular for its reasonable fixed-price menus.

**Shang Palace.** In the Shangri-La Hotel, 64 Mody Rd., Tsim Sha Tsui East. ☎ **852/2733 8754.** Reservations recommended. Main dishes HK$95–HK$280 ($12.35–$36.40). AE, CB, DC, MC, V. Mon–Sat noon–3pm, Sun and holidays 10am–3pm; daily 6:30–11pm. MTR: Tsim Sha Tsui. CANTONESE.

While many Chinese restaurants have ditched traditional red and gold for a more contemporary look, this remains one of Hong Kong's most elaborately decorated restaurants. The entryway, with its rows of red columns, is cleverly set with mirrors to give the illusion of a long corridor, as if you're entering a royal palace. The walls of the restaurant itself are of carved red lacquerware, and Chinese lanterns hang from the ceiling. All in all, it fits every expectation of how an "authentic" Chinese restaurant should look. If your mother's experience of Chinese food is limited to chop suey, this is a comfortable and memorable place to bring her, though you also can't go wrong if she's a Chinese-food connoisseur.

The dinner menu is quite extensive, with an emphasis on seafood but also serving chicken, duck, pigeon, beef, and pork Cantonese-style. Specialties include shark's-fin soup, flambéed drunken prawns, barbecued pork, Peking duck, and pan-fried minced pigeon with lettuce. If cost is no object, you might consider bird's nest with bamboo fungus, which runs HK$430 ($55.85) or more. Otherwise, expect to spend about

HK$500 ($65) per person for a royal feast. Lunch is more economical; although the menu changes often, it always includes a dozen or more varieties of dim sum.

**Tutto Bene.** 7 Knutsford Terrace, Tsim Sha Tsui. ☎ **852/2316 2116.** Reservations required. Main courses HK$170–HK$205 ($21.85–$28.35). AE, DC, MC, V. Sun–Thurs 6:30pm–midnight, Fri–Sat 6:30pm–1am. MTR: Tsim Sha Tsui. ITALIAN.

Located on the northern edge of Tsim Sha Tsui, on a tiny narrow lane known for its bars, this small but very popular eatery is always packed, which would lead you to believe that everything is indeed fine (*tutto bene*). However, noisy bar patrons and subsequent neighborhood complaints have unfortunately banished dining from the front terrace, and tight indoor quarters prevent it from being even remotely romantic (unless you speak some obscure language, your neighbor is going to hear every word you say). For these reasons, prices seem a bit high (about HK$400/$51.95 per person without drinks), but the imaginative Italian food, spiced with Asian ingredients, has clearly won over a faithful clientele. Start with the buffalo mozzarella with fresh tomatoes; salads, with homemade dressings, are also good. For a main course, consider the rack of lamb with black olives or the veal scallopini with shiitake mushrooms and marsala wine. A good choice if you wish to dine outside a hotel, but don't mind paying hotel prices.

**The Verandah.** In the Peninsula Hotel, Salisbury Rd., Tsim Sha Tsui. ☎ **852/2920 2888.** Reservations highly recommended at lunch or dinner. Main courses HK$210–HK$280 ($27.30–$36.35); fixed-price lunch HK$225 ($29.25); dinner buffet HK$350 ($45.45). AE, CB, DC, MC, V. Daily 7–11am, noon–2:30pm, and 6:30–10:30pm. MTR: Tsim Sha Tsui. INTERNATIONAL.

If you find Gaddi's too stuffy and Felix too pretentious, this restaurant, reminiscent of the colonial era, may be more to your liking. It's an airy, bright, and cheerful place, which gives the illusion of being a verandah, albeit a very elegant one. Ceiling fans whirl noiselessly overhead; graceful palms placed strategically between tables and cushioned rattan chairs give an air of privacy. The big windows wrap themselves around the U-shaped front of the hotel, offering a view that unfortunately has been spoiled by a monstrosity across the street (the Space Museum). However, the food is so good and the service so attentive that you'll soon forget to look any farther than your own table.

I love to start the day by coming here for breakfast—the attentive service makes me feel deliciously pampered. On Sundays, brunch is served for HK$340 ($44.20). Lunch and dinner feature home-cooked dishes and healthy, light cuisine, including imaginative salads and pastas, all with a blend of Asian and Western ingredients. Although dinner buffets, with an accent on Mediterranean food, are available nightly, diners can also choose à la carte, opting, perhaps, for the veal steak on spinach topped with mushrooms, onions, peppercorns, and a brandy sauce, or the garoupa shashlik with peppers and onions on vegetable rice with a light curry sauce. If you order à la carte, expect to spend about HK$400 to HK$500 ($51.95 to $64.95) per person without wine. Fixed-price lunches, which include salad bar, soup of the day, choice of entree, and dessert, are a bargain; on Saturday there is also a curry buffet.

## MODERATE

**Arirang Korean Restaurant.** Shop 2306, The Gateway (Level 2), Harbour City, 25 Canton Rd., Tsim Sha Tsui. ☎ **852/2956 3288.** Main courses with side dishes HK$90–HK$220 ($11.70–$28.55); fixed-price lunch HK$80–HK$110 ($10.40–$14.30). AE, DC, MC, V. Daily noon–3pm and 6–11pm. MTR: Tsim Sha Tsui. KOREAN.

This simple Korean restaurant with spacious seating and an accommodating staff is located in The Gateway section of Harbour City on Canton Road, not far from the

Omni Prince Hotel. The waiters and waitresses are not likely to speak much English, but the English menu presents photographs of more than a dozen choices of Korean barbecues, all of which come with side orders such as kimchee (cabbage spiced with red chilies) or noodles. My own personal favorites are the beef strips of *bulgogi* or the *kalbi*. The dishes tend to be small, so if there are two of you, you'll probably want to order three different platters (or order two and then see if you want to add a third). You'll do your own barbecuing at smokeless grills at your table, which can be great fun, somewhat like an indoor cookout.

There's another Arirang in Causeway Bay, up on the 11th-floor Food Forum of Times Square, 1 Matheson St. (☎ 852/2506 3298; MTR: Causeway Bay), open daily noon to 3pm and 6 to 11pm.

**City Chiuchow Restaurant.** East Ocean Centre, 98 Granville Rd., Tsim Sha Tsui East. ☎ 852/ 2723 6226. Main dishes HK$56–HK$120 ($7.25–$15.60). AE, DC, MC, V. Mon–Thurs 11am–3pm and 5pm–midnight, Fri–Sun 11am–midnight. MTR: Tsim Sha Tsui. CHIU CHOW.

Riding the crest of a wave of a newfound popularity for Chiu Chow food, this spacious restaurant overlooks gardens leading down to a major promenade in Tsim Sha Tsui East. Seating 500, it features a big tank with fish swimming about, soon to end up on the chopping block.

Famous dishes here include Chiu Chow shark's-fin soup, much thicker and stronger tasting than the Cantonese version; double-boiled shark's-fin-and-chicken soup, not as strong but equally popular; sliced soy goose; fried chicken with a black spicy sauce; and seafood dishes, including lobster. I particularly recommend the cold sliced lobster in a special honey sauce—it's not on the menu but it's available year-round. Dim sum is also served. And don't forget to try the Iron Buddha tea, a specialty of Chiuchow's, a tea that is so strong it will knock your socks off—and may keep you awake all night. Complete meals here average HK$200 ($26).

**Dan Ryan's Chicago Grill.** 200 Ocean Terminal, Harbour City, Tsim Sha Tsui. ☎ 852/ 2735 6111. Main courses HK$65–HK$230 ($8.45–$29.85) before 6pm, HK$95–HK$260 ($12.35–$33.75) after 6pm. AE, DC, MC, V. Mon–Fri 11am–midnight; Sat–Sun 10am– midnight. MTR: Tsim Sha Tsui. AMERICAN.

Located in the huge Ocean Terminal complex at its southernmost end, where cruise ships dock, this casual restaurant serves real American food, with portions big enough to satisfy a hungry cowboy. The decor is Anywhere, U.S.A., but with a difference— since it's located right by the Star Ferry, the Chicago Grill offers views of the famous harbor. The lunch menu is substantial, including such classic American favorites as buffalo chicken wings, potato skins, nachos, New England clam chowder, barbecued ribs, spaghetti, lasagne, chili, great hamburgers, and large deli sandwiches. There are also lunch specials, available Monday to Friday, priced at HK$65 and HK$75 ($8.45 to $9.75). The dinner menu is more limited, confined mainly to barbecued steaks, chops, fish, and pasta. Admittedly, most dishes here are a bit pricey, but if you're hungering for the real thing you might consider it a lifesaver. You can also come just for a drink at its bar, and there are English-language newspapers for customer perusal.

There's another Dan Ryan's at Pacific Place in Admiralty, 88 Queensway (☎ 852/ 2845 4600; MTR: Admiralty), open Monday to Thursday 11am to midnight, Friday 11am to 2am, Saturday 9am to 2am, and Sunday 9am to midnight.

**El Cid Spanish Restaurant.** 14 Knutsford Terrace, Tsim Sha Tsui. ☎ 852/2312 1898. Main courses HK$85–HK$170 ($11–$22.05). AE, DC, MC, V. Daily noon–2:30pm and 6pm– midnight. MTR: Tsim Sha Tsui. SPANISH.

This cheerful restaurant with its red-and-white-checkered tablecloths is one of the best places for a meal on Knutsford Terrace, a narrow lane lined with bars and a few restaurants and located on the northern edge of Tsim Sha Tsui. Recommended are the fresh oysters, stuffed baby squid with ink sauce, seafood paella, roast chicken with brandy chocolate and prawn sauce, and fish in salt paste.

There are also several dozen tapas on the menu, but if that's all you want, head to the more casual **El Cid Tapas & Wine Bar** next door, at 12 Knutsford Terrace (☎ **852/2367 2263**). Its variety of tapas, from HK$40 to HK$55 ($5.20 to $7.15), can make for wonderful nibbling or out-and-out feasts. There's a patio out back. It's open daily 5pm to 1am.

There's another El Cid at 9–11 Cleveland St., Causeway Bay (☎ **852/2511 0300; MTR: Causeway Bay**), open daily noon to midnight and offering the same menu of Spanish dishes and tapas.

✪ **Gaylord.** 23–25 Ashley Rd., Tsim Sha Tsui. ☎ **852/2376 1001.** Main dishes HK$62–HK$198 ($8.05–$25.70); lunch buffet HK$95 ($12.35). AE, DC, MC, V. Daily noon–2:30pm and 6–11pm. MTR: Tsim Sha Tsui. INDIAN.

This long-established, first-floor restaurant in the heart of Tsim Sha Tsui is classy and comfortable, with private booths and overstuffed sofas. It is popular for its authentic North Indian classics, including tandoori, lamb curry cooked in North Indian spices and herbs, chicken cooked in hot fiery vindaloo curry, prawns cooked with green pepper and spices, and fish with potatoes and tomatoes. There are a dozen vegetarian dishes, and the lunchtime buffet, served every day except Sundays and public holidays until 2:30pm, is a winner. There are also fixed-price dinners for two or more persons, beginning at HK$150 ($19.50) per person. Otherwise, expect to spend about HK$250 ($32.45) per person for dinner. Singers perform in the evening.

**Golden Bull.** In the New World Centre, Shop 17 on the 1st Level, 20 Salisbury Rd., ☎ **852/2369 4617;** and in Ocean Centre, Shop 101, Harbour City, 5 Canton Rd., ☎ **852/2730 4866;** both in Tsim Sha Tsui. Main dishes HK$66–HK$140 ($8.55–$18.20). AE, DC, MC, V. Daily noon–11:30pm. MTR: Tsim Sha Tsui. VIETNAMESE.

The two Golden Bull restaurants are both in shopping arcades; they have the same open hours and menu. If you're not familiar with Vietnamese cuisine, you might want to try the Golden Bull Platter for HK$150 ($19.50), which is actually an appetizer plate with a variety of dishes, including spring rolls, fish balls, and satay. Otherwise, typical Vietnamese items include crisp spring rolls wrapped in lettuce and dipped in a tangy sauce, hot-and-sour prawns, roast pig, various noodle dishes, barbecued fish Vietnamese style, grilled jumbo prawns in garlic butter, barbecued chicken in red bean curd sauce, and seafood. The lunch menu offers Vietnamese snacks such as various rolls of steamed pork or beef, cellophane noodles, vermicelli, and congee, most in the HK$40–HK$50 ($5.20–$6.50) price range.

There's a branch on the 11th floor of Times Square in Causeway Bay, 1 Matheson St. (☎ **852/2506 1028**), open Monday to Friday noon to 2:30pm and 6 to 11:30pm, and Saturday and Sunday noon to 11:30pm.

**Golden Elephant Thai Restaurant.** 17 Canton Rd., Tsim Sha Tsui. ☎ **852/2735 0733.** Main dishes HK$85–HK$235 ($11.05–$30.55); lunch buffet HK$78 ($10.10); dinner buffet HK$180 ($23.40). AE, DC, MC, V. Daily 11:30am–2:30pm and 6–9:30pm. MTR: Tsim Sha Tsui. THAI.

Thai food has long been popular in Hong Kong, and one of the first Thai restaurants to open was this place, recently ensconced in a new location beside the Marco Polo Hotel and not far from the Star Ferry. Affiliated with Thai Airways, it serves both spicy and mild foods that have been toned down, so if you want something authentically hot, be sure to tell the waitress. The lunch buffet is a great bargain, as is the dinner buffet; both attract hordes of the hungry. If you opt for an à-la-carte meal, you might want to start with Thai crispy rice served with minced pork and shrimp sauce or the spicy beef salad. Main courses include such delectables as beef satay, fried diced chicken with red chili and basil leaf, spicy shrimp, steamed fish with plum sauce and ginger, and grilled chicken. Most dishes cost less than HK$140 ($18.20).

There's another Golden Elephant restaurant on the 11th floor of Food Forum, Times Square, 1 Matheson St., Causeway Bay (☎ 852/2506 1333; MTR: Causeway Bay), open daily 11:30am to 2:30pm and 6:30 to 9:30pm, and also popular for its buffets.

**Golden Island Bird's Nest Chiu Chau Restaurant.** Star House (2nd floor), 3 Salisbury Rd., Tsim Sha Tsui. ☎ 852/2736 6228. Main dishes HK$60–HK$150 ($7.80–$19.50). AE, MC, V. Daily 11am–3pm and 5:30–11:30pm. MTR: Tsim Sha Tsui. CHIU CHOW.

This Chiu Chow restaurant is conveniently located—right in front of the Star Ferry terminus. As the prices above indicate, you can eat quite cheaply here if you order only one dish per person, but you'll pay more if you choose the house specialty—bird's nest, prepared 14 different ways and available as a soup, entree, and even dessert. This was Hong Kong's first restaurant to offer bird's nest as a specialty; although the prices for this dish have risen dramatically the past few years, here it costs around HK$380 ($49.40)—expensive, but less than what you'd pay elsewhere. Anyway, I would suggest that you try at least one of the bird's-nest dishes, along with such Chiu Chow preparations as oyster omelets, prawn balls, or roast soy goose, topping it off with a thimble-size cup of Chiu Chow tea, which is believed to aid digestion.

There's another branch in Tsim Sha Tsui on the third and fourth floors of the BCC Building, 25–31 Carnarvon Rd. (☎ 852/2369 5211), with the same menu and open hours. Other branches are at 249 Des Voeux Rd. Central, Sheung Wan (☎ 852/2544 1638; MTR: Sheung Wan); and the fifth floor of Causeway Bay Plaza, 489 Hennessy Rd., Causeway Bay (☎ 852/2838 6988; MTR: Causeway Bay). Both are open daily 11am to 12:30am.

✪ **Great Shanghai.** 26 Prat Ave., Tsim Sha Tsui. ☎ 852/2366 8158. Main dishes HK$75–HK$210 ($9.75–$27.25). AE, DC, MC, V. Daily 11am–2:30pm and 6:30–11pm. MTR: Tsim Sha Tsui. SHANGHAINESE.

Established in 1958, this well-known spot in Tsim Sha Tsui is a big old-fashioned dining hall up on the first floor. In addition to its bright lights, white tablecloths, and army of waiters in green shirts, it has a gigantic menu with more than 300 items, most in the HK$85–HK$140 ($11.05–$18.20) range. Since the Shanghai area has no cuisine of its own, it has developed an eclectic cuisine, borrowing from neighboring provinces, including Szechuan. However, this restaurant is about as close as you can get to food the way Mom used to cook in old Shanghai. Try the Shanghainese dumplings, prawns in chili sauce, vegetarian imitation goose, diced chicken with cashews, cold chicken in wine sauce, Szechuan soup, or Peking duck. The house specialty is beggar's chicken for HK$260 ($33.80), but it's available only at night; in addition, only a limited number are prepared daily, so call in your order by mid-afternoon if you want to be assured of getting a bird. My own particular favorite is braised shredded eel, which is cooked in an oily garlic sauce, but all eel dishes here are good. I've also left the ordering entirely up to the waiter and ended up with a well-rounded sampling of Shanghainese food.

**The Greenery.** In the Royal Garden Hotel, 69 Mody Rd., Tsim Sha Tsui East. ☎ 852/2721 5215. Lunch buffet HK$155 ($20.15) Mon–Sat, HK$175 ($22.70) Sun; dinner buffet HK$238 ($30.90) Sun–Thurs, HK$258 ($33.55) Fri–Sat. AE, DC, MC, V. Daily noon–2:30pm and 6:30–9:30pm. MTR: Tsim Sha Tsui. INTERNATIONAL.

If you're looking for a quick, filling feast in Tsim Sha Tsui East, look no farther than the lunch or dinner buffets offered in this popular, open restaurant, located in the hotel's 15-story atrium. The sounds of piano music, a waterfall, and multitudes of hungry diners make eating a rather noisy affair, but the food is good and varied, ranging from Chinese and Japanese to Western fare, from salads and vegetables to ribs and fish, and an efficient staff keeps water glasses filled and used plates whisked away.

**Gripps American Bar and Restaurant.** In the Hongkong Hotel, Harbour City, 3 Canton Rd., Tsim Sha Tsui. ☎ **852/2113 0088.** Main courses HK$85–HK$320 ($11.05–$41.60). AE, DC, MC, V. Daily 6pm–midnight. MTR: Tsim Sha Tsui. AMERICAN.

With a friendly staff and boasting a view of Central across the harbor, this is a fun, casual, and relaxed place for a hearty meal, with seating in overstuffed chairs in a living-roomlike setting. It has a varied menu that fits about every budget, from sandwiches, burgers, potato skins, and create-your-own pizzas to steaks, lobster, and garlic-marinated king prawns. Come early for the 2-hour happy hour beginning at 5pm, with reduced drink prices. It's just a few minutes' walk from the Star Ferry.

**Harbour Side.** In the Regent Hotel, Salisbury Rd., Tsim Sha Tsui. ☎ **852/2721 1211.** Main courses HK$125–HK$280 ($16.25–$36.35). AE, DC, MC, V. Daily 6am–midnight. MTR: Tsim Sha Tsui. CONTINENTAL.

Although located in the elegant Regent Hotel, this is an informal dining hall, rather plain and bare with a brick floor and wooden chairs, but bright and airy because of its three-story-high wall of glass facing the harbor. It offers nonstop all-day dining and views of people walking along the waterfront promenade. Its open kitchen emphasizes light continental dishes such as pasta and salads, but other vegetarian selections, sandwiches, pizza, seafood, and steak are included on a menu that changes daily. If you stick to one of the sandwiches, pizzas, or pasta dishes, you can dine for less than HK$170 ($22.10); there are also lunch and dinner salad buffets with soup and roast for HK$195 ($25.30). On Sundays, there's a champagne brunch 11am to 3pm costing HK$295 ($38.30) for adults and half price for children, who even get their own special buffet table and play area. Or, if you want to come just for the view, a cup of coffee is HK$46 ($5.45), and cocktails average HK$85 ($11.05).

**Jade Garden Restaurant.** Star House (4th floor), 3 Salisbury Rd., Tsim Sha Tsui. ☎ **852/ 2730 6888.** Main dishes HK$58–HK$138 ($7.55–$17.90). AE, DC, MC, V. Mon–Sat 10am–3pm and 5:30–11:30pm; Sun and holidays 8am–11:30pm. MTR: Tsim Sha Tsui. CANTONESE.

Jade Garden is part of a chain of restaurants owned by the Maxim's Group, a company that has been wildly successful throughout Hong Kong and is popular with large Chinese families (other establishments in the group include Sichuan Garden, Shanghai Garden, Peking Garden, and Chiu Chow Garden; the latter two also have branches in Star House). Jade Garden is the place to go if you don't know much about Chinese food, feel that you should try it, but still aren't very keen on the idea. A plus is the view of the harbor afforded by some of the windowside tables. As in most Cantonese restaurants, lunch is dim sum served from trolleys pushed through the aisles. If you'd rather order from the menu or come for dinner, you might consider drunken shrimp in soup, pan-fried stuffed bean curd, fried prawns with lemon peel and orange, or, if you feel like splurging, barbecued Peking duck, which costs HK$290 ($37.70).

In Tsim Sha Tsui, Jade Garden has another branch at 25–31 Carnarvon Rd. (☎ 852/ 2369 8311), open daily 7:30am to midnight. On the Hong Kong side, there's a Jade Garden in the Jardine House at 1 Connaught Place in Central (☎ 852/2524 5098; MTR: Central), open daily 11am to 3pm and 5:30 to 11:30pm.

**Osaka.** 14 Ashley Rd., Tsim Sha Tsui. ☎ **852/2376 3323.** Most main dishes HK$60–HK$95 ($7.80–$12.35); sukiyaki or shabu-shabu HK$220–HK$410 ($28.55–$53.25); kaiseki courses HK$400 ($51.95); fixed-price lunch HK$63–HK$80 ($8.20–$10.40). AE, DC, MC, V. Daily noon–3pm and 6–11pm. MTR: Tsim Sha Tsui. JAPANESE.

Japanese in the know have long headed to this reasonably priced restaurant, simple and uncluttered. It's divided into several dining areas, where you can feast on higher-priced kaiseki meals, sukiyaki or shabu-shabu (one-pot meals featuring beef and vegetables you cook at your own table), or sushi. If you're on a budget, order one of the noodle dishes such as tempura udon (breaded prawn on noodles), the tonkatsu (pork filet), fried fish, or barbecued eel; or come for lunch. Lunch specials are in written in Japanese only; ask for a translation.

There's another branch at 482 Jaffe Rd., Causeway Bay (☎ **852/2893 2988;** MTR: Causeway Bay), open the same hours.

**Peking Garden.** Star House (3rd floor), 3 Salisbury Rd., Tsim Sha Tsui. ☎ **852/2735 8211.** Main dishes HK$86–HK$175 ($11.15–$22.75). AE, DC, MC, V. Mon–Sat 11:30am–3pm and 5:30pm–midnight; Sun 11am–3pm and 5:30pm–midnight. MTR: Tsim Sha Tsui. PEKINGESE.

Another Maxim's Group of restaurants, Peking Garden specializes in Pekingese and northern Chinese dishes, including stir-fried Pekingese noodles with shredded pork, Hunan ham with Chinese cabbage, and beggar's chicken for HK$320 ($41.55; order it 24 hours in advance). Try to be here during its nightly presentation of handmade noodles at 8:30pm. It's located in the Star House right beside the Star Ferry.

You'll find other branches at the Empire Centre, 68 Mody Rd., Tsim Sha Tsui East (☎ **852/2721 8868;** MTR: Tsim Sha Tsui); 1st and 2nd basements of Alexandra House, 6 Ice House St., Central (☎ **852/2526 6456;** MTR: Central); shop 003 in Pacific Place, 88 Queensway in Central (☎ **852/2845 8452;** MTR: Central); and Hennessy Centre, 500 Hennessy Rd., Causeway Bay (☎ **852/2577 7231;** MTR: Causeway Bay); all have the same open hours.

✪ **The Pizzeria.** In the Kowloon Hotel, 19–21 Nathan Rd., Tsim Sha Tsui. ☎ **852/2929 2888,** ext. 3322. Pasta and pizza HK$115–HK$140 ($14.95–$18.20); main courses HK$150–HK$195 ($19.50–$25.30); lunch buffet HK$140 ($18.20); fixed-price dinner HK$318–HK$348 ($41.30–$45.20). AE, CB, DC, MC, V. Daily noon–3pm, and 6–11pm. MTR: Tsim Sha Tsui. ITALIAN.

Located on the second floor of the Kowloon Hotel (just behind The Peninsula), this casual and bustling dining hall with large windows is one of my favorite places in Tsim Sha Tsui for a relaxed meal at good prices, especially when I want great pizza or pasta and don't feel like getting dressed up. Despite its name, this restaurant specializes in pasta, with an à la carte menu that changes often but has included such mouthwatering choices as lobster lasagne enriched with fresh spinach and mushrooms, tortellini with mushrooms and truffles in an herb-cream sauce, and ink noodles in a lobster tarragon sauce. There are also eight different kinds of pizza, and main courses have included grilled prawns with thyme olive oil in a bed of spinach and saffron risotto, braised veal shank with red wine, and roasted spring chicken with pancetta, rosemary gravy, and pesto polenta. Save room for dessert—they're all delicious. For the budget-conscious, lunch is a great time to come, when a trip through the antipasto and salad bar, choice of main dish (meat, pasta, or pizza), and dessert and coffee, are available at a great price. Incidentally, to reach The Pizzeria, you have to walk past Window Café, which specializes in international buffets.

**Planet Hollywood.** 3 Canton Rd., Tsim Sha Tsui. ☎ **852/2377 7888.** Main courses HK$78–HK$198 ($10.15–$25.75). AE, DC, MC, V. Daily 11:30am–midnight. MTR: Tsim Sha Tsui. AMERICAN.

The escalator ride up to this establishment, accompanied by music, is like the entrance to a theme park, and that theme park is Hollywood. If you're star crazy, you can gawk at the handprints of Paul Newman, Clint Eastwood, or Marlee Matlin (who signed "I love you"), or such movie memorabilia as the doll Chuckie from *Child's Play,* and the car used by Bruce Lee in the *Green Hornet* TV series. When I ate lunch there, action star Jackie Chan was holding a press conference about his latest film. There are also large screens with continually running Hollywood hits. The menu includes everything from blackened shrimp and buffalo wings to sandwiches, burgers, pastas, pizzas, fajitas, steak, ribs, and fish and chips, as well as some local dishes such as Hainanese chicken rice and wok-fried beef in oyster sauce. On weekdays, a fixed-price lunch is available until 2pm for HK$50 ($6.50), which includes a trip through the salad bar and one of a dozen main dishes ranging from tequila lime chicken to black pepper beef linguine. Opened in 1994, this was the first of this chain to open in Asia.

**The Spice Market.** In the Prince Hotel, 23 Canton Rd., Tsim Sha Tsui. ☎ **852/2113 6046.** Lunch buffet HK$118 ($15.35) Mon–Thurs, HK$128 ($16.60) Fri–Sun; dinner buffet HK$218 ($28.35) Mon–Thurs, HK$228 ($29.60) Fri–Sun. AE, DC, MC, V. Daily noon–2:30pm and 6:30–10pm. MTR: Tsim Sha Tsui. ASIAN.

Accessible from both the Omni Prince Hotel and the third floor of the Gateway shopping mall, this dark and cozy restaurant specializes in buffets offering diners a culinary adventure throughout Asia. There's Japanese sushi and noodles; Indian curries; and Chinese, Thai, and Singaporean favorites. Included are steamed fish, chili crab, satays, soups, salads, appetizers, and desserts. True to its name, many of the foods are spicy. While none of the dishes are outstanding, most of them are good; with so many choices, you'll probably end up eating more than you should.

**✪ Spring Deer Restaurant.** 42 Mody Rd., Tsim Sha Tsui. ☎ **852/2366 4012.** Small dishes HK$50–HK$90 ($6.50–$11.70). AE, MC, V. Daily noon–2:30pm and 6–11pm. MTR: Tsim Sha Tsui. PEKINGESE.

An old favorite in Hong Kong, this long-established restaurant offers excellent Pekingese food at reasonable prices. Spring Deer is cheerful and very accessible to foreigners, but don't expect anything fancy; in fact, your tablecloth may have holes in it, but it will be clean—and the place is usually packed with groups of loyal fans. This is one of the best places to come if you want to try its specialty—honey-glazed Peking duck, which costs HK$280 ($36.40). Since you'll probably have to wait 40 minutes for the duck if you order it during peak time (7:30 to 9:30pm), it's best to arrive either before or after the rush. Chicken dishes are also well liked, including the deep-fried chicken in soy sauce, and the handmade noodles are excellent. Other recommendations include the hot and sour soup, fresh-water shrimp, and stewed ham and cabbage. Most dishes come in small, medium, and large sizes; the small dishes are suitable for two people. Remember, you'll want to order one dish apiece, plus a third to share. Unfortunately, since Spring Deer is crowded with groups, the lone diner is apt to be neglected in the shuffle; it's best to come here only if there are at least two of you.

**Super Star Seafood Restaurant.** 91–93 Nathan Rd., Tsim Sha Tsui. ☎ **852/2366 0878.** Main dishes HK$65–HK$120 ($8.45–$15.60); fixed-price menu HK$260–HK$300 ($33.80–$39). AE, DC, MC, V. Daily 8am–midnight. MTR: Tsim Sha Tsui. CANTONESE SEAFOOD.

Walk past the tanks filled with fish, lobsters, prawns, and crabs up to this lively Cantonese restaurant on the first floor. It's very popular with local Chinese, many of whom consider it one of Hong Kong's top Cantonese restaurants. Its menu includes pictures of major dishes; as its name implies, the restaurant specializes in fresh seafood. Recommended are the deep-fried stuffed crab claws, sliced sole with spice and chili, baked lobster with minced spinach, and fish in season. Prices for seafood vary with the season and depend on the size of the creature you desire. If you want a specific fish or something else in the tank, simply point, but be sure to ask the price first. Stone fish is popular with the Chinese. It's a rather ugly fish and poisonous to boot, if not prepared correctly. If this is what you want, you'll have to wait an hour for it to cook. Dim sum, served until 5pm, starts at HK$19 ($2.45) per plate.

**Tsui Hang Village Restaurant.** Miramar Plaza, 132–134 Nathan Rd., Tsim Sha Tsui. ☎ **852/ 2376 2882.** Main dishes HK$68–HK$200 ($8.85–$25.95). AE, DC, MC, V. Mon–Sat 11:30am– 11:30pm, Sun 10am–11:30pm. MTR: Tsim Sha Tsui. CANTONESE.

Tsui Hang is named after the home village of Dr. Sun Yat-sen. Located across the street from the Miramar Hotel on the ground floor of a new shopping complex called Miramar Plaza, it's a bright, clean, and modern place with a white jade statue of the goddess of mercy at its entrance. This restaurant specializes in its own Cantonese original creations but also serves traditional, home-style Chinese cooking. Dishes you might want to try include fresh lobster, deep-fried minced shrimp balls with crisp almond, sautéed minced pigeon with lettuce, barbecued Peking duck, deep-fried crispy chicken with green onion, roast goose, or fried milk fritters. Dim sum, served during lunch and afternoon teatime, Monday to Saturday 11:30am to 5:30pm and Sunday 10am to 5pm, is priced from HK$18 to HK$38 ($2.35 to $4.95) per plate.

There's another Tsui Hang Village in Central on the second floor of the New World Tower, 16–18 Queen's Rd., Central (☎ **852/2524 2012;** MTR: Central), open Monday to Friday 11am to 3pm and 5:30 to 11:30pm, Saturday 11am to 11:30pm, and Sunday 10am to 11:30pm.

**Wu Kong.** 27 Nathan Rd. (entrance on Peking Rd.), Tsim Sha Tsui. ☎ **852/2366 7244.** Menu items HK$50–HK$200 ($6.50–$25.95). AE, DC, MC, V. Daily 11:30am–3pm and 5:30pm–midnight. MTR: Tsim Sha Tsui. SHANGHAINESE.

This basement restaurant in the heart of Tsim Sha Tsui just off Nathan Road is often packed during mealtimes with locals who come for the good food at excellent prices. More upscale than many Shanghainese restaurants, with its stark-white walls and pond with goldfish in the foyer, it serves a variety of shark's-fin dishes, as well as the usual sautéed fresh prawns, braised shredded eels, braised eggplant with hot garlic sauce, stuffed bean curd, and other dishes common to Shanghai. Other selections include cold pigeon in wine sauce (its signature appetizer), sautéed freshwater shrimp, Peking duck, crispy duck, and sautéed sliced duck. If you've had your fill of the more readily available and popular Cantonese and Szechuan food and are ready to experiment with other types of Chinese cuisine, this is an excellent place to start.

There's another branch on the 12th floor of Food Forum, Times Square, 1 Matheson St., Causeway Bay (☎ **852/2506 1018;** MTR: Causeway Bay), open Monday to Friday 11:30am to 3pm and 5pm to 11:30pm; and Saturday and Sunday 11:30am to 11:30pm.

## INEXPENSIVE

**Banana Leaf Curry House.** Golden Crown Court (3rd floor), 68 Nathan Rd., Tsim Sha Tsui. ☎ **852/2721 4821.** Main dishes HK$60–HK$120 ($7.80–$15.60); lunch buffet HK$68 ($8.85) Mon–Fri, HK$88 ($11.45) Sat–Sun. AE, V. Mon–Fri noon–2:30pm, Sat–Sun noon–3pm, daily 6–11:30pm. MTR: Tsim Sha Tsui. MALAYSIAN/INDIAN/SINGAPOREAN.

This fast-growing local chain has a good idea—more than 100 choices, including chicken, mutton, beef, seafood, and vegetables, cooked in several varieties of curry; and a gimmick—dishes are presented on banana leaves. Add to that the brisk, efficient service and reasonable prices, and you've got the makings of a winner for cheap

# You Paid What?

47,000 hotels, 700 airlines,
50 rental car companies. And a few
million ways to save money.

## Travelocity.com
A Sabre Company

**Go Virtually Anywhere.**

AOL Keyword: Travel

**Will you have enough stories to tell your grandchildren?**

©2002 Yahoo! Inc.

Yahoo! Travel

DO YOU
YAHOO!
?

Malaysian, Singaporean, and South Indian food. You might want to start with chicken satay and peanut sauce, or samosas with a mint chutney. Main dishes run the gamut from Hainan chicken and Malaysian curry crab to vegetarian selections; the dilemma is in making a choice. Otherwise, come for the lunch buffet.

Other conveniently located branches include those on the 15th floor of Chong Hing Square, 601 Nathan Rd., Mong Kok (☎ 852/2332 2525; MTR: Mong Kok), open Monday to Friday noon to 2:30pm and 6 to 11:30pm, and Saturday and Sunday noon to 11:30pm; and 30 Percival St., Causeway Bay (☎ 852/2834 8889; MTR: Causeway Bay) and 440 Jaffe Rd., Causeway Bay (☎ 852/2573 8187; MTR: Causeway Bay), both open Monday to Friday 11am to 3pm and 6 to 11:30pm, and Saturday and Sunday 11am to 11:30pm.

**Fat Angelo's.** 33 Ashley Rd., Tsim Sha Tsui. ☎ **852/2730 4788.** Pastas HK$88–HK$126 ($11.45–$16.35); main courses HK$125–HK$165 ($16.25–$21.45). AE, MC, V. Daily noon–11:30pm. MTR: Tsim Sha Tsui. ITALIAN.

With its checkered tablecloths, black-and-white family photographs, wainscoting, half-size curtains, ceiling fans, and other decor reminiscent of a New World Italian restaurant from the first half of the 20th century, this new chain offers good value with its hearty, American renditions of Italian food, including pastas ranging from traditional spaghetti marinara to fettucini Alfredo and main courses that include rosemary roasted chicken, grilled salmon with pesto, eggplant Parmesan, and veal shank stewed in red wine, all of which come with salad and homemade rolls.

There are two branches on the other side of the harbor, at 414 Jaffe Rd., Causeway Bay (☎ 852/2574 6263; MTR: Causeway Bay), and 49A-C Elgin St., Central (☎ 852/2973 6808), open the same hours.

**Genki Sushi.** Shops G7–9, East Ocean Centre, 98 Granville Rd., Tsim Sha Tsui East. ☎ **852/2722 6689.** Main dishes HK$9–HK$35 ($1.15–$4.55). AE, DC, MC, V. Daily 11:30am–11:30pm. MTR: Tsim Sha Tsui. JAPANESE.

Taking advantage of Hong Kong's surge in popularity of everything Japanese, this simple and always crowded establishment offers plates of sushi, which circle around the counter via a conveyor belt. Customers, seated at the counter, simply reach out and take whatever they want. The plates, color coded, vary in price and include traditional selections such as tuna and shrimp sushi, along with more unusual combinations like corn sushi, crab salad sushi, and California Temaki (seaweed rolled around rice, crab, and avocado). During lunch and dinner, there's often a line of customers waiting at the door.

Other branches can be found on the ground floor of the Far East Finance Centre, 16 Harcourt Rd., Central (☎ 852/2865 2933; MTR: Admiralty); Shop B222 in the second basement of Times Square, 1 Matheson St., Causeway Bay (☎ 852/2506 9366; MTR: Causeway Bay); and Shop A, ground floor of the CRE Building, 303 Hennessy Rd., Wan Chai (☎ 852/2802 7018; MTR: Wan Chai); all with the same open hours given above.

**Happy Garden Noodles & Congee Kitchen.** 76 Canton Rd., Tsim Sha Tsui. ☎ **852/2377 2604.** Main dishes HK$22–HK$80 ($2.85–$10.40). No credit cards. Daily 7am–12:30am. MTR: Tsim Sha Tsui. CANTONESE.

If you've passed all those hole-in-the-wall Chinese restaurants, knowing that they're often much cheaper than establishments catering to tourists but hesitating to enter because no one speaks English, this is the place for you. Small, clean, and with old-fashioned booth seating, a high ceiling, and lacquered stools, it has an English menu and specializes in noodle dishes and congee (a rice porridge traditionally eaten for breakfast or a late-night snack and usually flavored with meat, fish, or vegetables). Approximately 40 different kinds of congee are available, as well as a wide variety of noodle dishes, from braised and stir-fried noodles to shrimp wonton noodles and noodles in soup with barbecued pork. Located about a 4-minute walk from the Star Ferry, it's good for a quick and inexpensive meal after visiting neighborhood bars.

✪ **Koh-I-Noor.** Peninsula Apartments, 16C Mody Rd., Tsim Sha Tsui. ☎ 852/2368 3065. Curries HK$44–HK$125 ($5.70–$16.25); tandoori HK$65–HK$120 ($8.45–$15.60). AE, DC, MC, V. Daily 11:30am–2:30pm and 6–11:30pm. MTR: Tsim Sha Tsui. INDIAN.

Don't let the dinginess of the Peninsula Apartments deter you from trying this restaurant. Located up on the first floor, it's modern and clean, with spotless tablecloths and a pleasant purple color scheme. What's more, service is prompt and courteous and the food is great and reasonably priced; the specialties here are North Indian tandoori and fresh seafood. It takes its name from a renowned diamond mined in central India years ago. The restaurant is especially proud of its king prawns, but there are also chicken, lamb, and vegetable curries; my favorites include the samosas, crab with coconut, and the Gosht vindaloo—a spicy mix of lamb and potatoes. There's mashed eggplant with onions and tomatoes; *palak paneer* (Indian cottage cheese with spinach); garlic-flavored *nan* (Indian flat bread) or nan stuffed with cheese, potatoes, or meat—well, all of it's good and recommendable. The dishes can be ordered mild, medium, or fiery hot, according to taste. If you like variety, there's a set menu for two persons costing HK$188 ($24.45). There's also a fixed-price vegetarian lunch for HK$45 ($5.85).

There's a branch on the other side of the harbor in the Lan Kwai Fong nightlife district, on the first floor of the California Entertainment Building, 34 D'Aguilar St., Central (☎ 852/2877 9706; MTR: Central), with the same hours.

**The Salisbury.** In the Salisbury YMCA, 41 Salisbury Rd., Tsim Sha Tsui. ☎ 852/2369 2211, ext. 1026. Lunch buffet HK$98 ($12.75); dinner buffet HK$218 ($28.35). AE, DC, MC, V. Mon–Sat noon–2:30pm, daily 6:30–9:30pm. MTR: Tsim Sha Tsui. INTERNATIONAL.

One of the cheapest places for a filling meal in Tsim Sha Tsui is the YMCA's main restaurant, a bright and cheerful dining hall located on the fourth floor of the south tower. It serves both Western and Asian food, with an à la carte menu offering sandwiches, pasta, and Asian dishes. Best, however, are the lunch and dinner buffets. The lunch buffet includes a roast beef wagon, as well as other meat dishes, soups, salads, and desserts, while the dinner buffet includes many more entrees plus unlimited soda or beer. If these prices are too high, there's a ground-floor cafeteria, the Mall Cafe, which offers sandwiches and daily specials, as well as a fixed-price lunch for HK$54 ($7) and a fixed-price dinner for HK$70 ($9.10).

**Spaghetti House.** 30–34 Nathan Rd., Tsim Sha Tsui. ☎ 852/2721 2082. Individual-size pizza and pasta HK$48–HK$83 ($6.25–$10.80). AE, DC, MC, V. Daily 11am–11pm. MTR: Tsim Sha Tsui. ITALIAN.

The Spaghetti House chain has a total of 16 branches throughout Hong Kong—and there will probably be more by the time you read this. They're popular with families, young Chinese couples on dates, and foreigners who have had their fill of Chinese food and crave something familiar but cheap. Spaghetti and pizza cooked American-style or with Asian ingredients are the specialties here, and the decor and atmosphere resemble those of an American pizza parlor. There are more than a half-dozen varieties of spaghetti as well as pizzas (in all sizes), lasagne, sandwiches, risotto, and fried chicken. Although the food is only average in quality, the quantity more than makes up for it; most orders can be taken out.

Two branches in Tsim Sha Tsui, accessible via the Tsim Sha Tsui MTR station, are located at 57 Peking Rd. (☎ 852/2367 1683) and 38 Haiphong Rd. (☎ 852/2376

---

> ## ❷ Did You Know?
>
> - The world's largest floating restaurant, the Jumbo Floating Restaurant, is moored in Aberdeen. It measures 265 feet long, 80 feet wide, and 90 feet high (see "Life on the Water in Aberdeen," in chapter 6).
> - Five of the world's 10 busiest McDonald's restaurants are in Hong Kong.
> - Hong Kong has one restaurant or cafe for every 700 inhabitants; an estimated 1.5 million people eat out daily.

---

1015). Other convenient locations include 221 Nathan Rd., Yau Ma Tei (☎ 852/2377 2005; MTR: Yau Ma Tei); 594 Nathan Rd., Mong Kok (☎ 852/2388 4379; MTR: Mong Kok); 10 Stanley St., Central (☎ 852/2523 1372; MTR: Central); Shop 2004 in the International Finance Centre above Hong Kong Station, Central (☎ 852/2147 5543); 68 Hennessy Rd., Wan Chai (☎ 852/2529 0901; MTR: Wan Chai); and Shop 8, PJ Plaza, Paterson St., Causeway Bay (☎ 852/2895 2928; MTR: Causeway Bay). All Spaghetti Houses have the same hours.

**Woodlands.** Mirror Tower, 61 Mody Rd., Tsim Sha Tsui East. ☎ 852/2369 3718. Main dishes HK$35–HK$48 ($4.55–$6.25); fixed-price meals HK$55–HK$70 ($7.15–$9.10). AE, DC, MC, V. Daily noon–3:30pm and 6:30–10:30pm. MTR: Tsim Sha Tsui. INDIAN/VEGETARIAN.

The focus of this very simple dining room, looking slightly out of place on the ground floor of the Mirror Tower building in Tsim Sha Tsui East, is clearly on the food—vegetarian dishes from southern India, along with some selections from northern India. Best are the thali fixed-price meals, served on a round metal plate commonly used in India and including Indian bread, rice, and tiny portions of various dishes. Strangely, although the restaurant specializes in food from southern India, the North Indian thali is tastier than its southern counterpart. Alcoholic drinks are not served, but there are fruit juice, milk shakes, Indian tea, and lassi (yogurt shake).

## 3 Central District

### VERY EXPENSIVE

**Lobster Bar.** In the Island Shangri-La, Pacific Place, 88 Queensway, Central. ☎ 852/2820 8560. Reservations recommended, especially for lunch. Main courses HK$270–HK$525 ($35.05–$68.20); fixed-price lunch HK$238–HK$268 ($30.90–$34.80); fixed-price dinner HK$368–HK$468 ($47.80–$60.80); Sun brunch HK$320 ($41.55). AE, DC, MC, V. Mon–Sat noon–2:30pm, Sun 11:30am–2:30pm; daily 6:30–11pm. MTR: Admiralty. SEAFOOD.

If you love lobster, this upscale yet relaxed restaurant will almost certainly be on your agenda. The entrance features a beautiful aquarium, while the interior has elegant overtones of mahogany, leather, and imported French fabrics covering deep comfortable chairs, making the setting seem more like a lounge than a restaurant. Evenings feature live music. The crustacean is king here, so you might want to start with lobster bisque, followed by lobster Thermidor or one of the seasonal dishes. Another good choice is the traditional seafood platter, which comes in three sizes, but the best value for the money is one of the fixed-price meals. The limited menu also features a few non-lobster dishes, such as fresh seafood, a handful of pasta selections, and steaks. Don't pass up one of the crème brûlée desserts. On Sundays, there's a sumptuous seafood brunch buffet.

# Central District Dining

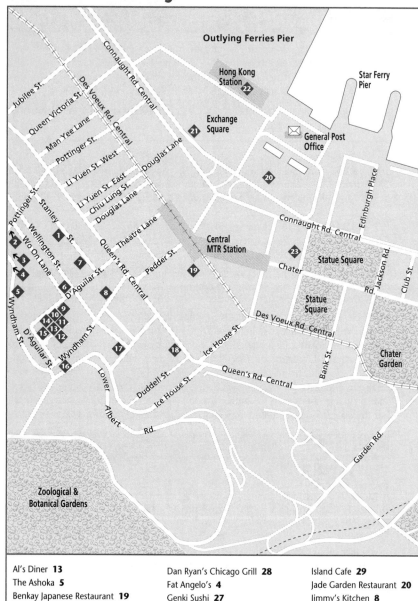

Al's Diner **13**
The Ashoka **5**
Benkay Japanese Restaurant **19**
Baci **9**
Baci Pizza **9**
Cafe des Artistes **11**
China Lan Kwai Fong **15**
City Hall Chinese Restaurant **24**

Dan Ryan's Chicago Grill **28**
Fat Angelo's **4**
Genki Sushi **27**
Grappa's **28**
Hanagushi **15**
Hunan Garden **21**
I Caramba! **3**
Indochine **11**

Island Cafe **29**
Jade Garden Restaurant **20**
Jimmy's Kitchen **8**
Joyce Cafe **21**
Koh-I-Noor **10**
La Ronda **25**
Landau's **17**

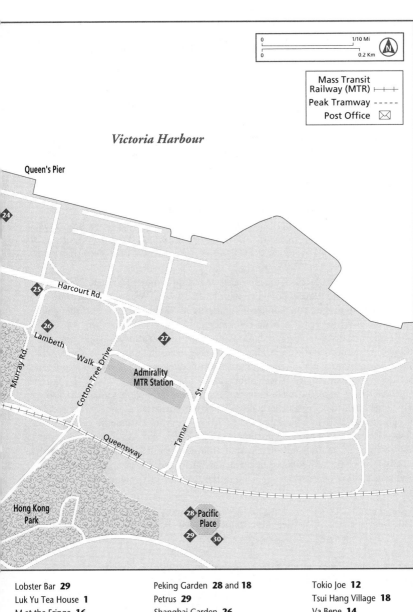

*Victoria Harbour*

Queen's Pier

Harcourt Rd.

Lambeth Walk

Murray Rd.

Cotton Tree Drive

Admirality
MTR Station

Tamar St.

Queensway

Hong Kong
Park

Pacific
Place

**Mass Transit
Railway (MTR)** ┼─┼─┼
**Peak Tramway** - - - - -
**Post Office** ⊠

0                    1/10 Mi
0                    0.2 Km

| | | |
|---|---|---|
| Lobster Bar **29** | Peking Garden **28** and **18** | Tokio Joe **12** |
| Luk Yu Tea House **1** | Petrus **29** | Tsui Hang Village **18** |
| M at the Fringe **16** | Shanghai Garden **26** | Va Bene **14** |
| Man Wah **23** | Sichuan Garden **19** and **28** | Vong **23** |
| Mandarin Grill **23** | Spaghetti House **7** and **22** | Ye Shanghai **28** |
| Nicholini's **30** | The Square **21** | Yung Kee **6** |
| Pavilion **2** | Thai Lemongrass **11** | Zen Chinese **28** |

**Mandarin Grill.** In the Mandarin Oriental Hotel, 5 Connaught Rd., Central. ☎ **852/2522 0111,** ext. 4020. Reservations required. Main courses HK$245–HK$385 ($31.85–$50). AE, DC, MC, V. Daily 7–11am, noon–3pm, and 6:30–11pm. MTR: Central. CONTINENTAL.

Decorated in dark green with details of gold, this is the Mandarin's most popular all-purpose restaurant, offering everything from breakfast (the Sunday brunch includes a special table for children) to steaks and seafood. But since this is the Mandarin, it caters to a well-heeled clientele, and the proper dress is smart casual. Both U.S. and Kobe beef are featured, as well as veal, lamb, a wide selection of seafood, and even vegetarian dishes. If you can't decide, order the mixed grill, which comes with beef, pork, veal, and lamb. Lobster is available prepared in a variety of styles, and there are also vegetarian dishes. Especially recommended is lobster bisque with cognac and tarragon; smoked Scottish salmon; spaghetti in a creamy vodka sauce with caviar; beef stroganoff; the U.S. Black Angus prime rib of beef; and the rack of lamb. The wine list is extensive, with more than 400 varieties available, and service is impeccable.

✪ **Man Wah.** In the Mandarin Oriental Hotel, 5 Connaught Rd., Central. ☎ **852/2522 0111,** ext. 4025. Reservations required. Main dishes HK$85–HK$258 ($11.05–$33.50); fixed-price meal HK$580–HK$860 ($75.30–$111.70). AE, DC, MC, V. Daily noon–3pm and 6:30–11pm. MTR: Central. CANTONESE.

Man Wah has long been one of the most elegant and sophisticated Chinese restaurants in Hong Kong. Traditionally decorated with local rosewood, wood carvings, lanterns that resemble birdcages, and painted silk portraits of Mandarins; and featuring gold tablecloths, exquisite Naruma bone chinaware, 24-carat gold cutlery, fresh flowers, and candles on every table—it's about as romantic as you can get. Unfortunately, although it's located on the 25th floor, only a few tables offer good views of the harbor, so be sure to request a harborside seat when making your reservation. And with a seating capacity of only 62, reservations here are a must.

Although the Cantonese menu changes seasonally, signature dishes usually available include the steamed crab claws with ginger and Chinese rice wine, sautéed filet of sole with green vegetables in a black bean sauce (complete with a wonderful carving of a dragon fashioned from carrots), anything with shark's fin, and beggar's chicken (order in advance) with its dramatic presentation and costing HK$460 ($59.80). Also, if available, the spicy-and-sour soup is divine—piquant and full of noodles, tofu, and mushrooms. Meals here average HK$700 ($91); the fixed-price menu requires a minimum of two persons.

**Nicholini's.** In the Conrad Hotel, Pacific Place, 88 Queensway Rd., Central. ☎ **852/2521 3838.** Reservations recommended. Main courses HK$240–HK$395 ($31.20–$51.35); fixed-price lunch HK$238 ($30.95). AE, DC, MC, V. Daily noon–3pm, 6:30–11pm. MTR: Central. ITALIAN.

Most of Hong Kong's Italian restaurants seem to fall into one of two categories—high-brow and sophisticated, or rustic and trattorialike. This one is neither and yet both, combining elegance and lightheartedness in keeping with the Conrad Hotel's overall playful style. Dress is casual to smart casual (though no jeans or tennis shoes are allowed), and the dining room bathes patrons in soothing colors of celadon green, pink, aquamarine, yellow, and plum rose. If you're a fan of Murano glass, be sure to check out the collection at the front of the restaurant. The cuisine here is northern Italian, combined with inventiveness. Lobster with herbs and Tuscan olive oil is the overwhelming first and most expensive entree on the extensive menu; other courses kinder to the pocketbook include salmon with a champagne and caviar sauce and grilled chicken breast. The wine list is extensive, and the service is beyond reproach. Too bad this restaurant doesn't have a view.

**Petrus.** In the Island Shangri-La (56th floor), Pacific Place, Supreme Court Rd., Central. ☎ **852/2820 8590.** Reservations recommended. Jacket required. Main courses HK$320–HK$520 ($41.55–$67.55); fixed-price lunch HK$278–HK$328 ($36.10–$42.60); fixed-price dinner HK$700–HK$850 ($90.90–$110.40). AE, DC, MC, V. Mon–Sat noon–3pm, daily 6:30–10:30pm. MTR: Admiralty. FRENCH.

Simply put, the views from this 56th-floor restaurant are breathtaking. In fact, they are probably the best of any hotel restaurant on the Hong Kong side; the only place with a better view is atop Victoria Peak. If you can bear to take your eyes off the windows, you'll find the restaurant decorated like a French castle, with the obligatory crystal chandeliers, black marble and gilded columns, statues, thick draperies, impressionist paintings, murals gracing dome-shaped ceilings, and a pianist playing softly in the background. Tables are spaced far enough apart for intimacy.

The cuisine emphasizes contemporary Alsatian creations, including light, healthy fare made with olive oil rather than the heavier cream and butter. The menu changes often but has included such intriguing combinations as eggplant cannelloni with tuna and anchovy tapenade; green asparagus fricassée with roasted prawn and deep-fried egg; and guinea fowl pie filled with mushroom and chestnut served with duck liver sauce and truffles. Probably the best way to sample the continuously new creations is with one of the fixed-price meals. As expected, the wine list—particularly Bordeaux—is among the best in Hong Kong. In any case, with the impressive blend of great views, refined ambience, and excellent cuisine, this restaurant is a top choice for a splurge, romantic dinner, or special celebration.

**Vong.** In the Mandarin Oriental Hotel (25th floor), 5 Connaught Rd., Central. ☎ **852/2825 4028.** Reservations required. Main courses HK$188–HK$308 ($24.40–$40); fixed-price lunch HK$228 ($29.60). AE, DC, MC, V. Daily noon–3pm and 6pm–midnight. MTR: Central. FRANCO-ASIAN.

Chef Jean-Georges Vongerichten, who made a name for himself with several well-known New York establishments, set Hong Kong abuzz when he opened his much-talked-about restaurant on the 25th floor of the Mandarin Oriental Hotel in 1997. Matching Petrus for its spectacular views of the harbor, this chic, black-and-gold venue serves what may well be the best interpretation of East-meets-West Franco-Asian cuisine this side of the hemisphere, with exquisite combinations that can set taste buds dancing with excitement. Appetizers range from shrimp satay dipped in a fresh oyster sauce to sautéed foie gras with ginger and mango. All main courses are tempting—perhaps you'll choose the spiny lobster with Thai herbs, the steamed sea bass in cardamon sauce with Savoy cabbage and watercress, or the chicken marinated in lemongrass with sweet rice steamed in banana leaf. If choosing only one dish causes anguish, order the Tasting Menu for HK$488 ($63.45) per person, though you'll have to convince everyone else at your table to do the same, since it's available only if the entire table chooses it. An alternative is to come early or late for the Theatre Menu, available daily 6 to 7pm and again at 10:30pm and costing HK$288 ($37.40) for a choice of appetizer, entree, and dessert. At lunch time, you can save money by ordering a plate with six exquisitely prepared items noon to 12:30pm or 1:30 to 3pm, at which time it costs HK$188 ($24.40) rather than the usual HK$228 ($29.60). My lunch plate contained crab spring roll, raw tuna and vegetables rolled in rice paper, prawn satays, lobster wrapped in daikon, quail rubbed with Thai spices, and crunch cress salad. The only complaint is that Vong is so popular and busy that its activity and noise level can be like an outdoor market, making it a good place for people-watching but not for a romantic tête-à-tête.

## ℹ️ Family-Friendly Restaurants

**Al's Diner** (see p. 134)    This may be the perfect antidote for restless teenagers who are threatening mutiny if they don't see any "real food" soon. It's located in Central's nightlife district (which might perk your teenager's interest) and offers burgers, hot dogs, sandwiches, sundaes, ice-cream floats, and banana splits. The jukebox is a good diversion, too, but make sure you come during the day or early evening, since the house specialty, vodka jelly shots, attracts a wild crowd at night that would provide a bit more excitement than your teenager is ready for.

**Dan Ryan's Chicago Grill** (see p. 112)    These two restaurant/bars serve the best burgers in town, as well as huge deli sandwiches. There are plenty of other American dishes as well, and the setting looks just like home.

**Harbour Side** (see p. 115)    Although located in the posh Regent Hotel, this casual restaurant has a view of people jogging and strolling the waterfront promenade and offers sandwiches, pizza, and pasta. Best, however, is the Sunday brunch, when kids pay half price for their own buffet table laden with food youngsters actually eat and there's also a play area. Still not sold? Adults get champagne.

**Island Cafe** (see p. 130)    An attractive place mat menu just for kiddies, crayons, and a coloring book are good diversions for a meal at the sumptuous lunch and dinner buffets offered at this pleasant, casual restaurant. Bribe your darlings with a promise to visit Hong Kong Park after your meal, visible from the restaurant.

**Mandarin Grill** (see p. 124)    For little ones who expect only the best, treat them to Sunday brunch at the comfortable but upscale Mandarin Grill, which boasts a children's table filled with standby favorites as well as exotic choices.

**Marché Mövenpick** (see p. 142)    If one of the best views of Hong Kong and inexpensive prices for self-serve international dishes doesn't impress your youngsters, this restaurant's children's corner surely will, with a toddler slide, toys, crayons, and other diversions. For older kids, there's a Ripley's Believe It or Not! Odditorium and a motion-simulation theater in the same building on the Peak.

**Planet Hollywood** (see p. 116)    Star-struck teenagers will like the drama of this tribute to celluloid, with movie memorabilia, TV screens showing Hollywood hits, and burgers and other American food.

**Spaghetti House** (see p. 120)    Locations all over town and low prices make this family chain a winner. There are more than a half dozen different kinds of spaghetti, as well as a wide range of pizza. Just like pizza parlors back home.

## EXPENSIVE

**Benkay Japanese Restaurant.** First basement of the Landmark, Des Voeux Rd. Central, Central. ☎ **852/2521 3344.** Reservations recommended, especially for lunch. Sukiyaki, shabu-shabu, teppanyaki, and kaiseki fixed-price meals HK$350–HK$750 ($45.50–$97.50). AE, CB, DC, MC, V. Mon–Sat 11:30am–3pm, Sun and holidays noon–3pm; daily 6–10:30pm. MTR: Central. JAPANESE.

A joint venture of Japan Airlines and the Maxim's restaurant chain, this restaurant is located among the expensive boutiques of the classy Landmark shopping complex and is popular with businesspeople in the area. Benkay uses screens and lighting to create a traditional atmosphere, complete with Japanese instrumental music in the background. If you are new to Japanese cuisine, the extensive menu might be overwhelming, as it offers all the usual Japanese favorites, including sukiyaki and shabu-shabu (one-pot beef dishes cooked at your table), teppanyaki (grilled steak), and kaiseki (a feast of seasonal dishes, artfully arranged). There are also reasonably priced fixed-price meals costing less than HK$300 ($39), including a Japanese *obento* lunch box (like a mini-kaiseki), grilled eel with rice, a sashimi set course, soba and udon noodles, and assorted tempura.

**✪ Cafe des Artistes.** California Tower (ground floor), 30–32 D'Aguilar St., Central. ☎ 852/ **2526 3880.** Main courses HK$118–HK$220 ($15.35–$28.60); fixed-price lunch HK$148 ($19.25). AE, DC, MC, V. Mon–Sat noon–2:30pm; Sun–Thurs 7–10:30pm, Fri–Sat 7–11pm. MTR: Central. FRENCH.

This pleasant and comfortable restaurant overlooks the action of Lan Kwai Fong with large open windows, making it great for people-watching and imparting a feeling of being above it all. But the real draw is the cuisine from southern France, expertly rendered by the chef imported from Nice into culinary masterpieces. The homemade goose liver terrine is not to be missed; other recommended dishes include the grilled sea bass, the pan-roasted duck breast, and spring chicken with brandy and goose liver sauce. Be sure to save room for dessert. Dinners average HK$500 ($46.95), without wine.

**China Lan Kwai Fong.** 17–22 Lan Kwai Fong, Central. ☎ 852/2536 0968. Reservations recommended. Main dishes HK$105–HK$245 ($13.65–$31.80); fixed-price lunch HK$128–HK$138 ($16.60). AE, DC, MC, V. Mon–Fri noon–3pm, Sat–Sun 11:30am–3pm; Sun–Thurs 6:30–11pm, Fri–Sat 6:30pm–midnight. MTR: Central. CANTONESE.

This retro-styled restaurant in trendy Lan Kwai Fong is one of Hong Kong's hottest and classiest Chinese restaurants, decorated with antiques, hanging lanterns, ceiling fans, and even birds giving song from inside wooden cages. While the emphasis is on Cantonese food, it offers specialties from other regions as well, including Shanghai, Beijing, and Szechuan. Prawns, for example, are available six variations, from stir fried with chilis (Szechuan) to sautéed with black bean and green pepper (Cantonese). Garoupa comes fresh from the restaurant's own tanks. Peking duck (costing HK$380/$49.35) and beggar's chicken (order in advance for HK$480/$62.35) are also available. Especially recommended is the deep-fried sole with black bean and pepper sauce. An all-you-can-eat dim sum brunch is available weekends and holidays for HK$128 ($16.60).

**Hanagushi.** 17–22 Lan Kwai Fong (1st floor), Central. ☎ 852/2521 0868. Yakitori, tempura, sashimi, and vegetarian yakitori fixed-price meals HK$280–HK$460 ($36.35–$59.75). AE, DC, MC, V. Mon–Sat 11am–3pm and 6–11:30pm. MTR: Central. JAPANESE.

The only thing missing at this traditionally styled Japanese restaurant with its gleaming woods, tansu chests, woodblock prints, and waitresses decked out in provincial Japanese clothing are tatami mats. It specializes in yakitori, morsels of food barbecued on a stick, with 46 different kinds available and costing HK$20 to HK$85 ($2.60 to $11.05) for a pair. My favorites include asparagus rolled in bacon, chicken meat balls, quail eggs, green pepper with minced chicken, and gingko nuts. You can also order fixed-price meals of yakitori, including a vegetarian version and yakitori meals that also include tempura or sashimi. Grilled fish, udon noodles, and other typical Japanese fare are also available, along with a dozen different kinds of sake to wash it all down.

**La Ronda.** In the Furama Kempinski Hotel (30th floor), 1 Connaught Rd., Central. ☎ 852/ **2848 7422.** Reservations required at dinner. Lunch buffet HK$240 ($31.20); dinner buffet HK$380 ($49.40). AE, CB, DC, MC, V. Daily noon–2:30pm and 6:30–10:30pm. MTR: Tsim Sha Tsui. INTERNATIONAL.

A revolving 30th-floor restaurant with stunning views! The buffets are quite a spread too, offering salads, desserts, appetizers, and international cuisine ranging from sushi and roast beef to curries and Chinese and Western dishes. The food, while mediocre, is more than compensated for by the view. Save money by coming for lunch. There's live entertainment nightly, and on Friday and Saturday nights from 9:30pm there's dancing for an additional HK$100 ($13), including two drinks.

○ **M at the Fringe.** 2 Lower Albert Rd., Central. ☎ **852/2877 4000.** Reservations strongly recommended. Main courses HK$188–HK$208 ($24.40–$27); fixed-price lunch HK$148–HK$168 ($19.25–$21.85). AE, MC, V. Mon–Fri noon–2:30pm; Sun–Thurs 7–10pm, Fri–Sat 7–10:30pm. MTR: Central. CONTINENTAL.

For a memorable, unusual dining experience, head for this delightful restaurant, located on the upper floor of a former dairy farm building, which is also home of the Fringe Theater. A meal here is a treat in more ways than one—the artsy furnishings are a feast for the eyes, while the food, influenced by cuisines along the Mediterranean, is to die for. The menu changes every 3 months but is always creative and always includes lamb and vegetarian selections. An example of the former is leg of lamb with spiced chickpeas and green peas, roasted eggplant, naan bread, and coriander paste and raita. For dessert, don't pass up the Pavlova.

○ **Va Bene.** 58–62 D'Aguilar St., Central. ☎ **852/2845 5577.** Reservations required. Pasta HK$178–HK$188 ($23.15–$24.45); main courses HK$188–HK$258 ($24.45– $33.55); fixed-price lunch HK$138 ($17.90). AE, DC, MC, V. Mon–Fri noon–3pm and daily 7pm–midnight (last order 10:30pm). MTR: Central. ITALIAN.

This upscale Italian restaurant, in the middle of Central's Lan Kwai Fong nightlife district, strives for the simplicity of a rustic Italian villa with its sponged, mustard-hued walls, a sky-blue ceiling, and rows of terra-cotta pots serving as the main decorations. With consistently excellent food and under the exuberant and watchful eye of maitre d' and co-owner Pino Piano, it's extremely popular with Hong Kong's well-heeled expat community, making it a lively and boisterous—though cramped—spot for a meal. Perhaps you'll want to start with carpaccio (wafer-thin beef tenderloin served with white mushrooms and shavings of Parmesan), artichokes cooked in olive oil and garlic, or ravioli with spinach and ricotta cheese. As a main course, you can choose from a number of veal, beef, and seafood offerings, including veal scallopini; braised sea bass with white wine, rosemary, garlic, and chickpeas; or pan-roasted sirloin steak served with artichokes and red wine sauce. Good Italian wines, great desserts, and attentive service round out the meal; expect to spend about HK$500 ($65) per person, without wine.

**Zen Chinese.** Pacific Place, 88 Queensway, Central. ☎ **852/2845 4555.** Reservations recommended. Main dishes HK$80–HK$220 ($10.40–$28.60). AE, DC, MC, V. Mon–Fri 11:30am–3pm, Sat 11:30am–5pm, Sun 10:30am–5pm; daily 6–11pm. MTR: Admiralty. CANTONESE.

Both its name and its appearance leave no doubt that this is no ordinary Cantonese restaurant. You won't find any reds and golds here, or any glittering chandeliers. Rather, the restaurant is somewhat austere in Zen Buddhist style, with a concrete ceiling, double-layered white tablecloths, fresh flowers on each table, and an open dining hall that allows customers to see and be seen. To offset the simplicity and starkness of the room, a succession of large glass bowls running the length of the restaurant are suspended from the ceiling, creating a never-ending cascade as water trickles from one bowl to the next; some think the arrangement looks like a dragon.

As for the food, there is a wide variety of Cantonese specialties that border on the nouvelle. Try the shark's-fin soup with shredded chicken, sautéed prawns with onions and black pepper, or baked fresh crab with bean vermicelli, ginger, and onion hot pot. Unlike those of most Chinese restaurants, the wine list is rather extensive. With most dishes averaging HK$90 to HK$130 ($11.70 to $16.90), you can easily dine here for around HK$300 to HK$400 ($39 to $51.95), not including drinks. For lunch you can even eat more cheaply, with dim sum available for HK$28 to HK$32 ($3.65 to $4.15) a plate.

## MODERATE

Several moderately priced restaurants already covered in the Tsim Sha Tsui section have branches in Central: **Dan Ryan's Chicago Grill,** located in Pacific Place and offering American classics; **Golden Island Bird's Nest Chiu Chau Restaurant** with its bird's nest specialties; **Jade Garden,** serving Cantonese food; **Peking Garden,** with two locations in Central and serving food from Peking; and **Tsui Hang Village Restaurant,** serving Cantonese fare.

**Baci.** 1 Lan Kwai Fong (2nd floor), Central. ☎ **852/2801 5885.** Reservations recommended. Pizza HK$98–HK$148 ($12.75–$19.20); main courses HK$170–HK$238 ($22.10–$30.90); fixed-price lunch HK$150 ($19.50). AE, DC, MC, V. Mon–Sat noon–2:30pm, daily 7–11pm. MTR: Central. ITALIAN.

On the second floor, above a less expensive pizzeria under the same ownership, this smart-looking restaurant with a crisp, white, minimalist interior boasts a friendly staff and an Italian chef. Ingredients are flown fresh from Italy; the pasta is homemade. Recommended are the grilled veal escalope rolls stuffed with ham, spinach, and mushrooms in a dressing of virgin oil, lemon juice, oregano, parsley, and garlic; and the oven-roasted salmon filet of white wine and artichokes. There's also a small bar, with windows that open to the madness of Lan Kwai Fong below.

**Grappa's.** Pacific Place, 88 Queensway, Central. ☎ **852/2868 0086.** Reservations recommended. Pizza and pasta HK$80–HK$155 ($10.40–$20.15); main courses HK$125–HK$245 ($16.25–$31.80); fixed-price lunch HK$145–HK$155 ($18.85–$20.15). AE, DC, MC, V. Daily 9:30am–10:30pm (last order). MTR: Admiralty. ITALIAN.

If you like to eat pizza or pasta to the accompaniment of noise, commotion, and lots of people parading past, this is the place for you. Grappa's is decorated like a trattoria, but with big glass windows overlooking the shops of Pacific Place—you can't escape the fact that this place is not a sidewalk cafe but is in a mall. The open kitchen, while providing some diversion, adds to the noise. Still, this is certainly the best place for Italian food anywhere in the area, even though it is strictly standard fare. Homemade bread, served with olive oil and fresh Parmesan, is brought swiftly to every table (and replenished if desired); it is so delicious that you may be tempted to eat your fill before the meal arrives, especially if the place is full and service is slow. The salads are good here, as are the dozen or so authentic Italian pizzas and the even larger selection of homemade pastas. The entrees lean toward the tried and true, from veal shank stew in Barolo red wine sauce to roasted lamb chops with rosemary. The Italian wines are affordable.

✪ **Hunan Garden.** The Forum (3rd floor), Exchange Sq., Central. ☎ **852/2868 2880.** Reservations recommended. Main dishes HK$78–HK$168 ($10.15–$21.80). AE, DC, MC, V. Daily 11:30am–3pm and 5:30pm–midnight. MTR: Central. HUNANESE.

Although the chili-rich cuisine of Hunan province is quite popular in Taiwan, this is one of the few Hunan restaurants in Hong Kong. It's puzzling, because Hunanese food is very spicy, and one would think that with the booming popularity of Thai and Szechuan food in the SAR, Hunanese food would catch on. Perhaps the next-door Hong Kong Station, terminus of the Airport Express Line, will bring a new popularity. In any case, this is a great restaurant, both in decor and food. It's decorated in hot pink and green, and the motif is clearly lotus (Hunan province is famous for its lotus). The dining area is spacious, with tables spread luxuriously far apart. Chinese folk music is performed live in the evening.

But the real treat is the food. The chefs were trained in both Hunan province and Taiwan and they don't tone down the spiciness of their authentic dishes (spicy items are marked on the menu). Start your meal with one of the soups. I tried the Hunan minced-chicken soup, a clear soup base with ginger and mousse of chicken, served piping hot in a length of bamboo. If you like hot-and-spicy foods, you'll love the braised bean curd with shredded meat and chili, developed by one of Hunan province's most famous chefs. Other recommended dishes include the honey-glazed Hunan ham served in pancakes and fried chicken with chili and garlic. As a special treat, try one of the Hunanese wines.

**Indochine 1929.** California Tower (2nd floor), 30–32 D'Aguilar, Central. ☎ **852/2869 7399.** Reservations recommended. Main dishes HK$115–HK$260 ($14.95–$33.75); fixed-price lunch HK$108–HK$148 ($14–$19.20). AE, DC, MC, V. Mon–Sat noon–3pm; daily 6:30–11pm. MTR: Central. VIETNAMESE.

Designed to resemble a breezy, 1920s veranda from Vietnam's French colonial era, this Lan Kwai Fong eatery serves delicious Indochinese cuisine to a consciously trendy crowd. Start with the spring rolls stuffed with shrimp, pork, and herbs; or the hot and sour fish soup. Other specialties are the fish prepared Hanoi style, with dill, turmeric, rice vermicelli, and peanuts; the salt and pepper soft shell crabs; the beef tenderloin with tomato; and grilled eggplant with scallion oil and soy sauce. If you've never had Vietnamese food, this restaurant should make you an instant convert.

**Island Cafe.** In the Island Shangri-La Hotel, Pacific Place, Supreme Court Rd., Central. ☎ **852/ 2877 3838,** ext. 8571. Lunch buffet HK$198 ($25.75) Mon–Fri, HK$240 ($31.20) Sat–Sun; dinner buffet HK$268 ($34.80) Sun–Thurs, HK$298 ($38.79) Fri–Sat. AE, DC, MC, V. Mon–Fri noon–2:30pm and 6:30–9:30pm; Sat–Sun noon–3pm and 7–10pm. MTR: Admiralty. INTERNATIONAL.

This bright and cheerful restaurant, with colorful paintings of flowers, trees, and fruit adorning the walls, overlooks the lush greenery of Hong Kong Park. Come here after shopping in Pacific Place or visiting the park's museum of tea ware. Its buffets offer a wide choice of Asian and Western dishes, allowing you to compose a meal from around the world.

**Jimmy's Kitchen.** 1 Wyndham St., Central. ☎ **852/2526 5293.** Main courses HK$116–HK$191 ($15.05–$24.80). AE, DC, MC, V. Daily 11:30am–3pm and 6–11pm. MTR: Central. CONTINENTAL.

This restaurant opened in 1928, a replica of a similar, American-owned restaurant in Shanghai. Now one of Hong Kong's oldest Western restaurants, Jimmy's Kitchen has had several homes before moving in the 1960s to its present site. Some of its waiters are descendants from the original staff. The atmosphere reminds me of an American steakhouse, with white tablecloths, dark-wood paneling, and elevator music, but it's a favorite with older foreigners living in Hong Kong and serves dependably good, unpretentious European food. The daily specials are written on a blackboard, and an extensive à la carte menu offers salads and soups, steaks, chicken, Indian curries, and a seafood selection that includes sole, scallops, and the local garoupa. It's a good place also for corned beef and cabbage, beef Stroganoff, and hearty German fare, including Wienerschnitzel (breaded veal), pig's knuckle, and Knockwurst sausage.

There's another branch at 29 Ashley Rd., Tsim Sha Tsui (☎ **852/2376 0327**), open daily noon to 11pm.

**Joyce Cafe.** The Atrium, One Exchange Sq., Central. ☎ **852/2810 0807.** Reservations required. Main courses HK$98–HK$168 ($12.75–$21.80). AE, DC, MC, V. Mon–Sat noon–2:30pm, tea time 3–5pm, happy hour 5–8pm. MTR: Central. EAST-MEETS-WEST CROSSOVER.

Located in an office building next to Hong Kong Station, this is *the* restaurant for beautiful professionals, who stay that way apparently by dining on the light and healthy food for which this sophisticated establishment is famous. Pastas, salads, and sandwiches are its mainstay, though by no means are they ordinary. Pastas, for example, prepared Western or Asian style, range from fusilli with asparagus, mozarella, sun-dried tomatoes, pine nuts, and chili al pesto to Shanghai vegetable wontons, made with eight different kinds of vegetables. Crab claws deep fried with prawns and spinach make a great beginning, followed, perhaps, by a Japanese obento lunch box, available as vegetarian or with fish. There are enough fruit and vegetable juices to make you sprout leaves. Who knows, after a few meals here, we might be able to actually fit into some of the designer clothing sold in neighboring Central. Pastries and finger foods are available during afternoon tea time, while snacks from a smaller menu are available in the evening.

**Landau's.** On Hing Building, 1–9 On Hing Terrace, Central. ☎ **852/2827 7901.** Main courses HK$140–HK$155 ($18.20–$20.15); fixed-price lunch HK$135–HK$155 ($17.55–$20.15). AE, DC, MC, V. Daily 12:30am–2:30pm and 6:30–10:30pm. MTR: Central. CONTINENTAL.

Owned by the same company as Jimmy's Kitchen and named after the original owner, Aaron Landau, this restaurant has had several reincarnations before reopening in this somewhat awkward location (to reach it, take the stairs off Wyndham Street). Losing its stodgier former self, it aims for a younger but successful expat crowd with a more adventuresome menu. Its decor is colonial-chic, with gold-washed walls, cushioned rattan furniture, shutters, and palm trees. There's a small bar, open throughout the day, with reduced prices for drinks during its 3-to-7:30pm happy hour. For starters, try the Scottish smoked salmon with avocado or the creamy mixed mushrooms on garlic toast. Also recommended are the filet of beef on a crispy crouton with salsa verde and red wine sauce; the slow-roasted swordfish with creamed potatoes, pak choi, and laksa sauce; or the madras-style curry of fresh prawns. Vegetarians might opt for the tomato and mozzarella salad with pistachios, balsamic vinegar and olive oil, followed by the mushroom stroganoff. It also offers a takeaway menu of deli items and sandwiches, popular with nearby businesspeople on the run.

✪ **Luk Yu Tea House.** 24–26 Stanley St., Central. ☎ **852/2523 5464.** Main dishes HK$100–HK$220 ($13–$28.60); dim sum HK$25–HK$55 ($3.25–$7.15). MC, V. Daily 7am–10pm. MTR: Central. CANTONESE.

Luk Yu, first opened in 1933, is the most famous teahouse remaining in Hong Kong. In fact, unless you have a time machine, you can't get any closer to old Hong Kong than this wonderful art deco–era Cantonese restaurant, with its ceiling fans, spittoons, individual wooden booths for couples, marble tabletops, wood paneling, and stained-glass windows. The cashier uses an abacus to figure bills. It's one of the best places to try a few Chinese teas, including bo lai, jasmine, lung ching (a green tea), and sui sin (narcissus or daffodil).

But Luk Yu is most famous for its dim sum, served 7am to 5:30pm. The problem for foreigners, however, is that the place is always packed with regulars who have their own special places to sit, and the staff is sometimes surly to newcomers. In addition, if you come after 11am, dim sum is no longer served by trolley but from an English menu with pictures but no prices, which could end up being quite expensive unless you ask before ordering. If you want to come during the day (certainly when Luk Yu is most colorful), try to bring along a Chinese friend. Otherwise, consider coming for dinner when it's not nearly so hectic. Also, at dinner there is an English menu listing more than 200 items, including all the Cantonese favorites. Dinner will average HK$250 to HK$300 ($32.50 to $38.95) a person.

**Pavilion.** 3 Tun Wo Lane, Central. ☎ **852/2869 7768** or 2973 0642. Main courses HK$180–HK$190 ($23.40–$24.65). AE, DC, MC, V. Mon–Sat noon–2:30pm and 7–10pm (last order). Closed holidays for lunch. MTR: Central. CONTINENTAL.

Although not south of Hollywood Road (from which SoHo derives its name), Pavilion is very much a part of the new SoHo dining and nightlife scene and may well qualify as the best restaurant in the area. You'll find it off Cochrane, at the end of a short alley. The restaurant, which adjoins the Petticoat Lane bar under the same ownership, is not much larger than a walk-in closet; on the wall is a quote by M.F.K. Fisher that proclaims provocatively "Almost everyone has something secret he likes to eat." If you're claustrophobic, try to get a seat alfresco in the romantic courtyard. The changing menu is limited (probably due to the size of a Lilliputian kitchen) to about three pastas and seven entrees, but they're always right on. Examples of past dishes include egg tagliatelle pasta topped with fresh crab meat and chive cream sauce topped by caviar; lightly grilled salmon on chili and coriander mashed potato, topped with grilled prawn and pink peppercorn sauce; and beef medallions wrapped in bacon served on new potatoes, with a warm salad of green beans, bell peppers, grilled shitake mushrooms and veal stock reduction. Whew! Encouraged by its success, the management has opened a tapas bar next door, equally diminutive and popular.

**Shanghai Garden.** Hutchinson House (1st floor), Murray Rd., Central. ☎ **852/2524 8181.** Reservations recommended. Main dishes HK$68–HK$158 ($8.85–$20.50). AE, CB, DC, MC, V. Daily 11:30am–3pm and 5:30–11pm. MTR: Central. SHANGHAINESE.

Located next to the Furama Hotel, the Shanghai Garden (part of the Maxim's group of restaurants) does a good job in presentation and cuisine. Since Shanghai does not have its own cuisine, the dishes served here are from Peking, Nanking, Sichuan, Hangchow, and Wuxi, as well as a few from Shanghai. The menu is extensive, including fish and vegetable potage or shark's-fin soup, such cold dishes as crispy shredded eel or chicken in wine sauce, and such main courses as sautéed prawns, beggar's chicken (which costs HK$250/$32.45), sautéed beef with green pepper, braised pig with vegetables, and fried noodles Shanghai style. Peking duck costs HK$125 ($16.25) for half a bird. This place, pleasantly and soothingly decorated, does a roaring business, especially for lunch. With most dishes priced around HK$80 to HK$120 ($10.40 to $15.60), you can expect your dinner here to cost about HK$200 to HK$250 ($26–$32.50), excluding drinks.

**Sichuan Garden.** Gloucester Tower (3rd floor), Landmark Building, Des Voeux Rd. Central, Central. ☎ **852/2521 4433.** Reservations recommended. Main dishes HK$78–HK$168 ($10.15–$21.80). AE, DC, MC, V. Daily 11:30am–3pm and 5:30–11pm. MTR: Central. SZECHUAN.

Another Maxim's restaurant, the Sichuan Garden is in the chic Landmark Building, which explains its high prices (someone has to pay the rent). The atmosphere is bright, spotless, and elegantly simple, the food excellent, and the service attentive. It's quite popular and almost always crowded, especially at lunch. The hot-and-spicy dishes are clearly marked on the 80-item menu to help the uninitiated, though those who appreciate fiery food will find that dishes here are only mildly hot. Recommended are the hot-and-sour soup, sautéed prawns with peanuts in chili sauce, pork in hot garlic sauce, bean curd with minced beef in a pungent sauce, smoked duck, and pigeon smoked in camphor wood and tea leaves. I ordered the pigeon and found it quite good, but I was not prepared to have the head brought out as well—perhaps as a decoration (at least, I assume it wasn't for consumption).

There's another Sichuan Garden in the Pacific Place mall at shop 004, 88 Queensway, Central (☎ **2845 8433;** MTR: Admiralty), open Monday to Saturday

11:30am to 3pm and 5:30pm to midnight, and Sunday 10:30am to 3pm and 5:30pm to midnight.

**The Square.** Exchange Square II, Central. ☎ **852/2525 1163.** Main dishes HK$85–HK$148 ($11.05–$19.20); fixed-price lunch HK$188–HK$238 ($24.40–$30.90). AE, DC, MC, V. Daily noon–2pm and 6–10pm. MTR: Central. CANTONESE.

Opened in 2000 with hopes of capturing some of the increased traffic in this area due to Hong Kong Station next door, this smartly decorated restaurant features jade napkin holders and flowers on each table, cabinets filled with Chinese antiques, and a view of the Star Ferry as it comes and goes from the Central pier. Recommended are the deep-fried boneless duck in mashed taro, homemade crispy chicken, barbecued pork in honey sauce, and Peking duck (HK$300/$38.95). Dim sum, costing HK$24 to HK$58 ($3.10 to 7.55), is also available for lunch.

**Thai Lemongrass.** 30–32 D'Aguilar St., Central. ☎ **852/2905 1688.** Main dishes HK$105–HK$235 ($13.65–$30.50); fixed-price lunch HK$138 ($17.90). AE, DC, MC, V. Mon–Sat noon–2:30pm; daily 7–11pm. MTR: Central. THAI.

Rattan furniture, fake banana trees, and calm statues of Buddha set the mood in this upscale Thai restaurant in Lan Kwai Fong. The menu, drawing from regional cuisines from throughout Thailand, includes such favorites as soft shelled crab with chili and garlic on fried basil leaves; chili crabs; lobster tails in sweet tamarind sauce with roasted garlic and shallots; and roast duck in red curry with grapes and aubergine. You should be able to dine here for less than HK$200 ($25.95), excluding drinks.

**Tokio Joe.** 16 Lan Kwai Fong, Central. ☎ **852/2525 1889.** Sushi à la carte HK$40–HK$65 ($5.20–$8.45); fixed-price lunch HK$110–HK$190 ($14.30–$24.70). AE, DC, MC, V. Mon–Sat noon–3pm; daily 6:30–11pm. MTR: Central. JAPANESE.

As its quirky name suggests, this is a hip sushi bar catering to Lan Kwai Fong's youthful nighttime revelers. Dimly lit even for lunch, it offers sushi (raw fish on vinegared rice) and sashimi (raw fish) à la carte, as well as combination platters. A platter of assorted sashimi large enough for two people to share as an appetizer costs HK$490 ($63.70); sushi combinations run from HK$150 to HK$360 ($19.50 to $46.80). Unique, however, are the California-style roll creations, like the deep-fried soft shell crab with avocado, cucumber, crab roe, and mayonnaise; or the roll with crab meat, asparagus, sliced fish, mushroom, and egg. Probably the best deal is one of the set lunches, featuring eel, sashimi, tempura, or a box lunch.

**Ye Shanghai.** Level 3, Pacific Place, Central. ☎ **852/2918 9833.** Main dishes HK$72–HK$200 ($9.35–$25.95). AE, MC, V. Daily 11:30am–3pm and 6–11pm. MTR: Admiralty. SHANGHAINESE.

Set in the Pacific Place mall but located in a removed corner, this classy restaurant with a nostalgic, 1930s decor offers such renowned specialties as smoked duck (HK$120/$15.60 for a half bird), Peking duck (which must be ordered 1 day in advance and costs HK$320/$41.55), and crispy skin chicken (HK$380/$49.35), which is served with sesame, mushrooms, seaweed rolls, crispy corn shoots, and crispy rice.

**✪ Yung Kee.** 32–40 Wellington St., Central. ☎ **852/2522 1624.** Main dishes HK$65–HK$150 ($8.45–$19.50); dim sum HK$12–HK$24 ($1.55–$3.10). AE, DC, MC, V. Daily 11am–11:30pm. MTR: Central. CANTONESE.

Popular for decades, Yung Kee started out in 1941 as a small shop selling roast goose, which did so well that it soon expanded into a very successful Cantonese enterprise. Through the years it has won numerous food awards and is the only restaurant in Hong Kong ever to be included in *Fortune* magazine's top 15 restaurants of the world.

Its specialty is still roast goose with plum sauce, cooked to perfection with tender meat on the inside and crispy skin on the outside and available only for dinner for HK$380 ($49.40). Other specialties include roasted suckling pig or duck, cold steamed chicken, barbecued pork, bean curd combined with prawns, sautéed filet of garoupa, any of the fresh seafoods, and thousand-year-old eggs (which are included with each meal). Dining is on one of the upper three floors, but if all you want is a bowl of congee or takeaway, join the office workers who pour in for a quick meal on the informal ground floor. This place is very Chinese, and unless you order the roast goose, you can dine here for as little as HK$200 ($25.95) per person.

## INEXPENSIVE

Several inexpensive restaurants reviewed in the previous Tsim Sha Tsui section have branches in Central: **Genki Sushi** offers conveyor-belt sushi at low prices; **Koh-I-Noor** is recommended for Indian curries; and **Spaghetti House** is a popular family restaurant.

In addition, many restaurants in the moderate category above offer lunches that even the budget-conscious can afford. Be sure, too, to check the section on "Dim Sum" later in this chapter.

Finally, another good place for a casual, inexpensive meal is in the basement of **Seibu department store** in Pacific Place, 88 Queensway, in Central (take the MTR to Admiralty), where a round counter offers Chinese, Thai, Korean, and Japanese food, including sushi, noodles, and other fare, daily 10:30am to 8pm. You can dine here for less than HK$100 ($13).

**Al's Diner.** 39 D'Aguilar St., Central. ☎ **852/2869 1869.** Main courses HK$75–HK$158 ($9.75–$20.50). AE, DC, MC, V. Mon–Thurs 11:30am–1am, Fri–Sat 11:30am–3am, Sun 11:30am–midnight. MTR: Central. AMERICAN.

This is one of the cheapest places for a late-night meal if you're carousing in Central's nightlife district around Lan Kwai Fong. Although it may not win any culinary awards, this informal diner, decorated in 1950s Americana style, definitely hits the spot with burgers, hot dogs, sandwiches, chili, meat loaf, macaroni and cheese, milk shakes, ice-cream floats, and banana splits. It serves breakfast anytime. Be aware, however, that this place really packs 'em in during the late hours, when the place pulsates with a DJ, people eating jelly shots (jelly laced with vodka), and revelers dancing on the table weekend nights.

**The Ashoka.** 57–59 Wyndham St., Central. ☎ **852/2524 9623** or 852/2525 5719. Main dishes HK$52–HK$95 ($6.75–$12.35); fixed-price lunch or dinner HK$98 ($12.75). AE, DC, MC, V. Daily noon–2:30pm and 6–10:30pm. MTR: Central. INDIAN.

Within walking distance of Central up on winding Wyndham Street, The Ashoka is just one of several Indian restaurants in the area but is among the best known and most popular. Opened in 1973, it claims to be the oldest Indian restaurant on Hong Kong Island. In any case, it's extremely tiny and crowded (only 60 seats), so be prepared to sit practically in your neighbor's lap. It's worth it, for the food, mainly northern Indian, is great, the service is enthusiastic, and the prices are even better, with ridiculously cheap fixed-price meals—there are two menus available, a vegetarian and a tandoori, available daily for both lunch and dinner. If you order à la carte, you will find such house specialties as fish or chicken tikka, chicken green masala (chicken served with green chili and tomatoes in a spicy green sauce), and creative vegetarian selections.

**Baci Pizza.** 1 Lan Kwai Fong (1st floor), Central. ☎ **852/2840 0153.** Pizzas and pastas HK$85–HK$156 ($11.05–$20.25). AE, DC, MC, V. Mon–Fri noon–2:45pm; Mon–Thurs 7–10:30pm, Fri–Sat 7–11:30pm, Sun 7:30–10pm. MTR: Central. PIZZA/PASTA.

This tiny, casual, welcoming pizzeria offers pasta dishes ranging from lasagna to penne pasta with scallops, asparagus, and tomatoes in a white wine sauce to various kinds of wafer-thin pizza, including a "four seasons" pizza with cheese, mushrooms, black olives, ham, and artichokes, and a pizza with four cheeses—Gorgonzola, Parmesan, mozzarella, and fontina.

**City Hall Chinese Restaurant.** City Hall (2nd floor), Low Block (the one closest to the harbor), Central. ☎ **852/2521 1303.** Reservations recommended, especially at lunch. Main dishes HK$70–HK$160 ($9.10–$20.80); dim sum HK$17–HK$38 ($2.20–$4.95). AE, V. Mon–Fri 10am–3pm and 5:30–11:30pm, Sat 10am–11:30pm, Sun and holidays 8am–11:30pm. MTR: Central. CANTONESE.

Decorated in Chinese red, this large restaurant on the second floor of city hall offers a view of the harbor and is so popular at lunchtime that you'll probably have to wait if you haven't made a reservation (report immediately to the woman at the desk near the door to get on the waiting list). The clientele is almost exclusively Chinese, and the food is Cantonese, with the usual shark's-fin, bird's-nest, abalone, pigeon, duck, vegetable, beef, and seafood dishes, most priced in the range of HK$75 to HK$110 ($9.75–$14.30). The food is fast and average; better, in my opinion, is the dim sum, served from trolleys until 3pm. Ask for the dim sum menu in English. Lunchtime fare also includes various noodle and rice dishes, all priced less than HK$100 ($13).

**I Caramba!** 26–30 Elgin St., Central. ☎ **852/2530 9963.** Reservations recommended. Main courses HK$101–HK$142 ($13.10–$18.45). AE, MC, V. Daily noon–10:45pm. MTR: Central. MEXICAN.

Located in the heart of Hong Kong's popular SoHo dining and nightlife district, down the street from the Mid-Levels escalator, this very narrow Mexican restaurant offers hearty dishes of tacos, burritos, enchiladas, chimichangas, fajitas, and fresh fish of the day, all served with side dishes of black beans and rice. Tables are too close together for intimate discussions, but after a few margaritas, who cares? On weekends and holidays, brunch is offered until 6pm for HK$99 ($12.85), including one drink. I caramba!

## 4 Causeway Bay & Wan Chai

### VERY EXPENSIVE

✪ **Grissini.** In the Grand Hyatt Hong Kong Hotel, 1 Harbour Rd., Wan Chai. ☎ **852/2588 1234,** ext. 7313. Reservations required. Main courses HK$250–HK$390 ($32.45–$50.65); fixed-price lunch HK$245 ($31.80). AE, DC, MC, V. Daily noon–2:30pm and 7–11pm. MTR: Wan Chai. ITALIAN.

This stylish, airy Italian restaurant echoes the palatial setting of the Grand Hyatt Hotel, with a tall ceiling, parquet floors, slick black furniture, and ceiling-to-floor windows offering a spectacular view of the harbor. Dining is on two levels, giving everyone a ringside seat. The menu offers some of the best Northern Italian fare in town. Although the menu changes often, it always includes the *antipasto misto,* a selection of appetizers, and if you're really hungry you might want to follow it with one of the pasta or risotto dishes, such as the eggplant and mozzarella filled ravioli with tomato, olives, and basil, or the saffron risotto with Marsala-glazed goose liver. Main dishes have included a very delicious baked filet of sea bass with black olive paste and pine nuts, and roast rack of lamb with goose liver in a black truffle sauce. Expect to spend a least HK$600 ($78) per person for dinner without wine, though the excellent Italian wines on hand are perfect accompaniments. At lunch there are lighter fare and more choices of pasta and risotto. Monday to Friday a fixed-price business lunch is

# Causeway Bay & Wan Chai Dining

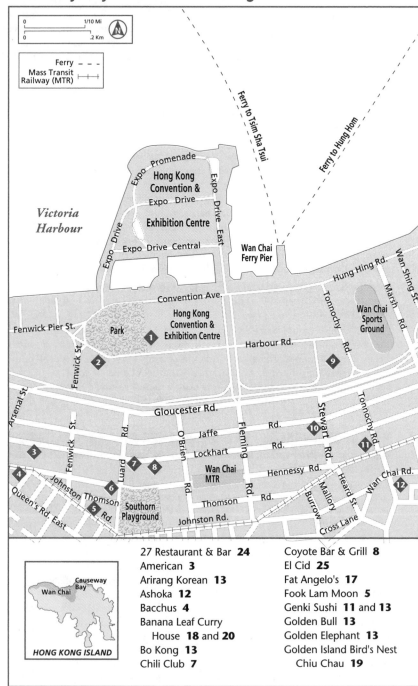

27 Restaurant & Bar **24**
American **3**
Arirang Korean **13**
Ashoka **12**
Bacchus **4**
Banana Leaf Curry
  House **18** and **20**
Bo Kong **13**
Chili Club **7**

Coyote Bar & Grill **8**
El Cid **25**
Fat Angelo's **17**
Fook Lam Moon **5**
Genki Sushi **11** and **13**
Golden Bull **13**
Golden Elephant **13**
Golden Island Bird's Nest
  Chiu Chau **19**

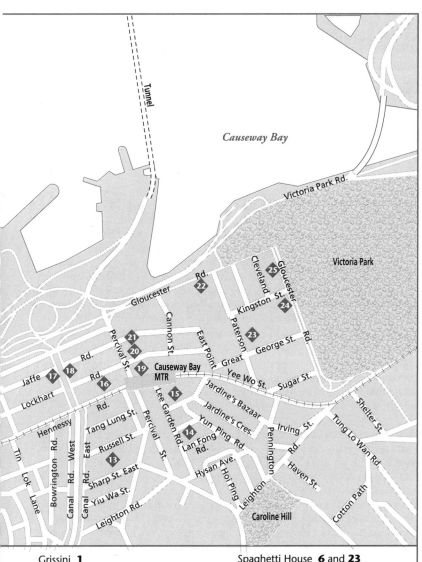

Causeway Bay

Victoria Park Rd.

Tunnel

Victoria Park

Gloucester Rd.

Cleveland

Gloucester St.

Kingston St.

Paterson

George St.

East Point

Great

Yee Wo St.

Sugar St.

Rd.

Cannon St.

Percival St.

Jaffe

Rd.

Lockhart

Rd.

Causeway Bay
MTR

Jardine's Bazaar

Jardine's Cres.

Irving St.

Shelter St.

Tung Lo Wan Rd.

Hennessy

Rd.

Tang Lung St.

Russell St.

Percival St.

Lee Garden Rd.

Yun Ping Rd.

Lan Fong Rd.

Pennington Rd.

Haven St.

Tin Lok Lane

Bowrington Rd.

Canal Rd. West

Canal Rd. East

Sharp St. East

Yiu Wa St.

Leighton Rd.

Hysan Ave.

Hoi Ping

Leighton

Caroline Hill

Cotton Path

**17** **18** **16** **21** **20** **19** **15** **14** **13** **22** **23** **24** **25**

available for HK$245 ($31.80), while the Pasta Live on Saturday features pasta cooked to order for HK$150 ($19.50). Sundays and holidays feature a lavish lunch antipasto buffet, choice of entree, and dessert for HK$335 ($43.50). Whether lunch or dinner, you can't go wrong dining here.

## EXPENSIVE

**Fook Lam Moon,** famous for its exotic Cantonese fare and already covered in the Tsim Sha Tsui dining section, has a branch in Wan Chai.

✪ **One Harbour Road.** In the Grand Hyatt Hong Kong Hotel, 1 Harbour Rd., Wan Chai. ☎ **852/2588 1234,** ext. 7338. Reservations required. Main dishes HK$130–HK$260 ($16.90–$33.75). AE, CB, DC, MC, V. Daily noon–2:30pm and 6:30–10:30pm. MTR: Wan Chai. CANTONESE.

For elegant Chinese dining in Wan Chai, head to the lobby of the Grand Hyatt Hotel, where a glass bubble elevator will deliver you directly to this eighth-floor restaurant. Designed to resemble the terrace of an elegant 1930s taipan mansion, it's bright and airy, with fresh flowers on every table and split-level dining, which offers views of the harbor. A profusion of plants, a large lotus pond, and the sound of running water give the illusion of outdoor dining; tables spread far apart provide privacy. The extensive Cantonese menu, adapted to Western tastes but wonderful just the same, offers the usual shark's-fin specialties, abalone, bird's nest, Peking duck (order in advance), beggar's chicken (order in advance), and roast goose (which costs substantially more than the prices given above). Specialties include braised shark's fin with crab roe, crispy duck with mango and grapefruit, deep-fried crispy eel with cinnamon leaves, and deep-fried crispy chicken skin. There are also fixed-price lunch and dinner menus, which require a minimum order for two people.

**TOTT'S Asian Grill & Bar.** In the Excelsior Hotel, 281 Gloucester Rd., Causeway Bay. ☎ **852/2837 6786.** Reservations recommended for dinner (request a window seat). Main courses HK$108–HK$288 ($14.05–$37.44); fixed-price lunch buffet HK$198 ($25.70). AE, DC, MC, V. Mon–Fri noon–2:30pm; daily 6:30–11pm. MTR: Causeway Bay. ASIAN/EAST-MEETS-WEST.

This flashy restaurant seems to suffer from an identity crisis: gigantic Chinese paint brushes at the entrance and a blood-red interior with zebra-striped chairs. I don't know whether I'm in Africa or China until I look at the fabulous view from the restaurant's 34th-floor perch. This is Hong Kong at its most eclectic, funky self, and though the setting seems contrived, the restaurant itself is relaxed, fun, and highly recommended for its innovative and varied fusion cuisine. Come early for a drink in the restaurant's bar (happy hour is 5 to 8pm), or retire there after dinner for live music and dancing nightly except Sunday. There's also an outdoor terrace where you can take your drinks with you to enjoy the view. A glass-enclosed kitchen reveals food being prepared in woks, over charcoal grills, and in tandoori and wood-burning pizza ovens. There's also a sushi bar. The menu is surprisingly diverse in cuisine and price, allowing diners to eat modestly priced dishes like smoked salmon pizza with roasted onions, capers, tomato, zucchini, and herbs; or angel hair pasta with char-grilled half Boston lobster and pesto; or go all out on tandoori-roasted salmon filet on basil whipped potatoes and crisp vegetable chips; or roasted chicken garam masala, served with spiced pumpkin, potatoes, and citrus yogurt. This place is a good choice for those who want dining and entertainment in one spot.

**27 Restaurant & Bar.** In the Park Lane Hotel (27th floor, 310 Gloucester Rd., Causeway Bay. ☎ **852/2293 8888.** Reservations recommended. Main courses HK$208–HK$298 ($27–$38.70); fixed-price lunch HK$188–HK$208 ($24.40–$27) or lunch buffet HK$218 ($28.30); fixed-price dinner HK$488–HK$528 ($63.40–$68.55). AE, DC, MC, V. Daily noon–3pm and 6pm–midnight. MTR: Causeway Bay. CONTINENTAL.

Using its location high over Victoria Park to full advantage, this restaurant boasts a clean, crisp, and elegant interior with great views beyond the park to the harbor. While it offers a variety of dishes ranging from lamb chops with baked olive-basted tomato and dried haricots beans to Matsuzaka beef with a pinot noir glaze, it is especially recommended for its clearly marked main courses that are low in calories, cholesterol, and fat: fresh dover sole with spinach, sea urchin beurre blanc, or free-range chicken marinated in honey and soy sauce and served on organic brown rice and vegetables. Lunch features international dishes ranging from sushi and dim sum to fried noodles.

## MODERATE

Several restaurants already covered in the Tsim Sha Tsui dining section have branches in Wan Chai or Causeway Bay. A few of these are located on the 11th and 12th floors of Times Square, 1 Matheson St. in Causeway Bay: **Arirang,** which serves Korean food; **Golden Bull,** serving Vietnamese food; **Golden Elephant Thai Restaurant;** and **Wu Kong,** which specializes in cuisine from Shanghai. Other Kowloon restaurants with branches in Wan Chai and Causeway Bay are **El Cid,** excellent for tapas and Spanish cuisine; **Golden Island Bird's Nest Chiu Chau Restaurant; Osaka,** with a variety of Japanese cuisines; and **Peking Garden,** which serves food from Peking.

**Bacchus.** China Hong Kong Tower (basement), 8–12 Hennessy Rd., Wan Chai. ☎ **852/ 2529 9032.** Main courses HK$140–HK$198 ($18.20–$25.70); fixed-price lunch HK$88– HK$118 ($11.45–$15.30). AE, DC, MC, V. Mon–Sat noon–3pm and 6pm–midnight. MTR: Wan Chai. GREEK/MEDITERRANEAN.

Decorated with antiques and exuding a warm, cozy atmosphere reminiscent of a rustic country home, this restaurant made its reputation serving excellent Greek food and has since expanded its menu to include other Mediterranean dishes as well. On Friday and Saturday nights, a vocal and piano duo entertain with popular love songs. With tables in several rooms, dining is romantic and intimate. The Mezze Platter is a great beginning, offering feta, dolmades, prosciutto and melon, leek and cheese filo rolls, olives, and roasted peppers. Follow it with paella, lobster risotto, Cornish game hen, or the mouthwatering moussaka.

**Lao Ching Hing.** In the Century Hong Kong Hotel, 238 Jaffe Rd., Wan Chai. ☎ **852/2598 6080.** Small dishes HK$60–HK$180 ($7.80–$23.40). AE, MC, V. Daily 11am–11pm. MTR: Wan Chai. SHANGHAINESE.

Located in the basement of a hotel, this unpretentious restaurant claims to serve the "best Shanghai food since 1955," when it first opened its doors in Shanghai. Today, Shanghai transplants in Hong Kong patronize Lao Ching Hing for its famous regional dishes, including steamed fresh-water eel marinated in Chinese wine, pork-filled buns, fried freshwater shrimp, and bamboo-shoot dishes (small dishes are good for two or three persons; remember to order several to share). But most popular are the Shanghai freshwater alcoholic crab, marinated in liquor for a year before being served cold; and the Shanghainese hairy crab, available September to the end of December.

**Milano.** Sun Hung Kai Centre (2nd floor), 30 Harbour Rd., Wan Chai. ☎ **852/2598 1222.** Pasta and pizza HK$88–HK$218 ($11.45–$28.30); main courses HK$148–HK$228 ($19.20–$29.60); fixed-price lunch HK$138–HK$268 ($17.90–$34.80). AE, DC, MC, V. Daily noon–3pm and 6–10pm. MTR: Wan Chai. ITALIAN.

With a hip, contemporary design and great views of the harbor, this restaurant offers pizzas with mozzarella, salami, ham, zucchini, pine nuts, goat's cheese, and Parmesan; pasta such as lobster spaghetti; and main courses ranging from dover sole to veal shank braised with saffron risotto. You can eat cheaply if you stick to pizza or come for lunch.

**☉ Red Pepper.** 7 Lan Fong Rd., Causeway Bay. ☎ **852/2577 3811.** Reservations recommended, especially at dinner. Small dishes HK$80–HK$125 ($10.40–$16.25). AE, DC, MC, V. Daily 11:30am–11:15pm (last order). MTR: Causeway Bay. SZECHUAN.

Open since 1970, the Red Pepper has a large following among the city's expatriates, many of whom seem to come so often that they know everyone in the place. It's a very relaxing, small restaurant, with a rather quaint decor of carved dragons on the ceiling and Chinese lanterns. Specialties include fried prawns with chili sauce on a sizzling platter, sour-pepper soup, smoked duck marinated with oranges, and shredded chicken with hot garlic sauce and dry-fried string beans. Most dishes are available in two sizes, with the small dishes suitable for two people. Lychee tea is a good accompaniment.

**Sze Chuen Lau Restaurant.** 466 Lockhart Rd., Causeway Bay. ☎ **852/2891 9027.** Reservations required. Small dishes HK$80–HK$180 ($10.40–$23.40). AE, MC, V. Daily 11:30am–11:30pm. MTR: Causeway Bay. SZECHUAN.

This is a small, rather nondescript restaurant, similar to many family-run neighborhood places all over Hong Kong and very popular with local Chinese for more than 30 years. It serves the usual Szechuan specialties, including chili prawns on a sizzling plate, smoked duck (excellent), shredded pork with hot garlic sauce, dry fried beans with minced beef, and cold chicken with chili-sesame sauce. Dishes come in three different sizes, which is nice for the lone diner. Try to get a table downstairs, but keep in mind that this place caters to the Chinese, not to foreign visitors, and the staff is not keen about explaining anything on the menu—assuming, of course, they understand English, which they may not. If you're already familiar with Szechuan food and know what you want, you'll find this place rewarding both price-wise and taste-bud–wise.

**The Viceroy.** Sun Hung Kai Centre (2nd floor), 30 Harbour Rd., Wan Chai. ☎ **852/2827 7777.** Main dishes HK$58–HK$148 ($7.55–$19.20); lunch buffet HK$108 ($14). AE, DC, MC, V. Daily noon–3pm and 6–11pm. MTR: Wan Chai. INDIAN.

Under the same management as the long-popular Gaylord in Tsim Sha Tsui, this contemporary restaurant has something its sister establishment doesn't—outdoor seating on a terrace with great views of the harbor, Wan Chai waterfront, and Kowloon. In the evening, the experience is almost magical, making it a good choice for a romantic dinner. On days when the weather doesn't cooperate (too cold, too hot, or rainy), indoor dining is a good second choice, with large windows offering the same views. Tandoori dishes range from lamb and prawns to whole roasted garoupa (the local fish). In addition to curries and dishes like roast chicken in yogurt and spices, there are also a fair number of vegetarian dishes, from potatoes cooked with curry leaves to yellow lentils with spinach. The lunch buffet, offered weekdays only, is a steal.

## INEXPENSIVE
The **Banana Leaf Curry House, Fat Angelo's, Genki Sushi,** and **Spaghetti House,** reviewed in the Tsim Sha Tsui section, all have branches in Wan Chai or Causeway Bay.

In addition to the recommendations below, be sure to go through the moderate section above for inexpensive buffet and fixed-price lunches; also see the "Dim Sum" section later in this chapter.

**American Restaurant.** 20 Lockhart Rd., Wan Chai. ☎ **852/2527 1000** or 852/2527 7277. Small dishes HK$50–HK$150 ($6.50–$19.50). AE, DC, MC, V. Daily 11:30am–11pm (last order). MTR: Wan Chai. PEKINGESE.

Despite its name, the American Restaurant serves hearty Pekingese food and has been doing so since it opened right after World War II. Recently renovated and often filled with noisy, celebratory patrons, it has an English menu listing almost 200 dishes (the small-size dishes are good for two or three persons), but the perennial specialties have always been barbecued Peking duck, beggar's chicken (which must be ordered a day in advance), sizzling prawns, and the sizzling beef hot plate. Of these, Peking duck, costing HK$275 ($35.70) remains the favorite and should be shared by two or more people.

**Bo Kong.** Times Square (12th floor), 1 Matheson St., Causeway Bay. ☎ **852/2506 3377.** Main dishes HK$58–$98 ($7.55–$12.75); fixed-price lunch HK$38 ($4.95). AE, MC, V. Daily 11am–10pm. MTR: Causeway Bay. VEGETARIAN.

A bit too bright for comfort but soothingly decorated, this pleasant restaurant, located in the Food Forum of Times Square with a dozen other restaurants and with branches in Canada, offers Chinese vegetarian fare that is so cleverly prepared, you'd swear it contained meat. There are braised vegetarian "shark's fin," vegetarian sashimi, an appetizer plate of "cold cuts" that looks like meat but isn't, sizzling vegetarian steak with a black bean sauce, vegetarian shish kebab, and vegetarian ham rolled with bean curd skin. There are also noodle, rice, and congee dishes. Neither smoking or the consumption of alcohol is allowed.

**Chili Club.** 88 Lockhart Rd., Wan Chai. ☎ **852/2527 2872.** Main dishes HK$50–HK$130 ($6.50–$16.90). AE, MC, V. Daily noon–3pm, 6–10:30pm. MTR: Wan Chai. THAI.

This simple upstairs restaurant wastes no money on decor. In fact, the only hint that you're in Asia comes from the rattan chairs, and the service is indifferent at best. But the seafood, curries, and noodles, which include all the Thai favorites, are as spicy as this national cuisine's should be. What's more, the price is right, making this one of Hong Kong's best dining values. Try to get a seat near the window where you can watch the action on the street below and, if possible, avoid the lunchtime rush.

**Coyote Bar & Grill.** 114–120 Lockhart Rd., Wan Chai. ☎ **852/2861 2221.** Main courses HK$111–HK$121 ($14.40–$15.70). AE, MC, V. Daily noon–2am. MTR: Wan Chai. MEXICAN.

"Mexican with attitude" is how this bar/restaurant describes its food and ambience. As popular for its drinks—sangria, Mexican beers, and more than 30 different kinds of margaritas—as for its food, it offers everything from tacos and burritos to fajitas. A facade that opens to the street beckons you to this party place, which can get quite packed on weekend nights.

✪ **Open Kitchen.** Hong Kong Arts Centre (6th floor), 2 Harbour Rd., Wan Chai. ☎ **852/ 2827 2923.** Main courses HK$68–HK$88 ($8.85–$11.45). AE, MC, V. Daily 11am–11pm. MTR: Wan Chai. INTERNATIONAL.

This self-serve cafeteria, bright with natural lighting, gets my vote as the best place in Wan Chai for an inexpensive and quick meal. Not only does it offer a good selection of food at very reasonable prices, but it also boasts a view of the harbor and even has a tiny outdoor terrace. True to its name, chefs working in an open kitchen prepare everything from lamb chops, grilled steak, and tandoori chicken to grilled Cajun salmon and spring chicken. Diners can also choose from four or five kinds of pasta, along with a choice of sauce. Lighter fare includes a salad bar, soups, sandwiches, sushi, quiche, and desserts. You can also come just for a drink, but the minimum charge per person is HK$20 ($2.60).

## 5 Around Hong Kong Island

### VICTORIA PEAK

✪ **Cafe Deco.** Peak Galleria, Victoria Peak. ☎ **852/2849 5111.** Reservations required (request window seat with view). Pizzas and pastas HK$94–HK$133 ($12.20–$17.25); main courses HK$94–HK$227 ($12.20–$29.50); fixed-price lunch, Mon–Fri only, HK$168 ($21.80). AE, DC, MC, V. Daily 10am–11pm (last order). Peak tram. INTERNATIONAL.

No expense was spared, it seems, in designing this chic, airy restaurant with its wood inlaid floor, authentic art deco trimmings (many imported from the U.S. and Europe), and open kitchen serving cuisines of China, Japan, Thailand, India, Italy, and Mexico. Ever since it opened in 1994, a nattily dressed crowd has been clamoring to get in. In the evening (except Sunday), diners are treated to live jazz. All this is secondary, however, to the restaurant's real attraction—the best view in town of Hong Kong. That alone is enough reason for dining here, though some of the view has been stolen with the completion of the Peak Tower's viewing platform. To assure a ringside window seat, be sure to make reservations for the second floor at least 2 weeks in advance, emphasizing that you don't want your view obstructed by the Peak Tower. The food, designed to appeal to visitors from around the world, is as trendy as the restaurant, with an eclectic mix of international dishes and ingredients, including tandoori kebabs and dishes, Asian noodles, grilled steaks and chops, oysters, pizzas, create-your-own pastas, soups, sandwiches, salads, ice creams, and desserts. Some of the entrees fall short of expectations; the pizzas, however, are great and may be the best items on the menu. The salads are generous enough for two to share.

**Marché Mövenpick.** Peak Tower (levels 6 and 7), 128 Peak Rd., Victoria Peak. ☎ **852/2849 2000.** Main courses HK$62–HK$75 ($8.05–$9.75); fixed-price lunch Mon–Fri HK$78 ($10.15); dinner buffet Mon–Thurs HK$278 ($36.10), Fri–Sun HK$298 ($38.70). AE, DC, MC, V. Daily 11am–11pm. Peak tram. INTERNATIONAL.

This Swiss chain has been very successful in Europe with its "marketplace" concept in self-service dining, and with the international crowds that visit the Peak, my guess is that it will do quite well here, too. For one thing, it's located in the newly completed Peak Tower and offers great views over Hong Kong. In addition, its food is reasonably priced and varied enough to please even fickle palates, the staff is efficient and friendly, and there's even a children's corner, with a small slide, toys, crayons, and other diversions, making it a good place for families. Upon entering, you'll be given a card, which is stamped each time you add a dish to your tray. There are various counters offering different foods, including salads, pizza, pasta, vegetables, sushi, Chinese dishes, and entrees ranging from grilled pork chops and roasted spring chicken to king prawns and sole. You can take as much or as little as you wish—if you're coming for drinks, try to hit the daily 4 to 7pm happy hour, with two beers or glasses of wine for the price of one. Otherwise, good dining deals are the three-course fixed-price lunches available weekdays only and the dinner buffets. From 9:30pm, there are also late-night buffets costing HK$108 ($14) Sunday to Thursday and HK$168 ($21.80) Friday and Saturday. The two-floor restaurant is divided into various themed rooms representing a different country; some views are better than others.

✪ **Peak Cafe.** 121 Peak Rd., Victoria Peak. ☎ **852/2849 7868.** Reservations required for dinner and weekends. Main courses HK$102–HK$255 ($13.25–$33.10); fixed-price lunch HK$138–HK$168 ($17.90–$21.80). AE, DC, MC, V. Mon–Fri 10:30am–11:30pm; Sat–Sun 8am–11:30pm. Peak tram. INTERNATIONAL.

Although it's on the Peak, located across the street from the Peak tram terminus, there are only limited views of the South China Sea from the Peak Cafe's terrace. And yet, it has long been a Hong Kong favorite; everyone seems to love it. A former tram station, it's a delightful place for a meal, with exposed granite walls, tall timber-trussed ceiling, open fireplace, wooden floor, Chinese antiques, and a greenhouselike room that extends into the garden. You can also sit outdoors amid the lush growth where you can actually hear birds singing—one of the best outdoor dining opportunities in Hong Kong (be sure to request a table outdoors if that's what you want). A jazz trio entertains Thursday evenings. The menu is eclectic, offering soups, sandwiches, and a combination of American, Chinese, Indian, Southeast Asian, and vegetarian dishes, including tandoori chicken tikka, Thai noodles, vegetable lasagne, grilled steaks and salmon, and curries like tiger prawns in green curry with coconut milk, white eggplant, seedless grapes, sweet basil, and rice.

## STANLEY

✪ **Stanley's French Restaurant.** Oriental Building (1st & 2nd floor), 90B Stanley Main St., Stanley. ☎ **852/2813 8873.** Reservations required. Main courses HK$165–HK$235 ($22.45–$30.50); fixed-price lunch HK$85–$155 ($11.05–$20.15). AE, DC, MC, V. Daily noon–3pm and 6:30–10:30pm. Bus: no. 6, 6A, 6X, or 260. FRENCH.

Whatever you save by bargain-shopping at Stanley Market may well go toward a meal at Stanley's Restaurant, and I can't think of a better place to spend it. This is an absolutely charming spot, refined, cozy, and romantic. There are two floors of dining, both with ceiling fans, wooden floors, and open windows facing the sea, making a dreamy, relaxed setting. Although the menu changes often, for starters you might try a Caesar salad, considered a house specialty, or the lobster and spinach bisque with sherry. Examples of what's been offered in the past include soya-flavored filet of black cod, roast quail with goose liver and chestnut filling, prime beef sirloin with Cajun spices on gratinéed spinach and crisp potatoes, and rack of lamb Provençal. There are also daily specials, written on a blackboard that will be brought to your table.

**Stanley's Oriental Restaurant.** Oriental Building (4th floor), 90B Stanley Main St., Stanley. ☎ **852/2813 9988.** Reservations required. Main dishes HK$68–HK$120 ($8.85–$15.60). AE, DC, MC, V. Daily noon–2:30pm, 6:30–10pm. Bus: no. 6, 6A, 6X, or 260. THAI/INDIAN.

Just around the corner from Stanley Market and facing the sea is this attractive place, decorated in breezy colonial style, with an open-fronted veranda cooled by ceiling fans. Dining here is relaxed and fun, almost like you're on some South Sea island rather than Hong Kong. Its menu lists various Thai curries and other dishes, including Thai chicken curry and fried prawns in chili sauce, as well as Indian curries and tandooris. All in all, a civilized and relaxing place to unwind after a hectic day of shopping.

**Tables 88.** 88 Stanley Village Rd., Stanley. ☎ **852/2813 6262.** Reservations required on weekends. Main courses HK$168–HK$228 ($21.80–$29.60); fixed-price lunch HK$88–HK$148 ($11.45–$19.20); fixed-price dinner HK$310–HK$370 ($40.30–$48.10). AE, DC, MC, V. Daily 11:30am–4pm, 6:30–10:30pm. Bus: no. 6, 6A, 6X, or 260. FRENCH CROSSOVER.

This restaurant, together with Cafe Deco on the Peak, was the hottest place in town when it opened in 1994. Now, of course, there are newer places that have garnered the spotlight in this scene-crazed town. Still, any competitor would have to be pretty outlandish to topple Tables 88's ranking as the most weirdly decorated restaurant in Hong Kong. From the outside, Tables 88 looks positively historic—a rather quaint-looking, century-old former police station. Inside, however, it's a different world—the decorating style might be called funky aboriginal, urban native, or upscale primitive. The management prefers to call it "rustic and raw." In any case, because the structure itself is historic, none of the walls could be knocked down (thank goodness), but that seems to have been the only restriction in decorating the warren of tiny rooms on two levels. Wooden floors, stone walls, exposed wooden beams, a tin roof, soft sofas, African wall prints, and modern artwork seem all the more mysterious by dim candlelight. You'll either love it or hate it. The menu has changed from the very expensive continental cuisine it sported in its first, heady year to more reasonably priced French food with an Asian twist. It includes Cornish game hen and chili prawns with asparagus and potatoes; filet mignon with lobster and mixed vegetables; tiger prawns wrapped in cabbage and served with ginger mayonnaise and new potatoes; and roast rack of lamb with honey mustard crust and Niçoise garnish. For lunch, you can dine for less than HK$100 ($13) on sandwiches, pastas, pizzas, and Asian dishes.

# ABERDEEN

**Jumbo Floating Restaurant.** Aberdeen Harbour, Hong Kong Island. ☎ **852/2553 9111.** Main dishes HK$80–HK$400 ($10.40–$52); dim sum HK$20–HK$30 ($2.60–$3.90). Table charge HK$8 ($1.05) per person. AE, DC, MC, V. Mon–Sat 11am–11pm; Sun 8am–11pm. Bus: no. 7 or 70 from Central to Aberdeen, then the restaurant's private boat. CANTONESE/ DIM SUM.

No doubt you've heard about Hong Kong's floating restaurants in Aberdeen. Although often included in Hong Kong's organized nighttime tours, they're no longer touted by the tourist office as something every visitor must see—there are simply too many other restaurants that are more authentic, are more affordable, and have better food. However, if you've always wanted to eat in a floating restaurant, the Jumbo Floating Restaurant is your best bet and claims to be the largest floating restaurant in the world. Simply take the bus to Aberdeen and then board one of the restaurant's own free shuttle boats, with departures every few minutes. In the evenings, the restaurant even offers free 20-minute sampan rides through the Aberdeen typhoon shelter on a first-come, first-serve basis. As for the restaurant, it has more reds, golds, and dragon motifs than you've ever seen in one place. The best views are from the large roof patio, designed like a traditional Chinese garden with a pagoda and pavilions. Be sure to stop by the "Seafood Exhibition" on the lower deck, where you'll see tanks of live creatures swimming about. Many diners like to make their seafood selections here. Dishes include everything from noodles and rice combinations to fresh lobster, scallops, garoupa balls, and fresh seafood (prawns are a particular favorite). Dim sum is served from trolleys until 4pm—certainly the least expensive way to enjoy the floating restaurant experience. For splurges, there are fixed-price meals for two persons costing HK$590 ($76.70).

# WESTERN DISTRICT

**Sammy's Kitchen.** 204–206 Queen's Rd. W., Sheung Wan. ☎ **852/2548 8400.** Main courses HK$35–HK$145 ($4.55–$18.85). AE, DC, MC, V. Daily 11:30am–11:30pm. MTR: Sheung Wan. CONTINENTAL.

There's no better place for Western food in the Western District than Sammy's Kitchen, recognizable by the sign in the shape of a cow outside its door. A simple and unpretentious place, it offers reasonably priced meals, but best yet is the presence of owner/chef Sammy Yip. Sammy, who has been cooking professionally for almost 50 years (including stints at The Peninsula and Mandarin Oriental hotels), opened this restaurant on his own in 1970. Sammy speaks good English and is happy to see foreign visitors; his sons have joined him in the family business. There are actually two menus, based on two different concepts. One is cheaper and quicker, available all day and offering rather mediocre main courses like spring chicken, lamb chops, and noodle and fried rice dishes; they're priced from HK$35 to HK$95 ($4.55 to $12.35). There are also fixed-price lunches for HK$35 to HK$85 ($4.55 to $11.05). In the evening, another, more expensive menu is also available (with entrees ranging from HK$83 to HK$145/$10.80 to $18.85), cooked by Sammy himself and served in a separate, more formal dining room. This menu includes fresh seafood, steaks from the United States and New Zealand, and such specialties as veal with Parmesan and marsala, chicken with special pepper sauce flaming with cognac, filet mignon, beef Wellington, ostrich steak, and chateaubriand for two. If you opt for seafood, you may wish to try garoupa dipped in egg and flour and then wrapped in paper with onion, garlic, shallots, tomato, parsley, mushrooms, hollandaise, and lemon and baked in the oven.

**Treasure Inn Seafood Restaurant.** Western Market, 323 Des Voeux Rd. Central, Sheung Wan. ☎ **852/2850 7780.** Main dishes HK$75–HK$128 ($9.75–$16.65); dim sum HK$28 ($3.65). AE, DC, MC, V. Daily 10:30am–midnight. MTR: Sheung Wan. Tram: Western Market. CANTONESE.

The food here is typical Cantonese food, with an English menu full of photographs, so that you can see the baked prawns with scallions and garlic, the stuffed asparagus with shrimp, lobster with bean curd and chili sauce, or pan-fried stuffed crab claws before ordering them. There are also pictures of the various dim sum available, served until 5pm. But what makes this place special is its setting—on the upper level of the restored Western Market, an attractive 1906 brick building once serving as a public market and now home to specialty shops, souvenir stands, and retailers selling bolts of cloth. The restaurant itself is quite spacious, with two tiers of dining under a tall ceiling with exposed beams, Chinese lanterns, and traditional Chinese music, all reminiscent of a 1920s teahouse setting. With its English menu, this is a good choice if you're exploring the very Chinese Western District.

# 6 Dim Sum

Everyone should try a dim sum meal at least once, as much for the atmosphere as the food. It's eaten primarily for breakfast or lunch, or as an afternoon snack with tea. On weekends, restaurants offering dim sum (mostly Cantonese restaurants) are packed with local families. On weekdays, they're popular with shoppers and businesspeople. Prices are low and you order only as much as you want. Simply look over the steaming baskets being pushed around by trolley and choose what appeals to you. Fancier restaurants, particularly those in hotels, offer dim sum from an English menu rather than carts; they claim that since the food is cooked to order it is fresher, but the prices are also higher. In most restaurants that offer dim sum, one pays by the basket, and each basket usually contains two to four items of dim sum; the average price is about HK$20 to HK$30 ($2.60 to $3.90). The prices given below, unless otherwise specified, are per basket; expect to spend HK$60 to HK$100 ($7.80 to $13) per person for a light meal.

## KOWLOON

**The Chinese.** In the Hyatt Regency Hotel, 67 Nathan Rd., Tsim Sha Tsui. ☎ **852/2311 1234,** ext. 2881. Dim sum HK$28–HK$45 ($3.65–$5.85). AE, DC, MC, V. Daily 11:30am–2:45pm for dim sum. MTR: Tsim Sha Tsui. CANTONESE.

A refined, modern, and fancy setting for dim sum, with correspondingly high prices. There are no trolleys here, but there's a dim sum menu.

**City Chiuchow Restaurant.** East Ocean Centre, 98 Granville Rd., Tsim Sha Tsui East. ☎ **852/2723 6226.** Dim sum HK$16–HK$25 ($2.10–$3.25). AE, DC, MC, V. Daily 11am–3pm for dim sum. MTR: Tsim Sha Tsui. CHIU CHOW.

Although it's a Chiu Chow restaurant, this place serves its own dim sum, which is not too surprising if you consider that Chiu Chow food has been greatly influenced by Cantonese food.

**Fook Lam Moon.** 53–59 Kimberley Rd., Tsim Sha Tsui. ☎ **852/2366 0286.** Dim sum HK$24–HK$50 ($3.10–$6.50). AE, DC, MC, V. Daily 11:30am–2:30pm. MTR: Tsim Sha Tsui. CANTONESE.

Another Hong Kong old-timer, with an atmosphere that is reminiscent of an earlier era. There aren't any trolleys here, however—just a Chinese menu. Ask an English-speaking waiter for translations.

**Golden Unicorn.** In the Hongkong Hotel, 3 Canton Rd., Tsim Sha Tsui. ☎ **852/2730 6565.** Dim sum HK$28 ($3.65). AE, DC, MC, V. Daily noon–2:30pm for dim sum. MTR: Tsim Sha Tsui. CANTONESE.

Twenty choices of dim sum are offered from a menu in this formal dining hall, complete with Wedgwood china and Christofle silverware.

**Jade Garden Chinese Restaurant.** Star House (4th floor), 3 Salisbury Rd., Tsim Sha Tsui. ☎ **852/2730 6888.** Dim sum HK$16–HK$38 ($2.10–$4.95). AE, DC, MC, V. Mon–Sat 10am–3pm, Sun and holidays 8am–3pm, for dim sum. MTR: Tsim Sha Tsui. CANTONESE.

An easy place for the uninitiated, this Cantonese chain is tourist-friendly and conveniently situated across from the Star Ferry terminus. It offers views of Victoria Harbour and trolleys of dim sum. There's another branch at 25–31 Carnarvon Rd. (☎ 852/2369 8311), serving dim sum daily 7:30am to 5pm, and another branch across the harbor in shop 5 of the Jardine House, 1 Connaught Place, Central (☎ 852/2524 5098), serving dim sum Monday to Saturday 11am to 3pm and Sunday and holidays 10am to 5pm.

**Lai Ching Heen.** In the Regent Hotel, Salisbury Rd., Tsim Sha Tsui. ☎ **852/2721 1211,** ext. 2243. Dim sum HK$26–HK$36 ($33.40nd]$4.70). AE, DC, MC, V. Daily noon–2:30pm for dim sum. MTR: Tsim Sha Tsui. CANTONESE.

One of Hong Kong's top Cantonese eateries, this elegant restaurant with large windows treats diners to views of the harbor. A daily changing menu offers about 30 varieties of dim sum.

**Shang Palace.** In the Shangri-La Hotel, 64 Mody Rd., Tsim Sha Tsui East. ☎ **852/2733 8754.** Dim sum HK$24–HK$38 ($3.10–$4.95). AE, CB, DC, MC, V. Mon–Sat noon–3pm, Sun and holidays 10am–3pm, for dim sum. MTR: Tsim Sha Tsui. CANTONESE.

One of Kowloon's most elaborate Chinese restaurants comes complete with red-lacquered walls and Chinese lanterns hanging from the ceiling. Because it provides a menu in English, this is a great place to try dim sum for the first time, not to mention the fact that its dim sum is among the best in town—a bit more expensive, but worth it. Choose your dim sum from the menu, which changes every 2 weeks and always includes more than a dozen varieties.

**Spring Moon.** In the Peninsula Hotel, Salisbury Rd., Tsim Sha Tsui. ☎ **852/2920 2888.** Dim sum HK$35–HK$52 ($4.55–$6.75). AE, DC, MC, V. Daily 11:30am–2:30pm for dim sum. MTR: Tsim Sha Tsui. CANTONESE.

As you'd expect from a restaurant in the venerable Peninsula Hotel, this is a very refined and civilized place for the humble dim sum, with an English menu that lists more than a dozen dim sum and more than two dozen varieties of Chinese teas. It's decorated in an art deco style reminiscent of how the restaurant would have looked in 1928, the year the Peninsula opened, with cuisine that changes with the season.

**Super Star Seafood Restaurant.** 83–97 Nathan Rd., Tsim Sha Tsui. ☎ **852/2366 0878.** Dim sum HK$19–HK$23 ($2.45–$3). AE, DC, MC, V. Daily 7am–5pm for dim sum. MTR: Tsim Sha Tsui. CANTONESE.

This lively and popular seafood restaurant is one of Tsim Sha Tsui's best places for trying authentic dim sum in a typical Chinese setting. There's no English menu, so you'll just have to look at the offerings of the various trolleys.

**Tsui Hang Village Restaurant.** Miramar Plaza, 1 Kimberley Rd., Tsim Sha Tsui. ☎ **852/ 2368 6363.** Dim sum HK$18–HK$38 ($2.35–$4.95). AE, MC, V. Mon–Sat 11:30am–5:30pm, Sun and holidays 10am–5:30pm, for dim sum. MTR: Tsim Sha Tsui. CANTONESE.

Tsui Hang Village, a modern restaurant located in a shopping complex across from the Miramar Hotel, offers inexpensive plates of dim sum. There's a branch across the harbor on the second floor of the New World Tower, 16–18 Queen's Rd., Central (☎ 852/2524 2012), serving dim sum Saturdays 11am to 5:30pm and Sundays and holidays 10am to 5:30pm.

## CENTRAL

**City Hall Chinese Restaurant.** City Hall (2nd floor), Low Block (the one closest to the harbor), Connaught Rd., Central. ☎ 852/2521 1303. Dim sum HK$17–HK$38 ($2.20–$4.95). AE, V. Mon–Sat 10am–3pm, Sun and holidays 8am–3pm for dim sum. MTR: Central. CANTONESE.

A popular place, City Hall Chinese Restaurant is often crowded, filled with shoppers and office workers. There's an English dim sum menu, trolleys deliver various steamed baskets of dim sum, and there are even views of the harbor.

**Luk Yu Tea House.** 24–26 Stanley St., Central. ☎ 852/2523 5464. Dim sum HK$25–HK$55 ($3.25–$7.15). No credit cards. Daily 7am–5:30pm for dim sum. MTR: Central. CANTONESE.

The most authentic dim sum teahouse in Hong Kong is often so packed with regulars that mere tourists can't get a seat. Furthermore, trolleys with dim sum are pushed through the place only until 11am, after which there's only a Chinese menu. Try to bring along a Chinese friend to help you with your selections.

**Shanghai Garden.** Hutchinson House (1st floor), Murray Rd., Central. ☎ 852/2524 8181. Dim sum HK$18–HK$48 ($2.35–$6.25). AE, CB, DC, MC, V. Daily 11:30am–3pm. MTR: Central. SHANGHAINESE.

Located next to the Furama Hotel and popular with area office workers for lunch, this pleasant restaurant offers dim sum from its lunchtime menu.

**The Square.** Exchange Square II, Central. ☎ 852/2525 1163. Dim sum HK$24–HK$58 ($3.10–$7.55). AE, DC, MC, V. Daily noon–2pm. MTR: Central. CANTONESE.

This smartly decorated restaurant, next to Hong Kong Station, offers dim sum for lunch, as well as views of the Star Ferry as it comes and goes from the Central pier.

**Yung Kee.** 32–40 Wellington St., Central. ☎ 852/2522 1624. Dim sum HK$12–HK$24 ($1.55–$3.10). AE, DC, MC, V. Mon–Sat 2–5pm, Sun and holidays 11am–5pm, for dim sum. MTR: Central. CANTONESE.

Famous for its roast goose, Yung Kee also offers dim sum weekday afternoons and throughout most of the day on Sunday, with an English dim sum menu.

**Zen Chinese.** The Mall, Pacific Place, 88 Queensway, Central. ☎ 852/2845 4555. Dim sum HK$28–HK$32 ($3.65–$4.15). AE, DC, MC, V. Mon–Fri 11:30am–3pm, Sat 11:30am–4:30pm, Sun 10:30am–4:30pm, for dim sum. MTR: Admiralty. CANTONESE.

Starkly modern and hip, this Cantonese restaurant offers dim sum daily, with more varieties available on the weekend.

## CAUSEWAY BAY/WAN CHAI

**Fook Lam Moon.** 35–45 Johnston Rd., Wan Chai. ☎ 852/2866 0663. Dim sum HK$24–HK$50 ($3.10–$6.50). AE, DC, MC, V. Daily 11:30am–3pm. MTR: Wan Chai. CANTONESE.

This well-known, expensive Cantonese restaurant offers dim sum from a Chinese menu only (no trolleys). Ask an English-speaking waiter for translations.

## 7 Afternoon Tea

**Clipper Lounge.** In the Mandarin Oriental Hotel, 5 Connaught Rd., Central. ☎ **852/2522 0111.** Fixed-price afternoon tea HK$145 ($18.85) for 1 person, HK$280 ($36.35) for 2. AE, DC, MC, V. Daily 3–6pm. MTR: Central. TEAS/CAKES.

If you're in Central in the afternoon, stop by the brass-and-teak-decorated Clipper Lounge for one of England's finest traditions—afternoon tea. Besides 11 varieties of tea (or, if you must, coffee), you'll have a choice of English tea sandwiches, "savoury puffs," homemade scones with Devonshire clotted cream and jam, brownies, fruit tartlets, Windsor cakes, and other goodies to sample. À la carte items are also available, but if there are two of you, you're better off getting the tea-for-two special. At any rate, you'll probably want to skip lunch or dinner if you indulge here.

**Peninsula Hotel Lobby.** In The Peninsula Hotel, Salisbury Rd., Tsim Sha Tsui. ☎ **852/2920 2888.** Fixed-price afternoon tea HK$155 ($20.15). AE, DC, MC, V. Daily 2–6:50pm. MTR: Tsim Sha Tsui. TEAS/CAKES.

The ornate lobby of The Peninsula Hotel, built in 1928, is the most famous lobby in Hong Kong. A popular place to see and be seen, the lobby features soaring columns topped with elaborate gilded ceilings and sculpted figures of gods and angels, palm trees, a Tai Ping carpet, and classically styled furniture. As late as the 1950s, the lobby was divided into east and west wings—one for the British and one for everyone else, including, as one pamphlet put it, women "seeking dalliance." The fixed-price tea includes finger sandwiches, French pastries, and scones with clotted cream. No reservations are accepted, so you may have to wait for a table. A classical string quartet serenades you from an upstairs balcony.

**Tiffin.** In the Grand Hyatt Hong Kong, 1 Harbour Rd., Wan Chai. ☎ **852/2588 1234,** ext. 7223. Fixed-price afternoon tea HK$99 ($12.85). AE, DC, MC, V. Daily 3:15–6pm. MTR: Wan Chai. TEA/CAKES.

The Grand Hyatt's lounge harkens back to the days of the British Empire, when high tea was known as a tiffin—a light meal to satisfy one's appetite. Here you can nibble on finger sandwiches, crepes Suzette, and desserts, and drink coffee or tea from bone chinaware while listening to live music and enjoying views of the harbor.

# Exploring Hong Kong 6

**M**ost people think of Hong Kong primarily as an exotic shopping destination. In the past decade, however, Hong Kong has revved up its sightseeing potential, opening new city parks and revamping older ones, constructing community art centers, expanding museums or developing new ones, and redesigning organized sightseeing tours to reflect the territory's changing demographics. Although a few attractions have closed since the handover, new ones are in the works. In 2005, Hong Kong will even get its own Disneyland. On the other hand, if all you want to do is hike or lie on the beach, you can do that, too.

To help you get the most out of your stay, this chapter will suggest sightseeing strategies; introduce you to top sights like Victoria Peak, museums, parks, and other attractions; and discuss organized tours, sports, and places of interest to children.

According to the Hong Kong Tourist Association, North Americans spend an average of 3.3 nights in Hong Kong. Although a week's stay would be better if you really want to do Hong Kong justice, you can see quite a bit of the city and its outlying islands in 3 to 5 days, especially if you're on the go from dawn until past dusk. One of the things that makes sightseeing easy is that Hong Kong is compact. In addition, transportation is efficient. To help you get the most out of your stay, the following suggested itineraries will guide you to the most important attractions.

## Suggested Itineraries

### If You Have 1 Day

If you have only 1 day to spend here, I feel sorry for you. I think I'd have a coronary racing around in a panic trying to see everything, growing more anxious by the minute as I realized that there were so many more things I wouldn't have time for. Start the morning with a breakfast of dim sum in a lively Chinese restaurant. For one-stop shopping, try one of the large stores specializing in Chinese products such as Chinese Arts and Crafts—you'll find one in Star House, right next to the Star Ferry in Tsim Sha Tsui (see chapter 8). Also in Tsim Sha Tsui, just a couple of minutes' walk from the ferry, is the Hong Kong Museum of Art, with its vast collection of Chinese antiquities and art. If you visit only one museum in Hong Kong, this should be it.

Afterward, take the famous Star Ferry across Victoria Harbour to the Central District. There, near the ferry pier, board the shuttle bus that will take you to the tram bound for Victoria Peak. Plan on spending at least an hour or more on the Peak, where you have fantastic views of Hong Kong if the weather is clear; if you have time, walk the 1-hour circular stroll around the Peak (see "Hong Kong's Top Attractions," below). If you still have time afterwards or the Peak is shrouded in clouds, board the double-decker tram in Central for a unique view of north Hong Kong Island or follow one of my walking tours for Central or the Western District (see chapter 7).

In the evening, visit the Temple Street Night Market with its festive atmosphere and outdoor stalls selling clothing and accessories, as well as its palm readers, fortune-tellers, and street opera singers (see chapter 9).

### If You Have 2 Days

After a dim sum breakfast and a ride on the famous Star Ferry, head straight to Victoria Peak for Hong Kong's best views, an hour's stroll around the Peak, or a visit to its several attractions. Next, head to Stanley Market on the south end of the island, with its many shops and stalls selling clothing and souvenirs. For dinner, consider going to Aberdeen with its famous floating restaurant. If you prefer to join an organized tour, you can join a sunset cruise that includes a meal at the Aberdeen floating restaurant. Tours can be booked through most tourist hotels in Hong Kong (for more information on evening tours, see chapter 9, "Hong Kong After Dark").

On your second day, board a ferry for one of the outlying islands. Cheung Chau is charming with its unhurried, small-village atmosphere; Lantau is famous for its giant outdoor Buddha and monastery. By mid-afternoon, try to be at the Hong Kong Museum of Art in Tsim Sha Tsui, Hong Kong's most important museum. Begin the evening with a cocktail at one of Hong Kong's many lounges that offer a view of the harbor, followed by dinner at a Chinese or Western restaurant. Afterward, visit Temple Street Night Market.

### If You Have 3 Days

Start your first day with a dim sum breakfast at a Chinese restaurant. Then, for your first breathtaking view of Hong Kong, ride the famous Star Ferry across Victoria Harbour. Afterward, for an even better perspective, take the tram to the top of Victoria Peak, where you'll be rewarded with a spectacular view of the city—that is, if the weather is clear. Take an hour's walk along the circular path around Victoria Peak, where you'll have changing vistas of Central, Kowloon, Aberdeen, and even Cheung Chau and other islands. If you have children, consider a visit to Ripley's Believe It or Not! Odditorium or the Peak Explorer, a motion-simulator theater with seats that move in accompaniment to the action on the screen.

Have lunch on the Peak or at one of Central's many restaurants or English-style pubs. In the afternoon, follow my do-it-yourself walking tour of the Western District, where you can observe traditional Chinese life firsthand, shop for antiques, and visit the Man Mo Temple (see chapter 7, "Hong Kong Strolls"). For your first evening, try one of Hong Kong's organized evening tours, such as a sunset cruise to Aberdeen.

On your second day, head to Stanley Market on south Hong Kong Island, where you can spend several hours shopping for clothing and souvenirs. After lunch in Stanley, head back to Tsim Sha Tsui for the Hong Kong Museum of Art with its great collection of Chinese antiquities and art. Explore the many shops along and around Nathan Road. If time permits, visit the newly opened Hong Kong Museum of History in Tsim Sha Tsui East, with its vivid representations of daily Chinese life through the ages. In early evening, head for a cocktail lounge that offers a view of the harbor,

# AT&T Direct® Service

## AT&T Access Numbers

| | | | |
|---|---|---|---|
| Aruba | 800-8000 | Czech Rep. ▲ | 00-42-000-101 |
| Australia● | 1-800-551-155 | Egypt●(Cairo)† | 510-0200 |
| Austria● | 0800-200-288 | France | 0-800-99-0011 |
| Bahamas | 1-800-872-2881 | Germany | 0800-2255-288 |
| Barbados+ | 1-800-872-2881 | Greece● | 00-800-1311 |
| Belgium● | 0-800-100-10 | Guam | 1-800-2255-288 |
| Bermuda+ | 1-800-872-2881 | Hong Kong | 800-96-1111 |
| Cayman Isl.+ | 1-800-872-2881 | Hungary | 06-800-01111 |
| China, PRC▲ | 10811 | India ✱.➤ | 000-117 |
| Costa Rica | 0-800-0-114-114 | Ireland ✓ | 1-800-550-000 |

# AT&T Direct® Service

## AT&T Access Numbers

| | | | |
|---|---|---|---|
| Aruba | 800-8000 | Czech Rep. ▲ | 00-42-000-101 |
| Australia● | 1-800-551-155 | Egypt●(Cairo)† | 510-0200 |
| Austria● | 0800-200-288 | France | 0-800-99-0011 |
| Bahamas | 1-800-872-2881 | Germany | 0800-2255-288 |
| Barbados+ | 1-800-872-2881 | Greece● | 00-800-1311 |
| Belgium● | 0-800-100-10 | Guam | 1-800-2255-288 |
| Bermuda+ | 1-800-872-2881 | Hong Kong | 800-96-1111 |
| Cayman Isl.+ | 1-800-872-2881 | Hungary | 06-800-01111 |
| China, PRC▲ | 10811 | India ✱.➤ | 000-117 |
| Costa Rica | 0-800-0-114-114 | Ireland ✓ | 1-800-550-000 |

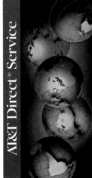

## FOR EASY CALLING WORLDWIDE

| | | | |
|---|---|---|---|
| Israel ● | 1-800-94-94-949 | Philippines ● | 105-11 |
| Italy ● | 172-1011 | Portugal ▲ | 0800-800-128 |
| Jamaica ● | 1-800-872-2881 | Singapore | 800-0111-111 |
| Japan ▲ ● | 005-39-111 | Spain | 900-99-00-11 |
| Malaysia ● | 1800-80-0011 | Switzerland ● | 0-800-89-0011 |
| Mexico ● ◇ ▽ | 01-800-288-2872 | Thailand ( | 001-999-111-11 |
| Neth. Ant. ● | 001-800-872-2881 | Turkey ● | 00-800-12277 |
| Netherlands ● | 0800-022-9111 | U.K. | 0800-89-0011 |
| New Zealand ● | 000-911 | U.K. | 0800-013-0011 |
| Panama | 800-001-0109 | Venezuela ● | 800-11-120 |

1. Just dial the AT&T Access Number for the country you are calling from.
2. Dial the phone number you're calling.   3. Dial your card number.

For access numbers not listed ask any operator for **AT&T Direct®** Service.
In the U.S. call 1-800-331-1140 for a wallet guide listing all worldwide AT&T Access Numbers.

Visit our **Web site** at: www.att.com/traveler
Bold-faced countries permit country-to-country calling outside the U.S.

● Public phones may require coin or card deposit to place call.
✦ Outside of Cairo, dial "02" first.
✚ May not be available from every phone/payphone.
✦ Public phones and select hotels.
◇ Use U.K. access number in N. Ireland.
✓ When calling from public phones, use phones marked "Lenso."
✗ Not available from public phones.
▽ Available from phones with international calling capabilities only
   from most Public Calling Centers.
○ From St. Maarten or phones at Bobby's Marina, use 1-800-872-2881.

When placing an international call *from* the U.S., dial 1 800 CALL ATT.

© 1/2000

## FOR EASY CALLING WORLDWIDE

| | | | |
|---|---|---|---|
| Israel ● | 1-800-94-94-949 | Philippines ● | 105-11 |
| Italy ● | 172-1011 | Portugal ▲ | 0800-800-128 |
| Jamaica ● | 1-800-872-2881 | Singapore | 800-0111-111 |
| Japan ▲ ● | 005-39-111 | Spain | 900-99-00-11 |
| Malaysia ● | 1800-80-0011 | Switzerland ● | 0-800-89-0011 |
| Mexico ● ◇ ▽ | 01-800-288-2872 | Thailand ( | 001-999-111-11 |
| Neth. Ant. ● | 001-800-872-2881 | Turkey ● | 00-800-12277 |
| Netherlands ● | 0800-022-9111 | U.K. | 0800-89-0011 |
| New Zealand ● | 000-911 | U.K. | 0800-013-0011 |
| Panama | 800-001-0109 | Venezuela ● | 800-11-120 |

1. Just dial the AT&T Access Number for the country you are calling from.
2. Dial the phone number you're calling.   3. Dial your card number.

For access numbers not listed ask any operator for **AT&T Direct®** Service.
In the U.S. call 1-800-331-1140 for a wallet guide listing all worldwide AT&T Access Numbers.

Visit our **Web site** at: www.att.com/traveler
Bold-faced countries permit country-to-country calling outside the U.S.

● Public phones may require coin or card deposit to place call.
✦ Outside of Cairo, dial "02" first.
✚ May not be available from every phone/payphone.
✦ Public phones and select hotels.
◇ Use U.K. access number in N. Ireland.
✓ When calling from public phones, use phones marked "Lenso."
✗ Not available from public phones.
▽ Available from phones with international calling capabilities only
   from most Public Calling Centers.
○ From St. Maarten or phones at Bobby's Marina, use 1-800-872-2881.

When placing an international call *from* the U.S., dial 1 800 CALL ATT.

© 1/2000

TIMBUKTU          KALAMAZOO

AT&T Direct® Service

The easy way to call home from anywhere.

Global
connection
with the AT&T
Network

**AT&T**
direct
service

For the easy way to call home, take the attached wallet guide.

# Make Learning Fun & Easy

## With IDG Books Worldwide

Frommer's®

FOR DUMMIES®

WEBSTER'S NEW WORLD™

Betty Crocker's®

the Unofficial Guide®

CliffsNotes™
www.cliffsnotes.com

BURPEE®

ARCO®

GUIDE TO
A HAPPY HEALTHY PET™

HOWELL BOOK HOUSE™

W E I G H T  W A T C H E R S®

## Available at your local bookstores

followed by dinner and then entertainment in a pub or disco, perhaps in the Lan Kwai Fong nightlife district.

For your last morning in Hong Kong, get up early and head for one of the outlying islands. Cheung Chau, with its small village, beach, and boat population, is good for a short excursion. Lamma is recommended if you want to do some hiking, swimming at a beach, or dining on seafood at a waterfront open-air restaurant. Lantau is a popular destination for its giant outdoor Buddha and adjoining monastery offering vegetarian lunches. (See chapter 10 for descriptions of the outlying islands.) Spend the afternoon following your own inclinations: a tram ride to Causeway Bay for more shopping; another museum; a walking tour of Central; Ocean Park with its aquarium, amusement rides, and Middle Kingdom; or an organized tour of the New Territories. After dinner at a traditional Chinese restaurant, take a stroll through Temple Street Night Market in Kowloon.

### If You Have 5 Days or More

Consider yourself lucky! Spend the first 3 days as outlined above. Note, however, that if you're having an article of clothing custom-made, you should visit the tailor on your first day to discuss needs and fittings. On the fourth day, take a trip to the New Territories (see chapter 10 for more information). Alternatively, consider taking one of the excellent tours offered by the Hong Kong Tourist Association or a private tour company. The 6-hour "Land Between" Tour of the New Territories allows you to see much more than you could possibly see on your own, while the Heritage Tour takes you to several far-flung Chinese historic buildings and homes, a must for architectural buffs. Other tours explore such local customs as the ancient Chinese principles for living in harmony with nature, *tai chi,* Chinese shadow boxing, and other traditions. If you're not too tired by evening, take the tram to Victoria Peak (if you haven't done so already) for a romantic, spectacular nighttime view of Hong Kong, ablaze with glittering lights. Alternatively, stroll the promenade along the Tsim Sha Tsui waterfront.

Devote the fifth day to all those things you haven't had time for—whether it's more shopping, sightseeing, or unstructured exploration. Visit another island, or, if you have children, make sure you visit Ocean Park with its performances by whales and dolphins, a shark aquarium, playground, and much more. If it's horse-racing season, try to get in on the action. If you've had something custom-made, don't forget to pick it up. For a memorable last evening in Hong Kong, splurge at one of Hong Kong's fine Chinese or Western restaurants with a view.

If you still have time to spare, I strongly urge you to cross the Pearl River Estuary by jetfoil to spend a day or two in the old Portuguese city of Macau, the first European settlement in the Far East (see chapter 11 on Macau). Not only is Macau cheaper than Hong Kong, but it is also very different, with its Mediterranean-influenced architecture in the old town, several great special-interest museums, fantastic Macanese cuisine, and more shopping opportunities. On December 20, 1999, Macau reverted back to Chinese rule, becoming a special administrative region similar to Hong Kong.

Or, if you wish, cross the border in the New Territories for a trip to China.

## 1 Hong Kong's Top Attractions

The four things I would recommend to every visitor to Hong Kong are: Ride the Star Ferry across the harbor; take the peak tram to the top of Victoria Peak; ride one of the rickety old trams on Hong Kong Island; and take a ferry to one of the outlying islands (see chapter 10, "Side Trips from Hong Kong," for information on the islands). Nothing can beat the thrill of these four experiences, nor give you a better insight into the essence of Hong Kong and its people. What's more, they're all incredibly inexpensive.

## THE STAR FERRIES

The stars of the Hong Kong show, of course, are the Star Ferries, green-and-white vessels that have been carrying passengers back and forth between Kowloon and Hong Kong Island since 1898. At only HK$1.70 (22¢) for the regular, lower-deck fare, it's one of the cheapest—and yet most dramatic—5-minute rides in the world. The entire trip from loading pier to unloading pier takes approximately 7 minutes in all; there are approximately 400 crossings a day. (For tips on using the Star Ferry, see "Getting Around" in chapter 3.)

Since a 5-minute ride isn't nearly enough time to soak up the ambience of Victoria Harbour, you may want to board a special Star Ferry for a 75-minute harbor cruise. These cruises depart several times daily from both the Kowloon and Hong Kong sides. (For more information on this and other cruises, see "Organized Tours," below.)

## VICTORIA PEAK

At 1,308 feet, Victoria Peak is Hong Kong Island's tallest hill and offers spectacular views of the city and surrounding area (if possible, go on a clear day). It's always been one of Hong Kong's most exclusive places to live, since the peak is typically cooler than the sweltering city below. Even just a one-bedroom apartment on the Peak goes for a purported HK$50,000 ($6,500) a month. More than a century ago, the rich reached the peak after a 3-hour trip in sedan chairs, transported to the top by coolies. Then, in 1888, the **peak tram** began operations, cutting the journey from a grueling 3 hours to a mere 8 minutes. In 1989 the older, cast-iron green funicular cars with mahogany seats were replaced by new, modern cars imported from Switzerland, which increased the passenger load from 72 to 120 people.

The easiest way to reach the Peak Tram Station, located on Garden Road, is to take the no. 15C open-top shuttle bus that operates between the tram terminal and the Star Ferry in Central. (After you exit from the Star Ferry, turn left; shuttle buses depart from a traffic island located between the parking garage and City Hall.) Shuttle buses cost HK$3 (40¢) and run every 10 to 15 minutes starting at 10am. Otherwise, it's about a 10-minute walk to Garden Road and the tram station. Alternatively, you can take Minibus no. 15 from in front of the Star Ferry in Central directly to the top of Victoria Peak, but then you'd miss the tram unless you opt to take it down.

As for the trams, they depart every 10 to 15 minutes between 7am and midnight. The tram climbs almost vertically for 8 minutes before reaching the top of the peak—don't worry, there's never been an accident in its entire 100-odd years of operation. For the best view, try to get a seat at the front on the right side. One-way tickets for the peak tram cost HK$20 ($2.60) for adults, HK$7 (90¢) for senior citizens, and HK$6 (80¢) for children. Round-trip tickets cost HK$30 ($3.90), HK$14 ($1.80), and HK$9 ($1.15), respectively. If you wish, you can also purchase combination tickets at the tram ticket window that include round-trip rides on the tram and entrances to the Peak's two main attractions: Ripley's Believe It or Not! Odditorium and the Peak Explorer. This combination ticket costs HK$110 ($14.30) for adults and HK$69 ($8.95) for children, a savings of HK$31 ($4) over tickets purchased separately. However, since these attractions appeal mostly to older children, I consider your time in Hong Kong better spent elsewhere, unless, of course, you have older children in tow.

Upon reaching the Peak, you'll find yourself at the very modern **Peak Tower,** designed by British architect Terry Farrell and looking for all the world like a Chinese cooking wok. Head straight for the viewing terrace on Level 5, where you have one of the world's most breathtaking views, with the skyscrapers of Central, the boats plying Victoria Harbour, Kowloon, and the many hills of the New Territories undulating in the background.

## Hong Kong Touring Tips

Although Hong Kong is compact and easy to navigate, it makes sense to divide the city into sections when planning your sightseeing. The following information on museums, parks, markets, and other attractions, therefore, is sub-divided according to area, making it easier to coordinate sightseeing and dining plans. Don't forget to read over the suggested walking tours in chapter 7, since they include stops at several of Hong Kong's top attractions.

Of the two attractions located in Peak Tower, most-well-known is **Ripley's Believe It or Not! Odditorium,** Level 3, Peak Tower, 128 Peak Rd., Victoria Peak (☎ 852/ 2849 0698). The 26th to open world-wide, it contains oddities (and replicas of oddities) collected by Robert L. Ripley on visits to 198 countries over 55 years, including a shrunken head from Ecuador, torture items from around the world, a two-headed calf, and models of the world's tallest and fattest men. Be forewarned that some of the items are purely grotesque, or, at best, out of date in a more socially correct world. Still, human nature being what it is, probably everyone wants to visit one of these museums at least once, and children, of course, are fascinated. The one here, open daily 9am to 10pm, costs HK$65 ($8.45) for adults and HK$46 ($5.95) for senior citizens and children.

**Peak Explorer,** Level 6 of the Peak Tower (☎ 852/2849 0866), is a 36-seat motion-simulator theater that features changing, 8-minute fast-paced films and seats that move, jerk, roll, and rock in accordance to the action on the screen. It's almost like being on board the roller coaster, race car, motorbike, or whatever is being shown. Definitely not for those with motion sickness. Admission here is HK$45 ($5.85) for adults and HK$32 ($4.15) for children and it's open daily 9am to 10pm.

Exit Peak Tower via Level 4. Across the street is the **Peak Galleria,** a three-story complex with shops, restaurants, a children's playground, and a viewing terrace.

But the best thing to do atop Victoria Peak, in my opinion, is to take a walk. If you're feeling particularly energetic, you might want to hike up Mount Austin Road to the former site of the governor's summer lodge—usually shrouded in mist. Only the formal gardens remain, carefully tended and offering a pleasant respite from the congestion of the city below.

My favorite walk on Victoria Peak, however, is the hour-long circular hike on Lugard Road and Harlech Road, both located just a stone's throw from the peak tram terminus. Mainly a footpath overhung with banyan trees and passing lush vegetation, it snakes along the side of the cliff, offering great views of the Central District below, the harbor, Kowloon, and then Aberdeen and the outlying islands on the other side. You will also pass Victoria Peak mansions. This is one of the best walks in Hong Kong; at night, the lighted path offers one of world's most romantic views. Don't miss it.

## RIDING A TRAM

Just as the Star Ferry is the best way to see the harbor, the tram is the most colorful and cheapest way to see the northern end of Hong Kong Island, including the Central District, Western District, Wan Chai, and Causeway Bay. In fact, the tram is so much a part of Hong Kong life that it was chosen for Hong Kong's exhibit at the Vancouver '86 Expo. Dating from 1904, the tram line follows what used to be the waterfront (before the days of land reclamation). Old, narrow, double-decker affairs, the trams cut through the heart of the city, from Kennedy Town in the west to Shau Kei Wan in the east. There's only one detour—off to Happy Valley—so it's impossible to get lost.

In any case, if you're in Central, you can board the tram on Des Voeux Road Central. Climb to the upper deck and try to get a seat in the front row. (For more information on the fare and how to ride the tram, see "Getting Around" in chapter 3.) I especially like to ride the tram at night, when neon signs are ablaze and the outdoor markets of Causeway Bay are in full swing. If you're a tram nut, you may even want to take an organized tram tour that includes drinks (see "Organized Tours," below).

## THE FERRIES TO OUTLYING ISLANDS

While most of Hong Kong's 260 outlying islands are uninhabited, ferry trips to the most interesting ones are described in chapter 10. These ferries, which depart from the Central District, are the cheapest way to see Hong Kong harbor, with most trips lasting less than an hour. Some even offer an outside deck, where you can sit with a coffee or beer and watch Hong Kong float past. In fact, part of the fun in visiting an outlying island is the ferry ride there and back.

# 2 Museums & Galleries

If you plan to visit all four of Hong Kong's museums—the Hong Kong Museum of Art, Hong Kong Museum of History, Hong Kong Space Museum, and Hong Kong Science Museum—you can save a minimal amount of money by purchasing the special Urban Council Museum "Monthly Pass" for HK$50 ($6.50), which allows unlimited admissions for 1 month and also entitles you to a 10% discount on selected items at the museums' gift shops. The total price of purchasing single tickets to all four is HK$55 ($7.15). You can purchase the pass at any of the four museums and at Hong Kong Tourist Association offices. Note that museum admissions are free on Wednesdays.

Keep in mind, too, that municipal museums are closed December 25 and 26, January 1, and the first 3 days of the Chinese New Year. Private museums are usually also closed on bank holidays.

## IN KOWLOON

✪ **Hong Kong Museum of Art.** Hong Kong Cultural Centre Complex, 10 Salisbury Rd., Tsim Sha Tsui. ☎ **852/2734 2167.** Admission HK$10 ($1.30) adults; HK$5 (65¢) children, students, and senior citizens. Free admission Wed. Fri–Wed 10am–6pm. MTR: Tsim Sha Tsui.

If you visit only one museum in Hong Kong, this should be it. Located on the Tsim Sha Tsui waterfront between the Cultural Centre and Space Museum and just a 2-minute walk from the Star Ferry terminus, this museum has a vast collection of Chinese antiquities and fine art, including ceramics, bronzes, jade, cloisonné, lacquerware, bamboo carvings, women's costumes (look for the fist-sized shoes for bound feet), and textiles, as well as paintings, wall hangings, scrolls, and calligraphy dating from the 16th century to the present. The works are arranged in five permanent galleries on three floors of exhibit space, plus two galleries devoted to changing exhibits. The Historical Pictures Gallery is especially insightful, with 1,000 works in oils, watercolors, pencil drawings, and prints that provide a visual account of life in Hong Kong, Macau, and Guangzhou (Canton) in the late 18th and 19th centuries. Another gallery displays contemporary Hong Kong works by local artists. A bonus is the beautiful backdrop of Victoria Harbour.

**Hong Kong Museum of History.** 100 Chatham Rd. S., Tsim Sha Tsui East. **852/ 2724 9042.** Admission HK$10 adults ($1.30), HK$5 (65¢) children and senior citizens. Free admission Wed. Tues–Sat 10am–6pm, Sun and holidays 1–6pm. MTR: Tsim Sha Tsui (a 20-min. walk from exit B2). Bus: 5 from the Star Ferry bus terminus.

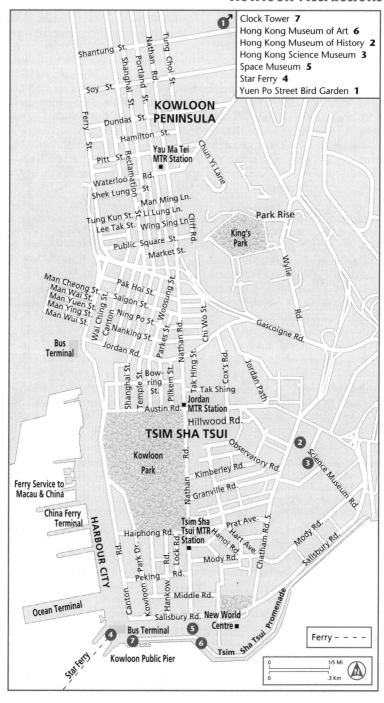

# Kowloon Attractions

Clock Tower **7**
Hong Kong Museum of Art **6**
Hong Kong Museum of History **2**
Hong Kong Science Museum **3**
Space Museum **5**
Star Ferry **4**
Yuen Po Street Bird Garden **1**

Shantung St.
Tung Choi St.
Nathan Rd.
Portland St.
Shanghai St.
Soy St.
Ferry St.
Dundas St.
**KOWLOON PENINSULA**
Hamilton St.
Pitt St.
Reclamation Rd.
Yau Ma Tei MTR Station
Chun Yi Lane
Waterloo Rd.
Shek Lung St.
Man Ming Ln.
Tung Kun St.
Li Lung Ln.
Lee Tak St.
Wing Sing Ln.
Cliff Rd.
Public Square St.
Market St.
Park Rise
King's Park
Wylie Rd.
Man Cheong St.
Man Wai St.
Man Yuen St.
Man Ying St.
Man Wui St.
Pak Hoi St.
Saigon St.
Wai Ching St.
Canton Rd.
Ning Po St.
Nanking St.
Parkes St.
Woosung St.
Nathan Rd.
Chi Wo St.
Gascoigne Rd.
Bus Terminal
Jordan Rd.
Shanghai St.
Temple St.
Bow-ring St.
Pilkem St.
Tak Hing St.
Cox's Rd.
Jordan Path
Austin Rd.
Tak Shing
Jordan MTR Station
Hillwood Rd.
**TSIM SHA TSUI**
Observatory Rd.
**2**
Kowloon Park
**3**
Science Museum Rd.
Ferry Service to Macau & China
Kimberley Rd.
Nathan Rd.
China Ferry Terminal
Granville Rd.
**HARBOUR CITY**
Haiphong Rd.
Tsim Sha Tsui MTR Station
Prat Ave.
Hart Ave.
Hanoi Rd.
Mody Rd.
Chatham Rd. S.
Mody Rd.
Salisbury Rd.
Park Dr.
Kowloon Rd.
Lock Rd.
Mody Rd.
Ocean Terminal
Peking Rd.
Canton Rd.
Kowloon Rd.
Hankow Rd.
Middle Rd.
Salisbury Rd.
New World Centre
Bus Terminal **5**
**4**
**7**
**6**
Tsim Sha Tsui Promenade
Star Ferry
Kowloon Public Pier
Tsim

Ferry – – – –

0        1/5 Mi
0        .3 Km

N

Having vacated its cramped quarters in Kowloon Park, the museum is scheduled to reopen in its new facility in summer 2001. The museum's exhibits outline 6,000 years of Hong Kong history, from its beginnings as a Middle Neolithic settlement to its development as a fishing village and then to a modern metropolis. Through displays that include replicas of fishing boats, furniture, clothing, and items from daily life, the museum introduces Hong Kong's ethnic groups and their traditional means of livelihood, customs, and beliefs. These include the Tanka, who lived their entire lives on boats, the Five Great Clans who settled in what is now the New Territories and built walled communities, and the Hakka, primarily rice farmers. My favorite part of the museum is a re-created street of old Hong Kong, complete with a Chinese herbal medicine shop actually located in Central until 1980, and reconstructed here. There are also 19th- and early-20th-century photographs, poignantly showing how much Hong Kong has changed through the decades.

**Hong Kong Science Museum.** 2 Science Museum Rd., Tsim Sha Tsui East. ☎ **852/ 2732 3232.** Admission HK$25 ($3.25) adults; HK$12.50 ($1.60) children, students, and senior citizens. Free admission Wed. Tues–Fri 1–9pm, Sat–Sun and holidays 10am–9pm. MTR: Tsim Sha Tsui (a 20-min. walk from exit B2). Bus: 5 from the Star Ferry bus terminus.

The mysteries of science and technology come to life here, with plenty of hands-on exhibits sure to appeal to children and adults alike. More than 500 exhibits cover four floors, with sections devoted to the life sciences; light, sound, and motion; virtual reality; meteorology and geography; electricity and magnetism; computers and robotics; construction; transportation and communication; occupational safety and health; energy efficiency; and food science and home technology. There is also an area specially designed for children 3 to 7. Visitors can play with different optical illusions, enter a rotating room to learn physics in a noninertial frame, "freeze" their shadows on a wall, pick up remote voices with a large parabolic disc, navigate a flight over retired Kai Tak Airport, and learn about herbs used in traditional Chinese medicine. There are exhibits designed to test a visitor's fitness, such as lung capacity, endurance, and blood pressure. In the computer section are more than 30 personal computers, where guests can learn about computer software, including word processing for children and graphics production, and surf the Internet for free.

**Hong Kong Space Museum.** Hong Kong Cultural Centre Complex, 10 Salisbury Rd., Tsim Sha Tsui. ☎ **852/2734 2722.** Admission to Exhibition Halls HK$10 ($1.30) adults; HK$5 (65¢) children, students, and senior citizens. Free admission on Wed. Space Theatre HK$24–HK$56 ($3.10–$7.25) adults; HK$12–HK$28 ($1.55–$3.65)) children, students, and senior citizens. Mon, Wed–Fri 1–9pm, Sat–Sun and holidays 10am–9pm. MTR: Tsim Sha Tsui.

Located in front of The Peninsula Hotel on the Tsim Sha Tsui waterfront, the Space Museum is easy to spot with its white-domed planetarium. It's divided into two parts: the Exhibition Halls with its Hall of Space Science and the Hall of Astronomy; and the Space Theatre. The Hall of Space Science explores the human journey into space, with exhibits on ancient astronomical history, science fiction, early rockets, manned spaceflights, and future space programs. There are also several interactive rides and exhibits, including a ride on a virtual paraglider, a harness that holds occupants aloft with the same approximate gravity they'd experience walking on the moon, and a multi-axis chair developed for astronaut training that gives the sensation of tumbling through space. The Hall of Astronomy presents information on the solar system, solar science, the stars, and the universe.

The Space Theatre, one of the largest planetariums in the world with a 75-foot domed roof, presents both Omnimax screenings with a projection system that produces an almost 360° panorama, and sky shows with a Zeiss star projector that can

---

**? Did You Know?**

- The 4,517-foot Tsing Ma Bridge, the world's second-longest road/rail suspension bridge that connects the new international airport with Kowloon, is 318 feet longer than San Francisco's Golden Gate Bridge and can withstand typhoon wind speeds up to 186 miles per hour.
- Hong Kong boasts several of the world's longest escalators. The world's two longest covered outdoor escalator systems are the four-section, 738-foot system at Ocean Park and the 2,600-foot Hillside Escalator Link connecting Central to the Mid-Levels. The Hongkong Bank headquarters in Central boasts the two longest freely supported escalators in the world.

---

project up to about 9,000 stars. Forty-minute to hour-long shows, ranging from such wonders of the world as the Great Barrier Reef to celestial phenomena like the Milky Way, are presented several times daily. Only a few are narrated in English, but for the others free headsets are available with simultaneous English translations. Try to buy your ticket at least a day in advance, either at the museum or any URBTIX outlet. Call ☎ 852/2734 2722 for show schedules.

## ON HONG KONG ISLAND

**Flagstaff House Museum of Tea Ware.** Hong Kong Park, 10 Cotton Tree Dr., Central. ☎ 852/2869 0690. Free admission. Thurs–Tues 10am–5pm. MTR: Admiralty; then follow the signs through Pacific Place to Island Shangri-La Hotel/Hong Kong Park.

Flagstaff House, located in Hong Kong Park, is the oldest colonial building in Hong Kong—the best place to go if you want to see typical Hong Kong architecture of 150 years ago. The house was completed in 1846 in Greek Revival style for the commander of the British forces. Now a museum devoted to the subject of tea culture in China, its collection includes about 500 pieces of tea ware ranging from earthenware to porcelain, primarily of Chinese origin, dating from the 7th century to the present day. With explanations in both English and Chinese, the exhibits also describe methods of making the various kinds of tea favored by the major dynasties. Don't miss the museum shop, which sells beautifully crafted teapots as well as teas.

**Hong Kong Arts Centre Pao Galleries.** Hong Kong Arts Centre (4th and 5th floors), 2 Harbour Rd., Wan Chai. ☎ 852/2582 0200. Free admission. Daily 10am–8pm. Closed during exhibition changes and some public holidays. MTR: Wan Chai.

Changing exhibitions of contemporary international and local art include paintings, graphic art, sculpture, photography, crafts, and calligraphy. This attraction is located about a 10-minute walk north of the Wan Chai MTR station, on the waterfront near the convention center.

**Hong Kong Museum of Coastal Defence.** 175 Tung Hei Rd., Shau Kei Wan. ☎ 852/2569 1500. Admission HK$10 ($1.30) adults; HK$5 (65¢) students, senior citizens, and children. Fri–Wed 10am–5pm. MTR: Schau Kei Wan (exit B2, then a 15-min. walk).

Located in Lei Yue Mun Fort, one of Hong Kong's oldest and best preserved British coastal fortresses dating from the Victorian period, this museum explores 600 years of the territory's coastal defense. Exhibits begin with the Ming and Qing dynasties, when coastal defenses guarded southern China against the invasion of pirates and western imperialists, and continue through the Opium War, Hong Kong's role as a major base

# Central District Attractions

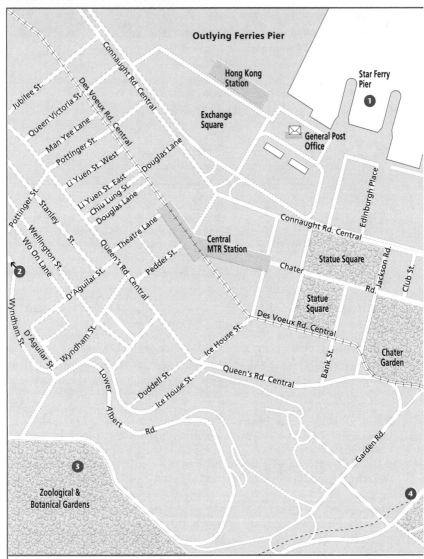

Outlying Ferries Pier

Hong Kong Station

Star Ferry Pier

Exchange Square

General Post Office

Connaught Rd. Central

Jubilee St.

Des Voeux Rd. Central

Queen Victoria St.

Man Yee Lane

Pottinger St.

Li Yuen St. West

Li Yuen St. East

Chiu Lung St.

Douglas Lane

Douglas Lane

Pottinger St.

Stanley St.

Wellington St.

Wo On Lane

Theatre Lane

D'Aguilar St.

Queen's Rd. Central

Pedder St.

Central MTR Station

Chater

Statue Square

Statue Square

Edinburgh Place

Jackson Rd.

Club St.

Wyndham St.

Des Voeux Rd. Central

Chater Garden

Wyndham St.

D'Aguilar St.

Ice House St.

Duddell St.

Ice House St.

Queen's Rd. Central

Bank St.

Lower Albert Rd.

Garden Rd.

Zoological & Botanical Gardens

Flagstaff House Museum of Teaware **5**
Hong Kong Museum of Medical Science **2**
Man Mo Temple **2**
Peak Tram Terminal **4**
Star Ferry **1**
Zoological & Botanical Gardens **3**

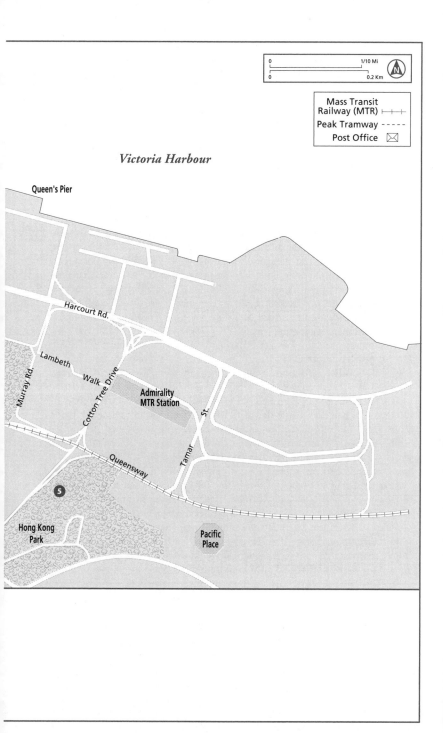

Victoria Harbour

Queen's Pier

Harcourt Rd.

Lambeth
Walk

Murray Rd.

Cotton Tree Drive

Admirality
MTR Station

Tamar St.

Queensway

⑤

Hong Kong
Park

Pacific
Place

0                              1/10 Mi
0                              0.2 Km

Mass Transit
Railway (MTR)
Peak Tramway
Post Office

# Life on the Water in Aberdeen

Situated on the south side of Hong Kong Island, Aberdeen is nestled around a naturally protected harbor. Famous for its colorful floating seafood restaurant and boat people who live on junks in Aberdeen Harbour, the town has undergone massive changes in recent years. Originally a typhoon shelter and land base for seafarers, it used to be a charming fishing village and boat-building port, supported primarily by several thousand junks and boat people. Many of the boat people, however, have been moved to massive housing projects, and the waterfront surrounding Aberdeen is now crowded with high-rises.

Still, Aberdeen continues to be popular with the tourist crowd because of its remaining boat population and floating restaurant. Women operating sampans will vie for your dollars to tour you around the harbor, which is definitely worth the price since it's about the only thing to do here and is the best way to see the junks. Although the boat population is shrinking, you'll pass huge boats that house extended families; you'll see men repairing fishing nets, women hanging out their laundry, dogs barking, children playing, and families eating. There was a time when a boat person could be born, live, marry, and die onboard, hardly ever setting a foot on shore. Nowadays, however, young people are moving on shore to seek more stable employment.

A 20-minute tour from a licensed operator will cost approximately HK$50 ($6.50) per person (or HK$15/$1.95 per person for a group of eight) and is offered daily between 9am and 5:30pm. There are also old women with wide-brimmed straw hats who will try to persuade you to board their sampan, with the price open to bargaining, and depending on the numbers of tourists around at the time. On one particularly slow day, for example, I was offered, and took, a sampan tour for HK$40 ($5.20), and I was the only one in the boat.

Other Aberdeen attractions include the largest floating restaurant in the world—the Jumbo Floating Restaurant, which offers its own free sampan ride (see chapter 5, "Where to Dine")—and a temple built in 1851. The temple is dedicated to Tin Hau, protectress of fishing folk, and is located at the junction of Aberdeen Main Road and Aberdeen Reservoir Road. Nearby is the huge Ocean Park amusement park with its thrill rides and aquarium.

To get to Aberdeen, take bus no. 7 from Central ferry pier no. 7; bus no. 70 from the Exchange Square Bus Terminal in the Central District; or bus no. 72 from Causeway Bay. For Ocean Park, take the special Ocean Park Citybus from either Admiralty MTR station or from in front of the Star Ferry pier in Central.

for the British navy, the Japanese 1941 invasion, and the recent handover to the People's Liberation Army. The fort itself, built in 1887 to defend the eastern approaches to the harbor against possible attacks by Russia or France, retains its batteries, underground magazines, protective ditch, caponiers, and torpedo station.

**Hong Kong Museum of Medical Sciences.** 2 Caine Lane, Mid-Levels. ☎ **852/2549 5123.** Admission HK$10 ($1.30) adults, HK$5 (65¢) children and senior citizens. Tues–Sat 10am–5pm, Sun and holidays 1–5pm. MTR: Central; then bus no. 26 from Des Voeux Rd. in front of Hongkong Bank headquarters to Man Mo Temple; walk up Ladder St. to Caine Lane.

This museum charts the historical development of medical science in Hong Kong. It's located in the century-old, Edwardian-style former Pathological Institute, which was founded to combat the colony's most horrific outbreak of bubonic plague. Back then,

British patients were treated upstairs, while the Chinese were relegated to the basement rooms. Several rooms remain almost exactly as they were, including an autopsy room and a laboratory filled with old equipment, while others serve as exhibition rooms devoted to such areas as the development of dentistry and radiology (note the X-ray of the bound foot). But what makes the museum particularly fascinating is its unique comparison of traditional Chinese and Western medicine, and its funding of research into Chinese medicine. Included are displays on acupuncture and traditional Chinese herbs.

**Police Museum.** 27 Coombe Rd., Wan Chai. ☎ **852/2849 7019.** Free admission. Tues 2–5pm, Wed–Sun 9am–5pm. Closed public holidays. Bus: no. 15 from Exchange Sq. or the Star Ferry terminal in Central; get off at the junction of Stubbs Rd. and Peak Rd.

Located on the site of the former Wan Chai Gap Police Station, this museum highlights the history of the Hong Kong Police Force (known as the Royal Hong Kong Police Force before the turnover) from its inception in 1844 to the present day. In addition to uniforms, historic documents, and descriptions of the development of the force, there are displays relating to the triad societies and narcotics (remember, Hong Kong was founded on the narcotics trade).

**University Museum and Art Gallery.** University of Hong Kong, 94 Bonham Rd., Sai Ying Pun. ☎ **852/2975 5600.** Free admission. Mon–Sat 9:30am–6pm, Sun 1:30–5:30pm. Closed public holidays and Mar 16. Bus: no. 3B from Jardine House on Connaught Rd. in Central; get off at the Bonham Rd. stop opposite St. Paul's College.

This museum, located west of Central in the midst of the University of Hong Kong with its Edwardian architecture, has collections of Chinese art, primarily ceramics and bronzes. The bronze collection includes Shang and Zhou ritual vessels, decorative mirrors, and 967 Nestorian crosses of the Yuan dynasty, the world's largest collection. The ceramics collection includes painted pottery of the third millennium B.C., tomb pottery of the Han dynasty, three-color glazes of the Tang dynasty, wares of the Song dynasty kilns, blue-and-white wares, monochromes and polychromes of the Ming and Qing dynasties, and recent works by Jingdezhen and Shiwan potters.

# 3  Temples

For more information on temples in Hong Kong, including the two listed below, contact the Hong Kong Tourist Association, ☎ **852/2508 1234.** For information on Po Lin Monastery and its adjacent Giant Tian Tan Buddha, see the section on Lantau island in "Side Trips from Hong Kong," chapter 10.

**Man Mo Temple.** Hollywood Rd. and Ladder St., Western District. ☎ **852/2803 2916.** Free admission. Daily 8am–6pm. Bus: no. 26 from Des Voeux Rd. Central (in front of the Hongkong Bank headquarters) to the second stop on Hollywood Rd., across from the temple.

Hong Kong Island's oldest and most important temple was built in the 1840s and is named after its two principal deities: Man, the god of literature, who is dressed in red and holds a calligraphy brush; and Mo, the god of war, wearing a green robe and holding a sword. Ironically, Mo finds patronage in both the police force (shrines in his honor can be found in all Hong Kong police stations today) and the infamous triad secret societies. Two ornately carved sedan chairs in the temple were once used during festivals to carry the statues of the gods around the neighborhood. But what makes the temple particularly memorable are the giant incense coils hanging from the ceiling, imparting a fragrant, smoky haze—these are purchased by patrons seeking fulfillment of their wishes, such as good health or a successful business deal, and may burn as long as 3 weeks.

**Wong Tai Sin.** Wong Tai Sin Estate. Temple daily 7am–5:30pm; gardens Tues–Sun 9am–4pm. Free admission to temple, though donations of about HK$1 (13¢) are expected at the temple's entrance and for Nine Dragon Wall Garden; admission to Good Wish Garden HK$2 (26¢) extra. MTR: Wong Tai Sin and then a 3-min. walk (follow the signs).

Located six subway stops northeast of Yau Ma Tei in the far north end of Kowloon Peninsula, Wong Tai Sin is Hong Kong's most popular Taoist temple. Although the temple itself dates only from 1973, it adheres to traditional Chinese architectural principles with its red pillars, two-tiered golden roof, blue friezes, yellow latticework, and multicolored carvings. The temple is very popular; everyone who comes here is seeking information about their fortunes—from advice about business or horse racing to determining which day is most auspicious for a wedding. Most worshippers make use of a bamboo container holding numbered sticks. After lighting a joss stick and kneeling before the main altar, the worshipper gently shakes the container until one of the sticks falls out. The number corresponds to a certain fortune, which is then interpreted by a soothsayer at the temple. You can wander around the temple grounds, where there are halls dedicated to the Buddhist Goddess of Mercy and to Confucius; the Nine Dragon Garden, a Chinese garden with a pond, waterfall, and a replica of the famous Nine Dragons mural (the original is in Beijing's Imperial Palace); the Good Wish Garden, a replica of the Yi He Garden in Beijing with circular, square, octagonal, and fan-shaped pavilions, ponds, an artificial waterfall, and rocks and concrete fashioned to resemble animals; and a clinic with both Western medical services and traditional Chinese herbal treatments. Wong Tai Sin takes its name, in fact, from a legendary shepherd who learned the art of healing. A visit to this temple, surrounded by vast, government housing estates, provides insight into Chinese religious practices and is well worth a stop despite its out-of-the-way location.

**Chi Lin Nunnery.** Chi Lin Rd., Diamond Hill. Free admission. Thurs–Tues 9am–3:30pm. MTR: Diamond Hill.

Just one subway stop away from Wong Tai Sin (above) is the newly renovated Chi Lin Buddhist Nunnery, founded in the 1930s to provide religious, cultural, educational, and elderly-care services to the Hong Kong community. Constructed using only wooden doweling and brackets rather than nails, the series of Tang Dynasty-style (A.D. 618–907) wooden halls house statues of Buddha and respected disciples made of bronze covered with gold, white jadeite, or precious wood. There's also a lotus pond garden, open daily 6:30am to 7pm.

## 4 Parks & Gardens

### IN KOWLOON

**KOWLOON PARK**   Occupying the site of an old military encampment first established in the 1860s, Kowloon Park is Tsim Sha Tsui's largest recreational and sports facility, boasting an indoor heated Olympic-size swimming pool, three outdoor leisure pools linked by a series of waterfalls, an open-air sculpture garden featuring works by local and overseas sculptors, a Chinese garden, a fitness trail, an aviary, a maze formed by hedges, a children's playground, and a bird lake with flamingos and other waterfowl. Not far from the Tsim Sha Tsui MTR station (take the A1 exit for Kowloon Park), it's easily accessible from Nathan, Haiphong, and Austin roads and is open daily 6am to midnight, with free admission. The swimming pools (☎ **852/2724 4522**) are open daily 6:30am to 9pm and charge HK$19 ($2.45) for adults and HK$9 ($1.15) for children.

**KOWLOON WALLED CITY PARK**  Hong Kong's newest park is perhaps its finest. Although it doesn't boast the attractions of the city's other parks, the Kowloon Walled City Park, on Tung Tau Tsuen Road, was designed to re-create the style of a classical Southern Chinese garden, and is the largest such garden outside China. Beautifully landscaped with man-made hills, ponds, streams, pines, boulders, bonsai, bamboo, and shrubs, it features winding paths through a sculpture garden, flower gardens, pavilions, and a playground.

Even more fascinating is the site's history, described through photographs in a former administration office. More than 150 years ago, the site was on the seashore, making it perfect in 1847 for the construction of a Chinese fort to defend Kowloon after the British takeover of Hong Kong Island. After 1898, when the British took over the New Territories, the 500 soldiers occupying the fort were expelled. But China did not consider the site part of the leased territories, and for most of the next century, the Kowloon Walled City remained in sovereign limbo, ignored by British authorities. It developed a lifestyle of its own, with its own set of laws. An enclave of tenements and secret societies that flouted Hong Kong's building regulations and health standards, it served as a haven for squatters, refugees, criminals, prostitutes, and drug addicts. Densely packed and infested with rats, many parts of the warrenlike city never saw the light of day. Hong Kong police ventured inside only in pairs. Following a special Sino-British agreement and years of lengthy negotiations over new housing for Walled City residents, the enclave was demolished in 1994. A few historic structures remain, however, including the Old South Gate entrance, wall foundations, and flagstone paths. To reach the park, take the MTR to Lok Fu station and then walk 15 minutes on Junction Road to Tung Tau Tsuen Road; or take bus no. 1 from the Star Ferry in Tsim Sha Tsui to the stop opposite the park. It's open daily 6:30am to 11:30pm, and admission is free.

**YUEN PO STREET BIRD GARDEN**  If you've been in Hong Kong for very long, you may have noticed wooden birdcages hanging outside shops or from apartment balconies, or perhaps you've even seen someone walking down the street with a cage. Birds are favorite pets in Chinese households, and the price of a bird is determined not by its plumage but by its singing talents. To see more of these prized songbirds, visit the fascinating Yuen Po Street Bird Garden, Prince Edward Road West, which consists of a series of Chinese-style gateways and courtyards lined with stalls selling songbirds, beautifully crafted wood and bamboo cages, live crickets and mealy worms, and tiny porcelain food bowls. Nothing, it seems, is too expensive for these tiny creatures. The lane is also crowded with scores of people buying and selling birds, or perhaps just taking their birds for an outing. This garden is very Chinese and a lot of fun to see; young children love it. Incidentally, next door is Flower Market Road, lined with flower shops. To reach the Bird Garden, open daily 7am to 8pm, take the MTR to Prince Edward Road station and walk 10 minutes west on Prince Edward Road West, turning left at the railway onto Yuen Po Street. Admission is free.

## ON HONG KONG ISLAND

**HONG KONG PARK**  Opened in 1991, Hong Kong Park, Supreme Court Road and Cotton Tree Drive, Central, features a dancing fountain at its entrance, Southeast Asia's largest greenhouse with more than 2,000 rare plant species, including desert and tropical jungle varieties, an aviary housing 800 exotic birds in a tropical rain-forest setting with an elevated walkway, various gardens, a children's playground, and a viewing platform reached by climbing 105 stairs. The most famous building on the park grounds is the Flagstaff House Museum of Tea Ware (described above). Since the marriage registry is located at the edge of the park, the gardens are a favorite place for wedding photographs, especially on weekends and auspicious days of the Chinese calendar. The park is open daily 6:30am to 11pm, the greenhouse and aviary are open daily 9am to 5pm, and the museum of tea ware is open every day except Wednesday 10am to 5pm. Admission is free to everything. To reach the park, take the MTR to Admiralty Station, then follow the signs through Pacific Place and up the escalators to Island Shangri-La Hotel and Hong Kong Park.

**VICTORIA PARK** This 19-acre park is one of Hong Kong's largest, located on Causeway and Gloucester roads in Causeway Bay and serving as the green lungs of the city. Constructed on reclaimed land formerly used for a typhoon shelter, it has tennis and squash courts, a 50-meter swimming pool, soccer fields, basketball courts, playgrounds, a skating rink, and a jogging track. It is also popular in early morning for those practicing *tai chi* or shadow boxing. The Mid-Autumn Festival is held here, as well as a flower market a few days before Chinese New Year. The park is open 24 hours and is free. To reach it, take the MTR to Causeway Bay station.

**ZOOLOGICAL & BOTANICAL GARDENS** Established in 1864, the Zoological and Botanical Gardens, Upper Albert Road, Central, are spread on the slope of Victoria Peak, making it a popular respite for Hong Kong residents. Come here early, around 7am, and you'll see Chinese residents going through the slow motions of *tai chi* (shadow boxing), a disciplined physical routine of more than 200 individual movements, designed to exercise every muscle of the body and bring a sense of peace and balance to its practitioners. In the gardens themselves, which retain some of their Victorian charm, flowers are almost always in bloom, from azaleas in the spring to wisteria and bauhinea in the summer and fall. More than 1,000 species of plants, most of them indigenous to tropical and sub-tropical regions and planted throughout the grounds, include Burmese rosewood trees, varieties of bamboo, Indian rubber trees, camphor trees, a variety of camellia, herbs, and the Hong Kong orchid. The small zoo houses 600 birds, 90 mammals and 20 reptiles, including jaguars, orangutans, tamarins, kangaroos, flamingos, a Burmese python, Palawan peacocks, birds of paradise from Papua New Guinea, cranes, and Mandarin ducks. The zoo is well known for its success in breeding birds on the verge of extinction and for supplying zoos around the world with new stock.

If you're tired of Central and its traffic, this is a pleasant place to regain your perspective. There's also a children's playground. Admission is free. The eastern part of the park, containing most of the botanical gardens and the aviaries, is open daily 6am to 10pm, while the western half with its reptiles and mammals is open daily 6am to 7pm. To reach it, take the MTR to Central and then walk 15 minutes up Garden Road to the corner of Upper Albert Road. Or take bus no. 3B or 12 from the Jardine House on Connaught Road Central.

## 5 An Amusement Park

✪ **Ocean Park.** Aberdeen, Hong Kong Island. ☎ **852/2552 0291.** Admission HK$150 ($19.50) adults, HK$75 ($9.75) children. Daily 10am–6pm. Bus: Ocean Park Citybus from the Admiralty MTR station every 10 min. or from the Central Star Ferry pier every half hour; you can buy round-trip tickets that include park admission. Or take no. 70 from Exchange Square in Central or no. 72 from Causeway Bay (get off at the first stop after the tunnel and then walk 20 min.).

If you're a kid or a kid at heart, you'll love Ocean Park, a combination marine park and amusement center, which also includes a replica of an old Chinese village called

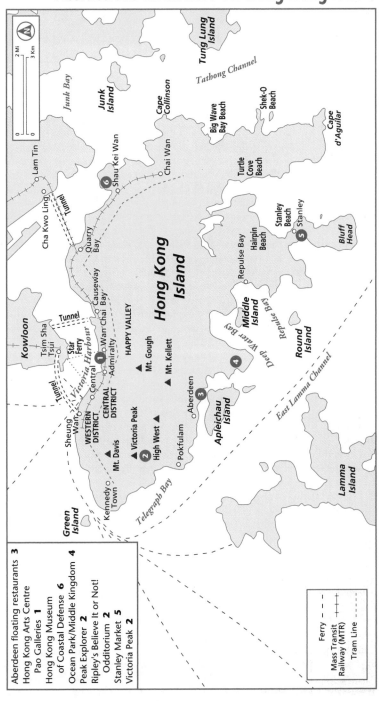

Aberdeen floating restaurants **3**
Hong Kong Arts Centre
  Pao Galleries **1**
Hong Kong Museum
  of Coastal Defense **6**
Ocean Park/Middle Kingdom **4**
Peak Explorer **2**
Ripley's Believe It or Not!
  Odditorium **2**
Stanley Market **5**
Victoria Peak **2**

Ferry
Mass Transit
  Railway (MTR)
Tram Line

the Middle Kingdom. Situated along a dramatic rocky coastline on the island's southern shore, the park is divided into three areas: a "lowland" and a "headland," connected by cable car, and the Middle Kingdom, connected by escalator. Because of the wide range of attractions, Ocean Park is interesting for children and senior citizens alike, as well as everyone in between.

The lowland is subdivided into several areas and attractions. The most popular residents of Ocean Park are An An and Jia Jia, a pair of pandas presented as gifts from China. Aimed at youngsters are the Dinosaur Discovery Trail, with 17 lifelike models of dinosaurs, and Kids' World, with its kiddie rides, playgrounds, remote-control cars and boats, shows geared toward children, shooting games arcade, and Dolphin University, where the audience can watch the training of dolphins at close range. Film Fantasia is a 100-seat theater with hydraulically actuated seats that move in time to the fast-paced action on the screen, kind of like riding a roller coaster without actually going anywhere but visually much more stimulating. There's also a high-dive show by professionals dressed in costumes. Much gentler are walks through the magical Butterfly House (shaped, interestingly enough, like a caterpillar) with 1,000 free-flying butterflies, and, my favorite, the Golden Pagoda set in a lush garden, with more varieties of goldfish than you ever imagined possible, most of them from China. The pompommed fish, for example, have large pompomlike growths on their heads, while the bubble eyes, with huge bubbles under their eyes, are too bizarre for words.

From the lowland, visitors board cable cars for a spectacular 8-minute ride over a hill to the headland, while being treated to great views of the coastline and the South China Sea along the way. The headland area, situated on a peninsula that juts into the sea, is also subdivided into several areas and attractions. Marine Land features an artificial wave cove that is home to sea lions, penguins, and a shark aquarium, with more than 250 sharks and rays representing more than 30 species, viewed from an underwater tunnel. Ocean Theatre features shows by talented dolphins, sea lions, and a killer whale. But my favorite is the Atoll Reef, one of the world's largest aquariums, with 4,000 fish of 400 different species. The observation passageway circles the aquarium on four levels, enabling you to view the sea life—everything from giant octopus to schools of tropical fish—from various depths and from different angles. There are also thrill rides, including a Ferris wheel, a roller coaster that turns upside down three times, another roller coaster that follows a Wild West theme, and a rather wet ride on a "raging river." Other exhibits include a Japanese Garden; a 230-foot-high Ocean Park Tower offering revolving, panoramic views of Aberdeen and outlying islands; and an aviary with more than 2,000 birds.

After touring the headland, take the long escalator down to the Middle Kingdom. Opened in 1989, this is a small, re-created village from China's past with full-size temples, shrines, pavilions, pagodas, street scenes, and public squares. Be sure to stop by the Exhibition Hall, which briefly describes China's history, a span of 4,000 years, and includes explanations on such subjects as the Great Wall, the principles of *fung shui* (also transliterated as *feng shui*), the Chinese writing system, and foot binding. Afterwards, a stroll through the Middle Kingdom's streets will lead you past buildings, statues, or objects, each representing one of China's 13 dynasties. For example, from the third century B.C. are replicas of Qin dynasty terra-cotta figures—soldiers, horses, and a chariot—unearthed near Xian. The Ming dynasty (A.D. 1368–1644) is represented by a replica of a boat used by Admiral Cheng Ho, who traveled as far west as the Red Sea. Several little shops sell a variety of Chinese products; these include a tea shop and a palm reader. There are also performances by Chinese acrobats and magicians. To do Ocean Park justice, plan on spending a minimum of 4 hours here.

## 6  Especially for Kids

Several attractions listed above especially appeal to children. On the Kowloon side, the **Space Museum** is very much oriented to children, with buttons to push, telescopes to look through, and computer quizzes to test what they've learned, not to mention the films featured in the Space Theatre. In the **Science Museum,** more than 60% of its 500-some displays are hands-on, and there's also a special play area for children between the ages of 3 and 7. Across the Plaza is the **Museum of History,** with life-size replicas and models that bring the history of Hong Kong to life. And don't forget **Kowloon Park** right on Nathan Road, which has a playground for children, a pond with flamingos and other waterfowl, an aviary, swimming pools, and lots of space to run. Another good destination for children is the **Yuen Po Street Bird Garden** with its thousands of birds.

On Hong Kong Island, the biggest draw for kids of all ages is Ocean Park, which boasts a wide mix of things to do and see, including thrill rides; a shark aquarium; animal performances; life-size dinosaurs; and a children's section with kiddie rides, a playground, shows geared to children, and lots more. Of all the things to do in Hong Kong, this is probably the one kids enjoy most. For free entertainment, visit the **Zoological and Botanical Gardens** with its jaguars, monkeys, birds, and other animals, and **Hong Kong Park** with its greenhouse, aviary, children's playground, and climbing tower.

## 7  Organized Tours

Hong Kong offers lots of organized tours, so if you're pressed for time this may be the best way to go. I especially recommend taking one of the special-interest tours that explores Hong Kong's history, architectural gems, or traditions, as they provide insight into areas or aspects of Hong Kong life not readily accessible to the individual traveler.

### CITY TOURS

For general sightseeing, the Gray Line offers a variety of tours, with bookings available through most Hong Kong hotels or by calling ☎ **852/2368 7111.** The Hong Kong Island Tour is a 5-hour trip offered both morning and afternoon and may include stops at Victoria Peak, Aberdeen, and Stanley. On the Kowloon side, there's the 4- to 5-hour Kowloon and New Territories Tour, which takes in the industrial area of Kowloon, views of the Tsing Ma Bridge (built for the new international airport), and the rural regions and satellite towns of the New Territories. Stops include a Tin Hau temple, the Tai Po Market, and a bird garden. Cost of both tours is HK$290 ($37.70) for adults and HK$190 ($24.70) for children.

For information about organized evening tours, see chapter 9, "Hong Kong After Dark."

### BOAT TOURS

Since so many of Hong Kong's attractions are on or near the water, a variety of boat tours are available. The most popular and frequent one is the harbor cruise; others that last 1 to 8 hours range from the harbor itself to Aberdeen and the outlying islands, including lunch, sunset, and evening cruises, as well as combination water-and-land tours. For complete information, consult the sightseeing desk at your hotel, a travel agent, or the HKTA; hotels and travel agents can help you with bookings.

One of the most popular cruises is the 1-hour trip aboard a **Star Ferry.** Departing from the Star Ferry piers in both Central and Tsim Sha Tsui, the cruise takes passengers past the Central District, Hong Kong Convention and Exhibition Centre, Causeway Bay Typhoon Shelter, and the old Kai Tak airport. There are four departures daily from the Tsim Sha Tsui pier: 12:30, 1:45, 3, and 7pm; departures from the Central ferry pier are 10 minutes later (for the first three departures only, as there is no pick up in Central at night; it would be wise to verify these times, however). The cruises, which include complimentary drinks, cost HK$150 ($19.50) for adults and HK$100 ($13) for children and can be booked at the Star Ferry terminals. For more information, call ☎ 852/2118 6235 or 852/2845 2324.

**Watertours** (☎ 852/2926 3868), Hong Kong's largest tour operator of boat and junk cruises, also offers a 2-hour cruise that includes a trip to a typhoon shelter and its junks and the firing of the Noon Day Gun in Causeway Bay by Jardine Matheson & Co., Hong Kong's oldest trading company. Cost of this tour, which departs at 10:15am from the Kowloon public pier and 10:30am from Queen's Pier in Central and includes a beer, soft drinks, coffee or tea, is HK$220 ($28.60) for adults and HK$130 ($16.90) for children. Watertours also schedules more than a half dozen other longer boat trips, including Chinese junk cruises to Aberdeen and sunset and evening cruises (for evening cruises, see chapter 9, "Hong Kong After Dark"). You can pick up a Watertours pamphlet at HKTA offices and in many hotels.

Otherwise, probably the unique boat tour is with **Hong Kong Dolphinwatch** (☎ 852/2984 1414), which offers 4-hour trips three or four mornings a week that includes a bus ride to the new satellite town of Tung Chung, followed by a luxury cruise to the natural habitat of the endangered Chinese white dolphins (Indo-Pacific Humpback dolphins), which live off Lantau island within sight of power plants, factories, Tung Chung, and the new airport. Advance booking is necessary, and the cost is HK$280 ($36.35) for adults and HK$140 ($18.20) for children.

## TRAM TOURS

Two of Hong Kong's original, double-decker, open-air trams from the early part of this century have been refurbished for the **Antique Tram Tour,** which lasts 1 hour. Costing HK$150 ($19.50) for adults and HK$100 ($13) for children, the price includes drinks for participants to enjoy while they rumble through colorful neighborhoods on Hong Kong Island. At last check, there were two tours a day, at noon and 3:30pm, from the Central ferry pier. For more information, call ☎ 852/2118 6235 or 852/2845 2324. Tickets are available at both the Tsim Sha Tsui and Central Star Ferry terminals.

## SPECIAL-INTEREST TOURS

The first three tours below, all organized and offered by the Hong Kong Tourist Authority, are highly recommended. The Heritage Tour would be very difficult, if not impossible, to do on your own. The "Land Between" Tour and the "Come Horse Racing" Tour make life easier because they leave the driving to HKTA. You can book these tours through your hotel tour desk, through HKTA offices, or by calling one of the HKTA booking hotlines below.

**"LAND BETWEEN" TOUR** This 6-hour excursion, offered by HKTA, takes visitors through the vast New Territories via air-conditioned motorcoach, enabling them to see how much this once-rural region has changed in the past decade, with traditional villages now overshadowed by huge government housing estates that house half of Hong Kong's population. Passing satellite towns with high-rise apartment buildings, farms, and villages, the bus stops at a Buddhist monastery, a lookout point on Hong Kong's tallest mountain, the traditional rural market at Luen Wo, a bird sanctuary, a fishing village to see how fisherfolk breed fish in submerged cages, the Sha Tin horse-racing track, and a Cantonese restaurant for lunch. The price of this tour, with departures daily, is HK$385 ($50.05) for adults, and HK$335 ($43.55) for children under 16 and seniors 60 and over. To book, call The Land Between Tour Reservations Hotline at ☎ **852/2110 1038.**

**HERITAGE TOUR**   This HKTA tour also takes in the New Territories, but its emphasis is on Hong Kong's past rather than the present and it makes stops at historic Chinese sites that even Hong Kong residents seldom see. It's a must for those who are interested in local historical architecture; it also gives insight into clan life in the New Territories long before the region became part of colonial Hong Kong. Not only does the tour visit scattered sites that would be impossible for the individual traveler to reach in 1 day (and in some cases even find), but the commentary provided by knowledge-able guides is much more informative than what you'd gain by visiting the sites on your own. Lasting approximately 5 hours, tours make stops at the Sam Tung Uk Museum, a 200-year-old walled village built by a Hakka clan and now a museum; Tai Fu Tai, a Chinese-style ornate mansion built in 1865 by a high-ranking official and fascinating for its insight into how the rich lived; Liu Man Shek Tong, an ancestral hall belonging to one of the Five Great Clans; and the Man Mo Temple and a traditional street mar-ket in Tai Po with stalls selling fresh produce and dried seafood. Tours depart every Monday, Wednesday, Friday, and Saturday (except public holidays), and cost HK$325 ($42.25) for adults and HK$275 ($35.75) for children younger than 16 and senior cit-izens 60 and older. Call the HKTA at ☎ **852/2508 1234** for more information.

**"COME HORSE RACING" TOUR**   Yet another HKTA-sponsored tour, this one allows visitors to experience the excitement of the races, at either Happy Valley or Sha Tin, an excitement that grows proportionally according to how much you bet. Tours are only scheduled during the horse-racing season—September to mid-June—usually on Wednesday evenings and on Saturday and/or Sunday afternoons. Two types of tours are available. The Classic Tour, costing HK$490 ($63.65), includes a pre-race Western-style buffet lunch or dinner, personal entry badge to the luxurious Visitors' Box in the Hong Kong Jockey Club's Members' Enclosure, transportation, guide ser-vices, and even hints to help you place your bets. The EZ Race Tour, costing HK$120 ($15.60), includes transportation and admission to the Betting Lounge within the Members' Enclosure. Tours are limited to individuals 18 years of age and older who have been in Hong Kong fewer than 21 days (be sure to bring your passport with you when booking and participating in this tour). For bookings, call the Come Horse Rac-ing Tour Reservations Hotline at ☎ **852/2366 3995.** More information on the horse races is presented in "Spectator Sports," below.

**HONG KONG LIFESTYLES TOUR**   Answering the oft-asked question, "Has life in Hong Kong changed since the handover?", this 5-hour tour offered by Gray Line (☎ **852/2368 7111**) explores life in this vibrant city, beginning with the raising of the Hong Kong SAR flag and a session of *tai chi* (shadow boxing), followed by a dim sum breakfast and visits to a produce and vegetable market and a temple. Tours depart every Tuesday and Friday mornings and cost HK$290 ($37.65) for adults and HK$190 ($24.65) for children.

**FUNG SHUI TOUR**   *Fung shui* (or *feng shui*), which translates literally as "wind water," is a 3,000-year-old form of divination that allows humans to live in harmony with the environment and nature, thus ensuring good luck, prosperity, wealth, health, and happiness. Even today, most office and apartment buildings in Hong Kong have been laid out in accordance to fung shui principles, aided by a geomancer. This 4-hour tour, offered by Sky Bird Travel (☎ **852/2736 2282**), describes the basic principles of fung shui and how it has been applied, with stops at Stubbs Road Lookout to see how Hong Kong is blessed with excellent fung shui, Repulse Bay to learn why the wealthy build homes facing the sea, and Statue Square in Central for a look at the Hongkong and Shanghai Bank and other famous skyscrapers. Tours depart every Tuesday and Friday and cost HK$280 ($36.35) for adults and HK$240 ($31.20) for children and senior citizens.

**WILDLIFE TOUR TO MAI PO WETLANDS**   The Mai Po Wetlands are an important stop and feeding ground for many migratory birds, including rare birds like the Black-Faced Spoonbill. As many as 325 species of birds, 400 species of insects, 90 species of marine invertebrates, and more than 50 species of butterflies have been recorded here. This 5-hour tour, offered by Gray Line (☎ 852/2368 7111) includes a leisurely walk into the nature reserve, bird-watching, a visit to a museum dedicated to traditional shrimp farming (still in practice), a walk via boardwalk through coastal mangroves, and a visit to the Mai Po Education Centre and adjacent waterfowl pond. Tours, offered Mondays and Thursdays, cost HK$345 ($44.80).

## 8 Outdoor Activities

Despite the fact that Hong Kong is densely populated, there's enough open space to pursue everything from golf to hiking to windsurfing. For the hardworking Chinese and expatriates, recreation and leisure are essential for relaxing and winding down. With that in mind, try to schedule your golfing, swimming, or hiking trips on weekdays unless you enjoy jostling elbows with the crowds.

### TAI CHI

*Tai chi* (shadow boxing) is an ancient Chinese regimen designed to balance body and soul and thereby release energy from within. By strengthening both the mind and the body through seemingly fluid, slow movements that mask the strength and control required to perform the balletlike exercise, tai chi fosters a sense of well-being and nurtures self-discipline. It also helps develop balance, improves muscle tone and breathing, and aids digestion. In Hong Kong, both young and old practitioners gather every morning in downtown parks and open public spaces to perform tai chi. Visitors, too, can join complimentary 1-hour **lessons** in English, offered by the Hong Kong Tourist Association every Tuesday, Friday, and Sunday at 8:15am. Available on a first-come, first-serve basis at the Garden Plaza located in Hong Kong Park near the Admiralty MTR station, lessons led by a tai chi master emphasize simple breathing and relaxation techniques. Participants are advised to wear casual clothing and comfortable sport shoes with rubber soles. For more information, contact the **Hong Kong Tourist Association** (☎ 852/2508 1234).

### GOLF

It's not as cheap to play golf as it used to be. Greens fees have tripled in the past decade, driven up no doubt by the flocks of golfing enthusiasts from Japan, where the cost of a game is through the roof. But compared with playing golf in Japan, Hong Kong is a giveaway, especially since the opening of the two, 18-hole public golf courses at Kau Sai Chau, near Sai Kung in the New Territories. Since courses can be crowded, it's recommended you call the clubs beforehand to check whether they're are open and what tee-off times are available. It's best to book a tee-time in advance.

The **Jockey Club Kau Sai Chau Public Golf Course** (☎ 852/2791 3388), carved out of an island formerly used by the British Army for shelling practice, offers great panoramic vistas and one of the world's finest public golfing facilities. There are two 18-hole courses, one for beginners that charges HK$500 ($64.95) on weekdays and HK$800 ($103.90) on weekends, and another course for advanced players that charges HK$550 ($71.45) and HK$850 ($110) respectively. To reach it, take the MTR to Choi Hung and then board a minibus for the special "golfer's ferry" to Kau Sai Chau.

The **Hong Kong Golf Club** maintains courses in both Fanling (☎ 852/2670 1211) and Deep Water Bay (☎ 852/2812 7070), and welcomes visitors Monday to Friday only (except public holidays). No advance reservations are taken, so visitors should first check availability by phone and then arrive early. There are three 18-hole courses in Fanling, in the New Territories, with greens fees at HK$1,400 ($182); you should begin playing between 7:28 and 11:26am. To reach it, take the KCR railway to Sheung Shui, followed by a 3-minute taxi ride. Deep Water Bay, on Hong Kong Island, is a 9-hole course, with greens fees at HK$450 ($58.50) for 18 holes. To reach it, take bus no. 260 or 262 from Exchange Square in Central.

The **Discovery Bay Golf Club,** on Lantau island (☎ 852/2987 7273), has a beautiful 18-hole course developed by Robert Trent Jones Jr., offering great views of Hong Kong and the harbor. Visitors are allowed to play here Monday, Tuesday, and Friday (except public holidays), and greens fees are HK$1,400 ($182) for 18 holes. To reach it, take the 20-minute ferry ride from Central (next to the Star Ferry) to Discovery Bay, followed by a ride in a special shuttle bus.

Another scenic 18-hole course and a 9-hole course, operated by the **Clearwater Bay Golf and Country Club** (☎ 852/2335 3885), is located in Sai Kung in the New Territories, on a picturesque headland overlooking the South China Sea. Visitors may play Tuesday to Friday (a 3-day advance booking is required), with HK$1,400 ($182) greens fees charged for the 18-hole course. To reach it, take the KCR railway to Sheung Shui, and then take a taxi.

## HIKING

With 23 country parks—amounting to more than 40% of Hong Kong's space—there are many trails of varying levels of difficulty throughout Hong Kong, including hiking trails, nature trails, and family trails. Serious hikers, for example, may want to consider the famous **MacLehose Trail** in the New Territories, which stretches about 60 miles through eight county parks, from the Sai Kung Peninsula in the east to Tuen Mun in the west. The **Lantau Trail** is a 43-mile circular trail on **Lantau island** that begins and ends at Mui Wo (also called Silvermine Bay), passing several popular scenic spots and campsites along the way and including a 2½-hour trek to the top of Lantau Peak. Both the MacLehose and Lantau Trails are divided into smaller sections of varying difficulty, which means that you can tailor your hike to suit your own abilities and time constraints. The Hong Kong Tourist Association has some trail maps, as well as a hiking and wildlife guide book called *Exploring Hong Kong Countryside: A Visitor's Companion.* In addition, the Hong Kong Government Publications Centre, located in the Low Block of the Government Offices at 66 Queensway, Central (☎ 852/2537 1910; MTR: Admiralty) has leaflets on country parks and maps, including the excellent "Countryside Series."

If you don't have a hiking partner or don't want to hassle with finding trailheads on your own, consider joining one of five **Guided Nature Walks,** led by experienced guides. Ranging from 3 to 4 hours and costing HK$275 to HK$320 ($35.70 to $41.55), these hikes cover different regions of Hong Kong, from the southeast coast of Hong Kong Island to Lantau Island or Sai Kung in the New Territories. For more information, pick up a brochure at one of the HKTA offices.

> ❓ **Did You Know?**
>
> Hong Kong won its first gold medal ever at the Centennial Olympic Games in Atlanta in 1996—in women's windsurfing.

## JOGGING

The best places to jog on Hong Kong Island without dodging traffic are **Victoria Park's jogging track** in Causeway Bay, **Harlech Road** on Victoria Peak, and **Bowen Road,** which stretches from Stubbs Road to Magazine Gap Road in the Mid-Levels and offers great views over the harbor. In addition, an inside track at the Happy Valley racecourse is open for runners when the horses aren't using the field. On the other side of the harbor, there's **Kowloon Park,** as well as the waterfront promenade along Tsim Sha Tsui and Tsim Sha Tsui East.

Remember that it can be quite hot and humid during the summer months, so try to jog in the early morning or in the evening.

## SWIMMING

In addition to the many outdoor and indoor swimming pools at Hong Kong's hotels that are available for hotel guests, there are numerous public swimming pools, including those at **Kowloon Park** and **Victoria Park.** Prices are HK$19 ($2.45) for adults and HK$9 ($1.15) for children and senior citizens. Avoid hot weekends, when the pools can become quite crowded.

There are also about 40 **beaches** in Hong Kong that are free for public use; most of them have lifeguards on duty April to October, changing rooms, and snack stands or restaurants. Even on Hong Kong Island itself you can find a number of beaches, including Big Wave Bay and Shek O on the east coast, and Stanley, Deep Water Bay, and Repulse Bay on the southern coast. Repulse Bay, by far the most popular beach in Hong Kong, becomes unbelievably crowded on summer weekends. There are prettier beaches on the outlying islands, including Hung Shing Ye and Lo So Shing on Lamma, Tung Wan on Cheung Chau, and Cheung Sha on Lantau. It is, however, advisable to check on water pollution before plunging in, especially on the islands. Furthermore, I wouldn't recommend the waters around Sai Kung peninsula. There seem to be fatal shark attacks here every couple of years; somehow they always seem to occur in June, exactly when I am visiting Hong Kong. I was beginning to feel guilty until I learned that the attacks were due to fish migration, not my presence, but I certainly wouldn't want to tempt fate. Most of the public beaches have shark nets and guards patrolling the water.

## 9 Spectator Sports

A popular sporting event is the **Seven-A-Side Rugby Tournament** (called the Sevens), held in March or April. During the cooler winter months, a number of marathons are held, of which the best known are the **Hongkong-Shenzhen Marathon** in February and the **China Coast Marathon** in March. There are also tennis tournaments, including the **Super Tennis Classic** and the **Marlboro Championship.** If you enjoy watching golf, the highlight of the year is the **Hong Kong Open Golf Championships,** held in December at the Hong Kong Golf Club in Fanling (the New Territories).

If you're here anytime from September to mid-June, join the rest of Hong Kong at the **horse races.** Horse racing got its start in the colony in Happy Valley more than

150 years ago, when British settlers introduced the sport, making the Happy Valley track the oldest racecourse in Asia outside China. There is also a newer, modern track in Sha Tin (the New Territories), which can accommodate 90,000 spectators.

Without a doubt, horse racing is by far the most popular sporting event in Hong Kong. It's not, perhaps, the sport itself that draws so much enthusiasm, but rather the fact that, aside from the local lottery, racing is the only legal form of gambling in Hong Kong. The Chinese love to gamble, and there are more than 100 off-course betting centers throughout Hong Kong. Winnings are tax free.

Races are held Wednesday evenings and some Saturday and Sunday afternoons. Both tracks feature giant color screens that show close-ups of the race in progress, photographs of jockeys and trainers, and videos of previous races. It's fun and easy to get in on the betting action, and you don't have to bet much—the minimum wager of HK$10 ($1.30) per race is enough.

The lowest admission price is HK$10 ($1.30), which is for the general public and is standing room only. If you want to watch from the more exclusive Hong Kong Jockey Club members' enclosure, are at least 18 years old, and have been in Hong Kong fewer than 21 days, you can purchase a temporary member's badge for HK$50 ($6.50). It's available upon showing your passport at either the Badge Enquiry Office at the main entrance to the members' private enclosure (at either track) or at the off-course betting center near the Star Ferry concourse in Central. Tickets are sold on a first-come, first-served basis.

To reach Happy Valley Racecourse, take the tram to Happy Valley or the MTR to Causeway Bay (take the Times Square exit and walk towards the Wong Nai Chung Road). To reach Sha Tin Racecourse, take the KCR railway to Racecourse Station.

If you don't want to go to the races but would still like to bet on the winning horses, you can place your bets at one of the off-course betting centers. There's a convenient one near the Star Ferry concourse in the Central District and another one at 2–4 Prat Ave. in Tsim Sha Tsui.

On the other hand, an easy way to see the races is to take an HKTA-sponsored tour to the tracks, described in "Organized Tours," above. For information on current sporting events and future dates, contact the Hong Kong Tourist Association.

# 7 Hong Kong Strolls

**S**urprisingly compact, Hong Kong is an easy city to explore on foot. If it weren't for the harbor, you could walk everywhere—Tsim Sha Tsui, Yau Ma Tei, the Central District, Wan Chai, and Causeway Bay. Walking affords a more intimate relationship with your surroundings, permits chance encounters with the unexpected, and lets you discover that vegetable market, temple, or shop you would have otherwise missed.

If, for example, you're in the Central District and want to have dinner in Causeway Bay, you can walk there in less than an hour, passing through colorful Wan Chai on the way. Causeway Bay is good for exploring since it's full of little sidewalk markets, Japanese department stores, restaurants, and shops patronized by the locals. Another great place for walking is the Western District, fascinating because it encompasses a wide spectrum of traditional Chinese shops, from chop makers to ginseng wholesalers. If you like panoramic views, nothing can beat the hour-long circular walk on Victoria Peak.

On the other side of the harbor, a walk up Nathan Road from the harbor to the Yau Ma Tei subway station takes less than 30 minutes, although you might want to browse in some of the shops and department stores along the way. And Yau Ma Tei itself is another good place for wandering about since it, too, offers insight into the Chinese way of life with its markets and traditional shops. For easy strolling with great views of the harbor, walk along the waterfront promenade that stretches from the Star Ferry all the way through Tsim Sha Tsui East.

What follows are three recommended strolls: one through the Central financial district where a few colonial-era buildings are sprinkled in among the modern skyscrapers; another through the Western District with its Chinese shops and antiques stores; the third along Nathan Road in Kowloon, from Tsim Sha Tsui to Mong Kok. If you're really interested in the history and architecture of Central and Kowloon, you may want to take one of the self-guided walking tours offered by the Hong Kong Tourist Association. Called the **Heritage and Architecture Walks,** these 2½- to 4-hour walks include a detailed audio commentary and a booklet that describes some of the city's most interesting buildings, sites, and monuments, and includes historical background and interesting events that have taken place. Two other self-guided walking tours lead participants through Tai Po and Lung Yeuk Tau, both in the New Territories. Cost for the walks is HK$50 ($6.50), plus a HK$500 ($65.95) refundable deposit for the audio system. For more information, contact the Hong Kong Tourist Association (☎ **852/2508 1234**).

## Walking Tour 1: The Central District

**Start:** Star Ferry terminus, Central District.
**Finish:** Pacific Place, 88 Queensway, Central.
**Time:** About 3 hours; more if you include Victoria Peak.
**Best Times:** Weekdays, when shops and restaurants are in full swing.
**Worst Times:** Wednesday, when the Flagstaff House Museum of Tea Ware is closed; Saturday afternoon, Sunday, and public holidays, when some stores and restaurants in the Central District are closed.

The birthplace of modern Hong Kong, the Central District used to be called "Victoria," after Queen Victoria; it boasted elegant colonial-style buildings with sweeping verandas and narrow streets filled with pigtailed men pulling rickshaws. That's hard to imagine nowadays. With Central's gleaming glass-and-steel skyscrapers, there's little left of its colonial beginnings. Still, this is the logical starting place for a tour of Hong Kong. The handful of historic buildings scattered among towering monoliths symbolize both the past and the future of this ever-changing city. Yet surprisingly, Central has several city parks, good for relaxation and sightseeing. If you have time, you can also take a trip to Victoria Peak from the tram terminus in Central.

If you're starting this tour from Tsim Sha Tsui, board the Star Ferry for an exhilarating ride across the world-famous harbor. You'll disembark in the heart of Central. Ahead of you—just outside the terminus—are all that remain of Hong Kong's once mighty fleet of:

1. **Rickshaw drivers.** First appearing in Japan (the name is derived from the Japanese *jinriksha,* which translates as "people-powered vehicle") and brought to Hong Kong in the 1870s, rickshaw drivers are now tourist attractions rather than providers of transportation. In all my days in Hong Kong, I've never once seen a driver plying the streets of Central, and since no new licenses are being issued, the tradition will soon end when the last of the remaining ancient-looking men give up their trade. Most tourists prefer to have their photos taken sitting in a rickshaw rather than riding in one, but even that is likely to cost HK$50 ($6.50). The drivers will also demand money if you take a picture of them. Negotiate the price beforehand.

   To your right, just outside the ferry wickets, is the General Post Office. Continue walking inland from the Star Ferry terminus (with the post office to your right) to the underground pedestrian passage leading straight to:

2. **Statue Square.** To your left after emerging from the underground passage is a cenotaph commemorating "The Glorious Dead" of both world wars. Across Chater Road is the larger part of the square. On the weekend, Statue Square and surrounding Central become the domain of Filipino housemaids, nannies, and waitresses, thousands of whom work in Hong Kong and send most of what they earn back home to their families. On their day off, they meet friends here, sitting on blankets spread on the concrete and sharing food, photographs, letters from home, and laughter, infusing the staid business district with a certain vitality and festivity. At any rate, a statue of Queen Victoria used to stand here, but it has been moved to Victoria Park. Perhaps appropriately for a town that was established to make money, the only statue remaining in the square is of a banker,

Sir Thomas Jackson, former manager of the Hongkong and Shanghai Bank. It's interesting to note that he stands facing the:

3. **Legislative Council Building,** formerly the Supreme Court and looking curiously out of place in modern Central. It was built in the early 1900s by architect Aston Webb, who later redesigned Buckingham Palace, and now houses Hong Kong's lawmaking body, popularly known as "Legco." With its local pink-and-gray granite, Ionic columns, and Chinese roof, the neoclassical structure is typical of late-Victorian colonial architecture and boasts a carved stone figure above the main portico of the Goddess of Justice holding scales. It carries two flags, one with the red star emblem of China and the other with the bauhinia flower of Hong Kong.

On the other side of the Legco building to the east is:

4. **Chater Garden,** former site of the Hong Kong Cricket Club until the 1960s. Today this is the only spot of green in the very heart of Central and is popular with those who practice *tai chi* (shadow boxing) in the early morning and among office workers on lunch break.

Running alongside the south edge of the garden is:

5. **Des Voeux Road Central,** easily recognizable by the tram lines snaking along it. What a contrast these quaint double-decker trams make when viewed against the high-rise banks on the other side of the street. Established in 1904 and now the city's oldest form of transportation, trams are the most colorful way to travel from the Western and Central Districts to Causeway Bay, especially at night when Hong Kong is ablaze in neon. Des Voeux Road itself was constructed as part of an early 1800s land reclamation project; before that the waterfront was situated farther inland—at Queen's Road. Land reclamation has been proceeding continuously throughout Hong Kong's history, slowly encroaching on the harbor itself. One Hong Kong resident I met joked that so much land was being reclaimed it wouldn't be long before you could walk across the harbor. With Central's most recent reclamation project—which extended the ferry piers for outlying islands far into the water—the joke no longer seems quite so funny.

☕ **TAKE A BREAK**   If it's before 3pm, consider having a typical Chinese snack of dim sum at **City Hall Chinese Restaurant** (☎ **852/2521 1303**), a casual Cantonese restaurant on the second floor of the City Hall's Low Block, located just a stone's throw from the Star Ferry terminus and Statue Square. It even has views of the harbor. For more spectacular views and a more substantial lunch, head up to the 30th-floor **La Ronda,** a revolving restaurant in the Furama Hotel, 1 Connaught Rd., Central (☎ **852/2848 7422**), north of Chater Garden. It offers buffet spreads of international dishes for both lunch and dinner, with incomparable views. If you're looking for one of Hong Kong's trendiest restaurants, however, look no further than **Vong,** located on the 30th floor of the Mandarin Oriental Hotel, 5 Connaught Rd., Central (☎ **852/2825 4028**), just west of Statue Square. Also with stunning views, this chic restaurant serves great Franco-Asian creations, but get carried away and you won't be able to finish this tour.

Across from Chater Garden, on the other side of Des Voeux Road Central, is the:

6. **Bank of China Tower,** rising like a glass finger pointing into the sky. Designed by I. M. Pei, this futuristic building with its crisscross pattern also observes the

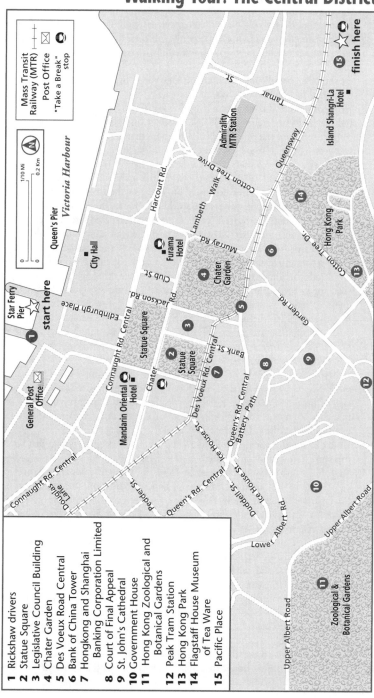

# Walking Tour: The Central District

Mass Transit Railway (MTR)

Post Office

"Take a Break" stop

*Victoria Harbour*

Queen's Pier

Star Ferry Pier

**start here**

City Hall

General Post Office

Connaught Rd. Central

Edinburgh Place

Statue Square

Mandarin Oriental Hotel

Chater

Connaught Rd. Central

Douglas Lane

Pedder St.

Queen's Rd. Central

Ice House St.

Duddell St.

Jackson Rd.

Club St.

Bank St. Central

Des Voeux Rd. Central

Battery Path

Queen's Rd. Central

Harcourt Rd.

Furama Hotel

Chater Garden

Murray Rd.

Lambeth Walk

Cotton Tree Drive

Admiralty MTR Station

Tamar St.

Queensway

Island Shangri-La Hotel

Hong Kong Park

Cotton Tree Dr.

Garden Rd.

Lower Albert Rd.

Upper Albert Road

Upper Albert Road

Zoological & Botanical Gardens

**finish here**

1 Rickshaw drivers
2 Statue Square
3 Legislative Council Building
4 Chater Garden
5 Des Voeux Road Central
6 Bank of China Tower
7 Hongkong and Shanghai
   Banking Corporation Limited
8 Court of Final Appeal
9 St. John's Cathedral
10 Government House
11 Hong Kong Zoological and
   Botanical Gardens
12 Peak Tram Station
13 Hong Kong Park
14 Flagstaff House Museum
   of Tea Ware
15 Pacific Place

1/10 Mi

0.2 Km

N

177

principles of *fung shui* (Chinese geomancy), as do all modern structures in Hong Kong in an effort to maintain harmony with their natural environment. Otherwise, disaster would surely strike—something no builder in Hong Kong wants to risk.

The most conspicuous building on Des Voeux Road Central, however, is farther west. It's the headquarters for the:

7. **Hongkong and Shanghai Banking Corporation Limited,** 1 Queen's Rd. Central, generally shortened to HSBC, which maintains offices in more than 20 countries around the world and employs more than 21,000 people. Hong Kong's first city hall once stood on this site. The Hongkong Bank, located here since 1865, issued the colony's first bank notes in 1881. The present building, designed in the mid-1980s by renowned British architect Sir Norman Foster and reputedly one of the most expensive buildings in the world (almost US$1 billion), attracts visiting architects the world over for its innovative external structure, rather than a central core. It was constructed from prefabricated components manufactured all over the world; the glass, aluminum cladding, and flooring came from the United States. Internal walls are removable, allowing for office reconfiguration. Walk underneath the bank's open ground plaza for a look up into this unique structure, or, if you choose, take the longest freely supported escalator in the world up to the first floor. Much care was given to the angle of these escalators, as well as to many other aspects of construction, in order not to disturb the spirits who reside here (altogether there are 62 escalators in the building, more than in any other office building in the world). Note, too, the two bronze lions you see at the entrance, which have been "guarding" the bank since 1935. You can rub their paws for good luck.

If you walk through the Hongkong Bank's open, ground-floor plaza to the other side, you'll find yourself on Queen's Road Central, where on the opposite side of the street are some stone steps leading up to a pathway overhung with branches, known as Battery Path, where you should turn left. Straight ahead is a handsome brick building, the 150-year-old:

8. **Court of Final Appeal,** and formerly the French Mission Building. Just beyond it is the cream-and-white colored, Gothic-style:

9. **St. John's Cathedral,** inaugurated in 1849 and thought to be the oldest Anglican church in the Far East. During the Japanese occupation, the church was used for Japanese social functions. You can enter the small church and take a look inside. It underwent extensive renovations following World War II, but still retains quaint tropical characteristics like the ceiling fans.

Take a left out of the church and walk around it to busy Garden Road, where you should turn right and walk uphill. After passing the U.S. Consulate, you'll come to Albert Road, where you should turn right. You'll soon see:

10. **Government House** on your right. Completed in 1855, it served as the official residence of 25 British governors, until 1997. During the World War II Japanese occupation, it also served as the headquarters of Lieutenant General Isogai, who ordered some extensive building renovations, a curious mix of Asian and Western architecture, including ceramic tile roofs and a tower reminiscent of Shinto shrines. Although presently closed, the grand, whitewashed edifice is being considered for transformation into a public events hall, with an art gallery for contemporary Hong Kong art, concerts, fund-raising events, and more.

Across the street, on the corner of Upper Albert Road and Garden Road, is a staircase leading up to the main entrance of the:

11. **Hong Kong Zoological and Botanical Gardens,** a wonderful oasis of plants and animals that was established in 1864 and still imparts a Victorian atmosphere with its wrought-iron bandstand and greenhouse. Entrance is free, and the grounds are not too extensive, so it's worth taking the time to wander through to see its tropical botanical gardens, aviaries, and apes. It opens daily at 6am, with the eastern half closing at 7pm and the western part at 10pm.

    Taking the same exit out of the gardens, cross to the other side of Garden Road and walk downhill, taking a right after passing the modern St. John's Building. Here, to your right, is the:

12. **Peak Tram Station,** which opened in 1888, reducing the travel time to the top of Victoria Peak from 3 hours (by sedan chair) to 8 minutes. Today the tram is the steepest funicular railway in the world, and the view from the peak is the best in Hong Kong. I suggest you visit the peak twice during your stay: during the day for the great panoramic view of the city, and again at night for its romantic atmosphere. There's a great, 1-hour circular walk around the peak, as well as attractions for children. In all, you'll probably want to spend at least an hour or 2 hours on the Peak, so you might want to save it for another day.

    On the other side of the tram station, on Cotton Tree Drive, is:

13. **Hong Kong Park,** once the grounds of Victoria Barracks and which opened as a park in 1991. On its grounds is the pink Rawlinson House, formerly the private residence of the Deputy General and now serving as a marriage registry. If it's a weekend or an auspicious day in the Chinese calendar, you'll find many newly-weds posing for pictures in the park. You'll also find a greenhouse, a great aviary with 800 birds, and a playground. Signs will direct you to the park's most important building and Hong Kong's oldest surviving colonial-style structure, the:

14. **Flagstaff House Museum of Tea Ware** (☎ **852/2869 0690**), built in 1846. It houses a small collection of tea utensils, with descriptions of tea-making through the various Chinese dynasties. It's open Thursday to Tuesday 10am to 5pm. Like everything else in the park, it's free. From here, walk past the fountain (a favorite backdrop for picture taking) to the escalators that will take you downhill to:

15. **Pacific Place,** a large complex filled with department stores, clothing boutiques, restaurants, and hotels. The nearest subway station from here is Admiralty Station, just a couple minutes' walk away.

    ☕ **WINDING DOWN**   There are many eating and drinking establishments in Pacific Place. **Dan Ryan's Chicago Grill** (☎ **852/2845 4600**) is a casual bar and grill that remains open throughout the day for drinks, burgers, and other American favorites. **Zen Chinese** (☎ **852/2845 4555**) is the ultimate in Chinese hip dining, with a Zenlike decor and specialties that border on Cantonese nouvelle. **Grappa's** (☎ **852/2868 0086**) is a moderately priced trattoria with an open kitchen and good food.

## Walking Tour 2: The Western District

**Start:** Star Ferry terminus, Central District.
**Finish:** Lan Kwai Fong, Central.
**Time:** About 4 hours.
**Best Times:** Weekday mornings, Monday to Friday, when markets are in full swing.
**Worst Times:** Sunday, when some shops are closed; Monday, when the Museum of Medical Sciences is closed.

While the Central District seems to be Western in style, with its banks, high-rises, and smart department stores, the Western District is very Chinese—a fascinating neighborhood of family-owned shops and businesses, with nary a tourist in sight. Traditional herbs, ginseng, antiques, preserved fish, name chops, coffins, funeral items, Hong Kong's oldest temple, and an interesting museum comparing traditional Chinese and Western medicine are just some of the things you'll see in my favorite area on Hong Kong Island.

As you exit from the Star Ferry terminus, take the first stairs you see on the right (by the post office) up to the elevated covered walkway that runs between the post office and the harbor. There are elevated walkways throughout Central, an efficient way of separating foot traffic from automobiles but also useful in rainy weather. This stretch, however, is a favored home—of the homeless, who create their own little sanctuaries with cardboard boxes and cots. At the end of this stretch, to the right, is the Outlying Districts Services Pier, where ferries depart for Lantau, Lamma, and Cheung Chau. Straight ahead are the IFC Mall, which houses Hong Kong Station, terminus for the Express Line, and Exchange Square, which houses the Stock Exchange and a major bus terminal.

You'll take a left here, however, and walk straight following the signs a couple of minutes until you reach our first destination, the:

1. **Landmark,** on the corner of Des Voeux Road Central and Pedder Street. This is an ultra-chic shopping complex with the boutiques of Gucci, Tiffany, Louis Vuitton, and Gianni Versace.

Return to Des Voeux Road Central, easily recognizable with its tram lines, and turn left (away from the harbor) onto Pedder Street. Just up the street on your right is the not-to-be-missed, smart-looking:

2. **Shanghai Tang,** in the Pedder Building (☎ **852/2525 7333**). This is a reproduction of a Shanghai clothing department store as it might have looked in the 1930s, with gleaming wooden and tiled floors, raised cashier cubicles, ceiling fans, and clerks wearing traditional Chinese clothing. This is a great place to shop for typical Chinese goods in mod colors, from cheongsams to Chinese jackets, as well as funky accessories like Mao watches, bathroom accessories, and gifts.

Just past Shanghai Tang is the main entrance to the:

3. **Pedder Building,** 12 Pedder St., a shopping center since 1926. It is now famous for its dozens of factory outlets and clothing boutiques; look for the elevator that services the first to seventh floors. Be aware, however, that just a handful of shops here are true factory outlets. The rest are simply taking advantage of the location to set up boutiques to sell their usual goods at regular prices. If you have the time, you might want to hunt for some bargains here. I usually take the elevator up to the sixth floor and then work my way down.

Return to Des Voeux Road Central, turn left, and continue west; in about 2 minutes you will come to:

4. **Li Yuen Street East and Li Yuen Street West,** two parallel pedestrian lanes that rise steeply to your left and are packed with stalls that sell clothing and accessories, including costume jewelry, handbags, belts, and even bras. If you see something you like, be sure to bargain for it. Walk up Li Yuen Street East, take a right, and then head back down Li Yuen Street West. If you wish to visit a couple of local department stores, however, at the top of Li Yuen Street East, to the left on Queens Road Central, is:

# Walking Tour: The Western District

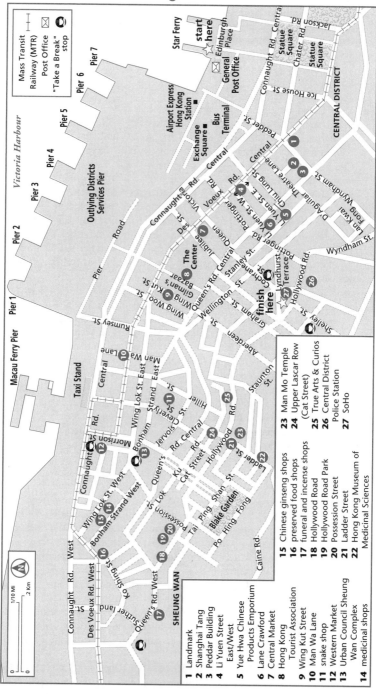

**Legend**
- ┤┼┤ Mass Transit Railway (MTR)
- ⊠ Post Office
- ◐ "Take a Break" stop

1 Landmark
2 Shanghai Tang
3 Peddar Building
4 Li Yuen Street East/West
5 Yue Hwa Chinese Products Emporium
6 Lane Crawford
7 Central Market
8 Hong Kong Tourist Association
9 Wing Kut Street
10 Man Wa Lane
11 snake shop
12 Western Market
13 Urban Council Sheung Wan Complex
14 medicinal shops
15 Chinese ginseng shops
16 preserved food shops
17 funeral and incense shops
18 Hollywood Road
19 Hollywood Road Park
20 Possession Street
21 Ladder Street
22 Hong Kong Museum of Medicinal Sciences
23 Man Mo Temple
24 Upper Lascar Row (Cat Street)
25 True Arts & Curios
26 Central District Police Station
27 SoHo

181

**5. Yue Hwa Chinese Products Emporium,** 39 Queen's. Rd., Central (☎ **852/ 2522 2333**), a great place to shop for Chinese souvenirs, furniture, arts and crafts, beaded purses, wooden vase stands, jewelry boxes, jade, traditional Chinese jackets, embroidery, Chinese medicines, and other products from the mainland. It's the next best thing to being in Beijing itself and is my favorite outlet for this popular chain.

Across the street is the:

**6. Lane Crawford** department store, 70 Queen's Rd. Central (☎ **852/2526 6121**), a very chic and upmarket clothing store and another Hong Kong favorite.

After walking down Li Yuen Street West, turn left onto Des Voeux Road Central and continue walking west a couple of blocks, until (on your left) you'll see the:

**7. Central Market,** a three-story building that serves as Hong Kong's largest public food market for everything from seafood and live poultry to fruits and vegetables. Although it's open 6am to 2pm and again 4:30 to 8pm, the market is at its best before 8am, with women buying the day's food for their families and chefs purchasing the daily specials. Following the Chinese penchant for freshness, chickens are killed on the spot, boiled, and then thrown into machines that pluck them. Almost every part of every animal is for sale, including the liver, heart, and intestines. Wicker baskets may contain the discarded horns and skulls of bulls, with even the brains carved out—not for the fainthearted. If all you want to see are fruit and vegetables, head for the second floor. If you're too late to see much action, however, don't despair—there's another public market later in this walk.

Central Market also marks the beginning of the 2,600-foot-long Hillside Escalator Link that connects Central with the Mid-Levels on Victoria Peak. Opened in 1993, it consists of a series of escalators and moving sidewalks, with 29 entrances, designed to accommodate commuters who live in the Mid-Levels but work in Central and beyond. As such, the escalators operate downhill 6am to 10am, and then reverse their direction and go uphill 10am to 11pm. Because of the foot traffic, the Link has spawned a number of easily accessible new restaurants and bars, most in an area dubbed SoHo (more on this later).

Continue walking west on Des Voeux Road Central, past Jubilee Street, to the next small, brick lane on your left, Gilman's Bazaar, where you should turn left. About halfway down on your left is a sign for the:

**8. Hong Kong Tourist Association,** located in The Center, 99 Queen's Rd. Central (☎ **852/2508 1234**). A bit off the beaten track, this new facility is nevertheless well equipped to help visitors with brochures, computers, and a knowledgeable staff, and is larger than the small office in the Star Ferry terminus in Kowloon. The Center, by the way, was supposed to end up the tallest building in Hong Kong but fell short of its goal; it is, however, the city's first building with a computer-controlled exterior lighting system capable of creating a million different colors and patterns, making it very visible indeed.

Back on Des Voeux Road Central, continue west 1 more block and turn left onto:

**9. Wing Kut Street,** another small lane lined with stalls that sell clothing, handbags, and other accessories for women. More interesting, however, are the small shops behind the stalls, which specialize in costume jewelry in a wide range of styles and prices. Some of the shops sell only wholesale, but others sell also to individual shoppers.

After walking through Wing Kut Street, take a right onto Queen's Road Central. This major thoroughfare will soon curve off to the left, but you'll want to keep walking straight westward onto Bonham Strand East. Soon, to your right, just after the Hongkong Bank, you'll see an interesting street:

10. **Man Wa Lane,** home since the 1920s of one of China's oldest trades—"chop" or carved-seal making. Sadly, the rise of recent high-rises makes the stalls look out of place. Made from stone, ivory, jade, clay, marble, bronze, porcelain, bamboo, wood, soapstone, and even plastic, these seals or stamps can be carved with a name and are used by the Chinese much like a written signature. You can have your own chop made at one of the several booths here, with your name translated into Chinese characters. It takes about an hour for a chop to be completed, so you may want to stop by again later after you've finished your walk. You can also have business cards made here with both English and Chinese characters; that takes about a day. Most stalls here are open Monday to Saturday 9am to 7pm.

Back on Bonham Strand East, continue westward. Just a few years ago, this area was known for its many snake shops, which did a roaring business from October to February. Now only a few remain, easily identifiable by cages of pythons, cobras, and banded kraits piled on the sidewalk, or by the wooden drawers lining the walls of the shop. Just past Mercer Street is Hillier Street, where you should turn left for the:

11. **Snake shop** at 13 Hillier St, an open-fronted shop recognizable by its many drawers lining the wall. Eaten as protection against the winter cold and as a cure for rheumatism, snakes are often served in soup. They are favored also for their gallbladders, which are mixed with Chinese wine as cures for rheumatism. Who knows, you might see a shopkeeper fill a customer's order by deftly grabbing a snake out of one of the drawers, extracting the gallbladder, and mixing it in yellow wine. The snake survives the operation, but who knows what other fate awaits it. The more poisonous the snake, so they say, the better the cure. The mixture is also believed to be an aphrodisiac.

You have now entered one of my favorite areas of the Western District. After continuing down Hillier Street, take the next right onto Jervois, walk 1 block, and then take the next right again on Cleverly Street; here you'll find several traditional, open-fronted, family-owned shops selling cookware, religious artifacts, joss sticks, and handcrafted birdcages. Take the first left again back onto Bonham Strand East, where you'll pass medicinal shops selling dried organic products such as mushrooms and roots; a tea merchant's shop; and, on the corner of Morrison Street, a rattan shop with handmade wares spilling out onto the sidewalks and hanging from hooks outside the shop. It takes an apprentice 3 years to learn the skills necessary to become a master rattan maker; the rattan itself comes from a climbing vine found throughout Asia. As a sign of the times, the shop has recently branched into plastic housewares.

Take a right here onto Morrison Street and walk to the end where, on the left, you'll find the handsome, redbrick:

12. **Western Market,** 323 Des Voeux Rd. Central. Built in 1906 and used as a public market until 1989, it escaped demolition when the decision was made to renovate the imposing Edwardian/Victorian landmark into a bazaar for shops and artisans. On the ground floor are souvenir and gift shops that sell everything from Chinese seals to children's toys; on the first floor retailers sell bolts of colorful cloth, buttons, clasps, and other sewing accessories. Most shops are open daily 10am to 7pm.

**TAKE A BREAK**   On the top floor of the Western Market is **Treasure Inn Seafood Restaurant** (☎ **852/2850 7780**), a Cantonese seafood restaurant open daily. In an atrium setting decorated in the style of a 1920s teahouse, it has an English menu with pictures, making ordering easy. If you're on a budget or like adventuresome dining, head to the **Cooked Food Centre** on the second floor of the Urban Council Sheung Wan Complex (described below), Bonham Strand East, where on the second floor are food stalls selling various noodle, vegetable, and other Chinese dishes. There are no English menus, and most of the patrons are neighborhood residents, vendors working inside the complex's market, or nearby blue-collar workers. It's open Monday to Saturday 6am to an astonishing 2am.

From Western Market, backtrack on Morrison Street to Bonham Strand East where, across the street, you'll see the large:

13. **Urban Council Sheung Wan Complex** (also called the Sheung Wan Civic Centre). One of Hong Kong's largest neighborhood markets, open 6am to 8pm, it features fish and poultry on the ground floor, meats and vegetables on the first floor, and a large dining hall with stalls selling cheap, cooked meals on the second floor. The market is at its liveliest before 11:30am, but you'll find butchers at their trade also in the afternoon.

Exit the market building back onto Bonham Strand East, turn left, and follow the road as it curves around the market's west side. Take the first right onto Bonham Strand West. This is where you'll find the Western District's most interesting enterprises:

14. **Medicinal shops.** Based on the Asian concept of maintaining a healthy balance between the yin and yang forces in the body, the range of medicinal herbs is startling, including roots, twigs, bark, dried leaves, seeds, pods, flowers, grasses, insects (such as discarded cicada shells), deer antlers, dried sea horses, dried fish bladders, and rhinoceros horns. The herbalist, after learning about the customer's symptoms and checking the pulses in both wrists, will prescribe an appropriate remedy, using perhaps a bit of bark here and a seed there, based on wisdom passed down over thousands of years.

The kings of trade on Bonham Strand are clearly the:

15. **Chinese ginseng shops.** More than 30 varieties of ginseng root are handled in this wholesale trading area. The most prized are the red ginseng from North Korea, white ginseng from North America, and a very rare ginseng that grows wild in the mountains of northeastern China. Red ginseng is supposed to aid male virility, while the white variety helps cure hangovers.

By the way, Bonham Strand has long had an exotic atmosphere—150 years ago it buzzed with activity as merchants from Shanghai, Canton (Guangzhou), Fujian, and other Chinese provinces and cities set up shop selling products from their native regions. At the end of Bonham Strand, turn left on Des Voeux Road West. Along this road you'll see:

16. **Shops selling preserved foods.** Dried and salted fish, flattened squid, oysters, scallops, abalone, sea slugs, fish bladders, starfish, shrimp, and many other kinds of seafood have been dried and preserved. You can buy bird's nest here, as well as shark's fin, and in winter there's also pressed duck and Chinese sausages made from pork and liver.

Continue west on Des Voeux Road; at shop no. 90 turn left onto Sutherland Street (if shop 90 is still under construction, you'll have to search for the street sign; if you reach shop no. 98, you'll have gone too far). A few years back, the neighborhood here was renovated and the Li Sing Street Playground was built in its midst, displacing some of the narrow alleys favored by one of Hong Kong's oldest professions—streetside barbers. Once plentiful, streetside barbers are now

# Chinese Gods

There are many gods in the Chinese world, each with different functions and abilities. There are household gods such as the kitchen god, as well as patron gods of various occupations and gods who protect worshippers through certain stages of their lives. There is an earth god, a goddess of pregnant women, 60 gods representing each year of the 60-year Chinese calendar, a god of riches popular with shopkeepers, and a scholar god whose favor is curried by students.

Most popular in Hong Kong is **Tin Hau,** goddess of the sea and protector of seafarers (in Macau she is known as **A-Ma**). As the patron goddess of fisherfolk, Tin Hau is honored by fishing communities throughout Hong Kong; there are more than two dozen Tin Hau temples, including those at Yau Ma Tei, Causeway Bay, Stanley, and Cheung Chau. According to popular lore, Tin Hau is the deification of a real girl who lived in Fujian Province around A.D. 900 or 1000 and who saved some fishermen during a storm. Her birthday is celebrated annually with gaily decorated junks and lion dances. Another popular goddess is **Kuan Yin** (called Kun Iam in Macau), the goddess of mercy, capable of delivering people from suffering or misery.

There are also several temples in Hong Kong devoted to **Man** (the god of literature and the patron of civil servants) and **Mo** (the god of war). Mo was a great warrior of the Han dynasty, deified not only for his integrity but his ability to protect from the misfortunes of war. Ironically, for this reason Mo is worshiped not only by soldiers and the Hong Kong police force but also by gang members of the underworld. Hong Kong's most famous Man Mo Temple is in the Western District on Hollywood Road.

One of the most popular gods in Hong Kong is **Wong Tai Sin,** believed to generously grant the wishes of his followers, cure sickness, and—best of all—dispense horse-racing tips. The Wong Tai Sin Temple, located in a district by the same name, is always crowded with worshippers, as well as fortune-tellers, making this one of the most interesting temple destinations in Hong Kong.

---

going the way of the rickshaw, but just past the playground, to the left, is the only makeshift barbershop remaining in this area. At the top of Sutherland Street, on busy Queen's Road West, there used to be an elderly woman who set up shop on the sidewalk, using only a couple of stools and a string. She used the string to pull out the facial hairs of her customers, an ancient method that few barbers can still perform. She wasn't there during my last couple of visits, but maybe you'll be lucky and see her. If you take a right from Sutherland onto Queen's Road West, you'll soon see—and hear—a bird shop, with hundreds of songbirds, exquisitely crafted wooden and bamboo cages, and tiny porcelain water bowls for sale.

☕ **TAKE A BREAK**   There's no better place for Western food in the Western District than **Sammy's Kitchen,** 204–206 Queen's Rd. West (reached from Sutherland Street by turning right and walking about 2 minutes; ☎ **852/2548 8400**). A landmark for almost 3 decades, it's owned by the gregarious and friendly Sammy Yip, who treats foreign guests like royalty. It's a good place for inexpensive lunchtime fare or, in the evenings, fresh seafood, steaks, chicken, and house-invented specialties.

From Sutherland Street, cross Queen's Road West and turn left, heading east. Here you'll pass several open-fronted:

**17. Funeral and incense shops.** Note the paper replicas of household goods and items that are sold to accompany the deceased into the afterlife: houses, cars, and even computers.

Shortly you will soon see a road leading uphill to the right. It's the famous:

**18. Hollywood Road,** with its strange mixture of shops selling coffins, funeral items, furniture, and antiques. In fact, there are more antiques shops concentrated here along this rather long road than anywhere else in Hong Kong, and you'll find everything from woodblock prints and rosewood tables to Neolithic pots, Ming dynasty ceramic figures, silk carpets, snuff bottles, porcelain, and round-bellied smiling Buddhas. Built in 1844 to accommodate British troops stationed here, the road takes its name from the woods of holly that used to adorn the area.

First, however, to your left will be:

**19. Hollywood Road Park,** a pleasant garden oasis with a children's playground, a pond with goldfish, and Chinese pagodas. Stop for a few moments of relaxation before continuing.

Just past the playground you'll soon pass a historic landmark:

**20. Possession Street,** to your left. There's no need to enter it, but you might be interested to know that it was here that the British first landed in 1841 and planted the Union Jack to claim the island for Britain. At the time, of course, this was part of the waterfront.

After passing more antiques and curio shops on Hollywood Road, you'll see to your right (just after shop no. 132–134):

**21. Ladder Street,** an extremely steep flight of stairs and once a common sight on steep Hong Kong Island. Now, of course, Hong Kong Island has escalators and the Peak Tram, but you're going to find out exactly how steep and tiring these stairs are by taking them almost to the top before turning right and following the sign down the short flight of steps to the:

**22. Hong Kong Museum of Medical Sciences,** 2 Caine Lane (☎ **852/2549 5123**). It's housed in a stately, 1905 Edwardian-style brick building that once served as the Pathological Institute, founded to combat Hong Kong's worst outbreak of bubonic plague, which eventually claimed 20,000 lives. With most rooms left intact and devoted to various aspects of early medicine practiced in colonial Hong Kong, it is the only museum in the world to compare both traditional Chinese and Western medicine. You'll see acupuncture needles, an autopsy room, an X ray of a bound foot (once considered a sign of beauty for Chinese women), Chinese medicinal herbs, and the Halvo Pelvic Distraction Apparatus, a Hong Kong invention for treating humped backs. Very fascinating. It's open Tuesday to Saturday 10am to 5pm and Sunday 1 to 5pm.

Head back down Ladder Street and turn right onto Hollywood Road, where you'll immediately see the:

**23. Man Mo Temple,** Hong Kong Island's oldest and most well-known temple. It was in this area that the movie *The World of Suzie Wong* was filmed. The temple, which dates back to the 1840s and is open daily 8am to 6pm, is dedicated to two deities: the god of literature (Man) and the god of war (Mo). Mo finds patronage both with the police force (shrines in his honor can be found in all Hong Kong police stations) and members of the underworld. Two ornately carved sedan chairs dating from the 1800s and kept in the temple were once used to carry the statues of the gods around the neighborhood during festivals. From the ceiling hang huge incense coils, which burn as long as 3 weeks, purchased by patrons seeking the fulfillment of their wishes.

If you follow the steps leading downhill opposite Ladder Street, you'll see:

**24.** **Upper Lascar Row,** better known as **Cat Street,** which leads off to the left. For almost a century Cat Street was famous for its antiques, which could be bought for a pittance; now, however, with the new antiques shops on Hollywood Road and the nearby Cat Street Galleries, Cat Street vendors offer a fantastic mix of curios and junk. Pleasantly dotted with potted palms, this pedestrian lane is worth a browse for jade, snuff bottles, watches, pictures, copper and brass kettles, old eyeglasses, birdcages, and odds and ends. You can bargain with the vendors who have laid their wares on the sidewalk; most of them do business Monday to Saturday 11am to about 5pm. You can also bargain at the surrounding antiques shops, where prices are rather high to begin with. If you're not an expert, be wary of purchasing anything of value. During one of my visits, it seemed that every shop was offering fossilized "dinosaur eggs" for sale. How many can there be?

At the end of Cat Street, return to Hollywood Road, where you should take a left and continue walking toward its eastern end. Here you'll find more chic and upscale antiques shops, selling furniture, blue-and-white porcelain, and goods from other countries, including Korean chests and Japanese hibachi. One of my favorites is:

**25.** **True Arts & Curios,** 89 Hollywood Rd. (☎ **852/2559 1485**), a tiny shop packed with all kinds of surprises, from antique children's pointed shoes to porcelain, jewelry, and snuff bottles. It also carries about 2,000 temple wood carvings, most of which are about 100 years old and small enough to carry with you on the plane.

Farther down, at 47 Hollywood Road, just before the Hillside Escalator Link, are a couple of ancient-looking hole-in-the-wall shops selling bric-a-brac, old photographs and postcards of Hong Kong (including portraits of women engaged in that ageless profession), snuff bottles, and other interesting stuff. Walk under the elevated people-mover, and just a bit beyond, to the right, on Old Bailey and Hollywood Road, is the:

**26.** **Central District Police Station,** originally built in 1864 and expanded in 1919 and 1925. It's one of Hong Kong's largest clusters of Victorian-era buildings, built in classical style.

Return to the Hillside Escalator. Here, on the steep lanes flanking the escalator and on narrow side alleys, is Hong Kong's newest nightlife and dining district:

**27.** **SoHo,** which stands for "south of Hollywood." Now, of course, SoHo has blossomed into side streets on both sides of Hollywood Road. Most establishments are tiny affairs, serving a great variety of ethnic cuisines at reasonable prices.

If you wish to return to Central, walk downhill on Cochrane Street (which runs underneath the escalator) to Queen's Road Central, where you should turn right.

☕ **WINDING DOWN**    Since establishments are opening up in SoHo literally overnight, I suggest you simply walk along Shelley and Cochrane streets and their side streets until something catches your fancy. Otherwise, for a place you can't miss, head downhill to the bright red exterior of **Dublin Jack,** 37 Cochrane St. (☎ **852/2543 0081**). It's elbow-to-elbow with working expats after offices close, especially during the 3-to-8pm happy hour. Uphill, on the corner of Shelley and Staunton streets, is **Staunton Bar & Cafe** (☎ **852/2973 6611**), one of the first venues to open in SoHo. On the ground floor is a casual bar, while the restaurant upstairs serves modern Mediterranean cuisine. One of my favorites is **Pavilion,** 3 Tun Wo Lane (just off Cochrane Street; ☎ **852/2869 7768**), which serves excellent Continental cuisine in a tiny, romantic courtyard and miniature restaurant; it adjoins **Petticoat Lane Bar,** under the same management. For Mexican food, head up Shelley street to I Caramba!, 26–30 Elgin St. (☎ **852/ 2530 9963**).

## Walking Tour 3: Kowloon

**Start:** Star Ferry Terminus, Tsim Sha Tsui.
**Finish:** Temple Street Night Market.
**Time:** About 4 hours.
**Best Time:** Early afternoon, when the Jade Market is open; or late in the day, when you can visit the Temple Street Night Market.
**Worst Times:** Thursday, when the Hong Kong Museum of Art is closed.

A stroll up Nathan Road through Tsim Sha Tsui and Yau Ma Tei will take you through the heart of Kowloon, past its famous hotels, restaurants, and shops and on to the fascinating Chinese shops and markets in Yau Ma Tei and Mong Kok. Because the Jade Market closes around 3pm and the nearby Temple Street Night Market is best visited after 7pm, you'll have to decide which is most important to you and plan your time accordingly. If you only choose one, I'd opt for the Temple Street Night Market. On the other hand, because the MTR is so efficient, you can always take in both by returning to the night market in the evening. Or, if you'd rather not visit Temple Street at night, a few vendors set up shop from 2 or 3pm. Alternatively, because this walk is such a long one, you might wish to either break it up into a 2-day stroll or cover only part of it, concentrating on those sights that interest you the most.

Otherwise, a logical tour of Tsim Sha Tsui begins with the Star Ferry since, for more than a century, it served as the only link with Hong Kong Island. Within the terminus itself is the Hong Kong Tourist Association office, where you can pick up free pamphlets, brochures, and maps of Hong Kong. In front of the Star Ferry concourse is Kowloon's main bus terminal; straight ahead, on the side of the bus terminal, is a large, nondescript building, Star House, which contains mostly offices but also restaurants and shops. Of most interest to visitors is:

1. **Chinese Arts & Crafts,** on the ground floor of Star House, 3 Salisbury Rd. (☎ **852/2735 4061**). Open daily 10am to 9:30pm, it is the most upscale store specializing in Chinese products, including embroidered tablecloths, jewelry, ceramics, arts and crafts, and clothing. It's also one of the safest places to buy jade.

Behind Star House is Ocean Terminal, the port of call for cruise liners docking in Hong Kong. It's probably no accident that it is immediately adjacent to:

2. **Harbour City,** Hong Kong's largest interconnected shopping mall and one of the largest shopping complexes in the world. Stretching more than a half mile along Canton Road, it contains more than 700 shops. Enter it and you might not escape during this lifetime; better save shopping for another day. Instead, look just east of the Star Ferry and bus terminals for the colonial-looking:

3. **Clock tower,** built in 1915. Now dwarfed by the buildings around it, it's the only structure remaining from Hong Kong's old train station, once the final stop

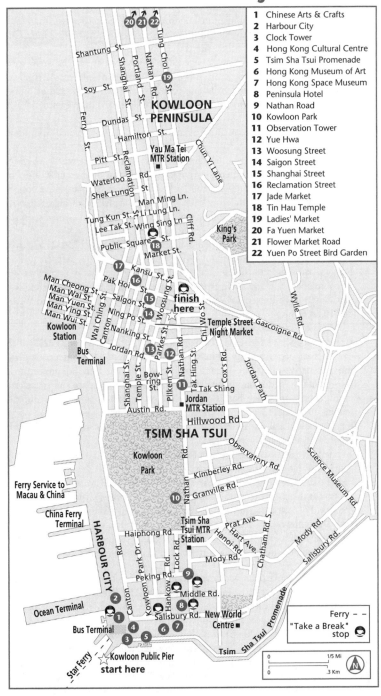

# Walking Tour: Kowloon

1 Chinese Arts & Crafts
2 Harbour City
3 Clock Tower
4 Hong Kong Cultural Centre
5 Tsim Sha Tsui Promenade
6 Hong Kong Museum of Art
7 Hong Kong Space Museum
8 Peninsula Hotel
9 Nathan Road
10 Kowloon Park
11 Observation Tower
12 Yue Hwa
13 Woosung Street
14 Saigon Street
15 Shanghai Street
16 Reclamation Street
17 Jade Market
18 Tin Hau Temple
19 Ladies' Market
20 Fa Yuen Market
21 Flower Market Road
22 Yuen Po Street Bird Garden

Shantung St.
Tung Choi St.
Shanghai St.
Portland St.
Nathan Rd.
Soy St.
Ferry St.
**KOWLOON PENINSULA**
Dundas St.
Hamilton St.
Chun Yi Lane
Pitt St.
Reclamation Rd.
Yau Ma Tei MTR Station
Waterloo Rd.
Shek Lung St.
Man Ming Ln.
Tung Kun St.
Li Lung Ln.
Lee Tak St.
Wing Sing Ln.
Cliff Rd.
Public Square St.
Market St.
King's Park
Kansu St.
Pak Hoi St.
Man Cheong St.
Man Wai St.
Man Yuen St.
Man Ying St.
Man Wui St.
Saigon St.
Ning Po St.
Wai Ching St.
Canton Rd.
**finish here**
Wylie Rd.
Gascoigne Rd.
Woosung St.
**Kowloon Station**
Nanking St.
Parkes St.
Chi Wo St.
**Bus Terminal**
Jordan Rd.
**Temple Street Night Market**
Shanghai St.
Temple St.
Bow-ring St.
Pilkem St.
Nathan Rd.
Tak Hing St.
Jordan Path
Austin Rd.
Jordan MTR Station
Tak Shing St.
Cox's Rd.
Hillwood Rd.
**TSIM SHA TSUI**
**Kowloon Park**
Kimberley Rd.
Observatory Rd.
Science Museum Rd.
Granville Rd.
Nathan Rd.
Ferry Service to Macau & China
China Ferry Terminal
**HARBOUR CITY**
Tsim Sha Tsui MTR Station
Prat Ave.
Hart Ave.
Mody Rd.
Chatham Rd. S.
Salisbury Rd.
Haiphong Rd.
Park Dr.
Hanoi Rd.
Mody Rd.
Peking Rd.
Kowloon Park Dr.
Hankow Rd.
Lock Rd.
Canton Rd.
Middle Rd.
**Ocean Terminal**
Salisbury Rd.
New World Centre
**Bus Terminal**
Tsim Sha Tsui Promenade
Tsim Sha Tsui
**Kowloon Public Pier**
Star Ferry
**start here**

Ferry – –
"Take a Break" stop

0    1/5 Mi
0    .3 Km

for those traveling overland from London on the Orient Express. In 1975, the Kowloon-Canton Railway moved to its present location in Hung Hom. Occupying the train station's former site is the modern:

4. **Hong Kong Cultural Centre,** opened in 1989 as the city's largest arena for the performing arts. In my opinion, however, it's terribly misplaced. After all, why situate concert and theater halls that have no windows on waterfront property with one of the world's most stunning views? Still, the Cultural Centre does offer first-rate concerts of both Western and Chinese music.

Walking between the clock tower and Victoria Harbour, you'll find yourself on the:

5. **Tsim Sha Tsui Promenade,** which hugs the shoreline all the way from the Star Ferry to Hung Hom. It offers a great vantage point of the harbor with its boat traffic, Hong Kong Island, and the Peak. It's also a good place for a romantic stroll at night, when the dazzling lights of Hong Kong Island are ablaze across the harbor. In just a couple of minutes' stroll along the promenade, you'll soon reach one of my favorite attractions in Hong Kong, the:

6. **Hong Kong Museum of Art,** 10 Salisbury Rd. (☎ **852/2734 2167**), which contains an excellent collection of Chinese porcelain, bronzes, jade, lacquerware, bamboo carvings, and paintings of old Hong Kong and Macau, as well as works by contemporary Hong Kong artists. If you see only one museum in Hong Kong, this should be it. It even has windows! Don't miss it. It's open Friday to Wednesday 10am to 6pm.

Beside the art museum, to the north, is the:

7. **Hong Kong Space Museum,** 10 Salisbury Rd. (☎ **852/2734 2722**), which is easy to spot because of its white-domed planetarium. The museum is divided into two parts—the Space Theatre's planetarium, where films are projected onto the 75-foot domed roof, and exhibition halls devoted to space and space exploration. There are many hands-on exhibitions, as well as some simulator rides, making it a good place for children. Shows at the Space Theatre are so popular that they often sell out in advance, so you might want to stop off now and buy your ticket for a later performance.

The Space Museum (also without windows) has stolen the view from Tsim Sha Tsui's most famous landmark, the venerable:

8. **Peninsula Hotel,** right across the street. Built in 1928 to serve guests disembarking at the old train station and guarded by the largest all-Rolls-Royce fleet in the world (13, at last count), The Peninsula is Hong Kong's grandest old hotel, with a new tower that restored harbor views to its front-facing rooms. Its lobby, reminiscent of a Parisian palace, with high gilded ceilings, pillars, and ferns, has long been a favorite spot for a cup of coffee and people-watching.

☕ **TAKE A BREAK**   Many visitors feel that their Hong Kong stay would not be complete without dropping by the lobby of **The Peninsula Hotel** (☎ **852/ 2920 2888**). Classical music serenades you noon to midnight, but the best time to stop by is between 2 and 6:30pm daily, when an English-style afternoon tea is served for HK$155 ($20.15). If it's lunchtime, there are so many options nearby that it's difficult to single any out. **The Verandah,** also located in The Peninsula, has a plush, colonial atmosphere and a moderately priced fixed lunch. If you're on a budget, two nearby standouts include **The Pizzeria,** located behind The Peninsula in the Kowloon Hotel, 19–21 Nathan Rd. (☎ **852/2369 8698**), which offers an inexpensive buffet lunch; and **The Salisbury,** located on the fourth floor of the Salisbury YMCA, beside The Peninsula at 41 Salisbury Rd. (☎ **852/2369 2211**), which has one of the cheapest buffets around. For Cantonese food, head to **Jade Garden,** on the fourth floor of Star House (☎ **852/2730 6888**); or **Peking Garden,** on the third floor of Star House (☎ **852/2735 8211**), for Pekingese specialties.

Just past The Peninsula Hotel, turn left on:

**9.** **Nathan Road,** Kowloon's most famous street. It is also one of Hong Kong's widest, and runs almost 2½ miles straight up the spine of Kowloon all the way to Boundary Road, the official border of the New Territories. Nathan Road is named after Sir Matthew Nathan, who served as governor at the time the road was constructed. After it was completed, it was nicknamed "Nathan's Folly." After all, why build such a wide road, seemingly leading to nowhere? Kowloon had very few people back then and even less traffic. Now, of course, Nathan Road is known as the "golden mile of shopping" because of all the boutiques and shops that line both sides.

You'll pass jewelry stores, electronics shops, optical shops, clothing boutiques, and many others as you head north on Nathan Road. The side streets are also good hunting grounds for inexpensive casual wear, at prices comparable to those of Stanley Market. You'll want to return here to explore this area at leisure; shops are open to 9pm or later. After about 10 minutes (assuming you don't stop to shop along the way), you'll see a mosque on your left, built in 1984 to replace an older mosque built before the turn of the century for Muslim Indian troops belonging to the British army. Today there are about 70,000 Muslims in Hong Kong; the mosque is not open to the public. Past the mosque is a string of shops called Park Lane Shopper's Boulevard. In the middle of the block are wide steps leading up to:

**10.** **Kowloon Park,** a good place to bring children for a romp through playgrounds and open spaces. It also boasts a water garden, Chinese garden, sculpture garden (with Scotland's Sir Eduardo Paolozzi's bronze version of William Blake's *Concept of Newton*), aviary, woodland trail, maze made of foliage, and swimming pools.

I suggest you walk through the park northward, past the indoor/outdoor public swimming pools, to Austin Road, where you should turn right, cross Nathan Road, and then continue north up Nathan Road. You will soon reach the Pruton Prudential Hotel on your right, 222 Nathan Rd. (with an entrance on Tak Shing St.), which towers above a shopping complex. On the hotel's roof, reached by taking the elevator to the 17th floor, is an:

**11.** **Observation tower,** 300 feet above the ground, which provides great views of surrounding Kowloon and is open free to the public until 7pm.

Back on Nathan Road, be on the lookout to the left for:

**12.** **Yue Hwa Chinese Products Emporium,** on the corner of Jordan Road at 301–309 Nathan Rd. (☎ **852/2384 0084**), which caters primarily to the local Chinese with traditional Chinese products. Its goods from China include silk, porcelain, jade, clothing, furniture, medicinal herbs, and everyday household goods. Hours here are 10am to 10pm daily.

Once you've passed Yue Hwa, you'll find yourself in Yau Ma Tei. Its name translates roughly as "the place for growing sesame plants," but you won't see any such cultivation today. Rather, like the Western District on Hong Kong Island, Yau Ma Tei offers a look at traditional Chinese life, with shops that sell tea, chopping blocks, joss, bamboo steamers, baked goods, embroidery, herbs, and dried seafood.

Just past the Yue Hwa store, take the first left onto Nanking Street and then a right onto:

**13. Woosung Street.** Here you'll pass restaurants with live seafood in tanks and glazed ducks hanging from windows, an herbalist shop, and other family-owned businesses. After a few blocks, take a left on:

**14. Saigon Street,** where in succession (on the left side of the street) you'll pass a mahjong parlor, a shop for herbal teas (on the corner of Saigon and Temple Streets), and a pawn shop. You'll also pass Temple Street, site of the famous night market (but more on that later). Take a right on:

**15. Shanghai Street,** where you'll pass more traditional shops, the most interesting of which, perhaps, is the shop selling embroidery at 190 Shanghai St. One block to the east is:

**16. Reclamation Street.** Here, as well as the nearby Yau Ma Tei Market, is an interesting stroll if you haven't yet visited a city market.

At Kansu Street, turn left for the:

**17. Jade Market.** This fascinating covered market, in two separate structures, consists of some 400 stalls selling jade, pearls, and collectibles and is open about 10am to approximately 3pm daily, though some vendors stay until 3:30pm or so if business warrants it. The jade on sale here comes in a bewildering range of quality. The highest quality should be cold to the touch and translucent, but unless you know your jade you're better off just coming here for a look. It's possible to infuse jade with color so that inferior stones acquire the brightness and translucence associated with more expensive stones. If you want a souvenir, get a pendant or bangle, but don't spend more than a few dollars on it. The freshwater pearls are also good buys. Although the Chinese here used to bargain secretly by using hand signals concealed underneath a newspaper so that none of the onlookers would know the final price, it appears that calculators have gained more popularity.

From the Jade Market, continue north on Shanghai Street, where you will soon see the:

**18. Tin Hau Temple,** shaded by banyan trees. One of many temples in Hong Kong dedicated to Tin Hau, the Goddess of the Sea, this popular community temple has a park, usually filled with people playing mahjong, and inner recesses, filled with people asking favors or giving thanks. The temple has sections dating back more than a century. It also reveres deities of the city, the earth, and mercy. It's open daily 8am to 6pm.

**TAKE A BREAK**    **The Pearl Seaview Hotel,** located across from the Tin Hau Temple in the heart of Yau Ma Tei at 262 Shanghai St. (☎ **852/2782 0882**), has a lounge on its 19th floor offering views of surrounding Kowloon. It's open daily 4pm to midnight; 4 to 8pm, you can get two drinks for the price of one. **The Eaton Hotel,** 380 Nathan Rd. (just south of Kansu Street; ☎ **852/ 2782 1818**), is another good place to stop by for lunch or a drink. **Planter's,** just off the hotel's lobby on the fourth floor (enter the hotel on Pak Hoi Street), offers a buffet lunch Monday to Saturday until 2:30pm, as well as a happy hour daily 3 to 8pm, with two drinks for the price of one and live music beginning at 6:40pm. Also off the lobby is an outdoor terrace, open noon to midnight for drinks and snacks; there's also a sophisticated lobby lounge. For a meal, in the basement of the Eaton Hotel is a Cantonese restaurant, **Yat Tung Heen Chinese Restaurant,** good for seafood and regional dishes.

# Temple Street Night Market

The Temple Street Night Market is named after the street where it's located. This market, with most stalls open about 7pm and busiest 8 to 11pm, is a wonderful place to spend an evening, with its countless stalls that sell clothing, watches, lighters, sunglasses, sweaters, cassettes, and more. The name of the game is bargaining. There are also many seafood stalls, where you can eat inexpensive meals of clams, shrimp, mussels, and crab. Be sure to follow Temple Street to its northern end past the overpass; in the vicinity of the Tin Hau Temple you'll find palm readers, musicians, and street singers (who favor Cantonese operas and pop songs). Several of the palm readers speak English.

The market is famous for its *dai pai dong* (Cantonese for "big rows of food stalls") that specialize in seafood. Fifty years ago, dai pai dong is where most Hong Kong families dined on an evening out, and they were found almost everywhere. Now the government has moved most food stalls into covered markets. The dai pai dong at this market are among the few remaining that retain their original ambience. You'll find several under one roof at the Temple Street Food Store at the intersection of Temple Street and Public Square Street, where you can dine inexpensively on clams, shrimp, mussels, and crab, sitting at simple tables in the middle of the action.

Depending on when you started this tour, at this point you may want to go back to your hotel room to rest and then take a taxi to visit Yau Ma Tei's most famous attraction, the **Temple Street Night Market** (see the box). The market doesn't get under way until after 7pm (a few vendors may start setting up stalls at around 2 or 3pm). Otherwise, if it's early, you like markets, and you're still feeling energetic, walk north on Nathan Road about 10 minutes, taking a right on Dundas Street and then a left onto Tung Choi, home of the so-called:

**19. Ladies' Market,** where daily about 10:30am to 10:30pm street vendors sell women's clothing and accessories, including handbags, sunglasses, and shoes, as well as some men's and children's clothing at low prices. Although most products are geared to local tastes (and sizes), you can spend at least an hour here, and maybe even pick up some bargains to boot. It's also a good alternative to the more touristy and crowded Temple Street Night Market.

The Ladies' Market, in the heart of Mong Kok, extends from Dundas to Argyle Street. However, for an even more local market, continue north on Tung Choi Street to Mong Kok Street, which you should cross and then turn right on Mong Kok, taking the first left for:

**20. Fa Yuen Street,** with stalls selling more clothing, handbags, socks, belts, cheap toys, and fruit, at very inexpensive prices. There probably won't be another tourist in sight.

At the end of Fa Yuen Street, turn right to cross Prince Edward Road West at the pedestrian light, turn left onto Sai Yee Street, and then take the first right for:

**21. Flower Market Road,** with shop after open-fronted shop selling orchids, roses, and other wonderfully aromatic flowers, at prices so inexpensive you'll wish you could take some home. More transportable but not nearly as appealing are the plastic flowers also sold on this street. Shops are open daily around 10am to 6pm. At the end of the road is the:

**22.** Yuen Po Street Bird Garden, an attractive series of Chinese-style open courtyards lined with shops selling songbirds, intricately fashioned birdcages, live crickets, and tiny porcelain water bowls. Note, too, the men who bring their pet birds here for an outing. This place is very Chinese and makes for some great photographs. It's open daily 7am till 8pm.

**WINDING DOWN**    After exploring this area of Mong Kok, either walk back to Nathan Road for the Prince Edward MTR station and take it three stations south to Jordan Station, or take a break at one of the suggestions above.

# Shopping 8

No doubt about it—one of the main reasons people come to Hong Kong is to shop. According to the Hong Kong Tourist Association (HKTA), visitors spend more than 50% of their money here on shopping. In fact, Hong Kong is such a popular shopping destination that many luxury cruise ships dock longer here than they do anywhere else on their tours. I doubt that there's ever been a visitor to Hong Kong who left empty-handed.

## 1 The Shopping Scene

### BEST BUYS

Hong Kong is a duty-free port, which means that imported goods are not taxed in Hong Kong with the exception of only a few luxury goods, such as tobacco, alcohol, and some petroleum products. What's more, there is no sales tax in Hong Kong. Thus, you can buy some goods in Hong Kong at a cheaper price than in the country where they were made. It's less expensive, for example, to buy Japanese products such as designer clothing, cameras, electronic goods, and pearls in Hong Kong than in Japan itself. In fact, all my friends who live in Japan try to visit Hong Kong at least once or twice a year to buy their business clothes, cosmetics, and other accessories.

Although not as cheap as it once was, clothing is probably one of the best buys in Hong Kong, simply because of the sheer quantity and variety. If you've looked at the labels of clothes sold in your own hometown, you've probably noticed that many say MADE IN HONG KONG. Hong Kong is one of the world's most foremost producers of knits. Both custom-made and designer garments remain affordable in Hong Kong, including three-piece business suits, leather outfits, furs, sportswear, and jeans. Even cheaper are factory outlets and small stores where you can pick up inexpensive fashions for a song. But even when I end up paying about as much for an outfit as I would back home, I'm satisfied—I can find unique clothing here that's impossible to find in the homogenized shopping malls in the United States.

Hong Kong is also a great place to shop for Chinese products, including porcelain, jade, cloisonné, silk handicrafts and clothing, hand-embroidery, jewelry, and artwork. You'll also find crafts and goods from other parts of Asia, including Thailand, India, the Philippines, and Indonesia.

Other good buys include Chinese antiques, shoes, jewelry, furniture, carpets, leather goods, luggage (you'll probably need a new bag just to lug your purchases home), handbags, briefcases, Chinese herbs, and eyeglasses. Hong Kong is also one of the world's largest exporters of watches and toys. As for electronic goods and cameras, they are not the bargains they once were. Make sure, therefore, to check prices on goods at home before you come to Hong Kong so that you will recognize a bargain. The best deals are in recently discontinued models, such as last year's Sony Discman.

If you're interested in fake name-brand watches, handbags, or clothing to impress the folks back home, you've come to the right place. Although illegal, fake name-brand goods were still being sold at Hong Kong's night markets during my last visit by vendors who were ready to flee at the first sight of an official. If customs officials spot these fake goods in your bags when you return home, however, they'll be confiscated.

## WHEN TO SHOP

Because shopping is such big business in Hong Kong, most stores are open 7 days a week, closing only for 2 or 3 days during the Chinese New Year. Most stores open at 10am, and remain open until 6pm in Central, 9pm in Tsim Sha Tsui and Yau Ma Tei, and 9:30pm in Causeway Bay. Street markets are open every day.

The biggest and best seasonal sale takes place around Chinese lunar New Year, generally in February. All the major department stores as well as shops in many of the huge shopping complexes hold sales at this time, with prices discounted about 40%. There is also a summer sale, usually in June or July, as well as end-of-season sales in the early spring and early autumn.

## GUARANTEES & RECEIPTS

It's always a good idea to obtain a receipt from the shopkeeper for your purchases, if for no other reason than as proof of value when going through customs upon returning home. You'll also need a receipt if the product you've purchased is defective. A receipt should give a description of your purchase, including the brand name, model number, serial number, and price for electronic and photographic equipment; for jewelry and gold watches, there should be a description of the precious stones and the metal content. If you're making a purchase using a credit card, you should also ask for the customer's copy of the credit-card slip, and make sure "HK$" appears before the monetary total.

If you're interested in a camera, electronic goods, watch, or any other expensive product, be sure first to inspect the product carefully and make sure its voltage is compatible with that of your home country. When purchasing, make sure that all parts, pieces, and the warranty card of your purchase are included in the box. Ask the shopkeeper for a manufacturer's guarantee, which should include the name and/or symbol of the sole agent in Hong Kong, a description of the model and serial number, date of purchase, name and address of the shop where you bought it, and the shop's official chop or stamp. Different products and models of the same brand may carry different warranties—some valid worldwide, others only in Hong Kong. Worldwide guarantees must carry the name and/or symbol of the sole agent in Hong Kong for the given product. If you're in doubt, check with the relevant Hong Kong sole agent.

## COMPARISON SHOPPING & BARGAINING

The cardinal rule of shopping in Hong Kong is to shop around. Unless you're planning to buy antiques or art, you'll probably see the same items in many different shops on both sides of the harbor. If you've decided to buy a washable silk blouse for that favorite niece, for example, check a few stores to get an idea of quality, color, and style.

# A Shopping Warning

Hong Kong is a buyer-beware market. Name brands are sometimes fakes, that cheap jade you bought may actually be glass, and electronic goods may not work. To make things worse, the general practice is that goods are usually not returnable, and deposits paid are not refundable.

To be on the safe side, try to make your major purchases at HKTA member stores, which display the HKTA logo (a round circle with a red Chinese junk in the middle) on their storefronts. Altogether there are more than 750 member stores, all listed in a directory called "The Official Dining, Entertainment & Shopping Directory" that you can get free from the HKTA. This booklet gives the names, addresses, and phone numbers of shops that sell everything from audio-video equipment to jewelry, tea, clothing, optical goods, antiques, and wines. Even more important, it lists the sole agents for specific products and brand names, such as Sony, Rolex, or Minolta, along with their telephone numbers (you can also find more information on sole agents by calling the **Consumer Council Shopping Hotline** at ☎ **852/2929 2222**). HKTA member stores are required to give accurate information on the products they sell and to respond promptly to justified complaints. If you have any complaints against a member store, call the HKTA (☎ **852/2508 1234**) multilingual hotline Monday to Friday 8am to 6pm and on Saturday, Sunday, and public holidays 9am to 5pm.

With the exception of department stores and designer boutiques, you may be able to bargain for your purchase, though I've noticed that some shopkeepers are less willing to bargain than they once were. Still, at some of the smaller, family-owned stores, a good strategy is to ask what the "best" price might be. You should also ask for a discount if you're buying several items from the same store, and generally speaking, you can get a better price if you pay with cash rather than by credit card. How much you pay will depend on your bargaining skills and how many items you intend to purchase. Begin your comparison-shopping as soon as you arrive in Hong Kong, so that you can get an idea of the differences in prices. As for street markets, you most certainly must bargain, though nowadays some vendors will just shake their heads and say their prices are fixed, especially in Stanley Market. If vendors are willing to bargain, sometimes just saying the item is too expensive and starting to walk away will suddenly get you that "special price."

## SHIPPING

Many stores, especially the larger ones, will pack and ship your purchases home for you. Since basic insurance usually insures only against loss, it's a good idea to buy an all-risk insurance for valuable or fragile goods, available at the store. However, since these policies can be expensive, find out whether using your credit card to make your purchase will provide automatic free insurance.

In addition, all upper-bracket and most medium-range hotels offer a parcel-wrapping and mailing service. If you decide to ship your purchase home yourself, the easiest thing to do is to stop by the post office and buy ready-made boxes, which come with everything you need to ship goods home. Packages sent to the United States or Europe generally take 6 to 8 weeks by surface mail and 1 week by airmail. For major purchases, you can also buy a postal insurance covering damage or loss in transit.

## 2  Great Shopping Areas

Hong Kong is so filled with shops, boutiques, street markets, department stores, and malls, it's hard to think of places where you *can't* shop. Still, there are specific hunting grounds for various products, as well as areas that have greater concentrations of shops than elsewhere.

**Tsim Sha Tsui** has the greatest concentration of shops in Hong Kong. Nathan Road, which runs through Kowloon for 2½ miles from the harbor to the border of the New Territories, is lined with stores selling clothing, jewelry, eyeglasses, cameras, electronic goods, crafts from China, shoes, handbags, luggage, watches, and more. There are also tailors, tattoo artists, and even shops that will carve your name into a wooden chop (a stamp used in place of a signature for official documents). Be sure to explore the side streets radiating off Nathan Road, especially Mody Road for shops specializing in washable silk and casual clothing, and Granville Road for export overruns of fun, youth-oriented fashions at modest prices and luggage shops. There are also department stores, Chinese emporiums, and shopping arcades, as well as several huge shopping malls. Harbour City on Canton Road, for example, is gigantic; it is comprised of Ocean Centre, Ocean Galleries, Ocean Terminal, the Hongkong Hotel Arcade, and the new Gateway Shopping Arcade. Palace Mall, stretching from the Space Museum to the New World Centre, is Hong Kong's first subterranean shopping complex. Farther north, in Yau Ma Tei, is Hong Kong's most famous outdoor market, the Temple Street Night Market, with vendors selling clothing, CDs, watches, toys, mobile phones, and accessories.

For upscale shopping, **Central** is the place where you'll find international designer labels. The Landmark and Prince's Building boast boutiques selling jewelry, clothing, leather goods and more, with names ranging from A Testoni, Aquascutum, Armani, Cartier, and Chanel to Christian Dior, Ferragamo, Gucci, Hermès, Lanvin, and Tiffany & Co. Central is also a good place to shop for Chinese imports and souvenirs, especially at the hip Shanghai Tang and the Yue Hwa Chinese Products Emporium.

Another happy hunting ground is **Causeway Bay** on Hong Kong Island. In contrast to Tsim Sha Tsui, it caters more to the local market than to tourists, and prices are often lower. In addition to small shops selling everything from shoes and clothing to Chinese herbs, there are a couple Japanese department stores and a large shopping complex called Times Square. Check the backstreets of Causeway Bay, such as Lockhart Road and Jaffe Road, as well as the area around Jardine's Crescent, an open-air market with cheap clothing, food, and produce.

One of my favorite places to shop for inexpensive fashions is **Stanley Market** on the southern end of Hong Kong Island, where vendors sell silk clothing and business and casual wear. In recent years, shops specializing in Chinese crafts and products have also opened in Stanley Market. For shoes, get on the tram and head for Happy Valley; on Leighton Road and Wong Nai Chung Road (near the racecourse) there are rows of shoe and handbag shops.

Antiques and curio lovers usually head for **Hollywood Road** and **Cat Street** in the Western District on Hong Kong Island, where everything from snuff bottles to jade carvings and Ming vases is for sale. Chinese handcrafts, including porcelain, furniture, silk clothing, and embroidery, are sold in Chinese-product department stores and Chinese arts and crafts shops located on both sides of the harbor. Several deluxe hotels boast arcades housing designer boutiques, most notably The Peninsula and Regent.

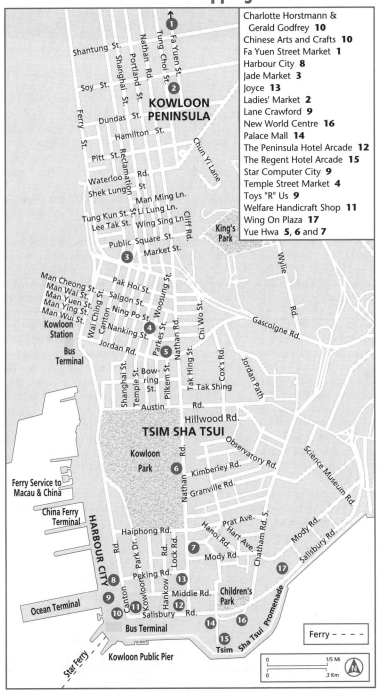

# Shopping in Tsim Sha Tsui

Charlotte Horstmann &
 Gerald Godfrey **10**
Chinese Arts and Crafts **10**
Fa Yuen Street Market **1**
Harbour City **8**
Jade Market **3**
Joyce **13**
Ladies' Market **2**
Lane Crawford **9**
New World Centre **16**
Palace Mall **14**
The Peninsula Hotel Arcade **12**
The Regent Hotel Arcade **15**
Star Computer City **9**
Temple Street Market **4**
Toys "R" Us **9**
Welfare Handicraft Shop **11**
Wing On Plaza **17**
Yue Hwa **5, 6** and **7**

## 3 Shopping A to Z

The stores listed below are just a few of the thousands upon thousands in Hong Kong. For more detailed coverage, see the booklet "The Official Dining, Entertainment & Shopping Directory," which lists more than 700 shops that are members of the HKTA.

### ANTIQUES & COLLECTIBLES

Several of the Chinese-product stores, listed below under "Chinese Craft Emporiums," stock antiques, especially porcelain. You can also find shops selling antiques and collectibles in Harbour City, a mega-mall in Tsim Sha Tsui, particularly along the so-called Silk Road arcade on level 3 of Zone D (the Hongkong Hotel Arcade). Many hotel shopping arcades have at least a few shops specializing in antiques. Antiques buffs should also inquire at HKTA whether international auctioneers Christie's or Sotheby's are holding one of their regular sales for antiques in Hong Kong.

The most famous area for antiques and chinoiserie, however, is around **Hollywood Road** and **Cat Street,** both above the Central District on Hong Kong Island. This area gained fame in the 1950s, following the 1949 revolution in China (which flooded the market with family possessions). Hollywood Road twists along for a little more than half a mile, with shops selling original and reproduction Qing and Ming dynasty Chinese furniture, original prints, scrolls, porcelain, clay figurines, silver, and rosewood and blackwood furniture, as well as fakes and curios. Near the western end is Upper Lascar Row, popularly known as Cat Street, where sidewalk vendors sell snuff bottles, curios, and odds and ends. At the eastern end of Hollywood Road near Pottinger Street is a cluster of chic antiques shops displaying furniture and blue-and-white porcelain, including goods from neighboring Asian countries, such as Korean chests and Japanese hibachi. If you're a real antiques collector, I suggest you simply walk through the dozens of shops on and around Hollywood Road.

If you cannot tell the difference between originals and reproductions, you are better off shopping at one of the HKTA member stores, which display HKTA's red junk logo. Be sure to ask whether an antique has been repaired or restored, as this can affect its value. If the piece is quite expensive, ask that it be tested. Wood, for example, can be tested using carbon-14 dating, while ceramics can be tested with the Oxford Test. The authenticiy of bronze, jade, glass, and stone can also be determined through testing. Finally, if you're purchasing anything older than 100 years old, request a Certificate of Antiquity, along with a receipt detailing your purchase. Although it is illegal to smuggle antiques out of mainland China, many smuggled items do in fact end up in Hong Kong, where it is legal to then sell, buy, and own them. Needless to say, this has caused some friction between China and Hong Kong, especially when international auction houses have sold well-documented, smuggled Chinese antiques.

**Cat Street Galleries.** 38 Lok Ku Rd., Central. ☎ **852/2543 1609.** MTR: Central. Bus: 26 (from Des Voeux Rd. Central in front of the Hongkong Bank) to the second stop on Hollywood Rd., at Man Mo Temple.

Cat Street Galleries, on Cat Street, houses several individually owned booths of arts and crafts and expensive antiques from the various dynasties, making it a good place to begin an antiques shopping odyssey. It's open Monday to Friday 11am to 6pm and Saturday 10am to 6pm.

**Charlotte Horstmann and Gerald Godfrey.** Shop 100D, Ocean Terminal, Harbour City, 3 Canton Rd., Tsim Sha Tsui. ☎ **852/2735 7167.** MTR: Tsim Sha Tsui.

A favorite of well-to-do antiques collectors for more than 40 years, this small shop, located in Zone C (Ocean Terminal) of the Harbour City shopping mall on Canton Road, is an emporium of expensive, top-quality Asian antiques, including rosewood furniture, wood carvings, and bronzes. Since the shop itself is rather small, be sure to make an appointment to see the adjoining 10,000-square-foot warehouse. Its stock varies, but Chinese art and jade are well represented; antiques from Indonesia, Thailand, Cambodia, India, and Korea are usually also available. It's open Monday to Saturday 9:30am to 6pm.

**China Art.** 15 Hollywood Rd., Central. ☎ **852/2542 0982** or 852/2840 0816. MTR: Central. Bus: 26 (from Des Voeux Rd. Central in front of the Hongkong Bank) to Hollywood Rd.

This family-owned shop, which has the elegance of an art gallery with its mixed displays of furniture and art, is one of Hong Kong's best for antique Chinese furniture, including chairs, tables, folding screens, chests, and wardrobes, mostly from the Ming dynasty (1368–1644). Located across from the Central Police Station, it's open Monday to Saturday 10:30am to 7pm and Sunday 11am to 7pm.

**Dragon Culture.** 231 Hollywood Rd., Sheung Wan. ☎ **852/2545 8098.** MTR: Central. Bus: 26 (from Des Voeux Rd. Central in front of the Hongkong Bank) to the second stop on Hollywood Rd., at Man Mo Temple.

One of the largest purveyors of antiques in Hong Kong, Victor Choi began collecting Chinese antiques in the 1970s, traveling throughout China from province to province and to all the major cities. With a second gallery nearby at 184 Hollywood Rd. (☎ **852/2815 5227**) and another one in New York, he carries Neolithic pottery, three-color glazed pottery horses from the Tang dynasty, Ming porcelains, bronzes, jade, wood carvings, snuff bottles, calligraphy, paintings, brush pots, stone carvings, and more, and also provides authenticity. The main shop is open Monday to Saturday 10am to 6pm.

**Friendship Trading Company.** 105–107 Hollywood Rd., Central. ☎ **852/2548 3830.** MTR: Central.

This small shop with a friendly staff specializes in antique and modern porcelain vases and lacquered boxes. It's open Monday to Saturday 9:30am to 6:30pm.

**True Arts & Curios.** 89 Hollywood Rd., Central. ☎ **852/2559 1485.** MTR: Central.

This tiny shop is so packed with antiques and curios that there's barely room for customers. Although everything from snuff bottles, porcelain, antique silver, earrings, hair pins, and children's shoes (impractical but darling, with curled toes) are stocked, the true finds here are some 2,000 intricate wood carvings, pried from the doors and windows of dismantled temples and homes. You'll find them hanging from the ceiling and in bins, many of them dusty and grimy from years of neglect. The best ones are carved from a single piece of wood, masterpieces in workmanship and available at modest prices. It's open Monday to Saturday 10:30am to 6:30pm and Sunday 2:30 to 6:30pm.

## CARPETS

Hong Kong is a good place to shop for Chinese, Indian, Persian, and other types of carpets and rugs. For those that are locally made, Tai Ping carpets are famous the world over, produced in Hong Kong with virgin wool imported from New Zealand.

For imported carpets from India and the Middle East, there are several shops along the **Hollywood Road** and **Wyndham Street** areas in Central. For hand-knotted wool or silk Chinese carpets, be sure to check out the **Chinese crafts and products stores** (see below), which stock hand-knotted wool or silk Chinese carpets.

**Harbour City,** the huge mega-mall that spreads along Canton Road in Tsim Sha Tsui, is another good place to browse. The shops here include Carpet World, Shop 271 in Zone C (Ocean Terminal; ☎ **852/2730 4275**); and Chinese Carpet Centre, in shops 164–168 also in Zone C (☎ **852/2730 7230**). The nearest MTR station to Harbour City is Tsim Sha Tsui.

For Tai Ping carpets, two conveniently located showrooms are in Wing On Plaza, 62 Mody Rd. in Tsim Sha Tsui East (☎ **852/2569 4061;** MTR: Tsim Sha Tsui), and shop 816 in Times Square, 1 Matheson St. in Causeway Bay (☎ **852/2522 7138;** MTR: Causeway Bay). If you don't see what you like, you can have one custom designed, specifying the color, thickness, and direction of the weave. It takes about 3 months to make a carpet, and the company will ship it to you.

## CHINA (PORCELAIN)

Chinaware, a fine, translucent earthenware, was first brought from China to Europe by the Portuguese in the 16th century. Its name was subsequently shortened to "china," and Hong Kong remains one of the best places in the world to shop for both antique (mainly from the Manchu, or Ching, dynasty, 1644–1911) and contemporary Chinese porcelain. Traditional motifs include bamboo, flowers, dragons, carp, and cranes, which adorn everything from dinner plates to vases, lamps, and jars. Also popular is translucent porcelain with a rice grain design. And of course, European and Japanese china is also available in Hong Kong, including Meissen, Wedgwood, and Noritake.

Probably the best place to begin looking for Chinese porcelain is at one of the Chinese-product stores, listed below under "Chinese Craft Emporiums." In addition, malls and shopping centers like Pacific Place in Admiralty, Times Square in Causeway Bay, and Harbour City in Tsim Sha Tsui also have porcelain shops. If you're looking for contemporary china or replicas, or wish to commission a design of your own, you might want to visit the porcelain factory below. Nowadays, contemporary china is generally both dishwasher- and microwave-safe.

**Friendship Trading Company.** 105–107 Hollywood Rd., Central. ☎ **852/2548 3830.** MTR: Central.

This small shop with a friendly staff specializes in antique and modern porcelain vases and lacquered boxes. It's open Monday to Saturday 9:30am to 6:30pm.

**Overjoy Porcelain Factory.** 1st floor, Block B of Kwai Hing Industrial Building, 10–18 Chun Pin St., Kwai Chung, New Territories. ☎ **852/2487 0615.** MTR: Kwai Hing station; then take a taxi.

With more than 400 stock designs, dinner services are the specialty here. You may also mix and match, or even create your very own design. Sets are usually commissioned for either 6, 8, or 12 diners and take 4 to 6 weeks to complete. It's open Monday to Saturday 10am to 6pm, but because it's in the New Territories, you'd be wise to call first.

**Wah Tung China Company.** 16th floor, Grand Marine Industrial Building, 3 Yue Fung St., Shek Pai Wan Rd., Aberdeen, Hong Kong Island. ☎ **852/2873 2272.** Bus: 70 from Exchange Square in Central.

This is reputedly the largest company specializing in hand-painted antique porcelain reproductions, especially huge pieces like vases and garden stools. Its vast collection covers all Chinese artistic periods, including Canton Rose, Chinoiserie, Chinese Imari, and 17th- and 18th-century Chinese export porcelain. It's open Monday to Saturday 9:30am to 6pm and Sunday 11am to 5pm. A smaller but more convenient branch is located at 59 Hollywood Rd., Central (☎ **852/2543 2823;** MTR: Central), open Monday to Saturday 10am to 7pm and Sunday 11am to 6pm.

## CHINESE CRAFT EMPORIUMS

In addition to the shops listed here, which specialize in traditional and contemporary arts, crafts, souvenirs, and gift items from China, there are several souvenir shops at Stanley Market, located in Stanley on the southern end of Hong Kong Island, that carry lacquered boxes, china, embroidered tablecloths, figurines, and other Chinese imports.

✪ **Chinese Arts and Crafts Ltd.** Shop 230, Pacific Place, 88 Queensway, Central. ☎ **852/2523 3933.** MTR: Admiralty.

In business for more than 30 years, this is the best upscale chain for Chinese arts and crafts and is one of the safest places to purchase jade. You can also buy silk dresses and blouses, arts and crafts, antiques, jewelry, watches, carpets, cloisonné, furs, Chinese herbs and medicine, rosewood furniture, chinaware, Chinese teas, and embroidered tablecloths or pillowcases—in short, virtually all upmarket items that China produces. It's a great place for gifts in all price ranges. This shop, located at Pacific Place, is open daily 10:30am to 7pm.

Other branches include: Star House, 3 Salisbury Rd., Tsim Sha Tsui (☎ **852/ 2735 4061;** MTR: Tsim Sha Tsui), open daily 10am to 9:30pm; and in the China Resources Building, 26 Harbour Rd., Wan Chai (☎ **852/2827 6667;** MTR: Wan Chai), open daily 10:30am to 7:30pm.

**CRC Department Store.** 488 Hennessy Rd., Causeway Bay. ☎ **852/2577 0222.** MTR: Causeway Bay.

Geared toward the local market rather than tourists, this no-nonsense store carries porcelain, teapots, vases, tea, Chinese medicinal products, embroidery, silk jackets, brushes, inkstones, and other traditional products in addition to luggage, shoes, TVs, and household goods. It's open daily 10am to 10pm. There are branches in Central at 92 Queen's Rd. Central (☎ **852/2524 1051;** MTR: Central) and in Mong Kok in the Argyle Centre Tower, 65 Argyle St. (☎ **852/2395 3191;** MTR: Mong Kok).

✪ **Shanghai Tang.** Pedder Building, 12 Pedder St., Central. ☎ **852/2525 7333.** MTR: Central.

You are stepping back into the Shanghai of the 1930s when you enter this upscale, two-level store with its gleaming wooden and tiled floors, raised cashier cubicles, ceiling fans, and helpful clerks wearing classical Chinese jackets. This is Chinese chic at its best, with neatly stacked rows of updated versions of traditional Chinese clothing, ranging from cheongsams and silk pajamas to padded jackets, caps, and shoes—all in bright, contemporary colors and styles. If you're looking for a lime-green or shocking pink padded jacket, this is the place for you. There are even Shanghai tailors on hand to custom-make something for you. You will also find funky accessories and home furnishings, from Mao-emblazoned watches to '30s-style alarm clock remakes, beaded picture frames, silver chopsticks, and fuchsia-colored serving trays. It's open Monday to Saturday 10am to 8pm and Sunday 11am to 7pm.

**Yue Hwa Chinese Products.** 301–309 Nathan Rd., Yau Ma Tei, Kowloon. ☎ **852/ 2384 0084.** MTR: Jordan.

Yue Hwa caters to a local clientele with both traditional Chinese and everyday products. This main shop in Yau Ma Tei stocks everything from household goods to clothing, jade jewelry, arts and crafts, china, medicinal herbs like dried seahorses, and even antlers. It was here that I bought some friends a gag wedding gift—Chinese whiskey with preserved lizards in it, all for only HK$25 ($3.25), definitely a bargain. The branch stores specialize primarily in Chinese handcrafts and jewels. My favorite is the one at 39 Queen's Rd. Central, in Central (☎ 852/2522 2333; MTR: Central), with a wealth of silk clothing and other traditional items. Other branches include: Park Lane Shopper's Boulevard at 143–161 Nathan Rd., Tsim Sha Tsui (☎ **852/ 2739 3888;** MTR: Tsim Sha Tsui), open daily 10am to 9:30pm; basement of Mirador Mansion, 54–64 Nathan Rd., Tsim Sha Tsui (☎ **852/2368 9165;** MTR: Tsim Sha Tsui), open daily 9:30am to 8:30pm; and in the Pearl City Plaza, 24–36 Paterson St., Causeway Bay (☎ **852/2808 1363;** MTR: Causeway Bay), open daily 10:30am to 10:30pm.

## DEPARTMENT STORES

It will probably come as no surprise to learn that Hong Kong has a great many department stores. Wing On and Lane Crawford, two upmarket local chain department stores, offer a nice selection of clothing, accessories, local and imported designer fashions, gift items, and cosmetics. Japanese department stores are also quite popular with the locals, with a couple located in Causeway Bay. Department store hours for the branches listed below are the same for other stores in the area (see "The Shopping Scene," above).

### LOCAL DEPARTMENT STORES

**Lane Crawford Ltd.** Lane Crawford House, 70 Queen's Rd. Central, Central. ☎ **852/ 2118 3388.** MTR: Central.

This upscale department store, with large clothing departments for the whole family, as well as shoes, handbags, silver, and crystal, has branches on both sides of the harbor (the branch at Pacific Place is probably the best) and is similar to established chain stores in England and the United States. This main store is open daily 10am to 7:30pm.

Other branches can be found at: Pacific Place, 88 Queensway, Central (☎ **852/ 2118 3668;** MTR: Admiralty); Times Square, 1 Matheson St., Causeway Bay (☎ 852/2118 3638; MTR: Causeway Bay); and Shop 100, Ocean Terminal, Harbour City, 3 Canton Rd., Tsim Sha Tsui (☎ **852/2118 3428;** MTR: Tsim Sha Tsui).

**Wing On.** 211 Des Voeux Rd., Central. ☎ **852/2852 1888.** MTR: Sheung Wan.

Founded in Shanghai almost a century ago and one of Hong Kong's oldest department stores, this main shop offers a wide selection of clothing, jewelry, accessories, and household items, with branches mostly in outlying areas. It's open Monday to Friday 10am to 7pm and Saturday and Sunday 10am to 6:30pm.

A convenient branch can be found at Wing On Plaza, 62 Mody Rd., Tsim Sha Tsui East (☎ **852/2723 2211;** MTR: Tsim Sha Tsui).

## JAPANESE DEPARTMENT STORES

**Mitsukoshi.** 500 Hennessy Rd., Causeway Bay. ☎ **852/2576 5222.** MTR: Causeway Bay.

Mitsukoshi is a long-established department store; it first opened as a kimono shop in Japan in the 1600s and is still one of Japan's most exclusive stores. Today it houses the boutiques of well-known designers of shoes, accessories, and clothing, with high prices to match; it also carries lingerie, cosmetics, household goods, and toys. It's open daily 10:30am to 10pm.

**Seibu.** Pacific Place, 88 Queensway, Central. ☎ **852/2868 0111.** MTR: Admiralty.

One of the largest department store chains in Japan (its Tokyo store is the third-largest department store in the world), this was Seibu's first store to open outside Japan. An upscale, sophisticated department store targeting Hong Kong's affluent yuppie population, it is the epitome of chic, from its art deco Italian furnishings to fashions from the world's top design houses. More than 65% of its merchandise is European, and 25% is from Japan. The Loft department carries well-designed housewares and gifts, while Seed is the place to go for the latest fashions. Junko Shimada, Kenzo, and Paul Smith have boutiques here. The food department in the basement is especially good, stocking many imported items that are not available elsewhere in Hong Kong. It's open Sunday to Wednesday 10:30am to 8pm and Thursday to Saturday 10:30am to 9pm.

**Sogo.** East Point Centre, 555 Hennessy Rd., Causeway Bay. ☎ **852/2833 8338.** MTR: Causeway Bay.

Sogo is much larger and more egalitarian than the other Japanese department stores listed above; its goods are cheaper and its prices lower. Consequently, the 12-story store is often packed (particularly on Sunday), filled with families shopping for clothing, toys, furniture, household goods, and electrical appliances. In the second basement is a large supermarket, as well as inexpensive Japanese restaurants. It's open daily 10am to 10pm.

## OTHER DEPARTMENT STORES

**Marks & Spencer.** Ocean Centre, Harbour City, Canton Rd., Tsim Sha Tsui. ☎ **852/ 2926 3330.** MTR: Tsim Sha Tsui.

Known in Britain for its great prices on clothing and affectionately nicknamed "Marks & Sparks," this import from the United Kingdom (but with smaller sizes) is open daily 10am to 8pm. It has several branches on the Hong Kong side, including at Pacific Place, 88 Queensway, Central (☎ **852/2921 8888;** MTR: Admiralty); and Times Square, 1 Matheson St., Causeway Bay (☎ **852/2923 7970;** MTR: Causeway Bay).

# ELECTRONICS

Because there is no import-duty or sales tax and because Hong Kong may offer the latest models months before they're available in other countries, shopping for electronic goods has long been a popular tourist pastime. However, prices have increased for electronic products in the past few years, so if you're interested in buying a digital camera, camcorder, laser disc player, computer, or other electronic product, be sure to check prices at home before you come to Hong Kong to make sure that what you would like to buy here is really a bargain. Then, head to Tsim Sha Tsui for the many shops along Nathan Road and surrounding streets specializing in electronics galore. Compare prices first, and to be on the safe side, shop in stores that are members of HKTA. Camera buffs may wish to check out the used camera stores at the Champagne Arcade, located beside the Miramar Hotel on Kimberley Road. For computers, try dedicated malls such as Star Computer City, located in the Star House across from the Tsim Sha Tsui Star Ferry terminal at 3 Salisbury Rd., or In Square, located at the Windsor House, 311 Gloucester Rd. in Causeway Bay. In any case, whatever you buy, be sure to inspect every piece of equipment before leaving the store (do not assume what's inside a box matches the picture on the outside), make sure equipment works and that its voltage is compatible with yours at home, and obtain warranties and receipts. For computers, look for complete packages that offer computer, printer, scanner, and software at competitive prices, and be sure that the loaded software is in English.

## FABRICS

Many tailors stock their own bolts of fabric, but for one-stop fabric shopping with larger selections, the place to go is the **Western Market,** 323 Des Voeux Rd. Central, in the Western District. The first floor of this 1906 renovated brick building is lined with shop after shop selling every imaginable type of cloth, from upholstery fabric and silk to linens and Indian cottons, with approximately 16 vendors in all. The salespeople can advise almost to the inch how much fabric you'll need for any outfit, even if all you have to show them is a drawing. The Western Market shops are open daily 10am to 7pm. The nearest MTR station is Sheung Wan, or take the tram to Sheung Wan.

Other good places to look for silk are the emporiums listed under "Chinese Craft Emporiums," above.

## FASHION

Ever since Hong Kong received a large influx of Shanghainese tailors following the revolution in China in 1949, Hong Kong has been a center for the fashion industry. Today, clothing remains one of Hong Kong's best buys, and many major international design houses have boutiques here; several have factories as well, either here or just across the border in Guangzhou. There are also a number of Hong Kong designers to watch out for, including Anna Sui, Vivienne Tam, Walter Ma, Lulu Cheung, and Barney Cheng.

If you're looking for international designer brands and don't care about price, there are several arcades and shopping centers known for their brand names. The **Landmark,** located on Des Voeux Road Central, Central, is an ultra-chic shopping complex boasting the highest concentration of international brand names in Hong Kong, including Gucci, Tiffany & Co., Polo/Ralph Lauren, Missoni, Helmut Lang, Versace, Sonia Rykiel, A Testoni, Louis Vuitton, Lanvin, Valentino, and Christian Dior, as well as restaurants and other shops. The shops here are generally open daily 10:30am to 7:30pm. Other shopping arcades with well-known international designer boutiques include **The Peninsula Hotel,** on Salisbury Road in Tsim Sha Tsui, with concessions for Hermès, Louis Vuitton, Loewe, Chanel, Gucci, Dior, Salvatore Ferragamo, and Manolo Blahnik, to name only a few. Nearby, the **Regent Hotel** also has a shopping arcade, with concessions for Louis Vuitton, Chanel, Nina Ricci, Lanvin, Salvatore Ferragamo, Cartier, and more. In Central, the **Prince's Building** next to the Mandarin Hotel carries international names like Dunhill, Cartier, and Chanel, while the nearby **Alexandra House** has boutiques for Giorgio Armani, Jil Sander, and Prada. Expect to spend a lot of money and you won't be disappointed.

For trendier designs catering to an upwardly mobile younger crowd, check out the **Joyce Boutique** chain, the first fashion house in Hong Kong, established in the 1970s by Joyce Ma to satisfy Hong Kong women's cravings for European designs. Today her stores carry clothing by Issey Miyake, Jean-Paul Gaultier, Yohji Yamamoto,

Rei Kawakubo (Comme des Garçons), and others on the cutting edge of fashion. You'll find Joyce shops at 16 Queen's Rd. Central, Central District (☎ **852/2810 1120;** MTR: Central) and 23 Nathan Rd. in Tsim Sha Tsui (☎ **852/2367 8128;** MTR: Tsim Sha Tsui).

For a wider range in prices, the department stores listed above are best for one-stop shopping for the entire family, as are Hong Kong's many malls and shopping centers. Otherwise, small, family-owned shops abound in both Tsim Sha Tsui and Stanley Market, offering casual wear, washable silk outfits, and other clothing at very affordable prices. Cheaper still are factory outlets and street markets (see below).

**FACTORY OUTLETS**   Savvy shoppers head for Hong Kong's factory outlets to buy at least some of their clothes. These outlets sell excess stock, overruns, and quality-control rejects; because these items have been made for the export market, the sizes are Western. Bargains include clothes made of silk, cashmere, cotton, linen, knitwear, and wool, and some outlets have men's and children's clothing as well. Some manufacturers even produce clothing for famous designer labels, though it's not unusual to find labels cut out. Although scattered throughout the territory, the most convenient outlets are in the Central District on Hong Kong Island or Hung Hom and Tsim Sha Tsui in Kowloon.

There are, however, a few caveats about shopping in factory outlets. For one thing, you never know in advance what will be on sale, and sometimes the selection is disappointing. If you do find something, it's important to examine garments inside out. What's more, some outlets are indistinguishable from upmarket boutiques, with prices to match. Unfortunately, it seems that some shops simply call themselves "factory outlets" because that's what tourists are looking for. Thus, unless you have lots of time, it may not be worth your while to go to the outlets in Hung Hom in search of a good deal.

On Hong Kong Island, the best-known building that houses factory-outlet showrooms is the **Pedder Building,** 12 Pedder St., Central. During my last visit I counted about 37 shops here located on six floors, but not all of these shops are factory outlets—many are just regular boutiques with the same merchandise at the same prices found at their other branches. In addition, a new trend seems to be shops selling used designer wear, making it good for bargains in last season's fashions. In any case, it's convenient to have so many shops in one building and it's fun to just poke around. Don't miss the Tian Art Design House in shop 107B on the first floor (☎ **852/ 2522 1773**), with unique designs by Flora Cheong-Leen that blend traditional Chinese styles with Western funk.

On the Kowloon side, there are a few factory outlets scattered in the heart of Tsim Sha Tsui, with a couple on **Granville Road.** The largest concentration of factory outlets, however, is in Hung Hom, clustered in a large group of warehouse buildings called **Kaiser Estates** on Man Yue Street. Although the Kaiser Estates themselves comprise huge concrete factory buildings, the many outlet shops inside look just like ordinary shops. To reach the Kaiser Estates, take bus no. 5C from the Tsim Sha Tsui Star Ferry bus terminal to Ma Tau Wai Road (the third stop after the KCR Kowloon Railway Station).

For a list of factory outlets along with their addresses, telephone numbers, and types of clothing, pick up the free pamphlet, "Factory Outlets for Locally Made Fashion and Jewellery," available at HKTA offices. Most outlets are open 9 or 10am to 6pm Monday to Friday, with shorter hours on Saturdays. Some are open Sunday as well.

## GIFTS & SOUVENIRS

The Chinese product emporiums listed above under "Chinese Craft Emporiums" offer a wide array of souvenirs and gifts. For one-stop shopping, I suggest a trip to **Chinese Arts and Crafts,** which has several branches in Hong Kong. Other places to look for souvenirs include hotel shopping arcades, Nathan Road in Tsim Sha Tsui, Stanley Market on Hong Kong Island, Western Market in the Western District, and the mega-malls.

I also make a point of stopping at one of the two **Welfare Handicrafts Shops,** which began more than 30 years ago as an outlet for crafts and goods made by Chinese refugees. Today, many of the items are made by local disadvantaged or disabled people and the proceeds go to charity, so I always stop by to see whether there are small items that might make nice stocking-stuffers or presents. Items for sale include T-shirts, porcelain, silk coin purses, pincushions, greeting cards, small cast-iron statues, and other souvenirs. You'll find one Welfare Handicrafts Shop conveniently located in Tsim Sha Tsui on Salisbury Road, between the YMCA and the Star Ferry Concourse (☎ **852/2366 6979;** MTR: Tsim Sha Tsui). It's open Monday to Saturday 9am to 5:30pm. The Central District branch is situated on the lower ground floor of Jardine House, Shop 7, 1 Connaught Place, Central (☎ **852/2524 3356;** MTR: Central), near the Star Ferry terminal. It's open Monday to Friday 9:30am to 6pm and Saturday 9:30am to 1pm.

## JEWELRY

According to the HKTA, Hong Kong has more jewelry stores per square mile than any other city in the world. Gems are imported duty free from all over the world, and Hong Kong is reputedly the world's third-largest trading center for diamonds. Gold jewelry, both imported and locally made, is required by law to carry a stamp stating the accurate gold content.

Jade, of course, remains the most popular item of jewelry for both visitors and Chinese. It's believed to protect wearers against illness and ward off bad luck. The two categories of jade are jadeite and nephrite. Jadeite (also called Burmese jade) is generally white to apple green in color, although it also comes in hues of brown, red, orange, yellow, and even lavender. It may be mottled, but the most expensive variety is a translucent emerald green. Nephrite, which is less expensive, is usually a dark green or off-white. In any case, true jade is so hard that supposedly even a knife leaves no scratch. Unless you know your jade, your best bet is to shop in one of the Chinese-product stores, listed above under "Chinese Craft Emporiums." For less expensive pieces and souvenirs, visit the Jade Market, described below under "Markets."

Pearls, almost all of which are cultured, are also popular among shoppers in Hong Kong. There are both sea- and freshwater pearls, available in all shapes, sizes, colors, and lusters. For inexpensive strands, check the vendors at the Jade Market. There are also many shops along Nathan Road in Tsim Sha Tsui that retail pearls.

If you're a real jewelry fan, you'll want to visit some of the jewelry factory outlets scattered throughout Hong Kong, including Tsim Sha Tsui, Hung Hom, and Aberdeen. At some outlets, visitors will be asked to register and then will be shown around the factory itself, where they can observe the designs being drawn, learn how the stones are graded, and see the final polishing. After the tour, visitors are taken to the shop that sells finished products. For a list of jewelry factory outlets, contact the Hong Kong Tourist Association.

## MARKETS

Markets offer the best deals in Hong Kong, though a lot depends on how well you can bargain. Be sure to scrutinize the items that interest you carefully, since you won't be able to return them. Check clothing for faults, tears, cuts, marks, and uneven seams and hemlines. Make sure electronic gadgets work; the cheap Pikachu alarm clock I bought my son lasted only a week. It's a buyer-beware market in Hong Kong.

# HONG KONG ISLAND

**STANLEY**   The Stanley Market is probably the most popular and best-known market in Hong Kong. Located on the southern coast of Hong Kong Island on a small peninsula, it's a great place to buy inexpensive clothing, especially sportswear, cashmere sweaters, casual clothing, silk blouses and dresses, and even linen blazers and outfits suitable for work. Men's, women's, and children's clothing are available. During my last visit, shopkeepers were not keen about bargaining, no doubt because tourists come here by the busload. In fact, Stanley is not as cheap as it once was, and many shops are remodeling and becoming more chic and expensive. In addition, souvenir shops selling Chinese paintings, handicrafts, and curios have encroached on the scene, reducing the number of clothing shops. Still, you're bound to find at least something you're wild about. I buy more of my clothes here than anywhere else in Hong Kong, especially when it comes to cheap, fun fashions. The inventory changes continuously—one year it seems everyone is selling tie-dyed shirts; the next year it's linen suits, washable silk, or Chinese traditional jackets. I usually walk through the market first, taking note of things I like and which stores they're in, and then I compare prices as I walk through. Most stores carry the same products, so it pays to comparison-shop.

To reach Stanley, take bus no. 6, 6A, 6X, or 260 from Central's Exchange Square bus terminal near the Star Ferry (bus no. 260 also makes a stop in front of the Star Ferry terminal). The bus ride to Stanley takes approximately 30 minutes. From Kowloon, take bus no. 973 from Mody Road in Tsim Sha Tsui East or from Canton Road in Tsim Sha Tsui. The shops are open daily 9 or 9:30am to 6pm (to 7pm Saturday and Sunday).

**LI YUEN STREET EAST & WEST**   These two streets are parallel pedestrian lanes in the heart of the Central District, very narrow and often congested with human traffic. Stalls are packed with handbags, clothes, scarves, sweaters, toys, baby clothes, watches, makeup, umbrellas, knickknacks, and even brassieres. Don't neglect the open-fronted shops behind the stalls. Some of these are boutiques selling fashionable but cheap clothing as well as shoes, purses, and accessories. These two streets are located just a couple of minutes' walk from the Central MTR station or the Star Ferry, between Des Voeux Road Central and Queen's Road Central. Vendors are open daily 10am to 6pm.

**JARDINE'S CRESCENT**   The open-air market that spreads along this narrow street in Causeway Bay is a traditional Chinese market for produce, cheap clothing, and accessories, including shoes, costume jewelry, handbags, hair accessories, children's clothing, and cosmetics. Though you may not find something worth taking home at this very local market, it's fun just to walk around. The nearest MTR station is Causeway Bay (take exit F), but you can also reach this area easily by tram. The best time to visit is between 11am and 6:30pm daily, though it's open until 10pm.

**WANCHAI MARKET**   This local market, centered on Spring Garden Lane and Wanchai Road (between Johnston Road and Queen's Road East), is very much a local market, attracting housewives with its wet markets and household goods but also young office workers with its stalls selling clothing originally meant for export. It's located near the Wanchai MTR Station and is open daily 7am to 7pm.

# KOWLOON

**JADE MARKET**   Jade, believed by the Chinese to hold mystical powers and to protect its wearer, is available in all sizes, colors, and prices at the Jade Market, located at the junction of Kansu Street and Battery Street in two temporary structures in the Yau Ma Tei District. The jade comes from Burma, China, Australia, and Taiwan. Unless you know your jade, you won't want to make any expensive purchases here, but the quality of jade sold here is great for bangles, pendants, earrings, and inexpensive gifts. This market is also recommended for pearls, especially inexpensive freshwater pearls from China. You can pick up some strands at a good price. Otherwise, this market is fun just for its unique atmosphere.

The Jade Market is open daily 10am to about 3pm (mornings are best), though some vendors stay until 3:30pm. It's located near the Jordan MTR station or less than a 30-minute walk from the Star Ferry.

**LADIES' MARKET**    If you want to shop at a market on the Kowloon side in the daytime, this large market, popular with Hong Kong Chinese, is your best bet. Stretching along Tung Choi Street (between Argyle and Dundas streets) in Mong Kok, it serves as a lively market for inexpensive women's and children's fashions, shoes, socks, hosiery, jewelry, sunglasses, watches, handbags (including fake designer handbags), and other accessories. Some men's clothing is also sold. Although many of the products are geared more to local tastes and sizes, an increasing number of tourists has brought more fashionable clothing and T-shirts, and you may find a few bargains. In any case, the atmosphere is fun and festive, especially at night. The nearest MTR station is Mong Kok. Vendors are open daily from about noon to 10:30pm.

**FA YUEN STREET MARKET**    Located just a few minutes' walk north of Ladies' Market, north of Mong Kok Road, this street market is geared to local residents rather than tourists and offers clothing for women and children, as well as toys and produce. With laundry fluttering from the apartments above, this is a typical Mong Kok Street, full of character. The nearest MTR station is Prince Edward, and stalls are open 10am to 8pm daily.

**✪ TEMPLE STREET NIGHT MARKET**    Temple Street in the Yau Ma Tei District of Kowloon is a night market that comes to life when the sun goes down. It offers the usual products sold by street vendors, including T-shirts, jeans, menswear, watches, lighters, pens, sunglasses, jewelry, CDs, mobile phones, electronic gadgets, alarm clocks, luggage, and imitation designer watches. Bargain fiercely, and check the products carefully to make sure they're not faulty or poorly made. The night market is great entertainment, a must during your visit to Hong Kong. North of Temple Street, near Tin Hau Temple, are fortune-tellers and sometimes even streetside performers singing Chinese opera.

Although some vendors begin setting up shop at 2 or 3pm, the night market is busiest from about 7pm until it closes at 10pm, and is located near the Jordan MTR station.

## MEGA-MALLS & SHOPPING CENTERS

Hong Kong boasts shopping complexes that are so huge I call them "mega-malls." They are literally everywhere and are open daily, with most businesses operating 10am to 8pm.

Aside from the more convenient ones listed below, other Hong Kong mega-malls include **Festival Walk** (located above Kowloon Tong MTR Station), the **New Town Plaza** in Sha Tin in the New Territories, and the **Taikoo Shing City Plaza,** located at the Taikoo MTR station on Hong Kong Island.

**Harbour City.** Canton Rd., Tsim Sha Tsui. MTR: Tsim Sha Tsui.

This is the largest of the mega-malls, and probably the largest in Asia. Conveniently located right next to the dock that disgorges passengers from cruise liners and just to the east of the Star Ferry, it encompasses several zoned areas: Zone A, Zone B (Ocean

Centre), Zone C (Ocean Terminal), and Zone D (the Hongkong Hotel Arcade), all interconnected by air-conditioned walkways and stretching more than half a mile along Canton Road. Altogether there are more than 700 outlets, with shops selling clothing, accessories, jewelry, cosmetics, antiques, electronic goods, furniture, housewares, toys, Asian arts and crafts, and much more. There's enough to keep you occupied for the rest of your life, but this is an especially good place to go on a rainy or humid day when you'd rather be inside than out. Outlets include Lane Crawford, Marks & Spencer, Burberry, DKNY, Front First (by local designer Walter Ma), Jean-Paul Gaultier, Plantation, Salvatore Ferragamo, Vivienne Tam, Bally, Louis Vuitton, Gold Pfeil, and Toys 'Я' Us. Some shops are closed on Sunday but otherwise the hours are about 10 or 11am to 8pm.

**New World Centre.** 18–24 Salisbury Rd., Tsim Sha Tsui. MTR: Tsim Sha Tsui.

Located next to the Regent Hotel on the waterfront and catering to a local market, this shopping complex has outlets on several floors, with shops selling curios, clothing, accessories, and more. There are two department stores and many restaurants.

**Pacific Place.** 88 Queensway, Central.

Pacific Place is the largest and most ambitious commercial project to hit Central; in fact, it has shifted the city center toward the east. Besides three hotels, Pacific Place has a mall with 200 retail outlets and restaurants and three major department stores (Marks & Spencer, Lane Crawford, and Seibu). Outlets include The Body Shop, Cartier, Cerruti 1881, Hermès, Hugo Boss, Kenneth Cole, Vivienne Tam, Plantation, Prada, Shu Uemura, Tiffany & Co., and Chinese Arts and Crafts Ltd. Most shops are open daily about 10:30am to 8pm.

**Times Square.** 1 Matheson St., Causeway Bay. MTR: Causeway Bay.

This stylish center offers nine "themed" floors of shopping, including the Casual Living floor, the Home Furnishings floor, the Sports and Leisure floor, the Electronics floor, the Family Land floor with a play area and shops selling toys and children's clothing, and even several Food Forum floors with branches of well-known restaurants. Marks & Spencer and Lane Crawford department stores are also here. Most shops are open daily 10am to 9:30pm.

## TAILORS

The 24-hour suit is a thing of the past, but you can still have clothes custom-made in a few days. Tailoring in Hong Kong really began in the 1950s, when tailor families from Shanghai fled China and set up shop in Hong Kong. Today, prices are no longer as low as they once were, but they're often about what you'd pay for a ready-made garment back home; the difference, of course, is that a tailor-made garment should fit you perfectly. The standards of the better, established shops rival even those of London's Savile Row—at less than half the price. A top-quality man's suit will run about HK$6,500 ($844) or more, including fabric, while a silk shirt can cost HK$600 ($78).

Tailors in Hong Kong will make anything you want, from business suits and evening gowns to wedding dresses, leather jackets, and monogrammed shirts. Some stores will allow you to provide your own fabric, while others require that you buy theirs. Many tailors offer a wide range of cloth from which to choose, from cotton and linen to very fine wools, cashmere, and silk. Hong Kong tailors are excellent at copying fashions, even if all you have is a picture or drawing of what you want.

On average, you should allow 3 to 5 days to have a garment custom-made, with at least two or three fittings. Be specific about what you want, such as lining, tightness of fit, buttons, and length. If you aren't satisfied during the fittings, speak up. Alterations should be included in the original price (ask about this during your first negotiations). If in the end you still don't like the finished product, you don't have to accept it. However, you will forfeit the deposit you are required to pay before the tailor begins working, usually about 50% of the total cost.

With more than 2,500 tailoring establishments in Hong Kong, it shouldn't be any problem finding one. Some of the most famous are located in hotel shopping arcades and shopping complexes, but the more upscale the location, the higher the prices. Tsim Sha Tsui abounds in tailor shops. In any case, your best bet is to deal only with shops that are members of the HKTA or those you have used before. Member shops are listed in "The Official Dining, Entertainment & Shopping Directory" booklet.

Once you've had something custom-made and your tailor has your measurements, you will more than likely be able to order additional clothing later after you've returned home.

## TOYS

Even though Hong Kong is one of the world's leading exporters of toys, they seem to be in short supply in Hong Kong itself. There is, however, an abundance of cheap plastic toys from mainland China; I've done some of my best (cheapest) shopping on Cheung Chau island, a popular weekend destination for families. In addition to the shop below, the ninth floor of Times Square in Causeway Bay (see "Mega-Malls & Shopping Centers" above) has several clothing and toy stores geared toward children.

**Toys 'Я' Us.** Shop 032, in Zone C (Ocean Terminal), Harbour City, 5 Canton Rd., Tsim Sha Tsui. ☎ **852/2730 9462.** MTR: Tsim Sha Tsui.

This is one of the largest, if not *the* largest, toy store in Hong Kong. A huge department store, it offers games, sporting goods, hobby goods, baby furniture, books, clothing, and, of course, toys galore. It's open daily 10am to 8pm.

# Hong Kong After Dark  9

Nightlife in Hong Kong seems pretty tame when compared with that in Tokyo or Bangkok. With the world of Suzie Wong in Wan Chai now a shadow of its former self, Hong Kong today seems somewhat reserved and, perhaps to some minds, yawningly dull. For the upper crust who live here, exclusive clubs are popular for socializing and entertaining guests, while the vast majority of Chinese are likely to spend their free evenings at one of those huge lively restaurants.

Yet it would be wrong to assume that Hong Kong has nothing to offer in the way of nightlife—it's just that you probably won't get into any trouble enjoying yourself. To liven things up, Hong Kong stages several annual events, including the City Festival in January, which celebrates alternative arts ranging from performance art to music, the Hong Kong Arts Festival held in February or March, and the Hong Kong International Film Festival held in April. There are cultural activities and entertainment throughout the year, including theater productions, pop concerts, and Chinese opera and dance performances. In addition, there are plenty of that finest of British institutions—the pub—not to mention sophisticated cocktail lounges, discos, hostess clubs, and topless bars. There are even a couple nightlife districts in the Central District: in the vicinity of Lan Kwai Fong Street and D'Aguilar Street, where a string of bars and restaurants have long added a spark to Hong Kong's financial district; and SoHo, along the Hillside Escalator Link servicing Central and the Mid-Levels, with its growing number of ethnic restaurants and bars.

Remember that a 10% service charge will be added to your bill. If you're watching your Hong Kong dollars, keep in mind that one of the best traditions in the city is its "happy hour," when many bars offer two drinks for the price of one or else drinks at lower prices. Actually, "happy hours" would be more appropriate, since the period is generally 5 to 7pm and often even longer than that. Furthermore, many pubs, bars, and lounges offer live entertainment, from jazz to Filipino combos, which you can enjoy simply for the price of a beer. There are also a variety of ways to enjoy yourself at night without spending money—for example, strolling along the Tsim Sha Tsui harbor waterfront or around Victoria Peak, or browsing at the Temple Street Night Market.

# Information, Please

To find out what's going on during your stay in Hong Kong, be sure to pick up "Hong Kong Diary," a HKTA leaflet published weekly that tells what's happening in theater, music, and the arts, including concerts. *HK Magazine,* distributed free at restaurants, bars, and other outlets around town and aimed at a young readership, is a weekly that lists what's going on at the city's theaters and other venues, including plays, concerts, the cinema, and events in Hong Kong's alternative scene. *Where Hong Kong* and *bc* are two other free magazines published monthly with nightlife information and special events. In addition, "Hong Kong Life," published as a supplement by the *Hong Kong Standard* newspaper on Sunday, describes what's going on in Hong Kong during next the week; the *South China Morning Post* carries an entertainment section on Friday. Finally, you can also find out what's going on for the upcoming week by visiting the Hong Kong Tourist Association online at **www.hkta.org**.

## 1 The Performing Arts

The busiest time of the year for the performing arts is the month-long **Hong Kong Arts Festival,** held every year in February and March. This international affair features artists from around the world performing with orchestras, dance troupes, opera companies, and chamber ensembles. Appearing at past festivals, for example, were the Hong Kong Philharmonic Orchestra, the London Philharmonic, the Empire Brass from Boston, the Hong Kong Chinese Orchestra, the Stuttgart Ballet, the Paul Taylor Dance Company, and the Georgian State Dance Company from the former USSR. City Hall, located in Central just east of the Star Ferry concourse, sells tickets to performances, which are priced from HK$55 to HK$650 ($7.15 to $84.50). For information about the Hong Kong Arts Festival programs and future dates, call ☎ **852/ 2824 2430.**

To obtain tickets for the Hong Kong Arts Festival, as well as tickets throughout the year for classical music performances (including the Hong Kong Philharmonic Orchestra and the Hong Kong Chinese Orchestra), Chinese opera, rock and pop concerts, theatrical productions, dance, and other major events, contact the **Urban Council Ticketing Office (URBTIX),** which has numerous easily accessible outlets throughout the city: City Hall, Low Block, 7 Edinburgh Place in Central, open daily 10am to 9:30pm; the Arts Centre, 2 Harbour Rd. in Wan Chai, open daily 10am to 6pm; and the Hong Kong Cultural Centre, 10 Salisbury Rd. in Tsim Sha Tsui, open daily 10am to 9:30pm. Simply drop by one of the outlets, or reserve a ticket in advance by calling URBTIX at ☎ **852/2734 9009.** Tickets reserved by phone must be picked up within 3 days of the order. You can even reserve tickets before arriving in Hong Kong by calling the URBTIX overseas hotline at ☎ **852/2734 9011** 10am to 8pm Hong Kong time. A booking form will be faxed to you to be completed and returned within 3 days (payment by Visa or MasterCard is accepted). Reservations will then be confirmed by fax and tickets can be collected at the performance venue on arrival in Hong Kong. Note that a HK$20 ($2.60) processing fee is charged for the service.

Incidentally, the Hong Kong Cultural Centre in Tsim Sha Tsui, City Hall in Central, and the Hong Kong Academy for Performing Arts in Wan Chai, all with URBTIX outlets described above, also serve as major venues for many concerts and productions.

# PERFORMING ARTS COMPANIES
## CHINESE OPERA

Chinese opera predates the first Western opera by about 600 years, although it wasn't until the 13th and 14th centuries that performances began to develop a structured operatic form, with rules of composition and fixed role characterization. Distinct regional styles also developed, and even today there are marked differences among the operas performed in, say, Peking, Canton, Shanghai, Fukien, Chiu Chow, and Szechuan.

Most popular in Hong Kong, however, is Peking-style opera, with its spectacular costumes, elaborate makeup, and feats of acrobatics and swordsmanship, and the less flamboyant but more readily understood Cantonese-style opera. Plots usually dramatize legends and historical events, and extol such virtues as loyalty, filial piety, and righteousness. Accompanied by seven or eight musicians, the performers sing in shrill, high-pitched falsetto, a sound Westerners sometimes do not initially appreciate. Although lyrics are in Chinese, body language helps translate the stories.

Another aspect of Chinese opera that surprises Westerners is its informality. No one minds if spectators arrive late or leave early; in fact, no one even minds if a spectator, upon spotting friends or relatives, makes his way through the auditorium for a chat.

For visitors, the easiest way to see a Chinese opera is during the **Hong Kong Arts Festival,** held from about mid-February to early March each year. Alternatively, Cantonese opera is a common feature of important Chinese festivals, such as the birthday of Tin Hau or the annual Bun Festival on Cheung Chau island, when temporary bamboo theaters are erected.

Otherwise, Cantonese opera is performed fairly regularly at Town Halls in the New Territories, as well as in City Hall in Central. However, Chinese opera is immensely popular in Hong Kong, so much so that tickets for these shows sell out well in advance, making it almost impossible for tourists to attend performances. If you're still determined to try, call the URBTIX overseas hotline well in advance before arriving in Hong Kong, or, once in Hong Kong, contact the HKTA or check with one of the tourist publications for information on what's playing and then call or drop by URBTIX. Alternatively, the concierge of your hotel may be able to secure seats. Prices generally range from HK$100 to HK$230 ($13 to $29.85).

## CLASSICAL MUSIC

**Hong Kong Chinese Orchestra.** Performing at the Hong Kong Cultural Centre, 10 Salisbury Rd., Tsim Sha Tsui (☎ **852/2734 2009**), and City Hall, Edinburgh Place, Central District (☎ **852/2921 2840**). Tickets HK$60–HK$120 ($7.80–$15.60). MTR: Tsim Sha Tsui for Cultural Centre, or Central for City Hall.

Established in 1977, the Hong Kong Chinese Orchestra is the world's largest professional Chinese-instrument orchestra. It features 85 musicians who perform both new works and traditional pieces, playing a wide range of traditional and modern Chinese instruments and combining them with Western orchestrations or Chinese music.

**Hong Kong Philharmonic Orchestra.** Performing at the Hong Kong Cultural Centre, 10 Salisbury Rd., Tsim Sha Tsui (☎ **852/2734 2009**), and City Hall, Edinburgh Place, Central District (☎ **852/2921 2840**). Tickets HK$60–HK$270 ($7.80–$35.05). MTR: Tsim Sha Tsui for Cultural Centre, or Central for City Hall.

The Hong Kong Cultural Centre is the home of the city's largest orchestra, the Hong Kong Philharmonic, founded in 1975 and performing regularly September to June and at other scheduled events throughout the year. Its conductor is David Atherton; guest conductors and soloists appear during the concert season. In addition to Western classical pieces, its repertoire is enriched by works commissioned from Chinese composers.

> ### ❓ Did You Know?
>
> - Hong Kong is home to the world's third most productive film industry.
> - The world's largest professional Chinese instrument orchestra is the 85-member Hong Kong Chinese Orchestra, which uses traditional and modern Chinese musical instruments.
> - Club Bboss, in Tsim Sha Tsui East, is the world's largest Japanese-style hostess club, occupying 70,000 square feet.

## DANCE

Both the **Hong Kong Ballet Company** and the **Hong Kong Dance Company** have extensive repertoires. The Hong Kong Ballet Company, founded in 1979, performs both classical works and modern pieces, usually at the Cultural Centre or the Hong Kong Academy for Performing Arts. The Hong Kong Dance Company specializes in the development of Chinese dance in modern forms. Finally, another troupe is the **City Contemporary Dance Company,** which expresses contemporary Hong Kong culture through dance. Performances are often held at the Hong Kong Academy for Performing Arts. Contact the HKTA for the current schedule.

## THEATER

Most plays presented in Hong Kong are performed in Cantonese. Hong Kong's leading local troupes are the **Chung Ying Theatre Company,** a community ensemble that plays in a wide range of venues, from schools and senior citizens' homes to Hong Kong's main theaters, often performing works by local writers, and the **Hong Kong Repertory Theatre,** which performs original Chinese works. Both perform in Cantonese at various venues, including City Hall in Central and the Hong Kong Cultural Centre in Tsim Sha Tsui. Prices range from about HK$100 to HK$160 ($13 to $20.80).

Otherwise, your best bet for English-language performances is at the **Fringe Club,** 2 Lower Albert Rd., Central (☎ 852/2521 7251; MTR: Central), a venue for experimental drama (in English and Cantonese), live music, comedy, art exhibitions, and other happenings, from mime to magic shows. Housed in a former dairy farm depot built in 1813 and consisting of two theaters, exhibition space, a restaurant, and a bar, it also sponsors the City Festival held in January, which celebrates Hong Kong's alternative arts scene.

## MAJOR CONCERT HALLS

**City Hall.** Connaught Rd. and Edinburgh Place, Central District. ☎ **852/2921 2840.** MTR: Central.

Located right beside the Star Ferry concourse, City Hall's Low Block has a 1,500-seat balconied concert hall, as well as a 470-seat theater used for plays and chamber music.

**Hong Kong Academy for Performing Arts.** 1 Gloucester Rd., Wan Chai. ☎ **852/ 2584 8500.** MTR: Wan Chai.

Located across the street from the Arts Centre, the academy is Hong Kong's institution for vocational training in the performing arts. It also features regular performances in theater and dance, by both local and international playwrights and choreographers. Its Theatre Block is composed of six venues, including the Lyric Theatre, Drama Theatre, Orchestral Hall, and Recital Hall.

**Hong Kong Arts Centre.** 2 Harbour Rd., Wan Chai. ☎ **852/2582 0200.** MTR: Wan Chai.

Built on Wan Chai's new waterfront of reclaimed land, the Arts Centre hosts the Hong Kong Arts Festival and other international presentations, as well as performances by Hong Kong's own amateur and professional companies. It offers a regular schedule of plays or dances, exhibition galleries, and showings of foreign films. There are three auditoriums: Shouson Theatre, McAulay Studio Theatre, and Lim Por Yen Film Theatre.

**Hong Kong Cultural Centre.** 10 Salisbury Rd., Tsim Sha Tsui. ☎ **852/2734 2009.** MTR: Tsim Sha Tsui.

Sandwiched in between the Space Museum and the Star Ferry concourse, the Hong Kong Cultural Centre is the territory's newest and largest arena for the arts. Opened in 1989, this complex boasts both a Western and a Chinese restaurant, exhibition areas, and practice and rehearsal rooms, but its pride is its 2,100-seat Concert Hall, home of the Hong Kong Philharmonic Orchestra. It features a 93-stop, 8,000-pipe Austrian Rieger organ—one of the world's largest. Two levels of seating surround the stage, which is set near the center of the oval hall.

There are also two theaters. The Grand Theatre, which seats 1,750, is used for musicals, large-scale drama, dance, film shows, and Chinese opera. It is fitted with a revolving stage wagon, an orchestra pit for 110 musicians, a five-language simultaneous interpretation system (for conventions and conferences), and cinematic projection equipment. The Studio Theatre, which can seat from 326 to 542 persons, was designed for experimental theater and dance. Its stage configuration can be changed to end, thrust, center, and transverse.

You can learn more about the history of the Cultural Centre and visit the Concert Hall, both theaters, and backstage areas by participating in a 30-minute tour of the Centre, given in English daily at 12:30pm. Cost of the tour is HK$10 ($1.30) for adults; half price for children, students, and senior citizens. For more information on tours, call ☎ **852/2734 2009.**

## 2 The Club & Music Scene

### LIVE MUSIC

Hong Kong does not have the kind of jazz-, rock-, or blues-club scene that many other cities do. On the other hand, live music is such a standard feature of many restaurants, hotel cocktail lounges, and bars, it would be hard *not* to hear live music in Hong Kong. Although some establishments levy a cover charge, most charge absolutely nothing.

Bars, lounges, and clubs offering live music include **Chasers, Club Shanghai, Delaney's, Ned Kelly's Last Stand, Sky Lounge,** and **Someplace Else,** all in Kowloon; the **Captain's Bar, Cyrano,** and **Insomnia** in Central; **Carnegie's** and **JJ's** in Wan Chai; and **TOTT's Asian Grill & Bar** in Causeway Bay.

Among the many restaurants with free live music are **Gaddi's, Hugo's, Margaux, Planet Hollywood,** and **Sabatini,** all in Kowloon; **Lobster Bar** and **Petrus** in Central;

---

**Impressions**

*Hong Kong illuminated . . . is wonderful. Imagine a giant Monte Carlo with a hundred times as many lights!*
　　　　　　　　—Alfred Viscount Northcliffe, *My Journey Round the World,* 1923

Cafe Deco and Peak Cafe on the Peak; Bacchus in Wan Chai; and TOTT's Asian Grill & Bar in Causeway Bay. For more information on all these establishments, refer to individual listings.

Because live music is regarded more as a sidelight than the raison d'être of most establishments, if you're serious about jazz you will want to head straight to one of the venues below.

**Blue Note.** In the Kowloon Shangri-La Hotel, 64 Mody Rd., Tsim Sha Tsui East. ☎ **852/ 2721 2111,** ext. 8916. No cover. MTR: Tsim Sha Tsui.

Offering live jazz performed by international (mostly American) musicians, this intimate, dimly lit bar is a great place to relax, listen to music, and enjoy good harbor views. Live music is featured Monday to Saturday 8:30pm to 12:30am, but you might wish to come early for happy hour, 5 to 8:30pm with reduced drink prices.

**Fringe Club.** 2 Lower Albert Rd., Central. ☎ **852/2521 7251.** No cover. MTR: Central.

Hong Kong's best known venue for alternative events offers free live music most Fridays and Saturdays from 10:30pm at its Nokia Gallery, including blues, jazz, folk, and funk. Call for an updated listing or pick up the Fringe Club's monthly calendar.

**The Jazz Club & Bar.** California Entertainment Building (second floor), 34–36 D'Aguilar, Central. ☎ **852/2845 8477.** Cover usually HK$60 to HK$150 ($7.80 to $19.50) for local acts and up to HK$300 ($39) for international bands. MTR: Central.

Small and intimate, with life-size photographs of such jazz greats as Billie, Dizzy, and Satchmo lining the walls, this is Hong Kong's most established jazz venue; Herbie Hancock, Jimmy Witherspoon, and Wynton Marsalis have performed here. Otherwise, local acts, such as the Victoria Jazz Band performing swing and jazz from Armstrong to Ellington, play regularly scheduled sets. If you're on a budget, no cover charge is levied for a drink in a separate bar, with closed-circuit TV capturing the show. It's open Tuesday to Thursday 7pm to 1:30am (live music 9pm to 12:30am) and Friday and Saturday 7pm to 2:30am (live music 10pm to 1am).

## DANCE CLUBS

Disco fever has cooled considerably since the heady days of the early 1980s, with only a couple of discos weathering the years. More prevalent are small, simple bars that metamorphose into miniature discos late at night or on weekends. Discos and dance clubs in Hong Kong generally charge more on weekend nights, but the admission price usually includes one or two free drinks. After that, beer and mixed drinks are often priced the same.

In addition to the discos below, check "The Bar Scene," for **California,** which transforms itself into a disco on Friday and Saturday nights, and for **Someplace Else,** which becomes a disco nightly at 11pm. In addition, both the **Captain's Bar,** located in the Mandarin Hotel, and **Cyrano,** located on the top floor of the Island Shangri-La, offer free live music nightly from 9pm and a small dance floor. **TOTT's Asian Grill & Bar,** a combination restaurant/bar located in the Excelsior Hotel, offers live music and dancing nightly except Sunday.

### KOWLOON

**Club Shanghai.** In the Regent Hotel, Salisbury Rd., Tsim Sha Tsui. ☎ **852/2721 1211,** ext. 2242. No cover. MTR: Tsim Sha Tsui.

Nostalgia for Shanghai of the 1930s and the decadence it represents have captured the collective imagination of Hong Kong's clubgoers, but few venues pull it off as successfully as this classy lounge in the Regent Hotel. Bathed in dim, red light, waitresses

## Mad About Mahjong

You don't have to be in Hong Kong long before you hear it—the clackity-clack of *mahjong,* almost deafening if it's emanating from a large mahjong parlor. You can hear it at large restaurants (there are usually mahjong parlors in side rooms), at wedding celebrations, in the middle of the day, and long into the night. In a land where gambling is illegal except at the horse races, mahjong provides the opportunity for skillful gambling. The Chinese, you might say, are mad about mahjong.

Although mahjong originated during the Sung dynasty almost 1,000 years ago, today's game is very different and more difficult, and is played with amazing speed. Essentially mahjong is played by four people, using tiles that resemble dominoes and bear Chinese characters and designs. Tiles are drawn and discarded (by slamming them on the table), until one player wins with a hand of four combinations of three tiles and a pair of matching tiles. But the real excitement comes with betting chips that each player receives and which are awarded to the winner based on his combination of winning tiles. Excitement is also heightened by the speed of the game—the faster tiles are slammed against the table and swooped up, the better. Technically, the mahjong game is over when a player runs out of chips, though it's not unusual to borrow chips to continue playing. There are lots of stories in Hong Kong of fortunes made and lost in a game of mahjong. Many hardcore players confess to an addiction.

wearing high-collared slit dresses glide past stuffed armchairs draped with lace antimacassars, potted palms, fringed lampshades, and decorative opium pipes. Although the focus is on live music and dancing, you can also come just for the harbor views. It's open Monday to Thursday 8pm to 1:30am and Friday and Saturday 8pm to 2am.

### CENTRAL DISTRICT

**Club 97.** 9 Lan Kwai Fong, Central. ☎ **852/2810 9333.** No cover Sun–Wed, HK$97 ($12.60) Thurs–Sat. MTR: Central.

One of the few full-fledged discos remaining in Hong Kong, this small, cavelike establishment, decorated in funky "Moroccan" style with black-and-white tiles, mirrors, and tiny lights reminiscent of stars, is fun and usually crowded to capacity. In fact, it's so small that it sometimes feels like a private party—even more so because it's officially a members-only disco. However, nonmembers are allowed in if the place isn't too crowded; plan for a weeknight and maybe even call ahead for a reservation. It's easy to strike up a conversation with your neighbors here, since they are generally a mixture of expatriates and Chinese. Wednesdays features music of the 1970s; Thursdays attract a mostly expat crowd with its Latin, soul, jazz, funk, and laid-back atmosphere; and a gay happy hour takes place every Friday 6 to 10pm. All in all, a very retro-hip joint. it's open Monday to Thursday 9pm to 4am, Friday 6 to 10pm and again 11pm to 6am, Saturday 10pm to 6am, and Sunday 10pm to 2am.

**Propaganda.** 1 Hollywood Rd., Central. ☎ **852/2868 1316.** Cover (including 1 drink) Thurs HK$80 ($10.40), Fri HK$120 ($15.60), Sat HK$200 ($25.95). No cover Mon–Wed, before 10:30pm Thurs, or after 3:30am Fri; reduced cover before 10:30pm Fri–Sat. MTR: Central.

Hong Kong's most popular gay disco, Propaganda recently moved into upgraded quarters in the new SoHo nightlife district, with a discreet entrance in a back alley (and a bit hard to find). Only about 5% of the people who come through the doors are straight, but everyone is welcome. Come late on a weekend if you want to see this alternative hot spot at its most crowded. It's open Monday to Wednesday 9pm to 3:30am, Thursday 9pm to 4am, Friday 9pm to 5am, and Saturday 9pm to 6am.

## CAUSEWAY BAY & WAN CHAI

**JJ's.** In the Grand Hyatt Hotel, 1 Harbour Rd., Wan Chai. ☎ **852/2588 1234,** ext. 7323. Cover HK$100 ($13) Mon–Thurs (including 1 drink), HK$200 ($26) Fri–Sat (including 2 drinks). No cover before 8:30pm. MTR: Wan Chai.

This upscale, glitzy entertainment complex was the first in Hong Kong to offer several diversions under one roof. It is decorated in a style that is part Victorian and part whimsical, giving it an eccentric and playful ambience. There's a main bar, a disco with house tracks and laser lights, a restaurant serving pizza and sandwiches, and a room with live jazz or rhythm-and-blues. This is the place for those who like to move from one scene to the next, without actually having to go anywhere. Note, however, that dress is smart casual (no tennis shoes, sandals, torn jeans, or shorts allowed). Monday to Friday, you can have two drinks for the price of one during happy hour 5:30 to 8:30pm, along with a free snack buffet 6 to 8pm. JJ's is open Monday to Thursday 5:30pm to 2am, Friday 5:30pm to 3am, and Saturday 6pm to 4am.

**Joe Bananas.** 23 Luard Rd., Wan Chai. ☎ **852/2529 1811.** No cover Sun–Wed; Thurs HK$50 ($6.50), including 1 drink; Fri–Sat HK$100 ($13), including 2 drinks. Free for women until 1am. MTR: Wan Chai.

Appealing to Hong Kong's single yuppies, this is a bar and restaurant that transforms itself into a happening disco every evening after 10pm, but the action doesn't kick in till late. There's dancing Sunday to Thursday 10pm to 5am, on Friday and Saturday 10pm to 6am.

## 3 The Bar Scene

## COCKTAIL LOUNGES

Although virtually all hotels in Hong Kong have cocktail lounges, I've limited my selection here to two with great views—since you're in one of the most romantically beautiful cities in the world, why settle for anything less?

### KOWLOON

✪ **Sky Lounge.** In the Sheraton Hotel and Towers, 20 Nathan Rd., Tsim Sha Tsui. ☎ **852/ 2369 1111.** MTR: Tsim Sha Tsui.

This plush and comfortable lounge is on the top floor of the Sheraton, affording one of the best and most romantic views of the harbor and glittering Hong Kong Island. There's soft live music nightly 9pm to midnight. Unless you're a hotel guest, from 8:30pm onward there's a minimum drink charge of HK$128 ($16.65) per person. Or, on weekends, come earlier for the afternoon tea buffet, available 2 to 6pm for $95 ($12.35). It's open Sunday to Thursday 2pm to 1am and Friday and Saturday 2pm to 2am.

### CENTRAL DISTRICT

**Cyrano.** In the Island Shangri-La, Pacific Place, 88 Queensway, Central. ☎ **852/ 2877 3838.** MTR: Admiralty.

This sophisticated, intimate lounge is Hong Kong's highest—on the 56th floor with great views of the harbor. Decorated in a style reminiscent of the 1930s, it offers live music every night from 9pm except Sunday and a small dance floor. On Friday and

Saturday, there's a minimum drink charge of HK$135 ($17.55; waived for hotel guests). Cocktails, averaging HK$75 ($9.75), are a specialty. It's open Sunday to Thursday 5pm to 1am and Friday and Saturday 5pm to 2am.

## PUBS & BARS
### KOWLOON

**Chasers.** 2–3 Knutsford Terrace, Tsim Sha Tsui. ☎ **852/2367 9487.** MTR: Tsim Sha Tsui.

One of several bars lining the narrow, alleylike Knutsford Terrace, which parallels Kimberley Road to the north, this is among the most popular, filled with a mixed clientele that includes both the young and the middle aged, foreign and Chinese. One of Hong Kong's first late-night haunts to actively promote the live music scene, it features a house Filipino band nightly from 11pm, playing rock, jazz, rhythm-and-blues, and everything in between. There is no cover charge. Happy hour is all day Sunday and the rest of the week 4 to 10pm. It's open Monday to Friday 3pm to 6am and Saturday and Sunday noon to 6am.

**Delaney's.** 71–77 Peking Rd., Tsim Sha Tsui. ☎ **852/2301 3980.** MTR: Tsim Sha Tsui.

This very successful, upmarket Irish pub is decorated in Old-World style with its old posters and photographs. Its convivial atmosphere gets an extra boost from live Irish bands playing 2 nights a week (at last check, Friday and Saturday), free of charge. Big soccer and rugby events are shown on a big screen. In addition to a set carvery lunch offered weekends, it also has an à-la-carte menu listing Irish stew, beef and Guinness pie, corned beef and cabbage, and other national favorites, and is open daily 10:30am to 2:30am. There's another Delaney's in Wan Chai at 18 Luard Rd. (☎ **852/ 2804 2880**).

**Kangaroo Pub.** 35 Haiphong Rd., Tsim Sha Tsui. ☎ **852/2376 0083.** MTR: Tsim Sha Tsui.

This Australian pub overlooking Kowloon Park, with dart boards and TVs often tuned to sporting events, is the place to go if you want a beer and fish-and-chips, an Aussie meat pie, bangers and mash (sausage and potatoes), samosas, chili, lasagne, grilled chicken, or other items from a mixed menu. Happy hour is 4 to 7pm, with draft beer going for half price. Open daily 11am–3am.

**Ned Kelly's Last Stand.** 11A Ashley Rd., Tsim Sha Tsui. ☎ **852/2376 0562.** MTR: Tsim Sha Tsui.

This is a lively Aussie saloon, with free live Dixieland jazz or swing Monday to Saturday 9pm to 2am and attracting a largely middle-aged crowd. It serves Australian chow, including juicy pork sausages with mashed potatoes and onion gravy; stew; chicken; Australian sirloin steak; hamburgers; and meat pie with mashed potatoes and onion gravy. Happy hour is 11:30am to 9pm, with reduced prices. It's open daily 11:30am to 2am.

**Schnurrbart.** 9–11 Prat Ave., Tsim Sha Tsui. ☎ **852/2366 2986.** MTR: Tsim Sha Tsui.

This is the Kowloon branch of a well-established Central bar, a cozy, small place offering great German beers and German food from a menu that changes weekly, including a daily fixed-price lunch. Happy hour, with reduced prices, is 3 to 8pm daily. Catering mostly to Germans in the evenings, it's open daily noon to 1am.

**Someplace Else.** Sheraton Hotel (basement), 20 Nathan Rd. (enter from Middle Rd.), Tsim Sha Tsui. ☎ **852/2369 1111.** MTR: Tsim Sha Tsui.

This is one of Tsim Sha Tsui's more popular watering holes, especially during happy hour (4 to 8pm, with two-for-one drinks) when it's standing room only on weekdays.

It's also worth checking back later in the evening, when late-night drink specials kick in—after midnight on weekdays, 1am on weekends. A combination restaurant/bar/disco, this two-level establishment, decorated with stained-glass lampshades and ceiling fans, offers a tempting menu of American and Tex-Mex food, including steaks, burgers, tacos, ribs, and fried chicken. Live music is featured Monday to Saturday 6 to 11pm. After that, it transforms into a disco, for which there's no cover charge. Hours here are Sunday to Thursday 11am to 2am and Friday and Saturday 11am to 3am.

## CENTRAL DISTRICT

**Al's Diner.** 39 D'Aguilar St., Central. ☎ **852/2869 1869.** MTR: Central.

Rather innocent-looking during the day, this hamburger joint transforms into one of Lan Kwai Fong's most extroverted party scenes on weekend nights, no doubt fueled by the house specialty, jelly shots (jelly laced with vodka), and music supplied by a DJ. A few shots, and you may find yourself joining the others dancing on the tables. It's open Monday to Thursday 11:30am to 1am, Friday and Saturday 11:30am to 3am, and Sunday 11:30am to midnight.

**Bull and Bear.** Hutchinson House, 10 Harcourt Rd., Central. ☎ **852/2525 7436.** MTR: Central.

The huge, sprawling, traditionally decorated Bull and Bear was at the forefront of Hong Kong's English-pub craze, opening back in 1974. Notorious from the beginning, it can get pretty rowdy on weekend nights, attracting everyone from business-men in suits to servicemen on leave. Since it attracts more men than women, one British expatriate described it as a "meat market." Maybe that's what you're looking for. I can confirm that it's not a particularly comfortable place for a woman alone at night, having had to fight off the attentions of a rather inebriated tattooed sailor. An alternative is to come for lunch or breakfast, when it attracts mainly business types. The menu includes fish and chips, steak-and-kidney pie, salads, sandwiches, and daily specials. Happy hour is daily 5 to 9pm. It's open Monday to Saturday 8am to midnight.

**California.** 24–26 Lan Kwai Fong St., Central. ☎ **852/2521 1345.** MTR: Central.

Located in Central's nightlife district, this chic bar was once the place to see and be seen—the haunt of young nouveaux riches in search of a definition. Newer establishments have since encroached upon California's exalted position, but it remains a respected and sophisticated restaurant/bar, with silent TV screens showing music videos or sporting events almost everywhere you look. You might consider starting your night on the town here with dinner and drinks—the innovative, young American chef has created a changing menu that ranges from spinach fettuccini with grilled artichokes, roasted tomatoes, red onions, and asparagus, to steak with wild mushrooms, smothered onions and red wine/balsamic thyme reduction, though hamburgers (the house specialty) remain hugely popular. A plus to coming early is happy hour, 5 to 9pm, with two drinks for the price of one. On Friday and Saturday nights 11pm to 4am, it becomes a happening disco, with hot DJs playing the latest hits and never a cover charge. It's open Monday to Thursday noon to midnight, Friday and Saturday noon to 4am, and Sunday 6 to midnight.

**Captain's Bar.** In the Mandarin Hotel, 5 Connaught Rd., Central. ☎ **852/2522 0111.** MTR: Central.

That this refined bar is popular with Hong Kong's professional crowd, especially at the end of the working day, comes as no surprise considering the fact that it's in the

Mandarin Hotel, a long-time favorite with business travelers. Well known for its martinis and its pints of beer served in aluminum and silver tankards, and its weekday lunch buffets, it's a small, intimate place, with seating at the bar or on couches. Live music begins nightly at 9pm; there's even a small dance floor for those inclined to shuffle around. It's open daily 11am to 2am.

**Dublin Jack.** 37 Cochrane St., Central. ☎ **852/2543 0081.** MTR: Central.

It's easy to spot this Irish pub with its bright red exterior, located right next to the Hillside Escalator Link in Central's SoHo entertainment district. It's so packed with expats on their way home to the Mid-Levels after a day's work in Central, it's hard to elbow your way in through the door. Maybe it's because of its whisky—more than 50 brands of Irish and 100 kinds of Scottish whiskies. Happy hour, with reduced drink prices, is noon to 8pm on weekdays, 3pm to 8pm on weekends. The multi-level bar is open daily noon to 2am.

**Insomnia.** 38–44 D'Aguilar St., Central. ☎ **852/2525 0957.** MTR: Central.

One of Lan Kwai Fong's most popular bars, it's aptly named, since live music by a Filipino band doesn't get underway until 11pm and it's at its most packed in the wee hours of the morning. Happy hour is 8am to 2pm and again 5 to 7pm. It's open daily 8am to 6am, leaving insomniacs 2 hours with nowhere to go.

**MadDogs.** 1 D'Aguilar St., Central. ☎ **852/2810 1000.** MTR: Central.

Catering to a mellow crowd of professional people during early evening hours and a wilder bunch at night, this is one of Hong Kong's long-standing, popular English pubs, with a traditional decor reminiscent of Britain during its imperial heyday. A wide variety of draft beers and Scotch malts is offered. It's often packed, especially during happy hour Monday to Friday 11am to 10pm and Saturday and Sunday 4 to 10pm. There's a DJ every night except Sunday. Incidentally, no shorts or flip-flops allowed; and since the owner is an animal-rights advocate, you must leave your furs at home. It's open Monday to Thursday 11am to 2am, Friday 10am to 3am, Saturday 11am to 3am, and Sunday 10am to 2am.

**Oscar's.** 2 Lan Kwai Fong, Central. ☎ **852/2804 6561.** MTR: Central.

This informal cafe/bar doesn't look like much inside, but then, hardly anyone goes inside. Rather, the youthful clientele fetches a beer, which begins at HK$42 ($5.45) for a can, and then stands around outside, giving the scene the atmosphere of a street party. Part of the establishment's success is its daily happy hour, when beer costs only HK$30 ($3.90) 3 to 8pm. A place to meet people, it's open Monday to Thursday 11am to 1am, Friday and Saturday 11am to 2am, and Sunday 11am to midnight.

**Pomeroy's Bar & Restaurant.** Pacific Place, Shop 349, 88 Queensway, Central. ☎ **852/ 2523 4772.** MTR: Admiralty.

This American-style bar/restaurant with its brick walls, low ceiling, and dim lighting is a good choice for a beer and a burger in the Pacific Place shopping center or if you're visiting nearby Hong Kong Park. If you have little ones, come for the special Kids Klub every Saturday noon to 3pm, featuring a children's menu, a clown, face-painting, and games. Otherwise, happy hour is 3 to 9pm daily. It's open daily 11am to 11pm.

**Post 97.** 9 Lan Kwai Fong, Central. ☎ **852/2186 1817.** MTR: Central.

Post 97 is a casual cafe with a name that's a cheeky reference to Hong Kong's handover. It's a good place to socialize, relax over a cup of coffee or a drink, or dine on such international fare as curried chicken salad; seafood and crab ravioli with a white wine truffle sauce; or barbecued tandoori salmon. Happy hour is 3 to 7pm daily. This is also a good place for breakfast. It's open Sunday to Thursday 9am to 2am and Friday and Saturday 9am to 3am.

**Schnurrbart.** 29 D'Aguilar St., Central. ☎ **852/2523 4700.** MTR: Central.

This is the place to come for German beer on tap, as well as a wide selection of bottled German beers. Popular with German expatriates, it serves sausages, sauerkraut, and other hearty German fare, with a menu that changes weekly. German beer begins at HK$38 ($4.95), except during happy hour (3 to 8pm daily) when the price of drinks is reduced. It's open Monday to Thursday noon to 1am, Friday and Saturday noon to 3am, and Sunday 6pm to midnight.

**Sherman's.** California Entertainment Building (ground floor), 34–36 D'Aguilar St., Central. ☎ **852/2801 4946.** MTR: Central.

This open-fronted establishment in the heart of Central's Lan Kwai Fong nightlife district has a sidewalk-cafe atmosphere and is always packed. Its menu lists tapas, create-your-own pasta dishes, and sandwiches. It's open Monday to Thursday noon to 2am, Friday and Saturday noon to 4am, and Sunday 4pm to 1am.

**Staunton's Bar & Cafe.** 10–12 Staunton St., Central. ☎ **852/2973 6611.** MTR: Central.

Located on the corner of Staunton and Shelley streets beside the Hillside Escalator Link, this was one of the first of many bars and restaurants that now give the SoHo district its unique, homey atmosphere. Above the ground-floor bar is a restaurant serving contemporary Mediterranean and Italian fare. Happy hour is 6 to 9pm daily, and open hours here are daily 9am to midnight.

## CAUSEWAY BAY & WAN CHAI

**Carnegie's.** 53–55 Lockhart Rd., Wan Chai. ☎ **852/2866 6289.** MTR: Wan Chai.

Imported from Singapore and dedicated to classic rock music, this bar attracts crowds with weekly promotions, DJs that play the Eagles and Springsteen, and a happy hour daily 11am to 10pm. Wednesday is ladies' night, featuring free champagne for women served by—ooh-la-la—topless waiters. On Sunday there's live music from 10pm. On Tuesdays you can drink vodka for free 10 to 11pm. It's open Monday 11am to 2am, Tuesday to Friday 11am to 5am, Saturday noon to 5am, and Sunday 5pm to 5am.

**Chinatown.** 78–82 Jaffe Rd., Wan Chai. ☎ **852/2861 3588.** MTR: Wan Chai.

Open to the street, this Shanghai-styled bar beguiles with its red and gold decor, red lanterns, Mao watching benevolently from a framed picture behind the bar, red star–emblazoned bar stools, and cheongsam-clad waitresses. Happy hour is daily 11:30am to 10pm, with two drinks for the price of one. It's open daily 11:30am to 3am.

**Devil's Advocate.** 48–50 Lockhart Rd., Wan Chai. ☎ **852/2885 7271.** MTR: Wan Chai.

This bar's open-to-the-street facade gives witness to the debauchery that takes place here late at night. Decorated like Hell, with a devilish motif, it offers happy hour daily noon to 9:30pm and is open daily noon to 2am or later.

**Joe Bananas.** 23 Luard Rd., Wan Chai. ☎ **852/2529 1811.** After 10pm, cover Thurs HK$50 ($6.50), including 1 drink; Fri–Sat HK$100 ($13), including 2 drinks. MTR: Wan Chai.

Under the same management as MadDogs, this has long been one of the most popular hangouts in Wan Chai, maybe because it's reportedly also one of Hong Kong's best pick-up bars. Called "JB's" by the locals, it's a tribute to the rock, pop, and movie greats of yesterday. It's decorated like an American diner, complete with jukebox, posters, and music memorabilia. This place is a combination bar/restaurant/disco, with an extensive menu that includes curries, fajitas, sandwiches, and fish-and-chips. There is dancing every evening after 10pm, but a cover is charged only Thursday to Saturday (though women get in free until 1am). Happy hour is 11am to 10pm Monday to Thursday, 1 to 10pm Friday and Saturday, and 5 to 10pm on Sunday. It's open Monday to Saturday 11am to 6am and Sunday 5pm to 5am.

**Old China Hand.** 104 Lockhart Rd., Wan Chai. ☎ **852/2527 9174.** MTR: Wan Chai.

This is one of the old-timers in Wan Chai, an informal English pub popular with older expats and with a picture of Queen Elizabeth and a lot of kitsch on the walls. A sign warns customers: SORRY, WE DON'T SERVE WOMEN—YOU HAVE TO BRING YOUR OWN. In the tradition of the pub lunch, meals include steak-and-kidney pie, fish-and-chips, sandwiches, salads, chili con carne, and spare ribs. Breakfast is available all day. Happy hour is daily 11am to 9pm. It's open Sunday to Thursday 10am to 2am and Friday and Saturday 10am to 7am.

**TOTT's Asian Grill & Bar.** In the Excelsior Hotel, Gloucester Rd., Causeway Bay. ☎ **852/ 2837 6786.** MTR: Causeway Bay.

This flashy bar and grill, with a blood-red interior and zebra-striped chairs, offers fabulous views of Victoria Harbour and Kowloon from its 34th-floor perch. There's live music and dancing every night except Sunday from 9:30pm, with a minimum drink/snack charge of HK$142 ($18.45) on weekends only (there's no minimum charge for hotel guests or diners who eat here). Happy hour is 5 to 8pm, with reduced prices for drinks. The bar is open Sunday to Thursday 5pm to 1am and Friday and Saturday 5pm to 2am.

## TOPLESS BARS & HOSTESS CLUBS

Hong Kong's world of hostess clubs and topless bars has changed in the past 30 years. Back in the 1950s and 1960s, Wan Chai was where the action was, buzzing with sailors fresh off their ships and soldiers on leave from Vietnam. It was a world of two-bit hotels, raunchy bars, narrow streets, and dark alleyways where men came to drink and brawl and spend money on women.

Today most of Wan Chai has become respectable (and a bit boring)—an area full of new buildings, mushrooming high-rises, and Hong Kong's expansive convention center. Although bars catering to young revelers have mushroomed in Wan Chai the past couple of years, Hong Kong's racier nightlife has moved across the harbor, where it has upscaled, accompanied, of course, by higher prices. Topless bars and hostess establishments still exist, but the Japanese have replaced the sailors and soldiers. Used to high-class hostess bars in their own country, they don't wince at the prices. At any rate, you've been warned.

**BBOSS.** New Mandarin Plaza, 14 Science Museum Rd., Tsim Sha Tsui East. ☎ **852/ 2369 2883.** Minimum drink/snack charge HK$460 ($59.75) until 9pm, HK$520 ($67.55) after 9pm. MTR: Tsim Sha Tsui; then take a taxi.

This dazzling, 70,000-square-foot hostess club can seat 3,000 people and claims to be the largest Japanese-style nightclub in the world. In fact, the place is so big that a full-size electric replica of an antique Rolls-Royce delivers customers along a "highway" to their seats. There are three nightly stage shows, at 9:30, 10:30, and 11:30pm, complete with a rotating stage so that everyone gets a chance to ogle the scantily clad performers. There's also a 20-member band, a smaller combo band, and a dance floor. Couples are welcome, though single women are not allowed, as they would compete with the scores of hostesses who flatter and chat with male customers. During the day, when entertainment consists of a pianist and singer, 2 hours spent with a hostess will set you back HK$450 ($58.45), including two drinks; in the evening a hostess sitting at your table for 2 hours will cost you HK$1,134 ($147). Big spenders can even take hostesses away from the club for the evening (escort services are big business in Hong Kong, as a perusal of any local newspaper will show). In any case, how much you end up spending will be determined by how many drinks you consume, how long you entertain a hostess at your table, and what time of the day or night you visit. If you're not careful, you could spend a fortune here. On the other hand, the place is so overdecorated in bows and the color pink, 1 hour may be all you can stand. It's open daily 1pm to 4am.

**Bottoms Up.** 14 Hankow Rd., Tsim Sha Tsui. ☎ **852/2367 5696.** MTR: Tsim Sha Tsui.

For years this basement establishment had explicit pictures of its namesake at the entranceway. These are now gone in the club's bid for respectability, and it's probably the best place to go if you want a topless joint. Welcoming tourists, couples, and unaccompanied men, Bottoms Up was used as a location shot in the James Bond movie *Man with the Golden Gun.* It features soft red lighting and four round counters with a topless waitress in the middle of each. I suggest that you come during happy hour (5:30 to 8:30pm daily), when drinks are cheaper. It's open daily 5:30pm to 3:30am.

## 4 Only in Hong Kong

### NIGHT TOURS

If you have only 1 or 2 nights in Hong Kong and you're uncomfortable roaming around on your own, I recommend an organized night tour. **Watertours** offers four evening tours that combine harbor cruises with various land activities. You can make reservations for these tours through your hotel or by calling Watertours directly ☎ **852/2926 3868.**

The Aberdeen & Harbour Night Cruise, for example, includes a sunset cruise on a traditional-style Chinese junk with unlimited drinks, dinner aboard a floating restaurant in Aberdeen, and a stop at a scenic overlook midway up Victoria Peak. This 4½-hour tour is offered nightly and costs HK$610 ($79.20), including dinner. There are also shorter evening cruises (without dinner). Watertours offers nightly cocktail cruises at 6:15pm and night cruises at 9:30pm. Both tours last approximately 90 minutes and cost HK$290 ($37.65), including unlimited free drinks.

There is also a 1-hour cruise aboard a famous Star Ferry, nightly at 7pm and costing HK$80 ($10.40). You can book the tour at the Star Ferry piers in Central and Tsim Sha Tsui.

If you're in Hong Kong anytime September to May on a Wednesday evening, you can go to the **horse races** in **Happy Valley** or **Sha Tin.** Although you can go on your own for as little as HK$10 ($1.30), you can also take an organized trip to the races offered by the Hong Kong Tourist Association; the tour includes a meal, a seat in the Royal Jockey Club members' stand, and racing tips. (For more information, see "Organized Tours" in chapter 6.)

### NIGHT STROLLS

One of the most beautiful and romantic sights in the world must be from **Victoria Peak** at night. The peak tram, which costs only HK$30 ($3.90) round-trip and runs daily until midnight, deposits passengers at the Peak Tower terminal. From the terminal, turn right, and then turn right again onto a pedestrian footpath. This path, which follows Lugard Road and Harlech Road, circles the peak, offering great views of glittering Hong Kong. Popular with both lovers and joggers, the path is lit at night and leads past expensive villas and primeval-looking jungles. Definitely the best stroll in Hong Kong, it takes about an hour.

On the other side of the harbor, there's a promenade along the **Tsim Sha Tsui waterfront,** which is popular among young Chinese couples. It stretches from the Star Ferry terminus all the way through Tsim Sha Tsui East, with very romantic views of a lit-up Hong Kong Island across the choppy waters.

## NIGHT MARKETS

If you're looking for colorful atmosphere, head for the **Temple Street Night Market,** near the Jordan MTR station in Kowloon. Extending for several blocks, it has stalls where clothing, accessories, toys, pens, watches, sunglasses, cassettes, household items, and much more are sold. Be sure to bargain fiercely if you decide to buy anything, and be sure to check the merchandise to make sure it isn't going to fall apart in 2 weeks. This is also a good place for an inexpensive meal at one of the *dai pai dong* (roadside food stalls), which specialize in seafood, including clams, shrimp, mussels, and crab.

But the most wonderful part of the market is its northern end, to the right around the white parking area. There, near the Tin Hau temple, you'll find palm readers and fortune-tellers, some of whom speak English, as well as street musicians and singers. You'll have to hunt for the tiny alleyway of musicians, where group after group has set up its own stage and is surrounded by an appreciative audience. Cantonese pop songs and operas are among the favorites, and when the musicians do an especially good job they are rewarded with tips. Get there before 9pm to see the musicians. Otherwise, although some vendors set up shop as early as 2 or 3pm, the market is in full swing about 7 to 10pm daily.

Farther north, near the Mong Kok MTR station, is the **Ladies' Market,** which stretches along Tung Choi Street between Argyle and Dundas streets. Locals come here for inexpensive women's and children's fashions and accessories; some men's clothing is also sold. It's not nearly as touristy as the Temple Street Night Market, and the atmosphere is fun and festive. It's open daily about noon to 10:30pm.

# 10

# Side Trips from Hong Kong

**M** ention Hong Kong and most people think of Hong Kong Island, Victoria Peak, the shops and neon of Tsim Sha Tsui, the Star Ferry crossing Victoria Harbour, and the high-rises of the Central District. What they don't realize is that Hong Kong Island and Kowloon comprise only 10% of the entire territory—the New Territories and the outlying islands make up the other whopping 90%.

If you have a day or two to spare, or even just an afternoon, I suggest that you spend it on a trip outside the city in one of Hong Kong's rural areas. Escape the bustle and chaos of the city to one of the region's small villages in the countryside, especially on the islands, and you'll have the chance to glimpse an older and slower way of life, where traditions still reign supreme and where lifestyles have a rhythm all their own.

## 1 The New Territories

Before the 1980s the New Territories were made up of peaceful countryside, with duck farms, fields, and old villages. No longer. A vast 389-square-mile region that stretches from Kowloon to the border of China, the New Territories are Hong Kong's answer to its growing population and the refugee crunch. Huge government housing projects have mushroomed throughout the New Territories, especially in towns along the railway and subway lines. Once-sleepy villages have become concrete jungles.

Close to one-half of Hong Kong's population—almost 3 million people—lives in the New Territories, mostly in subsidized housing. The New Territories, therefore, are vitally important to Hong Kong, its well-being, and its future. For visitors to ignore the area completely would be shortsighted; many find the housing projects, in some suburbs stretching as far as the eye can see, nothing short of astounding.

If, on the other hand, it's peace and quiet you're searching for, don't despair. The New Territories are so large and so mountainous that not all the land has been turned into housing, and the area still makes an interesting side trip—it's so different from the city itself that it's almost like visiting an entirely different country.

Be aware, however, that it takes time and patience to travel in the New Territories, especially by public bus. Distances are great, and the service is slow. If you are going for the adventure and don't care about inconvenience, fine. Otherwise, consider sticking to places easily reached by train or subway, as outlined below.

An even better tactic for seeing the New Territories is to leave the driving to someone else, namely, the Hong Kong Tourist Association, which offers a couple of excellent organized tours. The "Land Between" Tour emphasizes both the rural side of Hong Kong and its urban development, enabling visitors to learn about the lifestyle, customs, and beliefs of the local people. It visits a monastery, a rural market in Luen Wo, a fishing village, and the Sha Tin racecourse. The Heritage Tour, a must for architectural buffs, covers historic Chinese architectural sites spread throughout Kowloon and the New Territories, including the Sam Tung Uk Museum, a restored 18th-century walled village; a Man Mo temple; a traditional Chinese market; the Liu Man Shek Tong Ancestral Hall; and Tai Fu Tai, a stately country mansion. It's impossible for the individual traveler to cover as much ground in a single day as is covered in one of these tours. For more information on these and other tours offered by HKTA, as well as tours offered by other tour companies, see "Organized Tours" in chapter 6 or contact the HKTA.

If you decide to go it alone, be sure to stop by HKTA for a free copy of "Major Bus Routes in the New Territories," which tells which bus to take, the fare, and the frequency of buses along the route.

## SEEING THE NEW TERRITORIES BY KOWLOON-CANTON RAILWAY (KCR)

For years, every visitor to the New Territories took the train to the border for a look into forbidden and mysterious China. Now, of course, it's easy to get permission to enter China, and the border lookout has lost its appeal—the view was never very exciting anyway. Still, you might want to take the train up into the New Territories just for the experience, as well as for the interesting stops you can make on the way. From the KCR Kowloon-Canton Railway Station, located in Hung Hom, the trip costs only HK$9 ($1.15) one-way for ordinary class and HK$18 ($2.25) for first class and takes just 30 minutes to go to the end of the line—Sheung Shui. Trains depart every 3 to 10 minutes.

After leaving Kowloon KCR Railway Station, the Kowloon-Canton Railway (KCR) will take you along 20 miles of track, passing through such budding satellite towns as Sha Tin, University Station, Tai Po Market, and Fanling before reaching Sheung Shui—your last stop unless you have a visa to enter China. The train makes a total of 10 stops along the way, enabling you to get out and do some exploring on your own. (If you're staying in Tsim Sha Tsui East, an easier way to access the KCR is by taking the MTR as far as Kowloon Tong station and then transferring to the KCR there.)

Since it's impossible to visit all the attractions described below in 1 day, you should craft your individual tour according to personal preference. If I were making a day's excursion on this route, I would first go all the way to Sheung Shui for the ride, visit the Tai Fu Tai mansion or the Liu Man Shek Tong Ancestral Hall, and then stop at Luen Wo Market in Fanling before heading back south to Sha Tin. After lunch and visiting either the Monastery of 10,000 Buddhas or the art gallery at Chinese University, I would then board a ferry for a cruise through Tolo Harbour. For a more leisurely trip, I would limit my sightseeing to attractions in and around Sha Tin.

In any case, I have arranged the towns below in the order you'll reach them when traveling north from Kowloon. The names of the towns are also the names of the KCR stations.

### TAI WAI

Tai Wai, the first stop on the KCR after passing into the New Territories, was once a small village but has now been engulfed by Sha Tin, described below. Near the station are a couple of sights worth seeing if you're restricting your sightseeing to Sha Tin or have lots of time. **Che Kung Temple** is a modern Taoist temple honoring Che Kung, a general from the Song dynasty (A.D. 960–1279) credited with suppressing a revolt in southern China and safeguarding villagers from a plague. You'll find a giant statue of Che Kung inside, holding his sword, but the temple is popular with nearby residents mainly for the fortune-tellers on hand. To reach the temple, turn left from Tai Wai station onto Hung Mui Kuk Road, then left onto Che Kung Miu Road. The temple will be on your right, past Chui Tin Street. Admission is free, and it's open daily 7am to 6pm.

Just a few minutes' walk east of the temple, on the other side of Lion Rock Tunnel Road, is ✪ **Tsang Tai Uk,** a tiny, walled village built in 1840 for members of the Tsang clan (Tsang Tai Uk translates as "Mr. Tsang's Big House"). With its high, thick walls, four parallel rows, two side columns of houses, and central courtyard with the ancestral halls in the middle, it's typical of Hakka settlements in Guangdong Province (formerly Canton Province). Although not as old nor as famous as Kam Tin Walled Village (described below), Tsang Tai Uk is, in my opinion, more intriguing and interesting than Kam Tin because it has been spared the intrusion of the modern apartments that now plague Kam Tin. Still occupied by the Tsang clan, it looks like a vision of communal life from Hong Kong's not-so-distant past, with children playing in the grassy field out front and seniors sitting in doorways. Since Tsang Tai Uk is off the tourist pathway and serves as home to a number of families, visitors should be respectful of the inhabitants' privacy when visiting the compound.

North, across the river from Che Kung Temple and Tsang Tai Uk, is the **Hong Kong Heritage Museum,** Man Lam Road (☎ **852/2180 8107**). It is scheduled to open by 2001 with exhibitions on the history and culture of the New Territories, Cantonese opera, Chinese arts, and contemporary Hong Kong art and design. Contact the Hong Kong Tourist Association for open hours, admission prices, and other information.

## SHA TIN

This is Hong Kong's prime example of a budding satellite town, with a population approaching 640,000. Fewer than 8 miles north of Tsim Sha Tsui, it's also home to Hong Kong's new and modern **horse racetrack,** as well as a huge shopping mall called the **New Town Plaza,** located next to the Sha Tin KCR station and featuring a 10-minute performance by an illuminated, computer-controlled musical fountain. Shops here are open 10am to 10pm daily.

Most interesting for the visitor here, however, is the **Monastery of 10,000 Buddhas,** located on a hill west of the Sha Tin railway station (take the left-hand exit from the station and follow the signs). It will take about a half hour's energetic walk to get there—with more than 400 steps to climb before reaching the top. The temple was established in the 1950s by a monk named Yuet Kai, who wrote 96 books on Buddhism. He's still at the temple—well, actually, his body is still there. He's been embalmed and covered in gold leaf and sits behind a glass case for all to see. You'll find him in one of the outlying buildings farther up the hill from the main temple. Inside the main temple of the 10,000 Buddhas are more Buddha images than you've probably ever seen gathered in one place. In fact, there are almost 13,000 of them lining the walls, and no two are exactly alike. Also on the grounds is a nine-story pink pagoda. The temple affords a good view of Sha Tin's high-rise housing estates and the surrounding mountains. Admission is free, and it's open daily 9am to 5pm.

### Where to Dine

The **New Town Plaza,** Sha Tin's huge shopping mall located beside the Sha Tin KCR station, is a good place for a snack or quick meal, with cafeterias, fast-food outlets, and restaurants serving both Western and Chinese fare. The largest restaurant here is

**Maxim's Palace Chinese Restaurant** on the sixth floor (☎ 852/2693 6918), open daily 7:30am to 11:45pm and serving dim sum and Cantonese food, including barbecued Peking duck, roasted goose, deep-fried crispy chicken, and seafood. For inexpensive Western fare, head for the **Spaghetti House** (☎ 852/2697 9009), a chain of successful American-style spaghetti and pizza parlors open daily 11am to 11pm; or **Oliver's Super Sandwiches** (☎ 852/2692 7226), specializing in sandwiches, baked potatoes with various toppings, and bagels. It's open daily 7:30am to 10:30pm.

## UNIVERSITY

This stop, which is actually still within the boundaries of budding Sha Tin, serves students going to Chinese University. But your main interest will probably be its art museum and a ferry ride through Tolo Harbour.

The permanent collection of the **Chinese University Art Museum** at Chinese University (☎ 852/2609 7416) is made up of more than 1,000 paintings and examples of calligraphy by Guangdong artists dating from the Ming period to the present, as well as bronze seals, rubbings of stone inscriptions, jade flower carvings, Chinese ceramics, and other decorative arts, displayed on a rotating basis. There are also special exhibitions of art, sometimes on loan from China. The museum occupies four levels of a modern building with a Chinese garden in a central courtyard. It's open Monday to Saturday 10am to 4:45pm and on Sunday 12:30 to 5:30pm (closed on public holidays); admission is free. To reach it from KCR University Station, take one of the free, "Chinese University Hong Kong" shuttle buses departing every 20 or 30 minutes, getting off 5 minutes later near the administration building.

University is also where you get off if you want to take a ferry around **Tolo Harbour.** Located in the northeastern edge of the New Territories and surrounded by grassy low hills and lush woodlands, Tolo Harbour is home to several fishing villages, including Tap Mun. In the harbor itself are fishing boats and fish-breeding rafts. From University Station, it's a 15-minute walk to Ma Liu Shui, where you board the ferry for a leisurely trip to three villages around the harbor. The ferry departs Ma Liu Shui only twice a day, at 8:30am and 3pm. Since the first ferry may be a little too early, I would suggest taking the afternoon cruise. This ferry makes stops at Sham Chung and Lai Chi Chong before arriving at Tap Mun at 4:15pm. The ferry departs Tap Mun at 5:20pm for the return trip back to Ma Liu Shui. This gives you a little time to do some sightseeing, but make sure you return to the Tap Mun ferry dock by 5:20pm because there are no hotels here. The ferry gets back to Ma Liu Shui at 6:35pm. The entire round-trip ride costs HK$36 ($4.65) on weekdays and HK$50 ($6.50) on weekends and holidays. HKTA has a leaflet on Tolo Harbour with a timetable, but it would be wise to double-check with the Tsui Wah Ferry company itself by calling ☎ 852/2527 2513.

## TAI PO MARKET

One of the New Territories's new satellite towns, Tai Po was first settled by Tanka boat people more than 1,000 years ago because of its strategic location on a river that flows into Tolo Harbour. Just a short taxi ride from either the Tai Po Market or Tai Wo KCR station is the small **Hong Kong Railway Museum,** 13 Shung Tak St. (☎ 852/ 2653 3455). About halfway between both stations on the KCR line, it's located in what was formerly the very tiny Tai Po Market railway station, built in 1913 in traditional Chinese style with ceramic figurines cresting its gabled roof. Besides the station's original waiting hall and ticket office, the museum displays a few model trains, historic photographs of Tai Po, a narrow gauge steam locomotive, and some vintage railway coaches dating from the early 1900s; its main appeal is to railway fans. It is open free to the public every day except Tuesday from 9am to 5pm.

From the museum, you can visit the nearby **Man Mo Temple** by exiting from the museum's main entrance, walking downhill 1 block, and then turning left onto Fu Shin Street, a pedestrian lane that has been serving as Tai Po's market for more than a century. It bustles with activity from 7am to 6pm as housewives shop here twice daily to secure the freshest produce, fish, dried herbs, and other ingredients for the day's meals. At the end of Fu Shin Street is the small Man Mo Temple, founded in 1893 to commemorate the founding of Tai Po Market. Dedicated to the Taoist gods of war and literature, the temple is a popular spot for older residents to gather and play mahjong or simply pass the time. Note the two-storied compounds on both sides of the main entrance—they were once used by market administrators and for housing overnight guests. As at the Man Mo Temple on Hong Kong Island, huge incense coils suspended from the temple's ceiling are purchased by worshippers and burn more than 2 weeks.

## FANLING

A small farming settlement for several centuries, Fanling is now a huge satellite town. The **Luen Wo Market** in the middle of Fanling is interesting if you've never seen a rural Chinese country market. Covering 1 square block, this indoor market is a maze of tiny passageways and various stalls, selling everything from live lizards and frogs to turtles and chickens. There are also vendors of fruit, herbs, fish, dried seafood, goldfish (bred in astonishing varieties and thought to bring good luck), flowers, soybeans, clothing, and everyday necessities, including the characteristic black-fringed hats worn by Hakka women. Although the market is open daily 6am to noon and 3 to 6pm, the best time to visit is between 10:30am and noon, when it's at its busiest. In the mornings there's another, open-air market catty-corner across the street. To get to Luen Wo Market, take bus no. 78K from the Fanling KCR station for a short, 4-minute ride to Luen Wo Road, which runs right alongside the market. Luen Wo Market is also included in HKTA's the "Land Between" tour.

### Where to Dine

If looking at all those live and dried creatures has turned you ravenous, check out **Kwong Kee,** located on the perimeter of Luen Wo Market on Luen Shing Street across from the Sin Hua Bank (☎ **852/2675 8120**), for one of the cheapest meals you'll ever have. This is where the locals dine. With a very simple, open-fronted dining hall, it has the advantage of an English menu, offering fried noodles, steamed vermicelli roll with beef or pork, glutinous rice dumpling, and congee, with dishes priced from HK$5 to HK$14 (65¢ to $1.80). No credit cards are accepted, and it's open daily from 5:30am to 7pm.

## SHEUNG SHUI

Once its own market town, Sheung Shui, the last stop before the China border, has been swallowed up in the budding satellite town that now spreads out from Fanling. Although much of Sheung Shui's charm has been lost due to the construction of modern buildings all around, it's still more peaceful than other old villages that are closer to the beaten path. Of the five great clans that settled in the New Territories, the Lius were the most prominent in the Sheung Shui district. In 1688 as many as 500 members of the Liu clan were living here; more than 45 Lius passed the Imperial Civil Service Examination, making them high-ranking and respected officials. In 1751, at the height of the Liu clan's power and as a show of wealth, the clan erected an ancestral hall, **Liu Man Shek Tong,** which remains one of the largest and best preserved ancestral halls in Hong Kong. Set in a pleasant garden in the middle of the old village, it consists of three halls and two courtyards, embellished with wood carvings, traditional Chinese mural paintings, and pottery figurines on the ridge of the roof. In the ancestral hall, at the end of the compound, are more than 150 ancestral tablets, containing the name of the ancestor, his wife's name, the names of his sons, and an account of his good deeds. Liu Man Shek Tong is about a 25-minute walk from Sheung Shui station; take the Metropolis Plaza exit, walk along Lung Sum Avenue and San Fung Avenue to Jockey Club Road, and then along Jockey Club Road to Sheung Shui Wai. It's open Wednesday, Thursday, Saturday, and Sunday 9am to 1pm and 2 to 5pm. Admission is free.

Of all the historic, traditional Chinese buildings in the New Territories, none impresses me as much as ✪ **Tai Fu Tai,** built in 1865 and the only Mandarin mansion restored and remaining in Hong Kong. It belonged to Man Chung-luen, the 21st generation of the Man clan, a merchant and scholar who attained the highest grade in the Imperial Chinese Civil Service Examinations. Constructed of granite and bricks and adorned with ceramic figurines, fine plaster moldings, wood carvings, and murals, it is striking for its simplicity, a stark contrast to mansions being built by Westerners of the gentry class of the same period. Constructed like a miniature fort, without windows but with an inner courtyard to let in light, it contains a main hall, side chambers, bedrooms, study, kitchen, servants' quarters, and lavatory. In the back of the main hall is a portrait of Man Chung-luen, flanked by pictures of his two wives and two sons. Not shown are his eight daughters. Remarkably, the mansion was occupied by members of the Man clan until the 1980s. Tai Fu Tai is open free to the public every day except Tuesday 9am to 1pm and 2 to 5pm. To reach it, take bus no. 76K from Sheung Shui KCR station traveling in the direction of Yuen Long (West) about 30 minutes, followed by a 5-minute walk back along Castle Peak Road to the signposted entrance.

Remember, both Liu Man Shek Tong and Tai Fu Tai are a bit difficult finding on your own but are included in HKTA's Heritage Tour.

## ELSEWHERE IN THE NEW TERRITORIES
### TSUEN WAN

If I were to choose only one quick destination in the New Territories, it would be Tsuen Wan. The last stop on the MTR Tsuen Wan Line, which runs from Central through Tsim Sha Tsui, it is easily reached. Tsuen Wan was a small market town just 100 years ago, with a population of about 3,000 Hakkas and a thriving incense powder–producing industry. Then, as the first designated satellite town of the New Territories, it grew to a population of 282,000 residents, living mostly in high-rise housing estates. Tsuen Wan also serves as a convenient jumping-off point for bus trips through the New Territories, especially to the Kam Tin Walled Village (see below).

The main reason for visiting Tsuen Wan is its excellent ✪ **Sam Tung Uk Museum,** Kwu Uk Lane, Tsuen Wan (☎ **852/2411 2001**), located just a few minutes' walk from the MTR station. The museum is actually a restored Hakka walled village, built in the 18th century by members of the farming Chan clan. It consists of tiny lanes lined with tiny tiled-roofed homes, four houses that have been restored to their original condition, an ancestral hall, two rows of side houses, an exhibition hall, and an adjacent landscaped garden. The four windowless restored houses are furnished much as they would have been when occupied, with traditional Chinese furniture (including elegant blackwood furniture), and contain farm implements, kitchens, and lavatories. Although as many as 300 clan members once lived here, the village was abandoned in 1980. Today the museum is a tiny oasis in the midst of modern high-rise housing projects. The museum is open Wednesday to Monday 9am to 5pm, and admission is free.

About a 20-minute walk from the Tsuen Wan MTR station is **Chuk Lam Shim Yuen,** popularly known as the Bamboo Forest Monastery. Founded in 1927 and located on a hill with a view of Tsuen Wan's housing estates, it's one of Hong Kong's most picturesque, colorful, and ornate Buddhist monasteries and is famous for its three huge "Precious Buddha" gold statues. It's open daily 7am to 4pm, and admission is free.

## KAM TIN WALLED VILLAGE

Traveling in the New Territories, you quickly notice women wearing wide-brimmed hats with a black fringe and pajamalike clothing; many of them have gold-capped teeth as well. These women are Hakka, as are most of the farmers of the New Territories. They keep to themselves, preserving their customs and dialect. While most of them hate to have their photographs taken (they think it steals something from their spirit), some will oblige in return for payment. In fact, don't be surprised if you're instantly approached by Hakka women and asked to take their picture—they've learned that it's an easy way to make an extra Hong Kong dollar (be sure to settle on a price before you start clicking away).

At any rate, during the Ming dynasty (1368–1644) some of the Hakka clans in the area built walls around their homes to protect themselves against roving bandits and invaders. A handful of these walled villages still exist today, and are still inhabited by the Hakkas. Before visiting any of these villages, stop by the Sam Tung Uk Museum in Tsuen Wan (described above). It will enrich your visit to a lived-in walled village.

Hakka walled villages include Kat Hing Wai, Shui Tau, Kam Hing Wai, Kam Tsin Wai, and Shek Tsin Wai. Of these, Kat Hing Wai, just outside the town of Yuen Long, is the most famous. Popularly known as Kam Tin, it's home to about 400 descendants of the Tang clan, the first and largest of the "Five Great Clans" to settle in the New Territories. Built in the 1600s, the village is completely surrounded by 18-foot-thick walls, which provided protection against bandits, rival clans, and wild tigers; there is only one narrow entrance. A donation of HK$1 (13¢) is expected; you'll find a donation box located in the wall at the entrance. Also at the entrance are a few aged Hakka women asking you to take their pictures—for an extra HK$3 (40¢). Once inside Kam Tin, you'll find a lane that leads straight to the village's temple and ancestral hall. Unfortunately, on my last visit I was horrified to see that many of the ancient homes had been torn down to make way for shiny new flats. While such new apartments are undoubtedly more comfortable, an important part of Hong Kong's history has been lost forever. Although the wall and moat surrounding Kam Tin remains impressive, a visit here is worthwhile only if you combine it with a trip to Sam Tung Uk Museum.

To reach Kam Tin, first take the MTR to Tsuen Wan Station, then board bus no. 51 from the Tai Ho Road overpass (located above the Tsuen Wan MTR station). Your bus will travel 50 minutes, taking you over the hills along scenic Route Twisk. Get off at the last stop and then continue walking in the same direction the bus was going, past the open-fronted shops. Kam Tin is less than 5 minutes away, on your left.

## SAI KUNG

Located on the eastern coast of the New Territories, Sai Kung is the second largest and least populated of Hong Kong's 19 districts and encompasses three country parks. It's popular for its scenery, nature trails, and Sai Kung Town with its harborfront seafood restaurants.

To reach Sai Kung Town, take the MTR to Choi Hung Station, and then board maxicab no. 1A for a 20-minute ride to Sai Kung Town. The bus will deposit you at the bus terminal near the waterfront, where you should turn right and walk along the harbor to the local fish market. Here, too, are many seafood restaurants with outside tanks holding live prawn, crabs, lobster, abalone, moray eels, stone fish, garoupa, and other creatures of the sea. Behind the waterfront restaurants, on Sai Kung Tai Kai Street, is Sai Kung Old Town with its narrow, twisting lanes lined with shops selling incense, dried seafood, herbs, and provisions.

## Where to Dine

No trip to Sai Kung Town would be complete without dining on fresh seafood at one of the town's waterfront seafood restaurants. I suggest simply wandering from tank to tank of live fish, shellfish, and other delectables until something catches your fancy, but for a specific recommendation, try **Chuen Kee Seafood Restaurant,** 51 Hoi Pong St., Sai Kung Town (☎ **852/2791 1195**), a Cantonese restaurant with both indoor and outdoor seating. After selecting your lobster, prawns, or fish, you'll be given a number and your selections will be sent directly to the kitchen. As with most Cantonese restaurants, the seafood is mainly steamed. Prices depend on market price, with most meals costing about HK$250 to HK$300 ($32.50 to $38.95) per person (DC, MC, and V accepted). It's open daily 11:30am to 10:30pm.

## Hiking

For some hiking, board bus no. 94 (going in the direction of Wong Shek Pier) from Sai Kung's bus terminal and ride 20 minutes to Pak Tam Chung. Here you'll find the **Sai Kung Country Park Visitor Center,** open every day except Tuesday 9:30am to 4:30pm. In addition to displays on agriculture, fishing, rural culture, and village life, it has a model of Sai Kung Country Park, as well as a hiking map.

Beside the visitor center is a barrier gate, restricting vehicular access to Tai Mong Tsai Road. If you follow this road to its junction with Pak Tam Road, you'll find the starting point of the 62-mile-long **MacLehose Trail,** which winds through eight country parks and ends at Tuen Mun in the western part of the New Territories. It's divided into 10 stages of various difficulty; the beginning stage, which runs along the High Island Reservoir, is one of the easiest.

Alternatively, as you walk from the barrier gate on Tai Mong Tsai Road, keep your eyes peeled for the half-mile-long **Pak Tam Chung Nature Trail** on your left, which you'll reach in about 10 minutes. After crossing a small footbridge, you'll follow the pathway along a tidal creek and past groves of banana trees and bamboo. After about 10 minutes you'll reach a lime kiln, built by a Hakka family more than 150 years ago to secure lime from seashells and coral and used for manufacturing bricks and tiles. Just past the kiln is the **Sheung Yiu Folk Museum,** (☎ **852/2792 6365**), a small, fortified Hakka village built in the mid-19th century and abandoned in 1965. Composed of eight, joined houses facing a whitewashed courtyard, the village houses typical Hakka furnishings, including beds, cupboards and other wooden furniture, cooking utensils, and farm implements. It's open every day except Tuesday 9am to 4pm, and admission is free.

## 2 The Outlying Islands

There are 260 outlying islands, most of them barren and uninhabited. Because construction in the New Territories is booming and transportation to underpopulated areas there can be slow, the islands now offer the best opportunity to see something of rural Chinese life. What's more, they're easy to reach—hop on a ferry in Central and then sit back and enjoy the view. Taking a ferry to an outlying island is the cheapest harbor cruise there is, making getting there part of the fun.

Three of the most accessible and popular islands are **Lantau, Cheung Chau,** and **Lamma.** Each offers something different: Lantau is famous for its giant outdoor Buddha—one of Hong Kong's major attractions—and Po Lin Monastery; Cheung

Chau, with its beach, boat population, and thriving fishing community, is a popular destination for families and is the best choice for immersion into village life; and Lamma, known for its open-air seafood restaurants, hiking trail, and beaches, is the best place to go to get away from it all.

Ferries depart approximately every hour or so from the Central District—from new piers built out into the harbor on reclaimed land less than a 5-minute walk west of the Star Ferry (turn right after exiting the Star Ferry from Kowloon). You can purchase your ticket at the outlying-ferry piers just prior to departure or use the magnetic Octopus transportation card, but avoid going on Sunday when the ferries are packed with city folks on family outings. The fares are also slightly higher on Saturday afternoon and Sunday, though they're never very expensive—HK$14 to HK$15.70 ($1.80 to $2.05) for ordinary class depending on the destination, HK$25 to HK$31 ($3.25 to $4) for a deluxe ticket. On weekdays and before noon on Saturday, tickets cost just HK$10 ($1.30) for ordinary class and HK$16.80 ($2.20) for deluxe. If you're headed for Lantau or Cheung Chau, I highly recommend deluxe class, since this upper-deck ticket entitles you to sit on an open deck out back—a great place to sip coffee or beer when the weather is nice—and watch the harbor float past. In addition, deluxe cabins are the only ones that are air-conditioned, a plus when humidity is at its peak. Note that ferries to Lamma have no deluxe class or outside deck.

On Saturday afternoon and Sunday there is additional infrequent ferry service from Tsim Sha Tsui's Star Ferry concourse to Lantau and Cheung Chau, but it may not offer deluxe class. There is also a faster hoverferry service to Lantau and Cheung Chau used mostly by commuters, but I personally prefer the slower ferries because the view is better and they have outdoor decks. In any case, by ferry it takes only 30 to 35 minutes to reach Lamma, 50 minutes to reach Cheung Chau, and 45 minutes to reach Lantau.

For information on ferry schedules and prices, drop by the HKTA for a free copy of timetables and prices.

## LANTAU

Inhabited since Neolithic times and twice the size of Hong Kong Island, Lantau is Hong Kong's largest island. But while Hong Kong Island has a population of more than a million, Lantau has only about 45,000. Much of its population growth has occurred only recently, first with the founding of Discovery Bay, a large modern and expensive settlement of condominiums, and then with Hong Kong's new airport, which brought with it the creation of a new satellite town at Tung Chung. Although Tung Chung's present population is only 30,000, ambitious plans call for it to reach 200,000 by the year 2111.

Yet much of Lantau remains mountainous and lush. Country parks make up more than half of the island, with 43 miles of marked hiking trails. Lantau is an island of high peaks, remote and isolated beaches, small villages, temples, and monasteries. But the main reason visitors come here is to see its Giant Tian Tan Buddha, the largest seated outdoor Buddha in the world, and to eat a vegetarian meal at the nearby Po Lin Monastery.

Ferries, with both ordinary and deluxe class, depart from outlying-ferry pier no. 7 in Central approximately every 2 hours or less between 6:10am and 10:30pm and arrive about 50 minutes later at Silvermine Bay, known as *Mui Wo* in Chinese. There is also more frequent hoverferry service. In Mui Wo there are a hotel fronting the bay and some restaurants, but otherwise there isn't much of interest. As soon as you exit the ferry pier, you'll see a bus terminal with buses going to other parts of the island, with departures coinciding with the arrival of the ferries. For the Giant Buddha and Po Lin Monastery, take the bus bound for Ngong Ping (Po Lin Monastery). The exact bus fare of HK$16 ($2.05) Monday to Saturday and HK$25 ($3.25) on Sunday and public holidays is required, so come with lots of change. The bus hurtles around curves and up and down through lush countryside—not for the faint of heart.

If you don't wish to ride the ferry, you can also reach Lantau by taking the Tung Chung MTR Line, which was extended to Lantau to serve staff working and living near the new airport. It takes about 45 minutes to ride from Hong Kong Station in Central to Tung Chung, the end terminus. In Tung Chung, bus no. 23 reaches Ngong Ping in 45 minutes and the ride is no less hair-raising. In the future, a cable car may be built from Tung Chung directly to Ngong Ping, eliminating the roller coaster bus ride.

## EXPLORING LANTAU

The most famous attractions on Lantau are the **Giant Tian Tan Buddha** and **Po Lin Monastery,** both situated on the plateau of Ngong Ping at an elevation of 2,460 feet. The Buddha is so huge that you'll have your first glimpses of it en route on the bus. More than 100 feet tall and weighing 250 tons, it's the world's largest seated outdoor bronze Buddha and can be seen as far away as Macau (or so it is claimed) on clear days. There are 268 steps leading up to the Buddha itself, but first you should stop at the ticket office at the bottom of the steps to purchase a meal ticket, since the other reason people come to Po Lin is to eat. The monastery is famous for its vegetarian lunches, served in a big dining hall (see "Where to Dine" below). Your meal ticket, which specifies the time for your communal meal, doubles as your admission ticket to a small museum inside the base of the statue, but there isn't much to see here. Rather, the best part is the view of the surrounding countryside from the statue's platform, which is free. The Giant Buddha is open daily 10am to 6pm.

From here, walk a couple minutes to the colorful Po Lin Monastery, largest and best known of the dozens of Buddhist monasteries on Lantau. Po Lin (which means "precious lotus") was first established about 100 years ago by reclusive monks; the present buildings date from 1921 and 1970. The ornate main temple houses three magnificent bronze statues of Buddha, representing the past, present, and future; it also has a brightly painted vermilion interior with dragons and other Chinese mythical figures on the ceiling. You'll probably want to spend about a half hour wandering through the grounds here. If you're truly adventurous or energetic, you can climb to the top of nearby Lantau Peak, at 3,000 feet the second-tallest peak in Hong Kong; plan on 3 hours for the hike up and back.

From Po Lin, you can reboard the bus that will take you back to Mui Wo (Silvermine Bay) or Tung Chung, with departures once or twice an hour.

## WHERE TO DINE

**Mui Wo Cooked Food Market.** Chung Hau Rd., Silvermine Bay. Most menu items HK$20–HK$100 ($2.60–$13). No credit cards. Daily 10am–9pm. Take a right from the ferry dock; the market is to your right, a minute's walk away. VARIED.

This covered, open-air pavilion of food stalls (*dai pai dongs*) offers inexpensive dishes, such as noodles, vegetables, sandwiches, rice dishes, and fresh seafood. Fresh fish, kept alive in tanks in front of each stall, costs about HK$150 ($19.50). This is a good place to wait for the next ferry. If you want, just order a can of beer and sit at one of the tables next to the water.

**Po Lin Monastery.** Ngong Ping. ☎ **852/2985 5248.** Fixed-price lunch HK$60 or HK$100 ($7.80 or $13). No credit cards. Daily noon–4pm. VEGETARIAN.

Po Lin Monastery, offering fixed-price vegetarian meals, is the most famous place to eat on the island. Buy your lunch ticket from the counter at the base of the Giant Buddha or at the monastery itself; your ticket is for a specific time, at an assigned table.

Two different meals of soup, vegetarian dishes, and rice are available: the ordinary, HK$60 meal is served in an unadorned dining hall and the procedure is rather unceremonious, with huge dishes of vegetables, rice, and soup brought to communal tables covered with plastic tablecloths. Grab a Styrofoam bowl and chopsticks and help yourself. Packed with Chinese families, the dining hall here is certainly colorful. The HK$100 "Deluxe" meal, is served in an adjacent "VIP Room" and is popular mostly with foreign visitors. Meals here are served on china plates, and the food is a notch above the cheaper meal. Both, however, are good. There's also a snack menu offered for HK$28 ($3.65) available at an open-air counter at the monastery; it consists of fried noodles and bean curd; skip it.

## CHEUNG CHAU

If you have only a few hours to spare and don't want to worry about catching buses and finding your way around, Cheung Chau is your best bet. In fact, if I were forced to select only one island to show visiting friends on a limited time schedule, Cheung Chau would be it. Only 7½ miles from Hong Kong Island, it's a 50-minute ferry ride from outlying-ferry pier no. 6 in Central, with ferries leaving nearly every hour and offering scenic harbor views from the outdoor deluxe-class deck. Cheung Chau is a tiny, dumbbell-shaped island (only 1 square mile), but more than 25,000 people live here in a thriving fishing village. There are no cars on the island, making it a delightful place for walking around and exploring rural village life. The island is especially popular with Chinese families for its rental bicycles and beach, but my favorite thing to do here is to walk the tiny, narrow lanes of Cheung Chau village.

Inhabited for at least 2,500 years by fisherfolk and serving as a haven for smugglers and pirates until the 1920s, Cheung Chau still supports a sizable population of fishing families, and fishing remains the island's main industry. Junks are built on Cheung Chau after a design hardly changed through the centuries, entirely from memory and without the aid of blueprints. The waterfront where the ferry lands, known as the Praya, buzzes with activity as vendors sell fish, lobster, and vegetables. The village itself is a fascinating warren of narrow alleyways, food stalls, open markets, and shops selling everything from medicinal herbs and incense to noodles, rice, haircuts, and—a reflection of the island's increasing tourist trade—sun hats, sunglasses, and beach toys.

### EXPLORING CHEUNG CHAU

About 3% of Cheung Chau's population live on junks in the harbor, and one of the things to do here is take a *kai do,* or water taxi, past the junks to Sai Wan—it shouldn't cost more than HK$5 (65¢) for the 5-minute ride and may even be cheaper than that; board it at the public pier next to the ferry pier. I like this harbor more than Aberdeen because boats are moored right next to the waterfront, and I find it amazing how many families keep dogs aboard their boats. At Sai Wan, a tiny settlement with nary a tourist shop in sight, there's a temple dedicated to **Tin Hau,** goddess of the sea and protectress of fisherfolk. There's also Cheung Po Tsai Cave, reportedly a hideout of a 19th-century pirate. Steep, narrow, low, and dark, it should be skipped unless you're prepared to bring a flashlight or buy one from a vendor, and you're willing to inch your way through the tunnel with a queue of other tourists, exiting by climbing up a smooth-surfaced cliff. Definitely not for the faint-hearted, claustrophobic, or generously proportioned.

At any rate, from San Wai you can walk back to Cheung Chau village in less than 15 minutes by taking the road that hugs the harbor. Alternatively, you can take a longer, 45-minute hike back to the village via Peak Road, one of the main roads on the island and running along the crest of a lushly wooded hill with good vistas of the

# Cheung Chau

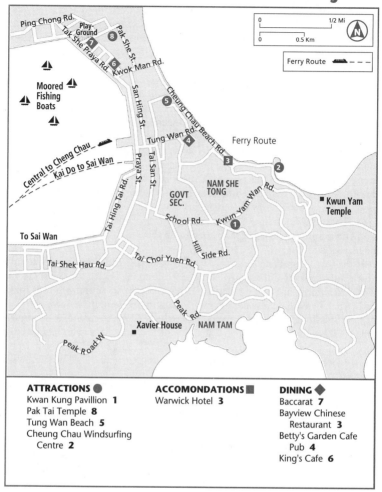

**ATTRACTIONS** ●
Kwan Kung Pavillion **1**
Pak Tai Temple **8**
Tung Wan Beach **5**
Cheung Chau Windsurfing
  Centre **2**

**ACCOMMONDATIONS** ■
Warwick Hotel **3**

**DINING** ◆
Baccarat **7**
Bayview Chinese
  Restaurant **3**
Betty's Garden Cafe
  Pub **4**
King's Cafe **6**

sea. Along the way you'll pass a huge Chinese cemetery on a hillside (blessed with excellent *fung shui*) and the Kwan Kung Pavilion, dedicated to the god of war and righteousness.

As for seeing Cheung Chau village, begin with a stroll along the **Praya**—the waterfront promenade right in front of the ferry pier. It's a good place from which to observe the many junks and fishing boats in the harbor. To the right as you leave the ferry pier are several open-air restaurants, as well as the unimaginative-looking Regional Council Cheung Chau Complex, which houses a library, post office, and city market (open daily 6am to 8pm) with more than 200 stalls that sell everything from fresh seafood to vegetables. On its upper floor are a few vendors selling clothing and toys, at prices much cheaper than those at Hong Kong's well-known markets.

On the opposite end of the Praya (to the left as you leave the ferry) are more waterfront restaurants, shops with bicycles to rent, and souvenir shops. After about a 3-minute walk, take a right at the playground onto Pak She Fourth, at the end of which is the **Pak Tai Temple,** guarded by two stone lions. Built in 1783, it's dedicated to the "Supreme Emperor of the Dark Heaven," long worshipped as a Taoist god of the sea. Inside is an iron sword measuring almost 5 feet in length that was found by local fishermen and thought to be 1,000 years old, as well as a sedan that is used to carry the statue of Pak Tai around the village during festivals. Beside the temple, on a shaded terrace, old villagers are almost always engaged in games of mahjong.

The most important festival here is the Bun Festival, held in late April or May. It originated a century ago following a terrible plague, and is famous throughout Hong Kong. It features 50-foot-tall towers of buns, but the biggest attraction is the parade of children who "float" through the streets suspended by hidden wires and rods.

Leaving the Pak Tai Temple, take a left onto Pak She Street, which later becomes San Hing Street. As you walk back to the center of the village, you'll pass open-fronted shops that sell incense, paper funeral objects such as cars (cremated with the deceased to accompany them to the next life), medicinal herbs, lotus-seed cakes, pungent shrimp paste, jade, rattan, and other local goods, vegetables, and meat. You'll also pass people's homes with the living rooms that hold the family altar opening onto the street. This is the traditional Chinese home, with the family business and communal rooms on the ground floor and the bedrooms up above. All day long you can hear people playing mahjong.

At the end of San Hing Street, at a small square, take a left onto Tung Wan Road, which cuts across the thinnest part of the island from the Praya with its ferry to Tung Wan Beach. Here, just past the square, is a gnarled old banyan tree, which is considered to be the dwelling place of the spirit of health and fertility. At the end of Tung Wan Road is **Tung Wan Beach,** the most popular beach on the island, with lifeguards and shark nets. Nearby, past the Warwick Hotel, is another, smaller public beach, home to the **Cheung Chau Windsurfing Centre** (☎ **852/2981 8316**), with a pleasant outdoor cafe and rental windsurfing boards beginning at HK$110 ($14.30) for 2 hours.

From Tung Wan Beach, it's only a few minutes' walk via Tung Wan Road back to the Praya and ferry pier.

## WHERE TO STAY

In addition to the hotel listed here, there are countless rooms and apartments for rent around the island, with deeply discounted weekly rates. Some of these are also available by the night or weekend. Upon leaving the ferry pier, you'll find several temporary counters and carts set up along the Praya, with vendors offering rooms. Most don't speak English, but they have photographs of all their available properties. Be sure you understand where the room is located (remember, you'll have to walk) and how much it costs, including tax and service charge.

**Warwick Hotel.** Tung Wan Beach, Cheung Chau. ☎ **852/2981 0081.** Fax 852/2981 9174. 71 units (all with bathroom). A/C MINIBAR TV TEL. HK$990–HK$1,190 ($129–$155) single or double. Winter discounts available. Children under 12 stay free in parents' room. AE, DC, MC, V. Take Tung Wan Rd. to Tung Wan Beach, about a 10-min. walk from the ferry pier.

If you want to spend a few nights away from the hustle and bustle of Hong Kong, this may be the place to do so. It's located on the south end of Cheung Chau's most popular beach; next to the hotel is a children's playground and a place where you can rent windsurfing boards and paddleboats, and there's an outdoor swimming pool, a pleasant restaurant with outdoor terrace, and a bar. The rooms facing the beach are slightly more expensive, but they're worth it, especially since all rooms have small balconies. If you come during the week or during off-season, ask whether you can receive a discount or be upgraded to a more expensive room. All rooms have hair dryers, radios, and cable TVs with pay movies.

## WHERE TO DINE

**Baccarat Restaurant.** 9A Pak She Praya St. ☎ **852/2981 0606** or 852/2981 0668. Main dishes HK$40–HK$170 ($5.20–$22). MC, V. Daily 11am–11pm. Turn left from the ferry and walk along the Praya about 4 min. CANTONESE.

On the Praya, the last of several open-air restaurants (located near the Pak Tai Temple on the corner of Pak She Street beside a playground), this simple spot offers outdoor seating under a canopy with a view of the harbor. Its English menu lists a variety of dishes, including veal spare ribs, fried chicken with mango, and various beef, pork, and rice dishes. The restaurant is best, however, for seafood, including crab, lobster, squid, scallop, and fish. The chili prawns are great. If you wish, you can buy fresh fish from the market and bring it here to be cooked to your specification for a fee of HK$60 ($7.80); if you're unsure about making such a purchase, the English-speaking staff here will even help you with the selection and is happy to make recommendations.

**Bayview Chinese Restaurant.** In the Warwick Hotel, Tung Wan Beach. ☎ **852/2981 0081.** Reservations recommended. Main dishes HK$55–HK$210 ($7.15–$27.30). AE, DC, MC, V. Daily noon–10pm. Take Tung Wan Rd. to Tung Wan Beach, about a 7-min. walk from the ferry pier. WESTERN/CANTONESE.

The Warwick Hotel, located on the beach, offers the most sophisticated dining on the island, yet its restaurant is rather casual. Although the Cantonese menu lists the usual chicken, duck, pigeon, pork, and beef dishes, most customers bring their own seafood from the market and have the kitchen prepare it for them. If you're interested in only a snack or drink, there's an outdoor terrace with a good view of the beach that is open daily in good weather 8am to 6pm. It offers a very limited menu: club sandwiches, hot dogs, fish-and-chips, desserts, and drinks.

**Betty's Garden Cafe Pub.** 84 Tung Wan Rd. ☎ **852/2981 4610.** Main courses HK$30–HK$90 ($3.90–$11.70); breakfast HK$38–HK$65 ($4.95–$8.45). No credit cards. Mon, Wed–Fri 6pm–2am; Sat–Sun 2pm–2am. WESTERN.

Located on the village's main passageway between the Praya and the beach, this simple cafe is the local hangout for foreigners and serves European food. Its specialty is British-style pub grub, including a ploughman's lunch for HK$33 ($4.30), toasted sandwiches, sausage or meat pies with "mushy" peas, salads, hamburgers, and curries. Breakfast is served all day. The best things about this place are the outdoor tables and the small beer garden across the street.

**King's Cafe.** 25 Praya St. ☎ **852/2981 0878.** Main dishes and sandwiches HK$10–HK$48 ($1.30–$6.25). No credit cards. Thurs–Tues 11am–11pm. WESTERN/CHINESE.

This simple establishment is on the Praya, to the left as you disembark from the ferry. It serves Western-style food and snacks such as sandwiches and omelets as well as fried rice and noodle dishes. Although the food isn't great, the prices are low, and there are tables and chairs outside where you have a wonderful view of the action on the Praya and the junks anchored close by. For a snack, try a fruit juice, shake or ice cream.

## LAMMA

Lamma is the island to visit if you want to do some pleasant hiking or eat fresh seafood on a peaceful waterfront. The closest of the outlying islands, only 30 or 35 minutes by ferry from outlying-ferry pier no. 5 in Central, Lamma is Hong Kong's third-largest island, has a population of about 12,000, and is still largely undeveloped. There are no cars on the island, and a 1½-hour hiking trail connects Lamma's two main villages—Yung Shue Wan and Sok Kwu Wan—both served by ferries from Hong Kong Island. Yung Shue Wan, with a large and youthful foreign population, has a decidedly Bohemian atmosphere, while much smaller Sok Kwu Wan is popular for its open-air seafood restaurants. If it's summer, don't forget to bring your bathing suit, since there are several beaches along the trails. You'd be smart, too, to buy bottled water from one of the many stores in either Sok Kwu Wam or Yung Shue Wan before setting out on the trail. In addition, try to avoid Sundays, when the trail is crowded with families, old people walking dogs, and even bicycles.

## EXPLORING LAMMA

Although ferries from Central will deposit you at both Yung Shue Wan or Sok Kwu Wan, I personally prefer to land at Sok Kwu Wan for a light seafood meal, hike 20 minutes to a nearby beach, and then continue onward to Yung Shue Wan for drinks or dinner before heading back to Central. The advantage of this route is that ferry service is more frequent from Yung Shue Wan, which means you're not constricted to a time schedule. However, you might choose to hike the trail in reverse from my description below. If you do, remember that ferries to and from Sok Kwu Wan are less frequent, so you'll have to time your arrival and departure with precision. In any case, the hike between the two villages along a marked, concrete footpath takes about 1½ hours and is a true delight, with great views of the surrounding sea and, in the distance, even Ocean Park and Aberdeen on Hong Kong Island.

Tiny **Sok Kwu Wan** is famous for its open-air seafood restaurants. They're aligned along the small waterfront, extended over the water on stilts and shaded by canopies; they offer views of the harbor (and, unfortunately, of denuded hills belonging to a cement factory across the harbor). I suggest that you simply walk along the waterfront and choose one that strikes your fancy (a recommendation is listed below). All restaurants here have tanks of fresh seafood where you can choose the creature that suits your fancy. Fresh seafood is available by the *catty* (one catty is about 1½ pounds). Prices for a catty vary each day, depending on supply and demand. One catty of prawns will cost approximately HK$150 to HK$175 ($19.50 to $22.75), with half a catty usually enough for two people. A catty of lobster will cost about HK$250 to HK$280 ($32.50 to $36.40). If you go all out, meals here will average about HK$250 ($32.50) a person.

Incidentally, as you dine you'll notice fish-breeding rafts in the harbor, many also supporting family homes. According to one restaurant manager, however, very little fishing is still done nowadays in local waters because of contamination. The manager assured me that only imported fish is served in Sok Kwu Wan's restaurants and that locally caught or bred fish is consumed only by local Chinese. Another restaurant owner, however, proudly told me that his fish came from the harbor fish farm. The restaurant I recommend serves only imported fish.

Turning right out of the ferry pier and walking past the many seafood restaurants of Sok Kwu Wan, you will soon come to a small, 150-year-old Tin Hau temple on the edge of town. Continue on the concrete path that hugs the harbor about 10 minutes to Lo So Shing School, where you should turn left and follow the dirt path another 10 minutes to **Lo So Shing Beach.** Prettily situated in a small bay, this is the island's nicest and least crowded beach, offering changing rooms and lifeguards on duty from April to October, daily 9am to 6pm.

From here, the main pathway takes you through lush and verdant valleys before ascending to a hillside pavilion overlooking the scandalous cement factory. From this point, the path climbs higher onto barren and windswept hills. About halfway along the trail, on the top of a peak, is a pagoda where you can take a rest and enjoy the view. After that, the barren hills give way to valleys and trees and then **Hung Shing Yeh Beach,** which also has changing facilities, showers, toilets, and lifeguards on duty in the summer. If it's hot, it may be hard to resist joining the throngs of families and taking another dip in the water. Regrettably, however, the beach is overshadowed by an unsightly power station.

The hiking path resumes on the other side of the beach. In less than 20 minutes you'll reach **Yung Shue Wan,** but it takes a while to walk past new development before reaching Yung Shue Wan Main Street and the center of town. Yung Shue Wan, which translates as "Banyan Tree Bay," is Lamma's main town. It used to be small and undeveloped, with old houses and small garden plots, but new apartment buildings and shops have sprung up on its hillsides in the past decade. A sizable population of expatriates has settled here (though the number has dwindled since the handover), and the town is unfortunately blighted by that unsightly power station. What's more, small motorized wagons carrying building supplies zip around as if they can't get to construction sites soon enough. Compared to how the village looked in the early 1980s, I can barely recognize the place. Still, the village has a laid-back, slow-paced tropical island atmosphere, making it a pleasant place to while away an hour or more at a local restaurant or bar.

## WHERE TO DINE

**Bookworm Cafe.** 79 Yung Shue Wan Main St., Yung Shue Wan. ☎ **852/2982 4838.** Main dishes HK$25–HK$60 ($3.25–$7.80). No credit cards. Daily 10am–10pm. VEGETARIAN.

Lined with shelves of used books and serving as an informal resource and meeting center for Yung Shue Wan's expat residents, and with occasional jam sessions, video nights, and other happenings, this casual restaurant is a great alternative to seafood. The interesting menu includes sandwiches—the Middle Eastern version has eggplant, feta cheese, and sundried tomatoes—vegi and tofu burgers, and salads like the "veg-out" salad plate with roasted eggplant, avocado, feta cheese, and black olives on a bed of mixed greens and herbs with Lebanese bread. There are also various teas and fresh juices. Dining is either in a small, air-conditioned room or across the street on an open terrace.

**Concerto Inn.** Hung Shing Yeh Beach, Yung Shue Wan. ☎ **852/2982 1668.** Main dishes HK$38–HK$68 ($4.95–$8.85). AE, DC, MC, V. Daily 8am–10pm. WESTERN/CHINESE/SNACKS.

Located right on Hung Shing Yeh Beach about a 30-minute walk from the ferry pier in Yung Shue Wan, this clean, low-key establishment offers both accommodations and a pleasant cafe, with outdoor, covered seating beside a running fountain and views of the beach. Its menu is limited, but the restaurant makes a comfortable stop along the hiking trail for a hamburger, sandwich, spaghetti, fish and chips, satays, rice and noodle dishes, ice cream, juice, or beer.

**Man Fung Restaurant.** 5 Yung Shue Wan Main St., Yung Shue Wan. ☎ **852/2982 0719.** Main dishes HK$50–HK$70 ($6.50–$9.10). AE, MC, V. Daily 10am–10pm. CANTONESE/SEAFOOD.

If you start your hike at Sok Kwu Wan and end up hungry on this side of the island, this restaurant is my number-one choice for a hearty meal. Located just a minute's walk from the ferry pier, it offers pleasant outdoor seating right by the water with a view of the harbor and town. Specialties are its fresh seafood straight from the tank, including lobster served with a cheese sauce; fried prawns with garlic and butter; steamed crab with chili; and various other fish, scallop, and seafood dishes available at market price (inquire first before ordering). Otherwise, the menu lists pork, beef, chicken, and pigeon dishes, as well as vegetarian dishes such as deep-fried bean curd with chili, fried broccoli and baby corn with garlic, sweet and sour bean curd, and braised eggplant in a hot pot. There are also pitchers of Carlsberg draft beer as well as wine from France and Portugal.

**Rainbow Seafood Restaurant.** 17 1st St., Sok Kwu Wan waterfront. ☎ **852/2982 8100.** Seafood dishes HK$70–HK$140 ($11.70–$18.20). AE, DC, MC, V. Daily 10am–10pm. CANTONESE/SEAFOOD.

This is the largest open-air restaurant on Sok Kwu Wan's waterfront, easily recognizable by its whir of ceiling fans and red lanterns. Farther from the pier (and the cement factory across the harbor) than many other restaurants, it therefore offers a better view of the harbor and boat rafts. A nice touch is the water sprayed over its canopy to cool the restaurant on hot summer days. A member of the HKTA and serving only imported fish from the South China Sea, it offers an English menu with photographs of its main dishes, including a variety of fresh seafood dishes, with prices for lobster, prawn, and fish clearly marked. Among its specialties are steamed garoupa, lobster available several ways (fried lobster with a cheese sauce is most popular), and fried crab with ginger and scallions. There are two fixed-price feasts for two persons or more, costing HK$320 and HK$380 ($41.55 and $49.35) per person. Incidentally, this restaurant also offers free ferry service to and from Queen's Pier (in Central, near Star Ferry) in the evenings from 5:30pm; be sure to call first and make a reservation.

### A LOCAL BAR

**The Island Bar.** 6 Yung Shue Wan Main St., Yung Shue Wan. ☎ **852/2982 1376.** Mon–Fri 6pm–2am, Sat–Sun and holidays noon–2am.

Located next to Man Fung Restaurant on the waterfront just a minute's walk from the ferry pier, this is a longtime bar and local *gwailo* (foreign) hangout. Owned by expats living in Yung Shue Wan, it's a comfortable place to wait for the next ferry, play darts, and meet the locals. Happy hour is 6 to 8pm daily.

## 3 China

Hong Kong is a major gateway to China. Most visitors to the mainland join an organized tour. Virtually all hotels in Hong Kong work with tour agencies that offer a variety of excursions to China, ranging from 1-day trips to Guangzhou to 5-day trips that include Guangzhou and Beijing in the itinerary. Most of these trips follow identical itineraries at similar prices. For example, I joined a 1-day guided tour of Shenzhen (Shekou) and Guangzhou. In Shenzhen, we were shown a small, musty museum containing three terra-cotta figures taken from the tomb of China's first emperor near the city of Xi'an; and in Guangzhou, a local market; an unenlightened zoo with cramped, littered cages and a couple of panda bears; a temple; and the outside of a concert hall built in 1931 as a memorial to Sun Yat-sen. What I most enjoyed about the trip, offered by Splendid Tours for HK$1,230 ($159.90) per person, was the journey by hoverferry to Shenzhen, the bus trip to Guangzhou, and the trip back by KCR railway, as these allowed good vistas of the surrounding countryside. Companies offering organized trips into China include **Splendid Tours** (☎ 852/2316 2151) and **Gray Line Tours** (☎ 852/2368 7111), or you can contact your hotel tour desk.

If you join one of these tours, your visa for China will be taken care of by the tour agency. But if you wish to visit China on your own, you'll need to obtain a visa. Your hotel or a travel agency may be able to arrange this for you; otherwise, one of your first stops should be at a **China Travel Service (CTS),** the official travel agency of the People's Republic of China (PRC), to get a visa. There are several branches in Hong Kong, including 78 Connaught Rd. Central, Central District (☎ 852/2853 3590; MTR: Central); 62 Sai Yee St., Mong Kok (☎ 852/2789 5970; MTR: Mong Kok); and 27–33 Nathan Rd., Tsim Sha Tsui (☎ 852/2315 7188), the most convenient with the most convenient hours: open Monday to Saturday 9am to 5pm and Sunday and holidays 9am to 12:30pm and 2 to 5pm.

To fill out an application for your visa, you will need your passport (with an expiration date of not less than 4 months) and one passport photograph (there's a portrait machine at CTS). It's best to make your visa application at least 2 business days prior to departure; cost of the visa is HK$160 ($20.80). However, if you're in a hurry, you can obtain a visa more quickly by paying more: For HK$210 ($27.30), your visa will be processed and available for pickup by 2pm the next day; for HK$320 ($41.60), visa applications made before noon will be available by 6pm the same day. Note that applications filed or picked up on Sunday or public holidays cost HK$50 ($6.50) more. CTS also organizes tours and makes hotel reservations in China.

If you're planning a 1-day trip to China, your destination will be either Shenzhen or Guangzhou. **Shenzhen,** located across the Hong Kong-China border, was established in the 1980s as one of China's first Special Economic Zones. Today, this experiment with capitalism looks almost like Hong Kong with its million people, concrete high-rises, traffic, industries, and relative prosperity. In recent years, it has become a shopping destination for day-trippers, who come for shoes, clothing, and fake name-brand handbags and watches at prices much cheaper than in Hong Kong. Even manicures and massages are cheaper there. You can travel to Shenzhen via the KCR Kowloon-Canton railway, with trains departing Kowloon KCR Railway Station in Hung Hom or Kowloon Tong Station every 3 to 10 minutes between 5:30am and 10:30pm. The border crossing (open daily 6:30am to 11:30pm) is at Lo Wu Station; cost of the KCR from Hung Hom to Lo Wu is HK$33 ($4.30) for ordinary class and HK$66 ($8.55) for first class. You can walk across the border into Shenzhen. Just across the border is a huge shopping mall. Tourist attractions are limited to Splendid China, a theme park with more than 80 miniatures of China's most historic buildings and sites, including the Great Wall, terra-cotta burial figures, and the Forbidden City; Window of the World, which recreates famous buildings and scenic spots from around the world, including the Taj Mahal, Eiffel Tower, and Grand Canyon; and China Folk Cultures Villages, which presents the art and cultures of China's various ethnic groups. All three are clustered together about 8 miles west of the border crossing.

Farther afield is **Guangzhou (Canton),** the capital of Guangdong Province with a population of 7.5 million. Guangzhou has a famous open-air market, Qingping Market, which has a somewhat lurid reputation for the exotic animals sold there for food, but it also has antiques, herbs, flowers, and a bird market. Otherwise, the sights are confined to a Buddhist temple and the monuments and statues in the city's largest park, Yuexiu Yuan, that include a memorial to Sun Yat-sen. You can reach Guangzhou by KCR railway in about 2 hours; cost of this trip is HK$230 ($29.85) for "premium" class, HK$190 ($24.70) for first class, and HK$180 ($23.40) for second class. At last check, through-train service to Guangzhou departed Kowloon KCR Railway Station in Hung Hom at 8:35am, 9:25am, 11:05am, 12:10pm, 1:25pm, and 4:45pm.

Be forewarned, however, that in Shenzhen and Guangzhou the tourist attractions hardly warrant the time spent in getting there (if your time in Hong Kong is extremely limited, I personally think you're better off staying in Hong Kong, with perhaps a side trip to Macau). The experience of going to China is most interesting for the contrast it provides with Hong Kong, especially in rural Guangdong Province with its duck and fish farms, rice fields and banana groves, and primitive living conditions. If you're really interested in a trip to China, you should plan on traveling at least as far as Shanghai or Beijing, both of which take about 28 hours by train from Hong Kong. Trips to Shanghai via KCR railway cost HK$1,039 ($135) one-way for a deluxe soft sleeper; trips to Beijing cost HK$1,191 ($155).

# 11 Macau

Hanging from China's gigantic underbelly on its southeastern coast, Macau covers all of 9.5 square miles. Forty miles west of Hong Kong across the Pearl River Estuary, it served as Portugal's last holdout in Asia until 1999, when it was handed back to China. Portugal's other former Asian strongholds, Goa and Malacca, had long before been claimed by neighboring powers.

In 1993, the *Guinness Book of World Records* declared Macau the most densely populated territory in the world, with more than 69,000 people per square mile. Today, due to a vigorous policy of land reclamation that has doubled its size, figures hover around 48,000 residents per square mile. Macau seems uncrowded compared with Hong Kong. With its mixture of Portuguese and Chinese elements, Macau feels different from Hong Kong, too, different from China—different from anywhere else. Maybe it's the jumble of Chinese signs and stores mixed in with freshly painted colonial-style buildings, or the temples alongside Catholic churches—Portuguese flair blended with Chinese practicality.

With its unique mixture of cultures, Macau makes an interesting day trip—or more, if you want to get away from the bustle of Hong Kong after a business trip or strenuous traveling itinerary. Consisting of a small peninsula and two tiny islands connected to the mainland by bridges, it's the ideal place to relax, and although the casinos are undoubtedly a major attraction (especially for Hong Kong's Chinese), there are also beaches, fortresses, churches, temples, gardens, and excellent museums to explore. What's more, although prices have risen in the past years, Macau's hotels are still cheaper than their counterparts in Hong Kong—you can bask in luxury in Macau for a fraction of what you'd pay in the former British colony; and as a duty-free port, Macau has also become something of a shopping mecca. And finally, Macanese cuisine, unique to Macau and combining ingredients from former Portuguese trading ports from around the world, is both inexpensive and delicious, especially when accompanied with Portuguese wine. If you're looking for a vacation from your vacation, I heartily recommend Macau.

Macau today is experiencing something of a revival with the lure of its resort hotels, spanking-new boutiques and restaurants, and increased transportation service both local and international. In fact, Macau is changing so rapidly that old-timers are right when they complain that the place isn't what it used to be—new construction has dramatically altered the city's skyline in just 10 short years, and there seems to be no end in sight. The small downtown, built in the era of pedicabs with its narrow lanes, is ill-equipped to deal with Macau's ever-increasing traffic. Indeed, city planners seem so intent on expansion, I fear that much of Macau's unique architectural legacy and charm will be lost in an ever-growing concrete jungle.

Even Macau's Portuguese legacy is under threat. The number of Portuguese remaining in Macau has fallen from 4,000 in the mid 1990s to about 1,000 residents today. There are approximately 20,000 Macanese, mixed Chinese and Portuguese. Although Portuguese was the only official language until as late as 1991, 96% of Macau's 455,000 residents are Chinese (half of whom were born in China), which means that you hardly ever hear Portuguese spoken. Though it remains an official language, Portuguese is in danger of losing ground outside official circles, as English and Putonghua (Mandarin) become the languages of choice for business and tourism.

Still, there have been many positive developments. Just a decade ago, Macau's downtown was crumbling and neglected, and there were few attractions beyond its casinos and a couple of ruined forts and churches. But in recent years, the small downtown has undergone a major renovation, with the restoration of its main plaza and its Mediterranean-influenced, colonial-era buildings with their arched, shuttered windows. In addition, the opening of several excellent, special-interest museums has greatly enhanced Macau's tourist circuit. Increased tourism has brought increased revenue, benefiting the local economy. Gambling in particular is a mainstay of Macau's economy, accounting for half the government's revenue.

## 1 Frommer's Favorite Macau Experiences

- **Following the Mosaic Pathway to St. Paul's Cathedral.** From Largo do Senado, Macau's main, colonial-era square, follow the wavy-patterned mosaic tiles through the old city uphill to St. Paul's Cathedral, Macau's most photographed facade.
- **Dining on Local Macanese and Portuguese Specialties.** African chicken, spicy prawns, sole, and codfish are just some of the culinary treats for the visitor to Macau, at very reasonable prices. Portuguese wine, the perfect accompaniment to both Macanese and Portuguese food, is also a bargain.
- **Splurging for a Room at a Resort Hotel.** After the traffic and crowds of Hong Kong, there's nothing more relaxing than gazing at the sea from your hotel room, sunning at an outdoor pool surrounded by greenery, and feeling tension and aches melt away under the expert care of a masseuse. Hong Kong has three resort hotels with extensive spa and fitness facilities.
- **Learning About Macau's History at the Museum of Macau.** Macau's history museum is a delight, built into the ruins of a fortress and highlighting not only the history of Macau but also the unique Macanese traditions, culture, architecture, and cuisine.
- **Visiting Lou Lim Iok Garden Early in the Morning.** Get to this Chinese garden early in the morning, when you're apt to see the locals going through the motions of *tai chi,* playing traditional Chinese music, and taking birds for walks in cages.
- **Strolling Around Guia Hill.** If you jog, you'll find the pathway that circles Guia Hill perfect—and even if you don't, this is a great place for a stroll. From the top of the hill, Macau's highest point, you have a panoramic view of the city. Here, too, are the remnants of a tiny fort, a chapel, a lighthouse, and a counter for the Macau Government Tourist Office.

# A Blending of Cultures

Macau was born centuries before Hong Kong was even conceived. Portuguese ships first landed in southern China in 1513, and in 1557 Portugal acquired Macau from China. Before long, Macau had achieved a virtual monopoly on trade between China, Japan, and Europe, making the city Portugal's most important trading center in Asia and the greatest port in the East in the early 1600s.

As the only Europeans engaged in trade in Asia, the Portuguese made a fortune acting as middlemen. Every spring, Portuguese ships laden with Indian goods and European crystal and wines sailed out of Goa, anchored in Malacca to trade for spices, stopped in Macau for silk brought down from China, and then traveled on to Nagasaki to trade the silk for silver, swords, and lacquerware. Using the monsoon winds, the ships returned to Macau to trade silver for more silk and porcelain, then sailed back to Goa where the exotic Asian goods were shipped to eager customers in Europe. The complete circuit from Goa and back took several years.

As Macau grew and prospered, it also served as an important base for the attempt to introduce Christianity to China and Japan, becoming a springboard for Jesuit missionaries to China, and a refuge for Asian Christians, including Japanese Christians who faced persecution and death at home. Many Portuguese married local Chinese, creating a new community of Macanese (Eurasian) families with a blend of the two cultures. This blending is still evident today in Macanese cuisine and architecture, as well as in the population. Macau represented a blending of European and Asian cultures that was rare in the Far East.

Needless to say, because of Macau's obvious prosperity, it attracted jealous attention from other European nations. Dutch invasions were repelled several times in the first decades of the 1600s. In response to the threat of invasion, the Portuguese built a series of forts, some of which still exist.

- **Stopping for Some Culture at the Leal Senado.** Macau's most outstanding example of Portuguese colonial architecture has a gallery where shows are mounted without much advance notice. Stop by and be surprised.
- **Cruising the Inner Harbour on a Junk.** Setting sail from the Maritime Museum are Chinese junks that explore either the Inner or Outer Harbours on 30-minute cruises. My favorite is of the busy Inner Harbour, with China on the other side and alive with fishing boats and cargo boats. Amazingly, the cruise costs only $10 ptcs ($1.30), making it one of the best cruising bargains in the world.
- **Swimming on Colôane Island.** Two public beaches, Cheoc Van and Hac Sa, feature lifeguards on duty, dining facilities, and public swimming pools. Afterward, retire for a drink or a Portuguese meal at Fernando's, a beach shack on Hac Sa.
- **Renting a Moke and Exploring the Islands.** A Moke is a small, jeeplike vehicle, perfect for exploring the islands of Taipa and Colôane. Visit the villages on Taipa and Colôane, hike through Seac Pai Van Park, stop for a swim at one of Colôane's beaches, and enjoy a relaxed meal at one of the many laid-back restaurants that dot the islands.
- **Trying Your Luck at the Horse and Dog Races.** Admission to the races in Macau is so cheap it's practically free. And who knows? You could strike gold. A great place to observe a local passion.

In the 1630s Japan closed its doors to foreign trade, granting a limited admittance only to the Dutch. This was a great blow for Macau, but the coup de grace came in 1841 when the British established their own colony on Hong Kong Island, only 40 miles away. As Hong Kong's deep natural harbor attracted trading ships, Macau lost its importance as a base for trade and slowly sank into obscurity.

In the 20th century, however, Macau gained a new foothold in the world of trade in the 1970s by producing electronics, clothing, toys, and other items for export. At the same time tourism began to grow, and with the establishment of casinos, Macau attracted a large number of Chinese gamblers from Hong Kong. In recent years the construction of ever larger resort hotels and apartment buildings has begun to bring in more leisure tourists, especially since the 1995 opening of Macau's international airport, which made Macau easily accessible for the first time in its history.

In 1998, however, with the end of Portuguese rule just around the corner, an outbreak of violence temporarily devastated the tourism industry. Rival triad gangs jockeying for power resorted to full-blown triad warfare—37 murders were committed in 1999, tied mostly to the lucrative gambling industry. Macau responded with increased police surveillance. Residents were hopeful that their new rulers would crack down on gang violence, and since the handover a number of key triad leaders have landed in jail.

On December 20, 1999, Portugal's 442 years of rule came to an end, with Macau's transition from colony to Special Administrative Region of China. Like Hong Kong, Macau is permitted its own internal government and economic system for another 50 years.

- **Observing the Chinese Gambling at the Ornate Floating Casino.** This moored boat is abuzz 24 hours a day with gambling fever. Drop by and observe the Chinese gambling, or try your luck with the slot machines on the upper deck.
- **People-Watching After Midnight.** After the sun goes down, Macau's nighttime revelers head to the Docks, a string of bars and discos with sidewalk seating. But the action doesn't really start hopping until after midnight.

## 2 Orientation

### ENTRY REQUIREMENTS

Entry procedures into Macau are very simple. If you are American, Canadian, Australian, Irish, British, or New Zealander, you do not need a visa for Macau for stays up to 20 days—all you need is your passport. What's more, even though the **pataca** (ptc) is Macau's official currency, you can use your Hong Kong dollars everywhere, even on buses and for taxis (though you are likely to receive change in patacas). The pataca is pegged to the Hong Kong dollar at the rate of $103.20 ptcs to HK$100; however, on the street and in hotels and shops, the Macau pataca and Hong Kong dollar are treated as having equal value. I suppose, therefore, that you could save a minuscule amount by exchanging your money for patacas, but I rarely have done so and don't consider it worth the hassle for short stays in Macau. You may wish to exchange a small amount—say, HK$20 ($2.60)—for taxis, buses, and admission fees, but keep in mind that the pataca is *not* accepted in Hong Kong. In addition, most Macau hotels and their restaurants, as well as restaurants catering largely to tourists, list room rates and menu items in Hong Kong dollars. For the sake of simplicity, the hotel rates given below are quoted in "HK$," but this could also read "patacas."

## VISITOR INFORMATION

**ON THE INTERNET**   You can obtain information on Macau through the Internet by visiting its Web site at **www.macautourism.gov.mo**. Its e-mail address is mgto@macautourism.gov.mo.

**IN THE UNITED STATES**   Macau has finally opened a U.S. office. Contact the **Macau Government Tourist Office,** 5757 West Century Blvd., Suite 660, Los Angeles, CA 90045 (☎ **877/MACAU-00,** or 310/670-2234; fax 310/338-0708).

**IN HONG KONG**   Your first stop for information about Macau should be as soon as you arrive in Hong Kong, at the new Hong Kong International Airport. In the arrivals lobby, at 3B, you'll find the **Macau Government Tourist Office (MTGO)** information counter (☎ **852/2769 7970**), open daily 9am to 10:30pm (closed for lunch 1 to 1:30pm and dinner 6 to 6:30pm). Stop here for a wealth of printed material about hotels and sightseeing in Macau. In addition, there's another MTGO information bureau at the Macau Ferry Terminal, the departure pier for most jetfoils and other craft bound for Macau. You'll find it on the third-floor Departure Floor, in room 336 of the Shun Tak Centre, 200 Connaught Rd., in Central (☎ **852/2857 2287**). It's open daily 9am to 5:30pm. Be sure to pick up a map of Macau, as well as the tourist tabloid *Macau Travel Talk.* If you enjoy do-it-yourself walking tours, be sure to get a copy of the free "Macau Walking Tours" pamphlet, which gives a street-by-street description of several easy hikes.

**IN MACAU**   Once in Macau, you'll find a **MGTO** at the Macau Ferry Terminal, located just outside customs and open daily 9am to 10pm; there is also a MGTO at Macau International Airport, open for all incoming flights. For complete information, however, your best bet is the **main Macau Government Tourist Office,** Largo do Senado, 9 (☎ **853/315566**). It's located in the center of town on the main plaza, just across from the water fountain, and is open daily 9am to 6pm. Other tourist information offices are located at St. Paul's Church and Macau Cultural Center, both open daily 9am to 6pm; and at Guia Fort and Lighthouse, both open daily 9am to 5:30pm.

## GETTING THERE

**BY BOAT**   Located only 40 miles from Hong Kong across the mouth of the Pearl River, Macau is most easily accessible from Hong Kong by high-speed jetfoil, with most departures from the **Macau Ferry Terminal,** located just west of the Central District in the Shun Tak Centre, 200 Connaught Rd., on Hong Kong Island. Situated above the Sheung Wan MTR station, the Shun Tak Centre houses booking offices for all forms of transportation to Macau, as well as the Macau Government Tourist Office (Room 336, on the same floor as boats departing for Macau). On the Kowloon side, limited service is available from the newer China Ferry Terminal on Canton Road, Tsim Sha Tsui, where boats also depart for China. The nearest MTR station for this terminal is Tsim Sha Tsui.

The fastest, most convenient way to travel to Macau is via sleek **jetfoils** and **catamarans,** operated by **TurboJET** (☎ **852/2859 3333**) and running 24 hours. The trip to Macau takes approximately 1 hour. Jetfoils depart from the Macau Ferry Terminal west of Central about every 15 minutes 7am to 5:30pm and every 30 to 60 minutes 5:45pm to 6am. One-way fares Monday to Friday are HK$232 ($30.15) for super class and HK$130 ($16.90) for economy class; fares on Saturday, Sunday, and holidays are HK$247 ($32.10) in super class and HK$141 ($18.35) in economy. Fares for night service (5:45pm to 6am) are HK$260 ($33.75) in super class and HK$161 ($20.95) in economy. Senior citizens older than 60 and children younger than 12 receive a HK$15 ($1.95) discount. Fares from the China Ferry Terminal in Tsim Sha Tsui are slightly cheaper.

Note that the Hong Kong government levies a HK$19 ($2.45) departure tax for those traveling to Macau. Likewise, passengers leaving Macau are charged a departure tax of $20 ptcs ($2.60). However, there's no need to worry about this, since departure taxes are already included in the price of your ticket. For this reason, tickets for travel from Macau to Hong Kong are $1 ptc (13¢) more than the ticket prices quoted above, reflecting the departure tax.

If you plan to travel on a weekend or holiday, it's wise to buy round-trip tickets well in advance. Tickets can be purchased at either the Macau Ferry Terminal on Hong Kong Island or the China Ferry Terminal in Kowloon, as well as at all China Travel Service branches in Hong Kong (see "China" in chapter 10) and at MTR Travel Service Centres located at Hong Kong, Admiralty, Causeway Bay, Tsim Sha Tsui, and Mong Kok stations. You can also book by credit card by calling ☎ **852/2921 6688** in Hong Kong. All tickets are for a specific time and cannot be changed. If, however, you've purchased your ticket in advance and then decide you'd like to leave at an earlier time, head for the special queue for standby passengers available at both Shun Tak Centre and in Macau. There is often a good chance that you can get a seat, even on weekends and during peak periods.

If you plan to spend only 1 or 2 nights in Macau, consider leaving most of your luggage at your Hong Kong hotel, or in computer-monitored lockers located at both the Hong Kong Island and Kowloon Macau ferry terminals. Then travel to Macau with only small, hand-carried bags. Otherwise, you could end up paying an extra charge. Passengers traveling on a TurboJET are allowed only one hand-carried bag, not to exceed 22 pounds. One additional piece of luggage may be checked in prior to departure, with charges ranging from HK$20 to HK$60 ($2.60 to $7.80) depending upon its weight. Additional checked-in luggage will be subject to the carrying capacity of the jetfoil. Baggage must be at the check-in counter 20 minutes before the jetfoil's departure. Obviously, your life will be easier if you leave heavy luggage in Hong Kong.

**BY HELICOPTER**   If traveling by boat is not fast enough for you, a helicopter can take you from Hong Kong to Macau in 15 minutes. I've never been in that much of a hurry, but one traveler I met said it was a hoot. **East Asia Airlines** operates flights from the Shun Tak Centre on Hong Kong Island, with flights every half hour 10am to 11pm. Fares from Hong Kong cost HK$1,206 ($156.80) on weekdays and HK$1,310 ($170.30) on weekends and holidays, including tax. Bookings can be made in Hong Kong at Counter 8 on the third floor of the Shun Tak Centre or by or by calling East Asia Airlines' Dial A Ticket Hotline at ☎ **852/2559 9800.**

**BY PLANE**   Macau's new **International Airport** opened in November 1995, heralding the birth of Air Macau, the territory's fledgling carrier. The airport is located on reclaimed land on Taipa Island and is conveniently connected to the peninsula by a new bridge and bus service. The airport serves flights mainly from China, including Beijing and Shanghai, as well as from several other cities, including Taipei, Singapore, Seoul, Manila, and Bangkok. Departure tax from Macau International Airport is $80 ptcs ($10.40) for adults and $50 ptcs ($6.50) for children for destinations in China. For other destinations the departure tax is $130 ptcs ($16.90) and $80 ptcs ($10.40) respectively. Contact your travel agent or the Macau Government Tourist Office for more information.

## ARRIVING IN MACAU

Passengers traveling by boat or helicopter arrive at the new Macau Ferry Terminal, located on the main peninsula. After going through customs, be sure to stop by the Macau Government Tourist Office for a map and brochures, including the useful "Macau Guide Book." In the arrivals hall is also a counter for hotels operating shuttle buses. Most expensive and moderately priced hotels operate free shuttle services from the terminal, including the Holiday Inn, Hyatt Regency, Mandarin Oriental, Lisboa, Pousada de São Tiago, Westin Resort Macau, and Sintra. Otherwise, city buses 3, 3A, and 10 travel from the terminal to Avenida Almeida Ribeiro, the main downtown street. The fare is $2.50 ptcs (30¢).

From the airport, several hotels offer complimentary transfer on request, including the Holiday Inn, Hyatt Regency, Westin, and Pousada de São Tiago. Otherwise, there's an airport bus, AP1, which travels from the airport to the ferry terminal, Lisboa Hotel, and the Border Gate. The fare for this is $6 ptcs (80¢). A taxi to the Lisboa costs approximately $40 ptcs ($5.20).

## CITY LAYOUT

Macau comprises a small peninsula and Taipa and Colôane, two small islands linked to the mainland by bridges and a causeway. The peninsula—referred to as Macau—is where you'll find the city of Macau, as well as the ferry terminal and most of its hotels, shops, and attractions. The ferry terminal is located on what is called the Outer Harbour, which faces Taipa and connects to the South China Sea. On the opposite side of the Peninsula is the Inner Harbour, which faces China. Although I used to love the Outer Harbour for its dreamy view of boats plying the Pearl River waterway and the tree-shaded Avenida da República which ran along the waterfront, land reclamation, including new highways and high-rises, has rendered the Outer Harbour a horror zone. I'd advise fleeing this side of the peninsula as hastily as possible for the downtown and the more colorful Inner Harbour. Walking along the Inner Harbour from Avenida Almeida Ribeiro to the Maritime Museum, you will see an unchanged Macau, with decaying buildings, small family businesses, streetside barbers, and occasionally fish laid out on sidewalks to dry.

Near the middle of the peninsula is Guia Hill, the highest point of Macau. Because of its strategic location, a fort was constructed atop the hill in the 1630s, followed in 1865 by a lighthouse, the first of its kind on the China coast. Also on the grounds of Guia Fort are a small chapel and a tourist-information counter (open daily 9am to 5:30pm). A jogging path, complete with exercise stations, circles the top of the hill. Although there's not much to do on Guia Hill, it does provide a good overview of Macau. You can reach it by taking bus no. 9 to Flora Garden and then boarding what must be the world's shortest ropeway to the top of the hill.

Connecting the two harbors is Macau's main road, Avenida Almeida Ribeiro. About halfway down its length is the attractive Largo do Senado, or Senate Square, Macau's main plaza. Lined with colonial-style buildings painted in hues of yellows and pinks, it is paved in a wave pattern of colored mosaic tiles, which lead from the square to St. Paul's Church crowning the crest of a hill. On the other side of the square is Leal Senado, Macau's most outstanding example of Portuguese colonial architecture.

Taipa, closest to the mainland and connected by two bridges, has witnessed a construction boom the past decade, with the addition of high-rise apartments and Macau's new airport. In its midst is the picturesque Taipa Village. Connected to Taipa by causeway and an ever-growing strip of reclaimed land is Colôane, largely undeveloped and site of Macau's best beaches. In fact, reclaimed land connecting the two islands is so extensive, in reality they are now just one fused island.

## GETTING AROUND

Because the peninsula is only 2½ miles in length and a mile at its greatest width, you can walk to most of the major sights. If you get tired, you can always jump into one of the licensed metered **taxis,** all painted black and beige and quite inexpensive. The charge is $10 ptcs ($1.30) at flagfall for the first 1.5 kilometer (0.9 miles), then $1 ptc (13¢) for each subsequent 250 meters (825 ft.). A taxi from the peninsula all the way to Hac Sa Beach on Colôane Island costs about $80 ptcs ($10.40). Luggage costs $3 ptc (4¢), and there's a surcharge of $5 ptcs (65¢) if you go all the way to Colôane. There is no surcharge, however, for the return journey to Macau.

**Public buses** run daily 7am to midnight, with fares costing $2.50 ptcs (30¢) for travel within the Macau peninsula, $3.30 ptcs (45¢) for travel to Taipa, and $4 to $5 ptcs (50¢ to 65¢) for travel to Colôane. Bus nos. 3, 3A, and 10, for example, travel from the front of the ferry terminal past the Lisboa Hotel to the main street, Avenida Almeida Ribeiro, in the city center and then continue to the Inner Harbour. Buses going to Taipa and Colôane islands stop for passengers at the bus stop in front of the Hotel Lisboa, located on the mainland near the Macau-Taipa Bridge. Bus nos. 11, 22, 28A, 33, and 34, as well as the airport bus AP1, travel between Macau and Taipa; bus nos. 15, 21, 21A, 25, 26, and 26A connect Macau, Taipa, and Colôane. The MGTO has a free map with bus routes.

There are also **pedicabs,** tricycles with seating for two passengers. Even as late as the early 1980s, this used to be one of the most common forms of transportation in Macau for the locals. But increased traffic and rising affluence have rendered pedicabs almost obsolete, and I suppose they will eventually vanish from the city scene much like the Hong Kong rickshaw. Today pedicab drivers vie mostly for the tourist dollar, charging about $150 ptcs ($19.50) for an hour of sightseeing, but keep in mind that there are many hilly sights you can't see by pedicab. The most popular route is along the Praia Grande Bay around the tip of the peninsula, and back via Rue do Almirante Sérgio. Be sure to settle on the fare, the route, and the length of the journey before climbing in.

And finally, if you want to drive around on your own, you can see Macau by **Moke,** a small, Jeeplike vehicle. However, because traffic on the Macau peninsula is so congested, I recommend hiring a Moke only for exploring the islands. Mokes rent for $480 ptcs ($62.40) per 24 hours Monday to Friday and $500 ptcs ($65) per 24 hours on Saturday, Sunday, and holidays. They are available from **Happy Mokes,** with a location at the Macau Ferry Terminal, level 1, counter 1025 (☎ **853/726868** or 853/439393). A map of Macau, leaflets, and a guidebook are provided. You can also see Macau via **rental car,** with a compact car HK$400 ($52) per day on weekdays and HK$520 ($67.60) on weekends, available from **Avis** with an office at the Mandarin Oriental (☎ **853/336789**). Drivers of a Moke or car must be at least 21 years old and must have held a driver's license for at least 2 years. Visitors from Australia, New Zealand, the United States, Ireland, and the United Kingdom need only a valid driver's license, but Canadians must have an international driver's license. Contact the Macau tourist office for more information. *Note:* Driving in Macau is on the left.

## Fast Facts: Macau

**Airport**    The Macau International Airport, located on reclaimed land on Taipa Island, opened in November 1995. From Hong Kong, however, the most convenient and economical mode of transportation is still by boat.

**American Express**   You'll find the main office of American Express near St. Paul's Church at 23B Rua de St. Paulo (☎ **853/363262**), open Monday to Friday 9am to 5pm. There's also a branch in the Hotel Lisboa, open 24 hours for all those gamblers (☎ **853/579898**).

**Area Code**   The international telephone country code for Macau is 853. From Hong Kong, dial 001/853 before the number. When dialing an international number from Macau, you must first dial 00, followed by the country code. However, when calling Hong Kong from Macau, you need only dial the prefix 01, though you can also dial 00/852.

**Currency**   Macau's currency is the pataca. Like the Hong Kong dollar, the pataca is identified by the "$" sign, sometimes also written "M$" or "MOP$." To avoid confusion, I have identified patacas by the shortened "ptcs." The pataca is composed of 100 avos. Coins come in 10, 20, and 50 avos and 1, 5, and 10 patacas. Banknotes are issued for 20, 50, 100, 500, and 1,000 patacas. The Macau pataca is pegged to the Hong Kong dollar (which is in turned pegged to the U.S. dollar) at a rate of $103.20 patacas to HK$100; if you're going to be in Macau for only a short time, there's no need to change your money into patacas since Hong Kong dollars are readily accepted everywhere in Macau. Hotel rates, in fact, are generally quoted only in Hong Kong dollars. If you do exchange U.S. dollars, you'll receive $8 patacas for each U.S.$1.

**Electricity**   Electricity in Macau is 220 volts AC, 50 cycles. Outlets accept British-type round or square three-pin plugs. If in doubt, check before using an electrical appliance.

**Emergencies**   For medical emergencies, dial **999.** Otherwise, dial ☎ **853/ 573333** for the police and ☎ **853/572222** for the fire department.

**Hospitals**   If you need to go to a hospital, contact the S. Januario Hospital, Estrada do Visconde de S. Januario (☎ **853/313731**), or Kiang Wu Hospital, Estrada Coelho do Amaral (☎ **853/371333**), both with 24-hour emergency service.

**Language**   Both Portuguese and Chinese are official languages, with Cantonese the most widely spoken language. Hotel and restaurant staff usually understand English.

**Mail**   Mailboxes are red in Macau. The main post office, located in the city center on Largo do Senado, is open Monday to Friday 9am to 6pm and Saturday 9am to 1pm. It costs $4.50 ptcs (60¢) to send a postcard or letter weighing up to 10 grams via airmail to the United States.

**Taxes**   Hong Kong levies a HK$19 ($2.45) tax for boat departures for Macau, while the Macau government levies a $20 ptc ($2.60) departure tax, but note that the tax is already included in the price of the ticket. Hotels levy a 5% government tax and a 10% service charge on room rates.

**Telephone**   For local calls made from public phone booths, it costs $1 ptc (13¢) for every 3 minutes. Telephones in Macau also offer international direct dialing, though in your hotel room you may have to go through the hotel operator. International direct-dial calls can also be made from the General Post Office, located at Largo do Senado, across from Leal Senado and the Macau Government Tourist Office (see open hours above, under "Mail"). It costs $5.50 ptcs (70¢) for a 1-minute phone call to the United States during peak hours (Monday to Saturday 6am to noon and 8am to midnight) and $4.50 ptcs (60¢) on Sundays and off-peak hours. For international directory assistance, dial 101; for local directory enquiries, dial 181.

**Time**    Macau is in the same time zone as Hong Kong.

**Water**    Macau's water is supplied from China and is purified and chlorinated. However, distilled water is supplied in restaurants and hotel rooms.

## 3 · Where to Stay

Most of Macau's hotels are located in the city of Macau on the peninsula, providing convenient access to most of Macau's sights. For a more relaxed getaway, however, there are a few hotels on the islands, mostly in a resort setting. Alas, the wonderful Hotel Bela Vista is a hotel no longer. Once Macau's most famous and oldest hotel, it closed at the end of March 1999, to serve as the Portuguese Embassy.

In addition to the room rates given below (which are the same whether you pay in Hong Kong dollars or in patacas), there is a 10% hotel service charge and a 5% government tax. Except for some of the moderate and inexpensive hotels, most charge the same price for single or double occupancy. However, as in Hong Kong, the prices given below are rack rates; you may be able to bargain for a better rate, especially in the off season. Since most of Macau's hotels have reservations facilities in Hong Kong, I've included the Hong Kong reservation telephone numbers when available. If you plan on visiting Macau in late November, when the Grand Prix is held, you should book well in advance. Weekends can also be quite busy. Otherwise, you shouldn't have any difficulty securing a room even on short notice, though if you have a specific hotel in mind it's always a good idea to reserve in advance. For more complete information about hotel restaurants, see "Where to Dine," below.

### EXPENSIVE

✪ **Hyatt Regency Macau.** 2 Estrada Almirante Marquês Esparteiro, Taipa Island, Macau. ☎ **800/233-1234** in the U.S. and Canada, 853/831234, or 852/2956 1234 for reservations in Hong Kong. Fax 853/830195. www.macauhyatt.com. E-mail: hyatt@macau.ctm.net. 326 units. A/C MINIBAR TV TEL. HK$1,600–HK$1,750 ($208–$227) single or double; HK$1,900 ($247) Regency Club; from HK$2,400 ($312) suite. Children under 12 stay free in parents' room (maximum 3 persons per room). AE, DC, MC, V. Free shuttle bus from ferry terminal and airport, or bus no. 28A from the ferry terminal.

If you're looking for a resort getaway with a tropical, Mediterranean atmosphere, extensive recreational facilities for the entire family, great restaurants, and comfortable rooms, the Hyatt is a good choice. It is located on Taipa Island near the horse-racing track and offers free shuttle service to the mainland. Adjoining the hotel is the Taipa Island Resort, a sprawling, 3-acre complex set amidst lush greenery with an outdoor heated pool open year-round, tennis and squash courts, fitness rooms, and more. For families, there's the children's wading pool, playground, games room, child-care center, baby-sitting services, and, for children ages 5 to 12, Camp Hyatt, with fun activities offered weekends and during school and public holidays. The guest rooms, which were shipped in units from the United States and then assembled in Macau like pieces of a jigsaw puzzle, have recently been refurbished with rattan furnishings, Asian artwork, shutters, and a cheerful turquoise or yellow color scheme, and offer all the usual amenities, including satellite TV with pay in-house movies, room safe, dataports, and a voice-mail system. The least expensive rooms face inland toward new apartment construction. The best rooms have views of the Outer Harbour and Macau's rapidly changing skyline. If you really feel like splurging, you might want to stay in the Regency Club, an executive floor that offers free continental breakfast, cocktails, and beverages. The hotel's restaurants are among the best in Macau. In short, you could easily spend days here, unwinding and relaxing. If you feel like exploring or dining on local cuisine, the quaint Taipa Village is only a 15-minute walk away, while Macau peninsula is just a 5-minute drive away. Note that the swimming pool, aerobics class, and exercise room are free, but there is a charge to use the health spa with its steam rooms, sauna, and Jacuzzi.

**Dining/Diversions: The Chinese** is a hip Cantonese restaurant specializing in country-style cooking, while the **Flamingo** is a Macanese restaurant with a tropical hot-pink setting, terrace seating, and views of a small lake. There's a swim-up bar in the swimming pool, a restaurant with themed lunch and dinner buffets and an international à-la-carte menu, a cocktail lounge serving high tea that has live entertainment in the evening, and a 24-hour casino.

**Amenities:** Outdoor heated swimming pool; children's pool; four floodlit tennis courts; two indoor squash courts; multi-purpose course for volleyball, basketball, and badminton; fitness center; aerobics class; rental bicycles; male and female spas with sauna, steam room, Jacuzzi, massage and solarium; hair salon; games room with table tennis and pool tables; business center; wonderful child-care center for children ages 2 to 8 (open Sunday to Friday 10:30am to 7:30pm and Saturday and holidays 9:30am to 9pm); playground; free shuttle to the ferry, airport, and Hotel Lisboa; same-day laundry; 24-hour room service; free newspaper; in-house nurse and doctor on call 24 hours; baby-sitting.

✪ **Mandarin Oriental Macau.** 956–1110 Avenida da Amizade, Macau. ☎ **800/526-6566** in the U.S. and Canada, 853/567888, or 852/2881 1288 for reservations in Hong Kong. Fax 853/594589. www.mandarinoriental.com. E-mail: mandarin@macau.ctm. net. 435 units. A/C MINIBAR TV TEL. HK$1,600–HK$1,900 ($208–$247) single or double; HK$2,000– HK$2,200 ($260–$286) Mandarin floors; from HK$4,600 ($597) suite. AE, DC, MC, V. Free shuttle bus from ferry terminal and airport.

A companion hotel of the Mandarin Oriental in Hong Kong and the Oriental in Bangkok, this is one of Macau's most exclusive hotels, with room rates much lower than you'd pay in Hong Kong. Conveniently located about a 7-minute walk from the ferry terminal in the direction of downtown, it used to enjoy a rather isolated spot right on the Outer Harbour, but a huge land-reclamation project has robbed the hotel of much of its view, not to mention peace and quiet. On the plus side, the hotel claimed a small portion of the new land for its new, state-of-the-art resort facility, which includes an outdoor swimming pool (heated in winter and chilled in summer) landscaped against a waterfall; a water slide, pool, playground, and children's center for the kids; a fitness room and aerobics studio; a spa offering five types of massage, body scrubs and wraps, facials and more; and the Outdoor Adventure Learning Centre that offers a rock climbing tower and a flying trapeze.

As for the hotel, although its exterior is rather nondescript, if not downright ugly, the interior is beautifully designed and elegantly decorated throughout with imports from Portugal, including blue-and-white tiles, chandeliers, tapestries, and artwork. The marble lobby features a carved teak staircase leading up to the second floor, where you'll find the hotel's small but sophisticated casino, with a separate room for slot machines. The guest rooms, equipped with safes, a voice-mail system, dataports, coffee/tea-making facilities, and satellite TVs with in-house movies, are decorated in soft pink or green with Portuguese fabrics and natural teak, and the bathrooms are marbled and spacious. The least expensive rooms face inland, while the best rooms (on the top four Mandarin executive floors) face the sea and feature large balconies. Privileges extended to those staying on the Mandarin executive floors include free continental breakfast and private lounge.

**Dining/Diversions:** Italian cuisine is offered at **Mezzaluna,** the hotel's premier restaurant. At the **Dynasty** you can eat dim sum and other Cantonese food, while the **Cafe Girassol** is open 24 hours a day except on Thursday and specializes in

# Macau Accommodations & Dining

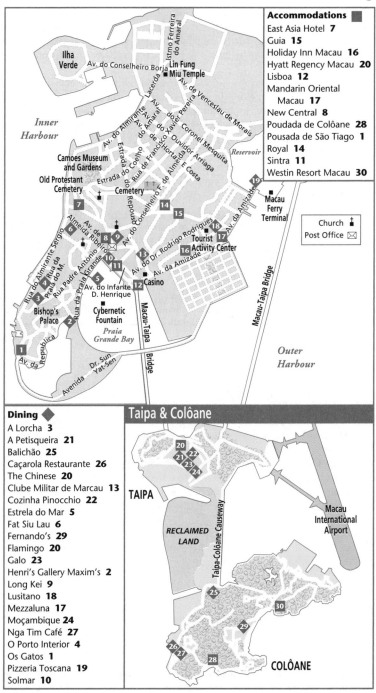

## Accommodations

East Asia Hotel **7**
Guia **15**
Holiday Inn Macau **16**
Hyatt Regency Macau **20**
Lisboa **12**
Mandarin Oriental
 Macau **17**
New Central **8**
Poudada de Colôane **28**
Pousada de São Tiago **1**
Royal **14**
Sintra **11**
Westin Resort Macau **30**

Church ✝
Post Office ✉

## Dining

A Lorcha **3**
A Petisqueira **21**
Balichão **25**
Caçarola Restaurante **26**
The Chinese **20**
Clube Militar de Marcau **13**
Cozinha Pinocchio **22**
Estrela do Mar **5**
Fat Siu Lau **6**
Fernando's **29**
Flamingo **20**
Galo **23**
Henri's Gallery Maxim's **2**
Long Kei **9**
Lusitano **18**
Mezzaluna **17**
Moçambique **24**
Nga Tim Café **27**
O Porto Interior **4**
Os Gatos **1**
Pizzeria Toscana **19**
Solmar **10**

## Taipa & Colôane

257

Macanese/Portuguese and Asian cuisine, with great breakfast, lunch, and dinner buffets. **Fresco MediterAsian Grill** offers alfresco dining with a view of the spa pool and low-fat cuisine that blends Thai, Greek, Italian, Chinese, and Portuguese ingredients. The **Embassy Bar** features a live band every night 10pm to 1am except Monday, while the casino is open 24 hours.

**Amenities:** Outdoor, year-round swimming pool; children's pool and water slide; playground; sauna; steam room; Jacuzzi; massage; two hard-court and two artificial-turf floodlit tennis courts; two indoor squash courts; multi-purpose court for basketball, badminton, and volleyball; fitness room; exercise studio with aerobics, body conditioning, and other classes; Outdoor Learning Center with a flying trapeze and rock-climbing wall; children's day-care center; business center; shopping arcade; book kiosk; beauty salon; 24-hour room service; car rental; doctor on call 24 hours; babysitting; parcel and packing service; same-day laundry and dry cleaning; free shuttle bus to the ferry and airport.

○ **Pousada de São Tiago.** Avenida da República, Fortaleza de São Tiago da Barra, Macau. ☎ **853/378111,** or 852/2739 1216 for reservations in Hong Kong. Fax 853/552170. www.saotiago.com.mo. E-mail: saotiago@macau.ctm.net. 24 units. A/C MINIBAR TV TEL. HK$1,540–HK$1,880 ($200–$244) single or double; from HK$2,100 ($273) suite. AE, DC, MC, V. Free shuttle bus (on request) or bus no. 28B from ferry terminal.

Built around the ruins of the Portuguese Fortress da Barra, which dates from 1629, this delightful small inn on the tip of the peninsula is guaranteed to charm even the most jaded of travelers. The entrance is dramatic—a flight of stone stairs leading through a cavelike tunnel that was once part of the fort, with water trickling in small rivulets on one side of the stairs. Once inside, guests are treated to the hospitality of a Portuguese inn, with bedroom furniture imported from Portugal and the use of stone, brick, and Portuguese blue tile throughout. Os Gatos, a terrace restaurant shaded by banyan trees, is a great place to while away an afternoon, as is the nearby outdoor swimming pool; and most of the rooms, all of which face the sea, have balconies. Although lacking the recreational resort facilities of other hotels in this category, this place is a true find, perfect for a romantic getaway. The Maritime Museum and A-Ma Temple are within easy walking distance; you can also walk to the city center in about a half hour.

**Dining: Cafe Da Barra,** with an elegant, drawing-room ambience, is open for dinner with a mix of classic Portuguese and continental cuisine. **Os Gatos,** which offers dining on either a tree-shaded outdoor patio with glimpses of the sea or in a glass-enclosed air-conditioned room, serves specialties from Macau, Portugal, and the Mediterranean region.

**Amenities:** Outdoor swimming pool, baby-sitting, same-day laundry and dry-cleaning, medical and dental service, free newspaper, parcel and postal service, room service (7:30am to 11:30pm), complimentary shuttle to and from the ferry pier on request.

○ **Westin Resort Macau.** 1918 Estrada de Hac Sa, Colôane Island, Macau. ☎ **800/ 228- 3000** in the U.S. and Canada, 853/871111, or 852/2803 2333 for reservations in Hong Kong. Fax 853/871122. www.westin.com. E-mail: Macau@westin.com. 208 units. A/C MINI-BAR TV TEL. HK$2,000–HK$2,250 ($260–$292.50) single or double; from HK$5,000 ($650) suite. Children under 19 stay free in parents' room. AE, DC, MC, V. Free shuttle bus from ferry terminal, airport, and Hotel Lisboa.

Opened in 1993, this is Macau's most stunning luxury resort hotel, complete with beautifully landscaped grounds, two outdoor swimming pools (one is a children's pool), an indoor pool, tennis courts, a health club, and Macau's first golf course (accessed from the top floor of the resort). Located just a stone's throw from Hac Sa

Beach on Colôane Island (with its popular Fernando's restaurant), it's a bit far from the center of town (about a 15-minute ride from the ferry pier on the hotel's complimentary shuttle bus, with departures every 30 to 60 min.), but the management is betting that most prospective guests are those who want to get away from it all. The hotel, Mediterranean in design and atmosphere, is spacious and airy, with a red terra-cotta tile roof and a comfortable lounge off the lobby, which takes advantage of the idyllic setting by providing lots of windows that overlook the sea. To assure tranquillity, there's a separate check-in counter for tour groups. For families, there's the Westin Kids Club, which provides children ages infant to 12 with appropriate amenities and activities, a child-care center, a wading pool, and playground.

Constructed in tiers to harmonize with the hillside overlooking Hac Sa Beach, each of the eight-storied hotel's very spacious rooms faces either the South China Sea or the beach (sea views are better) and features glass-sliding doors opening onto a huge 270-square-foot private terrace with plants and patio furniture. In-room amenities include room safe, satellite TV with in-house movies, computer hookups, a large desk, coffee/tea-making facility, hair dryer, shaving/makeup mirror, and separate areas for showering and bathing. The room rates are based on altitude, with the highest floors costing more.

**Dining/Diversions:** There are five restaurants and bars, including a Cantonese restaurant with an outdoor terrace overlooking the sea, a coffee shop offering both Portuguese and Macanese food, a Japanese restaurant, and a hotel bar with outdoor seating, all of which have no-smoking sections. There's also a poolside bar. The lounge off the lobby offers live music 6 nights a week.

**Amenities:** Outdoor swimming pool open year-round, outdoor children's pool, indoor pool, eight tennis courts, two squash courts, lawn bowling, jogging lanes, health club, sauna, steam room, massage, indoor and outdoor Jacuzzi, 18-hole golf course, golf-driving range, child-care center (HK$40 [$5.20] per hour), playground, games room, table tennis, minigolf course, lobby kiosk, small 24-hour business center with free access to the Internet, gift shop, 24-hour room service, same-day laundry, baby-sitting, complimentary shuttle bus.

## MODERATE

**Holiday Inn Macau.** Rua de Pequim, 82–86, Macau. ☎ **800/465-4329** in the U.S., 853/783333. Fax 853/782321. www.holiday-inn.com. 410 units. A/C MINIBAR TV TEL. HK$1,000–HK$1,480 ($130–$192) single or double; HK$1,680 ($218) executive floor; from HK$3,300 ($429) suite. Children under 12 stay free in parents' room. AE, DC, MC, V. Free shuttle bus from ferry terminal and airport.

Opened in 1993, this well-known chain is familiar to North American guests; however, though the hotel is comfortable enough, it falls short of what you've come to expect if you've stayed at other Holiday Inns in Asia, where the level of service and facilities is higher than in North American properties. The hotel is situated in a rather drab area of high-rises that is being developed between the ferry terminal and downtown (there are no views of the harbor). A plus is that it's about a 10-minute walk from the main downtown area of Avenida de Almeida Ribeiro. The rooms are somewhat plain and bare, although equipped with the usual satellite TV with in-house movies, safes, coffee-making facility, free bottled water, hair dryer, and, on the executive floor in addition, bathroom scales, makeup/shaving mirrors, and terry-cloth robes. Executive-floor guests also receive complimentary breakfast. Like most Macau hotels, it caters largely to gamblers and tour groups, mostly from Hong Kong, Taiwan, and China. The primary dining facility, open breakfast to dinner, specializes in Continental and Macanese cuisine. There's also a Chinese restaurant serving dim sum and Cantonese and Szechuan dishes, a very popular bar called Oskar's Pub, and a 24-hour casino. Other facilities and amenities include a small indoor swimming pool, sauna, steam room, whirlpool, exercise room, games room, 24-hour room service, same-day laundry, nightly turndown, and baby-sitting.

**Hotel Lisboa.** Avenida da Amizade, Macau. ☎ **800/44-UTELL** in the U.S. and Canada, 853/577666, or 852/2546 6944 for reservations in Hong Kong. Fax 853/567193. www. macau.ctm.net/~lisboa. E-mail: lisboa@macau.ctm.net. 928 units. A/C MINIBAR TV TEL. HK$1,350–HK$2,350 ($175–$305) single or double; from HK$3,800 ($493.50) suite. Children under 13 stay free in parents' room. AE, DC, MC, V. Free shuttle bus or bus no. 3, 3A, 10, 28A, 28B, or 28C from the ferry terminal.

The Lisboa is in a class by itself. Built in 1969, it's a Chinese version of Las Vegas—huge, flashy, and with a bewildering array of facilities that make it almost a city within a city. I always get lost in this hotel. Located near the water and one of the bridges to Taipa Island, it also has great *fung shui*, which may explain why its casino is one of the most popular in Macau. You certainly can't get much closer to the action than the Lisboa; it is very popular among the Hong Kong Chinese and tour groups from China and Taiwan, making its lobby rather noisy and crowded. Its casino, one of the largest, never closes, and there are countless restaurants, shops, and nighttime diversions, including the Crazy Paris Show with a revue of scantily clad European women. One advantage to staying here is that buses to the outlying islands and other parts of Macau stop at the front door. Downtown Macau is only a 5-minute walk away. As for the rooms, they're located in an older wing, a newer wing, and a tower that was completed in 1993. The tower, which added 14 floors, offers the best—and most expensive—harbor views, including rooms with traditional Chinese architecture and furniture. Otherwise, rooms seem rather old-fashioned and have been decorated in green, pink, or orange, but they do boast satellite TV with 18 channels and pay movies, room safes, and hair dryers. In short, this is the place to be if you want to be in the thick of it. I suspect some guests check in and never leave the premises.

There are more than a dozen restaurants (some open 24 hours) serving European, Portuguese, Japanese, Chiu Chow, Cantonese, and Shanghainese cuisine; plus cocktail lounges, bars, a nightclub, and a casino open 24 hours.

Guests enjoy 24-hour room service, same-day laundry, complimentary shuttle service, free newspaper on request, money-exchange banks, house doctor, and baby-sitting. The hotel also offers an outdoor heated swimming pool, sauna and massage, fitness center, large shopping arcade, electronic games room, beauty salon, and barbershop.

**Hotel Royal.** Estrada da Vitoria No. 2–4, Macau. ☎ **853/552222**, or 852/2543 6426 for reservations in Hong Kong. 380 units. A/C TV TEL. HK$750–HK$1,100 ($97–$143) single or double; from HK$2,200 ($286) suite. Children under 12 stay free in parents' room. AE, MC, V. Free hotel shuttle bus or bus no. 28C from ferry terminal.

Located at the foot of Guia Hill, a 15-minute walk from St. Paul's Church, Museum of Macau, Lou Lim Iok Garden, and downtown Macau, this older 19-story property is a popular choice for visitors of moderate means, with more facilities than other hotels costing the same. In addition to a restaurant serving Portuguese and Macanese cuisine, a cafe, a Cantonese restaurant, a lobby lounge with nightly entertainment, and a Japanese-style bar, it also offers an indoor-swimming pool, a sauna, a beauty salon, and a gaming room with slot machines. Rooms, with hair dryers, are rather simple; ask for one with a view of the harbor in the distance. The most expensive accommodations, which have the added convenience of minibars, are on the top floors. Services are limited to room service (7am to 1am), laundry service, and free shuttle service to the ferry pier every half hour or so, and, on request, Hotel Lisboa.

**Pousada de Colôane.** Praia de Cheoc Van, Colôane Island, Macau. ☎ **853/882143.** Fax 853/882251. 22 units. A/C MINIBAR TV TEL. HK$680–HK$750 ($88–$97.50) single or double. AE, MC, V. Bus: no. 21A, 25, or 26 from Lisboa Hotel (tell the bus driver you want to get off at the hotel).

This small, family-owned property, perched on a hill above Cheoc Van Beach with views of the sea, is a good place for couples and families in search of a reasonably priced isolated retreat. More than 30 years old but recently renovated, it's a relaxing, rather rustic place, with modestly furnished rooms, all of which have large balconies and face the sea and beach. There is are an outdoor swimming pool, a smaller children's pool, a playground, an outdoor terrace where you can have drinks, and a Portuguese restaurant that is especially popular for its Sunday lunch buffet offered during peak season. *Note:* The hotel was still undergoing renovation at press time; call to make sure it has reopened.

**Sintra.** Avenida de D. João IV, Macau. ☎ **800/44-UTELL** in the U.S. and Canada, 853/710111, or 852/2546 6944 for reservations in Hong Kong. Fax 853/567769. www.macau.ctm.net/~sintra. E-mail: bcsintra@macau.ctm.net. 240 units. A/C TV TEL. HK$680–HK$960 ($88–$125) single or double; HK$880–HK$1,080 ($114–$140) executive floor; from HK$1,480 ($192) suite. Children under 13 stay free in parents' room. AE, DC, MC, V. Free shuttle bus or bus no. 3A or 10 from the ferry terminal.

With the best central location of any of the moderately priced hotels, the Sintra, under the same management as Hotel Lisboa, enjoys a prime situation in the heart of Macau, within easy walking distance of Avenida de Almeida Ribeiro (Macau's main street), Largo do Senado, and the Hotel Lisboa. Originally built in 1975 but completely overhauled in the mid-1990s, it looks new. Its large rooms are nicely decorated with pastel-colored furnishings and the bathrooms have marble-topped counters; satellite TVs offer in-house pay movies. The higher-priced rooms are larger and occupy higher floors; individual bookings (not through a travel agency) are often upgraded to one of these rooms if space is available. The top floor, with 20 rooms, is the executive floor, with such extra services as complimentary buffet breakfast, free newspaper, a fruit basket, free shoe shine, a welcome drink, and discounts on laundry services and telephone calls. The hotel's one restaurant (open 24 hours!) serves Western and Chinese food, including dim sum breakfasts and buffet lunches, and there are a business center, a shopping center, a sauna (for men only), 24-hour room service, same-day laundry service, and free shuttle service to the ferry terminal and Hotel Lisboa.

## INEXPENSIVE

**East Asia Hotel.** Rua da Madeira 1–A, Macau. ☎ **853/922433,** or 852/2540 6333 for reservations in Hong Kong. Fax 853/922430. 98 units. A/C TV TEL. HK$260–HK$340 ($39–$44) single; HK$400–HK$500 ($52–$65) twin. Weekday discounts available. AE, MC, V. Bus: no. 3, 3A, or 10 from the ferry terminal.

This is one of Macau's better choices for inexpensive accommodation in the heart of the city (I've seen some pretty grim hotels and guesthouses in this category), located near the Inner Harbour just off Avenida de Almeida Ribeiro in an area filled with local color and atmosphere. More than 60 years old, the renovated hotel features a polite staff and large, somewhat tired rooms with tiled bathrooms and complimentary Chinese tea. The least expensive rooms are windowless, so be sure to ask for windows if that's important to you. The rooms on higher floors offer better views, including some of the Inner Harbour. There's one Chinese restaurant.

✪ **Hotel Guia.** Estrada do Engenheiro Trigo 1–5, Macau. ☎ **853/513888.** Fax 853/559822. 90 units. A/C MINIBAR TV TEL. HK$470–HK$600 ($61–$78) single or double; from HK$750 ($97.50) suite. AE, DC, MC, V. Free shuttle bus or bus no. 28C from ferry terminal.

Located on the slope of Guia Hill below the Guia Fort and Lighthouse and surrounded by traditional colonial architecture, this is one of Macau's more secluded inexpensively priced hotels. Opened in 1989, it's also one of the most modern and welcoming, small and personable with a friendly staff and spotless rooms that range from those facing inland to those with little balconies facing the sea. By far the best are those with a view of Guia Lighthouse and the harbor in the background—request a room on the highest (fifth) floor. The only drawback to its quiet residential location is that it's a bit far from the action, but a free shuttle bus makes runs every half hour or so to and from the boat pier and the Hotel Lisboa. Facilities include one Chinese restaurant offering seafood and specialties from different provinces in China and a disco/nightclub. Room service is available 7:30am to 10:30pm, and there's same-day laundry service. A nearby jogging path on Guia Hill makes this an ideal choice for joggers and walkers.

**Hotel New Central.** Avenida de Almeida Ribeiro, 26–28, Macau. ☎ **853/373888** or 853/372404. Fax 853/332275. 160 units. A/C TV TEL. HK$160–HK$268 ($21–$35) double. MC, V. Bus: no. 3, 3A, or 10 from the ferry terminal.

This landmark, with the best location of any hotel—right on Macau's main road beside Largo do Senado—first opened about 70 years ago and looks it, despite a promising new coat of bright-green exterior paint and the recent addition of "New" to its name. Inside, it's still the same run-down hotel, with one elevator serving 11 floors and with dark and narrow corridors. Although some rooms were refurbished with new carpets, wallpaper, and furniture a few years back, and have tiled bathrooms, most of the rooms are old and run-down, with discolored and peeling wallpaper and threadbare carpets. Furthermore, some rooms don't even have windows. Before deciding to take a room, ask to see it (though the staff seems reluctant to let prospective guests do so). Also, be aware that the renovated rooms are more expensive. If possible, try to get a room on the ninth floor; some rooms here boast balconies with a view over the rooftops to the harbor beyond; there are also upper-floor rooms with views of the harbor, though you'll have to open the glazed windows to see it. The hotel has one Cantonese restaurant and a coffee shop.

## 4  Where to Dine

As a former trading center for spices and a melting pot for Portuguese and Chinese cultures, it's little wonder that Macau developed its own very fine cuisine. The Portuguese settlers brought with them sweet potatoes, peanuts, and kidney beans from Brazil, piri-piri peppers from Africa, chilies from India, and codfish, coffee, and vegetables from Europe. In turn, the Chinese introduced rhubarb, celery, ginger, soy sauce, lychees, and other Asian foods. The result is Macanese cuisine. One of the most popular dishes is African chicken, grilled or baked with chilies and piri-piri peppers. Other favorites include Portuguese chicken (chicken baked with potatoes, tomatoes, olive oil, curry, coconut, saffron, and black olives), *bacalhau* (codfish), Macau sole, *caldeirada* (seafood stew), spicy giant shrimp, baked quail and pigeon, curried crab, Portuguese sausage, and *feijoada* (a Brazilian stew of pork, black beans, cabbage, and spicy sausage). There are also restaurants specializing in traditional Portuguese cuisine, and, of course, countless Chinese restaurants. And don't forget Portuguese wine, inexpensive and a great bargain. Most famous is the *vinho verde*, a young wine served very cold that is refreshing on hot summer days.

Restaurants will add a 10% service charge to your bill, but as you'll discover, even the "expensive" restaurants in Macau would be a bargain in Hong Kong.

# EXPENSIVE

**The Chinese.** In the Hyatt Regency Hotel, Taipa Island. ☎ **853/831234.** Reservations recommended. Main dishes HK$48–HK$120 ($6.25–$15.60). AE, DC, MC, V. Daily 10:30am–3pm and 6:30–11pm. Bus: no. 11, 21, 21A, 28A, or 33. CANTONESE.

Whereas just a few years ago it seemed no luxury hotel would dream of serving anything but Portuguese and Macanese food in its premier restaurant, nowadays hotel restaurants are happily diversifying into a broader spectrum of cuisines, making for much more variation. This very classy, modern Chinese restaurant, decorated in shades of green and yellow with black booths and views of a lily pond, serves traditional, country-style dishes, gleaned by the head chef as he traveled through Guangdong Province in search of authentic recipes. Many of the dishes will remind Cantonese diners of their grandmother's home cooking. An open kitchen features chefs in action. Particularly interesting are the combination specialties, allowing lone diners or couples to sample various two-dish combinations, including deep-fried prawns with sesame seed and lemon sauce, served with sautéed fish and honey peas; and sautéed beef tenderloin in spicy sauce, served with wok-fried green beans. Roast goose, Peking duck (costing HK$280/$36.35), seafood, and dim sum are also available.

**Clube Militar de Macau.** Avenida da Praia Grande, 795. ☎ **853/714009.** Reservations recommended for lunch. Main courses HK$90–HK$120 ($11.70–$15.60); fixed-price lunch or dinner HK$90 ($11.70); lunch buffet HK$130 ($16.90). AE, MC, V. Daily noon–3pm and 7–11pm. Bus: no. 3, 3A, 10, 10A, or 10. MACANESE/PORTUGUESE.

This is certainly one of Macau's most atmospheric dining halls, located in the century-old Military Club. Painted a bright pink, this striking colonial building behind the Hotel Lisboa opened its restaurant to the public in 1995, offering nonmembers the chance to dine in style in its old-fashioned dining hall with its tall ceilings, whirring ceiling fans, arched windows, wood floor, and displays of Chinese dishware. As for the food, it's best to stick to the classics, such as codfish, seafood stew in a white wine sauce, sirloin steak Portuguese style, stewed lamb leg in red wine, or African chicken. The lunch buffet is a downtown favorite, and the list of Portuguese wines is among the best in town.

**✪ Flamingo.** In the Hyatt Regency Hotel, Taipa Island. ☎ **853/831234.** Reservations recommended Sat–Sun. Main courses HK$68–HK$130 ($8.85–$16.90); fixed-price lunch HK$78 ($10.15). AE, DC, MC, V. Daily noon–3pm and 7–11pm. Bus: no. 11, 21, 21A, 28A, or 33. MACANESE/PORTUGUESE.

If I had time for only one memorable meal in Macau, this would be a serious contender. Decorated in hot pink, this restaurant has a great Mediterranean ambience, with ceiling fans, swaying palms, and a terrace overlooking lush landscaping and a duck pond. For lightweights unaccustomed to alfresco dining, an air-conditioned enclosure was recently added, but for me the real pleasure of dining here is the terrace. The bread is homemade, and the specialties are a unique blend of Portuguese, Chinese, African, Indian, and Malay spices, resulting in delicious Macanese fare as well as traditional Portuguese dishes. Try the spicy king prawns with chili sauce; curried crab; African chicken with chili-coconut sauce; grilled sardines; or Macanese fried rice with chorizo, shrimp, chicken, and vegetables. Meals here average HK$170 ($22)—a great value considering the ambience and the food. A strolling three-man band sets the mood.

**Mezzaluna.** In the Mandarin Oriental Hotel, Avenida da Amizade. ☎ **853/567888.** Reservations recommended. Main courses HK$110–HK$170 ($14.30–$22); pasta and pizza HK$52–HK$110 ($6.75–$14.30). AE, DC, MC, V. Tues–Sun 12:30–3pm and 6:30–11pm. Bus: no. 3A, 10, 10A, 10B, 12, 17, 23, 28A, 28B, or 28C. ITALIAN.

It was a bold move many years back to open an Italian restaurant as a premier hotel restaurant rather than Portuguese/Macanese, long favored by Macau's hotels, but for those looking for something different this is a welcome addition and is certainly the best Italian restaurant in town. With a modern setting of golds and greens and the casualness of wicker chairs, it evokes the sunny ambience of the Mediterranean. The focal point is the open kitchen with its charcoal grill and bell-shaped wood-burning oven, from which emerge tantalizing dishes—Neapolitan-style pizzas; pastas that include mouthwatering linguine with baby lobster, basil, garlic, and chili; and less than a dozen main courses ranging from grilled beef tenderloin to tuna loin. The pizzas and pasta dishes come in small and medium sizes, making them great as appetizers or as a main dish.

**Os Gatos.** In the Pousada de São Tiago Hotel, Avenida da República. ☎ **853/378111.** Main courses HK$116–HK$164 ($15.05–$21.30). AE, DC, MC, V. Daily 11am–11:30pm. Bus: no. 28B. MACANESE/MEDITERRANEAN.

Os Gatos occupies a wonderful tree-shaded brick terrace that faces the sea. It's a great place to stop for a meal, snack, or drink if you're walking around the tip of the peninsula (something I do on every trip to Macau) or visiting the nearby Maritime Museum or A-Ma Temple. If you wish, you can also sit in air-conditioned comfort inside a glass-enclosed room. The menu offers a blend of Mediterranean and Macanese food, including Macau sole, poached bacalhau with onions, seafood paella, baked salmon with garlic and basil, king crab in tomato sauce, and pastas. The restaurant itself is located in the delightful Pousada de São Tiago Hotel, a romantic and intimate getaway.

## MODERATE

**A Lorcha.** Rua do Almirante Sergio, 289. ☎ **853/313193.** Reservations recommended for lunch. Main courses HK$50–HK$82 ($6.45–$10.65). AE, MC, V. Wed–Mon 12:30–3:30pm and 7–11pm. Bus: no. 1, 1A, 2, 5, 6, 7, 8, 9, 10, 10A, 11, 18, 21, 21A, or 28B. PORTUGUESE.

Just a stone's throw from the Maritime Museum and A-Ma Temple, this is the best place to eat if you find yourself hungering for Portuguese food when you are in this area. Look for its whitewashed walls, an architectural feature repeated in the interior of the tiny restaurant with its arched, low ceiling. Casual yet often filled with businesspeople, it offers stewed broad beans Portuguese-style, codfish in a cream sauce, fried shrimp, clams prepared in garlic and olive oil, seafood rice, and other traditional dishes that are consistently good. Its name, by the way, refers to a type of Portuguese boat, which is appropriate for a colony founded by seafaring explorers.

**A Petisqueira.** Rua S. João, 15, Taipa Village, Taipa Island. ☎ **853/825354.** Main courses HK$50–HK$125 ($6.50–$16.25). MC, V. Mon–Fri noon–3pm and 6:30–11pm; Sat–Sun and holidays noon–11pm. Bus: no. 11, 22, 28A, 33, or 34. PORTUGUESE.

A small, unpretentious restaurant just off Taipa Village's main road, on the corner of Rua de S. João and Rua das Virtudes, it offers typical Portuguese fare, including codfish grilled, roasted, or boiled; grilled sole with lemon butter sauce; seafood beans; grilled quail; paella; fried tenderloin steak Portuguese style; and baked seafood casserole. All grilled dishes are cooked over a charcoal grill. The fresh cheeses are especially recommended. Of course, everything tastes better with Portuguese wine.

**Balichão.** Parque de Seac Pai Van, Colôane Island. ☎ **853/870098.** Main courses HK$45–HK$88 ($5.85–$11.45). AE, DC, MC, V. Daily noon–11pm. Bus: no. 21A, 25, 26, 26A. MACANESE/PORTUGUESE.

If you're off to explore the islands, I can't think of a more peaceful place for a meal than this, located amidst the greenery of Colôane Island's largest park and offering outdoor dining on a terrace. What's more, its excellent food is so reasonably priced that dining in this family-owned restaurant feels awfully close to exploitation. Yet it's easy to see that the food, which includes intriguing dishes based on family recipes that trace the history of Macanese cuisine, is cooked with love. Choices include *lacassa* (Macanese noodle stew), *minchi* (a very old Macanese dish of minced meat with potato and rice), pork spareribs with clove and cinnamon, pork casserole flavored with tamarind and shrimp paste, shrimp and crabmeat curry with quail eggs, and king prawn with white wine and garlic. There are also more common dishes like African chicken, Macau sole, and crab curry. After your meal, you might wish to stroll through the park's small, free zoo or museum dedicated to agriculture in Macau.

**Caçarola Restaurante.** Rua das Gaivotas, 8, Colôane Village, Colôane Island. ☎ **853/ 882226.** Reservations recommended on weekends. Main courses HK$42–HK$80 ($5.45– $10.40). AE, MC, V. Tues–Sun 12:30–3pm and 7:30–10pm. Bus: no. 21, 21A, 25, 26, or 26A. PORTUGUESE.

This is a tiny two-story restaurant, popular with the locals for its traditional, country-style Portuguese food. Located in a Chinese village house just off the main square in Colôane Village (Vila Colôane), just a few minutes' walk from the St. Francis Xavier Chapel, it offers a small menu that changes daily, drawn from more than 200 authentic recipes from all over Portugal. Some of the frequent specialties are an excellent baked codfish with cream, turkey Stroganoff, pork in wine sauce, duck rice, beefsteak Portuguese-style, and ministeak. Other dishes that have appeared on the menu include the following: shredded codfish with potatoes and egg, oven-roasted fish Portuguese style, stewed squid, grilled octopus, rabbit stew, or, for the more adventurous, "piglet paws stew with chickpea" or "chicken rice cooked in own blood." Cheese, sausage, ham, and wine are imported. In nice weather, you may want to sit at one of the three tables outside on the tiny balcony, where you can look upon ancient tiled roofs and listen to the clicking of mahjong.

**Cozinha Pinocchio.** Rua do Sol, Taipa Village, Taipa Island. ☎ **853/827128** or 853/827328. Main courses HK$48–HK$118 ($6.25–$15.35). MC, V. Daily noon–10pm. Bus: no. 11, 22, 28A, 33, or 34. PORTUGUESE/MACANESE.

Taipa Island's first Western restaurant is going strong, though some who have known it since its early days claim that the atmosphere became more staid when a roof was added to the original roofless two-story brick warehouse. Nevertheless, things are still hopping—people crowd its doors for specialties like curried crab, king prawns, charcoal-grilled sardines, fried codfish cakes, grilled spareribs, roast veal, roast quail, and Portuguese-style cooked fish. The wine list is extensive. It's located off the main street (Rua do Cunha) in Taipa Village and is not to be confused with the much smaller Pinocchio II, which lies directly on Rua do Cunha and is under different ownership.

**Fat Siu Lau.** Rua da Felicidade, 64. ☎ **853/573580.** Main courses HK$45–HK$135 ($5.85–$17.55). No credit cards. Daily 11:30am–11:30pm. Bus: no. 3, 3A, 5, 6, 7, 8, 10, 11, 18, 19, 21, or 21A. MACANESE.

This is Macau's oldest restaurant (dating from 1903), but its three floors of dining have been renovated in upbeat modern art deco. Its exterior matches all the other storefronts on this renovated street—whitewashed walls and red shutters and doors. Macanese cuisine is served here, including roast pigeon marinated according to a 90-year-old secret recipe; spicy African chicken; curried crab; garoupa stewed with tomatoes, bell pepper, onion, and potatoes; and grilled king prawns.

**✪ Fernando's.** Praia de Hac Sa, 9, Colôane. ☎ **853/882264** or 853/882531. Reservations not accepted. Main courses HK$60–HK$148 ($7.80–$19.20). No credit cards. Daily noon– 9:30pm. Bus: no. 21A, 25, or 26A. PORTUGUESE.

For years Fernando's was just another shack on Hac Sa Beach. Although outwardly there is nothing to distinguish it from the others (it's the one closest to the beach, below the vines), a brick pavilion was recently added on the back, complete with ceiling fans and an adjacent open-air bar with outdoor seating (open daily noon to midnight). Now everyone knows Fernando's, and even though there's no air-conditioning (that goes for the kitchen as well), it doesn't seem to deter the faithful who pilgrimage here, especially on weekends, when you'll probably have to wait for a table. Out-spoken Fernando is usually on hand, holding court. The menu is strictly Portuguese and includes prawns, crabs, mussels, codfish, feijoada, veal, chicken, pork ribs, suckling pig, beef, and salads. The bread all comes from the restaurant's own bakery, and the vegetables are grown on the restaurant's own garden plot across the border in China. Only Portuguese wine is served, stocked on a shelf for customer perusal (there is no wine list). Very informal, and not for those who demand pristine conditions.

✪ **Galo.** Rua dos Clérigos, 45, Taipa Village, Taipa Island. ☎ **853/827423** or 853/827318. Main courses HK$40–HK$140 ($5.20–$18.20). No credit cards. Daily 11:30am–3pm and 5:30–10:30pm. Bus: no. 11, 22, 28A, 33, or 34. PORTUGUESE/MACANESE.

A delightful, two-story house in Taipa Village has been converted into this informal and festively decorated restaurant specializing in local cuisines and unique creations of the talented owner/chef. "Galo" means rooster in Portuguese; look for the picture of the rooster outside the restaurant. Its menu, which includes photographs of each dish, offers such house specialties as Macau crabs, prepared with a mixture of Shanghainese and Macanese ingredients, rather than curry. You might also want to try giant prawns, mussels, African chicken, Portuguese broadbeans, or the mixed grill. In any case, be sure to start out with the *sopa da casa* (house soup), made from potatoes, red beans, onions, and vegetables simmered in broth from boiled beef and sausages. Delicious!

**Henri's Galley Maxim's.** Avenida da República, 4. ☎ **853/556251** or 853/562231. Main courses HK$47–HK$95 ($6.10–$12.35). MC, V. Daily 11am–11pm. Bus: no. 28B. MACANESE/PORTUGUESE.

Located on the Outer Harbour below the venerable Bela Vista (now the Portuguese Embassy), this 25-year-old restaurant was once *the* place to dine on the tree-shaded waterfront. Now the Bela Vista has closed as a hotel, the waterfront has been compromised with reclaimed land, and Macau's socially conscious have moved on to trendier restaurants. Still, this remains a good choice for Macanese and Portuguese cuisine. It's owned by Henri Wong, a jovial and friendly man who used to be chief steward in a galley at sea; he has decorated his restaurant as though he were still aboard ship. The waiters, dressed as stewards, are attentive and there are a few seats outdoors under umbrellas. Specialties of the house include fried Macau sole, Portuguese roast fish, African chicken, Portuguese baked chicken, bacalhau, feijoada, curry crab, spicy giant prawns, steaks, and stuffed crabmeat in its shell, but there are also sandwiches priced at less than HK$42 ($5.45). Expect to spend about HK$120 ($15.60) for dinner.

**O Porto Interior.** Rua do Almirante Sergio, 259B. ☎ **853/967770.** Main courses HK$50–HK$88 ($6.50–$11.45); fixed-price lunch HK$58 ($7.55). AE, DC, MC, V. Daily noon–3 and 6–11:30pm. Bus no. 1, 1A, 2, 5, 6, 7, 8, 9, 10, 10A, 11, 18, 21, 21A, or 28B. MACANESE/PORTUGUESE.

Located on the Inner Harbour not far from the Maritime Museum and A-Ma Temple, this comfortable, classy restaurant decorated in colonial style with woodwork carvings, a brick floor, and decorative birdcages offers surprisingly inexpensive fare, making it a good value. You might wish to start with grilled Portuguese sausage, spicy shrimp, or the seafood supreme soup, served inside a bread bowl. Main dishes range from Macau curry crab and Macanese garlic king prawns to African chicken, black pepper steak, and *minchi,* a Macanese dish prepared here with pork cubes, potatoes, onion, garlic, and fried egg.

**Solmar.** Avenida da Praia Grande, 8–10. ☎ **853/574391.** Main courses HK$62–HK$155 ($8.05–$20.15). MC, V. Daily 11am–11:30pm. Bus: no. 3, 3A, 10, 10A, 26, 26A, or 33. PORTUGUESE.

Everyone comes to this typical Portuguese cafe/restaurant to socialize and gossip. One of Macau's old-timers, this 40-year-old landmark is quite informal and has wasted no money on decor. Although specializing in seafood and African chicken, the menu also lists Macau sole, curried crab, Portuguese vegetable soup, prawns in hot sauce, bacalhau, steaks, and of course, Portuguese wines. Often crowded, it's located across from the Metropole Hotel.

## INEXPENSIVE

**Estrela do Mar.** Travessa do Paiva, 11. ☎ **853/322074.** Main courses HK$35–HK$95 ($4.55–$12.35). AE, MC, V. Daily 11:30am–11:30pm. PORTUGUESE/MACANESE.

Located on a side street off Rua da Praia Grande, across from the beautiful, pink-colored former colonial government palace, this small, unpretentious yet modern restaurant serves inexpensive Portuguese cuisine and is a longtime Macau favorite. The menu lists Portuguese or African chicken, Macau sole, spicy fried prawns, bacalhau, lamb dishes, and nine different kinds of curries, including curried crab and vegetarian curry. You can also dine on sandwiches, omelets, spaghetti, and snacks for less than HK$35 ($4.55). A couple of tables are outside on the sidewalk.

**Long Kei.** Largo do Senado, 7B. ☎ **853/573970.** Main dishes HK$38–HK$70 ($4.95–$9.10). AE, DC, V. Daily 11:30am–10:30pm. Bus: no. 3, 3A, 10. CANTONESE.

If you're in the mood for Cantonese food, this well-known Chinese restaurant is located in the heart of town, right off Avenida de Almeida Ribeiro near the Macau Government Tourist Office on the main plaza. The menu lists more than 350 items, including shark's fin, bird's nest, abalone, chicken, frog, duck, seafood, pigeon, noodles, and vegetable combinations. Try the double-boiled shark's fin with chicken in soup or the minced quail with lettuce.

**Nga Tim Cafe.** Rua Caetano, No. 8, Colôane Village, Colôane Island. ☎ **853/882086.** Main courses HK$32–HK$65 ($4.15–$8.45). MC, V. Daily 11:30am–1am. Bus: no. 21, 21A, 25, 26, or 26A. CHINESE/MACANESE.

This lively, open-air, pavilion restaurant is on the tiny main square of Colôane Village, dominated by the charming Chapel of St. Francis Xavier. Its popularity with the locals on weekends and holidays lends it a festive, community-affair atmosphere; it's a great place for relaxing and watching couples stroll the square and children playing. The food, which combines Chinese and Macanese styles of cooking and ingredients, is in a category all its own, with many unique dishes not available anywhere else. Try the salt and pepper shrimp, chicken in an earthen pot, grilled duck with lemon sauce, steamed chicken with garlic, scallops with broccoli, or crab curry, accompanied by Portuguese wine. A good place to rub elbows with the natives.

**Pizzeria Toscana.** Avenida da Amizade (in front of the ferry terminal). ☎ **853/726637.** Pasta and pizza HK$42–HK$68 ($5.45–$8.85); meat dishes HK$55–HK$90 ($7.15–$11.70). AE, MC, V. Daily 9:30am–11pm. Closed first Tues of the month. Bus: no. 1A, 3, 3A, 10, 10A, 10B, 17, 28A, 28B, 28C, 32, and AP1. ITALIAN.

This casual pizzeria is located across from the ferry terminal, making it a good place for a meal if you're shopping at New Yaohan department store or waiting for a ferry. Although it doesn't look like much from the outside, its interior is cheerful and welcoming. After trying the fresh or smoked mozzarella cheese served with homemade garlic bread, you might want to opt for one of the many kinds of pizza or 24 kinds of pasta, including the black spaghetti di mare (seafood spaghetti). For a hearty meal, consider ordering the saltimbocca (stuffed beef fillet) or T-bone steak.

## 5  Exploring Macau

### THE TOP ATTRACTIONS

✪ **St. Paul's Church.** Rua de São Paulo. ☎ **853/358444.** Free admission. Grounds open daily 24 hours; museum Wed–Mon 9am–6pm. Bus: no. 3, 3A, or 10 to Largo do Senado square (off Avenida Almeida Ribeiro), then follow the wavy, tiled sidewalk leading uphill to the northeast about 10 min.

The most famous structure in Macau is the ruin of St. Paul's Church. Crowning the top of a hill in the center of the city and approached by a grand sweep of stairs, only its ornate facade and some excavated sites remain. It was designed by an Italian Jesuit and built in 1602 with the help of Japanese Christians who had fled persecution in Nagasaki. In 1835, during a typhoon, the church caught fire and burned to the ground, leaving only its now-famous facade. The facade is adorned with carvings and statues depicting Christianity in Asia, a rather intriguing mix of images: a Virgin Mary flanked by a peony (representing China) and a chrysanthemum (representing Japan), and a Chinese dragon, a Portuguese ship, and a demon. Beyond the facade is the excavated crypt, where in glass-fronted cases are kept the bones of 17th-century Christian martyrs from Japan and Vietnam. Here, too, is the tomb of Father Allesandro Valignano, founder of the Church of St. Paul and instrumental in establishing Christianity in Japan. Next to the crypt is the underground Museum of Sacred Art, which contains religious works of art produced in Macau from the 17th to 20th centuries. Included are very interesting 17th-century oil paintings by exiled Japanese Christian artists, crucifixes of filigree silver, carved wooden saints, and other sacred objects. Incidentally, also at St. Paul's Church is a counter of the Macau Government Tourist Office, open daily 9am to 6pm.

✪ **Museum of Macau.** Citadel of São Paulo do Monte (St. Paul Monte Fortress). ☎ **853/357 911.** Admission $15 ptcs ($1.95) adults, $8 ptcs ($1.05) senior citizens and children. Tues–Sun 10am–6pm. Located next to St. Paul's Church.

Located in the bowels of ancient Monte Fortress, this very ambitious project opened in 1998 and provides an excellent overview of Macau's history, local traditions, and arts and crafts. If you see only one museum in Macau, it should be this. Entrance is via an escalator located near St. Paul's Church. Arranged chronologically, the first floor depicts the beginnings of Macau and the arrival of Portuguese traders and Jesuit missionaries. Particularly interesting is the room comparing Chinese and European civilizations at the time of their encounter in the 16th century, including descriptions of their different writing systems, philosophies, and religions. The second floor deals with the daily life and traditions of old Macau, including festivals, wedding ceremonies, and industries ranging from fishing to fireworks factories. Displays include paintings and photographs depicting Macau through the centuries, traditional games and toys, an explanation of Macanese cuisine and architecture, and a re-created street in Macau lined with colonial and Chinese facades and containing tea, pastry, and traditional Chinese pharmacy shops. The top floor, the only one above ground, is of modern Macau and its plans for the future. From here you can exit to the wall ramparts of the fort, which was built by the Jesuits about the same time as St. Paul's, and largely destroyed by the same fire.

## MORE MUSEUMS & GALLERIES

**Grand Prix Museum.** Centro de Actividades Turisticas Macau, Rua de Luis Gonzaga Gomes. ☎ **853/7984108.** Admission $10 ptcs ($1.30) adults, $5 ptcs (65¢) children 11 to 18, free for senior citizens and children younger than 11. Combination ticket to Grand Prix Museum and Wine Museum $20 ptcs ($2.60). Wed–Mon 10am–6pm. Bus: no. 1A, 3, 3A, 10, 10A, 12, 17, 23, 28A, 28B, 28C, 32, or AP1.

One of two museums located in the Tourist Activity Center (see the Wine Museum, below), the Grand Prix Museum opened in 1993 to celebrate the 40th anniversary of the Macau Grand Prix. Its display hall is filled mainly with cars and motorcycles that have competed in the race through the years. Most interesting for visitors, perhaps, are the two simulators, each of which costs $20 ptcs ($2.60) extra and gives visitors the thrill of "experiencing" the Grand Prix (participants must be 12 years or older). One lets you be the driver as you steer and race other drivers on the Guia Circuit (first-timers might want to request automatic transmission!); the other lets you be a passenger of a real car driven in the 1995 Grand Prix. Be warned—a closed-circuit TV outside the simulator allows spectators to watch your every facial expression.

**Macau Museum of Art.** Macau Cultural Centre (Novos Aterros do Porto Exterior/NAPE), Avenida Xian Xing Hai. ☎ **853/351741.** Admission $5 ptcs (65¢) adults, $3 ptcs (40¢) senior citizens and children. Tues–Sun 10am–7pm. Bus: no. 1A or 23.

Located in the new Macau Cultural Centre on reclaimed land in the Outer Harbour, this small but interesting museum displays historical paintings, Chinese calligraphy, pottery, and works by contemporary local artists. Particularly fascinating are paintings by Western artists such as British painter George Chinnery and others, who painted scenes, people, and customs of Macau and Guangdong, including depictions of the port town as it looked long ago. Their works were often copied and then sold to visiting foreigners as souvenirs. Also impressive is the collection of Shiwan ceramic figurines. The Cultural Centre, by the way, also has a tourist information counter.

**✪ Maritime Museum.** Largo do Pagode da Barra, 1. ☎ **853/595481.** Admission $10 ptcs ($1.30) adults, $5 ptcs (65¢) children, free for senior citizens and children under 10. Sun and holidays, half price. Wed–Mon 10am–5:30pm. Bus: no. 1, 1A, 2, 5, 6, 7, 8, 9, 10, 10A, 11, 18, 21, 21A, or 28B.

Macau's oldest museum, ideally situated on the waterfront of the Inner Harbour where visitors can observe barges and other boats passing by, does an excellent job of tracing the history of Macau's lifelong relationship with the sea. It's located at the tip of the peninsula, across from the Temple of A-Ma, in approximately the same spot where the Portuguese first landed. The museum begins with dioramas depicting the legend of A-Ma, protectress of seafarers and Macau's namesake, and continues with models of various boats, including trawlers, Chinese junks, Portuguese sailing boats, and even modern jetfoils. There are also life-size original boats on display, ranging from the sampan to an ornate festival boat. Various fishing methods are detailed, from trawling and gill netting to purse seining, as well as various voyages of discovery around the world. The museum also has nautical equipment, navigation instruments used by the Portuguese and Chinese, and a small aquarium, with tanks of exotic fish and a collection of shells. Outside, near the snack bar, is a simulator, which allows two passengers to explore a reef filled with sea life and costs $15 ptcs ($1.95) extra. The museum also operates 30-minute boat tours aboard a restored fishing junk, with sailings of the Inner Harbour at 10:30am and 3:30pm and of the Outer Harbour at 11:30am and 4pm daily except Tuesday and the first Sunday of the month. I personally find the cruise through the Inner Harbour more striking, as it gives views of modern China on one side and decaying Macau on the other. Cost of the boat trip is $10 ptcs ($1.30) for adults and $5 ptcs (65¢) for children. Senior citizens and children younger than 10 sail free. Note, however, that the junk sails only if a minimum of six persons show up.

**Wine Museum.** Centro de Actividades Turisticas Macau, Rua de Luis Gonzaga Gomes. ☎ **853/7984188.** Admission $15 ptcs ($1.95) adults, $5 (65¢) children 11 to 18, free for senior citizens and children younger than 11. Combination ticket to Wine Museum and Grand Prix Museum $20 ptcs ($2.60) adults, $10 ptcs ($1.30) children. Wed–Mon 10am–6pm. Bus: no. 1A, 3, 3A, 10, 10A, 12, 17, 23, 28A, 28B, 28C, 32, or AP1.

Located in the same building as the Grand Prix Museum, this is Asia's first museum dedicated to wine. Modeled like a wine cellar, it begins with a brief history of wine making, starting with its discovery by Egyptians and Phoenicians in 6000 to 4000 B.C. and its spread from Greece through the rest of Europe, reaching Portugal about A.D. 1100. On display are wine presses, storage barrels, harvesting tools, and other wine-making equipment, as well as descriptions of every wine-growing region in Portugal. Wine production in China is also presented. Highlight of the museum is the free wine tasting of red, white, or verde wine. Bottles of Portuguese wine can also be purchased.

**Gallery in the Provisional Municipal Council (formerly Leal Senado).** Largo do Senado. ☎ **853/573500.** Free admission. Daily 9am–9pm (exhibition rooms closed Mon).

The Leal Senado, located in the heart of the city just off Avenida Almeida Ribeiro, is considered Macau's most outstanding example of Portuguese colonial architecture. Once home of Macau's Loyal Senate, made up of leading citizens, it is now used for municipal offices. You can enter to see the carved stone plaques, blue-and-white tiled walls, wrought-iron gate, inner garden, and beautiful public library, which was built in the 1920s and boasts one of the world's best collections of English-language literature on China. Most interesting for visitors to Macau, however, is the gallery to the right of the main entrance that is used for changing exhibits of local interest. During one of my visits, there was a photographic essay of Macau during the last 150 years, providing fascinating insight into the history of the territory; another was an exhibit of contemporary art by Macau artists. Since admission is free, it's worth stopping by to see what's being shown. But be sure, too, to see the garden at the top of the stairs from the main entry. It features more examples of Portuguese tile, wrought-iron gates, and busts of the poet Luís de Camões (to the left) and Governor Amaral (to the right).

# TEMPLES

**Temple of Kun Iam Tong (Temple of the Goddess of Mercy).** Avenida do Coronel Mesquita. Free admission. Daily 8am–6pm (5pm in winter). Bus: no. 12, 17, 18, 19, 22, or 23.

Of the many temples in Macau, one of the most important is the Temple of Kun Iam Tong, founded in the 13th century. Its present buildings date from 1627. The most significant historical event that took place at this largest and wealthiest of Macau's Buddhist temples was the 1844 signing of the first treaty of trade and friendship between the United States and China; the round granite table where the treaty was signed is still here. The stairs of the main temple are guarded by stone lions; it's said that if you turn the stone ball they hold in their mouths three times to the left you'll have good luck, but now the lions are protected from the public by wire mesh. The temple houses images of Buddha, representing the past, present, and future, as well as the goddess of mercy (Kun Iam) dressed in the costume of a Chinese bride. She is attended by 18 gold-lacquered figures lining the walls that represent the 18 wise men of China. Curiously enough, the figure on the far left front, with bulging eyes and mustache, is identified here as Marco Polo, who, having embraced Buddhism, came

# Macau Attractions

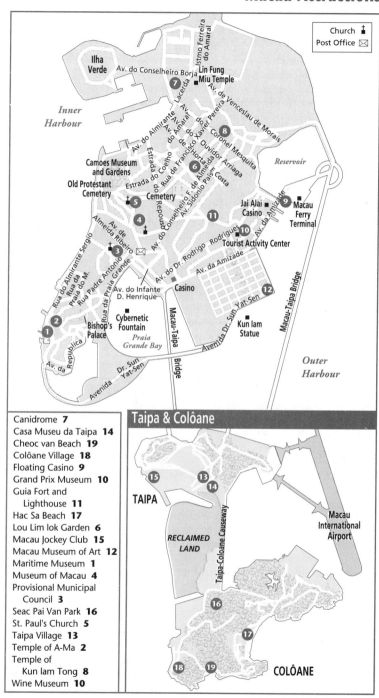

Church ✝
Post Office ✉

Ilha Verde

Inner Harbour

Av. do Conselheiro Borja

Istmo Ferreira do Amaral

Lin Fung Miu Temple

❼

Av. de Venceslau de Morais

❽

Reservoir

Camoes Museum and Gardens

Av. do Almirante Av.
Estrada do Coelho
Av. do Amaral
Av. dos Francisco Xavier Pereira
Rua de Francisco Xavier Pereira
Rua do Ouvidor Arriaga
de Hortala
Coronel Mesquita

Old Protestant Cemetery

Estrada do Repouso

Cemetery

❺

❻

Av. do Conselheiro F. de Almeida

Av. Sidónio Pais

❹

✝

❸ ✉

Av. de Almeida Ribeiro

Jai Alai Casino

Av. da Amizade

❾ Macau Ferry Terminal

❶❶

Av. do Dr. Rodrigo Rodrigues

❶⓪

Tourist Activity Center

Rua do Almirante Sergio
Rua da Praia do M.
Rua Padre Antonio
Rua da Praia Grande

❷

Av. do Infante D. Henrique

Casino

Av. da Amizade

❶❷

Bishop's Palace

Cybernetic Fountain

Praia Grande Bay

❶

Macau-Taipa Bridge

Kun Iam Statue

Outer Harbour

Av. da República

Avenida Dr. Sun Yat-Sen

Avenida Dr. Sun Yat-Sen

Macau-Taipa Bridge

Macau-Taipa Bridge

## Taipa & Colôane

❶❺

❶❸

TAIPA

❶❹

Macau International Airport

RECLAIMED LAND

Taipa-Colôane Causeway

❶❻

❶❼

COLÔANE

❶❽

❶❾

271

to be viewed as one of China's 18 wise men. Behind the temple is a landscaped Chinese garden; it has four banyan trees with intertwined branches, popularly known as the Lovers' Tree. According to local legend, the trees grew from the burial site of two lovers who committed suicide when they were forbidden to marry. But alas, the trees, considered symbols of marital fidelity, are now dying.

As you wander through the various buildings on the temple grounds, you will notice small funeral rooms with altars dedicated to the newly deceased, complete with photographs, offerings of fruit and other food, and paper money to assist the departed in the afterlife. You may even chance upon a funeral service, in which participants are dressed in white. Please show respect by being quiet, and refrain from taking photographs. It is also considered bad manners—not to mention bad luck—to take a picture of a monk without his permission.

**Temple of A-Ma.** Rua de S. Tiago da Barra. Free admission. Daily 8am–5pm. Bus: no. 1, 1A, 2, 5, 6, 7, 8, 9, 10, 10A, 11, 18, 21, 21A, or 28B.

Another important temple is situated at the bottom of Barra Hill at the entrance to the Inner Harbour, across from the Maritime Museum. It is Macau's oldest Chinese temple, with parts of it dating back more than 600 years. This temple is dedicated to A-Ma, goddess of seafarers. According to legend, a poor village girl sought free passage on a boat, but was refused until a small fishing boat came along and took her onboard. Once the boat was at sea, a typhoon blew in, destroying all boats except hers. Upon landing at what is now Barra Hill, the young girl revealed herself as A-Ma, and the fishermen repaid their gratitude by building this temple on the spot where they came ashore. At any rate, the temple was already here when the Portuguese arrived; they named their city A-Ma-Gao (Bay of A-Ma) after this temple. The name has been shortened to Macau now, of course. The temple has images of A-Ma and stone carvings of the Chinese fishing boat that carried A-Ma to Macau. The temple, spreading along the steep slope of a hill with views of the water, has good *fung shui*. There are several shrines set in the rocky hillside, linked by winding paths through moon gates. The uppermost shrine honors Kun Iam, the Goddess of Mercy, and affords good views of the Inner Harbour.

## A GARDEN

**Lou Lim Iok Garden.** Estrada de Adolfo Loureiro. Admission $1 ptc (13¢). Daily from dawn to dusk. Bus: no. 5, 9, 12, 22, or 28C.

Macau's most flamboyant Chinese garden was built in the 19th century by a wealthy Chinese merchant and modeled after the famous gardens in Soochow. Tiny, with narrow winding paths, bamboo groves, a nine-turn zigzag bridge (believed to deter evil spirits), and ponds filled with carp, it's a nice escape from the city. If possible, come in the morning, when the garden is filled with Chinese doing *tai chi chuan* exercises, musicians practicing traditional Chinese music, and bird lovers strolling with their birds in ornate wooden cages.

## TAIPA & COLÔANE ISLANDS

And of course, don't forget Macau's two islands—Taipa and Colôane. They are the city's breathing space, Macau's playground, a good place to get away from it all.

### TAIPA

Closest to the mainland, Taipa was accessible only by ferry until 1974, when the Macau-Taipa Bridge was finally completed. Now the second New Macau-Taipa Bridge, constructed for easy access to the airport, has led to increased development on Taipa, including new apartment blocks and booming suburbs that have pushed the

# Car Races & Fireworks—The Heat Is On!

Of Macau's several annual events, none is as popular or draws as many enthusiasts as the Macau Grand Prix, held in mid- to late November, and the Macau International Fireworks Display Contest, held on subsequent Saturdays from mid-September to the beginning of October.

The **Macau Grand Prix,** first staged in 1954, features races for motorcycles, production cars (international group A), and Formula Three racers, and attracts drivers from all over the world. Very similar to the famous circuit in Monaco, the 3.8-mile Guia Circuit, which winds through town near the ferry terminal and is lined with grandstands along the way, includes the winding roads of Guia Hill, hard corners around the waterfront, and the straightaway along the Outer Harbour. Champion drivers can complete a lap in as little as 2 minutes and 20 seconds. Tickets for stands during the 2 practice days cost HK$100 ($13), while race-day tickets range from HK$350 to HK$600 ($45.50 to $78). For ticket inquiries, contact the Macau Government Tourist Office. Note, however, that ferry tickets and hotel accommodations in Macau are tight during the races. Otherwise, race-car enthusiasts in Macau at other times of the year will want to visit the Grand Prix Museum, where simulators allow them to race the Guia Circuit.

Macau's other major competition, the **Macau International Fireworks Display Contest,** has a more universal appeal with its dazzling displays of fireworks, spread over 5 nights. Begun in 1988, it is now the world's biggest fireworks contest, with almost a dozen international teams competing. Displays last 20 minutes, and are judged using criteria such as the height reached by the fireworks, the explosive bang and spread of each firework, color and variety, and the overall choreographic effect of the each display. The best places to view the fireworks are along the Praia Grande, from Penha Hill, or from the Macau–Taipa Bridge.

---

population on this small, 2.5-square-mile island to 30,000. Taipa is also the home of several luxury hotels, Taipa Village with its popular restaurants and colonial architecture, a former firecracker factory, temples, the United Chinese Cemetery with its blend of Confucianist, Taoist, and Buddhist influences, a university, Macau Stadium, and the Macau Jockey Club for horse racing.

For history and architecture buffs, the first stop should be **Taipa Village,** a small traditional community of narrow lanes, alleys, and squares and two-story colonial buildings painted in hues of yellow, blue, and green. Although now almost completely engulfed by nearby housing projects, village life remains in full view here, with women sorting the day's vegetables on towels in the street, children playing, and workers carrying produce and goods in baskets balanced from poles on their shoulders. On or near Rua do Cunha, the picturesque main street with its hanging baskets of flowers, are a number of fine, inexpensive restaurants, making dining reason enough to come (see "Where to Dine," above).

But for sightseeing, the best place to visit is the **Casa Museu da Taipa (Taipa House Museum),** on Avenida da Praia (☎ 853/827088). It is one of five colonial-style buildings lining the street—homes that belonged to Macanese families in the early 1900s. Combining both European and Chinese design as a reflection of the families' Eurasian heritage, the Casa Museu has a dining and living room, study, kitchen, upstairs bedrooms, and large verandas that face banyan trees and the sea, reflecting the fact that most entertaining in this small colonial outpost took place at home. The home is filled with period furniture, paintings, art, and personal artifacts reflective of a dual heritage. The museum is open daily 10am to 8pm, and admission is free. Other buildings on the banyan-shaded Praia open to the public contain displays relating to the history of Taipa and its inhabitants, and traditional regional costumes of Portugal. Another building will eventually open as a restaurant. Next to the buildings, on a hill, is Our Lady of Carmel Church, built in the 19th century for the devout Macanese Catholics.

The easiest way to reach Taipa Village is via one of the buses that stops in front of the Hotel Lisboa near the bridge on the mainland. Bus nos. 11, 22, 28A, 33, and 34 all go to Taipa Village.

## COLÔANE

Farther away and connected to China via bridge and to Taipa via causeway and a huge added strip of reclaimed land that has essentially made the two islands one, Colôane once served as a haven for pirates who preyed upon the rich trading ships passing by. The last pirate raid was as late as 1910, when bandits kidnapped 18 children and demanded ransom. Government forces eventually overpowered the pirates, freeing all the children. At any rate, Colôane today, measuring 3 square miles but with a population of only 3,000, is less developed than Taipa and is known for its beaches, pine trees, hiking trails, golf course, and traditional village. Two of the most popular **beaches** are Cheoc Van and Hac Sa (which means "black sand"). Both beaches have lifeguards on duty in the summer, windsurfing boards for rent, restaurants, and nearby public swimming pools that are open until 10pm. To reach them, take bus no. 21A or 26A from Avenida de Almeida Ribeiro in the city center or from the Lisboa Hotel; bus no. 25 also runs from the Lisboa Hotel to both beaches.

For a bit of greenery, visit **Seac Pai Van Park** (☎ 853/870277), a 50-acre expanse on the island's western end with a walk-in aviary; a small zoo containing monkeys, cows, goats, geese, rabbits, and other animals; hillside trails; Chinese-style pavilions; a small botanical garden; a children's playground; a picnic area; and the excellent yet reasonably priced Balichão restaurant. There's also the Museum of Nature and Agriculture, dedicated to the geography, agriculture, flora, and fauna of Macau, including medicinal plants and displays on herbal remedies. On the grounds of the museum are life-size models of farmers and their families engaged in everyday tasks, such as rice farming, using traditional methods. The museum is open Tuesday to Sunday 10:30am to 4:30pm, while the park is open Tuesday to Sunday 8am to 6pm. Admission to both the park and the museum is free. To reach the park, take bus no. 21A or 26A from Avenida de Almeida Ribeiro in the city center or from the Lisboa Hotel; bus nos. 25 and 26 also stop at the park.

Farther along the coast is the laid-back, quaint community of **Colôane Village.** Now that Taipa Village has suffered so much surrounding development, I find Colôane Village much more picturesque and a worthy destination if exploring the islands. Located on the southwestern tip of the island, it is so close to China that it almost seems like you can reach out and touch it. Boats headed to and from China pass through the narrow waterway. The social center of the village revolves around a small, tiled square, which is lined on two sides with cloistered cafes. In its center is a monument erected in 1928 to commemorate those who fought in the 1910 battle against the pirates. At its end is the small but sweet **Chapel of St. Francis Xavier,** built in 1928 and dedicated to Asia's most important and well-known Catholic missionary. The church, built in classic Portuguese style, would seem rather plain if it weren't for its exuberant Asian artwork.

For more information on Taipa and Colôane, pick up a free pamphlet from the Macau tourist office called "Macau, Outlying Islands."

# 6 Gambling, Shopping & Nightlife

## GAMBLING

The Chinese so love gambling that it's often said that if two flies are walking on the wall, the Chinese will bet on which one will walk faster. It's not surprising, therefore, that Hong Kong Chinese make up about 80% of the 5.9 million annual visitors to Macau. Since the only legal gambling in Hong Kong are the horse races and mahjong, you can bet that most of the Chinese come to Macau to gamble, whether it's at the casinos or the tracks.

**CASINOS**    Altogether there are 12 casinos in Macau. Some are fancy, others aren't, but none allow photographs to be taken, and shorts may not be worn. Admission is free.

The most sophisticated casinos are those in hotels—the **Mandarin Oriental, Hyatt Regency, Kingsway Hotel, Holiday Inn,** and **Hotel Lisboa,** as well as at the **Jockey Club** on Taipa Island. The hotel casinos are open 24 hours and offer blackjack, baccarat, and Chinese games. The Hotel Lisboa, which has the busiest casino, also offers hundreds of slot machines (known, appropriately enough, as "hungry tigers" in Chinese) and roulette. Casinos that cater largely to Chinese include the **Casino Kam Pek,** on Avenida Almeida Ribeiro; the **Jai Alai,** once an arena for jai alai but now a popular casino because it is close to the ferry terminal; and the **Floating Macau Palace Casino,** moored in the Outer Harbour not far from the Mandarin Oriental Hotel. The ornately decorated Floating Casino is worth strolling through for a look at Chinese gambling. Open 24 hours, it has slot machines on the top floor.

**RACETRACKS**    The **Macau Jockey Club** has its racetrack on Taipa Island (☎ **853/820868**); it features horse racing most Saturdays and/or Sundays at 1pm and Tuesdays at 8pm, September to June. The minimum bet is $10 ptcs ($1.30). Transportation is available by both public buses and air-conditioned coaches, which depart from in front of the Hotel Lisboa; tickets for the coach and raceway are available in the hotel lobby. The grandstand, which is air-conditioned, charges an admission of $20 ptcs ($2.60); outdoor public stands are free. Call for more information or stop by the Macau Government Tourist Office. Take bus no. 11, 22, 28A, 33, 34, 38, or AP1.

For racing of a different sort, check out the greyhound races, held on Monday, Thursday, Saturday, and Sunday at 8pm at the open-air **Canidrome,** Avenida General Castelo Branco, located near the border gate to China (☎ **853/333399**). Admission is $10 ptcs ($1.30), and the minimum bet is $40 ($5.20). Take bus no. 1, 1A, 3, 4, 5, 16, 26A, 32, or 33.

## SHOPPING

A duty-free port, Macau has long been famous for its jewelry stores, especially those offering gold jewelry along Avenida do Infante D. Henrique and Avenida de Almeida Ribeiro. Market prices per tael (1.2 ounces) of gold are set daily; many Chinese consider them an investment. When buying gold or jewelry, always request a certificate of guarantee.

Portuguese wines are another good bargain, as are Chinese antiques and leather garments. In recent years, a number of fashionable clothing boutiques have also opened in the center of town. To my mind, they seem a bit out of place amid the crumbling colonial architecture; in any case, these boutiques can also be found in Hong Kong. More colorful are the clothing stalls near Largo do Senado square, many of which sell overruns and seconds from Macau's garment factories.

A significant indication of change was the 1993 opening of Macau's first full-fledged department store, **New Yaohan**—conveniently situated next to the ferry terminal (☎ **853/725338**). Modeled after Japanese department stores, New Yaohan features four floors of clothing, accessories, cosmetics, jewelry, toys, gifts, electronics, and household goods. It also has a Mister Minit for shoe repairs, an optical shop, a bakery, a liquor store, and even a children's playroom with games, rides, and activities fueled by $2 ptcs (25¢) tokens. On the third floor is the Food Plaza, where various counters offer grilled chicken, pizza, Japanese food, snacks, desserts, and drinks. New Yaohan is open daily 11am to 10:30pm.

Macau's first department store was followed in 1998 by **The Landmark,** located on Avenida da Amizade not far from the Hotel Lisboa. This fashionable complex houses approximately 60 shops, including designer boutiques, jewelry stores, interior decoration shops, and a duty-free department store.

## NIGHTLIFE

For many years, the only nighttime entertainment outside gambling and the horse races centered on hotel bars and lounges. While these are still recommendable for a drink and live entertainment, one of the few benefits to have arisen from the otherwise hideously sterile reclaimed-land development on the Outer Harbour is the Docks, an unofficial name given to a string of sidewalk cafes and bars lining Avenida Dr. Sun Yat-sen near the Kun Iam Statue. They're great places for a drink and watching the parade of people file past. True to Macau's Mediterranean roots, the action doesn't start until after 10pm and is at its most frenetic after 1am. For a suggestion, try **Opiarium** (☎ **853/750975**), which opens at 7pm and offers live bands on weekends.

# Appendix:
# Hong Kong in Depth

**A**lthough some people might erroneously believe that Hong Kong's history began after the British took control of the island in 1842, it actually begins millennia before that. Stone, bronze, and iron artifacts indicate that Hong Kong Island has been inhabited for at least 6,000 years, and more than 100 Neolithic and Bronze Age sites have been identified throughout the territory, including a 5,000-year-old kiln unearthed on Lantau Island, 4,000-year-old burial grounds, a 2,000-year-old brick tomb, and Neolithic rock carvings.

## 1 History 101

### EARLY SETTLERS
Although the area now called Hong Kong became part of the Chinese empire some 2,200 years ago during the Han dynasty, it was not until after the 12th century that the area became widely settled. Foremost were settler families, known as the "Five Great Clans," who built walled cities complete with moats and gatehouses to protect their homes against roving pirates; a few of these walled cities remain. First to arrive was the Tang clan, who built at least five walled villages and maintained imperial connections with Beijing for 800 years, until the end of the 19th century. The other four clans were the Hau, Pang, Liu, and Man. The clans were joined by the Tanka people, who lived their whole lives on boats anchored in sheltered bays throughout the territory, and by the Hoklos, another seafaring people who established coastal fishing villages. They were followed by the Hakka, primarily farmers who cultivated rice, pineapples, and tea. There were also garrison troops stationed at Tuen Mun and Tai Po (now major satellite towns in the New Territories) to guard pearls harvested from Tolo Harbour by Tanka divers, while forts to guard against invasion were constructed at Tung Chung and other coastal regions.

### TEA & OPIUM
Hong Kong's modern history, however, begins a mere 160 years ago, under conditions that were far less than honorable. During the 1800s the British were extremely eager to obtain Chinese silk and tea. Tea had become the national drink, but the only place it was grown was China, and it was being imported to England in huge quantities. The British tried to engage the Chinese in trade, but the Chinese were not interested in anything offered—only silver bullion would do. The

## Dateline

- **4,000–1,500 B.C.** Early settlers of Asian Mongoloid stock spread throughout South China, including Hong Kong, leaving behind Neolithic artifacts ranging from pottery and stone tools to burial grounds.
- **221 B.C.** Hong Kong becomes part of the Chinese empire with unification of China by the first emperor of Qin.
- **700 B.C.** Seafaring people of Malay-Oceanic stock set up floating communities in Hong Kong.
- **960–1500s** Pirates roam the seas around Hong Kong.
- **1514** Portuguese traders establish a base on Hong Kong.
- **1839** The Chinese emperor attempts to abolish the opium trade and destroys the British opium stockpile; the Royal Navy retaliates by firing on Chinese war junks, starting the first Opium War.
- **1841** British naval Capt. Charles Elliot seizes Hong Kong Island and declares himself governor.
- **1842** The first Opium War ends in the Treaty of Nanking, ceding Hong Kong Island to Britain in perpetuity.
- **1846** Hong Kong's population is 24,000. First horse races held at Happy Valley.
- **1856** Chinese officials searching for pirates arrest the crew of a British ship, prompting the second Opium War, which ends in 1858.
- **1857** A popular Chinese baker, Cheong Ah Lum, is accused of putting arsenic into his bread and poisoning nearly 300 Europeans in retaliation for the Opium Wars. He is acquitted but deported to China.

*continues*

Chinese also forbade the British to enter their kingdom, with the exception of a small trading depot in Canton.

But then the British hit upon a commodity that proved irresistible—opium. Grown in India and exported by the British East India Company, this powerful drug enslaved everyone from poor peasants to the nobility, and before long China was being drained of silver, traded to support a drug habit. The Chinese emperor, fearful of the damage being wreaked on Chinese society and alarmed by his country's loss of silver, declared a ban on opium imports in the 1830s. The British simply ignored the ban, smuggling their illegal cargo up the Pearl River. In 1839, with opium now India's largest export, the Chinese confiscated the British opium stockpiles in Canton and destroyed them. The British responded by declaring war and then winning the struggle. As a result of this first Opium War, waged until 1842, China was forced to open new ports for trade, agree to an exorbitant cash indemnity for the loss of the destroyed opium, and cede Hong Kong Island in perpetuity to the British in a treaty China never recognized. Not only was this Treaty of Nanking demoralizing to the Chinese, it also ensured that their country remain open to the curse of opium.

Following the second Opium War, waged from 1856 to 1858, the tip of Kowloon Peninsula and Stonecutters Island were added to the colony in 1860. In 1898, Britain decided it needed more land for defense and dictated a lease for the New Territories, including more than 200 outlying islands, for 99 years, until 1997. Approximately 100,000 Chinese were living in the New Territories at the time.

## THE PROMISED LAND

When the British took control of Hong Kong Island in 1842, some 7,000 Chinese lived on the island in farming and fishing communities. Britain's prospects for developing a thriving port, however, did not look rosy. Although Hong Kong had a deep and protected harbor, no one, including the Chinese, was much interested in the island itself, and many in the British government considered its acquisition an embarrassing mistake. Lord Palmerston, Queen Victoria's foreign secretary, dismissed Hong Kong as a "barren island with hardly a house upon it." What's more, no sooner had the island been settled than a typhoon tore through the settlement. Repairs were demolished only 5 days later by another tropical storm. Fever and fire followed, and the weather grew so oppressive and humid that the colony seemed to be enveloped in a giant steam bath.

Yet while the number of headstones in the hillside cemetery multiplied, so did the number of the living, especially as word spread of the fortunes being made by traders who built up the *hongs*, or trading houses. By 1846 the population had reached an astonishing 24,000. By the turn of the century the number had swelled to 300,000. British families lived along the waterfront and called it Victoria (now the Central District), slowly moving up toward the cooler temperatures of Victoria Peak. The Chinese, barred from occupying the Peak and other European-only neighborhoods, resided in a shantytown farther west, now called the Western District. In a typical Hong Kong dwelling, four Chinese families shared one room, along with their animals. Conditions were so appalling that when the bubonic plague struck in 1894, it raged for almost 30 years, claiming more than 20,000 lives.

Most of the newcomers to Hong Kong were mainland Chinese, who arrived with the shirts on their backs and nothing to lose. Every turmoil that sent a shudder through China—famine, flood, or civil war—flung a new wave of farmers, merchants, peasants, coolies, and entrepreneurs into Hong Kong. Everyone's dream was to make a fortune; it was just a matter of timing and good *joss* (luck). The Chinese philosophy of hard work and good fortune found fertile ground in the laissez-faire atmosphere of the colony.

Hong Kong's growth in the 20th century was no less astonishing in terms of both trade and population. In 1900, approximately 11,000 ships pulled into Hong Kong harbor each year; just a decade later, the number had doubled. In 1911 the overthrow of the Manchu dynasty in China sent a flood of refugees into Hong Kong, followed in 1938 by an additional 500,000 immigrants. Another mass influx of Chinese refugees arrived after the fall of Shanghai to the Communists in 1950. From this last wave of immigrants, including many Shanghai industrialists, emerged the beginnings of Hong Kong's now-famous textile industry. Throughout the 1950s, Hong Kong grew as a manufacturing and industrial center for electronics, watches, and other low-priced goods. By 1956, Hong Kong's population stood at 2.5 million.

- **1860** Victorious in the second Opium War and seeking a foothold on the mainland, Britain forces China to cede Kowloon Peninsula and Stonecutters Island to the British in perpetuity in the First Convention of Peking. Population reaches 94,000.
- **1865** Hongkong and Shanghai Bank founded.
- **1888** The Victoria Peak tram is completed, reducing the journey to the peak from 3 hours to 8 minutes.
- **1898** With the signing of the Second Convention of Peking, the New Territories are leased to Britain for 99 years, for which Britain pays nothing.
- **1900** Hong Kong's population is 263,000.
- **1904** The street tramway system is constructed along the waterfront on Hong Kong Island.
- **1910** The Kowloon Railway is completed, linking Hong Kong with China.
- **1911** The Manchu dynasty is overthrown by Sun Yat-sen's Nationalist revolution; refugees flood into Hong Kong.
- **1925** Hong Kong's first and only general strike; Nationalists and Communists join in a United Front, organizing anti-foreign strikes and boycotts in China that spread to Hong Kong, paralyzing the economy.
- **1938** Japan seizes Canton; Hong Kong becomes an arms-smuggling route for the Nationalist forces, now under Chiang Kai-shek; 500,000 Chinese refugees flee into Hong Kong.
- **1941** Japanese forces occupy Hong Kong.
- **1945** The British resume control of Hong Kong following World War II.

*continues*

- **1949** Mao declares the founding of the People's Republic; a subsequent flood of refugees to Hong Kong causes the Communist government to seal the Chinese–Hong Kong border.
- **1950** Mass influx of refugees continues following the fall of Shanghai to the Communists. Population of Hong Kong reaches 2 million.
- **1953** Following a huge fire in a squatter camp, Hong Kong begins an ambitious public housing program to house its still-growing population of refugees.
- **1966** A fare increase on the Star Ferry prompts clashes between Chinese and the police.
- **1967** The Cultural Revolution in China leads to pro-Communist riots in Hong Kong; 51 people are killed, and hundreds more are wounded or arrested in the fighting.
- **1972** First cross-harbor tunnel opens.
- **1978** Vietnamese refugees pour into Hong Kong at a rate of 600 a day.
- **1979** Hong Kong's Mass Transit Railway subway system opens. Hong Kong governor Sir Murray MacLehose goes to Beijing for the first Sino-British discussions on the return of Hong Kong to Chinese rule.
- **1981** British Parliament downgrades Hong Kong passports to prevent an exodus of Hong Kong Chinese to the United Kingdom.
- **1984** China and Britain sign the Joint Declaration for the handover of Hong Kong to China in 1997.
- **1989** Events at Tiananmen Square in Beijing send shock waves through Hong Kong. Some 80,000 demonstrators brave a typhoon in support

*continues*

# CHANGE, UNREST & THE LAST OF THE BRITISH

As a British colony, Hong Kong was administered by a governor appointed by the queen. There were no free elections, and the Legislative Council, Hong Kong's main governing body, was also appointed. As 1997 drew nearer, marking the end of the 99-year lease on the New Territories, it soon became clear that China had no intention of renewing the lease or renegotiating a treaty it had never recognized in the first place.

Finally, after more than 20 rounds of talks and meetings, Britain's Prime Minister Margaret Thatcher signed the Sino-British Joint Declaration of 1984, agreeing to transfer all of Hong Kong to Chinese Communist rule on June 30, 1997. For its part, China declared Hong Kong a "Special Administrative Region," granting it special privileges under a "one country, two systems" policy that guaranteed Hong Kong's capitalist lifestyle and social system for at least 50 years after 1997. Under provisions set forth in the Sino-British Joint Declaration and in Hong Kong's constitution, the Basic Law, Hong Kong would remain largely self-governing, and its people would retain rights to their property, to freedom of speech, and to travel freely in and out of Hong Kong. Throughout the negotiations concerning Hong Kong, its residents were never consulted about their future.

Then came the events of June 1989 in Tiananmen Square, in which hundreds of students and demonstrators were attacked by Chinese authorities in a brutal move to quash the pro-democracy movement. China's response to the uprising sent shock waves through Hong Kong and led to rounds of angry protest.

Those who could, emigrated, primarily to Australia, Canada, and the United States; at its height, more than 1,000 were emigrating each week. After all, nearly half of Hong Kong's Chinese are refugees from the mainland, and as one Hong Kong Chinese told me, his family had fled to escape Communist rule, so why should he remain after 1997? The vast majority of Chinese, however, remained, confident or at least hopeful that China realized it had more to gain by keeping Hong Kong as it was. In a move that angered Communist China, Hong Kong Chinese were granted more political autonomy during in the last few years of the colony's existence than in all the preceding 150 years, including various democratic reforms such as elections for the Legislative Council. Some early emigrants began returning to Hong Kong, confident they could do better in their native country and willing to wait to see how life might change under the Chinese.

On June 30, 1997, the last British governor of Hong Kong, Chris Patten, sailed out of Hong Kong, and Tung Chee-hwa, appointed by Beijing, became the new chief executive of the Special Administrative Region (SAR). Mainland China celebrated the event as the end of more than 100 years of shame. On July 1, it dissolved Hong Kong's elected Legislative Council and replaced it with a hand-picked Provisional Legislature until a new Legislative Council, with both elected and appointed members, could be formed. Hong Kong's first elections under Chinese rule, held in May 1998, allowed for one-third of the 60-member legislature to be elected by direct popular vote, with the Democrats, Hong Kong's largest party, winning the most seats. Although Democrat leader Martin Lee declared he would press for the entire legislature to be elected by popular vote in 2000 and for direct election of Hong Kong's chief executive, few believed it would happen, since the Basic Law's timeline for a fully elected legislature and democratically selected chief executive wasn't until after 2007.

At the end of May, an ominous foreshadowing of the future seemed to pass over Hong Kong when Yan Jiaqi, a Chinese dissident with a U.S. travel permit, was refused entry into Hong Kong after attending a meeting in Macau with other exiled activists. On the other hand, shortly thereafter Hong Kong police allowed 40,000 people to converge June 4 on Victoria Park to honor those killed in the 1989 military crackdown in Tiananmen Square.

## TRANSITION

On July 6, 1998, Hong Kong's new International Airport at Chek Lap Kok opened. This long-anticipated event, however, instead of giving Hong Kong a much needed boost of morale at a time when Asia was plunging deeper into a widespread financial crisis, shook public confidence when it was plagued with such problems as baggage delays, missed flights, poor cargo-handling service, and investigations into alleged bribery, corruption, and covering up of shoddy construction. Approval ratings for Tung and other government officials plunged, especially

of the pro-democracy uprising.

- **1992** Hong Kong governor Chris Patten announces new democratic reforms.

- **1995** Elections for the Legislative Council brings landslide victory for the Democrats; China announces it will dissolve the legislature after the handover.

- **1997** Britain transfers Hong Kong to Communist China, ending 156 years of British rule, in an agreement that allows Hong Kong—now a Special Administrative Region—to retain many of its freedoms for at least 50 years. Four thousand Chinese troops march in; Tung Chee-hwa becomes chief executive of the SAR. An outbreak of avian flu at the end of the year, killing four people, prompts the new government to order the slaughter of 1.3 million chickens.

- **1998** Hong Kong's first election under Chinese rule allows for one-third of the Legislative Council to be elected by popular vote; Democrats win the most seats. Hong Kong's new airport at Chep Lak Kok opens.

- **1999** Hong Kong's Court of Final Appeal rules that according to its constitution, Hong Kong residency can be extended to any mainland Chinese with one Hong Kong parent; Tung Chee-hwa invites Beijing to review the immigration ruling, which is subsequently overturned.

- **2000** Hong Kong's freedom of the press is threatened after a mainland official warns Hong Kong media against covering independence for Taiwan, followed by a crackdown on pornography.

after unemployment hit 4.5%, a 15-year high. Like the rest of Asia, Hong Kong was hit by economic recession, made worse by manufacturers moving across the Chinese border into Shenzhen to take advantage of cheaper land prices and cheaper wages.

In January 1999, Hong Kong's Court of Final Appeal ruled that the Basic Law granted Hong Kong residency to any mainland Chinese with one Hong Kong parent, even if that parent gained residency after the child was born. However, fearing unplanned population growth, with an estimated 1.6 million new immigrants potentially pouring in from the mainland, Tung Chee-hwa asked Beijing to review the immigration ruling. China responded by overturning the immigration judgment issued by Hong Kong's highest court and providing a narrower interpretation of the Basic Law, thereby cutting the number of potential immigrants over the next decade from 1.6 million to about 200,000. Mainland meddling with Hong Kong affairs continued in 2000, after a mainland official warned the Hong Kong media against covering independence for Taiwan. After elections in Taiwan swept in the Democratic Progressive Party over the Kuomintang, political activists in Hong Kong renewed calls for democratic elections in Hong Kong, saying 7 years was too long to wait for a Legislative Council and chief executive chosen by the people.

## 2 Hong Kong Today

Foremost in every visitor's mind today is, "How much has Hong Kong changed since the handover?" Actually, not much. In fact, if it hadn't dominated the news, I doubt the average tourist would even notice there'd *been* a handover. Entry formalities for Americans and most other nationalities remain unchanged. English remains an official language, and the English names of buildings, streets, and attractions have stayed the same. The Hong Kong dollar, pegged to the U.S. dollar, remains legal tender, and in most hotels, restaurants, and shops that cater to tourists, it's business as usual.

The differences? Most visible is the replacement of the Union Jack and colonial Hong Kong flag with China's starred flag and the new Hong Kong Special Administrative Region's flag emblazoned with the bauhinia flower. In addition, new coins bearing the bauhinia have been minted (the old coins with the queen's head remain valid but are being snapped up by collectors). There are also new stamps. Finally, the words "Royal" and "ER" (Elizabeth Regina) have disappeared throughout Hong Kong, along with royal crests, crowns, and coats of arms. The police wear new badges.

But there are other, more subtle differences. The British population dropped more than 10% in the first 6 months after the handover, due primarily to the completion of large construction projects such as the new airport and stricter regulations making it more difficult for casual workers to remain in the SAR. The decrease in Britons, including the military, has affected bars, restaurants, and other establishments that had long catered to the expatriate community; some of these have closed down. In fact, there are now more Americans (about 35,000) residing in Hong Kong than expats from the United Kingdom (about 22,000). Meanwhile, economic hardship throughout Asia has brought a new influx of expats looking for work, most notably Filipinos. And although border regulations between Hong Kong and China have remained largely unchanged, the SAR has been deluged with another flood of mainlanders—an estimated 50,000 a year, in addition to the 200,000 mainlanders recently given immigration status by authorities in Beijing.

## ❷ Did You Know?

- Hong Kong has more than 16,000 inhabitants per square mile, compared to 75 people per square mile in the United States.
- Although possessing only 400 square miles of land, Hong Kong is 70% rural, with about 40% preserved in country parks and reserves. About 60% of Hong Kong is mountainous.
- Hong Kong is the world's second-ranking reclaimer of land (after the Netherlands), with more than 15 square miles reclaimed over the past century. The new airport at Chek Lap Kok, occupying 5 square miles, is one of the largest reclamation projects in the world.
- Hong Kong is China's biggest overseas investor and second-largest trading partner. More than 50% of China's exports and one-third of its imports go through Hong Kong.

Yet even though Hong Kong has fared better than most of its neighbors, it has not been unaffected by the Asian financial crisis. Long-standing companies have gone bankrupt. Property and stock markets have nose-dived to unprecedented lows. Service industries, including hotels and restaurants, have had to downsize. Manufacturers have moved across the border to Shenzhen to take advantage of lower production costs. Other woes include fears that rights guaranteed by Hong Kong's constitution are being eroded by authorities in mainland China; every sign of hostility between Taiwan and Beijing sends shivers up the collective Hong Kong spine. Pollution, primarily from Hong Kong's increasing vehicular traffic and from regional diesel pollution in the Pearl River Delta, has reached an all-time high, threatening not only the health of its citizens but its status as a major tourist destination.

While there are indications that Asia is recovering from recession, and tourism shows signs of rebounding to its pre-1997 level, the past few years of hardship have worked to the benefit of tourists. For one thing, after tourism decreased following the 1997 handover, hotels were forced to offer attractive packages with much-reduced rates. Some budget hotels slashed their rates 30% or more. Restaurants also modified their meals and even lowered their prices, offering such bargains as all-you-can-eat buffets and fixed-price meals. In addition, ethnic and health-conscious restaurants have exploded onto the scene, offering good value and varied cuisine. Best of all, fewer tourists have meant smaller crowds. You may be able to get a seat in your favorite restaurant even without a reservation.

Still, no one can predict the future, as Hong Kong has always been a city in transformation. The Hong Kong I am writing about now is not the same city that existed just a few short years ago and is not the Hong Kong you'll probably experience when you go there. Changes occur at a dizzying pace: Relatively new buildings are torn down to make way for even newer, shinier skyscrapers; whole neighborhoods are obliterated in the name of progress; reclaimed land is taken from an ever-shrinking harbor; and traditional villages are replaced with satellite towns. Hong Kong's city skyline has surged upward and outward so dramatically since my first visit in 1983, it sometimes seems like decades rather than a year or two must have elapsed each time I see it anew. Change is commonplace, and yet it's hard not to lament the loss of familiar things that suddenly vanish; it's harder still not to brood over what's likely to come.

But these concerns are not new. Hong Kong, founded by the narcotics trade and created to make money, has always been a city on the go, obsessed with the present, worried but hopeful about the future, and indifferent to the past. Buildings have always been torn down to make way for the new, land reclamation has been ongoing almost from the beginning, and the population has exploded from a few thousand to more than six million in a mere 160 years. There are strikingly few monuments or statues to the city's past. Even the city's original settlement, once called Victoria but later renamed (less sentimentally) the Central District, long ago lost most of its colonial-age buildings.

But don't worry. If this is your first trip to Hong Kong, you're much more likely to notice its Chinese aspects than its Western elements. Ducks hanging by their necks in restaurant windows, bamboo scaffolding, herb medicinal shops, streetside markets, Chinese characters on huge neon signs, wooden fishing boats, shrines to the kitchen god, fortune-tellers, temples, laundry fluttering from bamboo poles, dim sum trolleys, and the clicking of mahjong tiles all conspire to create an atmosphere that is overwhelmingly Chinese.

But this is modern Hong Kong, so a picture of the city wouldn't be complete without mentioning the mobile cellular phone. Everyone, from housewives and students to sales clerks and business people, uses cell phones—more than 34% of Hong Kong's population. The phones are virtually everywhere, though some of the more enlightened restaurants forbid their use. You'll even see cell phones in the subway, since Hong Kong was the world's first to develop a mobile phone network that functions even underground. If you ask me, authorities missed the mark when they chose the bauhinia as the symbol of the new Hong Kong; it'd be much more appropriate to see a tiny cell phone in the middle of that flag.

## 3  Life in Hong Kong

### THE PEOPLE

With a population of approximately 6.8 million, Hong Kong is overwhelmingly Chinese—some 98% of its residents are Chinese, more than half of whom were born in Hong Kong. But the Chinese themselves are a diverse people and they hail from different parts of China. Most are Cantonese from southern China, the area just beyond Hong Kong's border—hence, Cantonese is one of the official languages of the region. Other Chinese include the Hakka, traditionally farmers whose women are easily recognizable by their hats with a black fringe, and the Tanka, the majority of Hong Kong's boat population. Hong Kong's many Chinese restaurants specializing in Cantonese, Szechuan, Chiu Chow, Pekingese, Shanghainese, and other regional foods are testaments of the city's diversity.

The Chinese are by nature a very hardworking, pragmatic people. There are many stories of refugees who arrived with nothing in their pockets, set up a small sidewalk stall, worked diligently until they had their own store, and then expanded it into a modest chain. In a land with virtually no raw materials, the people themselves have proved to be Hong Kong's greatest asset, geniuses at transforming imported raw goods into the electrical equipment, clothing, watches, toys, and other products that have made Hong Kong famous.

For the vast majority of Hong Kong's Chinese, there has been little—if any—discernible difference in their lives since the turnover. Many had little or no contact with their British rulers, and a long history of British racial discrimination prevented much intermingling. Not one Chinese I spoke to expressed regret that the British were gone; indeed, I had the distinct impression that more than a few were happy to see them go, as long as their own chances for making money were not affected. One government decision, however, impacted almost every young child in the SAR: Secondary school used to be taught in English throughout most of the colony, but most secondary schools now are taught in Chinese, with only a few English-language high schools remaining. While many Chinese welcome this change, others lament the decline in English proficiency, which is bound to follow, despite the hiring of native English speakers to teach English as a second language. Even at the new airport, signs are in Chinese, with English written underneath the Chinese characters, a stark contrast to the English-first policy of the old regime.

Hong Kong, with a total land area of slightly more than 400 square miles (about half the size of Rhode Island), is one of the most densely populated areas in the world. The best place to appreciate this is atop Victoria Peak, where you can feast your eyes on Hong Kong's famous harbor, and as far as the eye can see, mile upon mile of high-rise apartments. If Hong Kong were a vast plain, it would be as ugly as Tokyo. But it's saved by the undulating mountain peaks, which cover virtually all of Hong Kong and provide dramatic background to the cityscape and coastal areas.

Because of its dense population and limited land space, with more than 16,000 people per square mile, Hong Kong has long been saddled with acute housing deficiencies. Just a few decades ago, in an area called Mong Kok in northwestern Kowloon, there were an astounding 652,910 people per square mile. One house designed for 12 people had 459 living in it, including 104 people who shared one room and four people who lived on the roof.

Since 1953, when a huge fire left more than 50,000 squatters homeless, Hong Kong has pursued one of the world's most ambitious housing projects, with the aim of providing every Hong Kong family with a home of its own. By 1993, half of Hong Kong's population lived in government-subsidized public housing, a higher proportion than anywhere else in the world.

Most public housing is clustered in the New Territories, in a forest of high-rises that leaves foreign visitors aghast. Each apartment building is approximately 30 stories tall, containing about 1,000 apartments and 3,000 to 4,000 residents. Seven or eight apartment buildings comprise an estate, which is like a small town with its own name, shopping center, recreational and sports facilities, playgrounds, schools, and social services. A typical apartment is indescribably small by Western standards—approximately 250 square feet, with a single window. It consists of a combination living room/bedroom, a kitchen nook, and bathroom, and is typically shared by a couple with one or two children. According to government figures, every household in Hong Kong has at least one TV; many have one for each member of the household, even if the house consists of only one or two rooms. But as cramped, unimaginative, and sterile as these housing projects may seem, they're a vast improvement over the way much of the population used to live. They also account for most of Hong Kong's construction growth in the past 2 decades, especially in the New Territories. The town of Tung Chung, on Lantau, is a case in point. Constructed in connection with Hong Kong's new airport to provide homes for those working at the airport, the new town boasted some 20,000 residents in 1998; by 2111, the town is expected to house 200,000 people.

And where are these people coming from? Many are newly arrived from mainland China, an estimated 50,000 a year. Many Hong Kong Chinese look down on these newcomers as provincial, rude, and uneducated, and indeed, many of them now occupy the lowest rung on the economic ladder, accepting squalid living conditions in hopes of forging a better life, just as other Hong

# Tips for the Business Traveler to Hong Kong

- **Bring plenty of business cards.** They are exchanged constantly, and you'll be highly suspect without them (if you run out, hotel business centers can arrange to have new ones printed within 24 hours). When presenting your card, hold it out with both hands, turned so that the receiver can read it. Chinese names are written with the family name first, followed by the given name and then the middle name.

- **Use formal names for addressing business associates** unless told to do otherwise; you'll find that many Hong Kong Chinese used to dealing with foreigners have adopted a Western first name.

- **Shaking hands is appropriate** for greetings and introductions.

- **Business attire**—a suit and tie for men—is worn throughout the year, even in summer.

- **Avoid the Chinese New Year,** as all of Hong Kong shuts down for at least 3 days; based on the lunar calendar, it falls between late January and mid-February.

- **Entertainment** is an integral part of conducting business in Hong Kong, whether it's a meal in which the host orders the food and serves his guests, an evening at the race tracks, or a round of golf.

- If an invitation is extended, it is understood that **the host will treat.** Do not insist on paying; this will only embarrass your host. Accept graciously, and promise to pick up the tab next time around.

- Contact the **Hong Kong Trade Development Council,** 36–39 floors of the Office Tower at Convention Plaza, 1 Harbour Rd., Wan Chai (☎ **852/2584-4333**), for more information on conducting business in Hong Kong.

Kong Chinese did before them. There are also many young mainland Chinese wives in Hong Kong, since eligible Hong Kong bachelors often return to their parents' or ancestors' homeland in China in search of a bride. "Hong Kong girls are considered too materialistic," one Hong Kong resident told me, "and mainland Chinese will work harder." For those in mainland China, Hong Kong has long been the promised land.

## ARCHITECTURE

If you never ventured much beyond the waterfronts of Victoria Harbour, you might easily believe that Hong Kong is nothing more than chrome-and-glass skyscrapers, huge housing projects, shopping malls, and miles of glowing neon signs heralding countless open-fronted shops.

But Hong Kong was inhabited long before the British arrived, and some pre-colonial, Chinese architecture still survives in the hinterlands. Several rural villages boast buildings and temples with fine wood carving, and are examples of centuries-old Chinese craftsmanship. Especially fascinating are the walled villages in the New Territories, a few of which are still inhabited, and one of which has been meticulously restored and turned into a museum of traditional lifestyles (see chapter 10). These villages were built from the 14th to the 17th century by clan families to protect themselves from roving bandits, invaders, and even wild tigers. A few of the clans' ancestral halls, homes, and mansions also survive.

Also surviving are some of Hong Kong's temples. One of the oldest is a Tin Hau temple in Causeway Bay, dedicated to the seafarers' patron goddess. Hong Kong's most famous temple, however, is Man Mo, built in the 1840s and dedicated to the gods of literature and war.

Some colonial architecture also remains. One of Hong Kong's most familiar landmarks is the clock tower next to the Star Ferry terminus at Tsim Sha Tsui; it is all that remains of the old railway station that once linked the colony with China and beyond. On the Hong Kong Island side, the former Supreme Court in Central features Greco-Victorian columns and Chinese wood beam eaves. Today it houses the Legislative Council chamber. Nearby, in Hong Kong Park, is the Flagstaff House, Hong Kong's oldest surviving colonial-style building and now home to a museum of tea ware.

For the most part, however, there is precious little left to indicate Hong Kong has even had a past. Its architectural gems are scattered throughout the territory, and some are hard to reach. Many structures have also been compromised by the modern age. Kam Tin, the most famous of the walled villages, is a case in point, where inhabitants, understandably, have replaced centuries-old tiny homes in their walled village with larger, modern apartments. Hong Kong has shown far too little regard for history when it comes to renovating and preserving buildings.

Construction in Hong Kong has been going on at such a frenzied pace that if you haven't been here in 20 years (or even 10) you probably won't recognize the skylines of Central and Wan Chai. Among the most dramatic and notable newer buildings are the extension of the Hong Kong Convention and Exhibition Centre on reclaimed land on the Wan Chai waterfront, boasting the world's largest plate-glass window and a three-tiered roof said to resemble a gull's wings in flight; the Bank of China Tower by I. M. Pei, a showpiece of reflective triangles rising to a prism; and the Hongkong and Shanghai Bank, designed by British architect Norman Foster and featuring entire floors suspended from steel masts and a 160-foot-tall sun scoop on the roof that uses 480 mirrors to reflect sunlight down into the bank's atrium and public plaza. Atop Victoria Peak is the new Peak Tower, topped by a crescent-shaped bowl not unlike a wok. And Hong Kong's tallest building is the 78-story Central Plaza, located near the Wan Chai waterfront and boasting an art deco style with eye-catching nighttime lighting that changes color with each quarter hour, thereby giving the time. But this being Hong Kong, Central Plaza will undoubtedly be eclipsed by even taller buildings in the near future.

Even though Hong Kong's structures are Western, they were built using bamboo scaffolding and constructed according to ancient Chinese beliefs, especially the 3,000-year-old Taoist principle of *fung shui* that allows humankind to live in peace with the environment and nature, ensuring good luck, prosperity, wealth, health, and happiness. Even today, most office and apartment buildings in Hong Kong have been laid out in accordance to fung shui principles, aided by a geomancer (see "Fung Shui—Restoring a Balance with Nature").

## Impressions

*A barren Island with hardly a House upon it.*
—Lord Palmerston, Letter to Sir Charles Elliot, April 21, 1841

*A borrowed place living on borrowed time.*
—Anonymous, *The Times,* March 5, 1981

# CULTURAL LIFE

If you want to see Hong Kong's Chinese cultural life, simply step outside. Much of Hong Kong's drama is played in its streets, whether it's amateur Chinese opera singers at the famous Temple Street Night Market, a fortune-teller who has set up a chair and table at the side of the road or a Taoist temple, or a sidewalk calligrapher who will write letters for those who can't. Virtually everything the Chinese consider vital still thrives in Hong Kong, including ancient religious beliefs, superstitions, wedding customs, and festivals.

The first sign that Hong Kong's cultural life is not confined to its stages and concert halls can be observed if you get up early and stroll through a city park, where you'll see people practicing *tai chi* (Chinese shadow boxing), which looks like dance in slow motion. Originally a martial art developed about 1,000 years ago, tai chi today is a form of exercise that restores harmony in the body through 200 individual movements designed to use every muscle in the body. Good places to observe the art include Kowloon Park in Tsim Sha Tsui, as well as Victoria Park, Hong Kong Park, and the Zoological and Botanical Gardens on Hong Kong Island. If you wish, you can even partake in a free tai chi session held three mornings a week in Hong Kong Park (see chapter 6, "Outdoor Activities").

Hong Kong's many festivals are the most obvious expression of cultural life, most of which feature parades, dances, and observances of local customs. Lion dances, for example, may be performed to the accompaniment of drums, while in the evenings there may be puppet shows or Chinese opera performances.

Of the various Chinese performing arts, Chinese opera is the most popular and widely loved. Dating back to the Mongol period, it has always appealed to both the ruling class and the masses. Virtue, corruption, violence, and lust are common themes, and performances feature elaborate costumes and makeup, haunting atonal orchestrations, and crashing cymbals. The actor-singers train for many years. The costumes signify specific stage personalities; yellow is reserved for emperors, while purple is the color worn by barbarians. Unlike Western performances, Chinese operas are noisy affairs, with families coming and going during long performances, chatting with friends, and eating.

In Hong Kong you can also attend concerts of Western classical music, jazz, and pop, and performances of ballet, modern dance, and theater (see chapter 9).

# CHINESE MEDICINE

For most minor ailments, many Chinese are more likely to pay a visit to their neighborhood medicine store than see a doctor. Most traditional medicine stores cater solely to the practice of Chinese herbal medicine, with some cures dating back 2,000 years. The medicinal stock, however, includes much more than roots and plants—take a look inside one of Hong Kong's many medicinal shops and you'll find a bewildering array of jars and drawers containing everything from ginseng and deer's horn to fossilized bones and animal teeth. Deer's horn is said to be effective against fever; bones, teeth, and seashells are used as tranquilizers and cures for insomnia. In prescribing treatment, herbalists take into account the patient's overall mental and physical well-being, in the belief that disease and illness are caused by an imbalance in bodily forces. In contrast to Western medicine, treatment is often preventive rather than remedial. Visitors particularly interested in traditional Chinese medicine will want to visit the Hong Kong Museum of Medical Sciences.

Acupuncture is also alive and well in Hong Kong, with approximately 400 acupuncturists offering their services. With a history that goes back 4,000 years, acupuncture is based on 365 pressure points, which in turn act

# Fung Shui—Restoring a Balance with Nature

*Fung shui,* which translates literally as "wind water," is an ancient method of divination in which harmony is achieved with the spirits of nature. Virtually every Hong Kong Chinese believes that before a house or building can be erected, a tree chopped down, or a boulder moved, a geomancer must be called in to make certain that the spirits inhabiting the place aren't disturbed. The geomancer, who uses a compasslike device as an aid, determines the alignment of walls, doors, desks, and even beds, so as not to provoke the anger of the spirits residing there. He does this by achieving a balance among the eight elements of nature—heaven, earth, hills, wind, fire, thunder, rain, and ocean. Also considered are the spirit of yin (male-active) and yang (female-passive) forces that control our world.

Even non-Chinese-owned companies comply with fung shui principles, if only to appease their Chinese employees. But it doesn't hurt to be safe; tales abound of ill luck befalling those working or living inside buildings that ignored the needs of resident spirits.

Since facing the water is considered excellent fung shui, when the Regent Hotel was constructed it incorporated a huge glass window overlooking the harbor. While providing people with a great view of the harbor, the glass window also has another much more important function—it allows the nine dragons that inhabit Kowloon to pass through for their morning bath in Victoria Harbour. Dragons are unpredictable creatures, and who knows what might have happened if they had been barred from their favorite path to the harbor due to construction of a new building. They are lured to the hotel's entrance with a fountain, symbolizing a pearl (and a sign of wealth).

The next best thing, if you can't look out over water, is to bring the water inside, which is why many offices, shops, and restaurants have aquariums. Another way to deflect evil influences is to hang a small, eight-sided mirror outside your window. Other Chinese touches are incorporated into modern architecture—the Hongkong and Shanghai Bank, for example, are guarded by a pair of bronze lions, protecting their occupants.

If you wish to learn more about the principles of fung shui, consider joining an organized tour offered by Sky Bird Travel called the "Fung Shui Tour"; see chapter 6 for more details. Also note that *fung shui,* the transliteration used by the HKTA, is also transliterated as *feng shui.*

upon certain organs; slender stainless steel needles are used, which vary in length from half an inch to 10 inches. Most acupuncturists also use moxa (dried mugwort)—a slow-burning herb that applies gentle heat.

## RELIGION, MYTH & FOLKLORE

Most Hong Kong Chinese worship both Buddhist and Taoist deities, something they do not find at all incongruous. They also worship their family ancestors. There are ancestral altars in homes, and certain days are set aside for visiting ancestral graves. Many temples have large tablet halls, where Hong Kong families can worship the memorialized photographs of their dead. There are about 360 temples scattered throughout Hong Kong; some embody a mixture of both Buddhist and Taoist principles.

While Buddhism is concerned with the afterlife, Taoism is a folk faith whose devotees believe in luck and in currying its favor. Fortune-tellers, therefore, are usually found only at Taoist temples. Tao, essentially, is the way of the universe, the spirit of all things, and cannot be perceived. However, Taoist gods must be worshipped and Taoist spirits appeased. Most popular is Tin Hau, goddess of the sea and protectress of fishermen. Hong Kong has at least 24 temples that were erected in her honor. But each profession or trade has its own god—ironically, policemen and gangsters have the same one.

If you look for them, you'll find shrines dedicated to the earth god, Tou Ti, at the entrance to almost every store or restaurant in Hong Kong. They're usually below knee level, so that everyone pays homage upon entering and departing. Restaurants also have shrines dedicated to the kitchen god, Kwan Kung, to protect workers from knives and other sharp objects.

Although not a religion as such, another guiding principle in Chinese thought is Confucianism. Confucius, who lived in the 5th century B.C., devised a strict set of rules designed to create the perfect human being. Kindness, selflessness, obedience, and courtesy were preached, with carefully prescribed rules of how people should interact with one another. Since the masses were largely illiterate, Confucius communicated by means of easy-to-remember proverbs.

But despite the fact that many Hong Kong Chinese are both Buddhist and Taoist, they are not a particularly religious people in the Western sense of the word. They are too practical for that, too busy solving everyday problems, working, and earning money. There is no special day for worship, so devotees simply visit a temple whenever they want to pay their respects or feel the need for spiritual guidance. Otherwise, religion in Hong Kong plays a subtle role and is evident more in philosophy and action than in pious ceremony. To the Chinese, religion is a way of life and thus affects everyday living.

Almost every home has a small shrine, where lighted joss sticks are thought to bring good luck. In New Year's celebrations, door gods are placed on the front door for good luck, and all lights are switched on to discourage monster spirits. On New Year's Day, homes are not swept for fear of whisking away good luck. And during a full moon or major festival, housewives will often set fire to paper creations of homes, cars, or fake money to bring good luck.

But since no one can ever have too much good luck, superstitions abound in Hong Kong. Certain numbers, for example, have connotations. The most auspicious number is 8, because its pronunciation (*baht*) is similar to the word for wealth (*faht*). Likewise, the most inauspicious number is 4, since it sounds almost exactly like the Chinese word for death. Thirteen is also an unlucky number, with the result that many Hong Kong buildings simply skip it in their floor-numbering scheme.

The Chinese Almanac is another source for finding out which are the most auspicious days for getting married, when to visit the hairdresser, and information on fortune-telling, palmistry, and dates for various festivals held during the lunar year. Its origins date back to 2200 B.C.

To be on the safe side, Hong Kong Chinese will also visit fortune-tellers. Some read palms, while others study facial features, consult astrological birth charts, or let a little bird select a fortune card from a deck.

## 4  A Taste of Hong Kong

### MEALS & DINING CUSTOMS

Traditionally speaking, Chinese restaurants tend to be noisy and crowded affairs, the patrons much more interested in food than in decor. They range from simple diners where the only adornment is likely to be Formica-topped tables, to very elaborate affairs with Chinese lanterns, splashes of red and gold, and painted screens. In the 1980s, a new kind of Chinese restaurant exploded onto the scene—trendy, chic, and minimalist, many in art deco style, and catering to Hong Kong's young and upwardly mobile.

In any case, Chinese restaurants are places for social gatherings; since Hong Kong apartments are usually too small to entertain friends and family, the whole gang simply heads for their favorite restaurant.

Thus the Chinese usually dine in large groups; the more, the merrier. The basic rule is to order one dish per person, plus one extra dish or a soup, with all dishes placed in the center of the table and shared by everyone. The more people in your party, therefore, the more dishes are ordered and the more fun you'll have. Dishes usually come in two or three different sizes, so ask your waiter which size is sufficient for your group.

You shouldn't have any problem ordering, since many Chinese restaurants have English menus. If you want to be correct about it, a well-balanced meal should contain the five basic tastes of Chinese cuisine—acid, hot, bitter, sweet, and salty. The texture should vary as well, ranging from crisp and tender to dry and saucy. The proper order is to begin with a cold dish, followed by dishes of fish or seafood, meat (pork, beef, or poultry), vegetables, soup, and noodles or rice. Some dishes are steamed, while others may be fried, boiled, or roasted. Many of the dishes are accompanied by sauces, the most common being soy sauce, chili sauce, and hot mustard.

Because most Chinese restaurants cater to groups and Chinese food is best enjoyed if there's a variety of dishes, lone diners are at a distinct disadvantage when it comes to Chinese cuisine. Some modern restaurants, however, make life easier by offering fixed-price meals. An alternative is to dine at hotel buffets that offer Chinese and international dishes.

At any rate, at a Chinese restaurant, the beginning of your meal is heralded by a round of hot towels, a wonderful custom you'll soon grow addicted to and wish would be adopted by restaurants in the United States. Your eating utensils, of course, will be chopsticks, which have been around for 3,000 years and are perfect for picking up bite-size morsels. If you're eating rice, pick up the bowl and scoop the rice directly into your mouth with your chopsticks.

Keep in mind, however, that there are several superstitions associated with chopsticks. If, for example, you find an uneven pair at your table setting, it means you are going to miss a boat, plane, or train. Dropping chopsticks means you will have bad luck; laying them across each other is also considered a bad omen, except in dim sum restaurants where your waiter may cross them to show that your bill has been settled. You can do the same to signal the waiter that you've finished your meal and wish to pay the bill. When dining in a group, avoid ordering seven dishes, since seven dishes are considered food for ghosts, not humans.

As for dining etiquette, it's considered perfectly acceptable to slurp soup, since this indicates an appreciation of the food and also helps cool the soup so it doesn't burn the tongue. Toothpicks are also acceptable for use at the table during and after meals—they can even be used to spear foods too slippery or elusive for chopsticks, such as button mushrooms and jellyfish slices. As in most Asian countries, good manners call for covering your mouth with one hand while you dislodge food particles from your teeth.

A final custom you may see in Chinese restaurants is that of finger tapping—customers often tap three fingers on the table as a sign of thanks to the person pouring the tea.

# THE CUISINE

Chinese cooking has evolved over the course of several thousand years, dictated often by a population too numerous to feed. The prospect of famine meant that nothing should be wasted, and the scarcity of fuel meant that food should be cooked as economically as possible; thus, it was chopped into small pieces and quickly stir-fried. Food needed to be as fresh as possible to avoid spoiling. Among the many regional Chinese cuisines, the most common ones found in Hong Kong are from Canton, Beijing (or Peking), Shanghai, Szechuan, and Chiu Chow (Swatow).

Of course, there are many other dishes and styles of cuisine besides those outlined below. It's said that the Chinese will eat anything that swims, flies, or crawls; although that may not be entirely true, if you're adventurous enough you may want to try such delicacies as snake soup, pig's brain, bird's-nest soup (derived from the saliva of swallows), Shanghai freshwater hairy crabs (available only in autumn), tiny rice birds that are roasted and eaten whole, or eel heads simmered with Chinese herbs. One of the more common—albeit strange—items found on most Chinese menus is *bèche-de-mer,* which translates as sea cucumber but which is actually nothing more than a sea slug.

*A Word of Warning:* According to government authorities, you're safe eating anywhere in Hong Kong, even at roadside food stalls. However, don't eat local oysters—there have been too many instances of oyster poisoning. Eat oysters only if they're imported from, say, Australia. The good restaurants will clearly stipulate on the menu that their oysters are imported. Some expats, warning of cholera, also steer clear of local shellfish and fish caught from local waters. Nowadays, restaurants catering largely to tourists offer fresh seafood caught outside Hong Kong's waters.

Watch your reaction to monosodium glutamate (MSG), which is used to enhance the flavor in Chinese cooking. Some people react strongly to this salt, reporting bouts of nausea, headaches, and a bloated feeling. Fortunately, an awareness of the detrimental side effects of MSG has long prompted most Chinese upper- and medium-range restaurants, especially those in hotels, to stop using it altogether.

**CANTONESE FOOD**   The majority of Chinese restaurants in Hong Kong are Cantonese; this is not surprising since most Hong Kong Chinese are originally from Canton Province (now called Guangdong). It's also the most common style of Chinese cooking around the world and probably the one with which you're most familiar. Among Chinese, Cantonese cuisine is considered the finest, and many Chinese emperors employed Cantonese chefs in their kitchens.

Cantonese food, which is either steamed or stir-fried, is known for its fresh, delicate flavors. Little oil and few spices are used so that the natural flavors of the various ingredients prevail, and the Cantonese are sticklers for freshness (traditionalists may shop twice a day at the market). If you're concerned about cholesterol, Cantonese food is preferable. On the other hand, those with active taste buds may find it rather bland.

Since the Cantonese eat so much seafood, your best choice in a Cantonese restaurant is fish. I love steamed whole fish prepared with fresh ginger and spring onions, but equally good are slices of garoupa (a local fish), pomfret, red mullet, sole, and bream. It's considered bad luck to turn a fish over on your plate (it represents a boat capsizing), so the proper thing to do is to eat the top part of the fish, lift the bone in the air and then extract the bottom layer of meat with your chopsticks. Other popular seafood choices include shrimp and prawns, abalone, squid, scallops, crab, and sea cucumber. Shark's-fin soup is an expensive delicacy.

Other Cantonese specialties include roast goose, duck, and pigeon; pan-fried lemon chicken; stir-fried minced quail and bamboo shoots rolled in lettuce and eaten with the fingers; congee (thick rice porridge); crabmeat; sweet corn soup; and sweet-and-sour pork.

Another popular Cantonese dish is *dim sum,* which means "light snack" but whose Chinese characters literally translate as "to touch the heart." Dating back to the 10th century, dim sum is eaten for breakfast and lunch and with afternoon tea; in Hong Kong it is especially popular for Sunday family outings. It consists primarily of finely chopped meat, seafood, and vegetables wrapped in thin dough and then either steamed, fried, boiled, or braised. Dim sum can range from steamed dumplings to meatballs, fried spring rolls, and spareribs.

Many Cantonese restaurants offer dim sum from about 7:30am until 4pm, traditionally served from trolleys wheeled between the tables but nowadays just as often available from a written menu. The trolleys are piled high with steaming bamboo baskets, so ask the server to let you peek inside. If you like what you see, simply nod your head. There are nearly 100 different kinds of dim sum, but some of my favorites are *shiu mai* (steamed minced pork and shrimp dumplings), *har gau* (steamed shrimp dumplings), *au yuk* (steamed minced beef balls), *fun gwor* (steamed rice-flour dumplings filled with pork, shrimp, and bamboo shoots), and *tsuen guen* (deep-fried spring rolls filled with shredded pork, chicken, mushrooms, bamboo shoots, and bean sprouts). A serving of dim sum usually consists of two to four pieces on a plate and averages about HK$20 to HK$30 ($2.60 to $3.90) per plate. Your bill is calculated at the end of the meal by the number of plates on your table or by a card stamped each time you order a dish.

Since I can usually manage only two or three dishes, dim sum is one of the cheapest meals I eat in Hong Kong and is also the best when I'm dining alone. I often have it for breakfast with lots of tea. But it's more than just the price that draws me to traditional dim sum restaurants—they are noisy, chaotic, and the perfect place to read a newspaper or gossip. No one should go to Hong Kong without visiting a dim sum restaurant at least once.

For a light snack or late-night meal, try *congee,* which is a rice porridge popular for breakfast and usually topped with a meat, fish, or vegetable. Many of Hong Kong's countless, cheapest restaurants specialize in congee, as well as noodles in soup, the most famous of which is probably *wun tun meen,* noodle soup with shrimp dumplings.

**PEKINGESE FOOD**   Many Pekingese dishes originated in the imperial courts of the emperors and empresses and were served at elaborate banquets. This theatrical flamboyance is still evident today in the making of Pekingese noodles and the smashing of the clay around "beggar's chicken." Because of its northern source, the food of Peking (or Beijing) tends to be rather substantial (to keep the body warm), and it is richer than Cantonese food. Liberal amounts of peppers, garlic, ginger, leeks, and coriander are used. Noodles and dumplings are more common than rice, and roasting is the preferred method of cooking.

Most famous among Peking-style dishes is Peking duck (or Beijing duck), but unfortunately a minimum of six persons is usually required for this elaborate dish. The most prized part is the crisp skin, which comes from air-drying the bird and then coating it with a mixture of syrup and soy sauce before roasting. It's served by wrapping the crisp skin and meat in thin pancakes together with spring onion, radish, and sweet plum sauce.

Another popular dish prepared with fanfare is beggar's chicken: A whole chicken is stuffed with mushrooms, pickled Chinese cabbage, herbs, and onions, wrapped in lotus leaves, sealed in clay, and then baked all day. The guest of honor usually breaks open the hard clay with a mallet, revealing a tender feast more fit for a king than a beggar.

For do-it-yourself dining, try the Mongolian hot pot, where diners gather around a common pot in a scene reminiscent of campfires on the Mongolian steppes. One version calls for wafer-thin slices of meat, usually mutton, to be dipped in a clear stock and then eaten with a spicy sauce. Another variety calls for a sizzling griddle, over which thin-sliced meat, cabbage, bean sprouts, onions, and other vegetables are barbecued in a matter of seconds.

**SHANGHAINESE FOOD**   A big, bustling city, Shanghai does not technically have a cuisine of its own. Rather, it incorporates the food of several surrounding regions and cities, making it the most diverse cuisine in China. Because of the cold winters in Shanghai, its food is heavier, richer, sweeter, and oilier than Cantonese or Pekingese food, seasoned with sugar, soy sauce, and Shaoxing wine. In addition, because of hot summers, which can spoil food quickly, specialties include pickled or preserved vegetables, fish, shrimp, and mushrooms. Some dishes are rather heavy on the garlic, and portions tend to be enormous. The dishes are often stewed, braised, or fried.

The most popular Shanghainese delicacy in Hong Kong is freshwater hairy crab, flown in from Shanghai in autumn, steamed, and eaten with the hands. Other Shanghainese dishes include "yellow fish," braised eel with huge chunks of garlic, "drunken chicken" (chicken marinated in Chinese wine), sautéed shrimp in spicy tomato sauce over crispy rice, and sautéed shredded beef and green pepper. As for the famous hundred-year-old egg, it's actually only several months old, with a limey, pickled-ginger taste. Breads, noodles, and dumplings are favored over rice.

**SZECHUAN FOOD**   This is my favorite Chinese cuisine because it's the spiciest, hottest, and most fiery style of cooking. The fact that its spiciness recalls Thailand, India, and Malaysia is no coincidence, since this huge province (also called Sichuan) shares a border with Burma and Tibet.

The culprit is the Szechuan chili, fried to increase its explosiveness. Seasoning also includes chili-bean paste, peppercorns, garlic, ginger, coriander, and other spices. Foods are simmered and smoked rather than stir-fried. The most famous Szechuan dish is smoked duck, which is seasoned with peppercorns, ginger, cinnamon, orange peel, and coriander; marinated in rice wine; then steamed; and then smoked over a charcoal fire of camphor wood and tea leaves.

Other specialties include pan-fried prawns in spicy sauce, sour-and-peppery soup, sautéed diced chicken in chili-bean sauce, and dry-fried spicy string beans. Most Szechuan menus indicate which dishes are hot.

**CHIU CHOW FOOD**   Chiu Chow refers to the people, dialect, and food of the Swatow area in southeastern Canton. Chiu Chow chefs pride themselves on their talents for vegetable carvings—those incredible birds, flowers, and other adornments that are a part of every Chiu Chow banquet.

Influenced by Cantonese cooking, Chiu Chow food is rich in protein, light, and tasty. Sauces, often sweet and using tangerine or sweet beans for flavor, are liberally applied. A meal begins with a cup of *kwun yum* tea, popularly called Iron Buddha and probably the world's strongest and most bitter tea. It's supposed to cleanse the system and stimulate the taste buds. Drink some of this stuff and you'll be humming for hours.

Two very expensive Chiu Chow delicacies are shark's fin and birds' nests. Other favorites include steamed lobster, deep-fried shrimp balls, sautéed slices of whelk, fried goose blood, goose doused in soy sauce, stuffed eel wrapped in pickled cabbage, and crispy fried *chuenjew* leaves, which literally melt in the mouth.

## DRINKS

**Tea** is often provided regardless of whether you ask for it, often at a small charge. Grown in China for more than 2,000 years, tea is believed to help clear the palate and aid digestion. There are three main types: green or unfermented tea; black *bo lay* fermented tea (the most popular in Hong Kong); and *oolong,* or semifermented tea. These three teas can be further subdivided into a wide variety of specific types, with taste varying according to the region, climate, and soil. At any rate, if you want more tea at a restaurant, simply cock the lid of the teapot half open and someone will come around to refill it.

If you want something a bit stronger than tea, there are **Chinese wines.** Although there are Chinese red and white wines made from grapes, most Chinese wines aren't really wines in the Western sense of the word. Rather, they are spirits distilled from rice, millet, and other grains, as well as from herbs and flowers. Popular Chinese wines include *siu hing,* a mild rice wine that resembles a medium-dry sherry, goes well with all kinds of Chinese food, and is best served warm; *go leung* and *mao toi,* fiery drinks made from millet with a 70% alcohol content; and *ng ka pay,* a sweet herbal wine favored for its medicinal properties, especially against rheumatism.

As for **beer,** there's Tsingtao from mainland China, first brewed years ago by Germans and made from sparkling mineral water. San Miguel is also very popular. One thing to keep in mind, however, is that excess drinking is frowned upon by the Chinese, who often don't drink anything stronger than tea in restaurants. In fact, one waiter told me that Westerners spend much more in restaurants than Chinese simply because Westerners drink alcoholic beverages.

## 5 Recommended Books

If you want to read something about Hong Kong before setting out on your trip, a good place to start is *Fragrant Harbour: A Short History of Hong Kong* (Greenwood, 1977) by G. B. Endacott and A. Hinton, which is out of print but may be available at your library and which gives a thorough historical account of the colony's early beginnings to the mid-1960s; or *A Borrowed Place* (Kodansha, 1993) by Frank Welsh, which paints a more academic picture of Hong Kong's history from its ignoble beginning through the early 1990s. Likewise, *The Hong Kong Story* (Oxford University Press, 1997) by Caroline Courtauld and May Holdsworth presents Hong Kong's history from the beginning to the 1997 handover, complete with illustrations. Life in Hong Kong during the opium trade is chronicled in Nigel Cameron's *The Cultured Pearl* (Oxford University Press, 1978). And even though it is now dated, one of my favorite books is Jan Morris's *Hong Kong* (Random House, 1988), which traces the evolution of the British colony from its birth during the Opium Wars to the late 1980s. This book gives a unique perspective on the workings of the colony and imparts an astonishing wealth of information, making it fascinating armchair reading.

Readers interested in the legal aspects of the 1984 Joint Declaration should consult *Hong Kong, China* (McFarland & Company, 1995) by Steve Shipp. It discusses in detail the events from 1979 to 1995, along with the complete text of the Joint Declaration, the Basic Law issued by China concerning legal rights in Hong Kong, and the Hong Kong Bill of Rights. More insightful, perhaps, is Christopher Patten's *East and West: China, Power, and the Future of Asia* (Times Books, 1998), reflections from Hong Kong's last governor concerning the years leading up to the handover, negotiations with the Chinese, his struggle to assure Hong Kong's residents certain democratic rights, and what the future might bring.

I love looking at pictures of old Hong Kong, and especially fascinating is Nigel Cameron's *An Illustrated History of Hong Kong* (Oxford University Press, 1991), with photographs that show Hong Kong of yore and vividly illustrate how much the city has changed. Even more thorough pictorial histories are presented in Trea Wiltshire's *Old Hong Kong* (FormAsia Books, 1995 and 1997), available in three volumes and covering Hong Kong from 1860 through the June 1997 handover.

Lovers of architecture will enjoy reading *Building Hong Kong* (Formasia Books Ltd, 1998) by Jan Morris, which describes the history of the city through its architecture, from its early days through the 1990s, complete with photographs.

For an intimate view of Hong Kong, a recommended book is *Hong Kong: Borrowed Place, Borrowed Time* (Praeger, 1968) by Richard Hughes, a foreign correspondent who lived in Hong Kong for several decades and was said to have been the inspiration for several characters in John Le Carré's novels. Another good read and a great accompaniment to any guide book is *Travelers' Tales Hong Kong* (Travelers' Tales Inc., 1996), an anthology edited by James O'Reilly and filled with personal accounts and essays by well-known writers about life in Hong Kong. Likewise, *Hong Kong: Somewhere Between Heaven and Earth* (Oxford University Press, 1996), edited by Barbara-Sue White, is a collection of poems, short stories, novel excerpts, letters, speeches, and diaries with ties to Hong Kong, written by both Chinese and Europeans from all walks of life—soldiers, doctors, politicians, writers, and others, from Queen Victoria to Jules Verne and ranging from historic accounts dating from the Song Dynasty to the present day.

Fictional accounts that depict the character of Hong Kong are Richard Mason's *The World of Suzie Wong* (World Pub., 1957) and Han Suyin's *A Many-Splendored Thing* (Little Brown, 1952), an autobiographical account of life in Hong Kong shortly after the Chinese revolution in the late 1940s and early 1950s. James Clavell's *Tai-Pan* (Atheneum, 1966) is a novel about Hong Kong's beginnings; *Noble House* (Delacorte Press, 1981) is its sequel. John Le Carré's *The Honourable Schoolboy* (G. K. Hall, 1977) details the activities of George Smiley, acting head of the British Secret Service in Hong Kong. More recent is Paul Theroux's *Kowloon Tong* (Houghton Mifflin, 1997), the story of a British expatriate born and raised in Hong Kong but who lives as an outsider, never learning Chinese and failing to understand what's at stake when he's offered a large sum of money by a Chinese mainlander for his family business just before the handover. I also recommend *Hong Kong Collage* (Oxford University Press, 1998), edited by Martha P. Y. Cheung, which presents essays, short stories and other contemporary works by Chinese writers, most born in Hong Kong and presenting a dynamic view of their native land.

# Index

See also Accommodations and Restaurant indexes, below.

General Index

## ACCOMMODATIONS

Restaurant Index

## FROMMER'S® COMPLETE TRAVEL GUIDES

## FROMMER'S® DOLLAR-A-DAY GUIDES

## FROMMER'S® PORTABLE GUIDES

**FROMMER'S**

Family Vacati                                                          Grand Teton
  National Pa                                                      quoia/
Grand Canyo                                                        on
                                                                  Canyon

**FROMMER'S**

Chicago                    New York               San Francisco
London                     Paris                  Washington, D.C.

## FROMMER'S® GREAT OUTDOOR GUIDES

New England                Southern California & Baja   Washington & Oregon
Northern California        Southern New England

## FROMMER'S® BORN TO SHOP GUIDES

Born to Shop: France       Born to Shop: London    Born to Shop: Paris
Born to Shop: Italy        Born to Shop: New York

## FROMMER'S® IR

Amsterdam                                                          orld
Boston                                                             C.
Chicago
Las Vegas

**FROMMER'**

America
Britain
California

**THE UNOF**

Bed & Brea
  California
Bed & Brea                                                        ds
  New Engl                                                         d
Bed & Brea                                                        d
  the North
Bed & Brea                                                        d
  Southeast
Beyond Dis
Branson, M

**SPECIAL-**

Frommer's
  Country
Frommer's
The Civil V
  to the Ci
Frommer's
Frommer's
Frommer's

Frommer's Adventure Guide to Southeast Asia      Retirement Places Rated
Frommer's Food Lover's Companion to France       Frommer's Road Atlas Britain
Frommer's Gay & Lesbian Europe                   Frommer's Road Atlas Europe
Frommer's Exploring America by RV                Frommer's Washington, D.C., with Kids
Hanging Out in Europe                            Frommer's What the Airlines Never Tell You